The Israel-Arab Reader

*A Documentary History of the
Middle East Conflict*

SIXTH REVISED EDITION

**Walter Laqueur and
Barry Rubin, editors**

PENGUIN BOOKS

PENGUIN BOOKS

Published by the Penguin Group
Penguin Putnam Inc., 375 Hudson Street,
New York, New York 10014, U.S.A.
Penguin Books Ltd, 27 Wrights Lane,
London W8 5TZ, England
Penguin Books Australia Ltd, Ringwood,
Victoria, Australia
Penguin Books Canada Ltd, 10 Alcorn Avenue,
Toronto, Ontario, Canada M4V 3B2
Penguin Books (N.Z.) Ltd, 182–190 Wairau Road,
Auckland 10, New Zealand

Penguin Books Ltd, Registered Offices:
Harmondsworth, Middlesex, England

The *Israel-Arab Reader* edited by Walter Laqueur
first published by Citadel Press 1969
Revised edition published in Penguin Books (U.K.) 1970
Third revised edition published by Bantam Books 1976
Fourth revised and updated edition, edited by Walter Laqueur and Barry
Rubin, published in Pelican Books 1984
Published in Penguin Books (U.S.A.) 1991
Fifth revised and updated edition published 1995
This sixth revised and updated edition published 2001

5   7   9   10   8   6

ISBN 0-14-0.29713 8
(CIP data available)

Printed in the United States of America
Set in Times Roman

Contents

PART III: *FROM CAMP DAVID THROUGH THE MADRID CONFERENCE*

PART IV: THE APPARENT APPROACH OF PEACE

Preface to the Sixth Revised and Updated Edition

This collection of documents aims to provide a better understanding of the background, history, and efforts to resolve the Arab-Israeli conflict. The story is traced from the origins of Zionism and Arab nationalism, into the struggles both preceding and following Israel's independence in 1948, the wars and hostilities characterizing the following decades, and finally through the long diplomatic process and many initiatives made to resolve the issue.

We thank Eric Fredell and Yohai Sella for help in preparing earlier editions. Cameron Brown assisted greatly in preparing the current edition.

Walter Laqueur
Barry Rubin

Part I

From the Bilu to the British Mandate's End

Bilu Group: Manifesto (1882)

Bilu *are the first letters of a passage in Isaiah, Chapter 2, Verse 5: "House of Jacob, come, let us go." The Biluim, about five hundred young people mainly from the Kharkov region, were part of the wider movement of the "Lovers of Zion"* (Hovevei Zion), *which had developed in Russia in the early eighteen-eighties, mainly under the impact of the pogroms of 1881. This manifesto was issued by a Bilu group in Constantinople in 1882.*

To our brothers and sisters in Exile!
'If I help not myself, who will help me?'
Nearly two thousand years have elapsed since, in an evil hour, after a heroic struggle, the glory of our Temple vanished in fire and our kings and chieftains changed their crowns and diadems for the chains of exile. We lost our country where dwelt our beloved sires. Into the Exile we took with us, of all our glories, only a spark of the fire by which our Temple, the abode of our Great One, was engirdled, and this little spark kept us alive while the towers of our enemies crumbled into dust, and this spark leapt into celestial flame and shed light on the heroes of our race and inspired them to endure the horrors of the dance of death and the tortures of the *autos-da-fé*. And this spark is again kindling and will shine for us, a true pillar of fire going before us on the road to Zion, while behind us is a pillar of cloud, the pillar of oppression threatening to destroy us. Sleepest thou, O our nation? What hast thou been doing until 1882? Sleeping, and dreaming the false dream of Assimilation. Now, thank God, thou art awakened from thy slothful slumber. The Pogroms have awakened thee from thy charmed sleep. Thine eyes are open to recognise the cloudy delusive hopes. Canst thou listen silently to the taunts and mockeries of thine enemies? . . . Where is thy ancient pride, thine olden spirit? Remember that thou wast a nation possessing a wise religion, a law, a constitution, a celes-

3

tial Temple whose wall is still a silent witness to the glories of the past; that thy sons dwelt in palaces and towers, and thy cities flourished in the splendour of civilisation, while these enemies of thine dwelt like beasts in the muddy marshes of their dark woods. While thy children were clad in purple and fine linen, they wore the rough skins of the wolf and the bear. Art thou not ashamed?

Hopeless is your state in the West; the star of your future is gleaming in the East. Deeply conscious of all this, and inspired by the true teaching of our great master, Hillel, 'If I help not myself, who will help me?' we propose to form the following society for national ends.

1. The Society will be named 'BILU', according to the motto 'House of Jacob, come, let us go'. It will be divided into local branches according to the numbers of its members.

2. The seat of the Committee shall be Jerusalem.

3. Donations and contributions shall be unfixed and unlimited.

WE WANT:

1. A home in our country. It was given us by the mercy of God; it is ours as registered in the archives of history.

2. To beg it of the Sultan himself, and if it be impossible to obtain this, to beg that we may at least possess it as a state within a larger state; the internal administration to be ours, to have our civil and political rights, and to act with the Turkish Empire only in foreign affairs, so as to help our brother Ishmael in the time of his need.

We hope that the interests of our glorious nation will rouse the national spirit in rich and powerful men, and that everyone, rich or poor, will give his best labours to the holy cause.

Greetings, dear brothers and sisters!

HEAR, O ISRAEL! The Lord our God, the Lord is one, and our land Zion is our one hope.

GOD be with us! THE PIONEERS OF BILU

Theodor Herzl: The Jewish State (1896)

Theodor Herzl (1860–1904) was the founder of modern political Zionism. In the preface to Der Juden staat *(1896) he says: "The idea which I have developed in this pamphlet is a very old one: it is the restoration of the Jewish State."*

. . . The Jewish question still exists. It would be foolish to deny it. It is a remnant of the Middle Ages, which civilized nations do not even yet seem able to shake off, try as they will. They certainly showed a generous desire to do so when they emancipated us. The Jewish question exists wherever Jews live in perceptible numbers. Where it does not exist, it is carried by Jews in the course of their migrations. We naturally move to those places where we are not persecuted, and there our presence produces persecution. This is the case in every country, and will remain so, even in those highly civilized—for instance, France—until the Jewish question finds a solution on a political basis. The unfortunate Jews are now carrying the seeds of anti-Semitism into England; they have already introduced it into America.

I believe that I understand anti-Semitism, which is really a highly complex movement. I consider it from a Jewish standpoint, yet without fear or hatred. I believe that I can see what elements there are in it of vulgar sport, of common trade jealousy, of inherited prejudice, of religious intolerance, and also of pretended self-defence. I think the Jewish question is no more a social than a religious one, notwithstanding that it sometimes takes these and other forms. It is a national question, which can only be solved by making it a political world-question to be discussed and settled by the civilized nations of the world in council.

We are a people—one people.

We have honestly endeavored everywhere to merge ourselves in the social life of surrounding communities and to preserve the faith of our fathers. We are not permitted to do so. In vain are we loyal patriots, our loyalty in some places running to extremes; in vain do we make the same sacrifices of life and property as our fellow-citizens; in vain do we strive to increase the fame of our native land in science and art, or her wealth by trade and commerce. In countries where we have lived for centuries we are still cried down as strangers, and often by those whose ancestors were not yet domiciled in the land where Jews had already had experience of suffering. The majority may decide which are the strangers; for this, as indeed every point which arises in the relations between nations, is a question of might. I do not here surrender any portion of our prescriptive right, when I make this statement merely in my own name as an individual. In the world as it now is and for an indefinite period will probably remain, might precedes right. It is useless, therefore, for us to be loyal patriots, as were the Huguenots who were forced to emigrate. If we could only be left in peace . . . .

But I think we shall not be left in peace.

Oppression and persecution cannot exterminate us. No nation on earth has survived such struggles and sufferings as we have gone through. Jew-baiting has merely stripped off our weaklings; the strong among us were invariably true to their race when persecution broke out against them. This attitude was most clearly apparent in the period immediately following the emancipation of the Jews. Those Jews who were advanced intellectually and materially entirely lost the feeling of belonging to their race. Wherever our political well-being has lasted for any length of time, we have assimilated with our surroundings. I think this is not discreditable. Hence, the statesman who would wish to see a Jewish strain in his nation would have to provide for the duration of our political well-being; and even a Bismarck could not do that.

For old prejudices against us still lie deep in the hearts of the people. He who would have proofs of this need only listen to the people where they speak with frankness and simplicity: proverb and fairy-tale are both anti-Semitic. A nation is everywhere a great child, which can certainly be educated; but its education would, even in most favorable circumstances, occupy such a vast amount of time that we could, as already mentioned, remove our own difficulties by other means long before the process was accomplished.

Assimilation, by which I understood not only external conformity in dress, habits, customs, and language, but also identity of feeling and manner—assimilation of Jews could be effected only by intermarriage. But the need for mixed marriages would have to be felt by the majority; their mere recognition by law would certainly not suffice. . . .

No one can deny the gravity of the situation of the Jews. Wherever they live in perceptible numbers, they are more or less persecuted. Their equality before the law, granted by statute, has become practically a dead letter. They are debarred from filling even moderately high positions, either in the army, or in any public or private capacity. And attempts are made to thrust them out of business also: "Don't buy from Jews!"

Attacks in Parliaments, in assemblies, in the press, in the pulpit, in the street, on journeys—for example, their exclusion from certain hotels—even in places of recreation, become daily more numerous. The forms of persecutions vary according to the countries and social circles in which they occur. In Russia, imposts are levied on Jewish villages; in Rumania, a few persons are put to death; in Germany, they get a good beating occasionally; in Austria, anti-Semites exercise terrorism over all public life; in Algeria, there are travelling agitators; in Paris, the Jews are shut out of the so-called best social circles and excluded from clubs. Shades of anti-Jewish feeling are innumerable. But this is not to be an attempt to make out a doleful category of Jewish hardships.

I do not intend to arouse sympathetic emotions on our behalf. That would be a foolish, futile, and undignified proceeding. I shall content myself with putting the following questions to the Jews: Is it not true that, in countries where we live in perceptible numbers, the position of Jewish lawyers, doctors, technicians, teachers, and employees of all descriptions becomes daily more intolerable? Is it not true, that the Jewish middle classes are seriously threatened? Is it not true, that the passions of the mob are incited against our wealthy people? Is it not true, that our poor endure greater sufferings than any other proletariat? I think that this external pressure makes itself felt everywhere. In our economically upper classes it causes discomfort, in our middle classes continual and grave anxieties, in our lower classes absolute despair.

Everything tends, in fact, to one and the same conclusion, which is clearly enunciated in that classic Berlin phrase: *"Juden Raus!"* (Out with the Jews!)

I shall now put the Question in the briefest possible form: Are we to "get out" now and where to?

Or, may we yet remain? And, how long?

Let us first settle the point of staying where we are. Can we hope for better days, can we possess our souls in patience, can we wait in pious resignation till the princes and peoples of this earth are more mercifully disposed towards us? I say that we cannot hope for a change in the current of feeling. And why not? Even if we were as near to the hearts of princes as are their other subjects, they could not protect us. They would only feel popular hatred by showing us too much favor. By "too much," I really mean less than is claimed as a right by every ordinary citizen, or by every race. The nations in whose midst Jews live are all either covertly or openly anti-Semitic.

The common people have not, and indeed cannot have, any historic comprehension. They do not know that the sins of the Middle Ages are now being visited on the nations of Europe. We are what the Ghetto made us. We have attained pre-eminence in finance, because medieval conditions drove us to it. The same process is now being repeated. We are again being forced into finance—now it is the stock exchange—by being kept out of other branches of economic activity. Being on the stock exchange, we are consequently exposed afresh to contempt. At the same time we continue to produce an abundance of mediocre intellects who find no outlet, and this endangers our social position as much as does our increasing wealth. Educated Jews without means are now rapidly becoming socialists. Hence we are certain to suffer very severely in the struggle between classes, because we stand in the most exposed position in the camps of both socialists and capitalists . . .

The Plan

The whole plan is in its essence perfectly simple, as it must necessarily be if it is to come within the comprehension of all.

Let the sovereignty be granted us over a portion of the globe large enough to satisfy the rightful requirements of a nation; the rest we shall manage for ourselves.

The creation of a new State is neither ridiculous nor impossible. We have in our day witnessed the process in connection with nations which were not largely members of the middle class, but poorer, less educated, and consequently weaker than ourselves. The governments of all countries scourged by anti-Semitism will be keenly interested in assisting us to obtain the sovereignty we want.

The plan, simple in design, but complicated in execution, will be carried out by two agencies: The Society of Jews and the Jewish Company.

The Society of Jews will do the preparatory work in the domains of science and politics, which the Jewish Company will afterwards apply practically.

The Jewish Company will be the liquidating agent of the business interests of departing Jews, and will organize commerce and trade in the new country.

We must not imagine the departure of the Jews to be a sudden one. It will be gradual, continuous, and will cover many decades. The poorest will go first to cultivate the soil. In accordance with a preconceived plan, they will construct roads, bridges, railways and telegraph installations; regulate rivers; and build their own dwellings; their labor will create trade, trade will create markets and markets will attract new settlers, for every man will go voluntarily, at his own expense and his own risk. The labor expended on the land will enhance its value, and the Jews will soon perceive that a new and permanent sphere of operation is opening here for that spirit of enterprise which has heretofore met only with hatred and obloquy.

If we wish to found a State today, we shall not do it in the way which would have been the only possible one a thousand years ago. It is foolish to revert to old stages of civilization, as many Zionists would like to do. Supposing, for example, we were obliged to clear a country of wild beasts, we should not set about the task in the fashion of Europeans of the fifth century. We should not take spear and lance and go out singly in pursuit of bears; we would organize a large and active hunting party, drive the animals together, and throw a melinite bomb into their midst.

If we wish to conduct building operations, we shall not plant a mass of stakes and piles on the shore of a lake, but we shall build as men build now. Indeed, we shall build in a bolder and more stately style than was ever adopted before, for we now possess means which men never yet possessed.

The emigrants standing lowest in the economic scale will be slowly followed by those of a higher grade. Those who at this moment are living in despair will go first. They will be led by the mediocre intellects which we produce so superabundantly and which are persecuted everywhere.

This pamphlet will open a general discussion on the Jewish Question, but that does not mean that there will be any voting on it. Such a result would ruin the cause from the outset, and dissidents must remember that allegiance or opposition is entirely voluntary. He who will not come with us should remain behind.

Let all who are willing to join us, fall in behind our banner and fight for our cause with voice and pen and deed.

Those Jews who agree with our idea of a State will attach themselves to the Society, which will thereby be authorized to confer and treat with governments in the name of our people. The Society will thus be acknowledged in its relations with governments as a State-creating power. This acknowledgment will practically create the State.

Should the Powers declare themselves willing to admit our sovereignty over a neutral piece of land, then the Society will enter into negotiations for the possession of this land. Here two territories come under consideration, Palestine and Argentine. In both countries important experiments in colonization have been made, though on the mistaken principle of a gradual infiltration of Jews. An infiltration is bound to end badly. It continues till the inevitable moment when the native population feels itself threatened, and forces the government to stop a further influx of Jews. Immigration is consequently futile unless we have the sovereign right to continue such immigration.

The Society of Jews will treat with the present masters of the land, putting itself under the protectorate of the European Powers, if they prove friendly to the plan. We could offer the present possessors of the land enormous advantages, assume part of the public debt, build new roads for traffic, which our presence in the country would render necessary, and do many other things. The creation of our State would be beneficial to adjacent countries, because the cultivation of a strip of land increases the value of its surrounding districts in innumerable ways.

The First Zionist Congress:
The Basle Declaration (August 1897)

The aim of Zionism is to create for the Jewish people a home in Palestine secured by public law. The Congress contemplates the following means to the attainment of this end:

1. The promotion, on suitable lines, of the colonization of Palestine by Jewish agricultural and industrial workers.
2. The organization and binding together of the whole of Jewry by means of appropriate institutions, local and international, in accordance with the laws of each country.
3. The strengthening and fostering of Jewish national sentiment and consciousness.

4. Preparatory steps towards obtaining government consent, where necessary, to the attainment of the aim of Zionism.

Negib Azouri: Program of the League of the Arab Fatherland (1905)*

N. Azouri, a Christian Arab, edited the journal L'Indépendence Arabe *in Paris before the first world war. His* "Réveil de la Nation Arabe dans l'Asie Turque . . . " *(1905) from which this excerpt is drawn was the "first open demand for the secession of the Arab lands from the Ottoman Empire." (Sylvia G. Haim:* Arab Nationalism*)*

. . . There is nothing more liberal than the league's program. The league wants, before anything else, to separate the civil and the religious power, in the interest of Islam and the Arab nation, and to form an Arab empire stretching from the Tigris and the Euphrates to the Suez Isthmus, and from the Mediterranean to the Arabian Sea.

The mode of government will be a constitutional sultanate based on the freedom of all the religions and the equality of all the citizens before the law. It will respect the interests of Europe, all the concessions and all the privileges which had been granted to her up to now by the Turks. It will also respect the autonomy of the Lebanon, and the independence of the principalities of Yemen, Nejd, and Iraq.

The league offers the throne of the Arab Empire to that prince of the Khedivial family of Egypt who will openly declare himself in its favor and who will devote his energy and his resources to this end.

It rejects the idea of unifying Egypt and the Arab Empire under the same monarchy, because the Egyptians do not belong to the Arab race; they are of the African Berber family and the language which they spoke before Islam bears no similarity to Arabic. There exists, moreover, between Egypt and the Arab Empire a natural frontier which must be respected in order to avoid the introduction, in the new state, of the germs of discord and destruction. Never, as a matter of fact, have the ancient Arab caliphs succeeded for any length of time in controlling the two countries at the same time. . . .

*Translated by Sylvia G. Haim.

Sir Henry McMahon:
The McMahon Letter (October 24, 1915)

Sir Henry McMahon (1862–1949), British High Commissioner in Cairo, negotiated in 1915–16 with Hussein Ibn Ali, the Sherif of Mecca. The British government promised to support his bid for the restoration of the Caliphate (and leadership in the Arab world) if Hussein supported the British war effort against Turkey. Palestine was not mentioned by name in this exchange: the Arabs subsequently claimed that it had been included in the promise of an independent Arab state. The British denied this—as evidenced by McMahon's letter published in the London Times *in 1937.*

I have received your letter of the 29th Shawal, 1333, with much pleasure and your expression of friendliness and sincerity have given me the greatest satisfaction.

I regret that you should have received from my last letter the impression that I regarded the question of limits and boundaries with coldness and hesitation; such was not the case, but it appeared to me that the time had not yet come when that question could be discussed in a conclusive manner.

I have realised, however, from your last letter that you regard this question as one of vital and urgent importance. I have, therefore, lost no time in informing the Government of Great Britain of the contents of your letter, and it is with great pleasure that I communicate to you on their behalf the following statement, which I am confident you will receive with satisfaction.

The two districts of Mersina and Alexandretta and portions of Syria lying to the west of the districts of Damascus, Homs, Hama and Aleppo cannot be said to be purely Arab, and should be excluded from the limits demanded.

With the above modification, and without prejudice to our existing treaties with Arab chiefs, we accept those limits.

As for those regions lying within those frontiers wherein Great Britain is free to act without detriment to the interests of her ally, France, I am empowered in the name of the Government of Great Britain to give the following assurances and make the following reply to your letter:

(1) Subject to the above modifications, Great Britain is prepared to recognise and support the independence of the Arabs in all the regions within the limits demanded by the Sherif of Mecca.

(2) Great Britain will guarantee the Holy Places against all external aggression and will recognise their inviolability.

(3) When the situation admits, Great Britain will give to the Arabs her advice and will assist them to establish what may appear to be the most suitable forms of government in those various territories.

(4) On the other hand, it is understood that the Arabs have decided to seek the advice and guidance of Great Britain only, and that such European advisers and officials as may be required for the formation of a sound form of administration will be British.

(5) With regard to the *vilayets* of Baghdad and Basra, the Arabs will recognise that the established position and interests of Great Britain necessitate special administrative arrangements in order to secure these territories from foreign aggression to promote the welfare of the local populations and to safeguard our mutual economic interests.

I am convinced that this declaration will assure you beyond all possible doubt of the sympathy of Great Britain towards the aspirations of her friends the Arabs and will result in a firm and lasting alliance, the immediate results of which will be the expulsion of the Turks from the Arab countries and the freeing of the Arab peoples from the Turkish yoke, which for so many years has pressed heavily upon them.

I have confined myself in this letter to the more vital and important questions, and if there are any other matters dealt with in your letters which I have omitted to mention, we may discuss them at some convenient date in the future.

It was with very great relief and satisfaction that I heard of the safe arrival of the Holy Carpet and the accompanying offerings which, thanks to the clearness of your directions and the excellence of your arrangements, were landed without trouble or mishap in spite of the dangers and difficulties occasioned by the present sad war. May God soon bring a lasting peace and freedom of all peoples.

I am sending this letter by the hand of your trusted and excellent messenger, Sheikh Mohammed ibn Arif ibn Uraifan, and he will inform you of the various matters of interest, but of less vital importance, which I have not mentioned in this letter.

(Compliments) A. HENRY MCMAHON

British and French Governments:
The Sykes-Picot Agreement (May 15–16, 1916)

Sir Mark Sykes (1873–1919), a distinguished British orientalist, and Charles Georges-Picot, formerly French Consul in Beirut, prepared a draft agreement in 1915–16 about the post-war division of the Middle East, which was also approved in principle by Russia.

1. Sir Edward Grey to Paul Cambon, 15 May 1916

I shall have the honour to reply fully in a further note to your Excellency's note of the 9th instant, relative to the creation of an Arab State, but I should meanwhile be grateful if your Excellency could assure me that in those regions which, under the conditions recorded in that communication, become entirely French, or in which French interests are recognised as predominant, any existing British concessions, rights of navigation or development, and the rights and privileges of any British religious, scholastic, or medical institutions will be maintained.

His Majesty's Government are, of course, ready to give a reciprocal assurance in regard to the British area.

2. Grey to Cambon, 16 May 1916

I have the honour to acknowledge the receipt of your Excellency's note of the 9th instant, stating that the French Government accept the limits of a future Arab State, or Confederation of States, and of those parts of Syria where French interests predominate, together with certain conditions attached thereto, such as they result from recent discussions in London and Petrograd on the subject.

I have the honour to inform your Excellency in reply that the acceptance of the whole project, as it now stands, will involve the abdication of considerable British interests, but, since His Majesty's Government recognise the advantage to the general cause of the Allies entailed in producing a more favourable internal political situation in Turkey, they are ready to accept the arrangement now arrived at, provided that the cooperation of the Arabs is secured, and that the Arabs fulfill the conditions and obtain the towns of Homs, Hama, Damascus, and Aleppo.

It is accordingly understood between the French and British Governments—

1. That France and Great Britain are prepared to recognise and protect an independent Arab State or a Confederation of Arab States

in the areas (A) and (B) marked on the annexed map [*map not re-produced: Ed.*] under the suzerainty of an Arab chief. That in area (A) France, and in area (B) Great Britain, shall have priority of right of enterprise and local loans. That in area (A) France, and in area (B) Great Britain, shall alone supply advisers or foreign functionaries at the request of the Arab State or Confederation of Arab States.

2. That in the blue area France, and in the red area Great Britain, shall be allowed to establish such direct or indirect administration or control as they desire and as they may think fit to arrange with the Arab State or Confederation of Arab States.

3. That in the brown area there shall be established an international administration, the form of which is to be decided upon after consultation with Russia, and subsequently in consultation with the other Allies, and the representatives of the Shereef of Mecca.

4. That Great Britain be accorded (1) the ports of Haifa and Acre, (2) guarantee of a given supply of water from the Tigris and Euphrates in area (A) for area (B). His Majesty's Government, on their part, undertake that they will at no time enter into negotiations for the cession of Cyprus to any third Power without the previous consent of the French Government.

5. That Alexandretta shall be a free port as regards the trade of the British Empire, and that there shall be no discrimination in port charges or facilities as regards British shipping and British goods; that there shall be freedom of transit for British goods through Alexandretta and by railway through the blue area, whether those goods are intended for or originate in the red area, or (B) area, or area (A); and there shall be no discrimination, direct or indirect, against British goods on any railway or against British goods or ships at any port serving the areas mentioned.

That Haifa shall be a free port as regards the trade of France, her dominions and protectorates, and there shall be no discrimination in port charges or facilities as regards French shipping and French goods. There shall be freedom of transit for French goods through Haifa and by the British railway through the brown area, whether those goods are intended for or originate in the blue area, area (A), or area (B), and there shall be no discrimination, direct or indirect, against French goods on any railway, or against French goods or ships at any port serving the areas mentioned.

6. That in area (A) the Baghdad Railway shall not be extended southwards beyond Mosul, and in area (B) northwards beyond Samarra, until a railway connecting Baghdad with Aleppo via the Euphrates Valley has been completed, and then only with the concurrence of the two Governments.

7. That Great Britain has the right to build, administer, and be sole owner of a railway connecting Haifa with area (B), and shall have a perpetual right to transport troops along such a line at all times.

It is to be understood by both Governments that this railway is to facilitate the connexion of Baghdad with Haifa by rail, and it is further understood that, if the engineering difficulties and expense entailed by keeping this connecting line in the brown area only make the project unfeasible, that the French Government shall be prepared to consider that the line in question may also traverse the polygon Banias-Keis Marib-Salkhab Tell Otsda-Mesmie before reaching area (B).

8. For a period of twenty years the existing Turkish customs tariff shall remain in force throughout the whole of the blue and red areas, as well as in areas (A) and (B), and no increase in the rates of duty or conversion from *ad valorem* to specific rates shall be made except by agreement between the two Powers.

There shall be no interior customs barriers between any of the above-mentioned areas. The customs duties leviable on goods destined for the interior shall be collected at the port of entry and handed over to the administration of the area of destination.

9. It shall be agreed that the French Government will at no time enter into any negotiations for the cession of their rights and will not cede such rights in the blue area to any third Power, except the Arab State or Confederation of Arab States without the previous agreement of His Majesty's Government, who, on their part, will give a similar undertaking to the French Government regarding the red area.

10. The British and French Governments, as the protectors of the Arab State, shall agree that they will not themselves acquire and will not consent to a third Power acquiring territorial possessions in the Arabian peninsula, nor consent to a third Power installing a naval base either on the east coast, or on the islands, of the Red Sea. This, however, shall not prevent such adjustment of the Aden frontier as may be necessary in consequence of recent Turkish aggression.

11. The negotiations with the Arabs as to the boundaries of the Arab State or Confederation of Arab States shall be continued through the same channel as heretofore on behalf of the two Powers.

12. It is agreed that measures to control the importation of arms into the Arab territories will be considered by the two Governments.

I have further the honour to state that, in order to make the agreement complete, His Majesty's Government are proposing to the Russian Government to exchange notes analogous to those exchanged by the latter and your Excellency's Government on the 26th April last. Copies of these notes will be communicated to your Excellency as soon as exchanged.

I would also venture to remind your Excellency that the conclusion of the present agreement raises, for practical consideration, the question of the claims of Italy to a share in any partition or rearrangement of Turkey in Asia, as formulated in article 9 of the agreement of the 26th April, 1915, between Italy and the Allies.

His Majesty's Government further consider that the Japanese Government should be informed of the arrangement now concluded.

British Foreign Minister Arthur Balfour: The Balfour Declaration (November 2, 1917)

British policy during the war years became gradually committed to the idea of the establishment of Jewish home in Palestine. After discussions on cabinet level and consultation with Jewish leaders, the decision was made known in the form of a letter by Lord Arthur James Balfour (1848–1930) to Lord Rothschild.

Foreign Office
November 2nd, 1917.

Dear Lord Rothschild,

I have much pleasure in conveying to you, on behalf of His Majesty's Government, the following declaration of sympathy with Jewish Zionist aspirations which has been submitted to, and approved by, the Cabinet.

"His Majesty's Government view with favour the establishment in Palestine of a national home for the Jewish people, and will use their best endeavours to facilitate the achievement of this object, it being clearly understood that nothing shall be done which may prejudice the civil and religious rights of existing non-Jewish communities in Palestine, or the rights and political status enjoyed by Jews in any other country."

I should be grateful if you would bring this declaration to the knowledge of the Zionist Federation.

Yours sincerely,
ARTHUR JAMES BALFOUR

Emir Feisal and Chaim Weizmann: Agreement (January 3, 1919)

During the peace conference Emir Feisal (1855–1933), the son of Hussein, the Sherif of Mecca, met various Jewish leaders and signed an agreement with Dr. Chaim Weizmann (1877–1952), leader of the Zionist movement. Feisal, who in 1921 became King of Iraq, had it announced ten years later that "His Majesty does not remember having written anything of that kind with his knowledge."

His Royal Highness the Emir Feisal, representing and acting on behalf of the Arab Kingdom of Hedjaz, and Dr. Chaim Weizmann, representing and acting on behalf of the Zionist Organisation, mindful of the racial kinship and ancient bonds existing between the Arabs and the Jewish people, and realising that the surest means of working out the consummation of their national aspirations is through the closest possible collaboration in the development of the Arab State and Palestine, and being desirous further of confirming the good understanding which exists between them, have agreed upon the following Articles:

ARTICLE I

The Arab State and Palestine in all their relations and undertakings shall be controlled by the most cordial goodwill and understanding, and to this end Arab and Jewish duly accredited agents shall be established and maintained in the respective territories.

ARTICLE II

Immediately following the completion of the deliberations of the Peace Conference, the definite boundaries between the Arab State and Palestine shall be determined by a Commission to be agreed upon by the parties hereto.

ARTICLE III

In the establishment of the Constitution and Administration of Palestine all such measures shall be adopted as will afford the fullest guarantees for carrying into effect the British Government's Declaration of the 2nd of November, 1917.

ARTICLE IV

All necessary measures shall be taken to encourage and stimulate immigration of Jews into Palestine on a large scale, and as quickly as possible to settle Jewish immigrants upon the land through closer settlement and intensive cultivation of the soil. In taking such measures the Arab peasant and tenant farmers shall be protected in their rights, and shall be assisted in forwarding their economic development.

ARTICLE V

No regulation nor law shall be made prohibiting or interfering in any way with the free exercise of religion; and further the free exercise and enjoyment of religious profession and worship without discrimination or reference shall forever be allowed. No religious test shall ever be required for the exercise of civil or political rights.

ARTICLE VI

The Mohammedan Holy Places shall be under Mohammedan control.

ARTICLE VII

The Zionist Organisation proposes to send to Palestine a Commission of experts to make a survey of the economic possibilities of the country, and to report upon the best means for its development. The Zionist Organisation will place the aforementioned Commission at the disposal of the Arab State for the purpose of a survey of the economic possibilities of the Arab State and to report upon the best means for its development. The Zionist Organisation will use its best efforts to assist the Arab State in providing the means for developing the natural resources and economic possibilities thereof.

ARTICLE VIII

The parties hereto agree to act in complete accord and harmony on all matters embraced herein before the Peace Congress.

ARTICLE IX

Any matters of dispute which may arise between the contracting parties shall be referred to the British Government for arbitration.

Given under our hand at London, England, the third day of January, one thousand nine hundred and nineteen.

CHAIM WEIZMANN
FEISAL IBN-HUSSEIN

RESERVATION BY THE EMIR FEISAL

If the Arabs are established as I have asked in my manifesto of January 4th addressed to the British Secretary of State for Foreign Affairs, I will carry out what is written in this agreement. If changes are made, I cannot be answerable for failing to carry out this agreement.

FEISAL IBN-HUSSEIN

Emir Feisal and Felix Frankfurter: Correspondence (March 3–5, 1919)

Delegation Hedjazienne, *Paris*
3rd March, 1919.
Dear Mr. Frankfurter:

I want to take this opportunity of my first contact with American Zionists to tell you what I have often been able to say to Dr. Weizmann in Arabia and Europe.

We feel that the Arabs and Jews are cousins in race, having suffered similar oppressions at the hands of powers stronger than themselves, and by a happy coincidence have been able to take the first step towards the attainment of their national ideals together.

We Arabs, especially the educated among us, look with the deepest sympathy on the Zionist movement. Our deputation here in Paris is fully acquainted with the proposals submitted yesterday by the Zionist Organization to the Peace Conference, and we regard them as moderate and proper. We will do our best, in so far as we are concerned, to help them through: we will wish the Jews a most hearty welcome home.

With the chiefs of your movement, especially with Dr. Weizmann, we have had and continue to have the closest relations. He has been a great helper of our cause, and I hope the Arabs may soon be in a position to make the Jews some return for their kindness. We are working together for a reformed and revived Near East, and our two movements complete one another. The Jewish movement is national and not imperialist. Our movement is national and not imperialist, and there is room in Syria for us both. Indeed I think that neither can be a real success without the other.

People less informed and less responsible than our leaders and yours, ignoring the need for cooperation of the Arabs and Zionists have been trying to exploit the local difficulties that must necessarily arise in Palestine in the early stages of our movements. Some of them have, I am afraid, misrepresented your aims to the Arab peasantry, and our aims to the Jewish peasantry, with the result that interested parties have been able to make capital out of what they call our differences.

I wish to give you my firm conviction that these differences are not on questions of principle, but on matters of detail such as must inevitably occur in every contact of neighbouring peoples, and as are easily adjusted by mutual goodwill. Indeed nearly all of them will disappear with fuller knowledge.

I look forward, and my people with me look forward, to a future in which we will help you and you will help us, so that the countries in which

we are mutually interested may once again take their places in the community of civilised peoples of the world.
Believe me,
Yours sincerely,
FEISAL

5th March, 1919.

Royal Highness:
Allow me, on behalf of the Zionist Organisation, to acknowledge your recent letter with deep appreciation.

Those of us who come from the United States have already been gratified by the friendly relations and the active cooperation maintained between you and the Zionist leaders, particularly Dr. Weizmann. We knew it could not be otherwise; we knew that the aspirations of the Arab and the Jewish peoples were parallel, that each aspired to reestablish its nationality in its own homeland, each making its own distinctive contribution to civilisation, each seeking its own peaceful mode of life.

The Zionist leaders and the Jewish people for whom they speak have watched with satisfaction the spiritual vigour of the Arab movement. Themselves seeking justice, they are anxious that the just national aims of the Arab people be confirmed and safeguarded by the Peace Conference.

We knew from your acts and your past utterances that the Zionist movement—in other words the national aims of the Jewish people—had your support and the support of the Arab people for whom you speak. These aims are now before the Peace Conference as definite proposals by the Zionist Organisation. We are happy indeed that you consider these proposals "moderate and proper," and that we have in you a staunch supporter for their realisation. For both the Arab and the Jewish peoples there are difficulties ahead—difficulties that challenge the united statesmanship of Arab and Jewish leaders. For it is no easy task to rebuild two great civilisations that have been suffering oppression and misrule for centuries. We each have our difficulties we shall work out as friends, friends who are animated by similar purposes, seeking a free and full development for the two neighbouring peoples. The Arabs and Jews are neighbours in territory; we cannot but live side by side as friends.
Very respectfully,
FELIX FRANKFURTER

The General Syrian Congress: Memorandum Presented to the King-Crane Commission (July 2, 1919)

This is one of the first Arab statements on record opposing Jewish migration to Palestine.

We the undersigned members of the General Syrian Congress, meeting in Damascus on Wednesday, July 2nd, 1919, made up of representatives from the three Zones, viz., the Southern, Eastern, and Western, provided with credentials and authorizations by the inhabitants of our various districts, Moslems, Christians, and Jews, have agreed upon the following statement of the desires of the people of the country who have elected us to present them to the American Section of the International Commission; the fifth article was passed by a very large majority; all the other articles were accepted unanimously.

1. We ask absolutely complete political independence for Syria within these boundaries: the Taurus System on the North; Rafah and a line running from Al Jauf to the south of the Syrian and the Hejazian line to Akaba on the south; the Euphrates and Khabur Rivers and a line extending east of Abu Kamal to the east of Al Jauf on the east; and the Mediterranean on the west.

2. We ask that the Government of this Syrian country should be a democratic civil constitutional Monarchy on broad decentralization principles, safeguarding the rights of minorities, and that the King be the Emir Feisal, who carried on a glorious struggle in the cause of our liberation and merited our full confidence and entire reliance.

3. Considering the fact that the Arabs inhabiting the Syrian area are not naturally less gifted than other more advanced races and that they are by no means less developed than the Bulgarians, Serbians, Greeks, and Roumanians at the beginning of their independence, we protest against Article 22 of the Covenant of the League of Nations, placing us among the nations in their middle stage of development which stand in need of a mandatory power.

4. In the event of the rejection by the Peace Conference of this just protest for certain considerations that we may not understand, we, relying on the declarations of President Wilson that his object in waging war was to put an end to the ambition of conquest and colonization, can only regard the mandate mentioned in the Covenant of the League of Nations as equivalent to the rendering of economical and technical assistance that does not prejudice our complete inde-

pendence. And desiring that our country should not fall a prey to colonization is farthest from any thought of colonization and has no political ambition in our country, we will seek the technical and economical assistance from the United States of America, provided that such assistance does not exceed 20 years.

5. In the event of America not finding herself in a position to accept our desire for assistance, we will seek this assistance from Great Britain, also provided that such assistance does not infringe the complete independence and unity of our country and that the duration of such assistance does not exceed that mentioned in the previous article.

6. We do not acknowledge any right claimed by the French Government in any part whatever of our Syrian country and refuse that she should assist us or have a hand in our country under any circumstances and in any place.

7. We oppose the pretensions of the Zionists to create a Jewish commonwealth in the southern part of Syria, known as Palestine, and oppose Zionist migration to any part of our country; for we do not acknowledge their title but consider them a grave peril to our people from the national, economical, and political points of view. Our Jewish compatriots shall enjoy our common rights and assume the common responsibilities.

8. We ask that there should be no separation of the southern part of Syria, known as Palestine, nor of the littoral western zone, which includes Lebanon, from the Syrian country. We desire that the unity of the country should be guaranteed against partition under whatever circumstances.

9. We ask complete independence for emancipated Mesopotamia and that there should be no economical barriers between the two countries.

10. The fundamental principles laid down by President Wilson in condemnation of secret treaties impel us to protest most emphatically against any treaty that stipulates the partition of our Syrian country and against any private engagement aiming at the establishment of Zionism in the southern part of Syria; therefore we ask the complete annulment of these conventions and agreements.

The noble principles enunciated by President Wilson strengthen our confidence that our desires emanating from the depths of our hearts, shall be the decisive factor in determining our future; and that President Wilson and the free American people will be our supporters for the realization of our hopes thereby proving their sincerity and noble sympathy with the aspiration of the weaker nations in general and our Arab people in particular.

We also have the fullest confidence that the Peace Conference will realize that we would not have risen against the Turks, with whom we had participated in all civil, political, and representative privileges, but for their violation of our national rights, and so will grant us our desires in full in order that our political rights may not be less after the war than they were before, since we have shed so much blood in the cause of our liberty and independence.

We request to be allowed to send a delegation to represent us at the Peace Conference to defend our rights and secure the realization of our aspirations.

The King-Crane Commission: Recommendations (August 28, 1919)

The King-Crane Commission was appointed by President Woodrow Wilson, following a suggestion by Dr. Howard Bliss, President of the American University in Beirut and a sympathizer with the Arab cause. Its main function was to determine which of the Western nations should act as the mandatory power for Palestine.

We recommend . . . serious modification of the extreme Zionist program for Palestine of unlimited immigration of Jews, looking finally to making Palestine distinctly a Jewish State.

(1) The Commissioners began their study of Zionism with minds predisposed in its favor, but the actual facts in Palestine, coupled with the force of the general principles proclaimed by the Allies and accepted by the Syrians have driven them to the recommendation here made.

(2) The Commission was abundantly supplied with literature on the Zionist program by the Zionist Commission to Palestine; heard in conferences much concerning the Zionist colonies and their claims and personally saw something of what had been accomplished. They found much to approve in the aspirations and plans of the Zionists, and had warm appreciation for the devotion of many of the colonists, and for their success, by modern methods, in overcoming great natural obstacles.

(3) The Commission recognized also that definite encouragement had been given to the Zionists by the Allies in Mr. Balfour's often quoted statement, in its approval by other representatives of the Allies. If, however, the strict terms of the Balfour Statement are adhered to—favoring "the establishment in Palestine of a national home for the Jewish people," "it being clearly understood that nothing shall be done which may prejudice the civil and religious rights of existing non-Jewish communities in Palestine"—it can hardly be doubted that the extreme Zionist Program must be greatly modified. For "a national home for the Jewish people" is

not equivalent to making Palestine into a Jewish State; nor can the erection of such a Jewish State be accomplished without the gravest trespass upon the "civil and religious rights of existing non-Jewish communities in Palestine." The fact came out repeatedly in the Commission's conference with Jewish representatives, that the Zionists looked forward to a practically complete dispossession of the present non-Jewish inhabitants of Palestine, by various forms of purchase.

In his address of July 4, 1918, President Wilson laid down the following principle as one of the four great "ends for which the associated peoples of the world were fighting": "The settlement of every question, whether of territory, of sovereignty, of economic arrangement, or of political relationship upon the basis of the free acceptance of that settlement by the people immediately concerned, and not upon the basis of the material interest or advantage of any other nation or people which may desire a different settlement for the sake of its own exterior influence or mastery." If that principle is to rule, and so the wishes of Palestine's population are to be decisive as to what is to be done with Palestine, then it is to be remembered that the non-Jewish population of Palestine—nearly nine-tenths of the whole—are emphatically against the entire Zionist program. The tables show that there was no one thing upon which the population of Palestine were more agreed than upon this. To subject a people so minded to unlimited Jewish immigration, and to steady financial and social pressure to surrender the land, would be a gross violation of the principle just quoted, and of the peoples' rights, though it kept within the forms of law.

It is to be noted also that the feeling against the Zionist program is not confined to Palestine, but shared very generally by the people throughout Syria, as our conferences clearly showed. More than 72 percent—1350 in all—of all the petitions in the whole of Syria were directed against the Zionist program. Only two requests—those for a united Syria and for independence—had a larger support. This general feeling was only voiced by the "General Syrian Congress," in the seventh, eighth and tenth resolutions of their statement.

The Peace Conference should not shut its eyes to the fact that the anti-Zionist feeling in Palestine and Syria is intense and not lightly to be flouted. No British officer, consulted by the Commissioners, believed that the Zionist program could be carried out except by force of arms. The officers generally thought that a force of not less than fifty thousand soldiers would be required even to initiate the program. That of itself is evidence of a strong sense of the injustice of the Zionist program, on the part of the non-Jewish populations of Palestine and Syria. Decisions, requiring armies to carry them out, are sometimes necessary, but they are surely not gratuitously to be taken in the interests of a serious injustice. For the initial claim, often submitted by Zionist representatives, that they have a "right" to Palestine, based on an occupation of two thousand years ago, can hardly be seriously considered.

There is a further consideration that cannot justly be ignored, if the world is to look forward to Palestine becoming a definitely Jewish state, however gradually that may take place. That consideration grows out of the fact that Palestine is "the Holy Land" for Jews, Christians, and Moslems alike. Millions of Christians and Moslems all over the world are quite as much concerned as the Jews with conditions in Palestine, especially with those conditions which touch upon religious feelings and rights. The relations in these matters in Palestine are most delicate and difficult. With the best possible intentions, it may be doubted whether the Jews could possibly seem to either Christians or Moslems proper guardians of the holy places, or custodians of the Holy Land as a whole. The reason is this: the places which are most sacred to Christians—those having to do with Jesus—and which are also sacred to Moslems, are not only not sacred to Jews, but abhorrent to them. It is simply impossible, under those circumstances, for Moslems and Christians to feel satisfied to have these places in Jewish hands, or under the custody of Jews. There are still other places about which Moslems must have the same feeling. In fact, from this point of view, the Moslems, just because the sacred places of all three religions are sacred to them, have made very naturally much more satisfactory custodians of the holy places than the Jews could be. It must be believed that the precise meaning, in this respect, of the complete Jewish occupation of Palestine has not been fully sensed by those who urge the extreme Zionist program. For it would intensify, with a certainty like fate, the anti-Jewish feeling both in Palestine and in all other portions of the world which look to Palestine as "the Holy Land".

In view of all these considerations, and with a deep sense of sympathy for the Jewish cause, the Commissioners feel bound to recommend that only a greatly reduced Zionist program be attempted by the Peace Conference and even that, only very gradually initiated. This would have tomean that Jewish immigration should be definitely limited, and that the project for making Palestine distinctly a Jewish commonwealth should be given up.

There would then be no reason why Palestine could not be included in a united Syrian State, just as other portions of the country, the holy places being cared for by an International and Inter-religious Commission, somewhat as at present, under the oversight and approval of the Mandatory and of the League of Nations. The Jews, of course, would have representation upon this Commission. . . .

Winston Churchill:
The Churchill White Paper (June 1922)

In view of growing opposition to Zionism, a new statement of policy was drafted in 1922 by the then British Colonial Secretary, which, while not explicitly opposing the idea of a Jewish state, "redeemed the

Balfour promise in depreciated currency" to quote a contemporary British source.

Statement of British Policy
in Palestine Issued

The Secretary of State for the Colonies has given renewed consideration to the existing political situation in Palestine, with a very earnest desire to arrive at a settlement of the outstanding questions which have given rise to uncertainty and unrest among certain sections of the population. After consultation with the High Commissioner for Palestine the following statement has been drawn up. It summarizes the essential parts of the correspondence that has already taken place between the Secretary of State and a Delegation from the Moslem Christian Society of Palestine, which has been for some time in England, and it states the further conclusions which have since been reached.

The tension which has prevailed from time to time in Palestine is mainly due to apprehensions, which are entertained both by sections of the Arab and by sections of the Jewish population. These apprehensions, so far as the Arabs are concerned, are partly based upon exaggerated interpretations of the meaning of the Declaration favouring the establishment of a Jewish National Home in Palestine, made on behalf of His Majesty's Government on 2nd November, 1917. Unauthorized statements have been made to the effect that the purpose in view is to create a wholly Jewish Palestine. Phrases have been used such as that Palestine is to become "as Jewish as England is English." His Majesty's Government regard any such expectation as impracticable and have no such aim in view. Nor have they at any time contemplated, as appears to be feared by the Arab Delegation, the disappearance or the subordination of the Arabic population, language, or culture in Palestine. They would draw attention to the fact that the terms of the Declaration referred to do not contemplate that Palestine as a whole should be converted into a Jewish National Home, but that such a Home should be founded *in Palestine*. In this connection it has been observed with satisfaction that at the meeting of the Zionist Congress, the supreme governing body of the Zionist Organization, held at Carlsbad in September, 1921, a resolution was passed expressing as the official statement of Zionist aims "the determination of the Jewish people to live with the Arab people on terms of unity and mutual respect, and together with them to make the common home into a flourishing community, the upbuilding of which may assure to each of its peoples an undisturbed national development."

It is also necessary to point out that the Zionist Commission in Palestine, now termed the Palestine Zionist Executive, has not desired to possess, and does not possess, any share in the general administration of the country. Nor does the special position assigned to the Zionist Organization in Article IV of the Draft Mandate for Palestine imply any such functions.

That special position relates to the measures to be taken in Palestine affecting the Jewish population, and contemplates that the Organization may assist in the general development of the country, but does not entitle it to share in any degree in its Government.

Further, it is contemplated that the status of all citizens of Palestine in the eyes of the law shall be Palestinian, and it has never been intended that they, or any section of them, should possess any other juridical status.

So far as the Jewish population of Palestine are concerned it appears that some among them are apprehensive that His Majesty's Government may depart from the policy embodied in the Declaration of 1917. It is necessary, therefore, once more to affirm that these fears are unfounded, and that that Declaration, re-affirmed by the Conference of the Principal Allied Powers at San Remo and again in the Treaty of Sèvres, is not susceptible of change.

During the last two or three generations the Jews have recreated in Palestine a community, now numbering 80,000, of whom about one-fourth are farmers or workers upon the land. This community has its own political organs; an elected assembly for the direction of its domestic concerns; elected councils in the towns; and an organization for the control of its schools. It has its elected Chief Rabbinate and Rabbinical Council for the direction of its religious affairs. Its business is conducted in Hebrew as a vernacular language, and a Hebrew Press serves its needs. It has its distinctive intellectual life and displays considerable economic activity. This community, then, with its town and country population, its political, religious, and social organizations, its own language, its own customs, its own life, has in fact "national" characteristics. When it is asked what is meant by the development of the Jewish National Home in Palestine, it may be answered that it is not the imposition of a Jewish nationality upon the inhabitants of Palestine as a whole, but the further development of the existing Jewish community, with the assistance of Jews in other parts of the world, in order that it may become a centre in which the Jewish people as a whole may take, on grounds of religion and race, an interest and a pride. But in order that this community should have the best prospect of free development and provide a full opportunity for the Jewish people to display its capacities, it is essential that it should know that it is in Palestine as of right and not on sufferance. That is the reason why it is necessary that the existence of a Jewish National Home in Palestine should be internationally guaranteed, and that it should be formally recognized to rest upon ancient historic connection.

This, then, is the interpretation which His Majesty's Government place upon the Declaration of 1917, and, so understood, the Secretary of State is of opinion that it does not contain or imply anything which need cause either alarm to the Arab population of Palestine or disappointment to the Jews.

For the fulfilment of this policy it is necessary that the Jewish community in Palestine should be able to increase its numbers by immigration. This immigration cannot be so great in volume as to exceed whatever may be the economic capacity of the country at the time to absorb new arrivals. It is essential to ensure that the immigrants should not be a burden upon the people of Palestine as a whole, and that they should not deprive any section of the present population of their employment. Hitherto the immigration has fulfilled these conditions. The number of immigrants since the British occupation has been about 25,000.

It is necessary also to ensure that persons who are politically undesirable are excluded from Palestine, and every precaution has been and will be taken by the Administration to that end.

It is intended that a special committee should be established in Palestine, consisting entirely of members of the new Legislative Council elected by the people, to confer with the administration upon matters relating to the regulation of immigration. Should any difference of opinion arise between this committee and the Administration the matter will be referred to His Majesty's Government, who will give it special consideration. In addition, under Article 81 of the draft Palestine Order in Council, any religious community or considerable section of the population of Palestine will have a general right to appeal, through the High Commissioner and the Secretary of State, to the League of Nations on any matter on which they may consider that the terms of the Mandate are not being fulfilled by the Government of Palestine.

With reference to the Constitution which it is now intended to establish in Palestine, the draft of which has already been published, it is desirable to make certain points clear. In the first place, it is not the case, as has been represented by the Arab Delegation, that during the war His Majesty's Government gave an undertaking that an independent national government should be at once established in Palestine. This representation mainly rests upon a letter dated the 24th October, 1915, from Sir Henry McMahon, then His Majesty's High Commissioner in Egypt, to the Sherif of Mecca, now King Hussein of the Kingdom of the Hejaz. That letter is quoted as conveying the promise to the Sherif of Mecca to recognise and support the independence of the Arabs within the territories proposed by him. But this promise was given subject to a reservation made in the same letter, which excluded from its scope, among other territories, the portions of Syria lying to the west of the district of Damascus. This reservation has always been regarded by His Majesty's Government as covering the vilayet of Beirut and the independent Sanjak of Jerusalem. The whole of Palestine west of the Jordan was thus excluded from Sir H. McMahon's pledge.

Nevertheless, it is the intention of His Majesty's Government to foster the establishment of a full measure of self-government in Palestine. But they are of opinion that, in the special circumstances of that country, this should be accomplished by gradual stages and not suddenly. The first step was taken when, on the institution of a Civil Administration, the nominated Advisory Council, which now exists, was established. It was stated at the time by the High Commissioner that this was the first step in the development of self-governing institutions, and it is now proposed to take a second step by the establishment of a Legislative Council containing a large proportion of members elected on a wide franchise. It was proposed in the published draft that three of the members of this Council should be non-official persons nominated by the High Commissioner, but representations having been made in opposition to this provision, based on cogent considerations, the Secretary of State is prepared to omit it. The Legislative Council would then consist of the High Commissioner as President and twelve elected and ten official members. The Secretary of State is of opinion that before a further measure of self-government is extended to Palestine and the Assembly placed in control over the Executive, it would be wise to allow some time to elapse. During this period the institutions of the country will have become well established; its financial credit will be based on firm foundations, and the Palestinian officials will have been enabled to gain experience of sound methods of government. After a few years the situation will be again reviewed, and if the experience of the working of the constitution now to be established so warranted, a larger share of authority would then be extended to the elected representatives of the people.

The Secretary of State would point out that already the present Administration has transferred to a Supreme Council elected by the Moslem community of Palestine the entire control of Moslem religious endowments (Wakfs), and of the Moslem religious Courts. To this Council the Administration has also voluntarily restored considerable revenues derived from ancient endowments which had been sequestrated by the Turkish Government. The Education Department is also advised by a committee representative of all sections of the population, and the Department of Commerce and Industry has the benefit of the cooperation of the Chambers of Commerce which have been established in the principal centres. It is the intention of the Administration to associate in an increased degree similar representative committees with the various Departments of the Government.

The Secretary of State believes that a policy upon these lines, coupled with the maintenance of the fullest religious liberty in Palestine and with scrupulous regard for the rights of each community with reference to its Holy Places, cannot but commend itself to the various sections of the population, and that upon this basis may be built up that spirit of cooperation upon which the future progress and prosperity of the Holy Land must largely depend.

League of Nations:
The British Mandate (July 24, 1922)

The San Remo Conference decided on April 24, 1920, to assign the mandate under the League of Nations to Britain. The terms of the mandate were also discussed with the United States, which was not a member of the League. An agreed text was confirmed by the Council of the League of Nations on July 24, 1922, and it came into operation in September 1923.

The Council of the League of Nations:

Whereas the Principal Allied Powers have agreed, for the purpose of giving effect to the provisions of Article 22 of the Covenant of the League of Nations, to entrust to a Mandatory selected by the said Powers the administration of the territory of Palestine, which formerly belonged to the Turkish Empire, within such boundaries as may be fixed by them; and

Whereas the Principal Allied Powers have also agreed that the Mandatory should be responsible for putting into effect the declaration originally made on November 2nd, 1917, by the Government of His Britannic Majesty, and adopted by the said Powers, in favour of the establishment in Palestine of a national home for the Jewish people, it being clearly understood that nothing should be done which might prejudice the civil and religious rights of existing non-Jewish communities in Palestine, or the rights and political status enjoyed by Jews in any other country; and

Whereas recognition has thereby been given to the historical connexion of the Jewish people with Palestine and to the grounds for reconstituting their national home in that country; and

Whereas the Principal Allied Powers have selected His Britannic Majesty as the Mandatory for Palestine; and

Whereas the mandate in respect of Palestine has been formulated in the following terms and submitted to the Council of the League for approval; and

Whereas His Britannic Majesty has accepted the mandate in respect of Palestine and undertaken to exercise it on behalf of the League of Nations in conformity with the following provisions; and

Whereas by the aforementioned Article 22 (paragraph 8), it is provided that the degree of authority, control or administration to be exercised by the Mandatory, not having been previously agreed upon by the Members of the League, shall be explicitly defined by the Council of the League of Nations;

Confirming the said Mandate, defines its terms as follows:

ARTICLE 1.

The Mandatory shall have full powers of legislation and of administration, save as they may be limited by the terms of this mandate.

ARTICLE 2.

The Mandatory shall be responsible for placing the country under such political, administrative and economic conditions as will secure the establishment of the Jewish national home, as laid down in the preamble, and the development of self-governing institutions, and also for safeguarding the civil and religious rights of all the inhabitants of Palestine, irrespective of race and religion.

ARTICLE 3.

The Mandatory shall, so far as circumstances permit, encourage local autonomy.

ARTICLE 4.

An appropriate Jewish agency shall be recognized as a public body for the purpose of advising and cooperating with the Administration of Palestine in such economic, social and other matters as may affect the establishment of the Jewish national home and the interests of the Jewish population in Palestine, and, subject always to the control of the Administration, to assist and take part in the development of the country.

The Zionist Organization, so long as its organization and constitution are in the opinion of the Mandatory appropriate, shall be recognized as such agency. It shall take steps in consultation with His Britannic Majesty's Government to secure the cooperation of all Jews who are willing to assist in the establishment of the Jewish national home.

ARTICLE 5.

The Mandatory shall be responsible for seeing that no Palestine territory shall be ceded or leased to, or in any way placed under the control of, the Government of any foreign Power.

ARTICLE 6.

The Administration of Palestine, while ensuring that the rights and position of other sections of the population are not prejudiced, shall facilitate Jewish immigration under suitable conditions and shall encourage, in cooperation with the Jewish agency referred to in Article 4, close settlement by Jews on the land, including State lands and waste lands not required for public purposes.

ARTICLE 7.

The Administration of Palestine shall be responsible for enacting a nationality law. There shall be included in this law provisions framed so as to facilitate the acquisition of Palestinian citizenship by Jews who take up their permanent residence in Palestine.

ARTICLE 8.

The privileges and immunities of foreigners, including the benefits of consular jurisdiction and protection as formerly enjoyed by Capitulation or usage in the Ottoman Empire, shall not be applicable in Palestine.

Unless the Powers whose nationals enjoyed the aforementioned privileges and immunities on August 1st, 1914, shall have previously renounced the right to their re-establishment, or shall have agreed to their non-application for a specified period, these privileges and immunities shall, at the expiration of the mandate, be immediately re-established in their entirety or with such modifications as may have been agreed upon between the Powers concerned.

ARTICLE 9.

The Mandatory shall be responsible for seeing that the judicial system established in Palestine shall assure to foreigners, as well as to natives, a complete guarantee of their rights.

Respect for the personal status of the various peoples and communities and for their religious interests shall be fully guaranteed. In particular, the control and administration of Waqfs shall be exercised in accordance with religious law and the dispositions of the founders.

ARTICLE 10.

Pending the making of special extradition agreements relating to Palestine, the extradition treaties in force between the Mandatory and other foreign Powers shall apply to Palestine.

ARTICLE 11.

The Administration of Palestine shall take all necessary measures to safeguard the interests of the community in connexion with the development of the country, and, subject to any international obligations accepted by the Mandatory, shall have full power to provide for public ownership or control of any of the natural resources of the country or of the public works, services and utilities established or to be established therein. It shall introduce a land system appropriate to the needs of the country having regard, among other things, to the desirability of promoting the close settlement and intensive cultivation of the land.

The Administration may arrange with the Jewish Agency mentioned in Article 4 to construct or operate, upon fair and equitable terms, any public works, services and utilities, and to develop any of the natural resources of the country, in so far as these matters are not directly undertaken by the Administration. Any such arrangements shall provide that no profits distributed by such agency, directly or indirectly, shall exceed a reasonable rate of interest on the capital, and any further profits shall be utilized by it for the benefit of the country in a manner approved by the Administration.

ARTICLE 12.

The Mandatory shall be entrusted with the control of the foreign relations of Palestine, and the right to issue exequaturs to consuls appointed by foreign Powers. He shall also be entitled to afford diplomatic and consular protection to citizens of Palestine when outside its territorial limits.

ARTICLE 13.

All responsibility in connexion with the Holy Places and religious buildings or sites in Palestine, including that of preserving existing rights and of securing free access to the Holy Places, religious buildings and sites and the free exercise of worship, while ensuring the requirements of public order and decorum, is assumed by the Mandatory, who shall be responsible solely to the League of Nations in all matters connected herewith, provided that nothing in this article shall prevent the Mandatory from entering into such arrangements as he may deem reasonable with the Administration for the purpose of carrying the provisions of this article into effect; and provided also that nothing in this Mandate shall be construed as conferring upon the Mandatory authority to interfere with the fabric or the management of purely Moslem sacred shrines, the immunities of which are guaranteed.

ARTICLE 14.

A special Commission shall be appointed by the Mandatory to study, define and determine the rights and claims in connexion with the Holy Places and the rights and claims relating to the different religious communities in Palestine. The method of nomination, the composition and the functions of this Commission shall be submitted to the Council of the League for its approval, and the Commission shall not be appointed or enter upon its functions without the approval of the Council.

ARTICLE 15.

The Mandatory shall see that complete freedom of conscience and the free exercise of all forms of worship, subject only to the maintenance of public order and morals, are ensured to all. No discrimination of any kind shall be made between the inhabitants of Palestine on the ground of race, religion or language. No person shall be excluded from Palestine on the sole ground of his religious belief.

The right of each community to maintain its own schools for the education of its own members in its own language, while conforming to such educational requirements of a general nature as the Administration may impose, shall not be denied or impaired.

ARTICLE 16.

The Mandatory shall be responsible for exercising such supervision over religious or eleemosynary bodies of all faiths in Palestine as may be required for the maintenance of public order and good government. Subject to such supervision, no measures shall be taken in Palestine to obstruct or interfere with the enterprise of such bodies or to discriminate against any representative or member of them on the ground of his religion or nationality.

ARTICLE 17.

The Administration of Palestine may organize on a voluntary basis the forces necessary for the preservation of peace and order, and also for the defence of the country, subject, however, to the supervision of the Mandatory, but shall not use them for purposes other than those above specified save with the consent of the Mandatory. Except for such purposes, no military, naval or air forces shall be raised or maintained by the Administration of Palestine.

Nothing in this article shall preclude the Administration of Palestine from contributing to the cost of the maintenance of the forces of the Mandatory in Palestine.

The Mandatory shall be entitled at all times to use the roads, railways and ports of Palestine for the movement of armed forces and the carriage of fuel and supplies.

ARTICLE 18.

The Mandatory shall see that there is no discrimination in Palestine against the nationals of any State Member of the League of Nations (including companies incorporated under its laws) as compared with those of the Mandatory or of any foreign State in matters concerning taxation, commerce or navigation, the exercise of industries or professions, or in the treatment of merchant vessels or civil aircraft. Similarly, there shall be no discrimination in Palestine against goods originating in or destined for any of the said States, and there shall be freedom of transit under equitable conditions across the mandated area.

Subject as aforesaid and to the other provisions of this mandate, the Administration of Palestine may, on the advice of the Mandatory, impose such taxes and customs duties as it may consider necessary, and take such steps as it may think best to promote the development of the natural resources of the country and to safeguard the interests of the population. It may also, on the advice of the Mandatory, conclude a special customs agreement with any State the territory of which in 1914 was wholly included in Asiatic Turkey or Arabia.

ARTICLE 19.

The Mandatory shall adhere on behalf of the Administration of Palestine to any general international conventions already existing, or which may be concluded hereafter with the approval of the League of Nations, respecting the slave traffic, the traffic in arms and ammunition, or the traffic in drugs, or relating to commercial equality, freedom of transit and navigation, aerial navigation and postal, telegraphic and wireless communication or literary, artistic or industrial property.

ARTICLE 20.

The Mandatory shall co-operate on behalf of the Administration of Palestine, so far as religious, social and other conditions may permit, in the execution of any common policy adopted by the League of Nations for preventing and combating disease, including diseases of plants and animals.

ARTICLE 21.

The Mandatory shall secure the enactment within twelve months from this date, and shall ensure the execution of a Law of Antiquities based on the following rules. This law shall ensure equality of treatment in the matter of excavations and archaeological research to the nationals of all States Members of the League of Nations. . . .

ARTICLE 22.

English, Arabic and Hebrew shall be the official languages of Palestine. Any statement or inscription in Arabic on stamps or money in Palestine shall be repeated in Hebrew and any statement or inscription in Hebrew shall be repeated in Arabic.

ARTICLE 23.

The Administration of Palestine shall recognize the holy days of the respective communities in Palestine as legal days of rest for the members of such communities.

ARTICLE 24.

The Mandatory shall make to the Council of the League of Nations an annual report to the satisfaction of the Council as to the measures taken during the year to carry out the provisions of the mandate. Copies of all laws and regulations promulgated or issued during the year shall be communicated with the report.

ARTICLE 25.

In the territories lying between the Jordan and the eastern boundary of Palestine as ultimately determined, the Mandatory shall be entitled, with the consent of the Council of the League of Nations, to postpone or withhold application of such provisions of this mandate as he may consider inapplicable to the existing local conditions, and to make such provision for the administration of the territories as he may consider suitable to those conditions, provided that no action shall be taken which is inconsistent with the provisions of Articles 15, 16 and 18.

ARTICLE 26.

The Mandatory agrees that if any dispute whatever should arise between the Mandatory and another Member of the League of Nations relating to the interpretation or the application of the provisions of the mandate, such dispute, if it cannot be settled by negotiation, shall be submitted to the Permanent Court of International Justice provided for by Article 14 of the Covenant of the League of Nations.

ARTICLE 27.

The consent of the Council of the League of Nations is required for any modification of the terms of this mandate.

ARTICLE 28.

In the event of the termination of the mandate hereby conferred upon the Mandatory, the Council of the League of Nations shall make such arrangements as may be deemed necessary for safeguarding in perpetuity, under guarantee of the League, the rights secured by Articles 13 and 14, and shall use its influence for securing, under the guarantee of the League, that the Government of Palestine will fully honour the financial obligations legitimately incurred by the Administration of Palestine during the period of the mandate, including the rights of public servants to pensions or gratuities.

The present instrument shall be deposited in original in the archives of the League of Nations and certified copies shall be forwarded by the Secretary General of the League of Nations to all Members of the League.

DONE AT LONDON the twenty-fourth day of July, one thousand nine hundred and twenty-two.

British Prime Minister Ramsay MacDonald: The MacDonald Letter (February 13, 1931)

Following the Arab riots of 1929, the British Labor government published a new statement of policy (the Passfield White Paper), which urged the restriction of immigration and of land sales to Jews. It was bitterly denounced by Zionist leaders as a violation of the letter and the spirit of the Mandate. The MacDonald letter, while not openly repudiating the Passfield report, gave assurances that the terms of the Mandate would be fulfilled. It was rejected by the Arabs as the "Black Letter." James Ramsay MacDonald (1866–1937) was Prime Minister in 1931; Lord Passfield (Sidney Webb, 1859–1947) was Colonial Secretary in the Labor cabinet.

Dear Dr. Weizmann:

In order to remove certain misconceptions and misunderstandings which have arisen as to the policy of his Majesty's Government with regard to Palestine, as set forth in the White Paper of October, 1930, and which were the subject of a debate in the House of Commons on Nov. 17, and also to meet certain criticisms put forward by the Jewish Agency, I have pleasure in forwarding you the following statement of our position, which will fall to be read as the authoritative interpretation of the White Paper on the matters with which this letter deals.

It has been said that the policy of his Majesty's Government involves a serious departure from the obligations of the mandate as hitherto understood; that it misconceives the mandatory obligations, and that it foreshadows a policy which is inconsistent with the obligations of the mandatory to the Jewish people.

His Majesty's Government did not regard it as necessary to quote in extenso the declarations of policy which have been previously made, but attention is drawn to the fact that, not only does the White Paper of 1930 refer to and endorse the White Paper of 1922, which has been accepted by the Jewish Agency, but it recognizes that the undertaking of the mandate is an undertaking to the Jewish people and not only to the Jewish population of Palestine. The White Paper places in the foreground of its statement my speech in the House of Commons on the 3rd of April, 1930, in which I announced, in words that could not have been made more plain, that it was the intention of his Majesty's Government to continue to administer Palestine in accordance with the terms of the mandate as approved by the Council of the League of Nations. That position has been reaffirmed and again made plain by my speech in the House of Commons on the 17th of November. In my speech on the 3rd of April I used the following language:

His Majesty's Government will continue to administer Palestine in accordance with the terms of the mandate as approved by the Council of the League of Nations. This is an international obligation from which there can be no question of receding.

Under the terms of the mandate his Majesty's Government are responsible for promoting the establishment of a national home for the Jewish people, it being clearly understood that nothing shall be done which might prejudice the civil and religious rights of existing non-Jewish communities in Palestine or the rights and political status enjoyed by Jews in any other country.

A double undertaking is involved, to the Jewish people on the one hand and to the non-Jewish population of Palestine on the other; and it is the firm resolve of his Majesty's Government to give effect, in equal measure, to both parts of the declaration and to do equal justice to all sections of the population of Palestine. That is a duty from which they will not shrink and to discharge of which they will apply all the resources at their command.

That declaration is in conformity not only with the articles but also with the preamble of the mandate, which is hereby explicitly reaffirmed.

In carrying out the policy of the mandate the mandatory cannot ignore the existence of the differing interests and viewpoints. These, indeed, are not in themselves irreconcilable, but they can only be reconciled if there is a proper realization that the full solution of the problem depends upon an understanding between the Jews and the Arabs. Until that is reached, considerations of balance must inevitably enter into the definition of policy.

A good deal of criticism has been directed to the White Paper upon the assertion that it contains injurious allegations against the Jewish people and Jewish labor organizations. Any such intention on the part of his Majesty's Government is expressly disavowed. It is recognized that the Jewish Agency have all along given willing cooperation in carrying out the policy of the mandate and that the constructive work done by the Jewish people in Palestine has had beneficial effects on the development and well-being of the country as a whole. His Majesty's Government also recognizes the value of the services of labor and trades union organizations in Palestine, to which they desire to give every encouragement.

A question has arisen as to the meaning to be attached to the words 'safeguarding the civil and religious rights of all inhabitants of Palestine irrespective of race and religion' occurring in Article II, and the words 'insuring that the rights and position of other sections of the population are not prejudiced' occurring in Article VI of the mandate. The words 'safeguarding the civil and religious rights' occurring in Article II cannot be read as meaning that the civil and religious rights of individual citizens are unalterable. In the case of Suleiman Murra, to which reference has been made, the Privy Council, in construing these words of Article II said 'It does not mean . . . that all the civil rights of every inhabitant of Palestine which existed at the date of the mandate are to remain unaltered throughout its duration; for if that were to be a condition of the mandatory jurisdiction, no effective legislation would be possible.' The words, accordingly, must be read in another sense, and the key to the true purpose and meaning of the sentence is to be found in the concluding words of the article, 'irrespective of race and religion.' These words indicate that in respect of civil and religious rights the mandatory is not to discriminate between persons on the ground of religion or race, and this protective provision applies equally to Jews, Arabs and all sections of the population.

The words 'rights and position of other sections of the population,' occurring in Article VI, plainly refer to the non-Jewish community. These rights and position are not to be prejudiced; that is, are not to be impaired or made worse. The effect of the policy of immigration and settlement on the economic position of the non-Jewish community cannot be excluded from consideration. But the words are not to be read as implying that existing economic conditions in Palestine should be crystallized. On the contrary, the obligation to facilitate Jewish immigration and to encourage close settlement by Jews on the land remains a positive obligation of the mandate and it can be fulfilled without prejudice to the rights and position of other sections of the population of Palestine.

We may proceed to the contention that the mandate has been interpreted in a manner highly prejudicial to Jewish interests in the vital matters of land settlement and immigration. It has been said that the policy of the White Paper would place an embargo on immigration and would suspend, if not indeed terminate, the close settlement of the Jews on the land, which is a primary purpose of the mandate. In support of this contention particular stress has been laid upon the passage referring to State lands in the White Paper, which says that 'it would not be possible to make available for Jewish settlement in view of their actual occupation by Arab cultivators and of the importance of making available suitable land on which to place the Arab cultivators who are now landless.'

The language of this passage needs to be read in the light of the policy as a whole. It is desirable to make it clear that the landless Arabs, to whom it was intended to refer in the passage quoted, were such Arabs as can be shown to have been displaced from the lands which they occupied in consequence of the land passing into Jewish hands, and who have not obtained other holdings on which they can establish themselves, or other equally satisfactory occupation. The number of such displaced Arabs must be a matter for careful inquiry. It is to landless Arabs within this category that his Majesty's Government feels itself under an obligation to facilitate their settlement upon the land. The recognition of this obligation in no way detracts from the larger purposes of development which his Majesty's Government regards as the most effectual means of furthering the establishment of a national home for the Jews. . . .

Further, the statement of policy of his Majesty's Government did not imply a prohibition of acquisition of additional land by Jews. It contains no such prohibition, nor is any such intended. What it does contemplate is such temporary control of land disposition and transfers as may be necessary not to impair the harmony and effectiveness of the scheme of land settlement to be undertaken. His Majesty's Government feels bound to point out that it alone of the governments which have been responsible for the administration of Palestine since the acceptance of the mandate has declared its definite intention to initiate an active policy of development, which it is believed will result in a substantial and lasting benefit to both Jews and Arabs.

Cognate to this question is the control of immigration. It must first of all be pointed out that such control is not in any sense a departure from previous policy. From 1920 onward, when the original immigration ordinance came into force, regulations for the control of immigration have been issued from time to time, directed to prevent illicit entry and to define and facilitate authorized entry. This right of regulation has at no time been challenged.

But the intention of his Majesty's Government appears to have been represented as being that 'no further immigration of Jews is to be permitted so long as it might prevent any Arab from obtaining employment.' His Majesty's Government never proposed to pursue such a policy. They were concerned to state that, in the regulation of Jewish immigration, the following principles should apply: viz., that 'it is essential to insure that the immigrants should not be a burden on the people of Palestine as a whole, and that they should not deprive any section of the present population of their employment.' (White Paper 1922.)

In one aspect, his Majesty's Government have to be mindful of their obligations to facilitate Jewish immigration under suitable conditions, and to encourage close settlement by Jews on the land; in the other aspect, they have to be equally mindful of their duty to insure that no prejudice results to the rights and position of the non-Jewish community. It is because of this apparent conflict of obligations that his Majesty's Government have felt bound to emphasize the necessity of the proper application of the absorptive principle.

That principle is vital to any scheme of development, the primary purpose of which must be the settlement both of Jews and of displaced Arabs on the land. It is for that reason that his Majesty's Government have insisted, and are compelled to insist, that government immigration regulations must be properly applied. The considerations relevant to the limits of absorptive capacity are purely economic considerations.

His Majesty's Government did not prescribe and do not contemplate any stoppage or prohibition of Jewish immigration in any of its categories. The practice of sanctioning a labor schedule of wage-earning immigrants will continue. In each case consideration will be given to anticipated labor requirements for works which, being dependent upon Jewish or mainly Jewish capital, would not be or would not have been undertaken unless Jewish labor was available. With regard to public and municipal works failing to be financed out of public funds, the claim of Jewish labor to a due share of the employment available, taking into account Jewish contributions to public revenue, shall be taken into consideration. As regards other kinds of employment, it will be necessary in each case to take into account the factors bearing upon the demand for labor, including the factor of unemployment among both the Jews and the Arabs.

Immigrants with prospects of employment other than employment of a purely ephemeral character will not be excluded on the sole ground that the employment cannot be guaranteed to be of unlimited duration.

In determining the extent to which immigration at any time may be permitted it is necessary also to have regard to the declared policy of the Jewish Agency to the effect that 'in all the works or undertakings carried out or furthered by the Agency it shall be deemed to be a matter of principle that Jewish labor shall be employed.' His Majesty's Government do not in any way challenge the right of the Agency to formulate or approve and endorse this policy. The principle of preferential, and indeed exclusive, employment of Jewish labor by Jewish organizations is a principle which the Jewish Agency are entitled to affirm. But it must be pointed out that if in consequence of this policy Arab labor is displaced or existing unemployment becomes aggravated, that is a factor in the situation to which the mandatory is bound to have regard.

His Majesty's Government desire to say, finally, as they have repeatedly and unequivocally affirmed, that the obligations imposed upon the mandatory by its acceptance of the mandate are solemn international obligations from which there is not now, nor has there been at any time, any intention to depart. To the tasks imposed by the mandate, his Majesty's Government have set their hand, and they will not withdraw it. But if their efforts are to be successful, there is need for cooperation, confidence, readiness on all sides to appreciate the difficulties and complexities of the problem, and, above all, there must be a full and unqualified recognition that no solution can be satisfactory or permanent which is not based upon justice, both to the Jewish people and to the non-Jewish communities of Palestine.

RAMSAY MACDONALD

The Palestine Royal Commission
(Peel Commission): Report (July 1937)

A Royal Commission headed by Lord Peel was appointed in 1936, following the outbreak of fresh Arab riots earlier that year. Its report, published in July 1937, stated that the desire of the Arabs for national independence and their hatred and fear of the establishment of the Jewish National Home were the underlying causes of the disturbances. It found that Arab and Jewish interests could not be reconciled under the Mandate and it suggested, therefore, the partition of Palestine. The Jewish state was to comprise Galilee, the Yezreel Valley and the Coastal Plain to a point midway between Gaza and Jaffe, altogether

about twenty percent of the area of the country. The rest, Arab Pales-
tine, was to be united with Transjordan. Jerusalem, Bethlehem, a corri-
dor linking them to the sea, and, possibly, Nazareth and the Sea of
Genezareth would remain a British mandatory zone. The Arab lead-
ership rejected the plan, the Zionist Congress accepted it with quali-
fications—against the wish of a substantial minority. The British
government which had initially favored partition eventually rejected it
in November 1938. (See page 43.)

. . . To foster Jewish immigration in the hope that it might ultimately
lead to the creation of a Jewish majority and the establishment of a Jewish
State with the consent or at least the acquiescence of the Arabs was one
thing. It was quite another to contemplate, however remotely, the forcible
conversion of Palestine into a Jewish State against the will of the Arabs.
For that would clearly violate the spirit and intention of the Mandate System. It would mean that national self-determination had been withheld
when the Arabs were a majority in Palestine and only conceded when the
Jews were a majority. It would mean that the Arabs had been denied the
opportunity of standing by themselves: that they had, in fact, after an interval of conflict, been bartered about from Turkish sovereignty to Jewish
sovereignty. It is true that in the light of history Jewish rule over Palestine
could not be regarded as foreign rule in the same sense as Turkish; but the
international recognition of the right of the Jews to return to their old
homeland did not involve the recognition of the right of the Jews to govern
the Arabs in it against their will. The case stated by Lord Milner against an
Arab control of Palestine applies equally to a Jewish control. . . .

An irrepressible conflict has arisen between two national communities
within the narrow bounds of one small country. About 1,000,000 Arabs are
in strife, open or latent, with some 400,000 Jews. There is no common
ground between them. The Arab community is predominantly Asiatic in
character, the Jewish community predominantly European. They differ in
religion and in language. Their cultural and social life, their ways of
thought and conduct, are as incompatible as their national aspirations.
These last are the greatest bar to peace. Arabs and Jews might possibly
learn to live and work together in Palestine if they would make a genuine
effort to reconcile and combine their national ideals and so build up in time
a joint or dual nationality. But this they cannot do. The War and its sequel
have inspired all Arabs with the hope of reviving in a free and united Arab
world the traditions of the Arab golden age. The Jews similarly are inspired by their historic past. They mean to show what the Jewish nation
can achieve when restored to the land of its birth. National assimilation between Arabs and Jews is thus ruled out. In the Arab picture the Jews could
only occupy the place they occupied in Arab Egypt or Arab Spain. The
Arabs would be as much outside the Jewish picture as the Canaanites in

the old land of Israel. The National Home, as we have said before, cannot be half-national. In these circumstances to maintain that Palestinian citizenship has any moral meaning is a mischievous pretense. Neither Arab nor Jew has any sense of service to a single State. . . .

British Government: Policy Statement Against Partition (November 1938)

. . . .

4. His Majesty's Government, after careful study of the Partition Commission's report, have reached the conclusion that this further examination has shown that the political, administrative and financial difficulties involved in the proposal to create independent Arab and Jewish States inside Palestine are so great that this solution of the problem is impracticable.

5. His Majesty's Government will therefore continue their responsibility for the government of the whole of Palestine. They are now faced with the problem of finding alternative means of meeting the needs of the difficult situation described by the Royal Commission which will be consistent with their obligations to the Arabs and the Jews. His Majesty's Government believe that it is possible to find these alternative means. They have already given much thought to the problem in the light of the reports of the Royal Commission and of the Partition Commission. It is clear that the surest foundation for peace and progress in Palestine would be an understanding between the Arabs and the Jews, and His Majesty's Government are prepared in the first instance to make a determined effort to promote such an understanding. With this end in view, they propose immediately to invite representatives of the Palestinian Arabs and of neighbouring States on the one hand and of the Jewish Agency on the other, to confer with them as soon as possible in London regarding future policy, including the question of immigration into Palestine. As regards the representation of the Palestinian Arabs, His Majesty's Government must reserve the right to refuse to receive those leaders whom they regard as responsible for the campaign of assassination and violence.

6. His Majesty's Government hope that these discussions in London may help to promote agreement as to future policy regarding Palestine. They attach great importance, however, to a decision being reached at an early date. Therefore, if the London discussions should not produce agreement within a reasonable period of time, they will take their own decision in the light of their examination of the problem and of the discussions in London, and announce the policy which they propose to pursue.

7. In considering and settling their policy His Majesty's Government will keep constantly in mind the international character of the Mandate with which they have been entrusted and their obligations in that respect.

British Government:
The White Paper (May 17, 1939)

*After the failure of the partition scheme and a subsequent attempt
to work out an agreed solution at a Conference in London (February–March 1939), the British government announced its new policy in
a White Paper published on May 17, 1939. The Arab demands were
largely met: Jewish immigration was to continue at a maximum rate of
15,000 for another five years. After that it was to cease altogether unless the Arabs would accept it. Purchase of land by Jews would be prohibited in some areas, restricted in others. Jewish reaction was bitterly
hostile (see page 49), but the Arab leaders also rejected the White Paper: according to their demands, Palestine was to become an Arab
state immediately, no more Jewish immigrants were to enter the country, and the status of every Jew who had immigrated since 1918 was to
be reviewed.*

. . . .

2. The Mandate for Palestine, the terms of which were confirmed by the
Council of the League of Nations in 1922, has governed the policy of successive British Governments for nearly 20 years. It embodies the Balfour
Declaration and imposes on the Mandatory four main obligations. These
obligations are set out in Article 2, 6 and 13 of the Mandate. There is no
dispute regarding the interpretation of one of these obligations, that touch-
ing the protection of and access to the Holy Places and religious building
or sites. The other three main obligations are generally as follows:

(i) To place the country under such political, administrative and economic conditions as will secure the establishment in Palestine of a national
home for the Jewish people, to facilitate Jewish immigration under suitable
conditions, and to encourage, in co-operation with the Jewish Agency,
close settlement by Jews on the land.

(ii) To safeguard the civil and religious rights of all the inhabitants of
Palestine irrespective of race and religion, and, whilst facilitating Jewish
immigration and settlement, to ensure that the rights and position of other
sections of the population are not prejudiced.

(iii) To place the country under such political, administrative and economic conditions as will secure the development of self-governing institutions.

3. . . . but the establishment of self-supporting independent Arab and
Jewish States within Palestine has been found to be impracticable. It has
therefore been necessary for His Majesty's Government to devise an alternative policy which will, consistently with their obligations to Arabs and

Jews, meet the needs of the situation in Palestine. Their views and proposals are set forth below under the three heads, (I) The Constitution, (II) Immigration, and (III) Land.

I. THE CONSTITUTION

4. It has been urged that the expression "a national home for the Jewish people" offered a prospect that Palestine might in due course become a Jewish State or Commonwealth. . . . But, with the Royal Commission, His Majesty's Government believe that the framers of the Mandate in which the Balfour Declaration was embodied could not have intended that Palestine should be converted into a Jewish State against the will of the Arab population of the country. . . .

His Majesty's Government therefore now declare unequivocally that it is not part of their policy that Palestine should become a Jewish State. They would indeed regard it as contrary to their obligations to the Arabs under the Mandate, as well as to the assurances which have been given to the Arab people in the past, that the Arab population of Palestine should be made the subjects of a Jewish State against their will. . . .

7. In the recent discussions the Arab delegations have repeated the contention that Palestine was included within the area in which Sir Henry McMahon, on behalf of the British Government, in October 1915, undertook to recognise and support Arab independence. . . . His Majesty's Government . . . can only adhere . . . to the view that the whole of Palestine west of Jordan was excluded from Sir Henry McMahon's pledge, and they therefore cannot agree that the McMahon correspondence forms a just basis for the claim that Palestine should be converted into an Arab State.

8. His Majesty's Government are charged as the Mandatory authority "to secure the development of self-governing institutions" in Palestine. Apart from this specific obligation, they would regard it as contrary to the whole spirit of the Mandate system that the population of Palestine should remain forever under Mandatory tutelage. It is proper that the people of the country should as early as possible enjoy the rights of self-government which are exercised by the people of neighbouring countries. His Majesty's Government are unable at present to foresee the exact constitutional forms which government in Palestine will eventually take, but their objective is self-government, and they desire to see established ultimately an independent Palestine State. It should be a State in which the two peoples in Palestine, Arabs and Jews, share authority in government in such a way that the essential interests of each are secured.

9. The establishment of an independent State and the complete relinquishment of Mandatory control in Palestine would require such relations between the Arabs and the Jews as would make good government possible. Moreover, the growth of self-governing institutions in Palestine, as in other

countries, must be an evolutionary process. A transitional period will be required before independence is achieved, throughout which ultimate responsibility for the Government of the country will be retained by His Majesty's Government as the Mandatory authority, while the people of the country are taking an increasing share in the Government, and understanding and co-operation amongst them are growing. It will be the constant endeavour of His Majesty's Government to promote good relations between the Arabs and the Jews.

10. In the light of these considerations His Majesty's Government make the following declaration of their intentions regarding the future government of Palestine:

(1) The objective of His Majesty's Government is the establishment within ten years of an independent Palestine State in such treaty relations with the United Kingdom as will provide satisfactorily for the commercial and strategic requirements of both countries in the future. The proposal for the establishment of the independent State would involve consultation with the Council of the League of Nations with a view to the termination of the Mandate.

(2) The independent State should be one in which Arabs and Jews share in government in such a way as to ensure that the essential interests of each community are safeguarded.

(3) The establishment of the independent State will be preceded by a transitional period throughout which His Majesty's Government will retain responsibility for the government of the country. During the transitional period the people of Palestine will be given an increasing part in the government of their country. Both sections of the population will have an opportunity to participate in the machinery of government, and the process will be carried on whether or not they both avail themselves of it.

(4) As soon as peace and order have been sufficiently restored in Palestine steps will be taken to carry out this policy of giving the people of Palestine as increasing part in the government of their country, the objective being to place Palestinians in charge of all the Departments of Government, with the assistance of British advisers and subject to the control of the High Commissioner. With this object in view His Majesty's Government will be prepared immediately to arrange that Palestinians shall be placed in charge of certain Departments, with British advisers. The Palestinian heads of Departments will sit on the Executive Council which advises the High Commissioner. Arab and Jewish representatives will be invited to serve as heads of Departments approximately in proportion to their respective populations. The number of Palestinians in charge of Departments will be increased as circumstances permit until all heads of Departments are Palestinians, exercising the administrative and advisory functions which are at present performed by British officials. When

that stage is reached consideration will be given to the question of converting the Executive Council into a Council of Ministers with a consequential change in the status and functions of the Palestinian heads of Departments.

(5) His Majesty's Government make no proposals at this stage regarding the establishment of an elective legislature. Nevertheless they would regard this as an appropriate constitutional development, and, should public opinion in Palestine hereafter show itself in favour of such a development, they will be prepared, provided that local conditions permit, to establish the necessary machinery.

(6) At the end of five years from the restoration of peace and order, an appropriate body representative of the people of Palestine and of His Majesty's Government will be set up to review the working of the constitutional arrangements during the transitional period and to consider and make recommendations regarding the constitution of the independent Palestine State.

(7) His Majesty's Government will require to be satisfied that in the treaty contemplated by sub-paragraph (1) or in the constitution contemplated by sub-paragraph (6) adequate provision has been made for:

(*a*) the security of, and freedom of access to, the Holy Places, and the protection of the interests and property of the various religious bodies.

(*b*) the protection of the different communities in Palestine in accordance with the obligations of His Majesty's Government to both Arabs and Jews and for the special position in Palestine of the Jewish National Home.

(*c*) such requirements to meet the strategic situation as may be regarded as necessary by His Majesty's Government in the light of the circumstances then existing.

His Majesty's Government will also require to be satisfied that the interest of certain foreign countries in Palestine, for the preservation of which they are at present responsible, are adequately safeguarded.

(8) His Majesty's Government will do everything in their power to create conditions which will enable the independent Palestine State to come into being within ten years. If, at the end of ten years, it appears to His Majesty's Government that, contrary to their hope, circumstances require the postponement of the establishment of the independent State, they will consult with representatives of the people of Palestine, the Council of the League of Nations and the neighbouring Arab States before deciding on such a postponement. If His Majesty's Government come to the conclusion that postponement is unavoidable, they will invite the co-operation of these parties in framing plans for the future with a view to achieving the desired objective at the earliest possible date.

11. During the transitional period steps will be taken to increase the powers and responsibilities of municipal corporations and local councils.

II. IMMIGRATION

. . . If immigration has an adverse effect on the economic position in the country, it should clearly be restricted; and equally, if it has a seriously damaging effect on the political position in the country, that is a factor that should not be ignored. Although it is not difficult to contend that the large number of Jewish immigrants who have been admitted so far have been absorbed economically, the fear of the Arabs that this influx will continue indefinitely until the Jewish population is in a position to dominate them has produced consequences which are extremely grave for Jews and Arabs alike and for the peace and prosperity of Palestine. The lamentable disturbances of the past three years are only the latest and most sustained manifestation of this intense Arab apprehension. The methods employed by Arab terrorists against fellow-Arabs and Jews alike must receive unqualified condemnation. But it cannot be denied that fear of indefinite Jewish immigration is widespread amongst the Arab population and that this fear has made possible disturbances which have given a serious setback to economic progress, depleted the Palestine exchequer, rendered life and property insecure, and produced a bitterness between the Arab and Jewish populations which is deplorable between citizens of the same country. If in these circumstances immigration is continued up to the economic absorptive capacity of the country, regardless of all other considerations, a fatal enmity between the two peoples will be perpetuated, and the situation in Palestine may become a permanent source of friction amongst all peoples in the Near and Middle East. . . .

13. In the view of the Royal Commission the association of the policy of the Balfour Declaration with the Mandate system implied the belief that Arab hostility to the former would sooner or later be overcome. It has been the hope of British Governments ever since the Balfour Declaration was issued that in time the Arab population, recognizing the advantages to be derived from Jewish settlement and development in Palestine, would become reconciled to the further growth of the Jewish National Home. This hope has not been fulfilled. . . .

14. It has been urged that all further Jewish immigration into Palestine should be stopped forthwith. His Majesty's Government cannot accept such a proposal. It would damage the whole of the financial and economic system of Palestine and thus affect adversely the interests of Arabs and Jews alike. Moreover, in the view of His Majesty's Government, abruptly to stop further immigration would be unjust to the Jewish National Home. But, above all, His Majesty's Government are conscious of the present unhappy plight of large numbers of Jews who seek a refuge from certain European countries, and they believe that Palestine can and should make a further contribution to the solution of this pressing world problem. In all these circumstances, they believe that they will be acting consistently with

their Mandatory obligations to both Arabs and Jews, and in the manner best calculated to serve the interests of the whole people of Palestine, by adopting the following proposals regarding immigration:

(1) Jewish immigration during the next five years will be at a rate which, if economic absorptive capacity permits, will bring the Jewish population up to approximately one-third of the total population of the country. Taking into account the expected natural increase of the Arab and Jewish populations, and the number of illegal Jewish immigrants now in the country, this would allow of the admission, as from the beginning of April this year, of some 75,000 immigrants over the next five years. These immigrants would, subject to the criterion of economic absorptive capacity, be admitted as follows:

(*a*) For each of the next five years a quota of 10,000 Jewish immigrants will be allowed on the understanding that a shortage in any one year may be added to the quotas for subsequent years, within the five-year period, if economic absorptive capacity permits.

(*b*) In addition, as a contribution towards the solution of the Jewish refugee problem, 25,000 refugees will be admitted as soon as the High Commissioner is satisfied that adequate provision for their maintenance is ensured, special consideration being given to refugee children and dependants.

(2) The existing machinery for ascertaining economic absorptive capacity will be retained, and the High Commissioner will have the ultimate responsibility for deciding the limits of economic capacity. Before each periodic decision is taken, Jewish and Arab representatives will be consulted.

(3) After the period of five years no further Jewish immigration will be permitted unless the Arabs of Palestine are prepared to acquiesce in it.

(4) His Majesty's Government are determined to check illegal immigration, and further preventive measures are being adopted. The numbers of any Jewish illegal immigrants who, despite these measures, may succeed in coming into the country and cannot be deported will be deducted from the yearly quotas.

15. His Majesty's Government are satisfied that, when the immigration over five years which is now contemplated has taken place, they will not be justified in facilitating, nor will they be under any obligation to facilitate, the further development of the Jewish National Home by immigration regardless of the wishes of the Arab population.

III. LAND

16. The Administration of Palestine is required, under Article 6 of the Mandate, "while ensuring that the rights and position of other sections of the population are not prejudiced," to encourage "close settlement by Jews on the land," and no restriction has been imposed hitherto on the transfer of land from Arabs to Jews. The Reports of several expert Commissions

have indicated that, owing to the natural growth of the Arab population and the steady sale in recent years of Arab land to Jews, there is now in certain areas no room for further transfers of Arab land, whilst in some other areas such transfers of land must be restricted if Arab cultivators are to maintain their existing standard of life and a considerable landless Arab population is not soon to be created. In these circumstances, the High Commissioner will be given general powers to prohibit and regulate transfers of land. These powers will date from the publication of this statement of policy and the High Commissioner will retain them throughout the transitional period . . . .

The Jewish Agency for Palestine: Zionist Reaction to the White Paper (1939)

1. The new policy for Palestine laid down by the Mandatory in the White Paper now issued denies to the Jewish people the right to rebuild their national home in their ancestral country. It transfers the authority over Palestine to the present Arab majority and puts the Jewish population at the mercy of that majority. It decrees the stoppage of Jewish immigration as soon as the Jews form a third of the total population. It puts up a territorial ghetto for Jews in their own homeland.

2. The Jewish people regard this policy as a breach of faith and a surrender to Arab terrorism. It delivers Britain's friends into the hands of those who are biting her and must lead to a complete breach between Jews and Arabs which will banish every prospect of peace in Palestine. It is a policy in which the Jewish people will not acquiesce. The new regime now announced will be devoid of any moral basis and contrary to international law. Such a regime can only be established and maintained by force.

3. The Royal Commission invoked by the White Paper indicated the perils of such a policy, saying it was convinced that an Arab Government would mean the frustration of all their (Jews') efforts and ideals and would convert the national home into one more cramped and dangerous ghetto. It seems only too probable that the Jews would fight rather than submit to Arab rule. And repressing a Jewish rebellion against British policy would be as unpleasant a task as the repression of the Arab rebellion has been. The Government has disregarded this warning.

4. The Jewish people have no quarrel with the Arab people. Jewish work in Palestine has not had an adverse effect upon the life and progress of the Arab people. The Arabs are not landless or homeless as are the Jews. They are not in need of emigration. Jewish colonization has benefited Palestine and all its inhabitants. Insofar as the Balfour Declaration contributed to British victory in the Great War, it contributed also, as was pointed out by the Royal Commission, to the liberation of the Arab peo-

ples. The Jewish people has shown its will to peace even during the years of disturbances. It has not given way to temptation and has not retaliated to Arab violence. But neither have the Jews submitted to terror nor will they submit to it even after the Mandatory has decided to reward the terrorists by surrendering the Jewish National Home.

5. It is in the darkest hour of Jewish history that the British Government proposes to deprive the Jews of their last hope and to close the road back to their Homeland. It is a cruel blow, doubly cruel because it comes from the government of a great nation which has extended a helping hand to the Jews, and whose position must rest on foundations of moral authority and international good faith. This blow will not subdue the Jewish people. The historic bond between the people and the land of Israel cannot be broken. The Jews will never accept the closing to them of the gates of Palestine nor let their national home be converted into a ghetto. The Jewish pioneers who, during the past three generations, have shown their strength in the upbuilding of a derelict country, will from now on display the same strength in defending Jewish immigration, the Jewish home and Jewish freedom.

German Chancellor Adolf Hitler and Grand Mufti Haj Amin al-Husseini: Zionism and the Arab Cause (November 28, 1941)*

Haj Amin al-Husseini, the most influential leader of Palestinian Arabs, lived in Germany during the Second World War. He met Hitler, Ribbentrop and other Nazi leaders on various occasions and attempted to coordinate Nazi and Arab policies in the Middle East.

Record of the Conversation Between the Führer and the Grand Mufti of Jerusalem on November 28, 1941, in the Presence of Reich Foreign Minister and Minister Grobba in Berlin

The Grand Mufti began by thanking the Führer for the great honor he had bestowed by receiving him. He wished to seize the opportunity to convey to the Führer of the Greater German Reich, admired by the entire Arab world, his thanks for the sympathy which he had always shown for the Arab and especially the Palestinian cause, and to which he had given clear

Documents on German Foreign Policy 1918–45, Series D, Vol. XIII, London, 1964, pp. 881 ff.

expression in his public speeches. The Arab countries were firmly convinced that Germany would win the war and that the Arab cause would
then prosper. The Arabs were Germany's natural friends because they had
the same enemies as had Germany, namely the English, the Jews, and the
Communists. They were therefore prepared to cooperate with Germany
with all their hearts and stood ready to participate in the war, not only negatively by the commission of acts of sabotage and the instigation of revolutions, but also positively by the formation of an Arab Legion. The Arabs
could be more useful to Germany as allies than might be apparent at first
glance, both for geographical reasons and because of the suffering inflicted
upon them by the English and the Jews. Furthermore, they had had close
relations with all Moslem nations, of which they could make use in behalf
of the common cause. The Arab Legion would be quite easy to raise. An
appeal by the Mufti to the Arab countries and the prisoners of Arab, Algerian, Tunisian, and Moroccan nationality in Germany would produce a great
number of volunteers eager to fight. Of Germany's victory the Arab world
was firmly convinced, not only because the Reich possessed a large army,
brave soldiers, and military leaders of genius, but also because the Almighty could never award the victory to an unjust cause.

In this struggle, the Arabs were striving for the independence and unity
of Palestine, Syria, and Iraq. They had the fullest confidence in the Führer
and looked to his hand for the balm on their wounds which had been inflicted upon them by the enemies of Germany.

The Mufti then mentioned the letter he had received from Germany,
which stated that Germany was holding no Arab territories and understood
and recognized the aspirations to independence and freedom of the Arabs,
just as she supported the elimination of the Jewish national home.

A public declaration in this sense would be very useful for its propa-
gandistic effect on the Arab peoples at this moment. It would rouse the
Arabs from their momentary lethargy and give them new courage. It would
also ease the Mufti's work of secretly organizing the Arabs against the moment when they could strike. At the same time, he could give the assurance
that the Arabs would in strict discipline patiently wait for the right moment
and only strike upon an order from Berlin.

With regard to the events in Iraq, the Mufti observed that the Arabs in
that country certainly had by no means been incited by Germany to attack
England, but solely had acted in reaction to a direct English assault upon
their honor.

The Turks, he believed, would welcome the establishment of an Arab
government in the neighboring territories because they would prefer
weaker Arab to strong European governments in the neighboring countries,
and, being themselves a nation of 7 million, they had moreover nothing
to fear from the 1,700,000 Arabs inhabiting Syria, Transjordan, Iraq, and
Palestine.

France likewise would have no objections to the unification plan because she had conceded independence to Syria as early as 1936 and had given her approval to the unification of Iraq and Syria under King Faisal as early as 1933.

In these circumstances he was renewing his request that the Führer make a public declaration so that the Arabs would not lose hope, which is so powerful a force in the life of nations. With such hope in their hearts the Arabs, as he had said, were willing to wait. They were not pressing for immediate realization of their aspirations; they could easily wait half a year or a whole year. But if they were not inspired with such a hope by a declaration of this sort, it could be expected that the English would be the gainers from it.

The Führer replied that Germany's fundamental attitude on these questions, as the Mufti himself had already stated, was clear. Germany stood for uncompromising war against the Jews. That naturally included active opposition to the Jewish national home in Palestine, which was nothing other than a center, in the form of a state, for the exercise of destructive influence by Jewish interests. Germany was also aware that the assertion that the Jews were carrying out the function of economic pioneers in Palestine was a lie. The work there was done only by the Arabs, not by the Jews. Germany was resolved, step by step, to ask one European nation after the other to solve its Jewish problem, and at the proper time direct a similar appeal to non-European nations as well.

Germany was at the present time engaged in a life and death struggle with two citadels of Jewish power: Great Britain and Soviet Russia. Theoretically there was a difference between England's capitalism and Soviet Russia's communism; actually, however, the Jews in both countries were pursuing a common goal. This was the decisive struggle; on the political plane, it presented itself in the main as a conflict between Germany and England, but ideologically it was a battle between National Socialism and the Jews. It went without saying that Germany would furnish positive and practical aid to the Arabs involved in the same struggle, because platonic promises were useless in a war for survival or destruction in which the Jews were able to mobilize all of England's power for their ends.

The aid to the Arabs would have to be material aid. Of how little help sympathies alone were in such a battle had been demonstrated plainly by the operation in Iraq, where circumstances had not permitted the rendering of really effective, practical aid. In spite of all the sympathies, German aid had not been sufficient and Iraq was overcome by the power of Britain, that is, the guardian of the Jews.

The Mufti could not but be aware, however, that the outcome of the struggle going on at present would also decide the fate of the Arab world. The Führer therefore had to think and speak coolly and deliberately, as a rational man and primarily as a soldier, as the leader of the German and allied armies. Everything of a nature to help in this titanic battle for the common cause, and thus also for the Arabs, would have to be done. Anything, however, that might contribute to weakening the military situation must be put aside, no matter how unpopular this move might be.

Germany was now engaged in very severe battles to force the gateway to the northern Caucasus region. The difficulties were mainly with regard to maintaining the supply, which was most difficult as a result of the destruction of railroads and highways as well as of the oncoming winter. If at such a moment, the Führer were to raise the problem of Syria in a declaration, those elements in France which were under de Gaulle's influence would receive new strength. They would interpret the Führer's declaration as an intention to break up France's colonial empire and appeal to their fellow countrymen that they should rather make common cause with the English to try to save what still could be saved. A German declaration regarding Syria would in France be understood to refer to the French colonies in general, and that would at the present time create new troubles in western Europe, which means that a portion of the German armed forces would be immobilized in the west and no longer be available for the campaign in the east.

The Führer then made the following statement to the Mufti, enjoining him to lock it in the uttermost depths of his heart:

1. He (the Führer) would carry on the battle to the total destruction of the Judeo-Communist empire in Europe.

2. At some moment which was impossible to set exactly today but which in any event was not distant, the German armies would in the course of this struggle reach the southern exit from Caucasia.

3. As soon as this had happened, the Führer would on his own give the Arab world the assurance that its hour of liberation had arrived. Germany's objective would then be solely the destruction of the Jewish element residing in the Arab sphere under the protection of British power. In that hour the Mufti would be the most authoritative spokesman for the Arab world. It would then be his task to set off the Arab operations which he had secretly prepared. When that time had come, Germany could also be indifferent to French reaction to such a declaration.

Once Germany had forced open the road to Iran and Iraq through Rostov, it would be also the beginning of the end of the British world empire. He (the Führer) hoped that the coming year would make it possible for Germany to thrust open the Caucasian gate to the Middle East. For the good of their common cause, it would be better if the Arab proclamation were put off for a few more months than if Germany were to create difficulties for herself without being able thereby to help the Arabs.

He (the Führer) fully appreciated the eagerness of the Arabs for a public declaration of the sort requested by the Grand Mufti. But he would beg him to consider that he (the Führer) himself was the Chief of State of the German Reich for five long years during which he was unable to make to his own homeland the announcement of its liberation. He had to wait with that until the announcement could be made on the basis of a situation brought about by the force of arms that the Anschluss had been carried out.

The moment that Germany's tank divisions and air squadrons had made their appearance south of the Caucasus, the public appeal requested by the Grand Mufti could go out to the Arab world.

The Grand Mufti replied that it was his view that everything would come to pass just as the Führer had indicated. He was fully reassured and satisfied by the words which he had heard from the Chief of the German State. He asked, however, whether it would not be possible, secretly at least, to enter into an agreement with Germany of the kind he had just outlined for the Führer.

The Führer replied that he had just now given the Grand Mufti precisely that confidential declaration.

The Grand Mufti thanked him for it and stated in conclusion that he was taking his leave from the Führer in full confidence and with reiterated thanks for the interest shown in the Arab cause.

SCHMIDT

The Biltmore Program: Towards a Jewish State (May 11, 1942)

During a visit to the United States by David Ben Gurion, Chairman of the Executive of the Jewish Agency, Zionist policy was reformulated. At a conference at the Biltmore Hotel in New York, in May 1942, the establishment of a Jewish state was envisaged to open the doors of Palestine to Jewish refugees escaping from Nazi terror and to lay the foundations for the establishment of a Jewish majority.

*Declaration Adopted by the Extraordinary
Zionist Conference, Biltmore Hotel,
New York City*

1. American Zionists assembled in this Extraordinary Conference reaffirm their unequivocal devotion to the cause of democratic freedom and international justice to which the people of the United States, allied with the other United Nations, have dedicated themselves, and give expression to

their faith in the ultimate victory of humanity and justice over lawlessness and brute force.

2. This Conference offers a message of hope and encouragement to their fellow Jews in the Ghettos and concentration camps of Hitler-dominated Europe and prays that their hour of liberation may not be far distant.

3. The Conference sends its warmest greetings to the Jewish Agency Executive in Jerusalem, to the Va'ad Leumi, and to the whole Yishuv in Palestine, and expresses its profound admiration for their steadfastness and achievements in the face of peril and great difficulties. The Jewish men and women in field and factory, and the thousands of Jewish soldiers of Palestine in the Near East who have acquitted themselves with honor and distinction in Greece, Ethiopia, Syria, Libya and on other battlefields, have shown themselves worthy of their people and ready to assume the rights and responsibilities of nationhood.

4. In our generation, and in particular in the course of the past twenty years, the Jewish people have awakened and transformed their ancient homeland; from 50,000 at the end of the last war their numbers have increased to more than 500,000. They have made the waste places to bear fruit and the desert to blossom. Their pioneering achievements in agriculture and in industry, embodying new patterns of cooperative endeavor, have written a notable page in the history of colonization.

5. In the new values thus created, their Arab neighbors in Palestine have shared. The Jewish people in its own work of national redemption welcomes the economic, agricultural and national development of the Arab peoples and states. The Conference reaffirms the stand previously adopted at Congresses of the World Zionist Organization, expressing the readiness and the desire of the Jewish people for full cooperation with their Arab neighbors.

6. The Conference calls for the fulfilment of the original purpose of the Balfour Declaration and the Mandate which "*recognizing the historical connection of the Jewish people with Palestine*" was to afford them the opportunity, as stated by President Wilson, to found there a Jewish Commonwealth.

The Conference affirms its unalterable rejection of the White Paper of May 1939 and denies its moral or legal validity. The White Paper seeks to limit, and in fact to nullify Jewish rights to immigration and settlement in Palestine, and, as stated by Mr. Winston Churchill in the House of Commons in May 1939, constitutes "a breach and repudiation of the Balfour Declaration." The policy of the White Paper is cruel and indefensible in its denial of sanctuary to Jews fleeing from Nazi persecution; and at a time when Palestine has become a focal point in the war front of the United Nations and Palestine Jewry must provide all available manpower for farm and factory and camp, it is in direct conflict with the interests of the allied war effort.

7. In the struggle against the forces of aggression and tyranny, of which Jews were the earliest victims, and which now menace the Jewish National Home, recognition must be given to the right of the Jews of Palestine to play their full part in the war effort and in the defense of their country, through a Jewish military force fighting under its own flag and under the high command of the United Nations.

8. The Conference declares that the new world order that will follow victory cannot be established on foundations of peace, justice and equality, unless the problem of Jewish homelessness is finally solved.

The Conference urges that the gates of Palestine be opened; that the Jewish Agency be vested with control of immigration into Palestine and with the necessary authority for upbuilding the country, including the development of its unoccupied and uncultivated lands; and that Palestine be established as a Jewish Commonwealth integrated in the structure of the new democratic world.

Then and only then will the age-old wrong to the Jewish people be righted.

The Arab Office: The Arab Case for Palestine (March 1946)

Evidence submitted to the Anglo-American Committee of Inquiry.

The Problem of Palestine

1. The whole Arab people is unalterably opposed to the attempt to impose Jewish immigration and settlement upon it, and ultimately to establish a Jewish State in Palestine. Its opposition is based primarily upon right. The Arabs of Palestine are descendants of the indigenous inhabitants of the country, who have been in occupation of it since the beginning of history; they cannot agree that it is right to subject an indigenous population against its will to alien immigrants, whose claim is based upon a historical connection which ceased effectively many centuries ago. Moreover they form the majority of the population; as such they cannot submit to a policy of immigration which if pursued for long will turn them from a majority into a minority in an alien state; and they claim the democratic right of a majority to make its own decisions in matters of urgent national concern . . . .

2. In addition to the question of right, the Arabs oppose the claims of political Zionism because of the effects which Zionist settlement has al-

ready had upon their situation and is likely to have to an even greater extent in the future. Negatively, it has diverted the whole course of their national development. Geographically Palestine is part of Syria; its indigenous inhabitants belong to the Syrian branch of the Arab family of nations; all their culture and tradition link them to the other Arab peoples; and until 1917 Palestine formed part of the Ottoman Empire which included also several of the other Arab countries. The presence and claims of the Zionists, and the support given them by certain Western Powers have resulted in Palestine being cut off from the other Arab countries and subjected to a regime, administrative, legal, fiscal and educational, different from that of the sister-countries. Quite apart from the inconvenience to individuals and the dislocation of trade which this separation has caused, it has prevented Palestine participating fully in the general development of the Arab world.

First, while the other Arab countries have attained or are near to the attainment of self-government and full membership of the U.N.O., Palestine is still under Mandate and has taken no step towards self-government; not only are there no representative institutions, but no Palestinian can rise to the higher ranks of the administration. This is inacceptable on grounds of principle, and also because of its evil consequence. It is a hardship to individual Palestinians whose opportunities of responsibility are thus curtailed; and it is demoralizing to the population to live under a government which has no basis in their consent and to which they can feel no attachment or loyalty.

Secondly, while the other Arab countries are working through the Arab League to strengthen their ties and coordinate their policies, Palestine (although her Arab inhabitants are formally represented in the League's Council) cannot participate fully in this movement so long as she has no indigenous government; thus the chasm between the administrative system and the institutions of Palestine and those of the neighbouring countries is growing, and her traditional Arab character is being weakened.

Thirdly, while the other Arab countries have succeeded in or are on the way to achieving a satisfactory definition of their relations with the Western Powers and with the world-community, expressed in their treaties with Great Britain and other Powers and their membership of the United Nations Organization, Palestine has not yet been able to establish any definite status for herself in the world, and her international destiny is still obscure.

3. All these evils are due entirely to the presence of the Zionists and the support given to them by certain of the Powers; there is no doubt that had it not been for that, Arab Palestine would by now be a self-governing member of the U.N.O. and the Arab League. Moreover, in addition to the obstacles which Zionism has thus placed in the way of Palestine's development, the presence of the Zionists gives rise to various positive evils which will increase if Zionist immigration continues.

The entry of incessant waves of immigrants prevents normal economic and social development and causes constant dislocation of the country's life; in so far as it reacts upon prices and values and makes the whole economy dependent upon the constant inflow of capital from abroad it may even in certain circumstances lead to economic disaster. It is bound moreover to arouse continuous political unrest and prevent the establishment of that political stability on which the prosperity and health of the country depend. This unrest is likely to increase in frequency and violence as the Jews come nearer to being the majority and the Arabs a minority.

Even if economic and social equilibrium is re-established, it will be to the detriment of the Arabs. The superior capital resources at the disposal of the Jews, their greater experience of modern economic technique and the existence of a deliberate policy of expansion and domination have already gone far towards giving them the economic mastery of Palestine. The biggest concessionary companies are in their hands; they possess a large proportion of the total cultivable land, and an even larger one of the land in the highest category of fertility; and the land they possess is mostly inalienable to non-Jews. The continuance of land-purchase and immigration, taken together with the refusal of Jews to employ Arabs on their lands or in their enterprises and the great increase in the Arab population, will create a situation in which the Arab population is pushed to the margin of cultivation and a landless proletariat, rural and urban, comes into existence. This evil can be palliated but not cured by attempts at increasing the absorptive capacity or the industrial production of Palestine; the possibility of such improvements is limited, they would take a long time to carry out, and would scarcely do more than keep pace with the rapid growth of the Arab population; moreover in present circumstances they would be used primarily for the benefit of the Jews and thus might increase the disparity between the two communities.

Nor is the evil economic only. Zionism is essentially a political movement, aiming at the creation of a state: immigration, land-purchase and economic expansion are only aspects of a general political strategy. If Zionism succeeds in its aim, the Arabs will become a minority in their own country; a minority which can hope for no more than a minor share in the government, for the state is to be a Jewish state, and which will find itself not only deprived of that international status which the other Arab countries possess but cut off from living contact with the Arab world of which it is an integral part.

It should not be forgotten too that Palestine contains places holy to Moslems and Christians, and neither Arab Moslems nor Arab Christians would willingly see such places subjected to the ultimate control of a Jewish Government.

4. These dangers would be serious enough at any time, but are particularly so in this age, when the first task of the awakening Arab nation is to

come to terms with the West; to define its relationship with the Western Powers and with the westernized world community on a basis of equality and mutual respect, and to adapt what is best in Western civilization to the needs of its own genius. Zionist policy is one of the greatest obstacles to the achievement of this task: both because Zionism represents to the Arabs one side of the Western spirit and because of the support given to it by some of the Western Powers. In fact Zionism has become in Arab eyes a test of Western intentions towards them. So long as the attempt of the Zionists to impose a Jewish state upon the inhabitants of Palestine is supported by some or all of the Western Governments, so long will it be difficult if not impossible for the Arabs to establish a satisfactory relationship with the Western world and its civilization, and they will tend to turn away from the West in political hostility and spiritual isolation; this will be disastrous both for the Arabs themselves and for those Western nations which have dealings with them. . . .

8. In the Arab view, any solution of the problem created by Zionist aspirations must satisfy certain conditions:

(i) It must recognize the right of the indigenous inhabitants of Palestine to continue in occupation of the country and to preserve its traditional character.

(ii) It must recognize that questions like immigration which affect the whole nature and destiny of the country, should be decided in accordance with democratic principles by the will of the population.

(iii) It must accept the principle that the only way by which the will of the population can be expressed is through the establishment of responsible representative government. (The Arabs find something inconsistent in the attitude of Zionists who demand the establishment of a free democratic commonwealth in Palestine and then hasten to add that this should not take place until the Jews are in a majority.)

(iv) This representative Government should be based upon the principle of absolute equality of all citizens irrespective of race and religion.

(v) The form of Government should be such as to make possible the development of a spirit of loyalty and cohesion among all elements of the community, which will override all sectional attachments. In other words it should be a Government which the whole community could regard as their own, which should be rooted in their consent and have a moral claim upon their obedience.

(vi) The settlement should recognize the fact that by geography and history Palestine is inescapably part of the Arab world; that the only alternative to its being part of the Arab world and accepting the implications of its position is complete isolation, which would be disastrous from every point of view; and that whether they like it or not the Jews in Palestine are dependent upon the goodwill of the Arabs.

(vii) The settlement should be such as to make possible a satisfactory definition within the framework of U.N.O. of the relations between Palestine and the Western Powers who possess interests in the country.

(viii) The settlement should take into account that Zionism is essentially a political movement aiming at the creation of a Jewish state and should therefore avoid making any concession which might encourage Zionists in the hope that this aim can be achieved in any circumstances.

9. In accordance with these principles, the Arabs urge the establishment in Palestine of a democratic government representative of all sections of the population on a level of absolute equality; the termination of the Mandate once the Government has been established; and the entry of Palestine into the United Nations Organization as a full member of the working community.

Pending the establishment of a representative Government, all further Jewish immigration should be stopped, in pursuance of the principle that a decision on so important a matter should only be taken with the consent of the inhabitants of the country and that until representative institutions are established there is no way of determining consent. Strict measures should also continue to be taken to check illegal immigration. Once a Palestinian state has come into existence, if any section of the population favours a policy of further immigration it will be able to press its case in accordance with normal democratic procedure; but in this as in other matters the minority must abide by the decision of the majority.

Similarly, all further transfer of land from Arabs to Jews should be prohibited prior to the creation of self-governing institutions. The Land Transfer Regulations should be made more stringent and extended to the whole area of the country, and severer measures be taken to prevent infringement of them. Here again once self-government exists matters concerning land will be decided in the normal democratic manner. . . .

14. The Arabs believe that no other proposals would satisfy the conditions of a just and lasting settlement. In their view there are insuperable objections of principle or of practice to all other suggested solutions of the problem.

(i) The idea of partition and the establishment of a Jewish state in a part of Palestine is inadmissible for the same reasons of principle as the idea of establishing a Jewish state in the whole country. If it is unjust to the Arabs to impose a Jewish state on the whole of Palestine, it is equally unjust to impose it in any part of the country. Moreover, as the Woodhead Commission showed, there are grave practical difficulties in the way of partition; commerce would be strangled, communications dislocated and the public finances upset. It would also be impossible to devise frontiers which did not leave a large Arab minority in the Jewish state. This minority would not willingly accept its subjection to the Zionists, and it would not allow itself to be transferred to the Arab state. Moreover, partition would not satisfy the Zionists. It cannot be too often repeated that Zionism is a political movement aiming at the domination at least of the whole of Palestine; to give it a foothold in part of Palestine would be to encourage it to press for more and to provide it with a base for its activities. Because of this, because of the pressure of population and in order to escape from its isolation it would inevitably be thrown into enmity with the surrounding Arab states and this enmity would disturb the stability of the whole Middle East.

(ii) Another proposal is for the establishment of a bi-national state, based upon political parity, in Palestine and its incorporation into a Syrian or Arab Federation. The Arabs would reject this as denying the majority its normal position and rights. There are also serious practical objections to the idea of a bi-national state, which cannot exist unless there is a strong sense of unity and common interest overriding the differences between the two parties. Moreover, the point made in regard to the previous suggestion may be repeated here: this scheme would in no way satisfy the Zionists, it would simply encourage them to hope for more and improve their chances of obtaining it. . . .

The Anglo-American Committee of Inquiry: Recommendations and Comments (May 1, 1946)

An Anglo-American Inquiry Committee was appointed in November, 1945, to examine the status of the Jews in former Axis-occupied countries and to find out how many were impelled by their conditions to migrate.

The European Problem

Recommendation No. 1: We have to report that such information as we received about countries other than Palestine gave no hope of substantial assistance in finding homes for Jews wishing or impelled to leave Europe.

But Palestine alone cannot meet the emigration needs of the Jewish victims of Nazi and Fascist persecution; the whole world shares responsibility for them and indeed for the resettlement of all "displaced persons."

We therefore recommend that our Governments together, and in association with other countries, should endeavor immediately to find new homes for all such "displaced persons," irrespective of creed or nationality, whose ties with their former communities have been irreparably broken. . . .

Our investigations have led us to believe that a considerable number of Jews will continue to live in most European countries. In our view the mass emigration of all European Jews would be of service neither to the Jews themselves nor to Europe. Every effort should be made to enable the Jews to rebuild their shattered communities, while permitting those

Jews who wish to do so to emigrate. In order to achieve this, restitution of Jewish property should be effected as soon as possible. Our investigations showed us that the Governments chiefly concerned had for the most part already passed legislation to this end. A real obstacle, however, to individual restitution is that the attempt to give effect to this legislation is frequently a cause of active anti-Semitism. We suggest that, for the reconstruction of the Jewish communities, restitution of their corporate property, either through reparations payments or through other means, is of the first importance. . . .

Refugee Immigration into Palestine

Recommendation No. 2: We recommend (a) that 100,000 certificates be authorized immediately for the admission into Palestine of Jews who have been the victims of Nazi and Fascist persecution; (b) that these certificates be awarded as far as possible in 1946 and that actual immigration be pushed forward as rapidly as conditions will permit.

Comment. The number of Jewish survivors of Nazi and Fascist persecution with whom we have to deal far exceeds 100,000: indeed there are more than that number in Germany, Austria and Italy alone. Although nearly a year has passed since their liberation, the majority of those in Germany and Austria are still living in assembly centers, the so-called "camps," island communities in the midst of those at whose hands they suffered so much. . . .

Since the end of hostilities, little has been done to provide for their resettlement elsewhere. Immigration laws and restrictions bar their entry to most countries and much time must pass before such laws and restrictions can be altered and effect given to the alterations. . . .

We know of no country to which the great majority can go in the immediate future other than Palestine. Furthermore, that is where almost all of them want to go. There they are sure that they will receive a welcome denied them elsewhere. There they hope to enjoy peace and rebuild their lives.

We believe it is essential that they should be given an opportunity to do so at the earliest possible time. Furthermore, we have the assurances of the leaders of the Jewish Agency that they will be supported and cared for. . . .

Principles of Government: No Arab, No Jewish State

Recommendation No. 3: In order to dispose, once and for all, of the exclusive claims of Jews and Arabs to Palestine, we regard it as essential that a clear statement of the following principles should be made:

(I) That Jew shall not dominate Arab and Arab shall not dominate Jew in Palestine. (II) That Palestine shall be neither a Jewish state nor an Arab state. (III) That the form of government ultimately to be established, shall, under international guarantees, fully protect and preserve the interests in the Holy Land of Christendom and of the Moslem and Jewish faiths.

Thus Palestine must ultimately become a state which guards the rights and interests of Moslems, Jews and Christians alike and accords to the inhabitants, as a whole, the fullest measure of self-government consistent with the three paramount principles set forth above.

Palestine, then, must be established as a country in which the legitimate national aspirations of both Jews and Arabs can be reconciled without either side fearing the ascendancy of the other. In our view this cannot be done under any form of constitution in which a mere numerical majority is decisive, since it is precisely the struggle for a numerical majority which bedevils Arab-Jewish relations. . . .

Mandate and United Nations Trusteeship

Recommendation No. 4: We have reached the conclusion that the hostility between Jews and Arabs and, in particular, the determination of each to achieve domination, if necessary by violence, make it almost certain that, now and for some time to come, any attempt to establish either an independent Palestinian state or independent Palestinian states would result in civil strife such as might threaten the peace of the world. We therefore recommend that, until this hostility disappears, the Government of Palestine be continued as at present under mandate pending the execution of a trusteeship agreement under the United Nations. . . .

We recognize that, if they are adopted, they will involve a long period of trusteeship, which will mean a very heavy burden for any single Government to undertake, a burden which would be lightened if the difficulties were appreciated and the trustee had the support of other members of the United Nations.

Equality of Standards

Recommendation No. 5: Looking toward a form of ultimate self-government consistent with the three principles laid down in Recommendation No. 3, we recommend that the mandatory or trustee should proclaim the principle that Arab economic, educational and political advancement in Palestine is of equal importance with that of the Jews; and should at once prepare measures designed to bridge the gap which now exists and raise the Arab standard of living to that of the Jews and to bring the two peoples to a full appreciation of their common interest and common destiny in the land where both belong.

Further Immigration Policy

Recommendation No. 6: We recommend that pending the early reference to the United Nations and the execution of a trusteeship agreement, the mandatory should administer Palestine according to the mandate, which declares, with regard to immigration, that "the administration of Palestine, while insuring that the rights and position of other sections of the population are not prejudiced, shall facilitate Jewish immigration under suitable conditions.". . .

The well-being of all the people of Palestine, be they Jews, Arabs or neither, must be the governing consideration. We reject the view that there shall be no further Jewish immigration into Palestine without Arab acquiescence, a view which would result in the Arab dominating the Jew. We also reject the insistent Jewish demand that forced Jewish immigration must proceed apace in order to produce as quickly as possible a Jewish majority and a Jewish State. The well-being of the Jews must not be subordinated to that of the Arabs, nor that of the Arabs to the Jews. The well being of both, the economic situation of Palestine as a whole, the degree of execution of plans for further development, all have to be carefully considered in deciding the number of immigrants for any particular period. . . . The Arabs believe that no other proposals would satisfy the conditions of a just and lasting settlement. In their view there are insuperable objections of principle or of practice to all other suggested solutions of the problem.

UN Special Committee on Palestine: Summary Report (August 31, 1947)

British Foreign Secretary Ernest Bevin announced on February 14, 1947, that His Majesty's Government had decided to refer the Palestine problem to the United Nations. Tension inside Palestine had risen, illegal Jewish immigration continued, and there was growing restiveness in the Arab countries. Palestine, Bevin said, could not be so divided as to create two viable states. Since the Arabs would never agree to it, the Mandate could not be administered in its present form, and Britain was going to ask the United Nations how it could be amended.

The United Nations set up a U.N. Special Committee on Palestine (U.N.S.C.O.P.) composed of representatives of eleven member states. Its report and recommendations were published on August 31, 1947 (below). The Jewish Agency accepted the partition plan as the "indispensable minimum," the Arab governments and the Arab Higher Executive rejected it. On November 29, 1947, the U.N. General Assembly endorsed the partition plan by a vote of thirty-three to thirteen (see page 69). The two-thirds majority included the United States and the Soviet Union but not Britain.

(A) GENERAL RECOMMENDATIONS
OF THE COMMITTEE

The eleven unanimously-adopted resolutions of the Committee were:

That the Mandate should be terminated and Palestine granted independence at the earliest practicable date (recommendations I and II);

That there should be a short transitional period preceding the granting of independence to Palestine during which the authority responsible for administering Palestine should be responsible to the United Nations (recommendations III and IV);

That the sacred character of the Holy Places and the rights of religious communities in Palestine should be preserved and stipulations concerning them inserted in the constitution of any state or states to be created and that a system should be found for settling impartially any disputes involving religious rights (recommendation V);

That the General Assembly should take steps to see that the problem of distressed European Jews should be dealt with as a matter of urgency so as to alleviate their plight and the Palestine problem (recommendation VI);

That the constitution of the new state or states should be fundamentally democratic and should contain guarantees for the respect of human rights and fundamental freedoms and for the protection of minorities (recommendation VII);

That the undertakings contained in the Charter whereby states are to settle their disputes by peaceful means and to refrain from the threat or use of force in international relations in any way inconsistent with the purposes of the United Nations should be incorporated in the constitutional provisions applying to Palestine (recommendation VIII);

That the economic unity of Palestine should be preserved (recommendation IX);

That states whose nationals had enjoyed in Palestine privileges and immunities of foreigners, including those formerly enjoyed by capitulation or usage in the Ottoman Empire, should be invited to renounce any rights pertaining to them (recommendation X);

That the General Assembly should appeal to the peoples of Palestine to cooperate with the United Nations in its efforts to settle the situation there and exert every effort to put an end to acts of violence (recommendation XI);

In addition to these eleven unanimously approved recommendations, the Special Committee, with two members (Uruguay and Guatemala) dissenting, and one member recording no opinion, also approved the following twelfth recommendation:

"*Recommendation XII. The Jewish Problem in General*"

"It is recommended that

"In the appraisal of the Palestine question, it be accepted as incontrovertible that any solution for Palestine cannot be considered as a solution of the Jewish problem in general."

(b) Majority Proposal: Plan of Partition with Economic Union

According to the plan of the majority (the representatives of Canada, Czechoslovakia, Guatemala, Netherlands, Peru, Sweden and Uruguay), Palestine was to be constituted into an Arab State, a Jewish State and the City of Jerusalem. The Arab and the Jewish States would become independent after a transitional period of two years beginning on September 1, 1947. Before their independence could be recognized, however, they must adopt a constitution in line with the pertinent recommendations of the Committee and make to the United Nations a declaration containing certain guarantees, and sign a treaty by which a system of economic collaboration would be established and the economic union of Palestine created.

The plan provided, *inter alia*, that during the transitional period, the United Kingdom would carry on the administration of Palestine under the auspices of the United Nations and on such conditions and under such supervision as the United Kingdom and the United Nations might agree upon. During this period a stated number of Jewish immigrants was to be admitted. Constituent Assemblies were to be elected by the populations of the areas which were to comprise the Arab and Jewish States, respectively, and were to draw up the constitutions of the States.

These constitutions were to provide for the establishment in each State of a legislative body elected by universal suffrage and by secret ballot on the basis of proportional representation and an executive body responsible to the legislature. They would also contain various guarantees, e.g., for the protection of the Holy Places and religious buildings and sites, and for religious and minority rights.

The Constituent Assembly in each State would appoint a provisional government empowered to make the declaration and sign the Treaty of Economic Union, after which the independence of the State would be recognized. The Declaration would contain provisions for the protection of the Holy Places and religious buildings and sites and for religious and minority rights. It would also contain provisions regarding citizenship.

A treaty would be entered into between the two States, which would contain provisions to establish the economic union of Palestine and to provide for other matters of common interest. A Joint Economic Board would be established consisting of representatives of the two States and members appointed by the Economic and Social Council of the United Nations to organize and administer the objectives of the Economic Union.

The City of Jerusalem would be placed, after the transitional period, under the International Trusteeship System by means of a Trusteeship Agreement, which would designate the United Nations as the Administering

Authority. The plan contained recommended boundaries for the city and provisions concerning the governor and the police force.

The plan also proposed boundaries for both the Arab and Jewish States.

(c) Minority Proposal:
Plan of a Federal State

Three U.N.S.C.O.P. members (the representatives of India, Iran and Yugoslavia) proposed an independent federal state. This plan provided, *inter alia*, that an independent federal state of Palestine would be created following a transitional period not exceeding three years, during which responsibility for administering Palestine and preparing it for independence would be entrusted to an authority to be decided by the General Assembly.

The independent federal state would comprise an Arab State and a Jewish State. Jerusalem would be its capital.

During the transitional period a Constituent Assembly would be elected by popular vote and convened by the administering authority on the basis of electoral provisions which would ensure the fullest representation of the population.

The Constituent Assembly would draw up the constitution of the federal state, which was to contain, *inter alia*, the following provisions:

The federal state would comprise a federal government and governments of the Arab and Jewish States, respectively.

Full authority would be vested in the federal government with regard to national defence, foreign relations, immigration, currency, taxation for federal purposes, foreign and inter-state waterways, transport and communications, copyrights and patents.

The Arab and Jewish States would enjoy full powers of local self-government and would have authority over education, taxation for local purposes, the right of residence, commercial licenses, land permits, grazing rights, inter-state migration, settlement, police, punishment of crime, social institutions and services, public housing, public health, local roads, agriculture and local industries.

The organs of government would include a head of state, an executive body, a representative federal legislative body composed of two chambers, and a federal court. The executive would be responsible to the legislative body.

Election to one chamber of the federal legislative body would be on the basis of proportional representation of the population as a whole, and to the other on the basis of equal representation of the Arab and Jewish citizens of Palestine. Legislation would be enacted when approved by majority votes in both chambers; in the event of disagreement between the two chambers, the issue would be submitted to an arbitral body of five members including not less than two Arabs and two Jews.

The federal court would be the final court of appeal regarding constitutional matters. Its members who would include not less than four Arabs and three Jews, would be elected by both chambers of the federal legislative body.

The constitution was to guarantee equal rights for all minorities and fundamental human rights and freedoms. It would guarantee, *inter alia*, free access to the Holy Places and protect religious interests.

The constitution would provide for an undertaking to settle international disputes by peaceful means.

There would be a single Palestinian nationality and citizenship.

The constitution would provide for equitable participation of representatives of both communities in delegations to international conferences.

A permanent international body was to be set up for the supervision and protection of the Holy Places, to be composed of three representatives designated by the United Nations and one representative of each of the recognized faiths having an interest in the matter, as might be determined by the United Nations.

For a period of three years from the beginning of the transitional period Jewish immigration would be permitted into the Jewish State in such numbers as not to exceed its absorptive capacity, and having due regard for the rights of the existing population within the State and their anticipated natural rate of increase. An international commission, composed of three Arab, three Jewish and three United Nations representatives, would be appointed to estimate the absorptive capacity of the Jewish State. The commission would cease to exist at the end of the three-year period mentioned above.

The minority plan also laid down the boundaries of the proposed Arab and Jewish areas of the federal state.

UN General Assembly: Resolution on the Future Government of Palestine (Partition Resolution) (November 29, 1947)

The General Assembly,

Having met in special session at the request of the mandatory Power to constitute and instruct a special committee to prepare for the consideration of the question of the future government of Palestine at the second regular session;

Having constituted a Special Committee and instructed it to investigate all questions and issues relevant to the problem of Palestine, and to prepare proposals for the solution of the problem, and

Having received and examined the report of the Special Committee (document A/364) including a number of unanimous recommendations and a plan of partition with economic union approved by the majority of the Special Committee,

Considers that the present situation in Palestine is one which is likely to impair the general welfare and friendly relations among nations;

Takes note of the declaration by the mandatory Power that it plans to complete its evacuation of Palestine by 1 August 1948;

Recommends to the United Kingdom, as the mandatory Power for Palestine, and to all other Members of the United Nations the adoption and implementation, with regard to the future government of Palestine, of the Plan of Partition with Economic Union set out below;

Requests that

(a) The Security Council take the necessary measures as provided for in the plan for its implementation;

(b) The Security Council consider, if circumstances during the transitional period require such consideration, whether the situation in Palestine constitutes a threat to the peace. If it decides that such a threat exists, and in order to maintain international peace and security, the Security Council should supplement the authorization of the General Assembly by taking measures, under Articles 39 and 41 of the Charter, to empower the United Nations Commission, as provided in this resolution, to exercise in Palestine the functions which are assigned to it by this resolution;

(c) The Security Council determine as a threat to the peace, breach of the peace or act of aggression, in accordance with Article 39 of the Charter, any attempt to alter by force the settlement envisaged by this resolution;

(d) The Trusteeship Council be informed of the responsibilities envisaged for it in this plan;

Calls upon the inhabitants of Palestine to take such steps as may be necessary on their part to put this plan into effect;

Appeals to all Governments and all peoples to refrain from taking any action which might hamper or delay the carrying out of these recommendations, and

Authorizes the Secretary-General to reimburse travel and subsistence expenses of the members of the commission referred to in Part I, Section B, paragraph 1 below, on such basis and in such form as he may determine most appropriate in the circumstances, and to provide the Commission with the necessary staff to assist in carrying out the functions assigned to the Commission by the General Assembly.

Plan of Partition with Economic Union
Part I—Future Constitution and
Government of Palestine

A. Termination of Mandate Partition and Independence

1. The Mandate for Palestine shall terminate as soon as possible but in any case not later than 1 August 1948.

2. The armed forces of the mandatory Power shall be progressively withdrawn from Palestine, the withdrawal to be completed as soon as possible but in any case not later than 1 August 1948.

The mandatory Power shall advise the Commission, as far in advance as possible, of its intention to terminate the Mandate and to evacuate each area.

The mandatory Power shall use its best endeavours to ensure that an area situated in the territory of the Jewish State, including a seaport and hinterland adequate to provide facilities for a substantial immigration, shall be evacuated at the earliest possible date and in any event not later than 1 February 1948.

3. Independent Arab and Jewish States and the Special International Regime for the City of Jerusalem, set forth in part III of this plan, shall come into existence in Palestine two months after the evacuation of the armed forces of the mandatory Power has been completed but in any case not later than 1 October 1948. The boundaries of the Arab State, the Jewish State, and the City of Jerusalem shall be described in parts II and III below.

4. The period between the adoption by the General Assembly of its recommendation on the question of Palestine and the establishment of the independence of the Arab and Jewish States shall be a transitional period.

B. Steps Preparatory to Independence

1. A Commission shall be set up consisting of one representative of each of five Member States. The Members represented on the Commission shall be elected by the General Assembly on as broad a basis, geographically and otherwise, as possible.

2. The administration of Palestine shall, as the mandatory Power withdraws its armed forces, be progressively turned over to the Commission, which shall act in conformity with the recommendations of the General Assembly, under the guidance of the Security Council. The mandatory Power shall to the fullest possible extent co-ordinate its plans for withdrawal with the plans of the Commission to take over and administer areas which have been evacuated.

In the discharge of this administrative responsibility the Commission shall have authority to issue necessary regulations and take other measures as required.

The mandatory Power shall not take any action to prevent, obstruct or delay the implementation by the Commission of the measures recommended by the General Assembly.

3. On its arrival in Palestine the Commission shall proceed to carry out measures for the establishment of the frontiers of the Arab and Jewish States and the City of Jerusalem in accordance with the general lines of the recommendations of the General Assembly on the partition of Palestine. Nevertheless, the boundaries as described in part II of this plan are to be modified in such a way that village areas as a rule will not be divided by state boundaries unless pressing reasons make that necessary.

4. The Commission, after consultation with the democratic parties and other public organizations of the Arab and Jewish States, shall select and establish in each State as rapidly as possible a Provisional Council of Government. The activities of both the Arab and Jewish Provisional Councils of Government shall be carried out under the general direction of the Commission.

If by 1 April 1948 a Provisional Council of Government cannot be selected for either of the States, or, if selected, cannot carry out its functions, the Commission shall communicate that fact to the Security Council for such action with respect to that State as the Security Council may deem proper, and to the Secretary-General for communication to the Members of the United Nations.

5. Subject to the provisions of these recommendations, during the transitional period the Provisional Councils of Government, acting under the Commission, shall have full authority in the areas under their control, including authority over matters of immigration and land regulation.

6. The Provisional Council of Government of each State, acting under the Commission, shall progressively receive from the Commission full responsibility for the administration of that State in the period between the termination of the Mandate and the establishment of the State's indepen-dence.

7. The Commission shall instruct the Provisional Councils of Government of both the Arab and Jewish States, after their formation, to proceed to the establishment of administrative organs of government, central and local.

8. The Provisional Council of Government of each State shall, within the shortest time possible, recruit an armed militia from the residents of that State, sufficient in number to maintain internal order and to prevent frontier clashes.

This armed militia in each State shall, for operational purposes, be under the command of Jewish or Arab officers resident in that State, but general political and military control, including the choice of the militia's High Command, shall be exercised by the Commission.

9. The Provisional Council of Government of each State shall, not later

than two months after the withdrawal of the armed forces of the mandatory Power, hold elections to the Constituent Assembly which shall be conducted on democratic lines.

The election regulations in each State shall be drawn up by the Provisional Council of Government and approved by the Commission.

Qualified voters for each State for this election shall be persons over eighteen years of age who are: (*a*) Palestinian citizens residing in that State and (*b*) Arabs and Jews residing in the State, although not Palestinian citizens, who, before voting, have signed a notice of intention to become citizens of such State.

Arabs and Jews residing in the City of Jerusalem who have signed a notice of intention to become citizens, the Arabs of the Arab State and the Jews of the Jewish State, shall be entitled to vote in the Arab and Jewish States respectively.

Women may vote and be elected to the Constituent Assemblies.

During the transitional period no Jew shall be permitted to establish residence in the area of the proposed Arab State, and no Arab shall be permitted to establish residence in the area of the proposed Jewish State, except by special leave of the Commission.

10. The Constituent Assembly of each State shall draft a democratic constitution for its State and choose a provisional government to succeed the Provisional Council of Government appointed by the Commission. The constitutions of the States shall embody chapters 1 and 2 of the Declaration provided for in section C below and include *inter alia* provisions for:

(*a*) Establishing in each State a legislative body elected by universal suffrage and by secret ballot on the basis of proportional representation, and an executive body responsible to the legislature;

(*b*) Settling all international disputes in which the State may be involved by peaceful means in such a manner that international peace and security, and justice, are not endangered;

(*c*) Accepting the obligation of the State to refrain in its international relations from the threat or use of force against the territorial integrity or political independence of any State, or in any other manner inconsistent with the purposes of the United Nations;

(*d*) Guaranteeing to all persons equal and non-discriminatory rights in civil, political, economic and religious matters and the enjoyment of human rights and fundamental freedoms, including freedom of religion, language, speech and publication, education, assembly and association;

(*e*) Preserving freedom of transit and visit for all residents and citizens of the other State in Palestine and the City of Jerusalem, subject to considerations of national security, provided that each State shall control residence within its borders.

11. The Commission shall appoint a preparatory economic commission of three members to make whatever arrangements are possible for economic

co-operation, with a view to establishing, as soon as practicable, the Economic Union and the Joint Economic Board, as provided in section D below.

12. During the period between the adoption of the recommendations on the question of Palestine by the General Assembly and the termination of the Mandate, the mandatory Power in Palestine shall maintain full responsibility for administration in areas from which it has not withdrawn its armed forces. The Commission shall assist the mandatory Power in the carrying out of these functions. Similarly the mandatory Power shall cooperate with the Commission in the execution of its functions.

13. With a view to ensuring that there shall be continuity in the functioning of administrative services and that, on the withdrawal of the armed forces of the mandatory Power, the whole administration shall be in charge of the Provisional Councils and the Joint Economic Board, respectively, acting under the Commission, there shall be a progressive transfer, from the mandatory Power to the Commission, of responsibility for all the functions of government, including that of maintaining law and order in the areas from which the forces of the mandatory Power have been withdrawn.

14. The Commission shall be guided in its activities by the recommendations of the General Assembly and by such instructions as the Security Council may consider necessary to issue.

The measures taken by the Commission, within the recommendations of the General Assembly, shall become immediately effective unless the Commission has previously received contrary instructions from the Security Council.

The Commission shall render periodic monthly progress reports, or more frequently if desirable, to the Security Council.

15. The Commission shall make its final report to the next regular session of the General Assembly and to the Security Council simultaneously.

C. DECLARATION

A declaration shall be made to the United Nations by the provisional government of each proposed State before independence. It shall contain *inter alia* the following clauses:

General Provision

The stipulations contained in the declaration are recognized as fundamental laws of the State and no law, regulation or official action shall conflict or interfere with these stipulations, nor shall any law, regulation or official action prevail over them.

Chapter 1.—Holy Places, Religious Buildings and Sites

1. Existing rights in respect of Holy Places and religious buildings or sites shall not be denied or impaired.

2. In so far as Holy Places are concerned, the liberty of access, visit and transit shall be guaranteed, in conformity with existing rights, to all residents and citizens of the other State and of the City of Jerusalem, as well as to aliens, without distinction as to nationality, subject to requirements of national security, public order and decorum.

Similarly, freedom of worship shall be guaranteed in conformity with existing rights, subject to the maintenance of public order and decorum.

3. Holy Places and religious buildings or sites shall be preserved. No act shall be permitted which may in any way impair their sacred character. If at any time it appears to the Government that any particular Holy Place, religious building or site is in need of urgent repair, the Government may call upon the community or communities concerned to carry out such repair. The Government may carry it out itself at the expense of the community or communities concerned if no action is taken within a reasonable time.

4. No taxation shall be levied in respect of any Holy Place, religious building or site which was exempt from taxation on the date of the creation of the State.

No change in the incidence of such taxation shall be made which would either discriminate between the owners or occupiers of Holy Places, religious buildings or sites, or would place such owners or occupiers in a position less favourable in relation to the general incidence of taxation than existed at the time of the adoption of the Assembly's recommendation.

5. The Governor of the City of Jerusalem shall have the right to determine whether the provisions of the Constitution of the State in relation to Holy Places, religious buildings and sites within the borders of the State and the religious rights appertaining thereto, are being properly applied and respected, and to make decisions on the basis of existing rights in cases of disputes which may arise between the different religious communities or the rites of a religious community with respect to such places, buildings and sites. He shall receive full cooperation and such privileges and immunities as are necessary for the exercise of his functions in the State.

Chapter 2.—Religious and Minority Rights

1. Freedom of conscience and the free exercise of all forms of worship, subject only to the maintenance of public order and morals, shall be ensured to all.

2. No discrimination of any kind shall be made between the inhabitants on the ground of race, religion, language or sex.

3. All persons within the jurisdiction of the State shall be entitled to equal protection of the laws.

4. The family law and personal status of the various minorities and their religious interests, including endowments, shall be respected.

5. Except as may be required for the maintenance of public order and good government, no measure shall be taken to obstruct or interfere with the enterprise of religious or charitable bodies of all faiths or to discriminate against any representative or member of these bodies on the ground of his religion or nationality.

6. The State shall ensure adequate primary and secondary education for the Arab and Jewish minority, respectively, in its own language and its cultural traditions.

The right of each community to maintain its own schools for the education of its own members in its own language, while conforming to such educational requirements of a general nature as the State may impose, shall not be denied or impaired. Foreign educational establishments shall continue their activity on the basis of their existing rights.

7. No restriction shall be imposed on the free use by any citizen of the State of any language in private intercourse, in commerce, in religion, in the Press or in publications of any kind, or at public meetings.

8. No expropriation of land owned by an Arab in the Jewish State (by a Jew in the Arab State) shall be allowed except for public purposes. In all cases of expropriation full compensation as fixed by the Supreme Court shall be paid previous to dispossession.

Chapter 3.—Citizenship, International Conventions and Financial Obligations

1. *Citizenship.* Palestinian citizens residing in Palestine outside the City of Jerusalem, as well as Arabs and Jews who, not holding Palestinian citizenship, reside in Palestine outside the City of Jerusalem shall, upon the recognition of independence, become citizens of the State in which they are resident and enjoy full civil and political rights. Persons over the age of eighteen years may opt, within one year from the date of recognition of independence of the State in which they reside, for citizenship of the other State, providing that no Arab residing in the area of the proposed Arab State shall have the right to opt for citizenship in the proposed Jewish State and no Jews residing in the proposed Jewish State shall have the right to opt for citizenship in the proposed Arab State. The exercise of this right of option will be taken to include the wives and children under eighteen years of age of persons so opting.

Arabs residing in the area of the proposed Jewish State and Jews residing in the area of the proposed Arab State who have signed a notice of intention to opt for citizenship of the other State shall be eligible to vote in the elections to the Constituent Assembly of that State, but not in the elections to the Constituent Assembly of the State in which they reside.

2. *International conventions.* (*a*) The State shall be bound by all the international agreements and conventions, both general and special, to which Palestine has become a party. Subject to any right of denunciation pro-

vided for therein, such agreements and conventions shall be respected by the State throughout the period for which they were concluded.

(*b*) Any dispute about the applicability and continued validity of international conventions or treaties signed or adhered to by the mandatory Power on behalf of Palestine shall be referred to the International Court of Justice in accordance with the provisions of the Statute of the Court.

3. *Financial obligations.* (*a*) The State shall respect and fulfill all financial obligations of whatever nature assumed on behalf of Palestine by the mandatory Power during the exercise of the Mandate and recognized by the State. This provision includes the right of public servants to pensions, compensation or gratuities.

(*b*) These obligations shall be fulfilled through participation in the Joint Economic Board in respect of those obligations applicable to Palestine as a whole, and individually in respect of those applicable to, and fairly apportionable between, the States.

(*c*) A Court of Claims, affiliated with the Joint Economic Board, and composed of one member appointed by the United Nations, one representative of the United Kingdom and one representative of the State concerned, should be established. Any dispute between the United Kingdom and the States respecting claims not recognized by the latter should be referred to that Court.

(*d*) Commercial concessions granted in respect of any part of Palestine prior to the adoption of the resolution by the General Assembly shall continue to be valid according to their terms, unless modified by agreement between the concession-holder and the State.

[Section D has been deleted: "Economic Union and Transit." Part II of the Resolution deals with the borders of the new State; Part III with "Capitulations." Ed.]

1. The following stipulation shall be added to the declaration concerning the Jewish State: "In the Jewish State adequate facilities shall be given to Arabic-speaking citizens for the use of their language, either orally or in writing, in the legislature, before the Courts and in the administration."

2. In the declaration concerning the Arab State, the words "by an Arab in the Jewish State" should be replaced by the words "by a Jew in the Arab State."

Part II

From Israel's Independence Through the 1973 War's Aftermath

State of Israel: Proclamation of Independence (May 14, 1948)

The Proclamation of Independence was published by the Provisional State Council in Tel Aviv on May 14, 1948. The Provisional State Council was the forerunner of the Knesset, the Israeli parliament. The British Mandate was terminated the following day and regular armed forces of Transjordan, Egypt, Syria and other Arab countries entered Palestine.

The Land of Israel was the birthplace of the Jewish people. Here their spiritual, religious and national identity was formed. Here they achieved independence and created a culture of national and universal significance. Here they wrote and gave the Bible to the world.

Exiled from the Land of Israel the Jewish people remained faithful to it in all the countries of their dispersion, never ceasing to pray and hope for their return and the restoration of their national freedom.

Impelled by this historic association, Jews strove throughout the centuries to go back to the land of their fathers and regain their statehood. In recent decades they returned in their masses. They reclaimed the wilderness, revived their language, built cities and villages, and established a vigorous and ever-growing community, with its own economic and cultural life. They sought peace, yet were prepared to defend themselves. They brought the blessings of progress to all inhabitants of the country and looked forward to sovereign independence.

In the year 1897 the First Zionist Congress, inspired by Theodor Herzl's vision of the Jewish State, proclaimed the right of the Jewish people to national revival in their own country.

This right was acknowledged by the Balfour Declaration of November 2, 1917, and re-affirmed by the Mandate of the League of Nations, which gave explicit international recognition to the historic connection of the Jewish people with Palestine and their right to reconstitute their National Home.

The recent holocaust, which engulfed millions of Jews in Europe, proved anew the need to solve the problem of the homelessness and lack of independence of the Jewish people by means of the re-establishment of the Jewish State, which would open the gates to all Jews and endow the Jewish people with equality of status among the family of nations.

The survivors of the disastrous slaughter in Europe, and also Jews from other lands, have not desisted from their efforts to reach Eretz-Yisrael, in face of difficulties, obstacles and perils; and have not ceased to urge their right to a life of dignity, freedom and honest toil in their ancestral land.

In the second World War the Jewish people in Palestine made their full contribution to the struggle of the freedom-loving nations against the Nazi evil. The sacrifices of their soldiers and their war effort gained them the right to rank with the nations which founded the United Nations.

On November 29, 1947, the General Assembly of the United Nations adopted a Resolution requiring the establishment of a Jewish State in Palestine. The General Assembly called upon the inhabitants of the country to take all the necessary steps on their part to put the plan into effect. This recognition by the United Nations of the right of the Jewish people to establish their independent State is unassailable.

It is the natural right of the Jewish people to lead, as do all other nations, an independent existence in its sovereign State.

ACCORDINGLY WE, the members of the National Council, representing the Jewish people in Palestine and the World Zionist Movement, are met together in solemn assembly today, the day of termination of the British Mandate for Palestine; and by virtue of the natural and historic right of the Jewish people and of the Resolution of the General Assembly of the United Nations.

WE HEREBY PROCLAIM the establishment of the Jewish State in Palestine, to be called Medinath Yisrael (The State of Israel).

WE HEREBY DECLARE that, as from the termination of the Mandate at midnight, the 14th–15th May, 1948, and pending the setting up of the duly elected bodies of the State in accordance with a Constitution, to be drawn up by the Constituent Assembly not later than the 1st October, 1948, the National Council shall act as the Provisional State Council, and that the National Administration shall constitute the Provisional Government of the Jewish State, which shall be known as Israel.

THE STATE OF ISRAEL will be open to the immigration of Jews from all countries of their dispersion; will promote the development of the country for the benefit of all its inhabitants; will be based on the principles of liberty, justice and peace as conceived by the Prophets of Israel; will uphold the full social and political equality of all its citizens, without distinction of religion, race, or sex; will guarantee freedom of religion, conscience, education and culture; will safeguard the Holy Places of all religions; and will loyally uphold the principles of the United Nations Charter.

THE STATE OF ISRAEL will be ready to co-operate with the organs and representatives of the United Nations in the implementation of the Resolution of the Assembly of November 29, 1947, and will take steps to bring about the Economic Union over the whole of Palestine.

We appeal to the United Nations to assist the Jewish people in the building of its State and to admit Israel into the family of nations.

In the midst of wanton aggression, we yet call upon the Arab inhabitants of the State of Israel to preserve the ways of peace and play their part in the development of the State, on the basis of full and equal citizenship and due representation in all its bodies and institutions—provisional and permanent.

We extend our hand in peace and neighbourliness to all the neighbouring states and their peoples, and invite them to co-operate with the independent Jewish nation for the common good of all. The State of Israel is prepared to make its contribution to the progress of the Middle East as a whole.

Our call goes out to the Jewish people all over the world to rally to our side in the task of immigration and development, and to stand by us in the great struggle for the fulfillment of the dream of generations for the redemption of Israel.

With trust in the Rock of Israel, we set our hand to this Declaration, at this Session of the Provisional State Council, on the soil of the Homeland, in the city of Tel-Aviv. . . .

UN General Assembly: Resolution 194
(December 11, 1948)

The General Assembly,
　Having considered further the situation in Palestine,

1. Expresses its deep appreciation of the progress achieved through the good offices of the late United Nations Mediator in promoting a peaceful adjustment of the future situation of Palestine, for which cause he sacrificed his life; and extends its thanks to the Acting Mediator and his staff for their continued efforts and devotion to duty in Palestine;

2. Establishes a Conciliation Commission consisting of three States Members of the United Nations which shall have the following functions:

(a) To assume, in so far as it considers necessary in existing circumstances, the functions given to the United Nations Mediator on Palestine by the resolution of the General Assembly of 14 May, 1948;

(b) To carry out the specific functions and directives given to it by the present resolution and such additional functions and directives as may be given to it by the General Assembly or by the Security Council;

(c) To undertake, upon the request of the Security Council, any of the functions now assigned to the United Nations Mediator on Palestine or to the United Nations Truce Commission by resolutions of the Security Council; upon such request to the Conciliation Commission by the Security Council with respect to all the remaining functions of the United Nations Mediator on Palestine under Security Council resolutions, the office of the Mediator shall be terminated;

3. Decides that a Committee of the Assembly, consisting of China, France, the Union of Soviet Socialist Republics, the United Kingdom and the United States of America, shall present, before the end of the first part of the present session of the General Assembly, for the approval of the Assembly, a proposal concerning the names of the three States which will constitute the Conciliation Commission;

4. Requests the Commission to begin its functions at once, with a view to the establishment of contact between the parties themselves and the Commission at the earliest possible date;

5. Calls upon the Governments and authorities concerned to extend the scope of the negotiations provided for in the Security Council's resolution of 16 November, 1948, and to seek agreement by negotiations conducted either with the Conciliation Commission or directly with a view to the final settlement of all questions outstanding between them;

6. Instructs the Conciliation Commission to take steps to assist the Government and authorities concerned to achieve a final settlement of all questions outstanding between them;

7. Resolves that the Holy Places—including Nazareth—religious buildings and sites in Palestine should be protected and free access to them assured, in accordance with existing rights and historical practice that arrangements to this end should be under effective United Nations supervision; that the United Nations Conciliation Commission, in presenting to the fourth regular session of the General Assembly its detailed proposal for a permanent international regime for the territory of Jerusalem, should include recommendations concerning the Holy Places in that territory; that with regard to the Holy Places in the rest of Palestine the Commission should call upon the political authorities of the areas concerned to give appropriate formal guarantees as to the protection of the Holy Places and access to them; and that these undertakings should be presented to the General Assembly for approval;

8. Resolves that, in view of its association with three world religions, the Jerusalem area, including the present municipality of Jerusalem plus the surrounding villages and towns, the most Eastern of which shall be Abu Dis; the most Southern, Bethlehem; the most Western, Ein Karim (in-

cluding also the built-up area of Motsa); and the most Northern, Shu'fat, should be accorded special and separate treatment from the rest of Palestine and should be placed under effective United Nations control;

Requests the Security Council to take further steps to ensure the demilitarization of Jerusalem at the earliest possible date;

Instructs the Conciliation Commission to present to the fourth regular session of the General Assembly detailed proposals for a permanent international regime for the Jerusalem area which will provide for the maximum local autonomy for distinctive groups consistent with the special international status of the Jerusalem area;

The Conciliation Commission is authorized to appoint a United Nations representative who shall cooperate with the local authorities with respect to the interim administration of the Jerusalem area;

9. Resolves that, pending agreement on more detailed arrangements among the Governments and authorities concerned, the freest possible access to Jerusalem by road, rail or air should be accorded to all inhabitants of Palestine;

Instructs the Conciliation Commission to report immediately to the Security Council, for appropriate action by that organ, any attempt by any party to impede such access;

10. Instructs the Conciliation Commission to seek arrangements among the Governments and authorities concerned which will facilitate the economic development of the area, including arrangements for access to ports and airfields and the use of transportation and communication facilities;

11. Resolves that the refugees wishing to return to their homes and live at peace with their neighbours should be permitted to do so at the earliest practicable date, and that compensation should be paid for the property of those choosing not to return and for loss of or damage to property which, under principles of international law or in equity, should be made good by the Governments or authorities responsible;

Instructs the Conciliation Commission to facilitate the repatriation, resettlement and economic and social rehabilitation of the refugees and the payment of compensation, and to maintain close relations with the Director of the United Nations Relief for Palestine Refugees and, through him, with the appropriate organs and agencies of the United Nations;

12. Authorizes the Conciliation Commission to appoint such subsidiary bodies and to employ such technical experts, acting under its authority, as it may find necessary for the effective discharge of its functions and responsibilities under the present resolution;

The Conciliation Commission will have its official headquarters at Jerusalem. The authorities responsible for maintaining order in Jerusalem will be responsible for taking all measures necessary to ensure the security of the Commission. The Secretary-General will provide a limited number of guards for the protection of the staff and premises of the Commission;

13. Instructs the Conciliation Commission to render progress reports periodically to the Secretary-General for transmission to the Security Council and to the Members of the United Nations;

14. Calls upon all Governments and authorities concerned to cooperate with the Conciliation Commission and to take all possible steps to assist in the implementation of the present resolution;

15. Requests the Secretary-General to provide the necessary staff and facilities and to make appropriate arrangements to provide the necessary funds required in carrying out the terms of the present resolution.

UN General Assembly: Resolution 303, On the Internationalization of Jerusalem (December 9, 1949)

The General Assembly,

Having regard to its resolution 181 (II) of 29 November 1947 and 194 (III) of 11 December 1948,

Having studied the reports of the United Nations Conciliation Commission for Palestine set up under the latter resolution,

I. DECIDES

In relation to Jerusalem,

Believing that the principles underlying its previous resolutions concerning this matter, and in particular its resolution of 29 November 1947, represent a just and equitable settlement of the question,

1. To restate, therefore, its intention that Jerusalem should be placed under a permanent international regime, which should envisage appropriate guarantees for the protection of the Holy Places, both within and outside Jerusalem and to confirm specifically the following provisions of General Assembly resolution 181 (II):

(1) The City of Jerusalem shall be established as a *corpus separatum* under a special international régime and shall be administered by the United Nations; (2) The Trusteeship Council shall be designated to discharge the responsibilities of the Administering Authority . . . ; and (3) The City of Jerusalem shall include the present municipality of Jerusalem plus the surrounding villages and towns, the most eastern of which shall be Abu Dis; the most southern, Bethlehem; the most western, Ein Karim (including also the built-up area of Motsa); and the most northern, Shu'fat, as indicated on the attached sketch-map; (*map not reproduced: Ed.*)

2. To request for this purpose that the Trusteeship Council at its next session, whether special or regular, complete the preparation of the Statute of Jerusalem, omitting the now inapplicable provisions, such as articles 32

and 39, and, without prejudice to the fundamental principles of the international régime for Jerusalem set forth in General Assembly resolution 181 (II) introducing therein amendments in the direction of its greater democratization, approve the Statute, and proceed immediately with its implementation. The Trusteeship Council shall not allow any actions taken by any interested Government or Governments to divert it from adopting and implementing the Statute of Jerusalem;

II.

Calls upon the States concerned, to make formal undertakings, at an early date and in the light of their obligations as Members of the United Nations, that they will approach these matters with good will, and be guided by the terms of the present resolution.

State of Israel:
Law of Return (July 5, 1950)

1. Every Jew has the right to immigrate to the country.
2. (*a*) Immigration shall be on the basis of immigration visas.
   (*b*) Immigrant visas shall be issued to any Jew expressing a desire to settle in Israel, except if the Minister of Immigration is satisfied that the applicant:
   (i) acts against the Jewish nation; or
   (ii) may threaten the public health or State security.
3. (*a*) A Jew who comes to Israel and after his arrival expresses a desire to settle there may, while in Israel, obtain an immigrant certificate.
   (*b*) The exceptions listed in Article 2 (*b*) shall apply also with respect to the issue of an immigrant certificate, but a person shall not be regarded as a threat to public health as a result of an illness that he contracts after his arrival in Israel.
4. Every Jew who migrated to the country before this law goes into effect, and every Jew who was born in the country either before or after the law is effective enjoys the same status as any person who migrated on the basis of this law.
5. The Minister of Immigration is delegated to enforce this law and he may enact regulations in connection with its implementation and for the issue of immigrant visas and immigrant certificates.

UN Security Council: Resolution 619, Concerning Restrictions on the Passage of Ships Through the Suez Canal (September 1, 1951)

The Security Council,

1. *Recalling* that in its resolution of 11 August 1949 (S/1376) relating to the conclusion of Armistice Agreements between Israel and the neighbouring Arab States, it drew attention to the pledges, in these Agreements "against any further acts of hostility between the Parties";

2. *Recalling* further that in its resolution of 17 November 1950 (S/1907) it reminded the States concerned that the Armistice Agreements to which they were parties contemplated "the return of permanent peace in Palestine," and therefore urged them and the other States in the area to take all such steps as would lead to the settlement of the issues between them;

3. *Noting* the report of the Chief of Staff of the Truce Supervision Organization to the Security Council of 12 June 1951 (S/2194);

4. *Further noting* that the Chief of Staff of the Truce Supervision Organization recalled the statement of the senior Egyptian delegate in Rhodes on 13 January 1949, to the effect that his delegation was "inspired with every spirit of co-operation, conciliation and a sincere desire to restore peace in Palestine," and that the Egyptian Government has not complied with the earnest plea of the Chief of Staff made to the Egyptian delegate on 12 June 1951, that it desist from the present practice of interfering with the passage through the Suez Canal of goods destined for Israel;

5. *Considering* that since the Armistice regime, which has been in existence for nearly two and a half years, is of a permanent character, neither party can reasonably assert that it is actively a belligerent or requires to exercise the right of visit, search, and seizure for any legitimate purpose of self-defence;

6. *Finds* that the maintenance of the practice mentioned in paragraph 4 above is inconsistent with the objectives of a peaceful settlement between the parties and the establishment of a permanent peace in Palestine set forth in the Armistice Agreement;

7. *Finds further* that such practice is an abuse of the exercise of the right of visit, search and seizure;

8. *Further finds* that that practice cannot in the prevailing circumstances be justified on the ground that it is necessary for self-defence;

9. *And further noting* that the restrictions on the passage of goods through the Suez Canal to Israel ports are denying to nations at no time connected with the conflict in Palestine valuable supplies required for their economic reconstruction, and that these restrictions together with sanctions applied by Egypt to certain ships which have visited Israel ports represent

unjustified interference with the rights of nations to navigate the seas and to trade freely with one another, including the Arab States and Israel;

10. *Calls upon* Egypt to terminate the restrictions on the passage of international commercial shipping and goods through the Suez Canal wherever bound and to cease all interference with such shipping beyond that essential to the safety of shipping in the Canal itself and to the observance of international conventions in force.

Egyptian President Gamal Abdel Nasser: On Zionism and Israel (1960–1963)

The following excerpts are from Nasser's "The Philosophy of the Revolution," and speeches on various occasions between 1960 and 1963. Nasser served as an army officer in the Palestine War of 1948. The liberation of Palestine has been one of the chief planks of his political program, but there have been conflicting statements as to whether there was a definitive plan for the liberation. On several occasions, he announced that his army would soon be ready to enter Palestine on "a carpet of blood," on others that the time was not ripe yet.

As far as I am concerned I remember that the first elements of Arab consciousness began to filter into my mind as a student in secondary schools, wherefrom I went out with my fellow schoolboys on strike on December 2nd of every year as a protest against the Balfour Declaration whereby England gave the Jews a national home usurped unjustly from its legal owners.

When I asked myself at that time why I left my school enthusiastically and why I was angry for this land which I never saw I could not find an answer except the echoes of sentiment. Later a form of comprehension of this subject began when I was a cadet in the Military College studying the Palestine campaigns in particular and the history and conditions of this region in general which rendered it, throughout the last century, an easy prey ravaged by the claws of a pack of hungry beasts.

My comprehension began to be clearer as the foundation of its facts stood out when I began to study, as a student in the Staff College, the Palestine campaign and the problems of the Mediterranean in greater detail.

And when the Palestine crisis loomed on the horizon I was firmly convinced that the fighting in Palestine was not fighting on foreign territory. Nor was it inspired by sentiment. It was a duty imposed by self-defense.

Address by President Gamal Abdel Nasser in Aleppo (February 17, 1960)

Yesterday, the elderly Foreign Minister of Israel threatened the U.A.R. and said that Israel would not tolerate the ban on Israeli ships transiting the Suez Canal.

I would like to tell her and her master, Ben Gurion, as well as the Israeli people, that Israeli ships and cargoes will not, under any circumstances, transit the Canal.

Once these cargoes arrive in Port-Said or in any other port in the U.A.R. they become the property of the people of Palestine against whom Zionism and imperialism have conspired.

Eleven years after this tragedy, the people of Palestine have not changed. They, and we, are working for the restoration of their rights in their homeland. The rights of the people of Palestine are Arab rights above all. We feel it is our sacred duty to regain those rights for the people of Palestine.

By this unity which is binding you and the power of Arab unity and Arab nationalism, we can march along the road of freedom and liberation in order to get back the usurped rights of the Palestine Arabs.

Speech by President Gamal Abdel Nasser at a Mass Rally of the Youth Organisations in Damascus (October 18, 1960)

Now for the Palestinian issue. Wherever I have been in this or the Southern Region I hear the strong call for the liberation of this Arab territory of Palestine, and I would like to tell you, Brethren, that all that we are now doing is just a part of the battle for Palestine. Once we are fully emancipated from the shackles of colonialism and the intrigues of colonialist agents, we shall take a further step forward towards the liberation of Palestine.

When we have brought our armed forces to full strength and made our own armaments we will take another step forward towards the liberation of Palestine, and when we have manufactured jet aircraft and tanks we will embark upon the final stage of this liberation.

Address by President Gamal Abdel Nasser on the 11th Anniversary of the Revolution at the Republican Square, Cairo (July 22, 1963)

Work and readiness are the only means to protect the Arab's right in Palestine.

Arab unity is our hope of liberating Palestine and restoring the rights of the people of Palestine.

Arab unity is a sort of preparation, a human and national preparation as well as a preparation with weapons and plans in all fields. It is not enough to deliver speeches declaring that we would liberate Palestine and liberate it just on paper for political consumption. As I said before, we do not have any defined plan for the liberation of Palestine. I mention this because I find it my duty to say it. But we have a plan to be implemented in case of any Israeli aggression against us or against any Arab country.

In this case, we know well what to do. We have to be prepared. We have a plan for this preparation and for the unification of the Arab world which is the only means to protect the Arab land and safeguard Arab Nationalism.

God be with you and may his peace and mercy be upon you.

Speech Delivered by President Gamal Abdel Nasser at Alexandria on the Return of Another Contingent of U.A.R. Troops in Yemen (August 11, 1963)

The Armed Forces are getting ready for the restoration of the rights of the Palestine people because the Palestine battle was a smear on the entire Arab nation. No one can forget the shame brought by the battle of 1948. The rights of the Palestine people must be restored. Therefore, we must get ready to face Israel and Zionism as well as Imperialism which stands behind them.

United Arab Republic: Manifesto (April 1963)

The manifesto concerning the principles to govern the new Federal State of the United Arab Republic was published in April 1963. It was prepared in connection with an abortive attempt to establish federal union in the Arab world. Signed by Gamal Abdel Nasser and the presidents of Iraq and Syria, it is of interest mainly in view of the reference to Palestine.

In the name of the Merciful Compassionate God,
In the name of the Almighty God,
The three delegations representing the United Arab Republic, Syria and Iraq met in Cairo and in response to the will of the Arab people in the three regions and the great Arab fatherland, brotherly talks began between the three delegations on Saturday, April 6, and ended on Wednesday, April 17, 1963.

The delegations in all their discussions were inspired by faith that Arab unity was an inevitable aim deriving its principles from the oneness of language bearing culture and thought, common history-making sentiment and conscience, common national struggle deciding and defining destiny, common spiritual values stemming from Divine messages and common social and economic understanding based on liberty and socialism.

The delegations were guided by the will of the masses of the Arab peoples, demanding unity, struggling to attain it and sacrificing in its defence, and realising that the hard core of the union is to be formed by the unification of the parts of the homeland which have acquired their freedom and independence and in which nationalist, progressive governments have emerged with the determination to destroy the alliance of feudalism, capital, reaction and imperialism, and to liberate the working forces of the people in order to join them in alliance and to express their genuine will.

The revolution of July 23 was a historical turning point at which the Arab people in Egypt, discovering their identity and regaining their free will, set out on their quest for freedom, Arabism and union. The revolution of the 14th of Ramadan (February 8) illuminated the true Arab face of Iraq, and the path leading it to the horizons of unity, envisaged by the zealous elements of the July 14 revolution. The revolution of March 8 put Syria back into the line of the union destroyed by the setback of reactionary secession, having destroyed all the obstacles which the reactionaries and imperialism had determinedly put up in the path of union.

The three Revolutions thus met which affirmed again that unity is a revolutionary action deriving its conceptions from the people's faith, its power from their will, and its objectives from their aspirations for freedom and socialism.

Unity is a revolution—a revolution because it is popular, a revolution because it is progressive, and a revolution because it is a powerful tide in the current of civilisation.

Unity is especially a revolution because it is profoundly connected with the Palestine cause and with the national duty to liberate that country. It was the disaster of Palestine that revealed the conspiracy of the reactionary classes and exposed the treacheries of the hired regional parties and their denial of the people's objectives and aspirations. It was the disaster of Palestine that showed the weakness and backwardness of the economic and social systems that prevailed in the country, released the revolutionary energies of our people and awakened the spirit of revolt against imperialism, injustice, poverty and underdevelopment. It was the disaster of Palestine that clearly indicated the path of salvation, the path of unity, freedom and socialism. This was kept in mind by the delegations during their talks. If unity is a sacred objective, it is also the instrument of the popular struggle and its means to achieve its major objectives of freedom and security in liberating all the parts of the Arab homeland and in establishing a society of sufficiency and justice, a society of socialism, in continuing the revolutionary tide without deviation or relapse and its extension to embrace the greater Arab homeland, and in contributing to the progress of human civilisation and consolidation of world peace.

It was unanimously agreed that unity between the three regions would be based, as required by the Arab people, on the principles of democracy and socialism, would be a real and strong unity which would consider the regional circumstances to consolidate the ties of unity on a basis of practical understanding, not ignore the reasons for partitioning and separation, and make the power of each region a power for the Federal State of the Arab Nation, and make the Federal State a power for each of its regions as well as for the whole Arab Nation.

Palestine Liberation Organization: Draft Constitution (1963)

The charter of the Palestine Liberation Organization (PLO) was prepared under Egyptian auspices following an agreement at the Arab Summit Conference in 1963 by Ahmed Shukairy, a lawyer born in Palestine who represented Saudi Arabia and later Syria in the United Nations and ultimately became President of the PLO. The role of the PLO on the eve of the Arab-Israeli war was later criticized in the Arab capitals and Shukairy forced to resign in December 1967.

1. In accordance with this constitution, an organisation known as "The Palestine Liberation Organization" shall be formed, and shall launch its responsibilities in accordance with the principles of the National Charter and clauses of this constitution.

2. All the Palestinians are natural members in the Liberation Organization exercising their duty in the liberation of their homeland in accordance with their abilities and efficiency.

3. The Palestinian people shall form the larger base for this Organization; and the Organization, after its creation, shall work closely and constantly with the Palestine people for the sake of their organization and mobilization so they may be able to assume their responsibility in the liberation of their country.

4. Until suitable conditions are available for holding free general elections among all the Palestinians and in all the countries in which they reside, the Liberation Organization shall be set up in accordance with the rules set in this constitution.

5. Measures listed in this constitution shall be taken for the convocation of a Palestinian General Assembly in which shall be represented all Palestinian factions, emigrants and residents, including organisations, societies, unions, trade unions and representatives of (Palestinian) public opinions of various ideological trends; this assembly shall be called The National Assembly of the Palestine Liberation Organization.

6. In preparation and facilitation of work of the assembly, the Palestin-

ian representative at the Arab League (i.e., Ahmed Shukairy), shall, after holding consultations with various Palestinian factions, form:

a)—A Preparatory Committee in every Arab country hosting a minimum of 10,000 Palestinians; the mission of each one of these committees is to prepare lists according to which Palestinian candidates in the respective Arab country will be chosen as members of the assembly; these committees shall also prepare studies and proposals which may help the assembly carry out its work; these studies and proposals shall be presented to the Coordination Committee listed below.

b)—A Coordination Committee, with headquarters in Jerusalem; the mission of this committee shall be to issue invitations to the assembly, adopt all necessary measures for the holding of the assembly, and coordinate all proposals and studies as well as lists of candidates to the assembly, as specified in the clause above; also the committee shall prepare a provisional agenda—or as a whole, undertake all that is required for the holding and success of the assembly in the execution of its mission.

7. The National Assembly shall be held once every two years; its venue rotates between Jerusalem and Gaza; the National Assembly shall meet for the first time on May 14, 1964, in the city of Jerusalem.

8. To facilitate its work, the Assembly shall form the following committees:

a)—The Political Committee: shall be in charge of studying the political sides of the Palestine question in the Arab and international fields.

b)—The Charter By-laws and Lists Committee: shall consider the National Charter as well as the various by-laws and lists required by the Organization in the execution of its duties.

c)—The Financial Committee: shall formulate a complete plan for the National Palestinian Fund required for financing the Organization.

d)—Information Committee: shall work out a complete scheme for information and offices to be established in various parts of the world.

e)—The Juridical Committee: shall study the various legal aspects of the Palestine question, be it in relation to principles of International Law, U.N. Charter, or international documents pertaining to the Palestine question.

f)—Proposals and Nomination Committee: shall coordinate proposals and nominations submitted to the Assembly.

g)—Awakening Committee: shall study ways and means for the upbringing of the new generations both ideologically and spiritually so they may serve their country and work for the liberation of their homeland.

h)—The National Organization Committee: shall lay down general plans pertaining to trade unions, federations, sports organisations and scouts groups; this is in accordance with rules and laws in effect in Arab countries.

9. The National Assembly shall have a Presidency Office composed of the president, two vice presidents, a secretary, and a secretary general; these officers shall be elected by the National Assembly when it meets.

10. These (above-listed eight committees) shall submit their reports and recommendations to the National Assembly which, in turn, shall discuss them and issue the necessary resolutions.

11. The National Assembly shall have an executive apparatus to be called "The Executive Committee of the Liberation Organisation" which shall practice all responsibilities of the Liberation Organisation in accordance with the general plans and resolutions issued by the National Assembly.

12. The Executive Committee shall be formed of fifteen members elected by the National Assembly; the Committee shall in its turn elect a president, two vice presidents and a secretary general.

13. The Executive Committee can be called to a meeting in the time and place decided by the president, or by a proposal submitted by five members of the Committee.

14. The president of the Executive Committee shall represent the Palestinians at the Arab League; therefore, his office shall be in Cairo since the Arab League Headquarters is there.

15. The Executive Committee shall establish the following departments:

a)—Department of Political and Information Affairs.

b)—Department of the National Fund.

c)—Department of General Affairs.

Each one of these departments shall have a director general and the needed number of employees. Duties of each one of these departments shall be defined by special by-laws prepared by the Executive Committee.

16. The Executive Committee has the right of calling the National Assembly to meet in a place and time it specifies; it has the right also to call to a meeting any committee of the National Assembly to study certain subjects.

17. The Executive Committee shall have a consultative council to be known as "The Shura (Consultative) Council"; the Executive Committee shall select the president and members of this council from people of opinion and prestige among the Palestinians; prerogatives of the Consultative Council are in matters proposed to it by the Executive Committee.

18. The Arab states shall avail the sons of Palestine the opportunity of enlisting in their regular armies on the widest scale possible.

19. Private Palestinian contingents shall be formed in accordance with the military needs and plans decided by the Unified Arab Military Command in agreement and cooperation with the concerned Arab states.

20. A Fund, to be known as "The National Palestinian Fund," shall be established to finance operations of the Executive Committee: the Fund shall have a Board of Directors whose members shall be elected by the National Assembly.

21. Sources of the Fund are to be from:

a)—Fixed taxes levied on Palestinians and collected in accordance with special laws.

b)—Financial assistance offered by the Arab governments and people.

c)—A "Liberation Stamp" to be issued by the Arab states and be used in postal and other transactions.

d)—Donations on national occasions.

e)—Loans and assistance given by the Arabs or by friendly nations.

22. Committees, to be known as "Support Palestine Committees," shall be established in Arab and friendly countries to collect donations and to support the Liberation Organization.

23. The Executive Committee shall have the right to issue by-laws for fulfillment of provisions of this constitution.

24. This draft constitution shall be submitted to the National Assembly for consideration; what is ratified of it cannot be changed except by a two-thirds majority of the National Assembly.

Egyptian President Gamal Abdel Nasser: Speech at UAR Advanced Air Headquarters (May 25, 1967)

The Arab-Israeli conflict again escalated with the Egyptian decision in mid-May 1967 to concentrate troops in Sinai and the announcement that the Straits of Tiran would be closed to Israeli shipping.

. . .We are now face to face with Israel. In recent days Israel has been making aggressive threats and boasting. On 12th May a very impertinent statement was made. Anyone reading this statement must believe that these people are so boastful and deceitful that one simply cannot remain silent. The statement said that the Israeli commanders announced they would carry out military operations against Syria in order to occupy Damascus and overthrow the Syrian Government. On the same day the Israeli Premier, Eshkol, made a very threatening statement against Syria. At the same time the commentaries said that Israel believed that Egypt could not make a move because it was bogged down in Yemen. . . .

On 16th May we requested the withdrawal of the United Nations Emergency Force [UNEF] in a letter from Lt-Gen. Mahmud Fawzi. We requested the complete withdrawal of the UNEF. A major worldwide campaign, led by the United States, Britain and Canada, began opposing the withdrawal of the UNEF from Egypt. Thus we felt that attempts were being made to turn the UNEF into a force serving neo-imperialism. It is obvious that the UNEF entered Egypt with our approval and therefore cannot continue to stay in Egypt except with our approval. Until yesterday a great deal was said about the UNEF. A campaign is also being mounted against the UN Secretary-General because he made a faithful and honest decision and could not surrender to the pressure brought to bear upon him by the United States, Britain and Canada to make the UNEF an instrument for implementing imperialism's plans. . . .

Our forces are now in Sinai and we are fully mobilised both in Gaza and Sinai. We notice that there is a great deal of talk about peace these days. Peace, peace, international peace, international security, UN intervention, and so on and so forth, all appears daily in the press. Why is it that no one spoke about peace, the UN and security when on 12th May the Israeli premier and the Israeli commanders made their statements that they would occupy Damascus, overthrow the Syrian regime, strike vigorously at Syria, and occupy a part of Syria? It was obvious that the press approved of the statements made by the Israeli premier and commanders.

There is talk about peace now. What peace? If there is a true desire for peace we say that we also work for peace. But does peace mean ignoring the rights of the Palestinian people because of the passage of time? Does peace mean that we should concede our rights because of the passage of time? Nowadays they speak about a UN presence in the region for the sake of peace. Does a UN presence in the region for peace mean that we should close our eyes to everything? The UN has adopted a number of resolutions in favour of the Palestinian people. Israel has implemented none of these resolutions. This brought no reaction from the UN.

Today U.S. Senators, members of the House of Representatives, the press and the entire world speak in favour of Israel, of the Jews. But nothing is said in the Arabs' favour. The UN resolutions which favour the Arabs have not been implemented. What does this mean? No one is speaking in the Arabs' favour. How does the UN stand with regard to the Palestinian people? How does it stand with regard to the rights of the Palestinian people? How does it stand with regard to the tragedy which has continued since 1948? Talk of peace is heard only when Israel is in danger. But when Arab rights and the rights of the Palestinian people are lost, no one speaks about peace, rights, or anything like this. . . .

The armed forces' responsibility is now yours. The armed forces yesterday occupied Sharm ash-Shaykh. What does this mean? It is affirmation of our rights and our sovereignty over the Gulf of Aqabah which constitutes Egyptian territorial waters. Under no circumstances will we allow the Israeli flag to pass through the Gulf of Aqabah.

The Jews threaten war. We tell them you are welcome, we are ready for war. Our armed forces and all our people are ready for war, but under no circumstances will we abandon any of our rights. This water is ours. War might be an opportunity for the Jews, for Israel and Rabin, to test their forces against ours and to see that what they wrote about the 1956 battle and the occupation of Sinai was all a lot of nonsense.

With all this there is imperialism, Israel and reaction. Reaction casts doubt on everything and so does the Islamic alliance. We all know that the Islamic alliance is now represented by three states: the Kingdom of Saudi Arabia, the Kingdom of Jordan and Iran. They are saying that the purpose of the Islamic alliance is to reunite the Muslim against Israel. I would like the Islamic alliance to serve the Palestine question in only one way—by preventing the supply of oil to Israel. The oil which now reaches Israel, which reaches Eilat, comes from some of the Islamic alliance states. It goes to Eilat from Iran. Who then is supplying Israel with oil? The Islamic alliance—Iran, an Islamic alliance state. Such is the Islamic alliance. It is an imperialist alliance and this means it sides with Zionism because Zionism is the main ally of imperialism.

The Arab world, which is now mobilised to the highest degree, knows all this. It knows how to deal with the imperialist agents, the allies of Zionism and the fifth column.

They say they want to co-ordinate their plans with us. We cannot coordinate our plans in any way with Islamic alliance members because it would mean giving our plans to the Jews and to Israel. This is a vital battle. When we said that we were ready for the battle we meant that we would surely fight if Syria or any other Arab state was subjected to aggression.

The armed forces are now everywhere. The army and all the forces are now mobilised and so are the people. They are all behind you, praying for you day and night and believing that you are the pride of their nation, of the Arab nation. This is the feeling of the Arab people in Egypt and outside Egypt. We are confident that you will honour the trust. Everyone of us is ready to die and not give away a grain of his country's sand. This for us is the greatest honour. It is the greatest honour for us to defend our country. We are not scared by the imperialist, Zionist or reactionary campaigns. We are independent and we know the taste of freedom. We have built a strong national army and achieved our aims. We are building our country. There is currently a propaganda campaign, a psychological campaign, and a campaign of doubt against us. We leave all this behind us and follow the course of duty and victory. May God be with you.

Egyptian President Gamal Abdel Nasser: Speech to Arab Trade Unionists (May 26, 1967)

For several years, many people have raised doubts about our intentions towards Palestine. But talk is easy and action is difficult, very difficult. We emerged wounded from the 1956 battle. Britain, Israel and France attacked us then. We sustained heavy losses in 1956. Later, union was achieved.

The 1961 secession occurred when we had only just got completely together and had barely begun to stand firmly on our feet. . . .

We were waiting for the day when we would be fully prepared and confident of being able to adopt strong measures if we were to enter the battle with Israel. I say nothing aimlessly. One day two years ago, I stood up to say that we have no plan to liberate Palestine and that revolutionary action is our only course to liberate Palestine. I spoke at the summit conferences. The summit conferences were meant to prepare the Arab states to defend themselves.

Recently we felt we are strong enough, that if we were to enter a battle with Israel, with God's help, we could triumph. On this basis, we decided to take actual steps.

A great deal has been said in the past about the UN Emergency Force (UNEF). Many people blamed us for UNEF's presence. We were not strong enough. Should we have listened to them, or rather built and trained our Army while UNEF still existed? I said once that we could tell UNEF to leave within half an hour. Once we were fully prepared we could ask UNEF to leave. And this is what actually happened.

The same thing happened with regard to Sharm al Shaykh. We were also attacked on this score by some Arabs. Taking Sharm al Shaykh meant confrontation with Israel. Taking such action also meant that we were ready to enter a general war with Israel. It was not a separate operation. Therefore we had to take this fact into consideration when moving to Sharm al Shaykh. The present operation was mounted on this basis.

With regard to military plans, there is complete co-ordination of military action between us and Syria. We will operate as one army fighting a single battle for the sake of a common objective—the objective of the Arab nation.

The problem today is not just Israel, but also those behind it. If Israel embarks on an aggression against Syria or Egypt the battle against Israel will be a general one and not confined to one spot on the Syrian or Egyptian borders. The battle will be a general one and our basic objective will be to destroy Israel. I probably could not have said such things five or even three years ago. If I had said such things and had been unable to carry them out my words would have been empty and worthless.

Today, some 11 years after 1956, I say such things because I am confident. I know what we have here in Egypt and what Syria has. I also know that other states—Iraq, for instance, has sent its troops to Syria; Algeria will send troops; Kuwait also will send troops. They will send armoured and infantry units. This is Arab power. This is the true resurrection of the Arab nation, which at one time was probably in despair. Today people must know the reality of the Arab world. What is Israel? Israel today is the United States. The United States is the chief defender of Israel. As for Britain, I consider it America's lackey. Britain does not have an independent policy. Wilson always follows Johnson's steps and says what he wants him to say. All Western countries take Israel's view. . . .

The Soviet Union's attitude was great and splendid. It supported the Arabs and the Arab nation. It went to the extent of stating that, together with the Arabs and the Arab nation, it would resist any interference or aggression.

Muhammad Hassanain Haykal: An Armed Clash with Israel Is Inevitable—Why? (May 26, 1967)*

. . .The first observation is that I believe an armed clash between the UAR and Israel is inevitable. This armed clash could occur at any moment, at any place along the line of confrontation between the Egyptian forces and the enemy Israeli forces—on land, air or sea along the area extending from Gaza in the North to the Gulf of Aqabah at Sharm ash-Shaykh in the South. But why do I emphasise this in such a manner? There are many reasons, particularly the psychological factor and its effect on the balance of power in the Middle East.

Passage through the Gulf of Aqabah is economically important to Israel at a time when it is suffering the symptoms a man has on waking up after a long, boisterous and drunken party. The fountains of German reparations are drying up. Israel has also drained the sources of contributions and gifts. Although emergency sources will emerge as a result of the present crisis, particularly with the help of Western propaganda trumpets, people in the West, at least many of them, are getting tired of an entity which has been unable to lead a normal life, like a child who does not want to grow up, who cannot depend on himself and does not want to take on any responsibility. Israel is suffering from an economic crisis. There are over 100,000 unemployed, nearly one quarter of Israel's manpower. The new blow had added to the economic plight. Israel attached great importance to its trade with East Africa and Asia. This trade depended on one route: the Red Sea via the Gulf of Aqabah, to Eilat. There were many projects for enlarging the port of Eilat, which at present can handle 400,000 tons a year. In addition, there were the oil lines. Israel has built two pipelines to carry Iranian oil from Eilat to the Haifa oil refinery. Israel has also dreamed of digging a canal from Eilat to Ashdod to compete with or replace the Suez Canal. . . . .

From this aspect there is one answer: Yes. It is in the light of the compelling psychological factor that the needs of security, of survival itself, make acceptance of the challenge of war inevitable.

* Al Ahram, (May 26, 1967)

One thing is clear. The closure of the Gulf of Aqabah to Israeli navigation and the ban on the import of strategic goods, even when carried by
non-Israeli ships, means first and last that the Arab nation represented
by the UAR has succeeded for the first time, *vis-à-vis* Israel, in changing
by force a *fait accompli* imposed on it by force. This is the essence of the
problem, regardless of the complications surrounding it and future contin-
gencies.

As for the complications, we can find in the past ample justification for
Arab resistance. We could say that the British mandate in Palestine had
sold Palestine to Zionism in accordance with a resolution adopted by the
League of Nations. This is true. We could say that the UN betrayed Palestine, and this is true. We could say Arab reaction from the Jordanian King
Abdullah to the Saudi King Faysal connived at the plot against Palestine,
and this is true. We could say about the Gulf of Aqabah that in 1956 imperialism, represented by the British and French forces, imposed a *fait accompli* during this period from autumn 1956 to spring 1967. It was
imperialist not Israeli arms which imposed this *fait accompli*. We could say
all this is seeking to justify Arab resistance. But the naked and rocky truth
which remains after all this is that the accomplished fact was aggressively
imposed by force. The Arabs did not have the force to resist the accomplished fact, let alone to change it by force and to impose a substitute consistent with their rights and interests. . . .

Israel has built its existence, security and future on force. The prevalent
philosophy of its rulers has been that the Arab quakes before the forbid-
ding glance, and that nothing deters him but fear. Thus Israeli intimidation
reached its peak. Provocation went beyond tolerable bounds. But all of
this, from the Israeli point of view, had the psychological aim of convincing the Arabs that Israel could do anything and that the Arabs could do
nothing; that Israel was omnipotent and could impose any accomplished
fact, while the Arabs were weak and had to accept any accomplished fact.
Despite the error and danger in this Israeli philosophy—because two or
even three million Israelis cannot by military force or by myth dominate a
sea of 80 million Arabs—this philosophy remained a conviction deeply
embedded in Israeli thinking, planning and action for many disturbing
years, without any Arab challenge capable of restoring matters to their
proper perspective.

Now this is the first time the Arabs have challenged Israel in an attempt
to change an accomplished fact by force and to replace it by force with an
alternative accomplished fact consistent with their rights and interests. The
opening of the Gulf of Aqabah to Israel was an accomplished fact imposed
by the force of imperialist arms. This week the closure of the Gulf of
Aqabah to Israel was an alternative accomplished fact imposed and now
being protected by the force of Arab arms. To Israel this is the most dangerous aspect of the current situation . . . Therefore it is not a matter of the

Gulf of Aqabah but of something bigger. It is the whole philosophy of Israeli security. It is the philosophy on which Israeli existence has pivoted since its birth and on which it will pivot in the future.

Hence I say that Israel must resort to arms. Therefore I say that an armed clash between UAR and the Israeli enemy is inevitable.

As from now, we must expect the enemy to deal us the first blow in the battle. But as we wait for that first blow, we should try to minimise its effect as much as possible. The second blow will then follow. But this will be the blow we will deliver against the enemy in retaliation and deterrence. It will be the most effective blow we can possibly deal. Why do I say this now? My point of view is as follows: . . .

Israel cannot accept or remain indifferent to what has taken place. In my opinion it simply cannot do so. This means, and that is what I intend to say in the second observation of this inquiry, that the next move is up to Israel. Israel has to reply now. It has to deal a blow. We have to be ready for it, as I said, to minimise its effect as much as possible. Then it will be our turn to deal the second blow, which we will deliver with the utmost possible effectiveness.

In short, Egypt has exercised its power and achieved the objectives of this stage without resorting to arms so far. But Israel has no alternative but to use arms if it wants to exercise power. This means that the logic of the fearful confrontation now taking place between Egypt, which is fortified by the might of the masses of the Arab nation, and Israel, which is fortified by the illusion of American might, dictates that Egypt, after all it has now succeeded in achieving, must wait, even though it has to wait for a blow. This is necessitated also by the sound conduct of the battle, particularly from the international point of view. Let Israel begin. Let our second blow then be ready. Let it be a knockout.

Egyptian President Gamal Abdel Nasser: Speech to National Assembly Members (May 29, 1967)

. . . Brothers, the revolt, upheaval and commotion which we now see taking place in every Arab country are not only because we have returned to the Gulf of Aqabah or rid ourselves of the UNEF, but because we have restored Arab honour and renewed Arab hopes.

Israel used to boast a great deal, and the Western powers, headed by the United States and Britain, used to ignore and even despise us and consider us of no value. But now that the time has come—and I have already said in the past that we will decide the time and place and not allow them to decide—we must be ready for triumph and not for a recurrence of the 1948 comedies. We shall triumph, God willing.

Preparations have already been made. We are now ready to confront Israel. They have claimed many things about the 1956 Suez war, but no one believed them after the secrets of the 1956 collusion were uncovered—that mean collusion in which Israel took part. Now we are ready for the confrontation. We are now ready to deal with the entire Palestine question.

The issue now at hand is not the Gulf of Aqabah, the Straits of Tiran, or the withdrawal of the UNEF, but the rights of the Palestine people. It is the aggression which took place in Palestine in 1948 with the collaboration of Britain and the United States. It is the expulsion of the Arabs from Palestine, the usurpation of their rights, and the plunder of their property. It is the disavowal of all the UN resolutions in favour of the Palestinian people.

The issue today is far more serious than they say. They want to confine the issue to the Straits of Tiran, the UNEF and the right of passage. We demand the full rights of the Palestinian people. We say this out of our belief that Arab rights cannot be squandered because the Arabs throughout the Arab world are demanding these Arab rights.

We are not afraid of the United States and its threats, of Britain and her threats, or of the entire Western world and its partiality to Israel. The United States and Britain are partial to Israel and give no consideration to the Arabs, to the entire Arab nation. Why? Because we have made them believe that we cannot distinguish between friend and foe. We must make them know that we know who our foes are and who our friends are and treat them accordingly.

If the United States and Britain are partial to Israel, we must say that our enemy is not only Israel but also the United States and Britain and treat them as such. If the Western Powers disavow our rights and ridicule and despise us, we Arabs must teach them to respect us and take us seriously. Otherwise all our talk about Palestine, the Palestine people, and Palestinian rights will be null and void and of no consequence. We must treat enemies as enemies and friends as friends.

. . . .

Egyptian President Gamal Abdel Nasser: Resignation Broadcast (June 9, 1967)

Brothers, at times of triumph and tribulation, in the sweet hours and bitter hours, we have become accustomed to sit together to discuss things, to speak frankly of facts, believing that only in this way can we always find the right path however difficult circumstances may be.

We cannot hide from ourselves the fact that we have met with a grave setback in the last few days, but I am confident that we all can and, in a short time, will overcome our difficult situation, although this calls for much patience and wisdom as well as moral courage and ability to work on our part. . . .

Accurate calculations were made of the enemy's strength and showed us that our armed forces, at the level of equipment and training which they had reached, were capable of repelling the enemy and deterring him. We realised that the possibility of an armed clash existed and accepted the risk.

. . . In the morning of last Monday, 5th June, the enemy struck. If we say now it was a stronger blow than we had expected, we must say at the same time, and with complete certainty that it was bigger than the potential at his disposal. It became very clear from the first moment that there were other powers behind the enemy—they came to settle their accounts with the Arab national movement. Indeed, there were surprises worthy of note:

(1) The enemy, whom we were expecting from the east and north, came from the west—a fact which clearly showed that facilities exceeding his own capacity and his calculated strength had been made available to him.

(2) The enemy covered at one go all military and civilian airfields in the UAR. This means that he was relying on some force other than his own normal strength to protect his skies against any retaliatory action from our side. The enemy was also leaving other Arab fronts to be tackled with outside assistance which he had been able to obtain.

(3) There is clear evidence of imperialist collusion with the enemy—an imperialist collusion, trying to benefit from the lesson of the open collusion of 1956, by resorting this time to abject and wicked concealment. Nevertheless, what is now established is that American and British aircraft carriers were off the shores of the enemy helping his war effort. Also, British aircraft raided, in broad daylight, positions on the Syrian and Egyptian fronts, in addition to operations by a number of American aircraft reconnoitering some of our positions. The inevitable result of this was that our land forces, fighting most violent and brave battles in the open desert, found themselves at the difficult time without adequate air cover in face of the decisive superiority of the enemy air forces. Indeed it can be said without emotion or exaggeration, that the enemy was operating with an air force three times stronger than his normal force.

. . . We now have several urgent tasks before us. The first is to remove the traces of this aggression against us and to stand by the Arab nation resolutely and firmly; despite the setback, the Arab nation, with all its potential and resources, is in a position to insist on the removal of the traces of the aggression.

The second task is to learn the lesson of the setback. In this connection there are three vital facts, (1) The elimination of imperialism in the Arab world will leave Israel with its own intrinsic power; yet, whatever the circumstances, however long it may take, the Arab intrinsic power is greater and more effective. (2) Redirecting Arab interests in the service of Arab rights is an essential safeguard: the American Sixth Fleet moved with Arab oil, and there are Arab bases, placed forcibly and against the will of the peoples, in the service of aggression. (3) The situation now demands a united word from the entire Arab nation; this, in the present circumstances, is irreplaceable guarantee.

Now we arrive at an important point in this heartsearching by asking ourselves: does this mean that we do not bear responsibility for the consequences of the setback? I tell you truthfully and despite any factors on which I might have based my attitude during the crisis, that I am ready to bear the whole responsibility. I have taken a decision in which I want you all to help me. I have decided to give up completely and finally every official post and every political role and return to the ranks of the masses and do my duty with them like every other citizen.

The forces of imperialism imagine that Gamal Abdel Nasser is their enemy. I want it to be clear to them that their enemy is the entire Arab nation, not just Gamal Abdel Nasser. The forces hostile to the Arab national movement try to portray this movement as an empire of Abdel Nasser. This is not true, because the aspiration for Arab unity began before Abdel Nasser and will remain after Abdel Nasser. I always used to tell you that the nation remains, and that the individual—whatever his role and however great his contribution to the causes of his homeland is only a tool of the popular will, and not its creator.

In accordance with Article 110 of the Provisional Constitution promulgated in March 1964 I have entrusted my colleague, friend and brother Zakariya Muhiedin with taking over the point of President and carrying out the constitutional provisions on this point. After this decision, I place all I have at his disposal in dealing with the grave situation through which our people are passing. . . .

Israeli Foreign Minister Abba Eban: Speech at the Special Assembly of the United Nations (June 19, 1967)

Our Watchword Is 'Forward to Peace'

. . . In recent weeks the Middle East has passed through a crisis whose shadows darken the world. This crisis has many consequences but only one cause. Israel's rights to peace, security, sovereignty, economic development and maritime freedom—indeed its very right to exist—has been forcibly denied and aggressively attacked. This is the true origin of the tension which torments the Middle East. All the other elements of the conflict are the consequences of this single cause. There has been danger, there is still peril in the Middle East because Israel's existence, sovereignty and vital interests have been and are violently assailed. . . .

The General Assembly is chiefly pre-occupied by the situation against which Israel defended itself on the morning of June 5. I shall invite every peace-loving state represented here to ask itself how it would have acted on that day if it faced similar dangers. But if our discussion is to have any weight or depth, we must understand that great events are not born in a single instant of time. It is beyond all honest doubt that between May 14 and June 5, Arab governments led and directed by President Nasser, methodically prepared and mounted an aggressive assault designed to bring about Israel's immediate and total destruction. My authority for that conviction rests on the statements and actions of Arab governments themselves. There is every reason to believe what they say and to observe what they do. . . .

Israel's Policy, 1957–1967

From 1948 to this very day there has not been one statement by any Arab representative of a neighbouring Arab state indicating readiness to respect existing agreements or the permanent renunciation of force to recognize Israel's sovereign right of existence or to apply to Israel any of the central provisions of the United Nations Charter. . . .

President Nasser seemed for some years to be accumulating inflammable material without an immediate desire to set it alight. He was heavily engaged in domination and conquest elsewhere. His speeches were strong against Israel, but his bullets, guns and poison gases were for the time being used to intimidate other Arab states and to maintain a colonial war against the villagers of the Yemen and the peoples of the Arabian Peninsula.

But Israel's danger was great. The military build-up in Egypt proceeded at an intensive rate. It was designed to enable Egypt to press its war plans against Israel while maintaining its violent adventures elsewhere. In the face of these developments, Israel was forced to devote an increasing part of its resources to self-defence. With the declaration by Syria of the doctrine of a "day by day military confrontation," the situation in the Middle East grew darker. The Palestine Liberation Organization, the Palestine Liberation Army, the Unified Arab Command, the intensified expansion of military forces and equipment in Egypt, Syria, Lebanon, Jordan and more remote parts of the Arab continent—these were the signals of a growing danger to which we sought to alert the mind and conscience of the world.

The War Design, 1967

In three tense weeks between May 14, and June 5, Egypt, Syria and Jordan, assisted and incited by more distant Arab states, embarked on a policy of immediate and total aggression.

The clouds . . . gathered thick and fast. Between May 14 and May 23, Egyptian concentrations in Sinai increased day by day. Israel took corresponding measures. In the absence of an agreement to the contrary it is, of course, legal for any state to place its armies wherever it chooses in its territory. It is equally true that nothing could be more uncongenial to the prospect of peace than to have large armies facing each other across a narrow space, with one of them clearly bent on an early assault. For the purpose of the concentration was not in doubt. . . .

On May 25, Cairo Radio announced:

> The Arab people is firmly resolved to wipe Israel off the map and to restore the honour of the Arabs of Palestine.

On the following day, May 26, Nasser spoke again:

> The Arab people wants to fight. We have been waiting for the right time when we will be completely ready. Recently we have felt that our strength has been sufficient and that if we make battle with Israel we shall be able, with the help of God, to conquer. Sharm e-Sheikh implies a confrontation with Israel. Taking this step makes it imperative that we be ready to undertake a total war with Israel.

. . . . The troop concentrations and blockade were now to be accompanied by encirclement. The noose was to be fitted around the victim's neck. Other Arab states were closing the ring. On May 30 Nasser signed the Defence Agreement with Jordan, and described its purpose in these terms:

> The armies of Egypt, Jordan, Syria and Lebanon are stationed on the borders of Israel in order to face the challenge. Behind them stand the armies of Iraq, Algeria, Kuwait, Sudan and the whole of the Arab nation.
> This deed will astound the world. Today they will know that the Arabs are ready for the fray. The hour of decision has arrived.

. . . . Here we have the vast mass of the Egyptian armies in Sinai with seven infantry and two armoured divisions, the greatest force ever assembled in that Peninsula in all its history. Here we have 40,000 regular Syrian troops poised to strike at the Jordan Valley from advantageous positions in the hills. Here we have the mobilized forces of Jordan, with their artillery and mortars trained on Israel's population centres in Jerusalem and along the vulnerable narrow coastal plain. Troops from Iraq, Kuwait and Algeria converge towards the battle-front at Egypt's behest. Nine hundred tanks face Israel on the Sinai border, while 200 more are poised to strike the isolated town of Eilat at Israel's southern tip. The military dispositions tell their own story. The Northern Negev was to be invaded by armour and bombarded from the Gaza Strip. From May 27 onward, Egyptian air squadrons in Sinai were equipped with operation orders instructing them in detail on the manner in which Israeli airfields, pathetically few in number, were to be bombarded, thus exposing Israel's crowded cities to easy and merciless assault. Egyptian air sorties came in and out of Israel's southern desert to reconnoitre, inspect and prepare for the assault. An illicit blockade had cut Israel off from all her commerce with the eastern half of the world.

Blockade on Tiran Straits

Those who write this story in years to come will give a special place in their narrative to Nasser's blatant decision to close the Straits of Tiran in Israel's face. It is not difficult to understand why this outrage had a drastic impact. In 1957 the maritime nations, within the framework of the United Nations General Assembly, correctly enunciated the doctrine of free and innocent passage to the Straits. When that doctrine was proclaimed—and incidentally, not challenged by the Egyptian Representative at that time—it was little more than an abstract principle for the maritime world. For Israel it was a great but still unfulfilled prospect, it was not yet a reality. But during the ten years in which we and the other states of the maritime community have relied upon that doctrine and upon established usage, the principle had become a reality consecrated by hundreds of sailings under dozens of flags and the establishment of a whole complex of commerce and industry and communication. A new dimension has been added to the map of the world's communication. And on that dimension we have constructed Israel's bridge towards the friendly states of Asia and Africa, a network of relationships which is the chief pride of Israel in the second decade of its independence and on which its economic future depends.

All this, then, had grown up as an effective usage under the United Nations' flag. Does Mr. Nasser really think that he can come upon the scene in ten minutes and cancel the established legal usage and interests of ten years?

There was in his wanton act a quality of malice. For surely the closing of the Straits of Tiran gave no benefit whatever to Egypt except the perverse joy of inflicting injury on others. It was an anarchic act, because it showed a total disregard for the law of nations, the application of which in this specific case had not been challenged for ten years. And it was, in the literal sense, an act of arrogance, because there are other nations in Asia and East Africa that trade with the port of Eilat, as they have every right to do, through the Straits of Tiran and across the Gulf of Akaba. Other sovereign states from Japan to Ethiopia, from Thailand to Uganda, from Cambodia to Madagascar, have a sovereign right to decide for themselves whether they wish or do not wish to trade with Israel. These countries are not colonies of Cairo. They can trade with Israel or not trade with Israel as they wish, and President Nasser is not the policeman of other African and Asian States. . . .

An Act of War

. . . The blockade is by definition an act of war, imposed and enforced through violence

. . . To understand the full depth of pain and shock, it is necessary to grasp the full significance of what Israel's danger meant. A small sovereign State had its existence threatened by lawless violence. The threat to Israel was a menace to the very foundations of the international order. The State thus threatened bore a name which stirred the deepest memories of civilized mankind and the people of the remnant of millions, who, in living memory had been wiped out by a dictatorship more powerful, scarcely more malicious, than Nasser's Egypt. What Nasser had predicted, what he had worked for with undeflecting purpose, had come to pass—the noose was tightly drawn.

On the fateful morning of June 5, when Egyptian forces moved by air and land against Israel's western coast and southern territory, our country's choice was plain. The choice was to live or perish, to defend the national existence or to forfeit it for all time. . . .

Soviet Role in the Middle East Crisis

. . . When the Soviet Union initiates a discussion here, our gaze is inexorably drawn to the story of its role in recent Middle Eastern history. It is a sad and shocking story, it must be frankly told.

. . . Since 1961, the Soviet Union has assisted Egypt in its desire to conquer Israel. The great amount of offensive equipment supplied to the Arab States strengthens this assessment.

A Great Power which professes its devotion to peaceful settlement and the rights of states has for fourteen years afflicted the Middle East with a headlong armaments race, with the paralysis of the United Nations as an instrument of security and against those who defend it.

. . . It is clear from Arab sources that the Soviet Union has played a provocative role in spreading alarmist and incendiary reports of Israel intentions amongst Arab Governments. . . .

U.S.S.R. Attitudes at the United Nations

The U.S.S.R. has exercised her veto right in the Security Council five times. Each time a just and constructive judgment has been frustrated. . . . The Soviet use of veto has had a dual effect. First, it prevented any resolution which an Arab State has opposed, from being adopted by the Council. Secondly, it has inhibited the Security Council from taking constructive action in disputes between an Arab State and Israel because of the certain knowledge that the veto would be applied in what was deemed to be the Arab interest. The consequences of the Soviet veto policy have been to deny Israel any possibility of just and equitable treatment in the Security Council, and to nullify the Council as a constructive factor in the affairs of the Middle East.

. . . Your (the Soviet) Government's record in the stimulation of the arms race, in the paralysis of the Security Council, in the encouragement throughout the Arab World of unfounded suspicion concerning Israel's intentions, your constant refusal to say a single word of criticism at any time of declarations threatening the violent overthrow of Israel's sovereignty and existence—all this gravely undermines your claims to objectivity. You come here in our eyes not as a judge or as a prosecutor, but rather as a legitimate object of international criticism for the part that you have played in the sombre events which have brought our region to a point of explosive tension. . . .

The Vision of Peace

In free negotiation with each of our neighbours we shall offer durable and just solutions redounding to our mutual advantage and honour. The Arab states can no longer be permitted to recognize Israel's existence only for the purpose of plotting its elimination. They have come face to face with us in conflict. Let them now come face to face with us in peace.

Israeli Chief of Staff Yitzhak Rabin: The Right of Israel (June 28, 1967)*

Excellency, President of the State, Mr. Prime Minister, President of the Hebrew University, Rector of the University; Governors, Teachers, Ladies and Gentlemen:

I stand in awe before you, leaders of the generation, here in this venerable and impressive place overlooking Israel's eternal capital and the birthplace of our Nation's earliest history.

*The text of an address by Rabin on the occasion of receiving an honorary doctorate from the Hebrew University.

Together with other distinguished personalities who are no doubt worthy of this honour, you have chosen to do me great honour in conferring upon me the title of Doctor of Philosophy. Permit me to express to you here my feelings on this occasion. I regard myself, at this time, as a representative of the entire Israel Forces, of its thousands of officers and tens of thousands of soldiers who brought the State of Israel its victory in the Six-Day War. It may be asked why the University saw fit to grant the title of Honorary Doctor of Philosophy to a soldier in recognition of his martial activities. What is there in common to military activity and the academic world which represents civilisation and culture? What is there in common between those whose profession is violence and spiritual values? I, however, am honoured that through me you are expressing such deep appreciation to my comrades in arms and to the uniqueness of the Israel Defence Forces, which is no more than extension of the unique spirit of the entire Jewish People.

The world has recognised the fact that the Israel Defence Forces are different from other armies. Although its first task is the military task of ensuring security, the Israel Defence Forces undertakes numerous tasks of peace, tasks not of destruction but of construction and of the strengthening of the Nation's cultural and moral resources.

Our educational work has been praised widely and was given national recognition, when in 1966 it was granted the Israel Prize for Education, The Nahal, which combines military training and agricultural settlement, teachers in border villages contributing to social and cultural enrichment; these are but a few small examples of the Israel Defence Forces' uniqueness in this sphere.

However, today, the University has conferred this honorary title on us in recognition of our Army's superiority of spirit and morals as it was revealed in the heat of war, for we are standing in this place by virtue of battle which though forced upon us was forged into a victory astounding the world.

War is intrinsically harsh and cruel, bloody and tear-stained, but particularly this war, which we have just undergone, brought forth rare and magnificent instances of heroism and courage, together with humane expressions of brotherhood, comradeship, and spiritual greatness.

Whoever has not seen a tank crew continue its attack with its commander killed and its vehicle badly damaged, whoever has not seen sappers endangering their lives to extricate wounded comrades from a minefield, whoever has not seen the anxiety and the effort of the entire Air Force devoted to rescuing a pilot who has fallen in enemy territory, cannot know the meaning of devotion between comrades in arms.

The entire Nation was exalted and many wept upon hearing the news of the capture of the Old City. Our Sabra Youth and most certainly our soldiers do not tend to sentimentality and shy away from revealing it in public. However, the strain of battle, the anxiety which preceded it, and the sense of salvation and of direct participation of every soldier in the forging of the heart of Jewish history cracked the shell of hardness and shyness and released well-springs of excitement and spiritual emotion. The paratroopers, who conquered the Wailing Wall, leaned on its stones and wept, and as a symbol this was a rare occasion, almost unparalleled in human history. Such phrases and cliches are not generally used in our Army but this scene on the Temple Mount beyond the power of verbal description revealed as though by a lightning flash deep truths. And more than this, the joy of triumph seized the whole nation. Nevertheless we find more and more and more a strange phenomenon among our fighters. Their joy is incomplete, and more than a small portion of sorrow and shock prevails in their festivities. And there are those who abstain from all celebration. The warriors in the front lines saw with their own eyes not only the glory of victory but the price of victory. Their comrades who fell beside them bleeding. And I know that even the terrible price which our enemies paid touched the hearts of many of our men. It may be that the Jewish People never learned and never accustomed itself to feel the triumph of conquest and victory and therefore we receive it with mixed feelings.

The Six-Day War revealed many instances of heroism far beyond the single attack which dashes unthinkingly forward. In many places desperate and lengthy battles raged. In Rafiah, in El Arish, in Um Kataf, in Jerusalem, and in Ramat Hagollan, there, and in many other places, the soldiers of Israel were revealed as heroic in spirit, in courage, and in persistence which cannot leave anyone indifferent once he has seen this great and exalting human revelation. We speak a great deal of the few against the many. In this war perhaps for the first time since the Arab invasions of the spring of 1948 and the battles of Negba and Degania, units of the Israel Forces stood in all sectors, few against many. This means that relatively small units of our soldiers, often entered seemingly endless networks of fortification, surrounded by hundreds and thousands of enemy troops and faced with the task of forcing their way, hour after hour, in this jungle of dangers, even after the momentum of the first attack has passed and all that remains is the necessity of belief in our strength, the lack of alternative and the goal for which we are fighting, to summon up every spiritual resource in order to continue the fight to its very end.

Thus our armoured Forces broke through on all fronts, our paratroopers fought their way into Rafiah and Jerusalem, our sappers cleared minefields under enemy fire. The units which broke the enemy lines and came to their objectives after hours upon hours of struggle continuing on and on, while their comrades fell right and left and they continued forward, only forward. These soldiers were carried forward by spiritual values, by deep spiritual resources, far more than by their weapons or the technique of warfare.

We have always demanded the cream of our youth for the Israel Defence Forces when we coined the slogan "Hatovim l'Tayis"—The Best to Flying, and this was a phrase which became a value. We meant not only technical and manual skills. We meant that if our airmen were to be capable of defeating the forces of four enemy countries within a few short hours, they must have moral values and human values.

Our airmen, who struck the enemies' planes so accurately that no one in the world understands how it was done and people seek technological explanations of secret weapons; our armoured troops who stood and beat the enemy even when their equipment was inferior to his; our soldiers in all various branches of the Israel Defence Forces who overcame our enemies everywhere, despite their superior numbers and fortifications; all these revealed not only coolness and courage in battle but a burning faith in their righteousness, an understanding that only their personal stand against the greatest of dangers could bring to their country and to their families victory, and that if the victory was not theirs the alternative was destruction.

Furthermore, in every sector our Forces' commanders, of all ranks, far outshone the enemies' commanders. Their understanding, their will, their ability to improvise, their care for soldiers and above all, their leading troops into battle, these are not matters of material or of technique. They have no rational explanation, except in terms of a deep consciousness of the moral justice of their fight.

All of this springs from the soul and leads back to the spirit. Our warriors prevailed not by their weapons but by the consciousness of a mission, by a consciousness of righteousness, by a deep love for their homeland and an understanding of the difficult task laid upon them; to ensure the existence of our people in its homeland, to protect, even at the price of their lives, the right of the Nation of Israel to live in its own State, free, independent and peaceful.

This Army, which I had the privilege of commanding through these battles, came from the people and returns to the people, to the people which rises in its hour of crisis and overcomes all enemies by virtue of its moral values, its spiritual readiness in the hour of need.

As the representative of the Israel Defence Forces, and in the name of everyone of its soldiers, I accept with pride your recognition.

Egyptian President Gamal Abdel Nasser: We Shall Triumph (July 23, 1968)*

. . . We realised from the beginning, as we were trying a political solution, that it was a difficult and thorny road because the enemy was drunk with

*The text of a speech given at the National Congress of the Arab Socialist Union at Cairo University, Cairo.

victory. We know that the principle that what has been taken by force cannot be regained by anything but force is a sound and correct principle in all circumstances. But we tried sincerely and are still trying sincerely on a basis from which we do not deviate. This basis is clear and definite in UAR policy: no negotiations with Israel, no peace with Israel, no recognition of Israel, and no deals at the expense of Palestinian soil or the Palestinian people.

These are the foundations on which we proceeded in regard to solving the Middle East crisis peacefully. However, since 23rd November and until now, give and take has been going on with the UN representative. Have we achieved anything? We have achieved nothing. We co-operated to the maximum with the UN Secretary-General's representative. We accepted the Security Council resolution, but Israel did not.

No projects exist now for a peaceful solution, and it does not seem to me that there will be any in the future. We hear what the representative of the UN Secretary-General says, and we express our opinion on what we hear. So far our opinion has been clear. . . .

With regard to a political solution, we will not in any way agree to give away one inch of Arab territory in any Arab country. . . .

Because of its nature, the crisis cannot last long. We have been waiting for one year. Our area is a sensitive one. The status quo cannot be accepted. This status quo is against nature and creates a situation conducive to quick ignition and explosion at any time. . . .

Life will be meaningless and worthless to us however, until every inch of Arab soil is liberated. To us the liberation of Arab soil represents an indivisible whole. In no circumstances is there an alternative to the departure of the occupation forces from all occupied territory. Prior to this departure, there can be no peace in the Middle East in any circumstances. If there is no peace in the Middle East, it is very doubtful that the repercussions will be restricted to borders of the Middle East. . . .

[T]here is a fact which we must realise and know: Had it not been for the Soviet Union, we would now find ourselves facing the enemy without any weapons and compelled to accept his conditions. The United States would not have given us a single round of ammunition. It has given us and will give us nothing, but it gives Israel everything from guns to aircraft and missiles.

In reality, we have so far paid not one millieme for the arms we obtained from the Soviet Union to equip our armed forces. Actually, were it a question of payment, we have no money to buy arms. We all know the situation. We took part of the Soviet weapons as a gift and concluded a contract for the remainder for which we shall pay in the future in long-term installments. Had it not been for the Soviet Union and its agreement to supply us with arms, we should now be in a position similar to our position a year ago. We should have no weapons and should be compelled to accept Israel's condition under its threat. . . .

On this occasion, I may make a quick reference to our attitude towards the United States. U.S. policy has failed rapidly in this region. No one other than an obvious agent can openly declare friendship for the United States. The entire Arab world is aware of what the United States has done. We expected something different from the United States, or at least we did not expect all that has happened. However, that is the United States' business.

Giving arms to Israel while it is occupying Arab territory means that the United States supports Israel in the occupation of the Arab territory. Giving aircraft to Israel while it is occupying Arab territory means that the United States supports Israel in the occupation of the Arab territory. The complete U.S. support for Israel at the United Nations and the adoption and defence of the Israeli point of view means that the United States supports Israel's occupation of the Arab territory. The U.S. refusal to make a statement stipulating the need for the withdrawal of the Israeli forces to the positions they occupied before 5th June is proof that the United States supports Israel and, indeed, colludes with Israel in what it has done and is doing. Every member of the Arab nation is aware of this. . . .

There is one battle which is absorbing all our efforts in preparing for it; we have no time for anything else. It is the battle against the enemy. Our attitude towards any Arab State depends on that State's attitude towards the battle. Naturally, some states have sent us forces, Sudan and Algeria for instance. Their forces are with us. Other Arab countries such as Iraq and Kuwait have forces with us too. Some States have helped us to resist economically and have adhered to the Arab support agreement such as Saudi Arabia, Libya and Kuwait. I believe that Arab action can progress day after day in spite of the slow rate of progress. . . .

Our enemies have succeeded in winning a military victory, but our country has not fallen, has not accepted defeat, but has decided to stand fast. They have applied economic pressure to us and, despite this pressure, we have not surrendered but have marched on. We have imposed restrictions on ourselves and have accepted these restrictions. Our enemies have failed to destroy us economically. Hence, there remains one thing for them to do—to strike at the domestic front and to break up the alliance of the people's working forces because if the domestic front collapses the hostile imperialist forces and Israel will achieve the aims they have so far been unable to achieve. . . .

Brothers, there is no alternative to victory for our nation. The nation is capable of achieving victory provided it mobilises its forces and benefits properly from its energy and conditions, and also if we can build up and safeguard our domestic front according to the needs of the battle. The domestic front is the pillar of the fighting front. We must expose, defeat and crush all enemy attempts to influence the domestic front.

UN Security Council: Resolution 242
(November 22, 1967)

The Security Council,

Expressing its continuing concern with the grave situation in the Middle East,

Emphasizing the inadmissibility of the acquisition of territory by war and the need to work for a just and lasting peace in which every state in the area can live in security.

Emphasizing further that all member states in their acceptance of the Charter of the United Nations have undertaken a commitment to act in accordance with Article 2 of the Charter,

1. *Affirms* that the fulfillment of Charter principles requires the establishment of a just and lasting peace in the Middle East which should include the application of both the following principles:

(i) Withdrawal of Israel armed forces from territories occupied in the recent conflict;

(ii) Termination of all claims or states of belligerency and respect for and acknowledgment of the sovereignty, territorial integrity and political independence of every state in the area and their right to live in peace within secure and recognized boundaries free from threats or acts of force;

2. *Affirms further* the necessity

(a) For guaranteeing freedom of navigation through international waterways in the area;

(b) For achieving a just settlement of the refugee problem;

(c) For guaranteeing the territorial inviolability and political independence of every state in the area, through measures including the establishment of demilitarized zones;

3. *Requests* the Secretary General to designate a special representative to proceed to the Middle East to establish and maintain contacts with the states concerned in order to promote agreement and assist efforts to achieve a peaceful and accepted settlement in accordance with the provisions and principles in this resolution.

4. *Requests* the Secretary General to report to the Security Council on the progress of the efforts of the special representative as soon as possible.

Palestine National Council:
The Palestinian National Charter (July 1968)

1. Palestine is the homeland of the Arab Palestinian people; it is an indivisible part of the Arab homeland, and the Palestinian people are an integral part of the Arab nation.

2. Palestine, with the boundaries it had during the British Mandate, is an indivisible territorial unit.

3. The Palestinian Arab people possess the legal right to their homeland and have the right to determine their destiny after achieving the liberation of their country in accordance with their wishes and entirely of their own accord and will.

4. The Palestinian identity is a genuine, essential, and inherent characteristic; it is transmitted from parents to children. The Zionist occupation and the dispersal of the Palestinian Arab people, through the disasters which befell them, do not make them lose their Palestinian identity and their membership in the Palestinian community, nor do they negate them.

5. The Palestinians are those Arab nationals who, until 1947, normally resided in Palestine regardless of whether they were evicted from it or have stayed there. Anyone born, after that date, of a Palestinian father—whether inside Palestine or outside it—is also a Palestinian.

6. The Jews who had normally resided in Palestine until the beginning of the Zionist invasion will be considered Palestinians.

7. That there is a Palestinian community and that it has material, spiritual, and historical connection with Palestine are indisputable facts. It is a national duty to bring up individual Palestinians in an Arab revolutionary manner. All means of information and education must be adopted in order to acquaint the Palestinian with his country in the most profound manner, both spiritual and material, that is possible. He must be prepared for the armed struggle and ready to sacrifice his wealth and his life in order to win back his homeland and bring about its liberation.

8. The phase in their history, through which the Palestinian people are now living, is that of national struggle for the liberation of Palestine. Thus the conflicts among the Palestinian national forces are secondary, and should be ended for the sake of the basic conflict that exists between the forces of Zionism and of imperialism on the one hand, and the Palestinian Arab people on the other. On this basis the Palestinian masses, regardless of whether they are residing in the national homeland or in diaspora, constitute—both their organizations and the individuals—one national front working for the retrieval of Palestine and its liberation through armed struggle.

9. Armed struggle is the only way to liberate Palestine. Thus it is the overall strategy, not merely a tactical phase. The Palestinian Arab people

assert their absolute determination and firm resolution to continue their armed struggle and to work for an armed popular revolution for the liberation of their country and their return to it. They also assert their right to normal life in Palestine and to exercise their right to self-determination and sovereignty over it.

10. Commando action constitutes the nucleus of the Palestinian popular liberation war. This requires its escalation, comprehensiveness, and the mobilization of all the Palestinian popular and educational efforts and their organization and involvement in the armed Palestinian revolution. It also requires the achieving of unity for the national struggle among the different groupings of the Palestinian people, and between the Palestinian people and the Arab masses, so as to secure the continuation of the revolution, its escalation, and victory.

11. The Palestinians will have three mottoes: national unity, national mobilization, and liberation.

12. The Palestinian people believe in Arab unity. In order to contribute their share toward the attainment of that objective, however, they must, at the present stage of their struggle, safeguard their Palestinian identity and develop their consciousness of that identity, and oppose any plan that may dissolve or impair it.

13. Arab unity and the liberation of Palestine are two complementary objectives, the attainment of either of which facilitates the attainment of the other. Thus, Arab unity leads to the liberation of Palestine, the liberation of Palestine leads to Arab unity; and work toward the realization of one objective proceeds side by side with work toward the realization of the other.

14. The destiny of the Arab nation, and indeed Arab existence itself, depend upon the destiny of the Palestine cause. From this interdependence spring the Arab nation's pursuit of, and striving for, the liberation of Palestine. The people of Palestine play the role of the vanguard in the realization of this sacred national goal.

15. The liberation of Palestine, from an Arab viewpoint, is a national duty and it attempts to repel the Zionist and imperialist aggression against the Arab homeland, and aims at the elimination of Zionism in Palestine. Absolute responsibility for this falls upon the Arab nation—peoples and governments—with the Arab people of Palestine in the vanguard. Accordingly, the Arab nation must mobilize all its military, human, moral, and spiritual capabilities to participate actively with the Palestinian people in the liberation of Palestine. It must, particularly in the phase of the armed Palestinian revolution, offer and furnish the Palestinian people with all possible help, and material and human support, and make available to them the means and opportunities that will enable them to continue to carry out their leading role in the armed revolution, until they liberate their homeland.

16. The liberation of Palestine, from a spiritual point of view, will provide the Holy Land with an atmosphere of safety and tranquility, which in turn will safeguard the country's religious sanctuaries and guarantee freedom of worship and of visit to all, without discrimination of race, color, language, or religion. Accordingly, the people of Palestine look to all spiritual forces in the world for support.

17. The liberation of Palestine, from a human point of view, will restore to the Palestinian individual his dignity, pride, and freedom. Accordingly the Palestinian Arab people look forward to the support of all those who believe in the dignity of man and his freedom in the world.

18. The liberation of Palestine, from an international point of view, is a defensive action necessitated by the demands of self-defense. Accordingly, the Palestine people, desirous as they are of the friendship of all people, look to freedom-loving, and peace-loving states for support in order to re-store their legitimate rights in Palestine, to re-establish peace and security in the country, and to enable its people to exercise national sovereignty and freedom.

19. The partition of Palestine in 1947 and the establishment of the state of Israel are entirely illegal, regardless of the passage of time, because they were contrary to the will of the Palestinian people and to their natural right in their homeland, and inconsistent with the principles embodied in the Charter of the United Nations, particularly the right to self-determination.

20. The Balfour Declaration, the Mandate for Palestine, and everything that has been based upon them, are deemed null and void. Claims of historical or religious ties of Jews with Palestine are incompatible with the facts of history and the true conception of what constitutes statehood. Judaism, being a religion, is not an independent nationality. Nor do Jews constitute a single nation with an identity of its own; they are citizens of the states to which they belong.

21. The Arab Palestinian people, expressing themselves by the armed Palestinian revolution, reject all solutions which are substitutes for the total liberation of Palestine and reject all proposals aiming at the liquidation of the Palestinian problem, or its internationalization.

22. Zionism is a political movement organically associated with international imperialism and antagonistic to all action for liberation and to progressive movements in the world. It is racist and fanatic in its nature, aggressive, expansionist, and colonial in its aims, and fascist in its methods. Israel is the instrument of the Zionist movement, and a geographical base for world imperialism placed strategically in the midst of the Arab homeland to combat the hopes of the Arab nation for liberation, unity, and progress. Israel is a constant source of threat *vis-à-vis* peace in the Middle East and the whole world. Since the liberation of Palestine will destroy the Zionist and imperialist presence and will contribute to the establishment of peace in the Middle East, the Palestinian people look for the support of all

the progressive and peaceful forces and urge them all, irrespective of their affiliations and beliefs, to offer the Palestinian people all aid and support in their just struggle for the liberation of their homeland.

23. The demands of security and peace, as well as the demands of right and justice, require all states to consider Zionism an illegitimate movement, to outlaw its existence, and to ban its operations, in order that friendly relations among peoples may be preserved, and the loyalty of citizens to their respective homelands safeguarded.

24. The Palestinian people believe in the principles of justice, freedom, sovereignty, self-determination, human dignity, and in the right of all peoples to exercise them.

25. For the realization of the goals of this Charter and its principles, the Palestine Liberation Organization will perform its role in the liberation of Palestine in accordance with the Constitution of this Organization.

26. The Palestine Liberation Organization, representative of the Palestinian revolutionary forces, is responsible for the Palestinian Arab people's movement in its struggle—to retrieve its homeland, liberate and return to it and exercise the right to self-determination in it—in all military, political, and financial fields and also for whatever may be required by the Palestine case on the inter-Arab and international levels.

27. The Palestine Liberation Organization shall cooperate with all Arab states, each according to its potentialities; and will adopt a neutral policy among them in the light of the requirements of the war of liberation; and on this basis it shall not interfere in the internal affairs of any Arab state.

28. The Palestinian Arab people assert the genuineness and independence of their national revolution and reject all forms of intervention, trusteeship, and subordination.

29. The Palestinian people possess the fundamental and genuine legal right to liberate and retrieve their homeland. The Palestinian people determine their attitude toward all states and forces on the basis of the stands they adopt *vis-à-vis* the Palestinian case and the extent of the support they offer to the Palestinian revolution to fulfill the aims of the Palestinian people.

30. Fighters and carriers of arms in the war of liberation are the nucleus of the popular army which will be the protective force for the gains of the Palestinian Arab people.

31. The Organization shall have a flag, an oath of allegiance, and an anthem. All this shall be decided upon in accordance with a special regulation.

32. Regulations, which shall be known as the Constitution of the Palestine Liberation Organization, shall be annexed to this Charter. It shall lay down the manner in which the Organization, and its organs and institutions, shall be constituted; the respective competence of each; and the requirements of its obligations under the Charter.

33. This Charter shall not be amended save by [vote of] a majority of two-thirds of the total membership of the National Congress of the Palestine Liberation Organization [taken] at a special session convened for that purpose.

Y. Harkabi: Fatah's Doctrine (December 1968)*

Fatah's Major Conceptions

Fatah's prescription for facing the challenge inherent in [its] dilemma was Revolutionary War waged on guerrilla warfare lines. Its merit is that it does not require such long and tedious preparations as a conventional war, for it can be launched with small forces. Revolutions, *Fatah* reasons, once set in motion, generate their own forces and acquire momentum. "The armed struggle is the basic factor for expanding the revolution and its continuation; in short, causing a revolution in the life of this society. Such historic changes are usually achieved by wars, calamities and uncontrollable economic fluctuations. The nearest means of producing such a convulsion and a great historic change in the course of the national development of the Arab nation is by creating an appropriate environment for a decisive fateful battle between the Arabs and the Zionist enemy."

Arab politicians usually subordinated the Palestinian issue to their interests and policy, and manipulated it accordingly. *Fatah* signifies an attempt to reverse this trend and subordinate all other Arab problems to the goal of liberating Palestine. Before, the Palestinians orbited round the Arab state; now, *Fatah* tries to stage a Copernican revolution, and reverse the relationship.

The Objective of War

Fatah sets out the objective of the war against Israel in bold type: "The liberation action is not only the wiping out of an Imperialist base but, what is more important, the extinction of a society [*Inqirad mujtama*]. Therefore armed violence will necessarily assume diverse forms in addition to the liquidation of the armed forces of the Zionist occupying state, namely, it should turn to the destruction of the factors sustaining the Zionist society in all their forms: industrial, agricultural, and financial. The armed violence necessarily should also aim at the destruction of the various military, political, economic, financial and intellectual institutions of the Zionist occupation state, to prevent any possibility of a re-emergence of a new Zion-

*Reprinted by special permission from *Adelphi Papers* No. 53 (December, 1968), "Fedayeen Action and Arab Strategy." Institute of Strategic Studies, London.

ist society. Military defeat is not the sole goal in the Palestinian Liberation War, but it is the blotting out of the Zionist character of the occupied land, be it human or social." Or: "The Jewish state is an aberrant mistaken phenomenon in our nation's history and therefore there is no alternative but to wipe out the existential trace [*Alathar alwujudi*] of this artificial phenomenon."

Lt.-Col. Sha'ir, an officer in the command of the PLO Army, also expresses the objective in unmistakable terms: "The chief objective and the fundamental effort for the Popular War concerning the liberation of Palestine is the reoccupation of the usurped land regardless of the method, be it smashing or annihilation [*Ibada*], because the enemy when he usurped Palestine did not think of the fate of our people, of things holy to it and its lawful rights, in the lands of his forefathers."

Arab declarations of objectives frequently used extreme expressions like "throwing the Jews into the sea" which implied genocide. *Fatah* endeavours in its publications to avoid such notorious expressions, stressing that the purpose is limited to the destruction of the state, not of its people. The formula most frequently used in its writings is "liquidation, or the uprooting of the Zionist existence or entity." However, when the implications of this objective come to be spelled out, it is realised that Zionism is not only a political regime or a superstructure of sorts, but is embodied in a *society*. Therefore, this *society* has to be liquidated, which underlines that achieving it will require a great deal of killing. The Arabs' objective of destroying the state of Israel (what may be called a "politicide") drives them to genocide. Since the existence of Israel is founded on the existence of a concentration of Jews so their dispersion should precede the demise of the state. Thus, despite *Fatah*'s efforts, it comes back to the Arab objective in its extremist version.

Fatah stresses that Jews will be allowed to live in a democratic Arab Palestine after Israel's extinction. In order for the country to become Arab again, the sheer numerical predominance of Jews over Palestinian Arabs requires part of the Jewish population to disappear. How?

Fatah's recognition of the right of a Jewish minority to exist is nothing new. It recalls the fundamental Islamic position, which grants the Jews security on the condition of their subordination as a tolerated minority.

The Arab position is enmeshed in this complexity arising from the impossibility of destroying Israel as a state without destroying a considerable part of her inhabitants. To escape from this dilemma the Arab objective is sometimes expressed in another formula showing perhaps improved articulation without changing the issue: "the de-Zionization of Israel." Since the basic meaning of Zionism was the achievement of Jewish statehood, de-Zionizing Israel has only one implication, that Israel will cease being a Jewish state; not Israel but Palestine. Israel and Zionism are organically connected. De-Zionizing Israel is only a contradiction in terms.

Fatah senses the difficulties in the Arab position: "Examining the Palestinian issue from all its aspects, we realize the necessity to satisfy many parties by our solution. For instance, if we consider world public opinion has some weight and influence, we must put out a solution which will satisfy public opinion or be acceptable to it, even be it with difficulty. Of course, when we speak about the need for satisfying world opinion, we do not mean in the kind of solution to the Palestine issue, but in its method. Public opinion has no right to dispute the imperative necessity of its solution [i.e. by destruction of the state], but its right to know the method, so that public opinion will not castigate us with Fascism, anti-Semitism or other inhuman epithets."

What is more important for the present discussions is the influence of the objective on the nature of the war by which *Fatah* hopes to achieve its aim. Such a war is different from one directed towards a change of the political regime, or towards harassment of the representatives of a remote country until the government prefers to relinquish its rule in that area. In order to achieve the purpose of liquidating a society or wiping out its "existential trace," war must be of great extent and intensity and become really total.

The question that is crucial to any evaluation of *Fatah*'s position is the degree to which guerrilla warfare can suit such an objective. This will be taken up at the conclusion of this paper.

Palestinian Activism

Fatah exhorted the Palestinians to become the driving force in the conflict, not by agitation in the Arab countries as they had previously, not by pushing the Arab states to action, but by starting actual fighting themselves. *Fedayeen* action should be developed into a fully fledged War of National Liberation. Only by what *Fatah* terms an "armed struggle" can the Palestinians solve their problems and regain Palestine.

Fatah stressed its disbelief in the possibility of a political solution. Arab politics are treated, especially before the Six-Day War, with marked disapproval. Politics are sickening when juxtaposed with the sublimity of the "armed struggle." The Palestinians will be able to concentrate on their conflict only if they extricate themselves from inter-Arab rivalries and exercise neutrality. If they take sides in any Arab issue, they will antagonize the opponents of the side they support, who will then try to make things difficult for them. The Palestinian problem should be put above Arab politics. Only by freeing themselves from Arab rivalries will the Palestinians be able to acquire liberty of action in their affairs.

There are inconsistencies in the writings and pronouncements of *Fatah* on how far the Palestinians are capable of accomplishing by themselves the liberation of Palestine. On the one hand, there are announcements that the forces of the Palestinian masses are irresistible and can achieve this goal. On the other hand, there is recognition that the last stroke will have to be dealt by the concerted forces of the Arab armies.

The war *Fatah* aspires to wage is called, in its parlance, the "Palestinian Revolution," to signify as well the transformation it will cause in the Palestinians themselves who from passive onlookers will become dynamic fighters.

This trend towards Palestinian activism and the Palestinization of the conflict has to be seen against its historical background. Its psychological aspects should also be tackled, otherwise the human dimension of such developments will evade us. However, in offering psychological explanations, it should always be borne in mind how tentative they are so long as they are based on intuition, and how corrupting they may be by inspiring in the writer, and even the reader, a false sense of clairvoyance.

The mid-1960s saw the re-emergence of the Palestinians as contestants in the Arab-Israel conflict, after about seventeen years in which the confrontation was mainly at states level. The entry of the Arab armies into the war in 1948 transformed the conflict from a civil one between Jews and Arabs in Palestine, or an intra-state war, to an inter-state war. The activities surrounding the setting up of the Palestine Liberation Organization and the *Fedayeen* organizations signify in some respects an attempt to revert to the previous state of affairs. This development of the Palestinians' reassertion embodied elements of both protest and reproach towards the Arab states for their failure to fulfil their obligation towards the Palestinians. *Fatah*, by emphasizing that the "Palestinian people is the only true available stock [*Rasid*] for the war of return," insinuates that the others are not so trustworthy.

On the other hand, the Arab states handing over to the Palestinians the leading role in the conflict implied an abdication of sorts by the Arab states and an avowal of their failure. It is not mere coincidence that the Summit Meetings which established the PLO were convened as a result of, presumably, the most dismal of Arab failures between 1948 and the Six-Day War. All the Arab leaders had committed themselves to preventing Israel from completing her project of pumping water from Lake Tiberias (what Arabs called "the diversion of the Jordan"). When the time came, they realized their helplessness.

The relationship between the Palestinians and the Arabs has always been ambivalent, each accused the other of being responsible for their inadequacies in the conflict. The Arab states blamed the Palestinians for selling land to the Jews, for their feeble resistance during the Mandate, and for their acting as agents for Israel Intelligence. Their existence epitomized the calamities that befell the Arab world as a result of the Arab-Israel conflict, and the Palestinians were blamed for them.

The Palestinians blamed the Arab states for their half-hearted activities in the conflict, their irresolution, internal bickerings, the restrictions they imposed on the Palestinians, and their manipulation of the conflict to their narrow interests.

Despite that element of protest against the Arab states embodied in the Palestinians' organizations, they could be created only with the help of some Arab official quarters. The PLO did not come into being only by Palestinian spontaneity. It was established from above by the Summit Meetings and derived its authority and part of its finances from them. The *Fatah* acted under the aegis of the Syrian radical Baath. Thus protest and dependence intermingled.

Palestinian activism came in the early 1960s to be cherished widely in Palestinian circles. Palestinian initiative seemed vital after the Arab states' failure. Mr. Nashashibi ends his book as follows: "Oh Palestinians, if you do not restore the land, you will not return to it, and it will not return to you."

An important factor in the Palestinian move for the "re-Palestinization" of the conflict was the influence of the Algerian War. It was a source of both pride and inspiration. If the Algerians prevailed over a great power such as France, so it was argued, there was hope in defeating small Israel.

Hence the effort to draw analogies between Algeria and Palestine and the effort to describe Israel as only another colonialist case, whose fate is doomed as part of the general historical trend of the liquidation of colonies.

Palestinian ideologists argued that previous presentation of the conflict as an inter-state one was erroneous. It was an Imperialist ruse aimed at excluding the Palestinians from their natural role, thus "liquidating" the conflict. This argument was, too, an apologia for the Arabs themselves as they too described the conflict as international. They were only deluded and their failing was only naïvety. Both Israel and the Imperialists conspired to blur the "liberation" aspect of the conflict.

Naming the conflict a "War of National Liberation" after it had already reached a mature age, and the identification of "War of National Liberation" with guerrilla warfare, produced among Palestinians an inclination to project it backwards and describe the conflict as if the Palestinians had waged continuous popular guerrilla warfare against the Jews. The history of the events in Palestine from World War I is being rewritten to appear as a continuous popular resistance and heroic uprisings. The blame for failure is focused on the leadership. Naji Alush in his book *Arab Resistance in Palestine 1917–1948* gives a Marxist explanation for this failing. Because of its class interests the Palestinian leadership tied its destiny to colonialism, and betrayed the national cause.

Palestinian radio programmes abound with plays and descriptions of brave resistance against the Jews in Palestine. Small ambushes or attacks on Jewish settlers are elevated into heroic acts of guerrilla warfare. Thus, heroism anticipated in the future is reinforced by inspiration drawn from the past, and if the real past cannot be a source of such inspiration, some retouching is done. Such an account may have another merit: it implies that the Palestinians are not only imitators of Mao and Che, but preceded them.

The allure of activism is presumably very powerful for the Palestinians. The Palestinians suffered not only from the agony of defeat, deprivation, refugee status, living in camps, but from contempt by the other Arabs. Losing their land and property was a blow to their dignity, as traditionally the criterion for position and prestige in Arab society is ownership of real estate. Activism and "revolutionarism" are means of gaining self-respect, especially for the younger generation. This generation is ambivalent towards their parents—they reproach them for their weaknesses and failings, calling them "the generation of defeat," or "the defeated generation" (*Jil al-Hazima, Al-Jil al-Munhar*). Whereas the young generation dubbed itself (already before the Six-Day War) the "generation of resistance" or "the generation of revenge" (*Jil al-Muqawama, Jil-al-Naqma*). On the other hand, in order to bolster themselves up as Palestinians, they have to praise the Palestinian record and stress the continuity of the struggle.

Activism has the psychological function of atoning for past failings and inadequacies. It symbolizes the Palestinians' regeneration, and a reaction against fatalism, proverbial in Arab society, about which the young generation feels uneasy. Activism is a manly quality, hailed in a masculine society, and a reaction against emotionalism treated derogatorily in Arab political literature, including *Fatah*'s. "Revolutionarism" (*Thauria*) exerts a strong influence in most of the Arab world signifying a radical change, spectacular and forceful, a protest against the past, and a guarantee of success for the future. The adjective "revolutionary" is attached to all kinds of nouns in Arab political literature as a word of approbation and optimism.

Fatah described what this Palestinian revolution will accomplish: "The staging of the revolutionary movement is a conscious transcendence of the circumstances of the Arab Palestinian people, of the traditional leadership, of the stagnated situations, of the opportunism and the self-seeking political arrangements, or those directed from beyond the Palestinian pale, it is a rejection of this fragmented reality. The Palestinian revolutionary movement on this level is a social revolution and a mutation in the social relationship of the Palestinian Arab people."

Adulation of Violence

It is not by sheer accident that the third *Fatah* pamphlet entitled *The Revolution and Violence, the Road to Victory* is a selective précis of Frantz Fanon's book, *The Wretched of the Earth*. Fanon's influence is manifested in other *Fatah* writings, especially on the psychological impact of Israel on the Arabs and on the transformations that their armed struggle will produce in the Palestinians. "Violence," "Violent Struggle" and "Vengeance" are expressions of great frequency in *Fatah* literature. The reader of these texts is introduced to a world of simmering frustrated hatred and a drive for unquenchable vengeance.

Violence is described as imperative in wiping out colonialism, for between the colonialist and the colonized there is such a contradiction that no coexistence is possible. One of the two has to be liquidated. (Descriptions of the Arab-Israel conflict as both a zero-sum game and a deadly quarrel are frequent in Arab publications.) Such a conflict is "a war of annihilation of one of the rivals, either wiping out the national entity, or wiping out colonialism. . . . The colonized will be liberated from violence by violence. "The Palestinian Revolution" is such a cataclysmic event that it can only be achieved by violence.

Violence liberates people from their shortcomings and anxieties. It inculcates in them both courage and fearlessness concerning death. Violence has a therapeutic effect, purifying society of its diseases. "Violence will purify the individuals from venom, it will redeem the colonized from inferiority complex, it will return courage to the countryman." In a memorandum to Arab journalists, *Fatah* stated: "Blazing our armed revolution inside the occupied territory [i.e. Israel, it was written before the Six-Day War] is a healing medicine for all our people's diseases."

The praising of violence as purgative, may imply also an element of self-indictment for flaws which will now be rectified, and a desire to exorcize the record of failings. The praising of violence may have as well the function of giving cathartic satisfaction as a substitute for operational action.

Violence, *Fatah* asserts, will have a unifying influence on people, forging one nation from them. It will draw the individuals from the pettiness of their ego, and imbue them with the effusiveness of collective endeavour, as bloodshed will produce a common experience binding them together. Thus, "the territoriality, [i.e. the fragmentation into different Arab states] which was imposed by Imperialism and Arab leaderships and which was sustained by traditional circumstances in the societies, will end."

The struggle, besides its political goals, will have as a by-product an important impact on those who participate in it. It is "a creative struggling" (*Nidalia khallaqa*). Violence, Revolutionarism, Activism, "the battle of vengeance," "armed struggle," all coalesce in an apocalyptic vision of heroic and just aggression, meting out revenge on Israel.

Engineering a Revolution

Fatah ideologists have been inclined to deal with general ideas of guerrilla warfare, rather than specifying in detail how their objectives will be accomplished through it. Like the other exponents of guerrilla warfare *Fatah* deals with the more practical problems, by means of tracing the phases by which the war or the revolution will evolve. It is called "revolution" in which warfare proper is only a part of a larger complex of activities, mobilizing the support and the participation in the struggle of the masses, and their own transformation through it.

The pamphlet entitled *How Will the Armed Popular Revolution Explode?* dwells on the mechanism and process of this "revolution." It explains that a revolution originates when the oppressed people become aware of the evils of the present reality, and as a result of the growth of an urge to avenge themselves upon it. Needless to say, the reality here is Israel. Though the feelings of revolt against the oppressive reality are spontaneous, they have to be assisted and to be organized. The revolution has to be orchestrated by stages, by its leaders, the "Revolutionary Vanguard."

In *Fatah*'s descriptions of the stages and their names there are some inconsistencies. They may originate either from different authorship, reflecting diverse influences, or be caused by simple imprecision and vagueness. This vagueness is even more accentuated by the lack of differentiation between the organizational and the operational aspects of the stages, and the relationship between the two.

The parts of *Fatah*'s writings which deal with the phases of war make uneasy reading. *Fatah*'s terminology and formulation may seem both esoteric and highfalutin'. However, what may be more wearisome for the reader who is not versed in such parlance is the generality and abstraction of the discussion. It contains a mixture of a terminology influenced by Marxist literature, attempting to interpret developments in a rational way, with mythical overtones expressed in figures of speech like the "ignition" or "detonation" or a revolution, and leaves the reader wondering how it is to be done.

The organizational stages symbolize the expansion of the circles of those involved in the revolution or war. Stage one is the *Formation of the Revolutionary Vanguard.* This is achieved by "the movement of revolutionary gathering of the revengeful conscious wills." "The individual of the Revolutionary Vanguard is distinguished by his revolutionary intuition." His task is "to discover the vital tide in his society, for its own sake and for its usefulness for action and movement, and then to realize what obstacles hamper his movement in accordance with history's logic." Thus, "the Revolutionary Vanguard signifies the type of human who interacts positively with the reality [of his predicament], and so elevates himself by his consciousness until he releases himself from reality's grip, in order to pursue the superseding of this reality by another, which differs basically in its values and traits. To take a concrete example, the reality of Arab Palestinian people is fragmented, disfigured and corrupted, and shows signs of stagnation. However, despite this stagnation and immobility, the historical direction imposes the existence of a current of vitality among the Palestinian people, so long as the Palestinian man treasures vengeance on this reality. As this wish for vengeance grows, the current of vitality congeals in the form of a Revolutionary Vanguard."

The second stage is the *Formation of the Revolutionary Organization*. In it the Revolutionary Vanguard achieves a psychological mobilization of the Palestinian masses by stimulating their urge for revenge, until "the constructive revolutionary anxiety embraces all the Palestinian Arabs." It is thus called the stage of *Revolutionary Embracing (Al-Shumul al-Thauri)*. Indoctrination of the masses will not precede the staging of the armed struggle but will be achieved by it. "Mistaken are those who advocate the need for rousing a national consciousness before the armed struggle assumes a concrete form. . . . Ineluctably the armed struggle and mass consciousness will go side by side, because the armed struggle will make the masses feel their active personality and restore their selfconfidence." The Vanguard will galvanize the masses by means of its example and sacrifice in guerrilla activities.

Fatah's publications state that irresistible might is stored in the Arab masses. They are "latent volcanoes," they are the main "instrument" of the struggle. This explosive capacity has to be activated and this task is allotted to the Vanguard.

The revolution's success is dependent on co-operation between the Vanguard and the masses. "The Revolution in its composition has a leadership and a basis, necessitates the accomplishment of a conscious interaction between the basis, which is the masses, and the leadership, in order to ensure the revolution's success and continuation."

The third stage is the *Formation of the Supporting Arab Front*. Popular support for the "Palestinian Revolution" is to be secured in all Arab countries in order to safeguard rear bases in Arab countries for the war, and as a means of putting pressure on the Arab governments not to slacken or deviate from aiding the Palestinian Revolution by pursuit of their local interests. The Supporting Arab Front is thus expressed on two levels, the popular and the governmental. The popular support is used as an instrument of pressure against the Arab governments.

In the same publications the overall development of the revolution is divided into two major stages: one, *Organization and Mobilization*, called elsewhere the *Phases of Revolutionary Maturing*, comprises the organizational stages already enumerated. The second stage is called that of the *Revolutionary Explosion (Marhal atal-Tafjir al-Thauri)*. The stage of the Revolutionary Explosion is described in colourful language: "The hating revengeful masses plunge into the road of revolution in a pressing and vehement fashion as pouring forces that burn everything that stands in their way." In this stage "tempests of revenge" will be let loose. However, the Vanguard should ensure mass discipline to prevent violence going berserk. "The Revolution's Will should obey its regulating brain."

While the first stage is preparatory, the second is the main interesting stage. Unfortunately, *Fatah*'s description of it is rather rudimentary. Even the question of the timing of its beginning is not clear. *Fatah* specified: "Our operations in the occupied territory can never reach the stage of the aspired revolution unless all Palestinian groups are polarized around the revolution." *Fatah* does have an ambition to become the central leader of all the Palestinians, proving that the other movements, which have not matured round what has been described as a Revolutionary Vanguard like itself, are artificial and "counterfeited." Thus the stage of revolution will arrive only when *Fatah* has mobilized *all* the Palestinians.

Nevertheless, *Fatah*'s small action at the beginning of January 1965 is frequently hailed as the "detonation of the revolution," implying that the revolution started then. By the same token, at the beginning of 1968, *Fatah*'s official journal celebrated the fourth anniversary" of our Palestinian people's revolution in the occupied territory." Perhaps this ambiguity as to the timing of the revolutionary stage stems from *Fatah*'s emphasis of the need to precipitate action. Once action is launched the development proceeds spontaneously. . . .

Fatah: The Seven Points (January 1969)*

1. *Fatah,* the Palestine National Liberation Movement, is the expression of the Palestinian people and of its will to free its land from Zionist colonisation in order to recover its national identity.

2. *Fatah,* the Palestine National Liberation Movement, is not struggling against the Jews as an ethnic and religious community. It is struggling against Israel as the expression of colonisation based on a theocratic, racist and expansionist system and of Zionism and colonialism.

3. *Fatah,* the Palestine National Liberation Movement, rejects any solution that does not take account of the existence of the Palestinian people and its right to dispose of itself.

4. *Fatah,* the Palestine National Liberation Movement, categorically rejects the Security Council Resolution of 22 November 1967 and the Jarring Mission to which it gave rise.

This resolution ignores the national rights of the Palestinian people— failing to mention its existence. Any solution claiming to be peaceful which ignores this basic factor, will thereby be doomed to failure.

In any event, the acceptance of the resolution of 22 November 1967, or

Passed by the Central Committee of Fatah.

any pseudo-political solution, by whatsoever party, is in no way binding upon the Palestinian people, which is determined to pursue mercilessly its struggle against foreign occupation and Zionist colonisation.

5. *Fatah,* the Palestine National Liberation Movement, solemnly proclaims that the final objective of its struggle is the restoration of the independent, democratic State of Palestine, all of whose citizens will enjoy equal rights irrespective of their religion.

6. Since Palestine forms part of the Arab fatherland, *Fatah,* the Palestine National Liberation Movement, will work for the State of Palestine to contribute actively towards the establishment of a progressive and united Arab society.

7. The struggle of the Palestinian People, like that of the Vietnamese people and other peoples of Asia, Africa, and Latin America, is part of the historic process of the liberation of the oppressed peoples from colonialism and imperialism.

Muhammad Hassanain Haykal: The Strategy of the War of Attrition (March–April 1969)

. . . To my mind there is one chief method which cannot be ignored or avoided in tipping the balance of fear and assurance in the Arab-Israeli conflict in favour of the Arabs. This course, which meets all the requirements and necessities and is in harmony with logic and nature—this main course to tip the balance in our favour, or merely precisely to adjust it, is: to inflict a clear defeat on the Israeli Army in battle, in one military battle.

I should like to be more specific because there is no room under present conditions for irresponsible talk. I would make the following points: (1) I am not speaking about the enemy's defeat in the war, but his defeat in a battle. There is still a long way to go before the enemy can be defeated in the war. The possibilities for this are still not within sight. But the enemy's defeat in one battle presupposes capabilities which could be available at an early stage in the long period before the end of the war. (2) I am not speaking of a battle on the scale of that of 5th June 1967—a 5th June in reverse, with the Arabs taking the initiative and Israel taken by surprise. Most likely 5th June will not be repeated either in form or in effect. In the coming battle neither we nor the enemy will be taken by surprise . . . I am speaking about a limited battle which would result in a clear victory for the Arabs and a clear defeat for Israel—naturally within the limits of that battle. (3) The requirements and necessities I am speaking about, and which will impose the military battle, do not include any marked consideration for the so-called revenge for injured Arab dignity. . . .

To these three reservations regarding the battle, which I consider necessary and vital, I should like to add more, in the hope that they will give a clearer picture of what I am saying. (1) The current artillery exchanges along the Egyptian front are not the battle I am thinking of—the battle that I feel the requirements and necessities are imposing. What I am envisaging is far greater and broader. The artillery exchanges are important, indeed very important, but they are not the battle which can achieve the aim of inflicting a clear defeat on the Israeli Army. (2) Neither are the activities of the resistance organisations at their present level the battle I am thinking of or the battle imposed by the requirements and possibilities. . . . (3) In simple and general terms the battle I am speaking about . . . is one in which the Arab forces might, for example, destroy two or three Israeli Army divisions, annihilate between 10,000 and 20,000 Israeli soldiers, and force the Israeli Army to retreat from the positions it occupies to other positions, even if only a few kilometres back.

I am speaking, then, about a battle and not the war; about a battle that is limited as battles naturally are; about a real battle, however, resulting in a clear defeat for the Israeli Army. Such a limited battle would have unlimited effects on the war. . . .

1. It would destroy a myth which Israel is trying to implant in the minds—the myth that the Israeli Army is invincible. Myths have great psychological effect. . . .

2. The Israeli Army is the backbone of Israeli society. We can say that the greatest achievement placed on record by the Arab resistance against Zionism—an achievement resulting from the simple act of refusal—has been to dispel the Zionist dreams. Because of the Arab refusal, Israel has become a military stronghold and Israeli society has become the society of a besieged stronghold—a military garrison society. . . .

3. Such a battle would reveal to the Israeli citizens a truth which would destroy the effects of the battles of June 1967. In the aftermath of these battles, Israeli society began to believe in the Israeli Army's ability to protect it. Once this belief is destroyed or shaken, once Israeli society begins to doubt its Army's ability to protect it, a series of reactions may set in with unpredictable consequences.

4. Furthermore, such a battle would shake the influence of the ruling military establishment. The establishment has the whip hand in directing and implementing Israeli policy on the excuse of acting as Israel's sole protector and guardian of Zionist plans.

5. Such a battle would destroy the philosophy of Israeli strategy, which affirms the possibility of "imposing peace" on the Arabs. Imposing peace is in fact, a false expression which actually means "waging war."

6. Such a battle and its consequences would cause the U.S.A. to change its policy towards the Middle East crisis in particular, and towards the Middle East after the crisis in general.

There are two clear features of U.S. policy. One which concerns the Middle East crisis, is that the U.S.A. is not in a hurry to help in finding a solution to the crisis. No matter how serious or complicated the situation may become, the U.S.A. will continue to move slowly as long as Israel is militarily in a stronger position. This situation would surely change once the Israel position of strength was shaken.

The other phenomenon concerns the Middle East after its present crisis. It is that the U.S.A. sees in Israel an instrument for attaining its aims in the area. No matter how far the Arabs go in their revolt against the U.S. influence and how much they defy this influence, the U.S. aims are guaranteed as long as Israel remains capable of intimidating the Arabs. If Israel's ability to intimidate becomes doubtful, U.S. policy will have to seek another course. Israel has proved to the U.S.A. that for the time being it is more useful to it than the Arabs. Although all the U.S. interests in the Middle East lie with the Arabs, the U.S.A. continues to support Israel. The strange contradiction in the Middle East at present is that the U.S.A. is protecting its interests in the Arab world by supporting Israel. Israel is thus the gun pointed at the Arabs, the gun which the U.S.A. is brandishing to attain its aims and protect its interests. . . .

After all this, the question remains: is such a battle possible?

The answer is: I do not claim military experience, yet I say that there is no doubt or suspicion as to the possibilities of such a battle which could inflict defeat on the Israeli Army. My belief is based on the following considerations:

1. The only myths in the Israeli system are those fabricated by bold and daring propaganda or by great imagination. Israeli society is not a straw as some believe, nor a rock as others imagine. . . . Israeli society cannot live independently. It is a society which cannot produce any genuine economic or political force. What matters most is the intrinsic force and not the apparent force, which is deceptive in most cases. Myths that are based on apparent force are bound to be dispelled by experience, especially if met by a capable force.

2. Israel has lost its once-in-a-lifetime opportunity. After 5th June 1967 its myth acquired all the elements it needed. Yet Israel could not attain its goal of turning the end of the battle into the end of the war. Arab steadfastness proved that the battle has ended but the war will continue. Thus Israel has lost its opportunity.

3. In any future battle, the Israeli Army would fight under conditions different from those in all previous battles. The Israeli Army would not be able to advance easily from its present positions along the Jordan river, the Suez Canal and the Golan Heights without finding itself passing through densely populated Arab areas, with the danger that these would absorb all its striking forces, exhaust it and make it easy to pounce on the Israeli Army's scattered remains one by one. With the exception of the Air Force

effort, the Israeli Army would have to fight a sustained battle or a defensive battle, whereas it is accustomed to fighting offensive battles with its characteristic tactics of indirect approach and fast outflanking movements. The Israeli lines of communication between the bases and the fronts have become long and arduous, especially in times of operations. As a result of the long lines of communication it would be impossible for the Israeli Army to move quickly on the Arab fronts as it did in the past when it was able to strike on one front and then switch its forces by its short lines of communication to strike at another Arab front. . . .

4. In any future battle the Israeli Army would face Arab armies with different standards of fire power and its use, different command structures benefiting from past experience, and a higher morale, as the Arab forces would be aware of fighting for the heart of their homeland and not only for its borders.

At the beginning of my article I said that a battle ending in a clear defeat for the Israeli Army should be the chief method of tipping the balance of fear and assurance. . . . I did not say it is the only method because there are other secondary methods. . . . I will give the following examples in this respect:

1. Our acceptance of the Security Council resolution on the Middle East—the resolution which international society has endorsed—is a valuable step, particularly since Israel has rejected the resolution and thereby defied the whole of international society. Despite Israel's daily proclaimed disrespect for the international organisation, the question is not so simple. I mean that the Israeli citizens' awareness of being at odds with the entire world will undoubtedly influence their mood, and so affect the balance of fear and assurance in the Arab-Israeli conflict.

2. The Soviet Union's support for the Arabs and its continued help to them in rebuilding their military forces after the tragedy of June 1967 will undoubtedly affect the feelings of the Israeli people in the balance of fear and assurance.

3. France's stand cannot fail to affect the balance of fear and assurance for the Israeli inhabitants who realise that the greater part of their military power in 1967 came from France and that—from 1954 to 1964 at least—France was an ally of Israel joined by special ties.

4. The current four-power talks in New York arouse Israel's suspicions, to say the least, because they indicate clearly that the Middle East crisis cannot for long remain confined to the Middle East and that it might lead to a nuclear confrontation between the great Powers. The talks may produce a solution to the problem which—to put it at its lowest—will fail to give Israel everything it feels to be within its reach. Irrespective of their results and what the Arabs think of these results, the talks will play their part in affecting the balance of fear and assurance in the Israeli people's feelings.

PLO Chairman Yasir Arafat (Abu Ammar): An Interview (August 1969)

Q.—Fatah has offered an alternative to the Jews in Palestine—that is the creation of a progressive, democratic State for all. How do you reconcile this with the slogan "Long Live Palestine Arab and Free?"

Abu Ammar.—A democratic, progressive State in Palestine is not in contradiction to that State being Arab. The social, geographical and historical factors play a major role in determining the nature and identity of any State. Anyone who has tried to look at the Palestinian problem in its historic perspective would realise that the Zionist State has failed to make itself acceptable because it is an artificially created alien state in the midst of an Arab world.

Palestine has acquired its identity through the historical development of the area. It is impossible for any Palestinian State to isolate itself from its geographical surroundings. It has been proved historically that any State, created on the land of Palestine which had been alien to the area, was unable to survive.

It is claimed that the main reason for the establishment of the State of Israel was to find a solution to the Jewish problem, but the experience of the past twenty years has proved that the absorbing capacity of the State has been insufficient to solve the problem of the sixteen million Jews in the world.

The Zionist Movement has, as a result, to face one of two alternatives: either to carry on an expansionist policy which will enable it to absorb all the Jews of the world or to admit the failure of its experience and try and find a solution for those Jews who have been up-rooted from their countries of origin to be settled on the land of Palestine.

We have offered our solution: that is the creation of a democratic Palestinian State for all those who wish to live in peace on the land of peace. Such a State can only acquire stability and viability by forming a part of the surrounding area, which is the Arab area. Otherwise this State with its Jewish, Christian and Moslem citizens would be another alien and temporary phenomenon in the area, which will arouse the antagonism of its neighbours, exactly as did the first Jewish State and the Crusaders' State. Neither of these States lasted for more than seventy years.

The word Arab implies a common culture, a common language and a common background. The majority of the inhabitants of any future State of Palestine will be Arab, if we consider that there are at present 2,500,000 Palestinian Arabs of the Moslem and Christian faiths and another 1,250,000 Arabs of the Jewish faith who live in what is now the State of Israel.

Q.—The immediate objective of your Movement is the liberation of your occupied homeland. What are your long-term objectives after achieving liberation? How do you envisage the future State of Palestine?

Abu Ammar.—As you have rightly mentioned, the immediate objective of Fatah is the total liberation of Palestine from Zionism and the destruction of any racial or sectarian notion which might exist among the Arabs.

Accordingly, we believe the only way to realise our objective is by overcoming our differences and achieving national unity. Our struggle in its present stage is a struggle for survival and for recovering our national identity. We aim ultimately at the establishment of an independent, progressive, democratic State in Palestine, which will guarantee equal rights to all its citizens, regardless of race or religion.

We wish to liberate the Jews from Zionism, and to make them realise that the purpose behind the creation of the State of Israel, namely to provide a haven for the persecuted Jews, has instead thrown them into a ghetto of their own making.

We wish to help build a progressive society based on liberty and equality for all. We also aim at participating actively in any struggle led by any Arab nation to achieve freedom and independence and to help build the united progressive Arab society of the future.

We support the struggle of all oppressed peoples in the world and we believe in the right for self-determination to all nations. We do not know for how long our struggle will go on until the liberation of our homeland is achieved. It might be a few years, or perhaps tens of years. It will be up to the generation that will finally liberate Palestine to decide upon the structure of their State.

Q.—The Palestine National Liberation Movement has certainly been able to achieve a breakthrough in what used to be a Zionist domain: the Western Leftist movements. Fatah has become to many synonymous with freedom fighting and an expression of struggle against oppression everywhere. Yet the new Zionist propaganda tactic is to smear it, by accusing it of accepting help from what is termed by them as "reactionary sources." What have you to say to this?

Abu Ammar.—Our Revolution accepts help, whether technological, material or military, from all sources. We seek the support of all those who wish to see Palestine liberated from Zionism, provided it is unconditional. We address ourselves equally to those who wish to offer help because they wish to see the Holy places liberated or to those revolutionaries in Africa, Asia and Latin America who consider our struggle as part of the struggle against oppression everywhere.

We have formed very strong ties with the liberation movements all over the world—in Cuba, in China, in Algeria and in Vietnam. We must not forget that in a war of liberation we should make use of every available source and means that will help us reach our ultimate goal—that is the liberation of our homeland.

I would also like to point out that other nations who have entered a war of liberation have adopted the same methods: for example in Vietnam the National Liberation Front includes twenty-three different organisations ranging from the Catholics and Buddhists to the Communists.

Can anyone accuse the Vietnamese Revolution of being a reactionary force? Add to this that the Palestinian Revolution in undertaking to lead the struggle against the Zionists, and to prevent any further aggression against the rest of the Arab world is entitled to use all the resources available in the Arab area.

Q.—Plans for a "peaceful settlement" of what is termed as an "Arab-Israeli" conflict seem to be speeding up, with the Four Power talks going ahead. Both the United States and the Soviet Union are eager to impose such a solution. How will *Fatah* react or rather act?

Abu Ammar.—The United Nations Security Council and the Big Powers have chosen to call their solutions "peaceful," whereas, in fact they are political solutions which are in no way related to peace as they all aim at safeguarding the state of Israel and ignoring the Palestinian Revolution. As such we declare that we will not under any circumstances accept any so-called peaceful solution which is being concocted by either the "Big" States or the "Small" States. We regard any such settlement as a document of self-humiliation which our people are forcibly asked to accept.

I believe that if our generation is unable to liberate its homeland, it should not commit the crime of accepting a *fait accompli,* which will prevent the future generations from carrying on the struggle for liberation.

What seems strange is that the call for a peaceful settlement started to be heard only when the Zionist enemy began to feel the blows dealt him by our Revolution.

I would like to mention here that immediately following the June War 1967, when President Johnson was asked about the problem in the Middle East, he replied, "Is there a problem?" This goes to prove that a problem exists only when Israel considers it as existing. We, the Palestinian people, refuse to capitulate or to give legality to usurpation. As long as Israel is an invading, racialist, fascist State, it will be rejected. Let no one think that any resolution taken outside the will of the Palestinians will ever acquire viability or legality.

We have waited twenty years for world conscience to awaken, but it was at the cost of more dispersion. And here I would like to state that in this we do not only have the support of the Palestinian masses, but also of the whole Arab masses. We must also not forget that our Movement started before the 5th of June 1967, with the purpose of liberating Palestine and we will not throw our arms until victory, no matter who stands in our way.

Q.—Your Movement has on more than one occasion declared that it will not interfere in the affairs of other Arab countries. Don't you think that owing to recent developments in certain neighbouring Arab countries, this policy should be revised, especially as these developments aim at threatening the Palestinian Revolution?

Abu Ammar.—We will not interfere in the internal affairs of any Arab country that will not in its turn put obstacles in the way of our Revolution or threaten its continuation.

Q.—During her last visit to Britain, Golda Meir denied the existence of a Palestinian people or a Palestinian resistance movement. What is your answer?

Abu Ammar.—Her predecessor, Levi Eshkol, also denied our existence for a very long time. Yet before his death, in an interview with the American magazine *Newsweek*, he had to admit that we do exist. In 1967 Moshe Dayan claimed that the Palestinian resistance was like an egg in his hand, which he could crush any time. Yet in 1969 he was quoted as advising the Israelis to "deepen their graves." Our answer therefore to Golda Meir and to anyone who doubts our existence can be found in our actions inside the occupied territories, whether in Haifa or Jerusalem or Tel Aviv or Eilat or elsewhere. Besides, you are now living amongst us and you can judge whether a Palestinian Resistance Movement exists or not.

Q.—Besides the military field, what are Fatah's achievements, for example, in other fields such as the emancipation of women, the education of children, social services and so on?

Abu Ammar.—As a progressive revolution, we consider that all members of our society, whether men or women, should enjoy equal rights. We therefore encourage the total emancipation of all our women and we endeavour to give them every opportunity to participate actively in our struggle. The Palestinian woman has since the days of the Mandate fought side by side with our men. In the occupied territories at present, it is our valiant sisters who are leading the civilian resistance against the occupying forces.

We do not place any obstacles or restrictions in the face of any woman who wishes to join in our Movement. In fact, we are encouraging them to join both our military and political ranks.

As for the education of children, we have established schools for both girls and boys; we have the "Cubs" training centers, we have organisations for caring for the families of our martyrs. We have founded our own hospitals and clinics which provide free medical treatment to the displaced persons in their camps. In fact, we know that our struggle is a long-term one and we are preparing ourselves accordingly.

Q.—How many times did you personally cross the Jordan since 1967?

Abu Ammar.—I do not answer personal questions, but I have entered the occupied territories every time that my military command has asked me to do so.

Q.—Do you consider your struggle as part of the struggle against imperialism and colonialism everywhere and why?

Abu Ammar.—Our struggle is part and parcel of every struggle against imperialism, injustice and oppression in the world. It is part of the world revolution which aims at establishing social justice and liberating mankind. Outside the Palestinian and Arab masses our greatest support comes from all freedom-loving people who have realised the true nature of Zionism and its association with imperialism and neo-colonialism. Israel's natural allies are sufficient proof of this. We only have to look at the support it receives from the United States, at its close links with the racist Republics of South Africa and Rhodesia.

As for its ties with the puppet regime of South Vietnam, let us only remember that its defence minister Moshe Dayan found it necessary and useful to spend a few months there learning their methods. The 1956 aggression against Egypt is another very clear example of the reasons for the creation of a Zionist state in the area. To sum up, we consider Israel as playing the new role of the East India Company in the Middle East.

Q.—Do you accept non-Palestinians in your fighting forces?

Abu Ammar.—We have at present both Arab and non-Arab freedom fighters in our ranks.

Q.—Why do you think Fatah has had such an appeal on both the national and international levels?

Abu Ammar.—Fatah has revolutionised the approach to the Palestinian problem. It has been the active force behind the resurgence of the Palestinian entity, which has established itself as the major element in the conflict. It is a true expression of the new Arab determination to resist invasion and oppression. Above all, it is part of the world movements for liberation and as such must attract freedom-loving people everywhere. Fatah was the first movement which translated the Palestinian aspirations into actions and which by its nature represents the true Palestinian determination.

Popular Front for the Liberation of Palestine: Platform (1969)

1. Conventional War Is the War of the Bourgeoisie. Revolutionary War Is People's War

The Arab bourgeoisie has developed armies which are not prepared to sacrifice their own interests or to risk their privileges. Arab militarism has become an apparatus for oppressing revolutionary socialist movements within the Arab states, while at the same time it claims to be staunchly anti-imperialist. Under the guise of the national question, the bourgeoisie has used its armies to strengthen its bureaucratic power over the masses, and to prevent the workers and peasants from acquiring political power. So far it has demanded the help of the workers and peasants without organising them or without developing a proletarian ideology. The national bourgeoisie usually comes to power through military coups and without any activity on the part of the masses, as soon as it has captured power it reinforces its bureaucratic position. Through widespread application of terror it is able to talk about revolution while at the same time it suppresses all the revolutionary movements and arrests everyone who tries to advocate revolutionary action.

The Arab bourgeoisie has used the question of Palestine to divert the Arab masses from realising their own interests and their own domestic problems. The bourgeoisie always concentrated hopes on a victory outside the state's boundaries, in Palestine, and in this way they were able to preserve their class interests and their bureaucratic positions.

The war of June 1967 disproved the bourgeois theory of conventional war. The best strategy for Israel is to strike rapidly. The enemy is not able to mobilise its armies for a long period of time because this would intensify its economic crisis. It gets complete support from U.S. imperialism and for these reasons it needs quick wars. Therefore for our poor people the best strategy in the long run is a people's war. Our people must overcome their weaknesses and exploit the weaknesses of the enemy by mobilising the Palestinian and Arab peoples. The weakening of imperialism and Zionism in the Arab world demands revolutionary war as the means to confront them.

2. Guerrilla Struggle as a Form of Pressure for the "Peaceful Solution"

The Palestinian struggle is a part of the whole Arab liberation movement and of the world liberation movement. The Arab bourgeoisie and world imperialism are trying to impose a peaceful solution on this Palestinian problem but this suggestion merely promotes the interests of imperialism and of Zionism, doubt in the efficacy of people's war as a means of liberation and the preservation of the relations of the Arab bourgeoisie with the imperialist world market.

The Arab bourgeoisie is afraid of being isolated from this market and of losing its role as a mediator of world capitalism. That is why the Arab oil-producing countries broke off the boycott against the West (instituted during the June war) and for this reason McNamara, as head of the World Bank, was ready to offer credits to them.

When the Arab bourgeoisie strive for a peaceful solution, they are in fact striving for the profit which they can get from their role as mediator between the imperialist market and the internal market. The Arab bourgeoisie are not yet opposed to the activity of the guerrillas, and sometimes they even help them; but this is because the presence of the guerrillas is a means of pressure for a peaceful solution. As long as the guerrillas don't have a clear class affiliation and a clear political stand they are unable to resist the implication of such a peaceful solution; but the conflict between the guerrillas and those whose strive for a peaceful solution is unavoidable. Therefore the guerrillas must take steps to transform their actions into a people's war with clear goals.

3. No Revolutionary War Without a Revolutionary Theory

The basic weakness of the guerrilla movement is the absence of a revolutionary ideology, which could illuminate the horizons of the Palestinian fighters and would incarnate the stages of a militant political programme. Without a revolutionary ideology the national struggle will remain imprisoned within its immediate practical and material needs. The Arab bourgeoisie is quite prepared for a limited satisfaction of the needs of the national struggle, as long as it respects the limits that the bourgeoisie sets. A clear illustration of this is the material help that Saudi Arabia offers *Fatah* while *Fatah* declares that she will not interfere in the internal affairs of any Arab countries.

Since most of the guerrilla movements have no ideological weapons, the Arab bourgeoisie can decide their fate. Therefore, the struggle of the Palestinian people must be supported by the workers and peasants, who will fight against any form of domination by imperialism, Zionism or the Arab bourgeoisie.

4. The War of Liberation Is a Class War Guided by a Revolutionary Ideology

We must not be satisfied with ignoring the problems of our struggle, saying that our struggle is a national one and not a class struggle. The national struggle reflects the class struggle. The national struggle is a struggle for land and those who struggle for it are the peasants who were driven away from their land. The bourgeoisie is always ready to lead such a movement, hoping to gain control of the internal market. If the bourgeoisie succeeds in bringing the national movement under its control, which strengthens its position, it can lead the movement under the guise of a peaceful solution into compromises with imperialism and Zionism.

Therefore, the fact that the liberation struggle is mainly a class struggle emphasises the necessity for the workers and peasants to play a leading role in the national liberation movement. If the small bourgeoisie take the leading role, the national revolution will fall as a victim of the class interests of this leadership. It is a great mistake to start by saying that the Zionist challenge demands national unity for this shows that one does not understand the real class structure of Zionism.

The struggle against Israel is first of all a class struggle. Therefore the oppressed class is the only class which is able to face a confrontation with Zionism.

5. The Main Field of Our Revolutionary Struggle Is Palestine

The decisive battle must be in Palestine. The armed people's struggle in Palestine can help itself with the simplest weapons in order to ruin the economies and the war machinery of their Zionist enemy. The moving of the people's struggle into Palestine depends upon agitating and organising the masses, more than depending upon border actions in the Jordan valley, although these actions are of importance for the struggle in Palestine.

When guerrilla organisations began their actions in the occupied areas, they were faced with a brutal military repression by the armed forces of Zionism. Because these organisations had no revolutionary ideology and so no programme, they gave in to demands of self-preservation and re-treated into eastern Jordan. All their activity turned into border actions. This presence of the guerrilla organisations in Jordan enables the Jordanian bourgeoisie and their secret agents to crush these organisations when they are no longer useful as pressure for a peaceful solution.

6. Revolution in Both Regions of Jordan

We must not neglect the struggle in east Jordan for this land is connected with Palestine more than with the other Arab countries. The problem of the revolution in Palestine is dialectically connected with the problem of the revolution in Jordan. A chain of plots between the Jordanian monarchy, imperialism and Zionism have proved this connection.

The struggle in east Jordan must take the correct path, that of class struggle. The Palestinian struggle must not be used as a means of propping up the Jordanian monarchy, under the mask of national unity, and the main problem in Jordan is the creation of a Marxist-Leninist party with a clear action programme according to which it can organise the masses and enable them to carry out the national and class struggle. The harmony of the struggle in the two regions must be realised through co-ordinating organs whose tasks will be to guarantee reserves inside Palestine and to mobilise the peasants and soldiers in the border-territories.

This is the only way in which Amman can become an Arab Hanoi:—a base for the revolutionaries fighting inside Palestine.

Soviet General Secretary Leonid I. Brezhnev: Position on the 1973 War (October 9, 1973)

President Hawari Boumedien [of Algeria] late last night received the USSR Ambassador, who handed him an important message from the

CPSU Central Committee General Secretary on the Middle East situation. The message said:

The responsibility for the new military flare-up in the Middle East lies wholly and completely with the Tel Aviv leaders. While enjoying the support and protection of imperialist circles, Israel continues its aggression started in 1967 against the Arab countries, and foils every effort to establish a just peace in the Middle East and deliberately carries out provocations, including armed provocations, against Syria, Egypt and Lebanon, thus aggravating to the extreme the situation in this region.

I believe, dear comrade President, you agree that [in] the struggle at present being waged against Israeli aggression, for the liberation of Arab territories occupied in 1967 and the safeguarding of the legitimate rights of the Arab people of Palestine, Arab fraternal solidarity must, more than ever before, play a decisive role. Syria and Egypt must not be alone in their struggle against a treacherous enemy. There is an urgent need for the widest aid and support of the progressive regimes in these countries who, like Algeria, are the hope for progress and freedom in the Arab world.

The Central Committee of the CPSU and the Soviet Government are firmly convinced that the Algerian leaders, who are widely experienced in the anti-imperialist struggle, understand full well all the peculiarities of the present situation and that, guided by the ideals of fraternal solidarity, will use every means and take every step required to give their support to Syria and Egypt in the tough struggle imposed by the Israeli aggressor.

Dear comrade President, your high personal prestige in the Third World countries which in particular contributed to the great success of the fourth non-aligned conference, clearly gives you the indisputable means to act with the Arab states with a view to bringing about a united stand in the face of the common danger.

As for the Soviet Union, it gives to the friendly Arab states multilateral aid and support in their just struggle against the imperialist Israeli aggression.

Syrian President Hafiz al-Asad: Speech (October 15, 1973)

Brother compatriots, brother military men, sons of our Arab people, with great pride in you and your great steadfastness I address you today from the bastion of steadfastness, the immortal Damascus whose great steadfastness against the enemy's barbarous raids has become the symbol of the steadfastness of our entire Arab homeland and a cause for pride of all our Arab nation. This city will remain as towering as [Mount] Qasyun in the protection of its sons who are meeting the challenges with strong resolve and who are facing difficulties, no matter how big, with more resolve and iron will and increased determination to achieve victory.

The steadfastness of Damascus stems from the steadfastness of its sister towns of this struggling country; from the steadfastness of Homs, Latakia, Tartus and Baniyas, and also from the steadfastness of Cairo and every capital, town and village in the Arab homeland. This is because, basically, this steadfastness is the practical expression of the will of our people and their determination to live the life of dignity to which they aspire and to make bright the future that they wish for themselves and for all the peoples of the world.

Ten days ago I addressed you on the day which marked the end of a stage during which the enemy had wanted his repeated aggressions to consolidate occupation and expansion and pave the way for imposing his will on our nation. Today I address you as the battle takes its real shape as a full war of liberation. Its first achievement has been the liberation of the Arab will from the elements of pressure. God willing, it will end with the liberation of the land which its sons have long desired.

In those ten glorious days of ferocious battles waged by our armed forces with all their arms and with extreme manhood, bravery and unshakable faith in victory—in those days of magnificent, heroic steadfastness of our people we corrected many erroneous ideas which had almost become established abroad about our nation. We have restored self-confidence to the Arab individual after dressing his wounded dignity and proving to the enemy and all the world that our people are not an easy prey that the enemy thought it could easily swallow. We have proved that certain death awaits anyone who tries to humiliate our people or debase an inch of our land.

You have revived the traditions of our glorious nation, of the fathers and the forefathers. You have pleased God, the homeland and the sense of moral goodness. With chaste blood you have charted on the map of Arab struggle a road which will never change after today. It is a road to victory.

You have been supporting the cause of your nation and therefore your nation rose to support your steadfastness. You have been with the cause of freedom and therefore the free men in the world rushed to express their support for your giant stand. They have expressed it in various ways.

You have won the respect, appreciation and admiration of everyone. The reason for all this was our steadfastness, both by civilians and military, in our readiness to meet hardship with selflessness and in our insistence on proceeding steadily towards the goal, regardless of how costly the sacrifice or however long the road.

During these critical days I was, through my senses and feelings, with every individual. I was with the soldier, the NCO and officer while smashing the enemy tanks with his tank, shelling the concentrations of aggressors with his gun and directing precise fire at the enemy planes which fell in wreckage on the ground; I was with the pilot while defending the homeland's sky with his plane, chasing the enemy planes and smashing the legend of the invincible Israeli air force; I was with the sailor while protecting our coasts with his naval unit and gun and writing new chapters of Arab glory on the seas; I was with every citizen of our noble people; with the worker in his factory while operating the machine with one hand and carrying arms with the other; with the peasant while tilling the land and carrying his rifle; with the employee in his office while doing his duty towards his compatriots in the best manner and with a sense of responsibility; with the man responsible for security and civil defence while carrying out his duties with loyalty and devotion; with the doctor and the nurse as they stood in complete readiness and preparedness to fulfill humane and national duties; with the merchant in his shop as he met the needs of citizens with high patriotic spirit; with the housewives as they cared for the families and children; and with the army of loyal and sincere citizens in their various jobs as they managed the homeland's daily life.

Brothers, you may have questions on your mind which you would probably expect me to answer. Or perhaps you wish me to talk about national and international activities related to the battle, whether these were of a positive or negative nature. But you realize that war has its conditions and requirements which make it incumbent upon us to avoid discussing any matter that would not benefit the war effort.

Nevertheless, in this regard I am anxious to point out that our steadfastness in the war of liberation has begun to give the slogan, "pan-Arabism of the battle", a practical and real meaning. In this regard I would like to express, on your behalf, the greatest appreciation for the role of the sisterly Iraqi forces whose men fought heroically against the enemy and whose blood was mixed with that of their brothers in the Syrian forces. Their participation in the battle has been a true expression of the pan-Arabism of the battle. Greetings to the Iraqi Army and to our people in sisterly Iraq.

The day will come when the Saudi forces and the Jordanian forces will also take part in the battle and play their role in the national battle. Also, the two sisterly states Algeria and Libya, from the first moment [of the battle] took the initiative to give practical backing and actual support with various forms. The United Arab Amirates and the state of Qatar also extended a helping hand.

The support that was given to the northern front was matched by support to the western front where the valiant Egyptian forces are fighting major battles against the enemy after they humiliated him and defeated him. This defeat made the enemy resort to contradictions and exposed him to the entire world. This happened when the Egyptians crossed the Suez Canal, destroyed the enemy fortified positions and continued their advance into Sinai steadily and with strength.

If this indicates anything, it indicates Arab unity. It also indicates that our nation is alive. Our unity and vitality appear most gloriously during crises and hardships. We should not forget that our steadfastness is the fundamental and basic factor in every stand. On this rock all the enemy's attempts will be crushed. Continuous steadfastness increases the rally of the Arab nation around us and their support for us will double.

Our heroes have transformed Israel's aggression, since 6th October, to a retreat of the enemy forces. As I told you on that day, our forces rushed to repulse the aggression, forcing the occupation forces to withdraw before them. They continued their advance and expelled the enemy forces from Mount Hermon, Qunaytirah, Jibbin, Khushniyah, Jukhadar, Awl Al, Tall al-Faras and Rafid and other villages and positions in the Golan. They inflicted on the enemy losses which deeply shook the Zionist entity. At that time, while the enemy was hiding his losses and defeats from the people of Israel and from the outside world—a method which he is still following—we in turn kept quiet about the victories of our forces and postponed announcing them.

While the enemy's reports and statements exposed themselves day after day and uncovered more contradictions, we preferred to wait before announcing what we had achieved and until the repelling of the enemy forces is final and the liberation of the land is complete.

We could have announced the liberation of the greater part of the Golan on the fourth day of the battle. The faith of our armed forces in God—praise be to Him—as well as our armed forces' confidence in our people, their proper use of the good weapons in their possession, and their faith in the cause they are fighting for have all reflected on the course of fighting through the victories that our forces have achieved and are still achieving in every field and on every level. The heroic acts of our army have compelled the enemy to admit that the battle is tough and that the fighting is intense.

On our part, we have not anticipated an easy victory or that the enemy would accept his expulsion from our land without ferocious resistance. We know the enemy's expansionist ambitions and know that there are forces encouraging these ambitions and supporting the attempts to achieve these ambitions. In the aftermath of his losses and defeats in the first days of fighting, the enemy hastened to enlist the help of these forces, asking them for assistance and large numbers of foreigners to offset his losses in men in the various corps, particularly the air force as well as new weapons to offset his losses in weapons. With the quick supplies he received and which were added to the calculated reserve forces, the enemy heavily concentrated on one sector of our front and began to exert pressure with the larger part of his forces, tanks and planes and was able to achieve a limited penetration of our lines. Nevertheless, our forces initiated a quick reply and waged, from new positions, fierce fighting in which every member of our forces fought most valiantly and repulsed the enemy counter-offensive and inflicted heavy losses on his tanks and planes and forced him to retreat.

Our forces continue to pursue the enemy and strike at him and will continue to strike at enemy forces until we regain our positions in our occupied land and continue then until we liberate the whole land.

We know that our enemy has a source to supply him and offset his losses in men and weapons. However, we are confident of the resources of our people and nation and the sources of our support. I say to those who are supporting the falsehood and aggression of Israel that they should consider and think of the consequences that their hostile aggressive attitudes will have on their many interests in the Arab homeland. By gaining the animosity of the masses of our nation, they are arousing the anger of these masses. And when peoples become angry, no force can stand in their way.

Brother compatriots, brother soldiers, freedom and dignity have a price and the price is no doubt costly. However, we are ready to pay this price in order to preserve honour, to defend freedom, to liberate the land and to regain the rights so that we can give the coming Arab generations their right to an affluent life and a shining, smiling future in which they can enjoy freedom, security, reassurance and peace.

We are knocking at the door of freedom with our hands and with all our strength, realizing that the enemies of peoples do not voluntarily recognize the freedom of these peoples. We are determined that the liberation of the land and the achievement of victory in this war be the great goal from which we shall not budge, God willing. For the sake of the great goal, every sacrifice and effort will be cheap. As long as our goal is great and as long as we believe in this goal, our effort and struggle will be commensurate with our goal. As long as we believe in the goal, all enemy efforts and psychological warfare tactics will be defeated and fail and will definitely not affect the morale of our people and their ability to hold out and resist.

We are a people who, in the hour of decisiveness, are capable of creating miracles. The hour of decisiveness has come. Let us adapt ourselves to continue the war of liberation to its victorious end. Let us continue the war of liberation with a deep breath, believing in God, confident in ourselves and of our ability to make victory with our own hands.

Finally, on your behalf, I convey a greeting—coming from a heart full of love and appreciation—to all the men of our armed forces. I hail their courage, valour, high efficiency, firm faith in the cause of their homeland and their certain capability to wrest the right. Greetings from the heart to every Arab soldier who is helping to make victory in the battle of liberation certain. Greetings to every one of you. Let us all reiterate at all times: either martyrdom or victory.

Egyptian President Anwar Sadat:
Speech (October 16, 1973)

. . . The Egyptian armed forces have achieved a miracle by any military standard. They have fully devoted themselves to their duty. They have efficiently absorbed all the weapons and methods of training of the modern age, as well as its sciences.

When I gave them the order to reply to the enemy's provocation and to check his deceit, they proved themselves. After the orders were given them, these forces took the initiative, surprised the enemy and threw him off balance with their quick movement. I shall not be exaggerating to say that military history will make a long pause to study and examine the operation carried out on 6th October 1973 when the Egyptian armed forces were able to storm the difficult barrier of the Suez Canal which was armed with the fortified Bar Lev Line to establish bridgeheads on the east bank of the Canal after they had, as I said, thrown the enemy off balance in six hours.

The risk was great and sacrifices were big. However, the results achieved in the first six hours of the battle in our war were huge. The arrogant enemy lost its equilibrium at this moment. The wounded nation restored its honour.

The Middle East political map has changed. While we say so out of pride, as some of the pride is faith, we are duty bound to record here, on behalf of the people and this nation, our absolute confidence in our armed forces; our confidence in their command, which drew up the plan; our confidence in the officers and men who have implemented the plan with fire and blood. We record our confidence in the armed forces' faith and knowledge, our confidence in the armed forces' arms and in their capability of absorbing the arms. I say in brief that this homeland can be assured and feel secure, after fear, that it now has a shield and a sword.

From here I want to draw your attention with me to the northern front, where the great Syrian army is fighting one of the most glorious battles of the Arab nation under the loyal and resolute command of brother President Hafiz al-Asad.

I want to tell our brothers on the northern front: You made a promise and you were faithful to the promise. You made a friendship and you have turned out to be the most honest friends. You have fought and you have proved to be the most courageous fighters. You have fought like men and stood fast like heroes. We could not have found more reassuring and praiseworthy men in this comradeship in which we had to fight together against a common enemy, the enemy of the whole Arab nation.

We have been the vanguards of the battle. Together we have borne its brunt and paid most dearly with our blood and resources. We shall continue the fighting and defy danger. We shall continue, backed by our brothers who have sincerely and faithfully joined the battle, to pay the price in sweat and blood until we reach an objective acceptable to us and to our nation in this serious stage of its continuous struggle.

That was about war—and now that about peace. When we speak about peace we must remember and not forget—just as others also must not pretend to forget—the real reasons for our war. You will allow me specifically and categorically to put some of these reasons to you.

(1) We have fought for the sake of peace, the only peace that really deserves to be called peace—peace based on justice. Our enemy sometimes speaks about peace. But there is a vast difference between the peace of aggression and the peace of justice. David Ben Gurion was the one who formulated for Israel the theory of imposing peace. Peace cannot be imposed. The talk about imposing peace means a threat to wage war or actually waging it.

The great mistake our enemy has made is that he thought the force of terror could guarantee security. But the futility of this theory has been proved in practice on the battlefield. It has been proved that if this theory did work at one time, due to the weakness of the opposite side, it does not work if these people rally their forces every day. I do not know what David Ben Gurion would think if he were in command in Israel today. Would he have been able to understand the nature of history or would he be like the Israeli command today—in opposition to history?

Peace cannot be imposed. The peace of a fait accompli cannot exist and cannot last. There can only be peace through justice alone. Peace cannot be established through terror however oppressive and whatever illusions the arrogance of power or the stupidity of power might give. Our enemy has persisted in this arrogance and stupidity not only over the past six years, but throughout the past twenty-five years—that is, since the Zionist state usurped Palestine.

We might ask the Israeli leaders today: Where has the theory of Israeli security gone? They have tried to establish this theory once by violence and once by force in twenty-five years. It has been broken and destroyed. Our military power today challenges their military power. They are now in a long protracted war. They are facing a war of attrition which we can tolerate more and better than they can. Their hinterland is exposed if they think they can frighten us by threatening the Arab hinterland. I add, so they may hear in Israel: We are not advocators of annihilation, as they claim.

Our Zafir-type trans-Sinai Egyptian Arab rockets are now in their bases ready to be launched at the first signal to the deepest depth in Israel.

We could have given the signal and the order from the very first moment of the battle, particularly as the Israelis' haughtiness and vicious pride gave them the illusion that they could bear greater consequences that they really could sustain. But we are aware of the responsibility of using certain types of arms, and we ourselves restrain ourselves from using them. The Israelis should remember what I once said and still say: an eye for an eye, a tooth for a tooth and death for death.

(2) We do not fight to attack the territory of others, but we fought and will continue to fight for two objectives: (a) to restore our territory which was occupied in 1967; and (b) to find ways and means to restore and obtain respect for the legitimate rights of the people of Palestine.

These are our objectives in accepting the risks of the fighting. We have accepted them in reply to unbearable provocations. We were not the first to begin these, but we acted in self-defence to defend our land and our right to freedom and life.

Our war was not for aggression, but against aggression. In our war we did not depart from the values and laws of international society as stipulated in the UN Charter, which the free nations have written with their blood after their victory over Fascism and Nazism.

We may say that our war is a continuation of humanity's war against Fascism and Nazism; for, by its racist claims and its reasoning of expansion through brute force, Zionism is nothing but a feeble replica of Fascism and Nazism which is contemptible rather than frightening and calls for disdain more than for hatred. . . .

Brothers and sisters, the entire world has supported our rights and praised our courage in defending these rights. The world has realized that we were not the first to attack, but that we immediately responded to the duty of self-defence. We are not against but are for the values and laws of the international community. We are not warmongers but seekers of peace. The world has realized all this, and in the light of it sympathizes with our cause.

Today, the world sympathizes with us more out of its respect for our determination to defend this cause. We were sure of world sympathy, and now we are proud of its respect for us. I tell you in all sincerity and honesty that I prefer world respect, even without sympathy, to world sympathy that is without respect. I thank God.

Brothers and sisters, a single state has differed from the whole world—not just from us, but from the whole world, as I said. This state is the United States. The United States claims it was shocked because we tried to repulse the aggression. We do not understand how or why the United States was shocked. This state, it said, was not only shocked but has recovered from the shock without coming to its senses.

It is regrettable and sad that this should be the attitude of one of the two superpowers in this age. We were expecting, or perhaps wishing, despite all the indications and experiences, that the United States would recover from the surprise and come to its senses. But this did not happen. We have seen the United States recovering from the surprise and turning towards manoeuvres. Its first objective is to stop the fighting and bring a return to the lines that existed before 6th October. We could have been angered by this inverse logic, but we were not. This is because, on the one hand, we are confident of ourselves, and, on the other, we really do want to contribute to world peace.

The world is entering an era of detente between the two superpowers. Now we oppose the policy of detente. We had one reservation about this policy and this reservation still exists. If we want the world, after a world war has become impossible, to enter an era of peace, then peace is not an abstract or absolute meaning. Peace has one single meaning: that all the peoples of the world should feel that it is peace for them and not peace imposed on them.

I would like to say before you and to all the world that we want the policy of detente to succeed and to be consolidated. We are prepared to contribute to the success of this consolidation. But we rightly believe that this cannot happen while aggression is being committed against an entire Arab nation, which lies strategically in the heart of the world and possesses its most important economic resources. Any disregard of this logical fact is not only disregard but also an insult, which we do not accept, either for ourselves or for the world, which is aware of the importance and value of this area in which we live. Therefore, the world must realize now that this area can give and can withhold.

Brothers and sisters, the United States, after a manoeuvre we refused even to discuss—especially after we had forged the path of right with the force of arms—has resorted to a policy that neither we nor our Arab nation can keep silent about. It has established a quick bridge to transport military aid to Israel. The United States was not content with the fact that it was its arms that enabled Israel to obstruct all attempts for a peaceful solution of the Middle East question. It has now involved itself in something with more serious and more dangerous consequences. . . .

If you want to know our terms for peace, then here is our peace plan:

(1) We have fought and will fight to liberate our territories which the Israeli occupation seized in 1967 and to find a means to retrieve and secure respect for the legitimate rights of the Palestinian people. In this respect, we uphold our commitment to the UN resolutions, [those of] the General Assembly and the Security Council.

(2) We are prepared to accept a cease-fire on the basis of the immediate withdrawal of the Israeli forces from all the occupied territories, under international supervision, to the pre-5th June 1967 lines.

(3) We are prepared, as soon as the withdrawal from all these territories has been completed, to attend an international peace conference at the United Nations, which I will try my best to persuade my comrades, the Arab leaders directly responsible for running our conflict with the enemy [to accept]. I will also do my best to convince the Palestine people's representatives about this so that they may participate with us and with the as-

sembled states in laying down rules and regulations for a peace in the area based on the respect of the legitimate rights of all the peoples of the area.

(4) We are ready at this hour—indeed at this very moment—to begin clearing the Suez Canal and to open it for world navigation so that it may resume its role in serving world prosperity and welfare. I have actually issued an order to the head of the Suez Canal Authority to begin this operation on the day following the liberation of the eastern bank of the Canal. Preliminary preparations for this operation have already begun.

(5) In all this, we are not prepared to accept any ambiguous promises or loose words which can be given all sorts of interpretations and only waste time in useless things and put our cause back to the state of inaction, which we no longer accept whatever reasons the others may have or whatever sacrifices we have to make. What we want now is clarity: clarity of aims and clarity of means. . . .

UN Security Council: Resolution 338
(October 22, 1973)

The Security Council

1. Calls upon all parties to the present fighting to cease all firing and terminate all military activity immediately, no later than twelve hours after the moment of the adoption of this decision, in the positions they now occupy;

2. Calls upon the parties concerned to start immediately after the cease-fire the implementation of Security Council Resolution 242 (1967), in all of its parts;

3. Decides that immediately and concurrently with the cease-fire, negotiations start between the parties concerned under appropriate auspices aimed at establishing a just and durable peace in the Middle East.

Israeli Prime Minister Golda Meir:
Statement in the Knesset (October 23, 1973)

Members of the Knesset:

On 22 October the Government of Israel unanimously decided to respond to the approach of the U.S. Government and President Nixon and announce its readiness to agree to a cease-fire according to the resolution of the Security Council following the joint American-Soviet proposal.

According to this proposal, the military forces will remain in the positions they hold at the time when the cease-fire goes into effect.

The implementation of the cease-fire is conditional on reciprocity. Our decision has been brought to the notice of the Foreign Affairs and Security committee, and now to the notice of the Knesset.

As regards the second paragraph of the Security Council resolution, the Government decided to instruct Israel's representative at the United Nations to include in his address to the Security Council a passage clarifying that our agreement to this paragraph is given in the sense in which it was defined by Israel when it decided in August 1970 to respond positively to the United States Government's initiative for a cease-fire, as stated in the United Nations on 4 August, 1970, and by the Prime Minister in the Knesset on the same day. This was also made clear to the U.S. Government. Israel's acceptance of a cease-fire with Egypt is conditional upon Egypt's agreement, but is not conditional upon Syria's agreement to a cease-fire, and vice-versa.

The Government also decided to clarify with the U.S. Government a series of paragraphs intimately connected with the content of the Security Council resolution and the procedure required by it. It is our intention to clarify and ensure, *inter alia*, that:

The cease-fire shall be binding upon all the regular forces stationed in the territory of a State accepting the cease-fire including the forces of foreign States, such as the armies of Iraq and Jordan in Syria and also forces sent by other Arab States which took part in the hostilities.

The cease-fire shall also be binding upon irregular forces acting against Israel from the area of the States accepting the cease-fire.

The cease-fire shall assure the prevention of a blockade or interference with free navigation, including oil tankers in the Bab-el-Mandeb straits on their way to Eilat.

It shall ensure that the interpretation of the term referring to "negotiations between the parties" is direct negotiations—and, naturally, it must be assured that the procedures, the drawing up of maps and the subject of cease-fire supervision shall be determined by agreement.

A subject of great importance, one dear to our hearts, is the release of prisoners. The Government of Israel has decided to demand an immediate exchange of prisoners. We have discussed this with the Government of the United States, which was one of the initiators of the cease-fire.

I spoke about this with the Secretary of State, Dr. Kissinger. We will insist on an immediate exchange of prisoners. When Dr. Kissinger's plane arrived at Andrews Air Base, the State Department spokesman, Mr. McCloskey, made the following statement to newsmen:

"We believe one of the early priorities should be a release of prisoners on both sides, and we and the Soviet Union have pledged our efforts to obtain assurances that this will be done as a priority matter."

I stress again that this subject is one of the principal tests of the cease-fire, and that there will be no relaxation of our demand that the obligations undertaken by the initiators of the cease-fire be indeed carried out.

I will say several things about our military situation on the Syrian and Egyptian fronts before the cease-fire:

On the Syrian Front

The lines we are holding today on the Syrian front are better than those we held on the 6th of October.

Not only do we now hold all the territory which was under our control before, but our situation has been considerably improved by the holding of positions on the Hermon ridge and also on the front line in the east, which has shifted the previous cease-fire line to a better line supported by a strong flank in the north, on the Hermon ridge.

On the Egyptian Front

The Egyptians did indeed gain a military achievement in crossing the Canal, but in a daring counter-offensive by the Israel Defense Forces, our forces succeeded in regaining control of part of the Eastern Canal line, and to gain control of a large area west of the Canal, an area which opens before us both defensive and offensive possibilities:

(a) This deployment deprives the Egyptian army of its capacity to constitute an offensive threat in the direction of Sinai and Israel, and also prevents them from being able to attack essential installations or areas in our territory.

(b) The forces of the I.D.F. west of the Suez Canal constitute a strong military base for the development of operations initiated by us if required.

In connection with the cease-fire issue, the U.S. Secretary of State, Dr. Henry Kissinger, and his aides called here on their way from Moscow to Washington. The visit was an appropriate opportunity for a thoroughgoing discussion of questions arising from the cease-fire, as well as for an exchange of views, in a friendly spirit, on what was about to happen and what was called for as a result of Israel's response to the U.S. Government's request for agreement to a cease-fire. During this visit, we continued and strengthened the contacts which preceded the Security Council resolution.

In all our contacts with the United States, I learnt that not only does the U.S. have no plan for the borders and other components of peace, but that it is its view that those who offer their "good services" should see to it that the parties themselves—and they alone—should make proposals, plans, for the future.

Furthermore, I must emphasize that, in accordance with authoritative information to hand, the Moscow talks contained nothing more than is contained in the Security Council resolution. I have to inform you that the Syrian Government has so far not responded to the cease-fire resolution.

The fighting on that front continues, and the I.D.F. will operate there in accordance with its plans.

As for the Egyptian front—firing against our forces has not yet ceased, and the I.D.F. is obliged to operate as required as long as the firing continues.

At this stage, I will state only that we are examining the conduct of the Egyptians with close military and political attention. Should Egypt persist in belligerent activity, we shall deem ourselves free to take any action and move called for by the situation.

I shall not go into elaborate evaluations of the political activity which preceded the cease-fire. In any event, it was not we who made approaches concerning a cease-fire. As far as the situation on the fronts was concerned, there was no reason for such an approach on our part. It was not we who initiated the timing and clauses of the Security Council's resolution. On the fronts, our forces were not in an inferior battle position. As aforesaid, we deemed it right to respond to the call of the United States and its President, since:

(a) The State of Israel, by its nature, has no wish for war, does not desire loss of life. All Governments of Israel have been convinced that war would not promote peace.

(b) The cease-fire proposal has come when our position is firm on both fronts, when the achievements we hold are of great value and justify agreement to a cease-fire, despite the enemy's achievement east of the Suez Canal.

(c) We responded to the call by the United States and its President out of appreciation and esteem for its positive policy in the Middle East at this time.

Great importance attaches to our response insofar as concerns the continued strengthening of Israel, with particular reference to the continued military and political aid in the war that has been forced upon us. . . .

The Egyptian rulers' attitude to war and to loss of life is different from ours. On record is the statement by the Egyptian President concerning his readiness to sacrifice millions of his people. On 16 October, after the I.D.F. had succeeded in establishing a bridgehead west of the Canal, the Egyptian President delivered a boastful address, mocked at a cease-fire and said *inter alia:*

"We are prepared to agree to a cease-fire on the basis of withdrawal of the Israeli forces from all the occupied territories forthwith—under international supervision—to the pre 5 June 1967 lines." Only a few days passed and Egypt agreed to a cease-fire. Not one of the conditions raised by Sadat in his speech was included in the Security Council resolution.

Paragraph 3 of the Security Council resolution says:

The Security Council decides that immediately and concurrently with the cease-fire, negotiations start between the parties concerned under appropriate auspices aimed at establishing a just and durable peace in the Middle East.

According to the agreed version of representatives of the U.S.A., the meaning of negotiations between the parties is direct negotiations between Israel and her neighbors on the subject of a just and enduring peace. No such explicit statement was included in Resolution 242 of the Security Council. Moreover, the present resolution also specifies the timing of the beginning of these negotiations—immediately and concurrently with the cease-fire. And there is no need to stress that we attribute great importance to paragraph 3 of the Security Council resolution, if our neighbors will indeed carry it out. . . .

On various occasions the Government of Israel has officially defined its attitude towards Security Council Resolution 242. These statements were made from international platforms and at diplomatic meetings, and we have brought them to the knowledge of the Knesset, its Defense and Foreign Affairs Committee and the public at large.

At this time I shall refer to one statement made on 4 August, 1970, to the U.S. Government, to the United Nations and to the Knesset. This statement too, is connected with a cease-fire, and I shall not tire the Knesset by quoting it in full. However, I consider it necessary to quote from my statement in the Knesset on 5 August. This statement was made on the eve of possible talks with the Arab States, and it is still completely valid.

Israel has publicly declared that, by virtue of her right to secure borders, defensible borders, she will not return to the frontiers of 4 June 1967, which make the country a temptation to aggression and which, on various fronts, give decisive advantages to an aggressor. Our position was and still remains that, in the absence of peace, we will continue to maintain the situation as determined at the cease-fire. The cease-fire lines can be replaced only by secure, recognized and agreed boundaries demarcated in a peace treaty.

In accepting the American Government's peace initiative, Israel was not asked to, and did not, undertake any territorial commitments. On the contrary, the Government of Israel received support for its position that not a single Israeli soldier will be withdrawn from the cease-fire lines until a binding contractual peace agreement is reached.

This terrible war that was forced upon us reinforces our awareness of the vital need for defensible borders, for which we shall struggle with all our vigor.

It is worth noting that, since the outbreak of the war on Yom Kippur, the terrorists have also resumed activities from Lebanese territory. Up to this morning, during this period of 17 days, 116 acts of aggression have been perpetrated, 44 civilian settlements on the northern border have been attacked and shelled, and some 20 civilians and 6 soldiers were killed or wounded in these actions. Our people living in the border settlements may be confident that Israel's Defense Forces are fully alert to this situation. Despite the defensive dispositions operative on this front, it has been proved once again that defensive action alone is not sufficient to put an end to acts of terror.

The war in which we are engaged began with a concerted attack on two fronts. The aggressive initiative afforded our enemies preliminary achievements—but, thanks to the spirit and strength of Israel's Defense Army, which is backed by the entire nation, this attack was broken. The aggressors were thrown back. Considerable portions of their forces were destroyed, and the I.D.F. broke through and crossed the cease-fire lines. From holding battles our forces went over to the offensive and gained brilliant achievements.

On both fronts our forces are now holding strong positions beyond the cease-fire lines, unbroken in spirit. The people is united in support of our army.

Israel wants a cease-fire. Israel will observe the cease-fire on a reciprocal basis, and only on that basis. With all her heart Israel wants peace negotiation to start immediately and concurrently with the cease-fire. Israel is capable of evincing the inner strength necessary for the promotion of an honorable peace within secure borders.

We shall be happy if such readiness is also shown by the people and Government of Egypt. However, if the rulers of Egypt propose to renew the war, they shall find Israel prepared, armed and steadfast in spirit. . . .

Egyptian President Anwar Sadat: Speech (April 3, 1974)

. . . You recall that in 1971, I announced that this year must be the year of decision. You also recall that during the same year, 1971, only a few months had passed since I assumed my office. I made an initiative on 4th February 1971 after the termination of the second cease-fire, which was due to be ended on 5th February 1971, for the sake of peace.

The U.S. Secretary of State, Mr. Rogers, came in May 1971. You will also recall that he announced he had nothing to request from Egypt—nothing. After the announcement of the initiative in February, he announced in May that he had nothing to request from Egypt and that Egypt had fully done its part. At that time, we also answered Jarring's memorandum of 8th February 1971.

We waited. May and June passed. On 6th July 1971, I received notification from the U.S. Secretary of State that the United States would intervene to achieve a peaceful solution in accordance with the initiative I had submitted. They asked some questions, including a question about the Egyptian-Soviet treaty which was concluded at that time, May 1971.

After the U.S. Secretary of State had visited here, President Podgornyy came. We concluded the treaty in late May. They [the Americans] put questions, and I answered them. My answer has always been that all our decisions express our free will. Since 23rd July 1952, our will has been free to take whatever decision we see fit to take.

July passed without anything happening. August and September passed. On 11th October 1971 I went to the USSR. I had a long session with the three Soviet leaders. As I have told you before, and as you heard at the [ASU] Central Committee, we reached agreement. We removed the clouds that existed in our relations with the USSR. We agreed in October 1971 on specific deals, and the arms were to arrive before the end of 1971. They asked about the year of decision, why I held to this and why I insisted that the situation be reactivated militarily—because there was no other way.

I explained the matter to them very clearly and frankly and in a friendly manner. As I have said, we agreed on arms deals, and the arms were to arrive before the end of 1971.

Relations between ourselves and the United States at that time were not progressing well. On the contrary, their promises in May and July and their failure to fulfil all these promises prompted me to reveal the true American attitude to the people. I attacked them most violently.

This is because the attitude of the U.S. Secretary of State at that time was indeed regrettable. He had reason to feel ashamed and I did shame him before our people, the Arab nation and the whole world.

In 1971, when the first shipments began to arrive, we were supposed to be able to make a decision on the battle on 8th December. I was in the Soviet Union in October. October passed and so did November. And then December came, but there was absolutely no information about the arrival of any shipments or anything. On 8th December the battle between India and Pakistan began. As we all know, the Soviet Union had commitments towards India. We entered December and then more than half of December had gone by—nothing had arrived. The understanding was that these shipments would arrive in October, November and December so that before the end of 1971 we could make a decision and begin operations.

At that time I notified the Soviet Union. About the middle of December I told them that there were only fifteen days left before the end of the year and we did not yet even have the dates for the arrival of shipments or vessels. We had no information about them and they had not appeared. I had fixed the year as the year of decision, and therefore I asked if I could visit them in order to avert this situation and that we might solve it together. They fixed a date for my visit—not in January 1972 but in February 1972. This was so that the whole of December and January might have passed, and so would February. As a matter of fact, I almost rejected this date. However, I always place the sublime interest of the cause and the country above personal considerations.

As you have seen, in the past three years, I have experienced and suffered a great deal. I learned [something about the background] afterwards. I went [to the Soviet Union] in February and, as I understood it, their purpose in delaying the date was to let me calm down or cool off a little. This was because I had fixed 1971 as the year of decision and they did not approve of it. Actually they did not approve of any action other than political or diplomatic action.

I went in February, and two months after February in the same year—that is in April. This time they had asked that I visit them and insisted on it because Nixon was going to visit them in May. The first summit conference in Moscow was in May 1972. I visited the Soviet Union again late in April. It was the fourth time. The first was in March 1971. The second was in October 1971. The third in February 1972, and the fourth in April 1972.

The core of the discussion between us was—and I always said it—that the issue would not be activated or solved without military action. The Soviet Union's view was against military action. The discussions used to finish up with the view that even in order to reach a peaceful solution, Israel must be made to feel that we are in a position to talk about a peaceful solution from a position of strength, not weakness. This was the result that we used to end up with, and they used to promise to supply us with arms, etc. etc.

I am not saying this to belittle the arms that we have received. I am continuing the explanation. The April 1972 meeting was held, as I told you, and we agreed at that meeting that after the summit meeting between President Nixon and Secretary Brezhnev in May, [the process of] consolidating Egypt's capability would begin quickly because we agreed that there would be nothing new in the U.S. position in 1972 since it was an election year in the United States. We also agreed that after the elections, that is immediately after November, we had to be prepared. They agreed to this.

I returned from this visit, and in May the summit conference was held in Moscow. I waited for a notification, and after fourteen days, I received a notification, including an analysis by the Soviet Union similar to what we had predicted, that is, that there was nothing new in the U.S. position because the U.S. position viewed Egypt and the Arabs as a motionless corpse and they only respect force. So if Egypt and the Arabs were a motionless corpse, why should they [the Americans] act or change their position? The Soviet analysis was the same as our predictions before the April visit, and it came after fourteen days. I replied and said: All right, now that the analysis is the same as the one we agreed upon, the questions, as agreed upon with you, are the following:

There were seven clauses—this, that and the other thing. Therefore, as we agreed, these clauses were to have reached me by November. We would then be standing on solid ground after the U.S. elections in November. If they spoke about a peaceful solution, we would be standing on solid ground and in a position to speak and say yes or no—we reject or we agree. Why should a solution be proposed to us when we are weak? The solution proposed would exactly reflect the extent of our strength.

My reply was sent to them and I said simply that my reply was on its way. A whole month passed during which I received no answer. We calculated in days the period between the Moscow visit, that is the meeting, and November so as not to lose a single day for the seven clauses that I had requested and that we had agreed upon. A whole month passed. The first fifteen days passed before I received the analysis and one month before I received an answer. I was surprised by the answer I received. There was absolutely no mention of anything about the battle except in the last three lines of the answer.

Before that, there was the statement about the Moscow summit meeting between the two giants. The statement included the phrase military relaxation—military relaxation while Israel had complete superiority and we were short of several things. However, we were asked to embark on military relaxation. What did this mean? It meant that if such military relaxation took place in the area at a time when Israel was superior and we were at the level of our position at that time, the question would not be solved. It would be a case of the stronger side dictating conditions to us. We would either accept or reject. Whether we accepted or not, they would say: We are staying where we are and that is all.

When I received the answer a month later and it included absolutely no mention of what we had agreed upon in April, I made my decisions regarding the Soviet experts, a decision that you learned about in the summer. As I said afterwards, the real aim of these decisions was also strategic; analysts should have been more aware than they were—because anyone who had studied my decisions even a little would have understood that I intended to enter a battle when I ousted the Soviet experts. The Soviet experts were not fighters. They would not enter the battle with me. In fact, they were banned from going near the Canal. All of them were here in the interior as experts on arms and other types of training. Some were manning SAM-3 missiles after the Abu Za'bal raid.

Our sons were already trained and ready to take over everything. In fact, when the Soviet experts left, our sons took over the SAM-3 emplacements in a matter of seconds. There was no vacuum at all that would have left a gap in our air defences. This never happened because our sons took over immediately.

Actually, my purpose, as I have said, was a pause with the friend on the one hand and, on the other, to tell everyone that I was entering the battle—a 100 per cent Egyptian battle. No one at all can claim that anyone has fought it for me. I do not even have experts for weapons training. That was among the reasons for my decision at that time.

The situation continued. Our brothers in the Soviet Union took a long time despite the fact that I sent the Prime Minister, who was Dr. Aziz Sidqi at that time. I sent him because before we proclaimed the decision [on the Soviet experts] we had to agree on a joint declaration in order to cover anything that the West might exploit. They refused and we declared it unilaterally. The issue was settled and the decision was implemented.

Relations remained frozen between us and the Soviet Union all during the summer. The decisions were taken in July. Relations remained frozen all during the summer until October came, when our brother, President Hafiz al-Asad, went to Moscow and intervened in the matter. Dr. Aziz Sidqi left on 16th October and then returned. It was clearly apparent that relations had begun to move again. However, this was on the surface only. In fact and in essence, relations did not move at all.

It was necessary for the Soviet Union to take time to find out that I did not carry out the operation in agreement with the United States behind their backs. I allowed them to take enough time to find out that the matter was not a dagger in their back in agreement with the United States or others. Not at all. It was a national decision. It was a pause to tell them this procedure was unacceptable—a procedure which amounts to a kind of "wait a little, cool off a little, you cannot move until we want you to move." We do not accept this. We do not accept this procedure. It is not according to our will, which has been free since 23rd July 1952. No one at all can direct us or impose any trusteeship on us.

In December 1972 three months were left before the expiration of an agreement between us and them over facilities in the Mediterranean. We gave them facilities in the Mediterranean, not bases. We do not give bases to anyone. Since 23rd July no one has had bases here with us. We are nonaligned. However, we have extended facilities to them. The agreement was to end in March 1973. Five years would have passed of the agreement, for it was concluded in 1968. The agreement stipulates that three months before its expiry the two sides will agree either to terminate or renew it. At that time, relations were disrupted—exactly as I have told you, and everything was at a standstill.

I asked Field Marshal Isma'il to call the Russian General at the Embassy here and tell him that we had decided for our part, to extend the facilities for another period. This happened three months before the expiration of the agreement.

Nevertheless, I still say that the USSR stood by us in the dark moments of 1967. We are a grateful people. We do not forget past favours.

The Field Marshal called the General and told him about this. The facilities have remained ever since. Early in 1973, Field Marshal Isma'il and Hafiz Isma'il left for the USSR. The two of them concluded a deal. After February 1973 our relations began to be, or to become, normal. Some of [the arms included in] this deal began reaching us after Field Marshal Isma'il's return from the USSR.

As I have told you and as you have already heard from me, the decision on the battle was made last April, April 1973. As I have told you, some of the deal began reaching us after the Field Marshal's return in February. We were happy that our relations would return to normal. But the USSR persisted in the view that a military battle must be ruled out and that the question must await a peaceful solution.

The month of June came and with it the second summit conference between President Nixon and Brezhnev. The first meeting was held in Moscow in May 1972. As I have told you, that meeting resulted in military relaxation. This meant that everything must stop and that Israel would remain superior and that we would remain in our position. It was clear from the statement issued in June 1973 that the two super powers had taken another leap forward. They agreed that nothing should happen anywhere in the world. They agreed to abide by this. The only [trouble] spot left in the world was the Middle East. The Vietnam issue was decided. Nothing would happen there. So the Middle East was the only spot left. Nothing should happen here and everyone should await a peaceful solution. On reading the statement, we found that our issue had been put into cold storage pending a peaceful solution.

Palestine National Council: Resolutions (June 1974)

1. The PLO reaffirms its previous attitude concerning Security Council Resolution 242 which obliterates the patriotic and national rights of our people and treats our national cause as a refugee problem. It therefore refuses categorically any negotiations on the basis of this Resolution at any level of inter-Arab or international negotiation including the Geneva Conference.

2. The PLO will struggle by all possible means and foremost by means of armed struggle for the liberation of the Palestinian lands and the setting up of a patriotic, independent, fighting peoples regime in every part of the Palestine territory which will be liberated. It affirms that this will only be accomplished through major changes in the balance of forces to the advantage of our people and their struggle.

3. The PLO will struggle against any proposal to set up a Palestine entity at the price of recognition, peace and secure boundaries, giving up the historic right and depriving our people of its right to return and to self-determination on its national soil.

4. The PLO will consider any step toward liberation which is accomplished as a stage in the pursuit of its strategy for the establishment of a

democratic Palestinian state, as laid down in the decisions of previous National Council meetings.

5. The PLO will struggle together with patriotic Jordanian forces for the creation of a Jordanian-Palestinian patriotic front, the object of which will be the establishment of a patriotic, democratic regime in Jordan which will make common cause with the Palestinian entity which will arise as a result of struggle and conflict.

6. The PLO will struggle for the establishment of a fighting union between the Palestinian and Arab peoples and between all Arab liberation forces agreed on this program.

7. The Palestine national authority will strive to call on the Arab states in confrontation [with Israel] to complete the liberation of the whole of the soil of Palestine as a step on the way to comprehensive Arab unity.

8. The PLO will strive to strengthen its solidarity with the socialist countries and world forces of liberation and progress to thwart all Zionist, reactionary, and imperialist designs.

9. In the light of this program, the PLO will strive to strengthen patriotic unity and raise it to the level at which it will be able to fulfill its patriotic and national tasks and duties.

10. In the light of this program, the revolutionary command will prepare tactics which will serve and make possible the realization of these objectives.

The Agranat Commission: Report (1974)

Blocking Actions

. . . We have decided to concentrate our investigation of the blocking actions in the events of October 8 on the southern front and the events of October 6–7 (till the afternoon) on the northern front. The reasons, in brief, follow:

We had two alternatives—either to examine in a general way all the battles involved in the blocking stage or to analyse in depth the battle that was decisive. We chose the second. Our job was not to write the history of the blocking actions—that would have involved years of work—but to pinpoint the main defects uncovered in this stage.

Many of the defects in this stage derive from the element of surprise. A distinction must be made between the southern and the northern fronts. In the south, the surprise was complete both in time and method of attack so that no effective steps were taken beforehand. In the north, on the other hand, the surprise mainly involved the objectives of the enemy and his method, not so much the attack itself. We chose to examine the battle of October 8 in the south because these were to be the first time that the IDF took the initiative.

What caused this battle to go wrong, among other things, was the deviation from the objectives defined by the Chief of Staff as well as lack of control on the part of the command and its inability to correctly read the progress of the battle. Furthermore, some of the steps taken that day by various command echelons stemmed consciously or unconsciously from opinions formed by commanders a long time before the Yom Kippur War and not from an analysis of the current situation. It is not our purpose to contradict or endorse these assumptions but only to examine to what extent it was appropriate to apply them given the circumstances.

From this, it is clear that a detailed study should be of the lessons and implications of this battle. It had a far-reaching effect on the entire strategy adopted thereafter by the IDF in the war and it also had potential or actual political implications.

In the South

. . . In summing up the results of the battles of October 8, we note the following:

Although the battles failed inasmuch as they did not attain the objectives set by the Southern Command, they were of great significance in the progress of the war. They contained the enemy's bridgeheads, preventing him from completely achieving the first stage of his plan. Although one reserve division was unsuccessful in its attempt to wipe out the bridgeheads, its hard fight contributed to the containment of the enemy's advance and prepared the ground for counterattack. Although another reserve division did not fight for most of that same day due to reasons beyond its control and although it sustained heavy losses on the evening of October 8 and the morning of October 9, these battles opened the way for further moves.

On Tuesday afternoon, October 9, the division deployed for a westward advance. The attempt did not succeed. But when the battle ended towards evening, a battalion reached the vicinity of the canal and thereby exposed the weak spot in the Egyptian alignment through which the IDF would subsequently cross the canal.

Finally, it must again be stressed that on the battlefields where these fights were waged, there were unsurpassed manifestations of sacrifice and bravery on the part of officers and men alike.

At the conclusion of discussions of the October 8 battles, the Commission adds some reservations and remarks about the evidence submitted on this subject.

In the North

. . . The Command was aware that hostilities might break out and took appropriate measures. Reinforcements were sent in and although the number of units was fewer than considered necessary for the defence of the Golan Heights in the event of an overall war, the imbalance was not intolerable. Units on the Golan were on a relatively high state of alert, although they too were taken aback by the scope and timing of enemy operations when war broke out.

The regulars who fought on the Golan in the initial stages distinguished themselves generally by their stubborn fight and their perseverance, like the reserves who joined them later. Supreme courage was manifest at all levels. At the front itself, units led by junior officers showed great resource. Their sometimes independent and even lone operations influenced the tide of battle in certain cases.

After the Syrian attack had been stemmed, the Northern Command switched from a situation in which the enemy had penetrated to the vicinity of the River Jordan and endangered Eastern Galilee, over to a counter-offensive which left the troops close to the enemy capital and in control of the Hermon crest.

The interim reports issued last year covered the intelligence aspect in the days before the fighting began. The probe of the intelligence aspect after the fighting began, covered the quality and organization of intelligence work, which preceded and accompanied the October 8 offensive on the southern front, as well as the intelligence reaching the units which took part in the fighting itself.

Some of the lessons emerging from what the Intelligence Corps did on the eve of the war and how it functioned hold true for the course of the fighting as well. In the initial stages, field intelligence as such scarcely existed. The Intelligence Corps, moreover was shackled by preconceived patterns of thought.

On the southern front, faulty intelligence had a considerable influence on the battles to stem the Egyptian advance.

Future of the Defence Forces

. . . The true test of any army is not only in its being able to win when it has the initiative, but precisely when it starts from difficult circumstances and goes ahead to victory. However, having been witnesses to the brilliance with which the army of the people stood up to its difficult test, it is essential to ensure that it will not have to meet a similar test in the future and it was this that we bore in mind in drawing up the three reports. It is to be hoped that the lessons to which we have pointed will be assimilated and that our recommendations will be implemented. . . .

Final Remarks

It is generally accepted by the IDF that there were serious disciplinary faults. A minority of the commanders believed these did not adversely affect the IDF's fighting conduct during the Yom Kippur War. Our opinion on the basis of the evidence before us is different. We explained above that there is a strong link between the level of everyday discipline in the army and the quality of performance during the supreme test of war. The readiness to sacrifice and the ability to improvise as they were revealed during the Yom Kippur War—and these are not substitutes for discipline—to a large extent extricated the army from its straits. But who knows what hitches might have been prevented had a greater degree of discipline been added to the readiness to fight.

One cannot promote trust in the IDF, insofar as it has been impaired, by banal declarations and demands for an attitude of civilian trust in respect to the army. Our public is linked by a thousand threads to the army, and reserve soldiers know very well what is going on within it. If the soldier and the junior officer work in a climate in which there is proper discipline, fulfillment of standing army orders and proper administration based on fixed rules, there is a corresponding increase in mutual trust within the ranks, in willingness to join the permanent army and in devotion of soldiers at all levels. And there will disappear of its own accord the regrettable occurrence of reserve soldiers speaking badly of the army, and the army will gain the full public trust it enjoyed in the past.

There can be no postponing the effort to remedy things that are wrong; this must be integrated with the difficult task of broadening the forces and physically strengthening them, because between these two there is a strong reciprocal link. The IDF and Israel's people are indeed one. Thus it is precisely for the IDF, and primarily for its senior command, to pave the way for the elimination of faults which began to penetrate into its ranks from the civilian sector—and thus to make a decisive contribution to the improvement of society generally. The IDF is capable of meeting this difficult task for which it was given instruments and sanctions that are not at the disposal of civilian society.

George Habash: Interview (August 3, 1974)

Q.—What is your analysis of the Palestinian and Arab political situations after the October War?

A.—Almost nine months have elapsed since the cease-fire; during this time, some Arab and some international powers have worked from the principle of political struggle based on Security Council Resolutions 242 and 338 to insure the Israeli withdrawal from the Arab territories, on the one hand, and to achieve what was called giving the Palestinian people their full right to self-determination.

What are the results of this policy? Part of the Arab land was regained—on the Syrian and Egyptian fronts—but in lieu of what? What exactly is the price?

On the imperialistic level: the prominent achievement of American imperialism as a result of this policy is the return of American influence to the area, and the continuous expansion of this influence politically, economically and morally. This truth reaffirms the enemy's nature and its aggressive identity, in spite of all attempts by the subservient systems and reactionary forces to decorate imperialism's ugly face. The results of the return of imperialism's influence to the area affected the close relations between the USSR and the Arab people. These are the most important concrete truths that surfaced during the recent nine months.

On the Arab level: in return for the disengagement steps on the Egyptian and Syrian fronts, those systems sacrificed their power of military confrontation which enables them to continue the struggle and secures for them the complete extraction of their rights. Additionally, there was the step of lifting the oil embargo from the imperialistic countries which supported Zionism in its war against the Arab people.

Here, it must be indicated that the proposed plans of "settlement" might be affected by the internal developments in America (for example, the Watergate scandal) or any developments that may occur in the world. But what must be clear is that America will remain eager and will push in the direction of settlement as long as this "settlement" guarantees the return of its interests and their continuity for the longest possible interval. Therefore, efforts will continue in the direction of more steps towards "settlement." Based on this obvious principle, in return for every piece of land recovered by the Arab side, the Arabs are required to pay the price to the imperialistic powers and Israel—part of this price paid to imperialism and part to Israel.

Q.—What is the position of the Front toward the official visit of the PLO delegation, headed by Yasser Arafat, to the USSR in August of this year?

A.—The Front decided not to join the delegation. This position is not against the USSR despite our disagreemnts on many issues. Rather, we consider the USSR a power that is supporting our people's struggle. We also consider the Soviets friends of the Arab and Palestinian struggle. It is a mistaken position to put the Soviets and the Americans in one basket for only their general convergence of opinion concerning Resolution 242 and their agreement on the general lines of a political settlement. We consider the USSR a friend of the Palestinian struggle. We are convinced that the continuity of the Palestinian political and military struggle and our success in guaranteeing this continuity, eventually to the level that will mobilize the Arab masses according to a well-rooted revolutionary political line, will definitely lead to a reconsideration by the USSR of the nature of the existing struggle in the area, and the truths about the presence of the Zionist state which means no more than the existence of a racist, fascist and aggressive state. No peace will materialize as long as the Zionist state exists. This is the only conclusion that can be drawn by our masses based on this fact. The day will come when the Communist and leftist powers will uncover the true core and substance of the Zionist system.

We should not misinterpret international contradictions. The Front's decision not to participate in the PLO's delegation to Moscow does not express a position estranged from the Soviets, for whom we possess every appreciation, but it is a position against the PLO's leadership who wished the delegation travelling to Moscow to be "homogeneous." In our opinion, homogeneity means the common representation of a political line, which is the line leading towards political settlement. But we must keep in mind that within the Palestinian circle there exist two completely contradictory political lines, one on either end. One line wants the PLO to be a part of the political settlement and the other line considers this a dangerous national divergence, and considers the present mission of the struggle to keep the PLO outside the boundaries of the settlement. Based on this came our demand that the delegation be composed of all the member organizations of the Executive Council so that the delegation fairly represents the coexisting and contradictory political lines within the Liberation Organization.

There is another reason for our nonparticipation in the organization's delegation to Moscow: the delegation which was appointed to travel left without the Executive Council of the organization discussing the specific missions to be deliberated with our Soviet comrades, and without specifying a position on all the subjects proposed. The unilateral decision-making of the PLO must not continue. Our position is an expression of our rejection of the sense of unilateral decision-making that is predominant in the leadership of the PLO.

Q.—What practical steps will the "rejection front" take at the Palestinian and Arab levels?

A.—In fact what is called the rejection forces is nothing but an expression of Palestinian and Arab forces that emerged from an analysis, summarized as follows: the Palestinian revolution is strained and ends when it becomes a part of the political settlement presently proposed, and the continuity of the revolution is only ensured by resisting and fighting the proposed political settlement plans. These forces now work as though they are one front. But such a front did not arise until now. It is the duty of these forces to organize one front that has its own political programme, a list of specified organizational interrelationships and consolidated struggle programmes. Presently it is the duty of this front to work within the framework of the Liberation Organization to prevent its complete deviation, so that the Liberation Organization does not become part of the settlement.

But, in the event that the PLO goes to Geneva, the rejection front becomes the sole representative of the continuity of the revolution.

The subject that should be given chief priority is the necessity for the transformation of these Palestinian and Arab forces from the state of reflexive cooperation to the state of a clear frontal format according to a precise political programme.

Q.—What is the PFLP's understanding of the relationship between the resistance and the Arab masses for the near future?

A.—We believe that the Palestinian resistance will not be able to get out of the dilemma it is living in if it remains dependent on the masses of the Palestinian people, even if the revolutionary Palestinian party existed and the united Palestinian front existed. Even though important, it is not sufficient to defeat the plans of imperialism since the subject is really the balance of power. Because of this, the only true way out from the resistance's dilemma is for the Palestinian revolution to become an integral part of the Arab revolution, fused with it in all sections of the Arab nation. It is the Palestinian, Jordanian, Syrian, Egyptian, Iraqi and Lebanese masses who are able to guarantee the victory of our Palestinian people's struggle. When the Palestinian military struggle movement becomes able to move from a geographical and human depth that is not confined by the boundaries of the land of Palestine or the west and east banks, but extends to include all the lands surrounding Palestine, then the military struggle feature will rely upon such a human and geographical depth. At that time, it will be an impossibility for the oppressing forces to hit the Palestinian revolution.

Q.—What is the explanation of the Front's acceptance of the ten points during the recent Palestinian National Council?

A.—It is important for me to clarify what I heard and what reverberated during and after the convention—that I had personally, and in my own handwriting, initiated these ten points. All what was said are lies and it is sad that attempts to slander our position as a popular front in front of the Palestinian masses occurred, whether premeditatedly or not. I put together some points as a basis for a political programme that might be agreed upon by the National Council during its twelfth convention. These points cumulatively put the resistance movement outside the framework of the settlement by opposing it in a way that cannot be disputed. Among those points is the definitive rejection of Resolution 242 and the Geneva Conference. The points which I wrote in the name of the Popular Front are in line with the political line represented by the Popular Front. But the ten points which the Palestinian National Council adopted are a compromise position attempting to prevent the explosion within the Palestinian circle. There have been several attempts aimed at concealing the contradictions within the Palestinian circle. But I take this opportunity to declare at the top of my voice that two contradictory political lines exist within the PLO, and the necessity of maintaining the struggle against any attempt to cover or weaken this contradiction is imperative.

One political line says that the only way open for the resistance movement is to enter into the framework of the political solution and to struggle within this framework to achieve whatever is possible. On the other hand, there is another line that believes in the continuity of the revolution and in staying away from political settlements in spite of the imperialistic powers' proposed dissolution attempts and plots.

There can be no real and strong national unity, in the long run, based upon the ten points . . . National unity cannot exist except upon a unified political stand: the Liberation Organization must reject in a clear and firm way, free from ambiguity or misunderstanding, all the forms of the proposed settlements.

In this respect, I announce in the name of the PFLP that it is important for us to remain within the PLO inasmuch as the Liberation Organization remains outside the framework of the Geneva Conference. Participation in the Geneva Conference means to us a dangerous national deviation which we will fight with all our power, based on the strength of the masses. When the Organization is in Geneva, the subject becomes black and white . . .

The attempts to dissolve the contradictions in the Palestinian circle must not continue. It is incorrect to state that disagreements do not exist. We must not bury our heads in the sand. There is a line that is devoted to the subservient Arab bourgeois system's policy of trying to dampen and cover the Palestinian and Arab proletariat's line in its struggle against the subservient bourgeois policy, on the Arab and Palestinian level . . . .

Q.—What are the PFLP's expectations on the Lebanese front for the next phase?

A.—Of course, it is necessary to expect attacks on the resistance and especially in Lebanon. This is a scientific deduction. Why? Because the proposed settlement aims at containing the Palestinian resistance. This is a fact. And it is natural for the resistance movement to hesitate in front of the humiliating format that American imperialism will propose to contain the revolution. At the same time, there will be a plan drawn to direct political and military attacks on the Palestinian resistance movement so that the resistance is compelled at the end to enter into the framework of the settlement from a position of weakness, permitting the plan to achieve its aims. This point must be engrained in our minds because the resistance in Lebanon still constitutes a revolutionary feature. The Palestinian gun is still held up in this area. Through the ability of the resistance movement to express its political line to the Palestinian and Arab masses through its overt existence in this and other circles, it is natural for the enemy to work against the existence of this revolutionary feature until he reaches the position that enables him to contain the resistance movement within a format that does not conflict with the basic benefits of his imperialistic appendages and his long-range benefits. . . .

What do I mean exactly?

Any Israeli imperialistic reactionary plan against the resistance as a whole will face opposition from all the resistance movement. We will find ourselves in front of the picture of May again. In other words, all the resistance movement will have a united stand. Will the enemy be able to come and isolate and attack the Popular Front in Shatila? No. Because that will result in a confrontation with all the Palestinian guns, whether carried by a Popular Front or Fateh member. All will face this attempt. By this we see the difficulty of directing a military blow to the resistance movement. But what may happen is that some Palestinian forces, for some excuse or another, based upon the claim of enforcing discipline in the camps, will hit another Palestinian group with the blessing of the reactionary forces. Here occurs intact the painful blow to the resistance movement as a whole.

The area in this case will be full of action. Thus, we must keep our eyes open in order to prevent the enemy from achieving its objectives. Of course, the principal dependence or main line in facing any plots of any kind aiming to hit the Palestinian resistance in any form is that of complete fusion between the resistance and the Lebanese mass movement. It is only this format of fusion that can crush all the plots.

PLO Chairman Yasir Arafat: Address to the UN General Assembly (November 13, 1974)

Mr. President, I thank you for having invited the Palestine Liberation Organization to participate in this plenary session of the United Nations General Assembly. I am grateful to all those representatives of States of the United Nations who contributed to the decision to introduce the question of Palestine as a separate item of the agenda of this Assembly. That decision made possible the Assembly's resolution inviting us to address it on the question of Palestine.

The roots of the Palestinian question reach back into the closing years of the 19th century, in other words, to that period which we call the era of colonialism and settlement as we know it today. This is precisely the period during which Zionism as a scheme was born; its aim was the conquest of Palestine by European immigrants, just as settlers colonized, and indeed raided, most of Africa. This is the period during which, pouring forth out of the west, colonialism spread into the further reaches of Africa, Asia, and Latin America, building colonies everywhere, cruelly exploiting, oppressing, plundering the people of those three continents. This period persists into the present. Marked evidence of its totally reprehensible presence can be readily perceived in the racism practised both in South Africa and in Palestine.

Just as colonialism and its demagogues dignified their conquests, their plunder and limitless attacks upon the natives of Africa with appeals to a "civilizing and modernizing" mission, so too did waves of Zionist immigrants disguise their purposes as they conquered Palestine. Just as colonialism as a system and colonialists as its instrument used religion, color, race and language to justify the African's exploitation and his cruel subjugation by terror and discrimination, so too were these methods employed as Palestine was usurped and its people hounded from their national homeland.

Just as colonialism heedlessly used the wretched, the poor, the exploited as mere inert matter with which to build and to carry out settler colonialism, so too were destitute, oppressed European Jews employed on behalf of world imperialism and of the Zionist leadership. European Jews were transformed into the instruments of aggression; they became the elements of settler colonialism intimately allied to racial discrimination.

Zionist theology was utilized against our Palestinian people: the purpose was not only the establishment of Western-style settler colonialism but also the severing of Jews from their various homelands and subsequently their estrangement from their nations. Zionism is an ideology that is imperialist, colonialist, racist; it is profoundly reactionary and discriminatory; it is united with anti-Semitism in its retrograde tenets and is, when all is said and done, another side of the same base coin. For when what is proposed is that adherents of the Jewish faith, regardless of their national residence, should neither owe allegiance to their national residence nor live on equal footing with its other, non-Jewish citizens—when that is proposed we hear anti-Semitism being proposed. When it is proposed that the only solution for the Jewish problem is that Jews must alienate themselves from communities or nations of which they have been a historical part, when it is proposed that Jews solve the Jewish problem by immigrating to and forcibly settling the land of another people—when this occurs exactly the same position is being advocated as the one urged by anti-Semites against Jews.

Thus, for instance, we can understand the close connection between Rhodes, who promoted settler colonialism in southeast Africa, and Herzl, who had settler colonialist designs upon Palestine. Having received a certificate of good settler colonialist conduct from Rhodes, Herzl then turned around and presented this certificate to the British Government, hoping thus to secure a formal resolution supporting Zionist policy. In exchange, the Zionists promised Britain an imperialist base on Palestine soil so that imperial interests could be safeguarded at one of their chief strategic points.

The Jewish invasion of Palestine began in 1881. Before the first large wave of immigrants started arriving, Palestine had a population of half a million; most of the population was either Moslem or Christian, and only 20,000 were Jewish. Every segment of the population enjoyed the religious tolerance characteristic of our civilization.

Palestine was then a verdant land, inhabited mainly by an Arab people in the course of building its life and dynamically enriching its indigenous culture.

Between 1882 and 1917 the Zionist Movement settled approximately 50,000 European Jews in our homeland. To do that it resorted to trickery and deceit in order to implant them in our midst. Its success in getting Britain to issue the Balfour Declaration once again demonstrated the alliance between Zionism and imperialism. Furthermore, by promising to the Zionist movement what was not hers to give, Britain showed how oppressive the rule of imperialism was. As it was constituted then, the League of Nations abandoned our Arab people, and Wilson's pledges and promises came to nought. In the guise of a mandate, British imperialism was cruelly and directly imposed upon us. The mandate document issued by the League of Nations was to enable the Zionist invaders to consolidate their gains in our homeland.

In the wake of the Balfour Declaration and over a period of 30 years, the Zionist movement succeeded, in collaboration with its imperialist ally, in settling more European Jews on the land, thus usurping the properties of Palestine Arabs.

By 1947 the number of Jews had reached 600,000: they owned about 6 percent of Palestinian arable land. The figure should be compared with the population of Palestine which at that time was 1,250,000.

As a result of the collusion between the mandatory Power and the Zionist movement and with the support of some countries, this General Assembly early in its history approved a recommendation to partition our Palestinian homeland. This took place in an atmosphere poisoned with questionable actions and strong pressure. The General Assembly partitioned what it had no right to divide—an indivisible homeland. When we rejected that decision, our position corresponded to that of the natural mother who refused to permit King Solomon to cut her son in two when the unnatural mother claimed the child for herself and agreed to his dismemberment. Furthermore, even though the partition resolution granted the colonialist settlers 54 percent of the land of Palestine, their dissatisfaction with the decision prompted them to wage a war of terror against the civilian Arab population. They occupied 81 percent of the total area of Palestine, uprooting a million Arabs. Thus, they occupied 524 Arab towns and villages, of which they destroyed 385, completely obliterating them in the process. Having done so, they built their own settlements and colonies on the ruins of our farms and our groves. The roots of the Palestine question lie here. Its causes do not stem from any conflict between two religions or two nationalisms. Neither is it a border conflict between neighboring states. It is the cause of a people deprived of its homeland, dispersed and uprooted, and living mostly in exile and in refugee camps.

With support from imperialist and colonialist Powers, it managed to get itself accepted as a United Nations Member. It further succeeded in getting the Palestine Question deleted from the agenda of the United Nations and in deceiving world public opinion by presenting our cause as a problem of refugees in need either of charity from do-gooders, or settlement in a land not theirs.

Not satisfied with all this, the racist entity, founded on the imperialist-colonialist concept, turned itself into a base of imperialism and into an arsenal of weapons. This enabled it to assume its role of subjugating the Arab people and of committing aggression against them, in order to satisfy its ambitions for further expansion on Palestinian and other Arab lands. In addition to the many instances of aggression committed by this entity against the Arab States, it has launched two large-scale wars, in 1956 and 1967, thus endangering world peace and security.

As a result of Zionist aggression in June 1967, the enemy occupied Egyptian Sinai as far as the Suez Canal. The enemy occupied Syria's Golan Heights, in addition to all Palestinian land west of the Jordan. All these developments have led to the creation in our area of what has come to be known as the "Middle East problem." The situation has been rendered more serious by the enemy's persistence in maintaining its unlawful occupation and in further consolidating it, thus establishing a beachhead for world imperialism's thrust against our Arab nation. All Security Council decisions and appeals to world public opinion for withdrawal from the lands occupied in June 1967 have been ignored. Despite all the peaceful efforts on the international level, the enemy has not been deterred from its expansionist policy. The only alternative open before our Arab nations, chiefly Egypt and Syria, was to expend exhaustive efforts in preparing forcefully to resist that barbarous armed invasion—and this in order to liberate Arab lands and to restore the rights of the Palestinian people, after all other peaceful means had failed.

Under these circumstances, the fourth war broke out in October 1973, bringing home to the Zionist enemy the bankruptcy of its policy of occupation, expansion and its reliance on the concept of military might. Despite all this, the leaders of the Zionist entity are far from having learned any lesson from their experience. They are making preparations for the fifth war, resorting once more to the language of military superiority, aggression, terrorism, subjugation and, finally, always to war in their dealings with the Arabs.

It pains our people greatly to witness the propagation of the myth that its homeland was a desert until it was made to bloom by the toil of foreign settlers, that it was a land without a people, and that the colonialist entity caused no harm to any human being. No: such lies must be exposed from this rostrum, for the world must know that Palestine was the cradle of the most ancient cultures and civilizations. Its Arab people were engaged in farming and building, spreading culture throughout the land for thousands of years, setting an example in the practice of freedom of worship, acting as faithful guardians of the holy places of all religions. As a son of Jerusalem, I treasure for myself and my people beautiful memories and vivid images of the religious brotherhood that was the hallmark of our Holy City before it succumbed to catastrophe. Our people continued to pursue this enlightened policy until the establishment of the State of Israel and their dispersion. This did not deter our people from pursuing their humanitarian role on Palestinian soil. Nor will they permit their land to become a launching pad for aggression or a racist camp predicated on the destruction of civilization, cultures, progress and peace. Our people cannot but maintain the heritage of their ancestors in resisting the invaders, in assuming the privileged task of defending their native land, their Arab nationhood, their culture and civilization, and in safeguarding the cradle of monotheistic religion.

By contrast, we need only mention briefly some Israeli stands: its support of the Secret Organization in Algeria, its bolstering of the settler-colonialists in Africa—whether in the Congo, Angola, Mozambique, Zimbabwe, Azania or South Africa—and its backing of South Vietnam against the Vietnamese revolution. In addition, one can mention Israel's continuing support of imperialists and racists everywhere, its obstructionist stand in the Committee of Twenty-Four, its refusal to cast its vote in support of independence for the African States, and its opposition to the demands of many Asian, African and Latin American nations, and several other States in the Conferences on raw materials, population, the Law of the Sea, and food. All these facts offer further proof of the character of the enemy which has usurped our land. They justify the honorable struggle which we are waging against it. As we defend a vision of the future, our enemy upholds the myths of the past.

The enemy we face has a long record of hostility even towards the Jews themselves, for there is within the Zionist entity a built-in racism against Oriental Jews. While we were vociferously condemning the massacres of Jews under Nazi rule, Zionist leadership appeared more interested at that time in exploiting them as best it could in order to realize its goal of immigration into Palestine.

If the immigration of Jews to Palestine had had as its objective the goal of enabling them to live side by side with us, enjoying the same rights and assuming the same duties, we would have opened our doors to them, as far as our homeland's capacity for absorption permitted. Such was the case with the thousands of Armenians and Circassians who still live among us in equality as brethren and citizens. But that the goal of this immigration should be to usurp our homeland, disperse our people, and turn us into second-class citizens—this is what no one can conceivably demand that we acquiesce in or submit to. Therefore, since its inception, our revolution has not been motivated by racial or religious factors. Its target has never been the Jew, as a person, but racist Zionism and undisguised aggression. In this sense, ours is also a revolution for the Jew, as a human being, as well. We are struggling so that Jews, Christians and Moslems may live in equality enjoying the same rights and assuming the same duties, free from racial or religious discrimination.

We do distinguish between Judaism and Zionism. While we maintain our opposition to the colonialist Zionist movement, we respect the Jewish faith. Today, almost one century after the rise of the Zionist movement, we wish to warn of its increasing danger to the Jews of the world, to our Arab people and to world peace and security. For Zionism encourages the Jew to emigrate out of his homeland and grants him an artificially-created nationality. The Zionists proceed with their terrorist activities even though these have proved ineffective. The phenomenon of constant emigration from Israel, which is bound to grow as the bastions of colonialism and racism in the world fall, is an example of the inevitability of the failure of such activities.

We urge the people and governments of the world to stand firm against Zionist attempts at encouraging world Jewry to emigrate from their countries and to usurp our land. We urge them as well firmly to oppose any discrimination against any human being, as to religion, race, or color.

Why should our Arab Palestinian people pay the price of such discrimination in the world? Why should our people be responsible for the problems of Jewish immigration, if such problems exist in the minds of some people? Why do not the supporters of these problems open their own countries, which can absorb and help these immigrants?

Those who call us terrorists wish to prevent world public opinion from discovering the truth about us and from seeing the justice on our faces. They seek to hide the terrorism and tyranny of their acts, and our own posture of self-defense.

The difference between the revolutionary and the terrorist lies in the reason for which each fights. For whoever stands by a just cause and fights for the freedom and liberation of his land from the invaders, the settlers and the colonialists, cannot possibly be called terrorist; otherwise the American people in their struggle for liberation from the British colonialists would have been terrorists, the European resistance against the Nazis would be terrorism, the struggle of the Asian, African and Latin American peoples would also be terrorism, and many of you who are in this Assembly Hall were considered terrorists. This is actually a just and proper struggle consecrated by the United Nations Charter and by the Universal

Declaration of Human Rights. As to those who fight against the just causes, those who wage war to occupy, colonize and oppress other people—those are the terrorists, those are the people whose actions should be condemned, who should be called war criminals: for the justice of the cause determines the right to struggle.

Zionist terrorism which was waged against the Palestinian people to evict it from its country and usurp its land is registered in our official documents. Thousands of our people were assassinated in their villages and towns, tens of thousands of others were forced at gun-point to leave their homes and the lands of their fathers. Time and time again our children, women and aged were evicted and had to wander in the deserts and climb mountains without any food or water. No one who in 1948 witnessed the catastrophe that befell the inhabitants of hundreds of villages and towns—in Jaffa, Lydda, Ramle and Galilee—no one who has been a witness to that catastrophe will ever forget the experience, even though the mass blackout has succeeded in hiding these horrors as it had hidden the traces of 385 Palestinian villages and towns destroyed at the time and erased from the map. The destruction of 19,000 houses during the past seven years, which is equivalent to the complete destruction of 200 more Palestinian villages, and the great number of maimed as a result of the treatment they were subjected to in Israeli prisons, cannot be hidden by any blackout.

Their terrorism fed on hatred and this hatred was even directed against the olive tree in my country, which has been a proud symbol and which reminded them of the indigenous inhabitants of the land, a living reminder that the land is Palestinian. Thus they sought to destroy it. How can one describe the statement by Golda Meir which expressed her disquiet about "the Palestinian children born every day"? They see in the Palestinian child, in the Palestinian tree, an enemy that should be exterminated. For tens of years Zionists have been harassing our people's cultural, political, social and artistic leaders, terrorizing them and assassinating them. They have stolen our cultural heritage, our popular folklore and have claimed it as theirs. Their terrorism even reached our sacred places in our beloved and peaceful Jerusalem. They have endeavoured to de-Arabize it and make it lose its Moslem and Christian character by evicting its inhabitants and annexing it.

I must mention the fire of the Aksa Mosque and the disfiguration of many of the monuments, which are both historic and religious in character. Jerusalem, with its religious history and its spiritual values, bears witness to the future. It is proof of our eternal presence, of our civilization, of our human values. It is therefore not surprising that under its skies the three religions were born and that under that sky these three religions shine in order to enlighten mankind so that it might express the tribulations and hopes of humanity, and that it might mark out the road of the future with its hopes.

The small number of Palestinian Arabs who were not uprooted by the Zionists in 1948 are at present refugees in their own homeland. Israeli law treats them as second-class citizens—and even as third-class citizens since Oriental Jews are second-class citizens and they have been subject to all forms of racial discrimination and terrorism after confiscation of their land and property. They have been victims to bloody massacres such as that of Kfar Kassim; they have been expelled from their villages and denied the right to return, as in the case of the inhabitants of Ikrit and Kfar-Birim. For 26 years, our population has been living under martial law and has been denied the freedom of movement without prior permission from the Israeli military governor—this at a time when an Israeli law was promulgated granting citizenship to any Jew anywhere who wanted to emigrate to our homeland. Moreover, another Israeli law stipulated that Palestinians who were not present in their villages or towns at the time of the occupation were not entitled to Israeli citizenship.

The record of Israeli rulers is replete with acts of terror perpetrated on those of our people who remained under occupation in Sinai and the Golan Heights. The criminal bombardment of the Bahr-al-Bakar School and the Abou Zaabal factory are but two such unforgettable acts of terrorism. The total destruction of the Syrian city of Kuneitra is yet another tangible instance of systematic terrorism. If a record of Zionist terrorism in South Lebanon were to be compiled, the enormity of its acts would shock even the most hardened: piracy, bombardments, scorched earth, destruction of hundreds of homes, eviction of civilians and the kidnapping of Lebanese citizens. This clearly constitutes a violation of Lebanese sovereignty and is in preparation for the diversion of the Litani River waters.

Need one remind this Assembly of the numerous resolutions adopted by it condemning Israeli aggressions committed against Arab countries, Israeli violations of human rights and the articles of the Geneva Conventions, as well as the resolutions pertaining to the annexation of the city of Jerusalem and its restoration to its former status?

The only description for these acts is that they are acts of barbarism and terrorism. And yet, the Zionist racists and colonialists have the temerity to describe the just struggle of our people as terror. Could there be a more flagrant distortion of truth than this? We ask those who usurped our land, who are committing murderous acts of terrorism against our people and are practising racial discrimination more extensively than the racists of South Africa, we ask them to keep in mind the United Nations General Assembly resolution that called for the one-year suspension of the membership of the Government of South Africa from the United Nations. Such is the inevitable fate of every racist country that adopts the law of the jungle, usurps the homeland of others and persists in oppression.

For the past 30 years, our people have had to struggle against British occupation and Zionist invasion, both of which had one intention, namely the usurpation of our land. Six major revolts and tens of popular uprisings were staged to foil these attempts, so that our homeland might remain ours. Over 30,000 martyrs, the equivalent in comparative terms of 6 million Americans, died in the process.

When the majority of the Palestinian people was uprooted from its homeland in 1948, the Palestinian struggle for self-determination continued under the most difficult conditions. We tried every possible means to continue our political struggle to attain our national rights, but to no avail. Meanwhile, we had to struggle for sheer existence. Even in exile we educated our children. This was all a part of trying to survive.

The Palestinian people produced thousands of physicians, lawyers, teachers and scientists who actively participated in the development of the Arab countries bordering on their usurped homeland. They utilized their income to assist the young and aged amongst their people who remained in the refugee camps. They educated their younger sisters and brothers, supported their parents and cared for their children. All along the Palestinian dreamed of return. Neither the Palestinian's allegiance to Palestine nor his determination to return waned; nothing could persuade him to relinquish his Palestinian identity or to forsake his homeland. The passage of time did not make him forget, as some hoped he would. When our people lost faith in the international community which persisted in ignoring its rights and when it became obvious that the Palestinians would not recuperate one inch of Palestine through exclusively political means, our people had no choice but to resort to armed struggle. Into that struggle it poured its material and human resources. We bravely faced the most vicious acts of Israeli terrorism which were aimed at diverting our struggle and arresting it.

In the past 10 years of our struggle, thousands of martyrs and twice as many wounded, maimed and imprisoned were offered in sacrifice, all in an effort to resist the imminent threat of liquidation, to regain our right to self-determination and our undisputed right to return to our homeland. With the utmost dignity and the most admirable revolutionary spirit, our Palestinian people has not lost its spirit in Israeli prisons and concentration camps or when faced with all forms of harassment and intimidation. It struggles for sheer existence and it continues to strive to preserve the Arab character of its land. Thus it resists oppression, tyranny and terrorism in their ugliest forms.

It is through our popular armed struggle that our political leadership and our national institutions finally crystalized and a national liberation movement, comprising all the Palestinian factions, organizations, and capabilities, materialized in the Palestine Liberation Organization.

Through our militant Palestine national liberation movement, our people's struggle matured and grew enough to accommodate political and social struggle in addition to armed struggle. The Palestine Liberation Organization was a major factor in creating a new Palestinian individual, qualified to shape the future of our Palestine, not merely content with mobilizing the Palestinians for the challenges of the present.

The Palestine Liberation Organization can be proud of having a large number of cultural and educational activities, even while engaged in armed struggle, and at a time when it faced the increasingly vicious blows of Zionist terrorism. We established institutes for scientific research, agricultural development and social welfare, as well as centers for the revival of our cultural heritage and the preservation of our folklore. Many Palestinian poets, artists and writers have enriched Arab culture in particular, and world culture generally. Their profoundly humane works have won the admiration of all those familiar with them. In contrast to that, our enemy has been systematically destroying our culture and disseminating racist, imperialist ideologies; in short, everything that impedes progress, justice, democracy and peace.

The Palestine Liberation Organization has earned its legitimacy because of the sacrifice inherent in its pioneering role, and also because of its dedicated leadership of the struggle. It has also been granted this legitimacy by the Palestinian masses, which in harmony with it have chosen it to lead the struggle according to its directives. The Palestine Liberation Organization has also gained its legitimacy by representing every faction, union or group as well as every Palestinian talent, either in the National Council or in people's institutions. This legitimacy was further strengthened by the support of the entire Arab nation, and it was consecrated during the last Arab Summit Conference which reiterated the right of the Palestine Liberation Organization, in its capacity as the sole representative of the Palestinian people, to establish an independent national State on all liberated Palestinian territory.

Moreover, the Palestine Liberation Organization's legitimacy was intensified as a result of fraternal support given by other liberation movements and by friendly, like-minded nations that stood by our side, encouraging and aiding us in our struggle to secure our national rights.

Here I must also warmly convey the gratitude of our revolutionary fighters and that of our people to the nonaligned countries, the socialist countries, the Islamic countries, the African countries and friendly European countries, as well as all our other friends in Asia, Africa and Latin America.

The Palestine Liberation Organization represents the Palestinian people, legitimately and uniquely. Because of this, the Palestine Liberation Organization expresses the wishes and hopes of its people. Because of this, too, it brings these very wishes and hopes before you, urging you not to shirk a momentous historic responsibility towards our just cause.

For many years now, our people has been exposed to the ravages of war, destruction and dispersion. It has paid in the blood of its sons that which cannot ever be compensated. It has borne the burdens of occupation, dispersion, eviction and terror more uninterruptedly than any other people. And yet all this has made our people neither vindictive nor vengeful. Nor has it caused us to resort to the racism of our enemies. Nor have we lost the true method by which friend and foe are distinguished.

For we deplore all those crimes committed against the Jews, we also deplore all the real discrimination suffered by them because of their faith.

I am a rebel and freedom is my cause. I know well that many of you present here today once stood in exactly the same resistance position as I now occupy and from which I must fight. You once had to convert dreams into reality by your struggle. Therefore you must now share my dream. I think this is exactly why I can ask you now to help, as together we bring out our dream into a bright reality, our common dream for a peaceful future in Palestine's sacred land.

As he stood in an Israeli military court, the Jewish revolutionary, Ahud Adif, said: "I am no terrorist; I believe that a democratic State should exist on this land." Adif now languishes in a Zionist prison among his co-believers. To him and his colleagues I send my heartfelt good wishes.

And before those same courts there stands today a brave prince of the church. Bishop Capucci. Lifting his fingers to form the same victory sign used by our freedom-fighters, he said: "What I have done, I have done that all men may live on this land of peace in peace." This princely priest will doubtless share Adif's grim fate. To him we send our salutations and greetings.

Why therefore should I not dream and hope? For is not revolution the making real of dreams and hopes? So let us work together that my dream may be fulfilled, that I may return with my people out of exile, there in Palestine to live with this Jewish freedom-fighter and his partners, with this Arab priest and his brothers, in one democratic State where Christian, Jew and Moslem live in justice, equality, fraternity and progress.

Is this not a noble dream worthy of my struggle alongside all lovers of freedom everywhere? For the most admirable dimension of this dream is that it is Palestinian, a dream from out of the land of peace, the land of martyrdom and heroism, and the land of history, too.

Let us remember that the Jews of Europe and the United States have been known to lead the struggles for secularism and the separation of Church and State. They have also been known to fight against discrimination on religious grounds. How can they continue to support the most fanatic, discriminatory and closed of nations in its policy?

In my formal capacity as Chairman of the Palestine Liberation Organization and leader of the Palestinian revolution I proclaim before you that when we speak of our common hopes for the Palestine of tomorrow we include in our perspective all Jews now living in Palestine who choose to live with us there in peace and without discrimination.

In my formal capacity as Chairman of the Palestine Liberation Organization and leader of the Palestinian revolution I call upon Jews to turn away one by one from the illusory promises made to them by Zionist ideology and Israeli leadership. They are offering Jews perpetual bloodshed, endless war and continuous thraldom.

We invite them to emerge from their moral isolation into a more open realm of free choice, far from their present leadership's efforts to implant in them a Masada complex.

We offer them the most generous solution, that we might live together in a framework of just peace in our democratic Palestine.

In my formal capacity as Chairman of the Palestine Liberation Organization, I announce here that we do not wish one drop of either Arab or Jewish blood to be shed; neither do we delight in the continuation of killing, which would end once a just peace, based on our people's rights, hopes and aspirations had been finally established.

In my formal capacity as Chairman of the Palestine Liberation Organization and leader of the Palestinian revolution I appeal to you to accompany our people in its struggle to attain its right to self-determination. This right is consecrated in the United Nations Charter and has been repeatedly confirmed in resolutions adopted by this august body since the drafting of the Charter. I appeal to you, further; to aid our people's return to its homeland from an involuntary exile imposed upon it by force of arms, by tyranny, by oppression, so that we may regain our property, our land, and thereafter live in our national homeland, free and sovereign, enjoying all the privileges of nationhood. Only then can Palestinian creativity be concentrated on the service of humanity. Only then will our Jerusalem resume its historic role as a peaceful shrine for all religions.

I appeal to you to enable our people to establish national independent sovereignty over its own land.

Y. Harkabi: The Meaning of "A Democratic Palestinian State" (1974)*

1. The Internal Debate

The crux of the Arab conflict with Israel has been the problem of safeguarding the country's Arab character. Arab demands during the Mandate for the prohibition of the sale of land to Jews and curtailment of Jewish immigration served the same purpose: that of keeping the ownership of land

---

*From an article originally published in 1970, with a postscript of 1974. From Y. Harkabi: *Palestinians and Israel,* Jerusalem, 1974.

and Palestine's ethnic character inviolate. The difficulties confronting the Arabs in their attempt to halt Judaization were aggravated with the end of the Mandate and the foundation of the State of Israel: from then on it was a question of turning back the wheel of history and erasing the Jewish state.

The problem of eliminating the Jewish state is heightened by the presence of a considerable Jewish population. For a Jewish state depends upon the existence of Jewish citizens, and therefore elimination of the state requires in principle a "reduction" in their number. Hence the frequency and dominance of the motif of killing the Jews and throwing them into the sea in Arab pronouncements. Their position, insofar as it was *politicidal* (i.e., calling for annihilation of a state), was bound to have *genocidal* implications, even had the Arabs not been bent upon revenge.

When, after the Six-Day War, the Arabs realized that their wild statements had harmed their international reputation, they moderated their shrill demands for the annihilation of Israel. Arab propagandists denied that they had ever advocated the slaughter of the Jewish population, asserting that, at most, "Jewish provocations" had aroused their anger and wild statements which, they alleged, were not meant to be taken literally. Ahmed Shukeiry insisted that he never advocated throwing the Jews into the sea, that the whole thing was merely a Zionist libel. What he meant, he explained, was that the Jews would return to their countries of origin by way of the sea: "They came by the sea and will return by the sea" (*Palestine Documents for 1967,* p. 1084).

After the Six-Day War, Arab spokesmen put forward the concept of "a Democratic Palestinian State in which Arabs and Jews will live in peace." This slogan was well-received and regarded by the world at large as evidence of a new Arab moderation. Many people overlooked the ambiguity of the pronouncement and disregarded the fact that it did not contradict basic Arab contentions: for the wording might well imply the reduction of Jews to an insignificant minority, which would then be permitted to live in peace. Once this line was adopted, its meaning was keenly debated among the Palestinian Arabs.

An indication of the slogan's true significance, as understood by the Palestinian organizations, is found in a circular to its members sent by the Popular Democratic Front for the Liberation of Palestine, reporting on the deliberations of the sixth session of the Palestinian National Assembly. This fedayeen organization, headed by Na'if Hawatmeh, broke away from George Habash's Popular Front for the Liberation of Palestine in February 1969. A delegation of the Popular Democratic Front proposed to the Assembly that the slogan "Democratic State" should be given "a progressive content." The Assembly rejected their proposal suggesting that the main purpose of the "Democratic State" concept was to improve the Arab image. Moreover, the inclusion of this slogan in the national program would, it was stressed, impair the Arab character of Palestine. Nevertheless, since it had been well-received abroad, the Assembly considered it worth retaining. The relevant passage in the Popular Democratic Front's report entitled "Internal Circular concerning Debates and Results of the Sixth National Assembly" reads:

> The slogan "The Democratic Palestinian State" has been raised for some time within the Palestinian context. Fatah was the first to adopt it. Since it was raised, this slogan has met with remarkable world response. Our delegation presented the Congress [i.e., the Assembly] with a resolution designed to elucidate its meaning from a progressive aspect, opposing in principle the slogan of throwing the Jews into the sea, which has in the past seriously harmed the Arab position.

When the subject was first debated, it was thought that there was general agreement on it. But as the debate developed, considerable opposition showed itself. In the course of the discussion the following views came to light.

1. One which maintains that the slogan of "The Democratic Palestinian State" is a tactical one which we propagate because it has been well received internationally.

2. Another suggests that we consider this slogan to be strategic rather than tactical, but that it should be retained even though it is not a basic principle. This position, but for a mere play of words, corresponds to the previous one.

3. The third view was more straightforward in rejecting the slogan and its progressive content as proposed by our delegation. The position of this faction was based on the assertion that the slogan contradicts the Arab character of Palestine and the principle of self-determination enshrined in the National Covenant of the [Palestine] Liberation Organization, and that it also advocates a peaceful settlement with the Jews of Palestine. . . .

In this way the "democratic solution" is presented as a compromise between two chauvinistic alternatives—a Jewish state, and driving the Jews into the sea—as if these were comparable propositions. By this supposedly fair solution, the Arabs renounce the extermination of Jews, and the Jews renounce their state. Although the Palestinian state will become a popular democracy, its Arab character will be preserved by being part of a larger "democratic" Arab federation. The final paragraph is meant to repudiate objections that a democratic Palestine would remain, owing to its mixed population, an anomaly among the Arab states and difficult to digest within the framework of Arab unity.

The Democratic Front's pronouncement may be mistakenly interpreted as favoring a binational state: "The Palestinian state will eliminate racial discrimination and national persecution and will be based on a democratic solution to the conflict brought about by the coexistence (*ta'a-yush*) of the two peoples, Arabs and Jews" (*The Present Situation* . . . , p. 136). The recognition of "a Jewish people" is a significant innovation. Hitherto Arabs have mostly held that Jews constitute only a religion and do not therefore deserve a national state. However, this admission of a Jewish nationhood is qualified, for Jews as a people are not entitled to a state of their own but must settle for incorporation in a state of Palestinian nationality. Their nationhood, therefore, has only cultural and not national-political dimensions. Thus, Hawatmeh tells Lutfi al-Khuli, editor of *at-Tali'a*:

> We urged initiation of a dialogue with the Israeli socialist organization Matzpen, which advocates an Arab-Jewish binational state. But we have not been able to convince Matzpen to adopt a thoroughly progressive, democratic position on the Palestine question which would mean liquidation (*tasfiaya*) of the Zionist entity and establishment of a democratic Palestinian state opposed to all kinds of class and national suppression (*at-Tali'a*, November, 1969, p. 106).

The proposal for a binational state, as advocated by Matzpen, is not sufficiently progressive for Hawatmeh. In his view, Jewish nationhood implies only cultural autonomy for a religious community. But this is no innovation; Mr. Shukeiry was prepared to grant the same.

2. Bafflements and Contradictions

In Arab journalism, particularly in periodicals, interesting articles and symposia are often published concerning social problems, self-criticism and the Arab-Israel conflict. Israeli newspaper reporting usually skips over these articles because it is by its nature more concerned with political events, more with Arabs' actions and less with their ideas. Such journalistic portrayal of the Arab world becomes pallid because of the absence of the human-ideological dimension of events. Human beings not only operate, they also think about their actions. Furthermore, our concern for the opponent's reflections tends to humanize him by viewing him along with all his human problems. The Six-Day War and its aftermath raised questions for the Arabs and stimulated them to reassess their procedure in the conflict. They began to grapple with the question of their *objective* in the conflict. This wrestling is primarily concerned now with the slogan "Democratic Palestinian State."

In the weekly supplement of the Beirut newspaper *al-Anwar* (March 8, 1970), a long symposium was published concerning the meaning of the slogan "The Democratic State," in which the views of most of the prominent fedayeen organizations were represented. A translation of extracts (italicized text) from this symposium is here presented, along with comments by the author and a summary concerning its significance.

Representative of the Democratic Front: . . . The adoption of a particular slogan, in our estimation, does not stem from a subjective position or a subjective desire but from a study and analysis of the evolution of the objective situation, the objective possibilities present in society and within history—moving forces, as well as the nature of the potential evolution of these forces in the future. . . .

> *Coexistence* (ta'a-yush) *with this entity (Israel) is impossible, not because of a national aim or national aspiration of the Arabs, but because the presence of this entity will determine this region's development in connection with world imperialism, which follows from the objective link between it and Zionism. Thus, eradicating imperialist influence in the Middle East means eradicating the Israeli entity. This is something indispensable, not only from the aspect of the Palestinian people's right of self-determination, and in its homeland, but also from the aspect of protecting the Arab national liberation movement, and this objective also can only be achieved by means of armed struggle. . . .*

The representative of the Arab Liberation Front (a fedayeen organization under Iraqi influence):

> *There is no special [separate] solution for the Palestine issue. The solution must be within the framework of the Arab revolution, because the Palestine issue is not merely the paramount Arab issue but the substance and basic motivation of the Arab struggle. If the Arab nation suffers from backwardness, exploitation and disunity, these afflictions are much more severe in Palestine. That is, the Arab cause in the present historical stage is epitomized in the Palestine issue. . . .*
>
> *The liberation of Palestine will be the way for the Arabs to realize unity, not to set up regional State No. 15, which will only deepen disunity. The unified State will be the alternative to the Zionist entity, and it will be of necessity democratic, as long as we understand beforehand the dialectical connection between unity and Socialism. In the united Arab State all the minorities—denominational and others—will have equal rights . . .*

The intention is not to set up a Palestinian State as an independent unit, but to incorporate it within a unified Arab State which will be democratic because it is progressive, and which will grant the Israeli Jews minority rights.

Shafiq al-Hut (a leader of the PLO and head of its Beirut office):

. . . The Palestinian problem is that of a Zionist-colonialist invasion at the expense of a land and a people known for thirteen centuries as the Palestinian Arab people. . . . I side with Farid al-Khatib in holding that there is no benefit in expatiating upon the slogan "Democratic Palestinian State." I hope the fedayeen organizations will not do so, although I would encourage discussion of it by those who are not in responsible positions. Whatever discussion of it there is on the part of the fighting groups may cause a sense of helplessness, despair or weakness. . . .

As far as it concerns the human situation of the Jews, which Farid al-Khatib mentioned, we should expose the Zionist movement and say to the Jew: The Zionist movement which brought you to Palestine did not supply a solution to your problem as a Jew; therefore you must return whence you came to seek another way of striving for a solution for what is called "the problem of the persecuted Jew in the world." As Marx has said, he (the Jew) has no alternative but to be assimilated into his society. . . .

Even if we wished, by force of circumstances, a Democratic Palestinian State "period," this would mean its being non-Arab. Let us face matters honestly. When we speak simply of a Democratic Palestinian State, this means we discard its Arab identity. I say that on this subject we cannot negotiate, even if we possess the political power to authorize this kind of decision, because we thereby disregard an historical truth, namely, that this land and those who dwell upon it belong to a certain environment and a certain region, to which we are linked as one nation, one heritage and one hope—Unity, Freedom and Socialism. . . .

The implication that the Israeli Jews would be allowed to stay in the Democratic State raises difficulties concerning its Arab character.

If the slogan of the Democratic State was intended only to counter the claim that we wish to throw the Jews into the sea, this is indeed an apt slogan and an effective political and propaganda blow. But if we wish to regard it as the ultimate strategy of the Palestinian and Arab liberation movement, then I believe it requires a long pause for reflection, for it bears upon our history, just as our present and certainly our future.

Representative of as-Sa'iqa (a Syrian fedayeen organization): *I was among those who thought five years ago that we must slaughter the Jews. But now I cannot imagine that, if we win one night, it will be possible for us to slaughter them, or even one tenth of them. I cannot conceive of it, neither as a man, nor as an Arab.*

If so, what do we wish to do with these Jews? This is a problem for which I do not claim to have a ready answer. It is a problem which every Arab and Palestinian citizen has an obligation to express his opinion about, because it is yet early for a final, ripe formulation to offer the world and those living in Palestine.

Thus, I think that among many Jews, those living in Palestine, especially the Arab Jews, there is a great desire to return to their countries of origin, since the Zionist efforts to transform them into a homogeneous, cohesive nation have failed. There is a well-known human feeling—yearning for one's homeland, one's birthplace. There are a number of known facts concerning the Jews living in Palestine today which clearly point to this feeling among them. They desire to return to their countries of origin, especially Jews from the Arab region. . . .

Moderator: *. . . Can we consider the Kurdish problem and the manner of its solution as similar to the Jewish problem and its solution under the heading of the slogan of one Democratic State? . . .*

Representative of the Liberation Front: *Our view of the subject of Kurdish national rights follows from objective and historical considerations which substantially contradict the nature and objectives of the Zionist movement. The Kurds comprise a nationality having a distinct, well-known historical, geographical and human dimension. . . .*

Farid al-Khatib: *As far as the Arab character of the Democratic State is concerned, the Jews in Palestine have the right to express their view concerning the Arab character of the Democratic State in a democratic manner. And although it is possible to say that the Democratic State is Arab, and to say furthermore that it is a union, it is advisable to hold back additional information until the appropriate stages in the evolution of the resistance are reached. When the Zionist movement came to Palestine, it first sought a refuge, afterward a homeland, and then a State; and now it is striving to build an empire within and outside Palestine.*

Zionism also disclosed its objectives in stages.

There is nothing to be gained by summoning the Jews in the Zionist State to join the national liberation movement, as Shafiq al-Hut proposed, when he advocated convening the unified State at once. This will not convince the Jews of the world and world public opinion.

As far as it concerns the number of Palestinians, all those who emigrated to Latin America in the nineteenth century, and those who live in the desert, in exile, under conquest, or in prison, all are citizens in the State. For example: the number of Bethlehemite residents living in South America exceeds the number of those Bethlehemites living in occupied Palestine, and the combined total [of all Palestinians] is not less than that of the Jews now living in the Zionist State. . . .

The Palestinians are more numerous than the Israeli Jews and will determine the character of the State.

Shafiq al-Hut: *First, how can Farid (al-Khatib) think that the Jews and Zionists who came to set up an empire in our country have the privilege to express their democratic right in the Palestinian State? Second, how can he claim that it is difficult to convince Jewish citizens to join the liberation movement?*

Farid al-Khatib: *I think that most of the Jews living in Palestine are groups of people who were deceived by the Zionist movement and the world imperialist movement. And the Jew, as a man, has the right to express his opinion in a democratic manner regarding his future life after the collapse of the Zionist State, which is opposed to the Democratic State insofar as it discriminates between the Eastern Jew and the Western Jew and the Circassian Jew.*

The second point: The greatest ambition of the revolution is to draw the Jews of the Zionist State into the ranks of the resistance movement . . . . But what I wanted to say is that it is difficult to persuade the Jews to join the resistance movement because its immediate objective is to dissolve the Zionist contradiction within the Zionist State. . . .

Representative of the Democratic Front: *It seems to me that many of the disagreements that exist concerning this idea can be traced to some manner of misunderstanding or lack of communication. . . . This State is not bi-national in the sense that there would be two national States joined together in one form or another. This solution must be rejected, not only because it is inconsistent with our own desire, but also because it is not a true democratic solution. It is rather a solution that will represent the continuation of the national conflict which exists between the Jews and Arabs, not a solution of this conflict. It is impossible to speak of a democratic solution if it is powerless to eliminate the conflict between the different denominations and peoples within the Democratic State. When we speak of democracy it must be clear that we do not mean liberal democracy in the manner of "one man, one vote."*

OLD ILLUSIONS AND NEW AWARENESS

If the number of Jews living in Israel is not reduced, then, on a national level their quantitative and qualitative weight will dilute the Arab character of the liberated state, and on a personal level there will not be sufficient room for these Jews as well as for the Palestinians who supposedly *all* desire to return. In order to evade these difficulties, the spokesmen in the symposium try to breathe life into old ideas: that the Jews brought to the country were misguided by Zionist deceit (Zionism therefore not being a vital need), and that they remain by coercion (criticism by Israelis of themselves and their state, in a manner unknown in Arab countries, is interpreted as a sign of hatred for the state and a desire to emigrate). On these grounds it is believed that the Jews would rejoice at the opportunity to leave. An interesting element of self-deception is added, that the Jews from

Arab countries wish to return to their countries of origin. One may suspect that this illusion contains the psychological dimension of *amour-propre* and self-adulation: the Arabs are so good and were so kind to the Jews that it is inconceivable for the Jews not to desire ardently to return to live under their protection. However, along with these notions, there are signs of recognition that this is a false hope, and that the Jews have nowhere to return to, especially those born in the country, who will soon become the majority of the Jewish community. An attempt to grapple with these contradictory notions is most evident in the words of the as-Sa'iqa representative, who maintains at one and the same time that most Israeli Jews have nowhere to go, and yet that many will emigrate.

The spokesmen also try to evade this problem by claiming that the Israeli Jews are not a people. Their attachment to the country is therefore weak, and the hope that they will emigrate is reinforced. Moreover, in the clash between the Jewish group, whose cohesion is supposedly religious and not national, and the group whose cohesion is national, the latter will prevail, thereby determining the character of the country. Therefore, even if a considerable Jewish community remains there will be no such thing as a partnership between two homogeneous groups, creating a bi-national state. The Democratic Front, which stresses the Palestinianism of the Democratic State more than its Arab character, also regards membership in an Arab unity as inherent in the very idea of the Democratic State, while the Iraqi organization rejects the notion of the Palestinian State and regards it at best as a district within a unified state. (For this organization, the struggle in Palestine has the value of a catalyst for the rest of the changes in Arab countries, or a spark that will ignite a revolution that will spread to all of them.) Along with these hopes of reducing the number of Jews in the Democratic State there is the notion of tipping the population scales in the Arabs' favor by considering all Palestine Arabs, wherever they may live, as prospective citizens of the state according to an Arab Law of Return of sorts.

All the participants in the symposium agree that the Jews do not presently constitute a people. However, the recognition gnaws at some of them that nationalism is not something static but an evolution, and as time goes on, the Jews in Israel will become consolidated into a people and a nation. Hence the conclusion that this process must be forestalled by the founding of a Palestinian State. The temporal factor thus works against the idea that the Israelis are not a people, and against the possibility of founding a Palestinian State. It is no accident that Shafiq al-Hut vigorously maintains the essential and permanent nature of the Jewish status as non-people and non-nation. According to the view presented by Arabs, only a people has the right of political self-determination and deserves a state of its own. If the Jews are indeed becoming a people, this means that they are in the process of acquiring these rights.

AN ARAB PANDORA'S BOX

For most of the participants, the slogan "Democratic State" is merely tactical, the aim being to give the outside world a positive impression and to
enchant the Israelis who, as the speaker who describes *Fatah*'s views says,
will only eventually discover its full meaning. For the Democratic Front
this is presumably not merely a slogan, but a *principle* they sincerely hold
as an implication of the progressivism they profess. However, even they
wrestle with the slogan; they safeguard themselves by various qualifications or *hedges*: the state will be a member within an Arab federation, and
the democracy will not be formal, nor expressed in a numerical representation, but a "true" democracy of "the contents"—that is, its policy will represent progressiveness as expressed by "the Palestinian revolution." The
final qualification is their insistence upon the precondition for establishing
the Democratic State, that Israel be destroyed.

For those who regard the slogan "Democratic State" as merely a tactic,
the problem arises that it is impossible to lead the public only by tactical
slogans; one must present the objectives of a national vision. While the
slogan "Democratic State" may be helpful externally, it is quite destructive
internally, impairs the state's Arabism and undermines confidence in the
feasibility of "returning" to the country, if it would not be evacuated.
Shafiq al-Hut states bluntly that acceptance of this slogan means abandoning the idea of Arabism. From the Arab viewpoint another two-fold question arises: 1) if the Jews are a people, it is doubtful whether they will
consent to live in a non-Jewish state, and hence the expressed hope that
they will emigrate; 2) since the Palestinians are a people, they will certainly be opposed to returning to a state which is not Arab.

It appears that the Palestinians and Arabs are beginning to sense the difficulty of their ideological position. In the past they could be content with
the formulations "restoration of rights" and "restoration of the homeland,"
which were restricted to the meaning of the objective as bearing upon what
would be given to the Arabs, and the implication concerning what would
be taken away from the Jews was overlooked. Arab spokesmen in foreign
countries are still striving to focus on the need to rectify the injustice inflicted on the Palestinians, while evading the implication of this rectifica-
tion for the Jews. The necessity of defining the position in all its aspects
and the debate concerning the Democratic Palestinian State undermine the
Arab position. The slogan of a "Democratic State" seemed to be an escape
from a genocidal position, but it was revealed as the first step of retreat,
and the source of problems and bewilderment. I think it is no exaggeration
to say that this slogan opened a Pandora's box for the Arab position in the
conflict. Hence the deep apprehensions of all the participants in the discussion concerning this slogan, and the dramatic agreement of everyone at the
end of it that the slogan "Democratic State" is premature, even though this

contradicted the previous insistence by some on the need for a clear definition of the objective.

It appears that those who formulated the Palestinian Covenant of 1968 sensed the difficulties inherent in the Arab position and wished to anticipate them by nailing down the qualification that only a small Jewish minority (the descendants of those who came to the country before 1917) would be given citizenship in "the liberated state," thus assuring the Arab character of the country. If this stipulation manifests radicalization of the position, the reason was probably the apprehension that otherwise the ground would begin sliding beneath the Arab position.

The slogan of the "Democratic State" was offered as an escape from the odium that Article 6 of the 1968 Covenant brought upon the PLO stand, and as if the former superseded the latter, even without the formal act of amending the Covenant. It seems that the difficulties in which the idea of the Democratic State is enmeshed and the internal controversies it aroused, as expressed in this symposium, explain why Article 6 has not been amended, despite the fact that it damaged the Palestinian cause.

3. Postscript

The slogan of the "Democratic State" was hailed by Arab spokesmen as an all-important innovation demonstrating the liberal humanitarian nature of the Palestine movement. Yasser Arafat, to strengthen this impression, even said that its president can be Jewish. However, scrutiny shows that it is neither so liberal nor new.

The objective of setting up a Democratic Palestine was enshrined in the resolutions of the Eighth Palestinian National Assembly (March 1–5, 1971). The resolution was carefully formulated and it does not say, as Palestinian spokesmen purport to interpret the slogan, that *all* Israelis will be allowed to stay, but that the state will be based on equality of rights for all its citizens: "The future state in Palestine . . . will be Democratic, in which all will enjoy the same rights and obligations." This is quite compatible with the quantitative limitation included in the infamous Article 6 of the 1968 Covenant.

It is not new. All along the Palestinians have repeatedly declared that their state will be democratic. That is part of the spirit of the age, when even autocratic regimes call themselves democratic. For instance, the Congress, which set up the "All-Palestine Government" in Gaza and which unanimously elected the former Mufti of Jerusalem, Hajj Amin al-Husaini, as its president, proclaimed on October 1, 1948 "the establishment of a free and democratic sovereign state. In it the citizens will enjoy their liberties and their rights. . . . "

Even if the slogan of the "Democratic State" were free of inconsistency and insincerity it is not acceptable to the Israelis. The Israelis have no less a right to national self-determination than the Palestinian Arabs. They do not want to become Palestinians of Jewish faith; they intend to remain Israelis.

The difficulties for the Arabs inherent in the slogan of the "Democratic State" caused a decline in its discussion at subsequent Palestinian Congresses. This does not mean that it was discarded, as the alternative is to fall back on the brutality of the former, blatant, political-genocidal position.

No Need To Worry Now

Perhaps the most common attitude is to concentrate at this stage on the demand for "self-determination for the Palestinians in their homeland" and leave the rest. This demand is an objective that can be easily justified. Defining the final objective now, it is argued, is a waste of time, and only a source of bafflement. Political objectives should be set in a time sequence. The problem of reconciling the existence of a large Jewish community with the conversion of the country into a Palestinian state is one for the distant future and should not bother the Arabs and Palestinians now. Now they should exert all their efforts in the struggle against Israel and in attaining of their national and social objectives. The achievement of these and the return of the Palestinians will produce new conditions which may solve the entire problem.

This approach was already alluded to in the Symposium. It has been expressed with greater clarity by Alias Murqus in his book criticizing the platform of the Lebanese Communist Party (LCP) at its Second Congress in the summer of 1968. Murqus commends the LCP stand in defining that the "final solution to the Palestinian problem should be based on positions of principle, stemming from the inalienable right of the Palestinian Arabs in their land and homeland and hence their right to return there and achieve their self-determination . . . as the existence of the Jews in Palestine cannot impair the Palestinian natural and historical right in their homeland." He stresses that "the final solution to the Palestinian problem is Palestine as an Arab homeland," and as regards the future it calls for "the complete eradication of the State of Israel." He goes on:

> How shall we reconcile the existence of two million Jews and two million Palestinian Arabs? This is not our task or yours now. Let us define our objective in principle and nothing more. Let us define the present way to the goal: The fighting and the falling of hundreds of thousands from the Arabs and the Jews (from the Arab more than from the Jews). With the victory of the Algerian revolution the majority of the French, young and old, went, returned to France. With Arab victory in the Near East (the battle will be longer, fiercer and with heavier casualties), it is possible that the Jews in great numbers will return whence they came—

Baghdad, Aleppo, Yemen, Morocco, Tunisia, Algeria, Egypt, Poland and other places, to France, or they will settle in Canada, the USA and Australia. This problem should not worry us, as its solution is by the struggle. (*Marxism, Leninism and the World and Arab Development in the Platform of the Lebanese Communist Party,* (Arabic) Dar al-Haqiqa, Beirut, 1970, pp. 362–363).

Egyptian-Israeli Accord on Sinai (September 1, 1975)

The Government of the Arab Republic of Egypt and the Government of Israel have agreed that:

ARTICLE I

The conflict between them and in the Middle East shall not be resolved by military force but by peaceful means.

The agreement concluded by the parties Jan. 18, 1974, within the framework of the Geneva peace conference constituted a first step towards a just and durable peace according to the provisions of Security Council Resolution 338 of Oct. 22, 1973; and they are determined to reach a final and just peace settlement by means of negotiations called for by Security Council Resolution 338, this agreement being a significant step towards that end.

ARTICLE II

The parties hereby undertake not to resort to the threat or use of force or military blockade against each other.

ARTICLE III

(1) The parties shall continue scrupulously to observe the cease-fire on land, sea and air and to refrain from all military or paramilitary actions against each other.

(2) The parties also confirm that the obligations contained in the annex and, when concluded, the protocol shall be an integral part of this agreement.

ARTICLE IV

A. The military forces of the parties shall be deployed in accordance with the following principles:

(1) All Israeli forces shall be deployed east of the lines designated as lines J and M on the attached map.

(2) All Egyptian forces shall be deployed west of the line designated as line E on the attached map.

(3) The area between the lines designated on the attached map as lines E and F and the area between the lines designated on the attached map as lines J and K shall be limited in armament and forces.

(4) The limitations on armament and forces in the areas described by paragraph (3) above shall be agreed as described in the attached annex.

(5) The zone between the lines designated on the attached map as lines E and J will be a buffer zone. On this zone the United Nations Emergency Force will continue to perform its functions as under the Egyptian-Israeli agreement of Jan. 18, 1974.

(6) In the area south from line E and west from line M, as defined in the attached map, there will be no military forces, as specified in the attached annex.

B. The details concerning the new lines, the redeployment of the forces and its timing, the limitation of armaments and forces, aerial reconnaissance, the operation of the early warning and surveillance installations and the use of the roads, the U.N. functions and other arrangements will all be in accordance with the provisions of the annex and map which are an integral part of this agreement and of the protocol which is to result from negotiations pursuant to the annex and which, when concluded, shall become an integral part of this agreement.

ARTICLE V

The United Nations Emergency Force is essential and shall continue its functions, and its mandate shall be extended annually.

ARTICLE VI

The parties hereby establish a joint commission for the duration of this agreement. It will function under the aegis of the chief coordinator of the United Nations peace-keeping missions in the Middle East in order to consider any problem arising from this agreement and to assist the United Nations Emergency Force in the execution of its mandate. The joint commission shall function in accordance with procedures established in the protocol.

ARTICLE VII

Nonmilitary cargoes destined for or coming from Israel shall be permitted through the Suez Canal.

ARTICLE VIII

(1) This agreement is regarded by the parties as a significant step toward a just and lasting peace. It is not a final peace agreement.

(2) The parties shall continue their efforts to negotiate a final peace agreement within the framework of the Geneva peace conference in accordance with Security Council Resolution 338.

ARTICLE IX

This agreement shall enter into force upon signature of the protocol and remain in force until superseded by a new agreement.

The U.S. Proposal for Early-Warning System in Sinai

In connection with the early-warning system referred to in Article IV of the agreement between Egypt and Israel concluded on this date and as an integral part of that agreement (hereafter referred to as the basic agreement), the United States proposes the following:

[1]

The early-warning system to be established in accordance with Article IV in the area shown on the attached map will be entrusted to the United States. It shall have the following elements:

A. There shall be two surveillance stations to provide strategic early warning, one operated by Egyptian and one operated by Israeli personnel. Their locations are shown on the map attached to the basic agreement. Each station shall be manned by not more than 250 technical and administrative personnel. They shall perform the functions of visual and electronic surveillance only within their stations.

B. In support of these stations, to provide tactical early warning and to verify access to them, three watch stations shall be established by the United States in the Mitla and Gidi Passes as will be shown on the agreed map.

These stations shall be operated by United States civilian personnel. In support of these stations, there shall be established three unmanned electronic-sensor fields at both ends of each pass and in the general vicinity of each station and the roads leading to and from those stations.

[2]

The United States civilian personnel shall perform the following duties in connection with the operation and maintenance of these stations:

A. At the two surveillance stations described in paragraph 1A, above, United States personnel will verify the nature of the operations of the stations and all movement into and out of each station and will immediately report any detected divergency from its authorized role of visual and electronic surveillance to the parties to the basic agreement and the UNEF.

B. At each watch station described in paragraph 1B above, the United

States personnel will immediately report to the parties to the basic agreement and to UNEF any movement of armed forces, other than the UNEF, into either pass and any observed preparations for such movement.

C. The total number of United States civilian personnel assigned to functions under these proposals shall not exceed 200. Only civilian personnel shall be assigned to functions under these proposals.

[3]

No arms shall be maintained at the stations and other facilities covered by these proposals, except for small arms required for their protection.

[4]

The United States personnel serving the early-warning system shall be allowed to move freely within the area of the system.

[5]

The United States and its personnel shall be entitled to have such support facilities as are reasonably necessary to perform their functions.

[6]

The United States personnel shall be immune from local criminal, civil, tax and customs jurisdiction and may be accorded any other specific privileges and immunities provided for in the UNEF agreement of Feb. 13, 1957.

[7]

The United States affirms that it will continue to perform the functions described above for the duration of the basic agreement.

[8]

Notwithstanding any other provision of these proposals, the United States may withdraw its personnel only if it concludes that their safety is jeopardized or that continuation of their role is no longer necessary. In the latter case the parties to the basic agreement will be informed in advance in order to give them the opportunity to make alternative arrangements. If both parties to the basic agreement request the United States to conclude its role under this proposal, the United States will consider such requests conclusive.

[9]

Technical problems including the location of the watch stations will be worked out through consultation with the United States.

Annex to the Sinai Agreement

Within five days after the signature of the Egypt-Israel agreement, representatives of the two parties shall meet in the military working group of the Middle East peace conference at Geneva to begin preparation of a detailed protocol for the implementation of the agreement. In order to facilitate preparation of the protocol and implementation of the agreement, and to assist in maintaining the scrupulous observance of the cease-fire and other elements of the agreement, the two parties have agreed on the following principles, which are an integral part of the agreement, as guidelines for the working group.

1. DEFINITIONS OF LINES AND AREAS

The deployment lines, areas of limited forces and armaments, buffer zones, the area south from line E and west from line M, other designated areas, road sections for common use and other features referred to in Article IV of the agreement shall be as indicated on the attached map (1:100,000—U.S. edition).

2. BUFFER ZONES

(a) Access to the buffer zones shall be controlled by the UNEF, according to procedures to be worked out by the working group and UNEF.

(b) Aircraft of either party will be permitted to fly freely up to the forward line of that party. Reconnaissance aircraft of either party may fly up to the middle line of the buffer zone between E and J on an agreed schedule.

(c) In the buffer zone, between line E and J, there will be established under Article IV of the agreement an early-warning system entrusted to United States civilian personnel as detailed in a separate proposal, which is a part of this agreement.

(d) Authorized personnel shall have access to the buffer zone for transit to and from the early-warning system; the manner in which this is carried out shall be worked out by the working group and UNEF.

3. AREA SOUTH OF LINE E AND WEST OF LINE M

(a) In this area, the United Nations Emergency Force will assure that there are no military or paramilitary forces of any kind, military fortifications and military installations; it will establish checkpoints and have the freedom of movement necessary to perform this function.

(b) Egyptian civilians and third-country civilian oil-field personnel shall have the right to enter, exit from, work and live in the above-indicated area, except for buffer zones 2A, 2B and the U.N. posts. Egyptian civilian police shall be allowed in the area to perform normal civil police functions among the civilian population in such numbers and with such weapons and equipment as shall be provided for in the protocol.

(c) Entry to and exit from the area, by land, by air or by sea, shall be only through UNEF checkpoints. UNEF shall also establish checkpoints along the road, the dividing line and at other points, with the precise locations and number to be included in the protocol.

(d) Access to the airspace and the coastal area shall be limited to unarmed Egyptian civilian vessels and unarmed civilian helicopters and transport planes involved in the civilian activities of the area, as agreed by the working group.

(e) Israel undertakes to leave intact all currently existing civilian installations and infrastructures.

(f) Procedures for use of the common sections of the coastal road along the Gulf of Suez shall be determined by the working group and detailed in the protocol.

4. Aerial Surveillance

There shall be a continuation of aerial reconnaissance missions by the U.S. over the areas covered by the agreement following the same procedures already in practice. The missions will ordinarily be carried out at a frequency of one mission every seven to 10 days, with either party or UNEF empowered to request an earlier mission. The U.S. will make the mission results available expeditiously to Israel, Egypt and the chief coordinator of the U.N. peace-keeping mission in the Middle East.

5. Limitation of Forces and Armaments

(a) Within the areas of limited forces and armaments the major limitations shall be as follows:

(1) Eight (8) standard infantry battalions.

(2) Seventy-five (75) tanks.

(3) Sixty (60) artillery pieces, including heavy mortars (i.e., with caliber larger than 120 mm.), whose range shall not exceed 12 km.

(4) The total number of personnel shall not exceed eight thousand (8,000).

(5) Both parties agree not to station or locate in the area weapons which can reach the line of the other side.

(6) Both parties agree that in the areas between lines J and K, and between line A (of the disengagement agreement of Jan. 18, 1974) and line E, they will construct no new fortifications or installations for forces of a size greater than that agreed herein.

(b) The major limitations beyond the areas of limited forces and armament will be:

(1) Neither side will station nor locate any weapon in areas from which they can reach the other line.

(2) The parties will not place anti-aircraft missiles within an area of 10 kilometers east of line K and west of line F, respectively.

(c) The U.N. Force will conduct inspections in order to insure the maintenance of the agreed limitations within these areas.

6. PROCESS OF IMPLEMENTATION

The detailed implementation and timing of the redeployment of forces, turnover of oil fields and other arrangements called for by the agreement, annex and protocol shall be determined by the working group, which will agree on the stages of this process, including the phased movement of Egyptian troops to line E and Israeli troops to line J. The first phase will be the transfer of the oil fields and installations to Egypt. This process will begin within two weeks from the signature of the protocol with the introduction of the necessary technicians, and it will be completed no later than eight weeks after it begins. The details of the phasing will be worked out in the military working group.

Implementation of the redeployment shall be completed within five months after signature of the protocol.

Part III

From Camp David Through the Madrid Conference

Harold H. Saunders: U.S. Foreign Policy and Peace in the Middle East (November 12, 1975)*

Mr. Chairman, a just and durable peace in the Middle East is a central objective of the United States. Both President Ford and Secretary Kissinger have stated firmly on numerous occasions that the United States is determined to make every feasible effort to maintain the momentum of practical progress toward a peaceful settlement of the Arab-Israeli conflict.

We have also repeatedly stated that the legitimate interests of the Palestinian Arabs must be taken into account in the negotiation of an Arab-Israeli peace. In many ways, the Palestinian dimension of the Arab-Israeli conflict is the heart of that conflict. Final resolution of the problems arising from the partition of Palestine, the establishment of the State of Israel, and Arab opposition to those events will not be possible until agreement is reached defining a just and permanent status for the Arab peoples who consider themselves Palestinians. . . . The U.S. has provided some $620 million in assistance—about sixty-two percent of the total international support ($1 billion) for the Palestinian refugees over the past quarter of a century.

Today, however, we recognize that, in addition to meeting the human needs and responding to legitimate personal claims of the refugees, there is another interest that must be taken into account. It is a fact that many of the three million or so people who call themselves Palestinians today increasingly regard themselves as having their own identity as a people and desire a voice in determining their political status. As with any people in this situation, there are differences among themselves, but the Palestinians collectively are a political factor which must be dealt with if there is to be a peace between Israel and its neighbors.

---

*Prepared statement of Harold H. Saunders, Deputy Assistant Secretarty for Near Eastern and South Asian affairs, before the House Foreign Affairs Subcommittee on the Middle East.

The statement is often made in the Arab world that there will not be peace until the "rights of the Palestinians" are fulfilled, but there is no agreed definition of what is meant and a variety of viewpoints have been expressed on what the legitimate objectives of the Palestinians are.

Some Palestinian elements hold to the objective of a binational secular state in the area of the former mandate of Palestine. Realization of this objective would mean the end of the present state of Israel, a member of the United Nations, and its submergence in some larger entity. Some would be willing to accept merely as a first step toward this goal the establishment of a Palestinian state comprising the West Bank of the Jordan River and Gaza.

Other elements of Palestinian opinion appear willing to accept an independent Palestinian state comprising the West Bank and Gaza, based on acceptance of Israel's right to exist as an independent state within roughly its pre-1967 borders.

Some Palestinians and other Arabs envisage as a possible solution a unification of the West Bank and Gaza with Jordan. A variation of this which has been suggested would be the reconstitution of the country as a federated state, with the West Bank becoming an autonomous Palestinian province.

Still others, including many Israelis, feel that with the West Bank returned to Jordan, and with the resulting existence of two communities—Palestinian and Jordanian—within Jordan, opportunities would be created thereby for the Palestinians to find self-expression.

In the case of a solution which would rejoin the West Bank to Jordan or a solution involving a West Bank/Gaza state, there would still arise the property claims of those Palestinians who before 1948 resided in areas that became the State of Israel. These claims have been acknowledged as a serious problem by the international community ever since the adoption by the United Nations of Resolution 194 on this subject in 1948, a resolution which the United Nations has repeatedly reaffirmed and which the United States has supported. A solution will be further complicated by the property claims against Arab states of the many Jews from those states who moved to Israel in its early years after achieving statehood.

In addition to property claims, some believe they should have the option of returning to their original homes under any settlement.

Other Arab leaders, while pressing the importance of Palestinian involvement in a settlement, have taken the position that the definition of Palestinian interests is something for the Palestinian people themselves to sort out, and the view has been expressed by responsible Arab leaders that realization of Palestinian rights need not be inconsistent with the existence of Israel.

No one, therefore, seems in a position today to say exactly what Palestinian objectives are. . . . What is needed as a first step is a diplomatic process which will help bring forth a reasonable definition of Palestinian interests—a position from which negotiations on a solution of the Palestinian aspects of the problem might begin. The issue is not whether Palestinian interests should be expressed in a final settlement, but how. There will be no peace unless an answer is found.

Another requirement is the development of a framework for negotiations—a statement of the objectives and the terms of reference. The framework for the negotiations that have taken place thus far and the agreements they have produced involving Israel, Syria, and Egypt, has been provided by United Nations Security Council Resolutions 242 and 338. In accepting that framework, all of the parties to the negotiation have accepted that the objective of the negotiations is peace between them based on mutual recognition, territorial integrity, political independence, the right to live in peace within secure and recognized borders, and the resolution of the specific issues which comprise the Arab-Israeli conflict.

The major problem that must be resolved in establishing a framework for bringing issues of concern to the Palestinians into negotiation, therefore, is to find a common basis for the negotiation that Palestinians and Israelis can both accept. This could be achieved by common acceptance of the above-mentioned Security Council resolutions, although they do not deal with the political aspect of the Palestinian problem.

A particularly difficult aspect of the problem is the question of who negotiates for the Palestinians. It has been our belief that Jordan would be a logical negotiator for the Palestinian-related issues. The Rabat Summit, however, recognized the Palestinian Liberation Organization as the "sole legitimate representative of the Palestinian people."

However, the PLO does not accept the United Nations Security Council resolutions, does not recognize the existence of Israel, and has not stated its readiness to negotiate peace with Israel; Israel does not recognize the PLO or the idea of a separate Palestinian entity. Thus we do not at this point have the framework for a negotiation involving the PLO. We cannot envision or urge a negotiation between two parties as long as one professes to hold the objective of eliminating the other—rather than the objective of negotiating peace with it.

There is one other aspect to this problem. Elements of the PLO have used terrorism to gain attention for their cause. Some Americans as well as many Israelis and others have been killed by Palestinian terrorists. The international community cannot condone such practices, and it seems to us that there must be some assurance if Palestinians are drawn into the negotiating process that these practices will be curbed.

This is the problem which we now face. If the progress toward peace which has now begun is to continue, a solution to this question must be found. We have not devised an American solution, nor would it be appropriate for us to do so. This is the responsibility of the parties and the purpose of the negotiating process. But we have not closed our minds to any reasonable solution which can contribute to progress toward our overriding objective in the Middle East—an Arab-Israeli peace. The step-by-step approach to negotiations which we have pursued has been based partly on the understanding that issues in the Arab-Israeli conflict take time to mature. It is obvious that thinking on the Palestinian aspects of the problem must evolve on all sides. As it does, what is not possible today may become possible.

Our consultations on how to move the peace negotiations forward will recognize the need to deal with this subject. As Secretary Kissinger has said, "We are prepared to work with all the parties toward a solution of all the issues yet remaining—including the issue of the future of the Palestinians." We will do so because the issues of concern to the Palestinians are important in themselves and because the Arab governments participating in the negotiations have made clear that progress in the overall negotiations will depend in part on progress on issues of concern to the Palestinians. We are prepared to consider any reasonable proposal from any quarter, and we will expect other parties to the negotiation to be equally open-minded.

The Likud Party: Platform (March 1977)

The Right of the Jewish People to the Land of Israel (Eretz Israel)

a. The right of the Jewish people to the land of Israel is eternal and indisputable and is linked with the right to security and peace; therefore, Judaea and Samaria will not be handed to any foreign administration; between the Sea and the Jordan there will only be Israeli sovereignty.

b. A plan which relinquishes parts of western Eretz Israel, undermines our right to the country, unavoidably leads to the establishment of a "Palestinian State," jeopardizes the security of the Jewish population, endangers the existence of the State of Israel, and frustrates any prospect of peace.

Genuine Peace—Our Central Objective

a. The Likud government will place its aspirations for peace at the top of its priorities and will spare no effort to promote peace. The Likud will act as a genuine partner at peace treaty negotiations with our neighbors, as is customary among the nations. The Likud government will attend the Geneva Conference. . . .

d. The Likud government's peace initiative will be positive. Directly or through a friendly state, Israel will invite her neighbors to hold direct negotiations, in order to sign peace agreements without pre-conditions on either side and without any solution formula invented by outsiders ("invented outside").

At the negotiations each party will be free to make any proposals it deems fit.

Settlement

Settlement, both urban and rural, in all parts of the Land of Israel is the focal point of the Zionist effort to redeem the country, to maintain vital security areas and serves as a reservoir of strength and inspiration for the renewal of the pioneering spirit. The Likud government will call on the younger generation in Israel and the dispersions to settle and help every group and individual in the task of inhabiting and cultivating the wasteland, while taking care not to dispossess anyone.

Arab Terror Organizations

The PLO is no national liberation organization but an organization of assassins, which the Arab countries use as a political and military tool, while also serving the interests of Soviet imperialism, to stir up the area. Its aim is to liquidate the State of Israel, set up an Arab country instead and make the Land of Israel part of the Arab world. The Likud government will strive to eliminate these murderous organizations in order to prevent them from carrying out their bloody deeds.

Egyptian President Anwar Sadat: Peace with Justice (November 20, 1977)*

. . . I come to you today on solid ground to shape a new life and to establish peace. We all love this land, the land of God, we all, Moslems, Christians and Jews, all worship God.

Under God, God's teachings and commandments are: love, sincerity, security and peace.

I do not blame all those who received my decision when I announced it to the entire world before the Egyptian People's Assembly . . . with surprise and even with amazement. . . .

Many months in which peace could have been brought about have been wasted over differences and fruitless discussions on the procedure of convening the Geneva conference. All have shared suspicion and absolute lack of confidence.

*Speech delivered by the Egyptian President before the Israeli Knesset.

But to be absolutely frank with you, I took this decision after long thought, knowing that it constitutes a great risk, for God Almighty has made it my fate to assume responsibility on behalf of the Egyptian people, to share in the responsibility of the Arab nation, the main duty of which, dictated by responsibility, is to exploit all and every means in a bid to save my Egyptian Arab people and the pan-Arab nation from the horrors of new suffering and destructive wars, the dimensions of which are foreseen only by God Himself. . . .

Those who like us are shouldering the same responsibilities entrusted to us are the first who should have the courage to make determining decisions that are consonant with the magnitude of the circumstances. We must all rise above all forms of obsolete theories of superiority, and the most important thing is never to forget that infallibility is the prerogative of God alone.

If I said that I wanted to avert from all the Arab people the horrors of shocking and destructive wars I must sincerely declare before you that I have the same feelings and bear the same responsibility toward all and every man on earth, and certainly toward the Israeli people.

Any life that is lost in war is a human life, be it that of an Arab or an Israeli. A wife who becomes a widow is a human being entitled to a happy family life, whether she be an Arab or an Israeli.

Innocent children who are deprived of the care and compassion of their parents are ours. They are ours, be they living on Arab or Israeli land.

They command our full responsibility to afford them a comfortable life today and tomorrow.

For the sake of them all, for the sake of the lives of all our sons and brothers, for the sake of affording our communities the opportunity to work for the progress and happiness of man, feeling secure and with the right to a dignified life, for the generations to come, for a smile on the face of every child born in our land—for all that I have taken my decision to come to you, despite all the hazards, to deliver my address.

I have shouldered the prerequisites of the historic responsibility and therefore I declared on Feb. 4, 1971, that I was willing to sign a peace agreement with Israel. This was the first declaration made by a responsible Arab official since the outbreak of the Arab-Israeli conflict. Motivated by all these factors dictated by the responsibilities of leadership on Oct. 16, 1973, before the Egyptian People's Assembly, I called for an international conference to establish permanent peace based on justice. I was not heard.

I was in the position of man pleading for peace or asking for a ceasefire, motivated by the duties of history and leadership, I signed the first disengagement agreement, followed by the second disengagement agreement in Sinai.

Then we proceeded, trying both open and closed doors in a bid to find a certain road leading to a durable and just peace. . . .

How can we achieve permanent peace based on justice? Well, I have come to you carrying my clear and frank answer to this big question, so that the people in Israel as well as the entire world may hear it. All those devoted prayers ring in my ears, pleading to God Almighty that this historic meeting may eventually lead to the result aspired to by millions.

Before I proclaim my answer, I wish to assure you that in my clear and frank answer I am availing myself of a number of facts which no one can deny.

The first fact is that no one can build his happiness at the expense of the misery of others.

The second fact: never have I spoken, nor will I ever speak, with two tongues; never have I adopted, nor will I ever adopt, two policies. I never deal with anyone except in one tongue, one policy and with one face.

The third fact: direct confrontation is the nearest and most successful method to reach a clear objective.

The fourth fact: the call for permanent and just peace based on respect for United Nations resolutions has now become the call of the entire world. It has become the expression of the will of the international community, whether in official capitals where policies are made and decisions taken, or at the level of world public opinion, which influences policymaking and decision-taking.

The fifth fact, and this is probably the clearest and most prominent, is that the Arab nation, in its drive for permanent peace based on justice, does not proceed from a position of weakness. On the contrary, it has the power and stability for a sincere will for peace.

The Arab declared intention stems from an awareness prompted by a heritage of civilization, that to avoid an inevitable disaster that will befall us, you and the whole world, there is no alternative to the establishment of permanent peace based on justice, peace that is not swayed by suspicion or jeopardized by ill intentions.

In the light of these facts which I meant to place before you the way I see them, I would also wish to warn you, in all sincerity I warn you, against some thoughts that could cross your minds. . . .

First, I have not come here for a separate agreement between Egypt and Israel. This is not part of the policy of Egypt. The problem is not that of Egypt and Israel.

An interim peace between Egypt and Israel, or between any Arab confrontation state and Israel, will not bring permanent peace based on justice in the entire region.

Rather, even if peace between all the confrontation states and Israel were achieved in the absence of a just solution of the Palestinian problem, never will there be that durable and just peace upon which the entire world insists.

Second, I have not come to you to seek a partial peace, namely to terminate the state of belligerency at this stage and put off the entire problem to a subsequent stage. This is not the radical solution that would steer us to permanent peace.

Equally, I have not come to you for a third disengagement agreement in Sinai or in Golan or the West Bank.

For this would mean that we are merely delaying the ignition of the fuse. It would also mean that we are lacking the courage to face peace, that we are too weak to shoulder the burdens and responsibilities of a durable peace based upon justice.

I have come to you so that together we should build a durable peace based on justice to avoid the shedding of one single drop of blood by both sides. It is for this reason that I have proclaimed my readiness to go to the farthest corner of the earth.

Here I would go back to the big question:

How can we achieve a durable peace based on justice? In my opinion, and I declare it to the whole world, from this forum, the answer is neither difficult nor is it impossible despite long years of feuds, blood, faction, strife, hatreds and deep-rooted animosity.

The answer is not difficult, nor is it impossible, if we sincerely and faithfully follow a straight line.

You want to live with us, part of the world.

In all sincerity I tell you we welcome you among us with full security and safety. This in itself is a tremendous turning point, one of the land-marks of a decisive historical change. We used to reject you. We had our reasons and our fears, yes.

We refused to meet with you, anywhere, yes.

We were together in international conferences and organizations and our representatives did not, and still do not, exchange greetings with you. Yes. This has happened and is still happening.

It is also true that we used to set as a precondition for any negotiations with you a mediator who would meet separately with each party.

Yes. Through this procedure, the talks of the first and second disen-gagement agreements took place.

Our delegates met in the first Geneva conference without exchanging direct word, yes, this has happened.

Yet today I tell you, and I declare it to the whole world, that we accept to live with you in permanent peace based on justice. We do not want to encircle you or be encircled ourselves by destructive missiles ready for launching, nor by the shells of grudges and hatreds.

I have announced on more than one occasion that Israel has become a *fait accompli,* recognized by the world, and that the two superpowers have undertaken the responsibility for its security and the defense of its exis-tence. As we really and truly seek peace we really and truly welcome you to live among us in peace and security.

There was a huge wall between us which you tried to build up over a quarter of a century, but it was destroyed in 1973. It was the wall of an implacable and escalating psychological warfare.

It was a wall of the fear of the force that could sweep the entire Arab nation. It was a wall of propaganda that we were a nation reduced to immobility. Some of you had gone as far as to say that even for 50 years to come, the Arabs would not regain their strength. It was a wall that always threatened with a long arm that could reach and strike anywhere. It was a wall that warned us of extermination and annihilation if we tried to use our legitimate rights to liberate the occupied territories.

Together we have to admit that that wall fell and collapsed in 1973. Yet, there remains another wall. This wall constitutes a psychological barrier between us, a barrier of suspicion, a barrier of rejection; a barrier of fear, of deception, a barrier of hallucination without any action, deed or decision.

A barrier of distorted and eroded interpretation of every event and statement. It is this psychological barrier which I described in official statements as constituting 70 percent of the whole problem.

Today, through my visit to you, I ask you why don't we stretch out our hands with faith and sincerity so that together we might destroy this barrier? Why shouldn't our and your will meet with faith and sincerity so that together we might remove all suspicion of fear, betrayal and bad intentions? . . .

Ladies and gentlemen, to tell you the truth, peace cannot be worth its name unless it is based on justice and not on the occupation of the land of others. It would not be right for you to demand for yourselves what you deny to others. With all frankness and in the spirit that has prompted me to come to you today, I tell you you have to give up once and for all the dreams of conquest and give up the belief that force is the best method for dealing with the Arabs.

You should clearly understand the lesson of confrontation between you and us. Expansion does not pay. To speak frankly, our land does not yield itself to bargaining, it is not even open to argument. To us, the nation's soil is equal to the holy valley where God Almighty spoke to Moses. Peace be upon him.

We cannot accept any attempt to take away or accept to seek one inch of it nor can we accept the principle of debating or bargaining over it.

I sincerely tell you also that before us today lies the appropriate chance for peace. If we are really serious in our endeavor for peace, it is a chance that that may never come again. It is a chance that if lost or wasted, the resulting slaughter would bear the curse of humanity and of history.

What is peace for Israel? It means that Israel lives in the region with her Arab neighbors in security and safety. Is that logical? I say yes. It means that Israel lives within its borders, secure against any aggression. Is that logical? And I say yes. It means that Israel obtains all kinds of guarantees that will ensure these two factors. To this demand, I say yes.

Beyond that we declare that we accept all the international guarantees you envisage and accept. We declare that we accept all the guarantees you want from the two superpowers or from either of them or from the Big Five or from some of them. Once again, I declare clearly and unequivocally that we agree to any guarantees you accept, because in return we shall receive the same guarantees.

In short then, when we ask what is peace for Israel, the answer would be that Israel lives within her borders, among her Arab neighbors in safety and security, within the framework of all the guarantees she accepts and which are offered to her.

But, how can this be achieved? How can we reach this conclusion which would lead us to permanent peace based on justice? There are facts that should be faced with courage and clarity. There are Arab territories which Israel has occupied and still occupies by force. We insist on complete withdrawal from these territories, including Arab Jerusalem.

I have come to Jerusalem, the city of peace, which will always remain as a living embodiment of coexistence among believers of the three religions. It is inadmissible that anyone should conceive the special status of the city of Jerusalem within the framework of annexation or expansionism. It should be a free and open city for all believers.

Above all, this city should not be severed from those who have made it their abode for centuries. Instead of reviving the precedent of the Crusades, we should revive the spirit of Omar Emil Khtab and Saladin, namely the spirit of tolerance and respect for right.

The holy shrines of Islam and Christianity are not only places of worship but a living testimony of our interrupted presence here. Politically, spiritually and intellectually, here let us make no mistake about the importance and reverence we Christians and Moslems attach to Jerusalem.

Let me tell you without the slightest hesitation that I have not come to you under this roof to make a request that your troops evacuate the occupied territories. Complete withdrawal from the Arab territories occupied after 1967 is a logical and undisputed fact. Nobody should plead for that. Any talk about permanent peace based on justice and any move to ensure our coexistence in peace and security in this part of the world would become meaningless while you occupy Arab territories by force of arms.

For there is no peace that could be built on the occupation of the land of others, otherwise it would not be a serious peace. Yet this is a foregone conclusion which is not open to the passion of debate if intentions are sincere or if endeavors to establish a just and durable peace for our and for generations to come are genuine.

As for the Palestine cause—nobody could deny that it is the crux of the entire problem. Nobody in the world could accept today slogans propagated here in Israel, ignoring the existence of a Palestinian people and questioning even their whereabouts. Because the Palestine people and their legitimate rights are no longer denied today by anybody; that is nobody who has the ability of judgment, can deny or ignore it.

It is an acknowledged fact, perceived by the world community, both in the East and in the West, with support and recognition in international documents and official statements. It is of no use to anybody to turn deaf ears to its resounding voice, which is being heard day and night, or to overlook its historical reality.

Even the United States of America, your first ally, which is absolutely committed to safeguard Israel's security and existence and which offered and still offers Israel every moral, material and military support—I say, even the United States has opted to face up to reality and admit that the Palestinian people are entitled to legitimate rights and that the Palestine problem is the cause and essence of the conflict and that so long as it continues to be unresolved, the conflict will continue to aggravate, reaching new dimension.

In all sincerity I tell you that there can be no peace without the Palestinians. It is a grave error of unpredictable consequences to overlook or brush aside this cause.

I shall not indulge in past events such as the Balfour Declaration 60 years ago. You are well acquainted with the relevant text. If you have found the moral and legal justification to set up a national home on a land that did not all belong to you, it is incumbent upon you to show understanding of the insistence of the people of Palestine for establishment once again of a state on their land. When some extremists ask the Palestinians to give up this sublime objective, this in fact means asking them to renounce their identity and every hope for the future.

I hail the Israeli voices that called for the recognition of the Palestinian people's right to achieve and safeguard peace.

Here I tell you, ladies and gentlemen, that it is no use to refrain from recognizing the Palestinian people and their right to statehood as their right of return. We, the Arabs, have faced this experience before, with you. And with the reality of the Israeli existence, the struggle which took us from war to war, from victims to more victims, until you and we have today reached the edge of a horrible abyss and a terrifying disaster unless, together, we seize this opportunity today of a durable peace based on justice.

You have to face reality bravely, as I have done. There can never be any solution to a problem by evading it or turning a deaf ear to it. Peace cannot last if attempts are made to impose fantasy concepts on which the world has turned its back and announced its unanimous call for the respect of rights and facts.

There is no need to enter a vicious circle as to Palestinian rights. It is useless to create obstacles, otherwise the march of peace will be impeded or peace will be blown up. As I have told you, there is no happiness [based on] the detriment of others.

Direct confrontation and straightforwardness are the shortcuts and the most successful way to reach a clear objective. Direct confrontation concerning the Palestinian problem and tackling it in one single language with a view to achieving a durable and just peace lie in the establishment of that peace. With all the guarantees you demand, there should be no fear of a newly born state that needs the assistance of all countries of the world.

When the bells of peace ring there will be no hands to beat the drums of war. Even if they existed, they would be stilled.

Conceive with me a peace agreement in Geneva that we would herald to a world thristing for peace. A peace agreement based on the following points:

Ending the occupation of the Arab territories occupied in 1967.

Achievement of the fundamental rights of the Palestinian people and their right to self-determination, including their right to establish their own state.

The right of all states in the area to live in peace within their boundaries, their secure boundaries, which will be secured and guaranteed through procedures to be agreed upon, which will provide appropriate security to international boundaries in addition to appropriate international guarantees.

Commitment of all states in the region to administer the relations among them in accordance with the objectives and principles of the United Nations Charter. Particularly the principles concerning the nonuse of force and a solution of differences among them by peaceful means.

Ending the state of belligerence in the region.

Ladies and gentlemen, peace is not a mere endorsement of written lines. Rather it is a rewriting of history. Peace is not a game of calling for peace to defend certain whims or hide certain admissions. Peace in its essence is a dire struggle against all and every ambition and whim.

Perhaps the example taken and experienced, taken from ancient and modern history, teaches that missiles, warships and nuclear weapons cannot establish security. Instead they destroy what peace and security build.

For the sake of our peoples and for the sake of the civilization made by man, we have to defend man everywhere against rule by the force of arms so that we may endow the rule of humanity with all the power of the values and principles that further the sublime position of mankind.

Allow me to address my call from this rostrum to the people of Israel. I pledged myself with true and sincere words to every man, woman and child in Israel. I tell them, from the Egyptian people who bless this sacred mission of peace, I convey to you the message of peace of the Egyptian people, who do not harbor fanaticism and whose sons, Moslems, Christians and Jews, live together in a state of cordiality, love and tolerance.

This is Egypt, whose people have entrusted me with their sacred message. A message of security, safety and peace to every man, woman and child in Israel. I say, encourage your leadership to struggle for peace. Let all endeavors be channeled toward building a huge stronghold for peace instead of building destructive rockets.

Introduce to the entire world the image of the new man in this area so that he might set an example to the man of our age, the man of peace everywhere. Ring the bells for your sons. Tell them that those wars were the last of wars and the end of sorrows. Tell them that we are entering upon a new beginning, a new life, a life of love, prosperity, freedom and peace.

You, sorrowing mother, you, widowed wife, you, the son who lost a brother or a father, all the victims of wars, fill the air and space with recitals of peace, fill bosoms and hearts with the aspirations of peace. Make a reality that blossoms and lives. Make hope a code of conduct and endeavor . . .

PLO: Six-Point Program (December 4, 1977)*

In the wake of Sadat's treasonous visit to the Zionist entity, all factions of the Palestinian Resistance Movement have decided to make a practical answer to this step. On this basis, they met and issued the following document:

We, all factions of the PLO, announce the following:

FIRST: We call for the formation of a "Steadfastness and Confrontation Front" composed of Libya, Algeria, Iraq, Democratic Yemen, Syria and the PLO, to oppose all capitulationist solutions planned by imperialism, Zionism and their Arab tools.

SECOND: We fully condemn any Arab party in the Tripoli Summit which rejects the formation of this Front, and we announce this.

THIRD: We reaffirm our rejection of Security Council resolutions 242 and 338.

FOURTH: We reaffirm our rejection of all international conferences based on these two resolutions, including the Geneva Conference.

FIFTH: To strive for the realization of the Palestinian people's rights to return and self-determination within the context of an independent Palestinian national state on any part of Palestinian land, without reconciliation, recognition or negotiations, as an interim aim of the Palestinian Revolution.

SIXTH: To apply the measures related to the political boycott of the Sadat regime.

In the name of all the factions, we ratify this unificatory document.

*Signed by leaders of the PLO's constituent organizations in Tripoli, Libya.

Arab League: Summit Declaration
(December 5, 1977)*

With a sense of complete pan-Arab responsibility, the conference discussed the dimensions of the current phase through which the Arab cause in general and the Palestinian question in particular are passing and the American-Zionist plans aimed at imposing capitulatory settlements on the Arab nation, prejudicing the established national rights of the Palestinian people, liquidating the national Arab accomplishments and striking at the Arab liberation movement as a prelude to subduing the Arab area and controlling its destiny and tying it to the bandwagon of world imperialism.

The conference also discussed the visit made by President Sadat to the Zionist entity as being a link in the framework of the implementation of the hostile schemes. . . .

Those attending the conference studied the current situation with all of its dimensions and concluded that the objectives of the plot are as follows:

To undermine the possibility of the establishment of a just and honorable peace which would safeguard the national rights of the Arab nation and guarantee for it the liberation of its occupied territories, the foremost of which is Jerusalem, and for the Palestinian people their established national rights.

. . . To enable the forces hostile to the Arab nation, headed by the United States, to realize gains that will upset the international balance in favor of the Zionist-imperialist forces and Zionism and undermine the national independence of the Afro-Asian and Latin American countries.

To establish an alliance between the Zionist enemy and the current Egyptian regime aimed at liquidating the Arab issue and the issue of Palestine, split the Arab nation and forfeit its national interests.

Out of its belief in the nature of the Zionist and imperialist challenges aimed at weakening the Arab will for liberation and harming the firm national rights of the Palestinian people which have been confirmed by international legitimacy—the foremost of which is their right to return and decide their own destiny and build their independent state on the soil of their homeland under the leadership of the PLO, which is the sole legitimate representative of the Palestinian people—and proceeding from the reality of pan-Arab and historic responsibility, the summit conference decided the following:

1. To condemn President al-Sadat's visit to the Zionist entity since it constitutes a great betrayal of the sacrifices and struggle of our Arab people in Egypt and their armed forces and of the struggle, sacrifices and principles of the Arab nation. While appreciating the role of the great Egyptian

*The Arab League Summit Conference was held in Tripoli, Libya, December 2–5, 1977.

people in the national struggle of the Arab nation, the conference stresses that Egypt is not the beginning or the end and that if the Arab nation is great with Egypt, the latter's greatness is only possible within the Arab nation, without which it can only diminish in importance.

2. To work for the frustration of the results of President al-Sadat's visit to the Zionist entity and his talks with the leaders of the Zionist enemy and the subsequent measures including the proposed Cairo meeting. The conference warns that anyone who tries to pursue a similar line or to have any dealings with the said results shall be held responsible for his deed nationally and on the pan-Arab level.

3. To freeze political and diplomatic relations with the Egyptian Government, to suspend dealings with it on the Arab and international levels and to apply the regulations, provisions and decisions of the Arab Boycott against Egyptian individuals, companies and firms which deal with the Zionist enemy.

4. To decide not to take part in Arab League meetings which are held in Egypt and to undertake contacts with the Arab League member states to study the question of its headquarters and organs and the membership of the Egyptian regime.

5. The conference salutes the Palestinian Arab people, who are standing fast in the occupied homeland, including all of their national and other popular organizations which are struggling against the occupation and which reject the visit of al-Sadat to occupied Palestine. The conference also warns against any attempt to prejudice the legitimacy of the PLO representation of the Palestinian people.

6. The conference takes satisfaction in recording the preliminary positions taken by the Arab states which have denounced the visit and rejected its consequences. Out of its responsibility and in compliance with its commitment and collective resolutions, the conference calls on these states to adopt practical measures to face the serious character of this capitulatory policy, including the suspension of political and military support. The conference also condemns the disgraceful stands adopted by those who praise this visit or support it and warn them of the consequences of their despondent and defeatist policies.

7. The conference appeals to the Arab nation on the official and popular levels to provide economic, financial, political and military aid and support to the Syrian region, now that it has become the principal confrontation state and the base of steadfastness for dealing with the Zionist enemy and also to the Palestinian people represented by the PLO.

8. The conference greets our Arab people in sisterly Egypt and particularly their national and progressive forces, which have rejected the capitulatory policy being pursued by the Egyptian regime as being a betrayal of the sacrifices of the people and their martyrs and an insult to the dignity of their armed forces.

9. In asserting the importance of the relationship of struggle and nationalism between Syria and the Palestinians, the Syrian Arab Republic and the PLO announce the formation of a unified front to face the Zionist enemy and combat the imperialist plot with all its parties and to thwart all attempts at capitulation. The Democratic and Popular Republic of Algeria, the Socialist People's Libyan Arab Jamahiriyah and the PDRY [People's Democratic Republic of Yemen—South Yemen] have decided to join this front, making it the nucleus of a pan-Arab front for steadfastness and combat which will be open to other Arab countries to join.

10. Members of the pan-Arab front consider any aggression against any one member as an aggression against all members.

The conference pledges to the Arab nation that it will continue the march of struggle, steadfastness, combat and adherence to the objectives of the Arab struggle. The conference also expresses its deep faith and absolute confidence that the Arab nation, which has staged revolutions, overcome difficulties and defeated plots during its long history of struggle—a struggle which abounds with heroism—is today capable of replying with force to those who have harmed its dignity, squandered its rights, split its solidarity and departed from the principles of its struggle. It is confident of its own capabilities in liberation, progress and victory, thanks to God.

The conference records with satisfaction the national Palestinian unity within the framework of the PLO.

Israeli Prime Minister Menachem Begin: Autonomy Plan for the West Bank and Gaza Strip (December 28, 1977)*

. . . With the establishment of peace we shall propose the introduction of an administrative autonomy for the Arab residents of Judea, Samaria and the Gaza Strip on the basis of the following principles:

The administration of the military rule in Judea, Samaria and the Gaza Strip will be abolished. In Judea, Samaria and the Gaza Strip an administrative autonomy of, by and for the Arab residents will be established. The residents of Judea, Samaria and the Gaza Strip will elect an administrative council which will be composed of 11 members. The administrative council will act according to the principles postulated in this document. Every resident 18 years old or older, regardless of his citizenship or the lack of it, will be entitled to vote for the administrative council. Every resident who is 25 years old or older the day the list of candidates for the administrative council is presented will be entitled to be elected to the administrative

*Speech to the Israeli Knesset.

council. The administrative council will be elected in general, direct, personal, equal and secret elections. . . .

The administrative council will establish the following departments: department of education; department of transportation; department of construction and housing; department of industry, commerce and tourism; department of agriculture; department of health; department of labor and social betterment; department for the rehabilitation of refugees; department of legal administration and supervision of the local police force. The administrative council will issue regulations pertaining to the activities of those departments.

Security and public order in the areas of Judea, Samaria and Gaza will be entrusted to the Israeli authorities. . . .

Residents of Judea, Samaria and Gaza, regardless of their citizenship or lack of it, will have the free option to receive either Israeli or Jordanian citizenship. . . . A committee of representatives of Israel, Jordan and the administrative council will be established to examine the law in Judea, Samaria and the Gaza district and to determine which laws will remain valid, which will be abolished and what the authority of the administrative council will be to issue regulations. The decisions of this committee will be adopted unanimously.

Israeli residents will be entitled to purchase land and settle in the areas of Judea, Samaria and Gaza. Arab residents of Judea, Samaria and the Gaza district who become, in accordance with the free option granted them, Israeli citizens will be entitled to purchase land and settle in Israel. A committee of representatives of Israel, Jordan and of the administrative council will be established to determine immigration rules for the areas of Judea, Samaria and Gaza. The committee will postulate those rules which will permit Palestinian refugees outside Judea, Samaria and Gaza immigration in a reasonable volume into these areas. The decision of the committee will be adopted unanimously.

Israeli residents and the residents of Judea, Samaria and the Gaza district will be assured free movement and free economic activity in Israel, in Judea, in Samaria and in the Gaza district.

The administrative council will name one of its members to represent it before the Government of Israel for the purpose of discussing common issues, and one of its members will represent it before the Government of Jordan for the discussion of common issues.

Israel insists on its rights and demand for its sovereignty over Judea, Samaria and the Gaza Strip. Knowing that other demands exist, it proposes, for the sake of the agreement and of peace, to leave the question of sovereignty in those areas open.

Regarding the administration of the places holy to the three religions in Jerusalem, a special proposal will be prepared and presented, insuring free admission for all believers to the places sacred to them.

These principles will lend themselves to reexamination after a period of five years. . . .

We do not even dream of the possibility—if we are given the chance to withdraw our military forces from Judea, Samaria and Gaza—of abandoning those areas to the control of the murderous organization that is called the PLO. . . . This is history's meanest murder organization, except for the armed Nazi organizations. It also bragged two days ago about the murder of Hamdi al-Qadi, deputy director of the Education Bureau in Ramallah.

It is a frightening proposition that someone's solution to the problems in the Middle East might be a single bullet dispatched to the heart of Egyptian President as-Sadat as the PLO's predecessors did at Al-Aqsa Mosque to King Abdallah. One single bullet. No wonder that the Egyptian Government has declared that should such a single shot be fired, Egypt would retaliate with a million shots. We wish to say that under no condition will that organization be allowed to take control over Judea, Samaria and Gaza. If we withdraw our army, this is exactly what would happen. Hence, let it be known that whoever desires an agreement with us should please accept our announcement that the IDF will be deployed in Judea, Samaria and Gaza. And there will also be other security arrangements, so that we can give to all the residents, Jews and Arabs alike, in Eretz Yisrael a secure life—that is to say, security for all. . . .

. . . We have a right and a demand for sovereignty over these areas of Eretz Yisrael. This is our land and it belongs to the Jewish nation rightfully. We desire an agreement and peace. We know that there are at least two other demands for sovereignty over these areas. If there is a mutual desire to reach an agreement and to promote peace—what is the way?

Should these contradictory demands remain, and should there be no answer to the collision course between them, an agreement between the parties would be impossible. And for this reason, in order to facilitate an agreement and make peace, there is only one possible way. One way and no other: to agree to decide that the question of sovereignty remain open and to deal with people, with nations. That is to say, administrative autonomy for the Arabs of Eretz Yisrael; and for the Jews of Eretz Yisrael—genuine security. This is the fairness that is inherent in the content of the proposal. And in that spirit the proposal was also accepted abroad. . . .

U.S. President Jimmy Carter: Statement on Palestinian Rights (January 4, 1978)

It is an honor and a pleasure for us to be in this great country, led by such a strong and courageous man.

Mr. President, your bold initiative in seeking peace has aroused the admiration of the entire world. One of my most valued possessions is the warm, personal relationship which binds me and President Sadat together and which exemplifies the friendship and the common purpose of the people of Egypt and the people of the United States of America.

The Egyptian-Israeli peace initiative must succeed, while still guarding the sacred and historic principles held by the nations who have suffered so much in this region. There is no good reason why accommodation cannot be reached.

In my own private discussions with both Arab and Israeli leaders, I have been deeply impressed by the unanimous desire for peace. My presence here today is a direct result of the courageous initiative which President Sadat undertook in his recent trip to Jerusalem.

The negotiating process will continue in the near future. We fully support this effort, and we intend to play an active role in the work of the Political Committee of Cairo, which will soon reconvene in Jerusalem.

We believe that there are certain principles, fundamentally, which must be observed before a just and a comprehensive peace can be achieved.

First, true peace must be based on normal relations among the parties to the peace. Peace means more than just an end to belligerency.

Second, there must be withdrawal by Israel from territories occupied in 1967 and agreement on secure and recognized borders for all parties in the context of normal and peaceful relations in accordance with U.N. Resolutions 242 and 338.

Third, there must be a resolution of the Palestinian problem in all its aspects. The problem must recognize the legitimate rights of the Palestinian people and enable the Palestinians to participate in the determination of their own future.

Some flexibility is always needed to insure successful negotiations and the resolution of conflicting views. We know that the mark of greatness among leaders is to consider carefully the views of others and the greater benefits that can result among the people of all nations which can come from a successful search for peace.

Mr. President, our consultations this morning have reconfirmed our common commitment to the fundamentals which will, with God's help, make 1978 the year for permanent peace in the Middle East.

UN Security Council: Resolution 425, on Lebanon (March 19, 1978)

The Security Council,
Taking note of the letters from the Permanent Representative of Lebanon and the Permanent Representative of Israel, Having heard the statements of the Permanent Representatives of Lebanon and Israel,

Gravely concerned at the deterioration of the situation in the Middle East and its consequences to the maintenance of international peace,
Convinced that the present situation impedes the achievement of a just peace in the Middle East, Calls for the strict respect for the territorial integrity, sovereignty and political independence of Lebanon within its internationally recognized boundaries;
Calls upon Israel immediately to cease its military action against Lebanese territorial integrity and withdraw its forces from all Lebanese territory;
Decides, in light of the request of the Government of Lebanon, to establish immediately under its authority a United Nations interim force for Southern Lebanon for the purpose of confirming the withdrawal of Israeli forces, restoring international peace and security and assisting the Government of Lebanon in ensuring the return of its effective authority in the area, the force to be composed of personnel drawn from Member States;
Requests the Secretary-General to report to the Council within twenty-four hours on the implementation of the present resolution.

Camp David Summit Meeting: Frameworks for Peace (September 17, 1978)*

Preamble

The search for peace in the Middle East must be guided by the following:
—The agreed basis for a peaceful settlement of the conflict between Israel and its neighbors is United Nations Security Council Resolution 242, in all its parts.
—After four wars during thirty years, despite intensive human efforts, the Middle East, which is the cradle of civilization and the birthplace of three great religions, does not yet enjoy the blessings of peace. The people of the Middle East yearn for peace so that the vast human and natural resources of the region can be turned to the pursuits of peace and so that this area can become a model for coexistence and cooperation among nations.
—The historic initiative of President Sadat in visiting Jerusalem and the reception accorded to him by the Parliament, government and people of Israel, and the reciprocal visit of Prime Minister Begin to Ismailia, the peace proposals made by both leaders, as well as the warm reception of these missions by the people of both countries, have created an unprecedented opportunity for peace which must not be lost if this generation and future generations are to be spared the tragedies of war.

*This document was signed by Egyptian President Anwar Sadat and Israeli Prime Minister Menachem Begin and witnessed by President Jimmy Carter at Camp David, in Thurmont, Maryland.

—The provisions of the Charter of the United Nations and the other accepted norms of international law and legitimacy now provide accepted standards for the conduct of relations among the states.

—To achieve a relationship of peace, in the spirit of Article 2 of the United Nations Charter, future negotiations between Israel and any neighbor prepared to negotiate peace and security with it, are necessary for the purpose of carrying out all the provisions and principles of Resolutions 242 and 338.

—Peace requires respect for the sovereignty, territorial integrity and political independence of every state in the area and their right to live in peace within secure and recognized boundaries free from threats or acts of force. Progress toward that goal can accelerate movement toward a new era of reconciliation in the Middle East marked by cooperation in promoting economic development, in maintaining stability, and in assuring security.

—Security is enhanced by a relationship of peace and by cooperation between nations which enjoy normal relations. In addition, under the terms of peace treaties, the parties can, on the basis of reciprocity, agree to special security arrangements such as demilitarized zones, limited armaments areas, early warning stations, the presence of international forces, liaison, agreed measures for monitoring, and other arrangements that they agree are useful.

Framework

Taking these factors into account, the parties are determined to reach a just, comprehensive, and durable settlement of the Middle East conflict through the conclusion of peace treaties based on Security Council Resolutions 242 and 338 in all their parts. Their purpose is to achieve peace and good neighborly relations. They recognize that, for peace to endure, it must involve all those who have been most deeply affected by the conflict. They therefore agree that this framework as appropriate is intended by them to constitute a basis for peace not only between Egypt and Israel, but also between Israel and each of its other neighbors which is prepared to negotiate peace with Israel on this basis. With that objective in mind, they have agreed to proceed as follows:

A. West Bank and Gaza

1. Egypt, Israel, Jordan and the representatives of the Palestinian people should participate in negotiations on the resolution of the Palestinian problem in all its aspects. To achieve that objective, negotiations relating to the West Bank and Gaza should proceed in three stages:

(a) Egypt and Israel agree that, in order to ensure a peaceful and orderly transfer of authority, and taking into account the security concerns of all the parties, there should be transitional arrangements for the West Bank and Gaza for a period not exceeding five years. In order to provide full autonomy to the inhabitants, under these arrangements the Israeli military government and its civilian administration will be withdrawn as soon as a self-governing authority has been freely elected by the inhabitants of these areas to replace the existing military government. To negotiate the details of a transitional arrangement, the Government of Jordan will be invited to join the negotiations on the basis of this framework. These new arrangements should give due consideration both to the principle of self-government by the inhabitants of these territories and to the legitimate security concerns of the parties involved.

(b) Egypt, Israel, and Jordan will agree on the modalities for establishing the elected self-governing authority in the West Bank and Gaza. The delegations of Egypt and Jordan may include Palestinians from the West Bank and Gaza or other Palestinians as mutually agreed. The parties will negotiate an agreement which will define the powers and responsibilities of the self-governing authority to be exercised in the West Bank and Gaza. A withdrawal of Israeli armed forces will take place and there will be a redeployment of the remaining Israeli forces into specified security locations. The agreement will also include arrangements for assuring internal and external security and public order. A strong local police force will be established, which may include Jordanian citizens. In addition, Israeli and Jordanian forces will participate in joint patrols and in the manning of control posts to assure the security of the borders.

(c) When the self-governing authority (administrative council) in the West Bank and Gaza is established and inaugurated, the transitional period of five years will begin. As soon as possible, but not later than the third year after the beginning of the transitional period, negotiations will take place to determine the final status of the West Bank and Gaza and its relationship with its neighbors, and to conclude a peace treaty between Israel and Jordan by the end of the transitional period. These negotiations will be conducted among Egypt, Israel, Jordan, and the elected representatives of the inhabitants of the West Bank and Gaza. Two separate but related committees will be convened, one committee, consisting of representatives of the four parties which will negotiate and agree on the final status of the West Bank and Gaza, and its relationship with its neighbors, and the second committee, consisting of representatives of Israel and representatives of Jordan to be joined by the elected representatives of the inhabitants of the West Bank and Gaza, to negotiate the peace treaty between Israel and Jordan, taking into account the agreement reached on the final status of the West Bank and Gaza. The negotiations shall be based on all the provisions and principles of UN Security Council Resolution 242. The negotiations will resolve, among other matters, the location of the boundaries and the nature of the security arrangements. The solution from the negotiations must also recognize the legitimate rights of the Palestinian people and their just requirements. In this way, the Palestinians will participate in the determination of their own future through:

1) The negotiations among Egypt, Israel, Jordan and the representatives of the inhabitants of the West Bank and Gaza to agree on the final status of the West Bank and Gaza and other outstanding issues by the end of the transitional period.

2) Submitting their agreement to a vote by the elected representatives of the inhabitants of the West Bank and Gaza.

3) Providing for the elected representatives of the inhabitants of the West Bank and Gaza to decide how they shall govern themselves consistent with the provisions of their agreement.

4) Participating as stated above in the work of the committee negotiating the peace treaty between Israel and Jordan.

All necessary measures will be taken and provisions made to assure the security of Israel and its neighbors during the transitional period and beyond. To assist in providing such security, a strong local police force will be constituted by the self-governing authority. It will be composed of inhabitants of the West Bank and Gaza. The police will maintain continuing liaison on internal security matters with the designated Israeli, Jordanian, and Egyptian officers.

During the transitional period, representatives of Egypt, Israel, Jordan, and the self-governing authority will constitute a continuing committee to decide by agreement on the modalities of admission of persons displaced from the West Bank and Gaza in 1967, together with necessary measures to prevent disruption and disorder. Other matters of common concern may also be dealt with by this committee.

Egypt and Israel will work with each other and with other interested parties to establish agreed procedures for a prompt, just and permanent implementation of the resolution of the refugee problem.

B. Egypt-Israel

1. Egypt and Israel undertake not to resort to the threat or the use of force to settle disputes. Any disputes shall be settled by peaceful means in accordance with the provisions of Article 33 of the Charter of the United Nations.

2. In order to achieve peace between them, the parties agree to negotiate in good faith with a goal of concluding within three months from the signing of this Framework a peace treaty between them, while inviting the other parties to the conflict to proceed simultaneously to negotiate and conclude similar peace treaties with a view to achieving a comprehensive

peace in the area. The Framework for the Conclusion of a Peace Treaty between Egypt and Israel will govern the peace negotiations between them. The parties will agree on the modalities and the timetable for the implementation of their obligations under the treaty.

C. Associated Principles

1. Egypt and Israel state that the principles and provisions described below should apply to peace treaties between Israel and each of its neighbors—Egypt, Jordan, Syria and Lebanon.

2. Signatories shall establish among themselves relationships normal to states at peace with one another. To this end, they should undertake to abide by all the provisions of the Charter of the United Nations. Steps to be taken in this respect include:

(a) full recognition;

(b) abolishing economic boycotts;

(c) guaranteeing that under their jurisdiction the citizens of the other parties shall enjoy the protection of the due process of the law.

3. Signatories should explore possibilities for economic development in the context of final peace treaties, with the objective of contributing to the atmosphere of peace, cooperation and friendship which is their common goal.

4. Claims Commissions may be established for the mutual settlement of all financial claims.

5. The United States shall be invited to participate in the talks on matters related to the modalities of the implementation of the agreements and working out the timetable for the carrying out of the obligations of the parties.

6. The United Nations Security Council shall be requested to endorse the peace treaties and ensure that their provisions shall not be violated. The permanent members of the Security Council shall be requested to underwrite the peace treaties and ensure respect for their provisions. They shall also be requested to conform their policies and actions with the undertakings contained in this Framework.

. . . The following matters are agreed between the parties:

(a) the full exercise of Egyptian sovereignty up to the internationally recognized border between Egypt and mandated Palestine;

(b) the withdrawal of Israeli armed forces from the Sinai;

(c) the use of airfields left by the Israelis near El Arish, Rafah, Ras en Naqb, and Sharm el Sheikh for civilian purposes only, including possible commercial use by all nations;

(d) the right of free passage by ships of Israel through the Gulf of Suez and the Suez Canal on the basis of the Constantinople Convention of 1888 applying to all nations; the Strait of Tiran and the Gulf of Aqaba are international waterways to be open to all nations for unimpeded and nonsuspendable freedom of navigation and overflight;

(e) the construction of a highway between the Sinai and Jordan near Elat with guaranteed free and peaceful passage by Egypt and Jordan; and

(f) the stationing of military forces listed below.

STATIONING OF FORCES

A. No more than one division (mechanized or infantry) of Egyptian armed forces will be stationed within an area lying approximately 50 kilometers (km) east of the Gulf of Suez and the Suez Canal.

B. Only United Nations forces and civil police equipped with light weapons to perform normal police functions will be stationed within an area lying west of the international border and the Gulf of Aqaba, varying in width from 20 km to 40 km.

C. In the area within 3 km east of the international border there will be Israeli limited military forces not to exceed four infantry battalions and United Nations observers.

D. Border patrol units, not to exceed three battalions, will supplement the civil police in maintaining order in the area not included above.

The exact demarcation of the above areas will be as decided during the peace negotiations.

Early warning stations may exist to ensure compliance with the terms of the agreement.

United Nations forces will be stationed: (a) in part of the area in the Sinai lying within about 20 km of the Mediterranean Sea and adjacent to the international border, and (b) in the Sharm el Sheikh area to ensure freedom of passage through the Strait of Tiran; and these forces will not be removed unless such removal is approved by the Security Council of the United Nations with a unanimous vote of the five permanent members.

After a peace treaty is signed, and after the interim withdrawal is complete, normal relations will be established between Egypt and Israel, including: full recognition, including diplomatic, economic and cultural relations; termination of economic boycotts and barriers to the free movement of goods and people; and mutual protection of citizens by the due process of law.

Egypt and Israel: Peace Treaty (March 26, 1979)*

ARTICLE I

1. The state of war between the Parties will be terminated and peace will be established between them upon the exchange of instruments of ratification of this Treaty.

---

*This treaty was drawn up during the Camp David meetings.

2. Israel will withdraw all its armed forces and civilians from the Sinai behind the international boundary between Egypt and mandated Palestine, as provided in the annexed protocol . . . and Egypt will resume the exercise of its full sovereignty over the Sinai. . . .

ARTICLE II

The permanent boundary between Egypt and Israel is the recognized international boundary between Egypt and the former mandated territory of Palestine . . . without prejudice to the issue of the status of the Gaza Strip. The Parties recognize this boundary as inviolable. Each will respect the territorial integrity of the other, including their territorial waters and airspace.

ARTICLE III

. . . Each Party undertakes to ensure that acts or threats of belligerency, hostility, or violence do not originate from and are not committed from within its territory, or by any forces subject to its control or by any other forces stationed on its territory, against the population, citizens or property of the other Party. Each Party also undertakes to refrain from organizing, instigating, inciting, assisting or participating in acts or threats of belligerency, hostility, subversion or violence against the other Party, anywhere, and undertakes to ensure that perpetrators of such acts are brought to justice.

The Parties agree that the normal relationship established between them will include full recognition, diplomatic, economic and cultural relations, termination of economic boycotts and discriminatory barriers to the free movement of people and goods, and will guarantee the mutual enjoyment by citizens of the due process of law.

Arab League: Summit Communiqué (March 31, 1979)*

As the Government of the Arab Republic of Egypt has ignored the Arab summit conferences' resolutions, especially those of the sixth and seventh conferences held in Algiers and Rabat; as it has at the same time ignored the ninth Arab summit conference resolutions—especially the call made by the Arab kings, presidents and princes to avoid signing the peace treaty with the Zionist enemy—and signed the peace treaty on 26 March 1979;

It has thus deviated from the Arab ranks and has chosen, in collusion with the United States, to stand by the side of the Zionist enemy in one

*The communiqué was issued in Baghdad, Iraq.

trench; has behaved unilaterally in the Arab-Zionist struggle affairs; has violated the Arab nation's rights; has exposed the nation's destiny, its struggle and aims to dangers and challenges; has relinquished its pan-Arab duty of liberating the occupied Arab territories, particularly Jerusalem, and of restoring the Palestinian Arab people's inalienable national rights, including their right to repatriation, self-determination and establishment of the independent Palestinian state on their national soil.

. . . . The Arab League Council, on the level of Arab foreign ministers, has decided the following:

1. A. To withdraw the ambassadors of the Arab states from Egypt immediately.

B. To recommend the severance of political and diplomatic relations with the Egyptian Government. The Arab governments will adopt the necessary measures to apply this recommendation within a maximum period of one month from the date of issuance of this decision, in accordance with the constitutional measures in force in each country.

2. To consider the suspension of the Egyptian Government's membership in the Arab League as operative from the date of the Egyptian Government's signing of the peace treaty with the Zionist enemy. This means depriving it of all rights resulting from this membership.

3. To make the city of Tunis, capital of the Tunisian Republic, the temporary headquarters of the Arab League. . . .

Soviet Foreign Minister Andrei Gromyko: On the Camp David Agreement (September 25, 1979)*

The Middle East problem, if divested of the immaterial, boils down to the following—either the consequences of the aggression against the Arab states and peoples are eliminated or the invaders get a reward by appropriating lands that belong to others.

A just settlement and the establishment of durable peace in the Middle East require that Israel should end its occupation of all the Arab lands it seized in 1967, that the legitimate rights of the Arab people of Palestine including the right to create their own state be safeguarded and that the right of all states in the Middle East, including Israel, to independent existence under conditions of peace be effectively guaranteed.

The separate deal between Egypt and Israel resolves nothing. It is a means designed to lull the vigilance of peoples. It is a way of piling up on a still greater scale explosive material capable of producing a new confla-

*Speech delivered to the UN General Assembly by the Soviet Foreign Minister.

gration in the Middle East. Moreover, added to the tense political atmosphere in this and the adjacent areas is the heavy smell of oil.

It is high time that all states represented in the United Nations realized how vast is the tragedy of the Arab peoples of Palestine. What is the worth of declarations in defence of humanism and human rights—whether for refugees or not—if before the eyes of the entire world the inalienable rights of an entire people driven from its land and deprived of a livelihood are grossly trampled upon?

The Soviet policy with respect to the Middle East problem is one of principle. We are in favour of a comprehensive and just settlement, of the establishment of durable peace in the Middle East, a region not far from our borders. The Soviet Union sides firmly with Arab peoples who resolutely reject deals at the expense of their legitimate interests.

PLO Chairman Yasir Arafat: Interview on Camp David (November 19, 1979)*

First, we must consider the events in the occupied land, since it is one of the main fronts on which we are fighting the Camp David plot. At the same time, it is a front against which the tripartite alliance—Carter, Begin, al-Sadat—launched their counterattack in retaliation for the resolutions of the Front of Steadfastness and Confrontation and those of the Baghdad summit and the Arab foreign and economy ministers' conference, which implemented all resolutions that were agreed upon.

This attack centered on our people in the occupied land by means of fascist, mean and oppressive measures in addition to the confiscation of land, building of settlements and terrorism such as deportation of the population, arrest and mass punishment against towns and villages as well as confiscation of springs. Our kinfolk's reply was magnificent and is now crowned by this splendid popular uprising against the Zionist authorities, protesting against the Zionist authorities' decision to deport one of our cadres and leaders in the occupied land: Bassam ash-Shak'ah, the Nablus mayor.

The other face of the battle is the mounting war of attrition against the Lebanese and Palestinian peoples. The most modern weapons, even the internationally banned ones, are being used in this war. This is resulting in the destruction of many Lebanese towns and villages and Palestinian camps and in the eviction of hundreds of thousands of Lebanese and Palestinian people. Actually, this terrorist and hellish plan is still continuing, and the Zionist enemy leaders continue to implement it. This, however, will

*Interview in the Algerian newspaper *Al-Sha'b*.

neither intimidate us nor make us hesitate to reply to the enemy actions, both in the occupied land and in southern Lebanon, and with all forms of the military and political struggle. We have practiced this and we will never retreat. We have all the Arabs on our side. Our steadfastness has proved that the Arab nation does not lack will and steadfastness. . . .

Syrian President Hafiz al-Asad: Speech
(March 8, 1980)

To us, to the whole world and as outlined in the UN resolutions, peace means Israel's complete withdrawal from the occupied Arab territories and the acknowledgement of the Palestinians' inalienable rights, including their right to determine their own destiny and set up their independent state. Peace under the Camp David accords means Israel's false withdrawal from Sinai—and it has not yet withdrawn—so that eventually it would be in a position to take all Egypt.

To us, peace means that Arab flags should fly over the liberated territories. Under the Camp David accords, peace means that the Israeli flag should be hoisted in an official ceremony in Cairo, while Israel is still occupying Egyptian, Syrian and Palestinian territory and is still adamantly denying Palestinian rights.

To us, peace means we should exercise our free will. Under the Camp David accords, peace means that the al-Sadat regime should keep Egypt's doors wide open to a Zionist economic, cultural and psychological invasion. It also means that Israel should continue to expand settlements.

To us, peace means a step further toward Arab unity. Under the Camp David accords, peace means Egypt should disengage from the Arab nation and move closer to usurper and aggressor Israel.

We do not make any distinction between one Arab territory and another, while the Camp David partners insist on making a distinction between Egyptian territory and other Arab territories.

The whole world calls for the establishment of a Palestinian state, while al-Sadat and his two allies talk about autonomy. The whole world knows, and the Israeli opposition leaders confirm, that the autonomy farce is a figment of Begin's imagination which he presented during his visit to Ismailia. On the other hand, al-Sadat presents autonomy as the distillation of his genius and most ideal solution.

Israel stresses daily that it will not withdraw from the West Bank and Gaza at any time in the future, and al-Sadat does not stop speaking about great hopes for the success of the autonomy farce. Despite their meager means, our heroic people in the occupied territory are resisting and waging a mighty struggle against the plot. But al-Sadat is using every material and psychological pressure on these people to force them to surrender to the plot.

The world condemns Israel's policy and aggression and supports the just Arab cause. But al-Sadat considers his close friend Begin as the messenger of peace, and his own Arab nation as the enemy of peace. Al-Sadat makes peace with the Israeli leaders and slanders the Arab nation, to which he has turned his back, forgetting that Egypt is part of this nation.

As for the third party, or the full partner as they like to call it, or the honest broker as it likes to call itself, it is determined not to annoy the Israeli leaders even in words. It is not prepared to draw a line between U.S. and Israeli interests in this region. To the United States, therefore, Israeli interests must come first, before anything else.

The Palestine question is the central issue of our struggle and the substance of our cause. We consider the PLO the sole legitimate representative of the Palestinian people. We will continue to support and strengthen the Palestinian revolution against all potential dangers. Syria and the Palestinian revolution are in one trench, something which must be understood by both friend and foe.

I frankly and truly say that the Soviet Union is the real friend of all peoples fighting for their freedom and independence. In my opinion, the imperialists have discovered from experience that they cannot weaken this friendship. But this does not mean that they will stop their attempts to destroy this friendship if they can. We know that we need the assistance of this big friend in our current battle. We must not miscalculate. This is a big battle. Israel is backed by the United States with large quantities of sophisticated weapons. Therefore, how can we possibly shut our eyes to a maneuver aimed at dragging us into a conflict with this big friend and closing the door through which we obtain assistance in the fiercest confrontation that we and all Arabs have in this age?

European Council: Venice Declaration (June 13, 1980)*

The heads of state and government and the ministers of foreign affairs . . . agreed that growing tensions affecting this region constitute a serious danger and render a comprehensive solution to the Israeli-Arab conflict more necessary and pressing than ever.

. . . The time has come to promote the recognition and implementation of the two principles universally accepted by the international community: the right to existence and to security of all the states in the region, includ-

*Declaration by the European Council issued at the conclusion of a two-day conference in Venice.

ing Israel, and justice for all the peoples, which implies the recognition of the legitimate rights of the Palestinian people.

All of the countries in the area are entitled to live in peace within secure, recognized and guaranteed borders. The necessary guarantees for a peace settlement should be provided by the United Nations by a decision of the Security Council and, if necessary, on the basis of other mutually agreed procedures. The Nine declare that they are prepared to participate within the framework of a comprehensive settlement in a system of concrete and binding international guarantees, including guarantees on the ground.

A just solution must finally be found to the Palestinian problem, which is not simply one of refugees. The Palestinian people, which is conscious of existing as such, must be placed in a position, by an appropriate process defined within the framework of the comprehensive peace settlement, to exercise fully its right to self-determination.

. . . These principles apply to all the parties concerned, and thus the Palestinian people, and to the Palestine Liberation Organization, which will have to be associated with the negotiations.

. . . The Nine stress that they will not accept any unilateral initiative designed to change the status of Jerusalem and that any agreement on the city's status should guarantee freedom of access of everyone to the holy places.

The Nine stress the need for Israel to put an end to the territorial occupation which it has maintained since the conflict of 1967, as it has done for part of Sinai. They are deeply convinced that the Israeli settlements constitute a serious obstacle to the peace process in the Middle East. The Nine consider that these settlements, as well as modifications in population and property in the occupied Arab territories, are illegal under international law.

Concerned as they are to put an end to violence, the Nine consider that only the reunification of force or the threatened use of force by all the parties can create a climate of confidence in the area, and constitute a basic element for a comprehensive settlement of the conflict in the Middle East. . . .

Israeli Government: Fundamental Policy Guidelines (August 5, 1981)*

The right of the Jewish people to the land of Israel is an eternal right that cannot be called into question, and which is intertwined with the right to security and peace.

*Begin Government's Second Coalition agreement.

The Government will continue to place its aspirations for peace at the head of its concerns, and no effort will be spared in order to further peace. The peace treaty between Israel and Egypt is a historic turning point in Israel's status in the Middle East.

The Government will continue to use all means to prevent war.

The Government will diligently observe the Camp David agreements.

The Government will work for the renewal of negotiations on the implementation of the agreement on full autonomy for the Arab residents of Judea, Samaria and the Gaza Strip.

The autonomy agreed upon at Camp David means neither sovereignty nor self-determination. The autonomy agreements set down at Camp David are guarantees that under no conditions will a Palestinian state emerge in the territory of western "Eretz Yisrael."

At the end of the transition period, set down in the Camp David agreements, Israel will raise its claim, and act to realize its right of sovereignty over Judea, Samaria and the Gaza Strip.

Settlement in the land of Israel is a right and an integral part of the nation's security. The Government will act to strengthen, expand and develop settlement. The Government will continue to honor the principle that Jewish settlement will not cause the eviction of any person from his land, his village or his city.

Equality of rights for all residents will continue to exist in the land of Israel, with no distinctions [on the basis] of religion, race, nationality, sex, or ethnic community.

Israel will not descend from the Golan Heights, nor will it remove any settlement established there. It is the Government that will decide on the appropriate timing for the imposition of Israeli law, jurisdiction and administration on the Golan Heights.

Saudi Crown Prince Fahd ibn Abd al-Aziz: The Fahd Plan (August 7, 1981)

. . . There are a number of principles which may be taken as guidelines toward a just settlement; they are principles which the United Nations has taken and reiterated many times in the last few years. They are:

First, that Israel should withdraw from all Arab territory occupied in 1967, including Arab Jerusalem.

Second, that Israeli settlements built on Arab land after 1967 should be dismantled.

Third, a guarantee of freedom of worship for all religions in the holy places.

Fourth, an affirmation of the right of the Palestinian people to return to their homes and to compensate those who do not wish to return.

Fifth, that the West Bank and the Gaza Strip should have a transitional period, under the auspices of the United Nations, for a period not exceeding several months.

Sixth, that an independent Palestinian state should be set up with Jerusalem as its capital.

Seventh, that all states in the region should be able to live in peace.

Eighth, that the United Nations or member states of the United Nations should guarantee to execute these principles. . . .

I wish to reaffirm that the principles of a just comprehensive solution have become familiar and do not require great effort:

1. An end to unlimited American support for Israel.
2. An end to Israeli arrogance, whose ugliest facet is embodied in Begin's government. This condition will be automatically fulfilled if the first condition is fulfilled.
3. A recognition that, as Yasir Arafat says, the Palestinian figure is the basic figure in the Middle Eastern equation.

West Bank Palestinians: Reactions to Camp David (August 30, 1981)*

The Palestinian masses in the occupied West Bank and Gaza Strip continue to reject the declaration made by Sadat and Begin . . . that they had agreed to resume talks concerning so-called "autonomy" for the inhabitants of the West Bank and the Gaza Strip. A large number of Palestinian figures and personalities have commented . . . that the autonomy plan does not concern them in any respect, and that they consider the autonomy plan to be a conspiracy directed against the hopes and aspirations of the Palestinian people who are striving to attain their legitimate rights—which have been established by the international community, as represented by the UN. . . .

Dr. Amin al-Khatib, head of the Federation of Charity Associations in Jerusalem, said:

"I do not believe that any plan for a solution to the Palestine problem which does not include the establishment of an independent Palestinian state in the territory of Palestine will be successful, no matter how skillfully its sponsors choose names for it and think up methods of attempting to convince us to accept it. We are quite confident that a people such as the Palestinian people, who have gone through great hardships and have become seasoned concerning all different types of plans and half-

*Article in the Algerian newspaper *Al-Sha'b*.

solutions, will not be able to accept or be content with any solution other than a Palestinian state. . . .

"We have the following to say to Sadat: 'The Palestinian people, inside the occupied territories, do not wish to have you speak or negotiate in their behalf. Give both yourself and us some peace and do not bother us with this whirlpool which is called "autonomy." ' "

Zalikhah Shihabi, the head of the Jerusalem Women's Federation, said:

"Everything concerning autonomy—whether it be the autonomy talks, resumption of such talks, their cessation, or the breaking off of such talks altogether—does not concern us. The reason for this is that we know that it is merely a waste of time, and the objective of those who are calling for autonomy is to decrease the resentment of world public opinion against them, to attempt to outflank and encircle the PLO, and to flee from the truth which is shining as brightly as the sun. This truth is that the PLO is the only body authorized to discuss all matters which concern the Palestine question. All of us here agree that there should be an independent Palestinian state. Anything other than that will only meet with rejection and indifference on the part of the Palestinian people."

Mustafa 'Abd al-Nabi al-Natshah, deputy mayor of Hebron:

"Autonomy is a continuation of military occupation, only with a mask over it. Autonomy, which is tantamount to local rule, does not contain any of the elements of establishing an independent state. It is a deception utilized in order to impose permanent occupation and would confer permanent legitimacy upon the military occupation. This is something which we totally reject."

Ibrahim al-Tawil, mayor of al-Birah, said:

"Our people have not rejected autonomy for no reason. The rejection is based on the convictions of Palestinians living both inside and outside the occupied territories. What is called 'autonomy' is nothing more than a creation of the occupation and a part of it. Agreeing to this autonomy means conferring legitimacy upon the occupation."

Mr. al-Tawil then asked: "What kind of autonomy is it that does not grant our Palestinian people their legitimate rights—people who, like any other people, are demanding to live in peace and tranquility?" He added:

"Autonomy, as the Israelis understand it, means withdrawing army patrols and leaving [military] camps and settlements all over the West Bank. Furthermore, Begin has threatened to open the doors of his jails if any of the autonomy officials think about establishing their own state. So what is this autonomy which is nothing more than another version of the occupation? What it is is the deception and misleading of world public opinion and the other people of the world."

Mr. al-Tawil asserted that there are no people—and that there never will be people—who will participate in carrying out this step. He said that if there were any such mercenaries, they would not represent anybody and would not number even 1 person out of 10,000. He said that all [Palestinian] citizens reject this plan.

Egyptian President Hosni Mubarak: Egypt and Israel (October 14, 1981)*

Egypt, the state and the people, is continuing along the road to a lasting and comprehensive peace based upon the framework that has been agreed upon at Camp David and that is based on the peace treaty between Egypt and Israel in letter and in spirit. Egypt, the state and the people, will spare no effort or time in continuing the autonomy talks until we put the Palestinian people along the beginning of the correct course for achieving their legitimate rights.

We, as the late leader repeatedly declared, do not speak on behalf of the Palestinian people. We do not claim that we are achieving the final solution of the question. The Palestinian people are the owners of the right and owners of the first and last responsibility for solving their problem. However, we are continuing in our role, dictated by our historical responsibility. We will make all efforts and pave the way for a transitional period during which the Palestinian people will determine their fate.

Egypt, the state and the people, is implementing the peace treaty. Egypt's position before the complete Israeli withdrawal in April 1982 is the same as Egypt's position after the complete withdrawal.

It pleases me to announce to you that we have received categorical assurances that the final Israeli withdrawal will take place on schedule, without delay and without slowing down. This coming 25th of April will, God willing, not pass without Egypt's flag waving high over Rafah, Sharm ash-Shaykh and every foot of the sacred land of the Sinai. The martyr of justice will have thus given his country and nation the greatest fulfillment by liberating the territory, restoring dignity and opening the road to a great fu-

*The Egyptian President's inaugural address.

ture. With this historic event, the glorious Egyptian people and their valiant armed forces will have completed their most tremendous achievement in their contemporary history, lighting an eternal flame on the sands of Sinai that time cannot extinguish. Brothers, the historic peace initiative undertaken by our departed leader was the initiative of 42 million Egyptians. In fact, today that initiative does not belong only to the Egyptian people but also to all the peoples of the world.

Since President Reagan assumed power, the United States has announced the continuation of the U.S. commitment as a full partner in all the peace steps that are now taking their normal course.

I take this opportunity to declare to all the peoples of the world that the Egyptian people, who have faith in the peace miracle achieved by the hero of peace, today believe even more strongly in the continuation of the peace process, today they are more determined to protect all the fruits of peace.

The result of the referendum on my assumption of the responsibility on Sadat's road is the best evidence of the will and decision of the Egyptian people. It is a will for peace and it is a decision for peace.

U.S. and Israel: Memorandum of Understanding (November 30, 1981)

Preamble

This Memorandum of Understanding reaffirms the common bonds of friendship between the United States and Israel and builds on the mutual security relationship that exists between the two nations. The Parties recognize the need to enhance strategic cooperation to deter all threats from the Soviet Union in the region. Noting the long-standing and fruitful cooperation for mutual security that has developed between the two countries, the Parties have decided to establish a framework for continued consultation and cooperation to enhance their national security by deterring such threats in the whole region.

The Parties have reached the following agreements in order to achieve the above aims:

Article I

United States-Israeli strategic cooperation, as set forth in this Memorandum, is designed against the threat to peace and security of the region caused by the Soviet Union or Soviet-controlled forces from outside the region introduced into the region. It has the following broad purposes:

A. To enable the Parties to act cooperatively and in a timely manner to deal with the above mentioned threat;

B. To provide each other with military assistance for operations of their forces in the area that may be required to cope with this threat;

C. The strategic cooperation between the Parties is not directed at any State or group of States within the region. It is intended solely for defensive purposes against the above mentioned threat.

ARTICLE II

1. The fields in which strategic cooperation will be carried out to prevent the above mentioned threat from endangering the security of the region include:

A. Military cooperation between the Parties, as may be agreed by the Parties;

B. Joint military exercises, including naval and air exercises in the eastern Mediterranean Sea, as agreed upon by the Parties;

C. Cooperation for the establishment and maintenance of joint readiness activities, as agreed upon by the Parties;

D. Other areas within the basic scope and purpose of this agreement, as may be jointly agreed.

Israeli Law on the Golan Heights (December 14, 1981)

1. The law, jurisdiction and administration of the State shall apply to the Golan Heights. . . .

2. This law shall become valid on the day of its passage in the Knesset.

3. The Minister of the Interior shall be charged with the implementation of this law, and he is entitled, in consultation with the Minister of Justice, to enact regulations for its implementation and to formulate in regulations transitional provisions and provisions concerning the continued application of regulations, orders, administrative orders, rights and duties which were in force on the Golan Heights prior to the application of this law.

Israeli Defense Minister Ariel Sharon: Israel's Security (December 15, 1981)*

As I see them, our main security problems during the 1980's will stem from external threats to Israel, her integrity and her sovereign rights. . . .

One—The Arab confrontation.

*Speech by Defense Minister Ariel Sharon at the Center for Strategic Studies, Tel Aviv University.

Second—The Soviet expansion which both builds on the Arab confrontation and at the same time provides it with its main political and military tools.

Later on, I will comment on the implications in terms of political and military requirements in order to cope with the threat and to ensure Israel's national security in the 1980's.

Starting with the Arab challenge, I must touch upon the three major factors which, in my mind, contribute the most to sustain Arab enmity and confrontation at a level that presents an actual danger to our security and which, I believe, will continue to sustain it in the foreseeable future—at a level which might confront us with a potential threat to the existence and integrity of Israel.

Those factors are:

A. First, the national ideology of radical Arab regimes (such as in Syria, Libya, Iraq and South Yemen) and their political and strategic ambitions which motivate them to invest, on a first-priority basis, in the creation of a political-military setting designed to serve a strategy of political and military stages for the liquidation of the State of Israel.

The main elements of this strategy of stages can be summed up as follows:

1) A combined effort of sustained political pressure and, when needed, limited military action aimed at the harassment and weakening of Israel.

2) The build-up of a military power, conventional and eventually nonconventional, to be used in appropriate conditions in the future, for a decisive onslaught against Israel.

3) The third element of the strategy is the political and military reliance on the Soviet Union, to ensure the Arab capability to initiate and carry out the confrontation.

4) The fourth element is to maximize the political strategic impact of the oil weapon.

5) And the fifth is the political and military backing to the PLO as an instrument to carry out terrorist activities. This constitutes a central element in the strategy of stages, so long as Israel's deterrent posture and other political considerations prevent the formation of an Arab coalition, ready to wage war.

That brings me to the second major factor, which is the PLO. On the challenge presented by the PLO, I will say only this: The PLO poses a political threat to the very existence of the State of Israel and remains one of the main obstacles to the resolution of the Palestinian problem on the basis of the Camp David accords.

It constitutes a framework for terrorist organizations operating against Israel, in its territory or in the world at large, with the following purposes:

—To undermine the domestic stability in Israel and its security.

—To generate international pressure on Israel.

—To drag the confrontation states to war against Israel.

—To deter Arab countries and moderate Palestinian elements from negotiations with Israel on the basis of Camp David.

The third factor is one of growing concern to us and to the Western world, and might well develop as the main challenge of the 1980's. It has to do with the Soviet strategy of expansion in the Middle East and Africa. The Soviet strategy is under no pressure of time, but its achievements since the middle of the 1950's are really impressive. . . . It is a strategy of expansion which, if not checked, could eventually enable the Soviet Union:

—To ensure a sea-control capability in the Mediterranean, the Indian Ocean, the Red Sea and the Persian Gulf.

—To establish the military infrastructure for direct or indirect operations.

—To expand and penetrate other key countries in the Middle East and the Persian Gulf, from the direction of Afghanistan, Iraq, South Yemen and Syria.

—To outflank NATO's eastern tier (Turkey) through Iran, Iraq, Syria and Lebanon.

—To outflank NATO's southern tier in the Mediterranean, through Libya, Syria and Algeria.

—To gain control over other key countries in Africa, from the direction of Libya, Algeria, South Yemen, Ethiopia, Mozambique, Angola and Congo-Brazzaville. . . .

Today, as in the past two decades, the Soviet strategy of expansion in the area continues to build on:

—Arab regimes which Soviet political and military support enables to survive, to carry out their own ambitions and to maintain military confrontations—including the confrontation with Israel.

—Radical elements and terrorist organizations, which Soviet political and military support enables to create upheavals threatening to shift the region towards Soviet political-strategic patronage.

The shadow of Soviet presence in the Middle East and Africa endangers the stability of the region and vital interests of the free world. I want to stress this point with all possible emphasis. The greatest danger to the free world in the 1980's would be to continue to indulge in the wishful thinking and the inaction which have characterized Western attitudes to Soviet gradual expansion during the last two decades. . . .

Obviously, in order to be able to protect our national security interests, we will have to ensure our ability to maintain a balance of forces and a qualitative and technological edge over any combination of Arab war coalition; in other words:

—To prevent war by maintaining a deterrent posture against the threats to the existence of Israel.

—Should deterrence break down and war erupt, to ensure a military capability to preserve the integrity of Israel's territory, in any war-opening situation including a sudden Arab attack, and to disrupt the war coalition by damaging the core of its offensive capability.

To achieve these goals, we will have to structure our military strength on new approaches, taking into account:

—The lack of territorial depth and therefore the necessity to establish a strong territorial defense system, based on populous and high quality settlement of key border areas in Judaea, Samaria, the Gaza district, the Golan Heights, the Galilee and the Negev.

—The need to provide maximum protection to human life.

—The need to develop and produce weapon systems and equipment which should enable us to maintain a permanent qualitative advantage over Arab confrontation states—including with regard to advanced and sophisticated equipment they might get from Eastern and Western sources.

As a rule, while striving to establish ties of strategic cooperation with the United States to enhance stability and security in the region as a whole, we will continue to ensure our own independent ability to cope with the Arab military threats to our existence and security.

In order to cope with the threat, Israel cannot build on a balance of power based on a simple quantitative ratio of military forces. We cannot hope to match Arab numbers. Therefore, Israel's defense policy will have to ensure our ability to maintain a military balance based, beyond the quantitative ratio, on a clear qualitative and technological superiority. Israel is confronted by the challenge of maintaining a balance in peace of countries which have practically no limitations in funds to finance their military effort and furthermore in the . . . military technology and sophisticated weaponry they receive from all three sources—the Soviet, the American and the Western European supply sources, which are all competing by the same means for influence and economic advantages. Among the three sources of supply the United States remains sensitive to the need of maintaining a balance in the Arab-Israeli confrontation. But there is no control on the influx of armament from Soviet and European sources. Therefore, Israel has to build on her independent capability to develop and produce systems which are vital to ensure our qualitative advantage and our security. This puts a tremendous burden on our defense budget and on Israel's national economy. . . . The second "safety valve," if I can use that concept, in our defense policy, is our resolve and our ability to prevent the disruption of the territorial military status in neighboring countries. That includes our resolve.

One—To prevent the violation of security arrangements laid down in political agreements such as in the Sinai with Egypt, and the Golan with Syria. It must be crystal clear: We did sign the peace treaty with Egypt and we faithfully carry out its provisions of withdrawal to the international border, but we have no intention to accept any violation of the status and of the security arrangements in the Sinai as agreed between us.

Two—We will prevent any violation of the status quo ante in south Lebanon.

Three—We will prevent any change in the geographical-military status of the confrontation area which might present unacceptable threat such as the massive introduction of Iraqi forces into Jordan or southern Syria or Syrian forces into Jordan. Such an accumulation of forces in the confrontation area would endanger our very existence and is therefore unacceptable to Israel. . . .

The third element in our defense policy for the 1980's is our determination to prevent confrontation states or potentially confrontation states from gaining access to nuclear weapons. Israel cannot afford the introduction of the nuclear weapon. For us it is not a question of a balance of terror but a question of survival. We shall therefore have to prevent such a threat at its inception.

There are three major elements in our defense policy for the 1980's. We shall, of course, also maintain our freedom of action and our ability to act in order to overcome the terrorist threat. To sum up—in order to strengthen the foundation of its national security, in face of the direct Arab threat as well as in face of the challenge from outside the region, Israel will make special efforts:

One—To ensure our qualitative advantage and maintain the required balance of forces.

Two—To expand and consolidate our economic, industrial, scientific, demographic and physical infrastructure, so as to carry the burden of our national security.

Three—To hold political negotiations from a position of security for the purpose of continuing the peace process between Israel and her neighbors.

Four—To consolidate and nurture national unity in Israel, as well as the ties between Israel and the Jewish people in the Diaspora.

Five—To enhance strategic cooperation with the United States and to develop security relationships with Middle-Eastern and African countries and with other countries in the world. In that respect, I want to stress that Israel is not a liability but an asset, as the United States has gradually come to realize. For the common defense of the Free World, beyond our military capabilities, Israel has to offer an example of true democracy and stability in the midst of regional uncertainties and upheavals, and moreover the capability to contribute to the well-being of developed and less-developed nations, in many important fields such as science, medicine, food production and sophisticated agricultural technology in general.

Israeli Foreign Minister Yitzhak Shamir: Israel's Role in a Changing Middle East (Spring 1982)*

Traditionally, the twin goals of Israel's foreign policy have always been peace and security—two concepts that are closely interrelated: Where there is strength, there is peace—at least, shall we say, peace has a chance. Peace will be unattainable if Israel is weak or perceived to be so. This, indeed, is one of the most crucial lessons to be learned from the history of the Middle East since the end of the Second World War—in terms not only of the Arab-Israel conflict, but of the area as a whole.

The Middle East is a mosaic of peoples, religions, languages and cultures. Although the Muslim-Arab culture is predominant, it has not produced any homogeneity. A vast number of currents—religious and political—are vying with each other, cutting across political borders. The region is permanently in ferment, and frequently unrest flares up in violence, terror, insurrection, civil strife and open and sometimes prolonged warfare. . . .

The most remarkable feature, in our context, of these chronic manifestations of unrest and belligerence is the fact that the great majority of them have nothing to do with Israel or with the Arab-Israel conflict. There were some outsiders, 20 and 30 years ago, who sincerely, but out of ignorance, believed that a solution of the Arab-Israel conflict would lead to regional stability and open a new era of progress. Nothing could be further from the truth. There have, it is true, been four major wars between Israel and its Arab neighbors. However, a full count of the instances of trouble and strife, both domestic and international, in North Africa and Western Asia, would show that the overwhelming majority have no connection whatsoever with the Arab relationship to Israel. . . .

Reduced to its true proportions, the problem is clearly *not* that of a homeland for the Palestinian Arabs. That homeland is Trans-Jordan, or eastern Palestine. There are, however, 1.2 million Palestinian Arabs living in the territories which have been administered by Israel since 1967 in Judea, Samaria and Gaza. Their status and problems were discussed at great length at Camp David. The granting of sovereignty to those areas was ruled out by Israel. A second Palestinian Arab state to the west of the River Jordan is a prescription for anarchy, a threat to both Israel and Jordan, and a likely base for terrorist and Soviet penetration. Hence, it was finally resolved at Camp David to implement an Autonomy Plan for the inhabitants of those areas, on a five-year interim basis. The proposal was

*Excerpts from an article in *Foreign Affairs*, Spring 1982. Yitzhak Shamir became Israel's Foreign Minister in March 1980 and its Prime Minister in October 1983.

made by Israel and accepted by the other partners of the Camp David accords, Egypt and the United States. It is not intended as the ultimate solution of the problem represented by these areas and their inhabitants, but as an interim arrangement designed to achieve two objectives: (a) to allow the Arab inhabitants of these areas the fullest feasible freedom in running their own lives, and (b) to create optimal conditions of peaceful coexistence between Arab and Jew.

Israel has made it clear, at Camp David and since, that it has a claim to sovereignty over Judea, Samaria and Gaza. In order, however, to keep the door open to a solution that will be acceptable to the parties, as envisaged at Camp David, Israel has deliberately refrained from exercising its rights under this claim. The claim will undoubtedly be presented at the end of the five-year interim period, and, while it is realized that there will be a similar claim on the Arab side, by that time one would hope that the kind of atmosphere will have been created that will make it possible to reach an agreement involving a solution acceptable to both sides. It should be clearly understood, therefore, that just as Israel is refraining from pushing its own solution at this time, by the same token the Arab side must refrain from pushing now for measures or the adoption of principles (such as self-determination, an embryo parliament in the autonomous territories, and the like) that would clearly fall beyond the parameters of Camp David and that would tend to prejudge the ultimate outcome of the negotiations on the final status of these areas. Autonomy, in other words, must be allowed to perform the function it was intended to perform—namely, to serve as an interim arrangement, pending the ultimate solution that is to be addressed at a later stage.

Meanwhile, Israelis and Arabs are learning to coexist in Judea, Samaria and Gaza—ultimately the best way to reconciliation and peace. Israelis will continue to reside in those areas. As in the past, this will not be done, of course, at the expense of the Arab inhabitants and their property. But, as Judea and Samaria constitute the heartland of the Jewish people's birth and development as a nation, Israel will not be party to a design that would deny Jews residence in those areas.

No less important, the Israeli presence in these areas, both civilian and military, is vital to Israel's defense—as should be abundantly clear against the background of the recent history of the region and of Israel's patent inability to maintain a large standing army on its borders. The defunct pre-1967 armistice lines—which for nearly 20 years proved to be a prescription for chronic instability and warfare—have long since ceased to have any relevance in the context of the search for a viable Middle East peace. Certainly, Israel will not entertain any notion of a return to those lines or anything approximating them. On this point there is, in Israel, virtually universal agreement.

A final word on the Palestinian subject. There are some, no doubt well-intentioned but largely unaware of some very important facts, who have proposed that Israel negotiate with the PLO. They point to the absence of any organized voice, other than the PLO, representing "the Palestinians" and to the existence of ostensibly moderate elements in that organization that may be encouraged to seek a political solution that would include recognition of Israel.

The real problem is not whether to deal with the PLO or not, but whether it would serve any useful purpose whatsoever. Even if one were to overlook their bloodthirsty modus operandi, their subservience to Soviet aims and their key role in international terror, the PLO's very raison d'etre is the denial of Israel's right to exist, thinly veiled behind the cover of an ostensibly legitimate call for Palestinian statehood. The very act of granting the PLO a status—any status—in the political negotiations would be self-defeating. It would elevate its standing from that of a terrorist organization to that of a recognized aspirant to a totally superfluous political entity. Hence, association of the PLO with any aspect whatsoever of the political process and the prospects of peace are mutually exclusive.

On its part, Israel will do everything it can to ensure that the peace treaty with Egypt will serve as a solid base from which to expand the peace process toward a wider circle of participants. This can be achieved only by means of an Israel-Egypt partnership that is encouraged by active U.S. participation. It has a chance of success, provided that no alternative proposals and plans other than the Camp David accords are introduced into the process. No one is so naïve as to believe that this is a goal which will be easily attained. But this combination of states, working together toward a worthy and vital objective, has already proved its capacity to overcome obstacles and make progress. Together, they are a formidable force for stability that cannot be bypassed by any factor in the Middle East. In order for this policy to bear fruit, much patience and persistent effort are required. . . .

The magnitude of Israel's sacrifice for the achievement of the peace treaty has not been given proper recognition by the international community. From 1968 onward, Israel invested $17 billion in the Sinai Peninsula—in airfields, military installations, development of oilfields, infrastructure, towns and farm villages. The cost of the military redeployment to the Negev is estimated at $4.4 billion. Beyond the financial burden, and the strategic significance of the withdrawal from Sinai, the uprooting of several thousand Israelis who built their homes in the townships and villages along the eastern edge of Sinai is a traumatic event that has made a deep imprint on the entire nation.

With the transfer of the Sinai Peninsula to Egyptian sovereignty and the normalization of relations with Egypt under the peace treaty, Israel has gone a long way toward implementing the provisions of the 1967 U.N. Security Council Resolution 242. The Sinai Peninsula, it should be remembered, covers more than 90 percent of the territory that came into Israel's possession in the Six-Day War. Thus Israel has demonstrated, through concrete action and considerable risk and sacrifice, that it seeks peace and coexistence with its neighbors. It is now up to its neighbors to come forth with a similar demonstration of peaceful intent and readiness. . . .

Thus, within the context of a powerful, basically unchanging ideological rejection of Israel, there are two conflicting currents coursing through the Arab world. One—which is, as of now, the prevailing current—rejects the Jewish State wholly and without reservation, in theory and in practice. The other—only just beginning to crack the surface of developments in the Middle East—accepts the fact of Israel's existence and is ready, in some sort of pragmatic fashion, to come to terms with that existence. Israel is learning to live with this reality, and to try to build on the hope that, in the course of time, this pragmatism can be developed into something more permanent and more meaningful.

A crucial role in determining the future direction of events in the region can be played by forces and influences outside the region.

The history of the involvement of foreign governments in Middle Eastern politics is not a happy one. Attracted by the strategic importance of the region and, more recently, by its immense natural resources and bank deposits, most governments have sought to apply a political gloss to their perceived economic interests by making political statements on the Arab-Israel issue in response to Arab pressures.

. . . Arab hopes of exercising the military option against Israel would not have been sustained as they are if not for the immense supplies of sophisticated offensive military supplies from Russia. The Soviet Government has steadily increased its political and military support of the PLO in spite of, or perhaps because of, this organization's central role in international terror and its declared aim of destroying Israel and its population. This totally one-sided stand by the Soviet Union is compounded by its policy of boycotting Israel, and of persisting in its non-relations with Israel since 1967.

Soviet actions demonstrate clearly that the Soviet Union is opposed to peace in the Middle East, is bent on expanding its presence and influence in the region at the expense of regional stability, and has no problem in the choice of means to achieve its objective. Public opinion is far from being a factor in Soviet decisionmaking. . . .

Peace is fundamental to Israel's way of life, and Israel's determination to achieve it is permanent. Security is a vital guarantee of the viability and maintenance of peace. Together these two objectives provided the conceptual framework that produced the Camp David accords, and the march along this road must continue unabated.

A program for continued action to secure regional stability and peace must originate from the countries and governments that will have to implement the peace and live by it. Israel believes that it should include the following elements:

1. Negotiations between Israel and each of its neighbors, aimed at agreement on a just and lasting peace, laid out in formal peace treaties, that would provide for the establishment of normal diplomatic, economic and good-neighborly relations.

2. Recognition of the sovereignty and political independence of all existing states in the region, and of their right to live in peace within secure and recognized boundaries, free from threats or acts of force, including terrorist activity of any kind.

3. Autonomy for the Arab inhabitants of Judea, Samaria and the Gaza district for a five-year interim period, as set forth in the Camp David accords, and deferment of the final determination of the status of these areas until the end of this transitional period.

4. Restoration of the full independence of Lebanon, through the withdrawal of Syrian and PLO forces from Lebanese territory.

5. Negotiations, among all the states of the Middle East, aimed at declaring the region a nuclear-weapons-free zone, for the security and well-being of all its inhabitants.

Egyptian Foreign Minister Boutros Boutros-Ghali: The Foreign Policy of Egypt in the Post-Sadat Era (Spring 1982)*

. . . Broadly speaking, Egyptian foreign policy in the last three decades has been directed toward two main challenges: how to contain Israeli ambitions and how to solve the Palestinian problem, the core of the Middle East crisis. This task, difficult in itself and rendered more complex by virtue of the multifaceted nature of the conflict, has been further complicated by the differences among Arabs, and the inability of some to adopt a rational attitude or to discard shortsighted policies toward the problem.

Thus, Egypt's efforts to resolve the contradictions between Palestinian national rights and Israeli national aims had to take place in the framework of an equation that would strike a balance between Egypt's conviction that Arab initiative is an important factor in any peace process and the necessity for her to exercise her traditional leadership in order to break the deadlock that has existed for well over 30 years. . . .

President Sadat presented the elements of Egypt's peace plan before the Knesset, as follows:

*Excerpts from an article in *Foreign Affairs*, Spring 1982.

—the termination of the Israeli occupation of all the Arab territories occupied since 1967, including East Jerusalem;

—the realization of the inalienable rights of the Palestinian people and their rights to self-determination including the right to establish their own state;

—the right of all states in the area to live in peace within secure boundaries, based on the recognition that the security of international borders can be established through agreed-upon arrangements and international guarantees;

—the commitment by all states in the region to conduct relations among themselves according to the purposes and principles of the U.N. Charter, in particular the peaceful settlements of disputes and the abstention from the threat or use of force; and

—the termination of the state of belligerency in the area.

Thus it was abundantly clear that Egypt viewed the Palestinian problem as being at the very heart of the Middle East conflict and that an unjust peace that would not guarantee the rights of the Palestinian people would have no future. Indeed, Egypt is seeking a comprehensive peace and not a separate or bilateral agreement with Israel. And during long hours of negotiations with the Israelis, Egyptians have sought to link the withdrawal of Israeli forces from Egyptian territory to the withdrawal of Israeli forces from Palestinian territory. Every effort was exerted by Egypt to associate the solution of the Egyptian question with that of the Palestinian question, in order to lay special emphasis on her comprehensive approach to the peace process. . . .

What Egypt has in mind is that the Palestinians and other Arab parties concerned join these negotiations. It is obvious, however, that only tangible and positive results would induce them to do so. Hence the emphasis laid by Egypt on the necessity for the Israelis to adopt a number of confidence-building measures, to discard the policies of economic sabotage, psychological warfare and cultural frustration being conducted against the Palestinians in the occupied lands. . . .

Occupation by Israel of the West Bank and Gaza will have to end, for three million Israelis cannot go on forever governing one-and-a-half million Palestinians and ignoring their national rights and aspirations.

Needless to say, Egypt feels as strongly about ending the occupation of the Golan Heights as she does about ending the occupation of Gaza and the West Bank, including East Jerusalem. Egypt rejects totally both the annexation of East Jerusalem and that of the Golan, as illegal, unacceptable and obnoxious measures that are not conducive to the atmosphere that is necessary to reach a peaceful comprehensive solution. Such unilateral measures contradict the letter and the spirit of the Camp David accords. Egypt in an official statement on December 15, 1981, strongly condemned the Israeli decision to extend Israeli law, jurisdiction and administration to the occupied Syrian territory of the Golan Heights and termed it an illegal measure and a violation of international law and the Charter of the United Nations. In U.N. Security Council Resolution 242, which is the basis of the Camp David accords, it is stipulated that the acquisition of territory by war is inadmissible and that it is essential to respect the sovereignty and territorial integrity of every state in the area, including Syria.

When Saudi Arabia took the bold step of putting forward what has become known as the "Fahd Peace Plan," Egypt could only welcome the fact that a major Arab state would opt for a constructive approach that could end the indecisiveness that has plagued the Arab scene. The Saudi proposals are a set of principles derived from Security Council Resolution 242 and other U.N. resolutions. But to translate these principles into practical realities, one would still need a framework and a negotiating process, which Camp David has provided. In other words, the Saudi proposals are not an alternative to Camp David, but they need a "Camp David" to be implemented satisfactorily.

Thus, Egypt does not consider that peace in the Middle East is her own exclusive concern. Any proposals are welcomed by Egypt provided that they build upon what has already been achieved through Camp David, take into account what has already been acquired through the present negotiations, and meet with the approval of all the parties concerned. Until such a formula is proposed and accepted by these parties, Egypt under President Mubarak is intent on pursuing the negotiations and efforts to reach a comprehensive, peaceful solution that would bring justice and security for all. Egypt is equally intent on continuing to play her historical role in the peace process and in the negotiations that may take place between the Arabs and Israel to achieve that goal.

The diplomatic relations established between Egypt and Israel will, needless to say, continue at the same level. As stipulated in the peace treaty, relations between the two countries are "normal" relations, the word normal meaning exactly what it says and not implying in any way a concept of special relations, alliance or strategic cooperation. This kind of cooperation might be envisaged the day a comprehensive and just peace is achieved, but nothing in the peace treaty commits Egypt to anything that goes further than normal relations between any two given countries.

The role of the United States in establishing a just, comprehensive peace cannot be overemphasized. The full partnership role played by the United States in the negotiations between Egypt and Israel has borne fruit in the form of the peace treaty. It is expected that the United States would continue to play the same positive role in order to achieve a just and lasting solution to the Palestinian problem, the crux of the Middle East problem.

Egypt's conviction is that American participation in the peace negotiations is an essential element. This participation has been instrumental in reaching the Camp David accords and the peace treaty. But there is an even more vital role for U.S. diplomacy to play in helping to define the terms of full Palestinian autonomy and to convince the Israelis that only a self-governing Palestinian body with wide-ranging jurisdiction in all fields would have a chance to be accepted by the Palestinians. The United States can also play a part in convincing the Palestinians and the Palestine Liberation Organization (PLO) that their legitimate rights can be obtained by negotiation and that they can find their place in the family of nations through a peaceful and legitimate process. But to be able to do that, the United States would have to start talking to the Palestinians, to the organization that is accepted by the majority of them as representative of their aspirations, to the organization that is recognized by the majority of nations—namely the PLO. Contacts have to be established between the U.S. government and the PLO and not only through impromptu meetings in the corridors of the United Nations or at diplomatic parties. This was the gist of the message carried by President Sadat on his last trip to Washington in August 1981. This remains a strong belief of Egyptian diplomacy. . . .

Certain Arab governments criticize the peace process but have been unable to unite not only behind an alternative process but even behind the goals to be attained by such a process. This failure on the part of the Arab governments emphasizes the importance of Egypt's leadership. In playing a leading role in the search for a peaceful and just solution to the Arab-Israeli conflict, Egypt maintains a balance between her own national interests and the wider interests of the Arab nations. . . .

Sooner or later, Egypt's actions will make the other Arab governments grasp that the withdrawal of Israeli forces and the return of Sinai to full Egyptian sovereignty constitute a valuable precedent, in accordance with the text of the Egyptian-Israeli Treaty of Peace, which states in its preamble that: "The (Camp David) Framework is intended to constitute a basis for peace not only between Egypt and Israel, but also between Israel and each of its Arab neighbors. . . ." The success of the Camp David accords is bound to have a "snowball" effect and give the peace process more strength, more dynamism and more credibility in Arab eyes. Sooner or later, Arab governments are bound to join the peace process and Egypt's efforts to induce them to do so will be successful.

This is because the present disagreement between Egypt and a number of Arab countries is not in any way the first inter-Arab dispute and will not be the last.

In spite of the severance of diplomatic relations between Cairo and those Arab capitals, transnational relations have continued and even increased: more than two million Egyptian workers, technicians and experts, teachers, doctors and judges are performing a well-appreciated mission in these Arab countries; private Arab investment continues to flow into Egypt; and Cairo remains the favorite destination of Arab tourists. Thousands of Arabs of every nationality are learning in schools and colleges in Egypt, and Arab military and police officers are still being trained in Egyptian academies.

Reconciliation at the official level between Egypt and the governments of the other Arab states is bound to come and President Mubarak has made it quite clear that Egypt does not object to such a reconciliation. Ever since his accession to the presidency, he has underlined the futility of press campaigns among Arabs that can only exacerbate the differences, and he has urged Egyptian journalists and editors to refrain from attacking or abusing Arab governments.

There is hardly any doubt, however, that a rapprochement between Cairo and the dissenting Arab capitals will have to take into account the reality of the relations existing between Egypt and Israel. Egypt would not be the only country able to maintain relations both with Israel and the Arab states. A number of countries in the area itself manage to do that quite successfully, namely Turkey, a Muslim country, and Cyprus which has diplomatic representatives from both Israel and the PLO. Besides, the European and the Latin American countries and the United States all have excellent relations with both the Arab states and Israel. So why should the same thing be impossible to realize in Egypt's case? Certainly the fact that Egypt is an Arab country might seem to complicate the issue, but should not the Arabs accept from a sister state what they readily accept from others? . . .

U.S. Secretary of State George Shultz: Congressional Testimony (July 12, 1982)*

In late 1974 I visited Beirut, at the time a beautiful and thriving city, even then marked by the presence of Palestinian refugees. But since then Lebanon has been racked by destruction, enduring the presence of armed and assertive PLO and other forces.

Coherent life and government are impossible under those conditions and inevitably Lebanon became a state in disrepair. The Lebanese deserve a chance to govern themselves, free from the presence of the armed forces of any other country or group. The authority of the Government of Lebanon must extend to all its territory.

The agony of Lebanon is on the minds and in the hearts of us all. But in a larger sense Lebanon is but the latest chapter in a history of accumulated grief stretching back through decades of conflict. We are talking here about a part of the globe that has had little genuine peace for generations. A region with thousands of victims—Arab, Israeli and other families torn apart

---

*Confirmation hearing for the Secretary of State—designate before the Senate Foreign Relations Committee.

as a consequence of war and terror. What is going on now in Lebanon must mark the end of this cycle of terror rather than simply the latest in a continuing series of senseless and violent acts.

We cannot accept the loss of life brought home to us every day even at this great distance on our television screens; but at the same time we can, as Americans, be proud that once again it is the United States, working most prominently through President Reagan's emissary, Ambassador Philip Habib, that is attempting to still the guns, achieve an equitable outcome and alleviate the suffering.

Mr. Chairman, the crisis in Lebanon makes painfully and totally clear a central reality of the Middle East: The legitimate needs and problems of the Palestinian people must be addressed and resolved—urgently and in all their dimensions. Beyond the suffering of the Palestinian people lies a complex of political problems which must be addressed if the Middle East is to know peace. The Camp David framework calls as a first step for temporary arrangements which will provide full autonomy for the Palestinians of the West Bank and Gaza. That same framework then speaks eloquently and significantly of a solution that "must also recognize the legitimate rights of the Palestinian people."

The challenge of the negotiations in which the United States is, and during my tenure will remain, a full partner, is to transform that hope into reality. For these talks to succeed, representatives of the Palestinians themselves must participate in the negotiating process. The basis must also be found for other countries in the region, in addition to Israel and Egypt, to join in the peace process.

Our determined effort to stop the killing in Lebanon, resolve the conflict, and make the Government of Lebanon once again sovereign throughout its territory underscores the degree to which our nation has vital interests throughout the Arab world. Our friendly relations with the great majority of Arab states have served those interests and, I believe, assisted our efforts to deal with the current Lebanon crisis.

But beyond the issues of the moment, the importance to our own security of wide and ever-strengthening ties with the Arabs is manifest. It is from them that the West gets much of its oil; it is with them that we share an interest and must cooperate in resisting Soviet imperialism; it is with them, as well as Israel, that we will be able to bring peace to the Middle East.

Finally, and most important, Mr. Chairman, the Lebanese situation is intimately linked to the vital question of Israel's security. Israel, our closest friend in the Middle East, still harbors a deep feeling of insecurity. In a region where hostility is endemic, and where so much of it is directed against Israel, the rightness of her preoccupation with matters of security cannot be disputed. Nor should anyone dispute the depth and durability of America's commitment to the security of Israel or our readiness to assure that Israel has the necessary means to defend herself. I share in this deep and enduring commitment. And more, I recognize that democratic Israel shares with us a deep commitment to the security of the West.

Beyond that, however, we owe it to Israel, in the context of our special relationship, to work with her to bring about a comprehensive peace—acceptable to all the parties involved—which is the only sure guarantee of true and durable security.

Israeli Prime Minister Menachem Begin: The Wars of No Alternative and Operation Peace for the Galilee (August 8, 1982)*

Let us turn from the international example to ourselves. Operation Peace for Galilee is not a military operation resulting from the lack of an alternative. The terrorists did not threaten the existence of the State of Israel; they "only" threatened the lives of Israel's citizens and members of the Jewish people. There are those who find fault with the second part of that sentence. If there was no danger to the existence of the state, why did you go to war?

I will explain why. We had three wars which we fought without an alternative. The first was the War of Independence, which began on November 30, 1947, and lasted until January 1949. . . . We carried on our lives then by a miracle, with a clear recognition of life's imperative: to win, to establish a state, a government, a parliament, a democracy, an army—a force to defend Israel and the entire Jewish people.

The second war of no alternative was the Yom Kippur War and the War of Attrition that preceded it. What was the situation on that Yom Kippur day [October 6, 1973]? We had 177 tanks deployed on the Golan Heights against 1,400 Soviet-Syrian tanks; and fewer than 500 of our soldiers manned positions along the Suez Canal against five divisions sent to the front by the Egyptians.

It is any wonder that the first days of that war were hard to bear? I remember Gen. Avraham Yaffe came to us, to the Knesset Foreign Affairs and Defence Committee, and said: "Oy, it's so hard! Our boys, 18- and 19-year-olds, are falling like flies and are defending our nation with their very bodies."

In the Golan Heights there was a moment when the O/C Northern Command—today our chief of staff—heard his deputy say, "This is it." What that meant was: "We've lost: we have to come down off the Golan Heights." And the then O/C said, "Give me another five minutes."

---

*Speech delivered at the National Defense College in Israel.

Sometimes five minutes can decide a nation's fate. During those five minutes, several dozen tanks arrived, which changed the entire situation on the Golan Heights.

If this had not happened, if the Syrian enemy had come down from the heights to the valley, he would have reached Haifa—for there was not a single tank to obstruct his armoured column's route to Haifa. Yes, we would even have fought with knives—as one of our esteemed wives has said—with knives against tanks. Many more would have fallen, and in every settlement there would have been the kind of slaughter at which the Syrians are experts.

In the south, our boys in the outposts were taken prisoner, and we know what happened to them afterwards. Dozens of tanks were destroyed, because tanks were sent in piecemeal, since we could not organize them in a large formation. And dozens of planes were shot down by missiles which were not destroyed in time, so that we had to submit to their advances.

Woe to the ears that still ring with the words of one of the nation's heroes, the then defence minister, in whose veins flowed the blood of the Maccabees: "We are losing the Third Commonwealth."

Our total casualties in that war of no alternative were 2,297 killed, 6,067 wounded. Together with the War of Attrition—which was also a war of no alternative—2,659 killed, 7,251 wounded. The terrible total: almost 10,000 casualties.

Our other wars were not without an alternative. In November 1956 we had a choice. The reason for going to war then was the need to destroy the *fedayeen,* who did not represent a danger to the existence of the state.

However, the political leadership of the time thought it was necessary to do this. As one who served in the parliamentary opposition, I was summoned to David Ben-Gurion before the cabinet received information of the plan, and he found it necessary to give my colleagues and myself these details: We are going to meet the enemy before it absorbs the Soviet weapons which began to flow to it from Czechoslovakia in 1955.

In June 1967 we again had a choice. The Egyptian army concentrations in the Sinai approaches did not prove that Nasser was really about to attack us. We must be honest with ourselves. We decided to attack him.

This was a war of self-defence in the noblest sense of the term. The government of national unity then established decided unanimously: We will take the initiative and attack the enemy, drive him back, and thus assure the security of Israel and the future of the nation.

As for Operation Peace for Galilee, it does not really belong to the category of wars of no alternative. We could have gone on seeing our civilians injured in Metulla or Kiryat Shmona or Nahariya. We could have gone on counting those killed by explosive charges left in a Jerusalem supermarket, or a Petah Tikva bus stop.

All the orders to carry out these acts of murder and sabotage came from Beirut. Should we have reconciled ourselves to the ceaseless killing of civilians, even after the agreement ending hostilities reached last summer, which the terrorists interpreted as an agreement permitting them to strike at us from every side, besides Southern Lebanon? They tried to infiltrate gangs of murderers via Syria and Jordan, and by a miracle we captured them. We might also not have captured them. There was a gang of four terrorists which infiltrated from Jordan, whose members admitted they had been about to commandeer a bus (and we remember the bus on the coastal road).

And in the Diaspora? Even Philip Habib interpreted the agreement ending acts of hostility as giving them freedom to attack targets beyond Israel's borders. We have never accepted this interpretation. Shall we permit Jewish blood to be spilled in the Diaspora? Shall we permit bombs to be planted against Jews in Paris, Rome, Athens or London? Shall we permit our ambassadors to be attacked?

There are slanderers who say that a full year of quiet has passed between us and the terrorists. Nonsense. There was not even one month of quiet. The newspapers and communications media, including *The New York Times* and *The Washington Post*, did not publish even one line about our capturing the gang of murderers that crossed the Jordan in order to commandeer a bus and murder its passengers.

True, such actions were not a threat to the existence of the state. But they did threaten the lives of civilians whose number we cannot estimate, day after day, week after week, month after month.

During the past nine weeks, we have, in effect, destroyed the combat potential of 20,000 terrorists. We hold 9,000 in a prison camp. Between 2,000 and 3,000 were killed and between 7,000 and 9,000 have been captured and cut off in Beirut. They have decided to leave there only because they have no possibility of remaining there. The problem will be solved.

We have destroyed the best tanks and planes the Syrians had. We have destroyed 24 of their ground-to-air missile batteries. After everything that happened, Syria did not go to war against us, not in Lebanon and not in the Golan Heights.

For our part, we will not initiate any attack against any Arab country. We have proved that we do not want wars. We made many painful sacrifices for a peace treaty with Egypt. That treaty stood the test of the fighting in Lebanon; in other words, it *stood the test.*

The demilitarized zone of 150 kilometers in Sinai exists, and no Egyptian soldier has been placed there. From the experience of the 1930s, I have to say that if ever the other side violated the agreement about the demilitarized zone, Israel would be obliged to introduce, without delay, a force stronger than that violating the international commitment: not in order to wage war, but to achieve one of two results: restoration of the previous situation, i.e., resumed demilitarization, and the removal of both armies from the demilitarized zone; or attainment of strategic depth, in case the other side has taken the first step towards a war of aggression, as happened in Europe only three years after the abrogation of the demilitarized zone in the Rhineland.

Because the other Arab countries are completely incapable of attacking the State of Israel, there is reason to expect that we are facing a historic period of peace. It is obviously impossible to set a date.

It may well be that "The land shall be still for 40 years." Perhaps less: perhaps more. But from the facts before us, it is clear that, with the end of the fighting in Lebanon, we have ahead of us many years of establishing peace treaties and peaceful relations with the various Arab countries.

The conclusion—both on the basis of the relations between states and on the basis of our national experience—is that there is no divine mandate to go to war only if there is no alternative. There is no moral imperative that a nation must, or is entitled to, fight only when its back is to the sea, or to the abyss. Such a war may avert tragedy, if not a Holocaust, for any nation; but it causes it terrible loss of life.

Quite the opposite. A free, sovereign nation, which hates war and loves peace, and which is concerned about its security, must create the conditions under which war, if there is a need for it, *will not be* for lack of alternative. The conditions must be such—and their creation depends upon man's reason and his actions—that the price of victory will be few casualties, not many.

U.S. President Ronald Reagan: The Reagan Plan (September 1, 1982)

My fellow Americans, today has been a day that should make us proud. It marked the end of the successful evacuation of the Palestine Liberation Organization (PLO) from Beirut, Lebanon. This peaceful step could never have been taken without the good offices of the United States and, especially, the truly heroic work of a great American diplomat, Ambassador Philip Habib [President's special emissary to the Middle East]. Thanks to his efforts, I am happy to announce that the U.S. Marine contingent helping to supervise the evacuation has accomplished its mission. Our young men should be out of Lebanon within two weeks. They, too, have served the cause of peace with distinction, and we can all be very proud of them.

But the situation in Lebanon is only part of the overall problem of conflict in the Middle East. So, over the past two weeks, while events in Beirut dominated the front page, America was engaged in a quiet, behind-the-scenes effort to lay the groundwork for a broader peace in the region. For once, there were no premature leaks as U.S. diplomatic missions traveled to Mid-East capitals, and I met here at home with a wide range of experts to map out an American peace initiative for the long-suffering peoples of the Middle East, Arab and Israeli alike.

It seemed to me that, with the agreement in Lebanon, we had an opportunity for a more far-reaching peace effort in the region, and I was determined to seize that moment. In the words of the scripture, the time had come to "follow after the things which make for peace."

Tonight, I want to report to you on the steps we have taken and the prospects they can open up for a just and lasting peace in the Middle East. America has long been committed to bringing peace to this troubled region. For more than a generation, successive U.S. administrations have endeavored to develop a fair and workable process that could lead to a true and lasting Arab-Israeli peace. Our involvement in the search for Mid-East peace is not a matter of preference, it is a moral imperative. The strategic importance of the region to the United States is well known.

But our policy is motivated by more than strategic interests. We also have an irreversible commitment to the survival and territorial integrity of friendly states. Nor can we ignore the fact that the well-being of much of the world's economy is tied to stability in the strife-torn Middle East. Finally, our traditional humanitarian concerns dictate a continuing effort to peacefully resolve conflicts.

When our Administration assumed office in January 1981, I decided that the general framework for our Middle East policy should follow the broad guidelines laid down by my predecessors. There were two basic issues we had to address. First, there was the strategic threat to the region posed by the Soviet Union and its surrogates, best demonstrated by the brutal war in Afghanistan; and, second, the peace process between Israel and its Arab neighbors. With regard to the Soviet threat, we have strengthened our efforts to develop with our friends and allies a joint policy to deter the Soviets and their surrogates from further expansion in the region and, if necessary, to defend against it. With respect to the Arab-Israeli conflict, we have embraced the Camp David framework as the only way to proceed. We have also recognized, however, that solving the Arab-Israeli conflict, in and of itself, cannot assure peace throughout a region as vast and troubled as the Middle East.

Our first objective under the Camp David process was to insure the successful fulfillment of the Egyptian-Israeli Peace Treaty. This was achieved with the peaceful return of the Sinai to Egypt in April 1982. To accomplish this, we worked hard with our Egyptian and Israeli friends, and eventually with other friendly countries, to create the multinational force which now operates in the Sinai.

Throughout this period of difficult and time-consuming negotiations, we never lost sight of the next step of Camp David: autonomy talks to pave the way for permitting the Palestinian people to exercise their legitimate rights. However, owing to the tragic assassination of President Sadat and other crises in the area, it was not until January 1982 that we were able to make a major effort to renew these talks. Secretary of State Haig and Ambassador Fairbanks [Richard Fairbanks, Special Negotiator for the Middle East Peace Process] made three visits to Israel and Egypt this year to pursue the autonomy talks. Considerable progress was made in developing the basic outline of an American approach which was to be presented to Egypt and Israel after April.

The successful completion of Israel's withdrawal from Sinai and the courage shown on this occasion by Prime Minister Begin and President Mubarak in living up to their agreements convinced me the time had come for a new American policy to try to bridge the remaining differences between Egypt and Israel on the autonomy process. So, in May, I called for specific measures and a timetable for consultations with the Governments of Egypt and Israel on the next steps in the peace process. However, before this effort could be launched, the conflict in Lebanon preempted our efforts. The autonomy talks were basically put on hold while we sought to untangle the parties in Lebanon and still the guns of war.

The Lebanon war, tragic as it was, has left us with a new opportunity for Middle East peace. We must seize it now and bring peace to this troubled area so vital to world stability while there is still time. It was with this strong conviction that over a month ago, before the present negotiations in Beirut had been completed, I directed Secretary of State Shultz to again review our policy and to consult a wide range of outstanding Americans on the best ways to strengthen chances for peace in the Middle East. We have consulted with many of the officials who were historically involved in the process, with Members of the Congress, and with individuals from the private sector; and I have held extensive consultations with my own advisers on the principles I will outline to you tonight.

The evacuation of the PLO from Beirut is now complete. And we can now help the Lebanese to rebuild their war-torn country. We owe it to ourselves, and to posterity, to move quickly to build upon this achievement. A stable and revived Lebanon is essential to all our hopes for peace in the region. The people of Lebanon deserve the best efforts of the international community to turn the nightmares of the past several years into a new dawn of hope.

But the opportunities for peace in the Middle East do not begin and end in Lebanon. As we help Lebanon rebuild, we must also move to resolve the root causes of conflict between Arabs and Israelis. The war in Lebanon has demonstrated many things, but two consequences are key to the peace process:

First, the military losses of the PLO have not diminished the yearning of the Palestinian people for a just solution of their claims; and

Second, while Israel's military successes in Lebanon have demonstrated that its armed forces are second to none in the region, they alone cannot bring just and lasting peace to Israel and her neighbors.

The question now is how to reconcile Israel's legitimate security concerns with the legitimate rights of the Palestinians. And that answer can only come at the negotiating table. Each party must recognize that the outcome must be acceptable to all and that true peace will require compromises by all.

So, tonight I am calling for a fresh start. This is the moment for all those directly concerned to get involved—or lend their support—to a workable basis for peace. The Camp David agreement remains the foundation of our policy. Its language provides all parties with the leeway they need for successful negotiations.

• I call on Israel to make clear that the security for which she yearns can only be achieved through genuine peace, a peace requiring magnanimity, vision, and courage.

• I call on the Palestinian people to recognize that their own political aspirations are inextricably bound to recognition of Israel's right to a secure future.

• And I call on the Arab states to accept the reality of Israel and the reality that peace and justice are to be gained only through hard, fair, direct negotiation.

In making these calls upon others, I recognize that the United States has a special responsibility. No other nation is in a position to deal with the key parties to the conflict on the basis of trust and reliability.

The time has come for a new realism on the part of all the peoples of the Middle East. The State of Israel is an accomplished fact; it deserves unchallenged legitimacy within the community of nations. But Israel's legitimacy has thus far been recognized by too few countries and has been denied by every Arab state except Egypt. Israel exists; it has a right to exist in peace behind secure and defensible borders; and it has a right to demand of its neighbors that they recognize those facts.

I have personally followed and supported Israel's heroic struggle for survival ever since the founding of the State of Israel thirty-four years ago. In the pre-1967 borders, Israel was barely ten miles wide at its narrowest point. The bulk of Israel's population lived within artillery range of hostile Arab armies. I am not about to ask Israel to live that way again.

The war in Lebanon has demonstrated another reality in the region. The departure of the Palestinians from Beirut dramatizes more than ever the homelessness of the Palestinian people. Palestinians feel strongly that their cause is more than a question of refugees. I agree. The Camp David agreement recognized that fact when it spoke of the legitimate the Palestinian people and their just requirements. For peace to endure, it must involve all those who have been most deeply affected by the conflict. Only through broader participation in the peace process—most immediately by Jordan and by the Palestinians—will Israel be able to rest confident in the knowledge that its security and integrity will be respected by its neighbors. Only through the process of negotiation can all the nations of the Middle East achieve a secure peace

These then are our general goals. What are the specific new American positions, and why are we taking them?

In the Camp David talks thus far, both Israel and Egypt have felt free to express openly their views as to what the outcome should be. Understandably, their views have differed on many points.

The United States has thus far sought to play the role of mediator; we have avoided public comment on the key issues. We have always recognized—and continue to recognize—that only the voluntary agreement of those parties most directly involved in the conflict can provide an enduring solution. But it has become evident to me that some clearer sense of America's position on the key issues is necessary to encourage wider support for the peace process.

First, as outlined in the Camp David accords, there must be a period of time during which the Palestinian inhabitants of the West Bank and Gaza will have full autonomy over their own affairs. Due consideration must be given to the principle of self-government by the inhabitants of the territories and to the legitimate security concerns of the parties involved.

The purpose of the five-year period of transition, which would begin after free elections for a self-governing Palestinian authority, is to prove to the Palestinians that they can run their own affairs and that such autonomy poses no threat to Israel's security.

The United States will not support the use of any additional land for the purpose of settlements during the transition period. Indeed, the immediate adoption of a settlement freeze by Israel, more than any other action, could create the confidence needed for wider participation in these talks. Further settlement activity is in no way necessary for the security of Israel and only diminishes the confidence of the Arabs that a final outcome can be freely and fairly negotiated.

I want to make the American position well understood: The purpose of this transition period is the peaceful and orderly transfer of authority from Israel to the Palestinian inhabitants of the West Bank and Gaza. At the same time, such a transfer must not interfere with Israel's security requirements.

Beyond the transition period, as we look to the future of the West Bank and Gaza, it is clear to me that peace cannot be achieved by the formation of an independent Palestinian state in those territories. Nor is it achievable on the basis of Israeli sovereignty or permanent control over the West Bank and Gaza.

So the United States will not support the establishment of an independent Palestinian state in the West Bank and Gaza, and we will not support annexation or permanent control by Israel.

There is, however, another way to peace. The final status of these lands must, of course, be reached through the give-and-take of negotiations. But it is the firm view of the United States that self-government by the Palestinians of the West Bank and Gaza in association with Jordan offers the best chance for a durable, just and lasting peace.

We base our approach squarely on the principle that the Arab-Israeli conflict should be resolved through negotiations involving an exchange of territory for peace. This exchange is enshrined in U.N. Security Council Resolution 242, which is, in turn, incorporated in all its parts in the Camp David agreements. U.N. Resolution 242 remains wholly valid as the foundation stone of America's Middle East peace effort.

It is the United States' position that—in return for peace—the withdrawal provision of Resolution 242 applies to all fronts, including the West Bank and Gaza.

When the border is negotiated between Jordan and Israel, our view on the extent to which Israel should be asked to give up territory will be heavily affected by the extent of true peace and normalization and the security arrangements offered in return.

Finally, we remain convinced that Jerusalem must remain undivided, but its final status should be decided through negotiations.

In the course of the negotiations to come, the United States will support positions that seem to us fair and reasonable compromises and likely to promote a sound agreement. We will also put forward our own detailed proposals when we believe they can be helpful. And, make no mistake, the United States will oppose any proposal—from any party and at any point in the negotiating process—that threatens the security of Israel. America's commitment to the security of Israel is ironclad. And, I might add, so is mine.

During the past few days, our ambassadors in Israel, Egypt, Jordan, and Saudi Arabia have presented to their host governments the proposals in full detail that I have outlined here today. Now I am convinced that these proposals can bring justice, bring security, and bring durability to an Arab-Israeli peace. The United States will stand by these principles with total dedication. They are fully consistent with Israel's security requirements and the aspirations of the Palestinians. We will work hard to participation at the peace table as envisaged by the Camp David accords. And I fervently hope that the Palestinians and Jordan, with the support of their Arab colleagues, will accept this opportunity.

Tragic turmoil in the Middle East runs back to the dawn of history. In our modern day, conflict after conflict has taken its brutal toll there. In an age of nuclear challenge and economic interdependence, such conflicts are a threat to all the people of the world, not just the Middle East itself. It is time for us all—in the Middle East and around the world—to call a halt to conflict, hatred, and prejudice; it is time for us all to launch a common effort for reconstruction, peace, and progress.

It has often been said—and regrettably too often been true—that the story of the search for peace and justice in the Middle East is a tragedy of opportunities missed. In the aftermath of the settlement in Lebanon we now face an opportunity for a broader peace. This time we must not let it slip from our grasp. We must look beyond the difficulties and obstacles of the present and move with fairness and resolve toward a brighter future. We owe it to ourselves—and to posterity—to do no less. For if we miss this chance to make a fresh start, we may look back on this moment from some later vantage point and realize how much that failure cost us all.

These, then, are the principles upon which American policy toward the Arab-Israeli conflict will be based. I have made a personal commitment to see that they endure and, God willing, that they will come to be seen by all reasonable, compassionate people as fair, achievable, and in the interests of all who wish to see peace in the Middle East.

Tonight, on the eve of what can be a dawning of new hope for the people of the troubled Middle East—and for all the world's people who dream of a just and peaceful future—I ask you, my fellow Americans, for your support, and your prayers in this great undertaking.

Twelfth Arab Summit Conference: Final Statement (September 9, 1982)*

. . . In view of the grave conditions through which the Arab nation is passing and out of a sense of historical and pan-Arab responsibility, their majesties and excellencies and highnesses the kings, presidents and emirs of the Arab nation discussed the important issues submitted to their conference and adopted the following resolution in regard to them.

I. The Arab-Israeli Conflict

The conference greeted the steadfastness of the Palestine revolutionary forces, the Lebanese and Palestinian peoples and the Syrian Arab Armed

*The Twelfth Arab Summit Conference convened in Fez, Morocco, on November 25, 1981, was adjourned, and resumed again on September 6, 1982.

Forces and declared its support for the Palestinian people in their struggle for the retrieval of their established national rights.

Out of the conference's belief in the ability of the Arab nation to achieve its legitimate objectives and eliminate the aggression, and out of the principles and basis laid down by the Arab summit conferences, and out of the Arab countries' determination to continue to work by all means for the establishment of peace based on justice in the Middle East and using the plan of President Habib Bourguiba, which is based on international legitimacy, as the foundation for solving the Palestinian question and the plan of His Majesty King Fahd ibn 'Abd al-'Aziz which deals with peace in the Middle East, and in the light of the discussions and notes made by their majesties, excellencies and highnesses the kings, presidents and emirs, the conference has decided to adopt the following principles:

1. Israel's withdrawal from all Arab territories occupied in 1967, including Arab Jerusalem.

2. The removal of settlements set up by Israel in the Arab territories after 1967.

3. Guarantees of the freedom of worship and the performance of religious rites for all religions at the holy places.

4. Confirmation of the right of the Palestinian people to self-determination and to exercise their firm and inalienable national rights, under the leadership of the PLO, its sole legitimate representative, and compensation for those who do not wish to return.

5. The placing of the West Bank and Gaza Strip under UN supervision for a transitional period, not longer than several months.

6. The creation of an independent Palestinian state with Jerusalem as its capital.

7. Security Council guarantees for the implementation of those principles.

8. The drawing up by the Security Council of guarantees for peace for all the states of the region, including the independent Palestinian state.

9. Security Council guarantees for the implementation of these principles.

II. The Israeli Aggression Against Lebanon

The conference declares its strong condemnation of the Israeli aggression against the Palestinian people, and draws the attention of international public opinion to the gravity of this aggression and its consequences on stability and security in the region.

The conference has decided to back Lebanon in everything that will lead to the implementation of the Security Council resolutions, particularly Resolutions 508 and 509 calling for the withdrawal of Israel from Lebanese territory up to the recognized international borders.

The conference affirms the solidarity of the Arab states with Lebanon in its tragedy, and its readiness to render any assistance it demands to remedy and put an end to this tragedy. The conference has been notified of the decision of the Lebanese Government to end the task of the Arab Deterrent Forces in Lebanon provided that negotiations be conducted between the Lebanese and Syrian Governments to make the arrangements in the light of the Israeli withdrawal from Lebanon.

Jordanian Crown Prince Al-Hasan Bin Talal: Jordan's Quest for Peace (Fall 1982)*

. . . Because Jordan is a small country, we are often discounted as a major factor in what is clearly the greatest threat to international security. We do not have a large population like Egypt or Syria. We do not have a position of military superiority like Israel. We do not have oil like Saudi Arabia or Iraq. So, then, why is Jordan important? Do we assert its centrality because we are Jordanian?

No, Jordan's views are important. Apart from the Sinai, which is in the process of being returned to Egypt, most of the territory Israel occupied in 1967, and therefore which is referred to in U.N. Security Council Resolution 242, was Jordanian. East Jerusalem was Jordanian. There are more Palestinians in Jordan than in any other state, most of them refugees from the wars of 1948 and 1967. Jordan and Israel have outstanding territorial conflicts dating from 1948. Although it is our position and belief that the Palestine Liberation Organization is and can only be the sole representative of the Palestinian people, still it is incontestable that large numbers of Arabs in the West Bank continue to attend closely to Jordan's actions and policies.

It is clear today that the sine qua non of any general and effective settlement of the Arab-Israeli conflict must address and resolve the Palestinian issue. It is not our purpose here to posit the requirements for such a resolution; indeed, the requirements are part of the dispute. What is clear, however, is that all parties today recognize that, to use the words of former U.S. Assistant Secretary of State Harold Saunders, "The Palestinians collectively are a political factor which must be dealt with if there is to be a peace between Israel and its neighbors." Even a cursory review of Israeli statements demonstrates conclusively that there too is a recognition of the crucial nature of the Palestinian problem. Whether in terms of "autonomy" proposals or hints that the Palestinians already have their state in Jordan, it is evident that Israeli leaders, too, have come to accept, implicitly or ex-

*Excerpts from an article in *Foreign Affairs*, Fall 1982.

plicitly, the unavoidable fact that no settlement is possible without dealing with the Palestinian problem.

We Jordanians must add that, practically speaking, a settlement must also take into account our perceptions. Small as Jordan is, our country is politically, socially, economically, militarily and historically inseparable from the Palestinian issue. Not that we can speak in place of the Palestinians; we cannot. As His Majesty King Hussein has said recently, "Palestinians alone have the right to determine their future. There are no other options acceptable to Jordan nor is there any substitute for the Palestine Liberation Organization, the sole legitimate representative of the people of Palestine. . . ." We cannot speak in place of the Palestinians. At the same time, however, as a leading Jordanian social scientist has written, "The Jordanians and Palestinians are now one people, and no political loyalty, however strong, will separate them permanently."

Consider for a moment the following:

—Half Jordan's population is Palestinian.

—The West Bank and East Jerusalem, both captured by Israel in 1967, were part of Jordan.

—If there is large-scale Palestinian migration as a result of any regional settlement, Jordan will necessarily be greatly affected.

—Virtually all Palestinians currently resident in Jordan are Jordanian nationals.

—Israel and Jordan have vital interests in development of regional water resources in the Jordan River. Israel has already illegally diverted much of the Jordan River, but the importance of cooperation in the future cannot be overestimated. In other areas such as tourism, there is also substantial need for cooperation.

—After any settlement as before it, Jordan will share a long border with Israel. For us, development is not just an abstract goal, but a pressing need. We do not wish to continue to divert so much of Jordan's small resource base to a costly armaments program to defend our overexposed position or in order to reduce the risks along this extended border.

—Pending the creation of a Palestinian state, it is still Jordan which pays the salaries and pensions of West Bank officials; it is Jordan that bears some development costs of the territory and whose approval is necessary for such projects; it is in the Jordanian parliament that the inhabitants of the West Bank are represented; it is Jordanian law that has effect in the West Bank. This is not to deny that Israel is also involved in these activities, for that is true, albeit a clear violation of international law. Rather, we intend only to show how concrete and contemporary are Jordan's interests. . . .

. . . Yet lately we in Jordan have begun to hear and read that "Jordan opposes an Arab-Israeli settlement." Let us be clear on this point: no one, no country, no people wants a settlement more than we do. Certainly, no one pays a heavier price for the continuation of the conflict than do we here in Jordan.

After the 1967 War, other Arab governments learned—and what a costly lesson—what we had known for almost two decades: Israel was to be an enduring reality of the Middle East, and the issue was not to undo the 1947 injustice to Palestinians and all Arabs but rather to constrain an Israel hungry for territorial expansion and powerful enough to obtain it.

Perhaps it is germane to say at this point that we Jordanians do not have a precise blueprint of a settlement in mind. Indeed, I believe I can speak for all the Arab countries, and probably for Israel too, in saying that the range of ideas or alternatives or minimums or maximums that is advanced in any of our countries is appallingly varied. For us Jordanians, there are a few clear-cut requirements. Certainly, the same can be said for Egyptians, Israelis, Iraqis, Palestinians, Saudis and Syrians. We have learned through successive tragedies to keep our requirements few, to question them, to be sure they are truly vital. This is true also of other Arab parties. Sadly, it is not true for Israel, whose list of requirements has grown with each passing year. . . .

In spite of Israel's intransigence, which is growing apace with her appetite, the Arab governments including Jordan still seek a settlement. We have to, for let us be candid: Israel has designs on the West Bank, East Jerusalem, the Golan Heights, and southern Lebanon—whose territories are these? Arab territories. We do not want to provide a pretext for further Israeli expansion. So, yes Jordan, and, yes, the other Arab states near Israel favor a settlement.

Yet it is true that we do not favor *any* settlement. Neither Jordan, nor Syria nor Lebanon nor Saudi Arabia nor Egypt nor Israel—none of the Middle East countries—is prepared to accept, or should be prepared to accept, "peace at any price." Again, let us all be honest. A "settlement" that did not resolve the Palestinian problem, or the question of the Golan, or Israel's or Jordan's or Lebanon's or Syria's rights to exist with reasonable security within a recognized territory—such an outcome would be no settlement at all, for natural forces would be at work to overturn it before it was signed. We understand Israel's needs, and believe Israel's truly vital requirements can be met, but we too have a few vital requirements. Each nation must enjoy some security as a result of a settlement, and none of us can have perfect security, for as has often been shown, one nation's perfect security is another's perfect insecurity.

It is true that agreement on what a settlement should look like is lacking both within and among Arab states, as it is lacking in fact within Israel and between Israel and other states. But a resolution to the conflict is much less likely to be found

—if Israel continues to expand what are clearly illegal settlements in the occupied territories;

—if Israel continues to decide unilaterally to annex Arab land;

—if private land is confiscated to be handed out to Israeli settlers;

—if peace agreements are made in the name of rather than with other parties;

—if Israel continues to play with internal vulnerabilities of Arab states, increasing instability and distrust;

—if Israel continues to play with internal vulnerabilities of seeing her role as a regional policeman.

Let there be no mistake. I am not holding the Arabs blameless for the depth and duration of the Arab-Israeli conflict. For too long Arab states thought the monumental injustice perpetrated against the Palestinian people in 1948 was the only reality. For too long many Arabs held that justice would be served in the end, that justice would triumph, and could see only a return to their lands by the refugees as just. After all, we knew the Palestinian Arabs, native to the land, as our Arab brothers. We did not know the Jews who had suddenly seized it. What was to happen to them? Arabs didn't care; they cared deeply, though, about the Palestinians. This was unrealistic. Today, we understand that the Palestinian problem must be dealt with *in the context* of the existence of Israel. Nevertheless, that problem *must* be resolved. We Arabs too have some requirements, but there is no question that we seek, favor, and deeply desire a resolution to this disastrous conflict.

It must be noted that the Israeli annexation of Arab Jerusalem and the Golan have both taken place in the aftermath of the Egyptian-Israeli peace treaty. Even Israelis never claimed historic rights to the Golan. Now that they have purported to annex the Golan Heights, can anyone doubt that the next step will be the West Bank? Never mind the concept of autonomy. Never mind the ideas of Palestinian self-rule. It is clear that Israel is intent upon adding this Arab territory to Greater Israel.

It was the inevitability of this result to the Camp David separate peace that led us to remain outside the discussions. We ask for a process of peace, not a process of annexation. Jordan and other Arab governments want a true peace, a peace of compromise, a peace that will allow Arab and Jew and Christian to live side by side in this region so important to all three faiths and the many peoples who embrace them. We seek a peace that will not force us to divert our meager resources to a constant cycle of arming to deter others and defend ourselves, a peace that will allow us to develop our land, our people, and our society both economically and spiritually, not bury the people in the land with continuing bitterness and hatred.

And what are the essentials of such a peace? Clearly, the modalities must be negotiated, but several prerequisites are manifestly central to bring about a peace that can endure. Happily, the prerequisites are few. Sadly, they are more elusive today than they were when President Sadat traveled to Jerusalem.

First, it is clear that the Palestinians must be allowed to freely exercise their national right of self-determination. The whole world, including the

United States, and implicitly even Israel, has recognized that the Palestinian problem is at the core of the continuing Middle East tragedy. Put another way, there will never be a true peace in the region until this first requirement is met.

The second requirement is Israeli withdrawal from territories occupied in the 1967 War. Indeed, these two requirements may be viewed as related. We understand that timing can be important, that security measures (such as arms or forces limitations, observers, and the like) may be an integral part of any agreement. Issues such as security measures, juridical status, corridors of transit and communication, representation, foreign nationals, and so forth are important and are proper subjects of negotiation. Moreover, it is clear that in some cases security requirements may dictate minor modifications to specific lines previously disputed. Yet, such exchanges must result from negotiations aimed at *mutual* security and based on the two principles we have identified, not as a result of force or threat. . . .

The United States has important—some would say, vital—interests in the Middle East. It is also true that we have critical interests in the West, not least with the United States. Much in our tradition is shared, from our great monotheistic traditions to our prolonged and close association with Western Europe. We have resources of faith as well as of minerals; America has resources of science and technology as well as capital. The world is interdependent, and those Arabs who ignore or castigate our interdependence with the West, like their counterparts here, are out of step with more than their compatriots—they are out of step with reality itself.

Thus, when some Arabs say that American or Western interests are at risk in the continued failure to achieve a settlement, what they are really saying is that world interests, our interests as well as yours, are at stake. A future that condemns us to pervert the nature and value of our relationship into that of a gunrunner's, that forces America's friends to confront and even do violence to other friends, that perpetuates poverty and ignorance and narrowly limits the resources to overcome these common enemies— this is not a hopeful destiny, this is not a humane destiny, this is not an acceptable destiny. . . .

The Kahan Commission: Report
(February 7, 1983)*

Before we discuss the essence of the problem of the indirect responsibility of Israel, or of those who operated at its behest, we perceive it to be neces-

*Excerpts from the report of the Kahan Commission to investigate the massacre at the Sabra and Shatila refugee camps, which was signed by Chairman Yitzhak Kahan and members Aharon Barak and Yona Efrat.

sary to deal with objections that have been voiced on various occasions, according to which if Israel's direct responsibility for the atrocities is negated—i.e., if it is determined that the blood of those killed was not shed by I.D.F. [Israel Defense Force] soldiers and forces, or that others operating at the behest of the state were not parties to the atrocities—then there is no place for further discussion of the problem of indirect responsibility. The argument is that no responsibility should be laid on Israel for deeds perpetrated outside of its borders by members of the Christian community against Palestinians in that same country, or against Muslims located within the area of the camps. A certain echo of this approach may be found in statements made in the Cabinet meeting of 9.19.82, and in statements released to the public by various sources.

We cannot accept this position. If it indeed becomes clear that those who decided on the entry of the Phalangists into the camps should have foreseen—from the information at their disposal and from things which were common knowledge—that there was danger of a massacre, and no steps were taken which might have prevented this danger or at least greatly reduced the possibility that deeds of this type might be done, then those who made the decisions and those who implemented them are indirectly responsible for what ultimately occurred, even if they did not intend this to happen and merely disregarded the anticipated danger. A similar indirect responsibility also falls on those who knew of the decision: it was their duty, by virtue of their position and their office, to warn of the danger, and they did not fulfill this duty. It is also not possible to absolve of such indirect responsibility those persons who, when they received the first reports of what was happening in the camps, did not rush to prevent the continuation of the Phalangists' actions and did not do everything within their power to stop them.

. . . We would like to note here that we will not enter at all into the question of indirect responsibility of other elements besides the State of Israel. One might argue that such indirect responsibility falls, *inter alia*, on the Lebanese Army, or on the Lebanese government to whose orders this army was subject, since despite Major General Drori's urgings in his talks with the heads of the Lebanese Army, they did not grant Israel's request to enter the camps before the Phalangists or instead of the Phalangists, until 9.19.82. It should also be noted that in meetings with U.S. representatives during the critical days, Israel's spokesmen repeatedly requested that the U.S. use its influence to get the Lebanese Army to fulfill the function of maintaining public peace and order in West Beirut, but it does not seem that these requests had any result. One might also make charges concerning the hasty evacuation of the multi-national force by the countries whose troops were in place until after the evacuation of the terrorists.

. . . As has already been said above, the decision to enter West Beirut was adopted in conversations held between the Prime Minister and the Defense Minister on the night between 14–15 September 1982. No charge may be made against this decision for having been adopted by these two alone without convening a Cabinet session. On that same night, an extraordinary emergency situation was created which justified immediate and concerted action to prevent a situation which appeared undesirable and even dangerous from Israel's perspective. There is great sense in the supposition that had I.D.F. troops not entered West Beirut, a situation of total chaos and battles between various combat forces would have developed, and the number of victims among the civilian population would have been far greater than it ultimately was. The Israeli military force was the only real force nearby which could take control over West Beirut so as to maintain the peace and prevent a resumption of hostile actions between various militias and communities. The Lebanese Army could have performed a function in the refugee camps, but it did not then have the power to enforce order in all of West Beirut. Under these circumstances it could be assumed that were I.D.F. forces not to enter West Beirut, various atrocities would be perpetrated there in the absence of any real authority; and it may be that world public opinion might then have placed responsibility on Israel for having refrained from action.

The demand made in Israel to have the Phalangists take part in the fighting was a general and understandable one; and political, and to some extent military, reasons existed for such participation. The general question of relations with the Phalangists and cooperation with them is a saliently political one, regarding which there may be legitimate differences of opinion and outlook. We do not find it justified to assert that the decision on this participation was unwarranted or that it should not have been made.

It is a different question whether the decision to have the Phalangists enter the camps was justified in the circumstances that were created.

In our view, everyone who had anything to do with events in Lebanon should have felt apprehension about a massacre in the camps, if armed Phalangist forces were to be moved into them without the I.D.F. exercising concrete and effective supervision and scrutiny of them. All those concerned were well aware that combat morality among the various combatant groups in Lebanon differs from the norm in the I.D.F., that the combatants in Lebanon belittle the value of human life far beyond what is necessary and accepted in wars between civilized peoples, and that various atrocities against the noncombatant population had been widespread in Lebanon since 1975. It was well known that the Phalangists harbor deep enmity for the Palestinians, viewing them as the source of all the troubles that afflicted Lebanon during the years of the civil war.

The decision on the entry of the Phalangists into the refugee camps was taken on Wednesday (9.15.82) in the morning. The Prime Minister was not then informed of the decision. The Prime Minister heard about the decision, together with all the other ministers, in the course of a report made by the Chief of Staff at the Cabinet session on Thursday (9.16.82) when the Phalangists were already in the camps. Thereafter, no report was made to the Prime Minister regarding the excesses of the Phalangists in the camps, and the Prime Minister learned about the events in the camps from a BBC broadcast on Saturday (9.18.82). With regard to the following recommendations concerning a group of men who hold senior positions in the Government and the Israel Defense Forces, we have taken into account [the fact] that each one of these men has to his credit [the performance of] many public or military services rendered with sacrifice and devotion on behalf of the State of Israel. If nevertheless we have reached the conclusion that it is incumbent upon us to recommend certain measures against some of these men, it is out of the recognition that the gravity of the matter and its implications for the underpinnings of public morality in the State of Israel call for such measures.

The Prime Minister, the Foreign Minister, and the Head of the Mossad

We have heretofore established the facts and conclusions with regard to the responsibility of the Prime Minister, the Foreign Minister, and the head of the Mossad. In view of what we have determined with regard to the extent of the responsibility of each of them, we are of the opinion that it is sufficient to determine responsibility and there is no need for any further recommendations.

The Minister of Defense, Mr. Ariel Sharon

We have found, as has been detailed in this report, that the Minister of Defense bears personal responsibility. In our opinion, it is fitting that the Minister of Defense draw the appropriate personal conclusions arising out of the defects revealed with regard to the manner in which he discharged the duties of his office—and if necessary, that the Prime Minister consider whether he should exercise his authority under Section 21-A(a) of the Basic Law of the Government, according to which "the Prime Minister may, after informing the Cabinet of his intention to do so, remove a minister from office."

The Chief of Staff, Lt.-Gen. Rafael Eitan

We have arrived at grave conclusions with regard to the acts and omissions of the Chief of Staff, Lt.-Gen. Rafael Eitan. The Chief of Staff is about to complete his term of service in April, 1983. Taking into account the fact that an extension of his term is not under consideration, there is no [practical] significance to a recommendation with regard to his continuing in office as Chief of Staff, and therefore we have resolved that it is sufficient to determine responsibility without making any further recommendation.

Closing Remarks

In the witnesses' testimony and in various documents, stress is laid on the difference between the usual battle ethics of the I.D.F. and the battle ethics of the bloody clashes and combat actions among the various ethnic groups, militias, and fighting forces in Lebanon. The difference is considerable. In the war the I.D.F. waged in Lebanon, many civilians were injured and much loss of life was caused, despite the effort the I.D.F. and its soldiers made not to harm civilians. On more than one occasion, this effort caused I.D.F. troops additional casualties. During the months of the war, I.D.F. soldiers witnessed many sights of killing, destruction, and ruin. From their reactions (about which we have heard) to acts of brutality against civilians, it would appear that despite the terrible sights and experiences of the war and despite the soldier's obligation to behave as a fighter with a certain degree of callousness, I.D.F. soldiers did not lose their sensitivity to atrocities that were perpetrated on noncombatants either out of cruelty or to give vent to vengeful feelings. It is regrettable that the reaction by I.D.F. soldiers to such deeds was not always forceful enough to bring a halt to the despicable acts. It seems to us that the I.D.F. should continue to foster the consciousness of basic moral obligations which must be kept even in war conditions, without prejudicing the I.D.F.'s combat ability. The circumstances of combat require the combatants to be tough—which means to give priority to sticking to the objective and being willing to make sacrifices—in order to attain the objectives assigned to them, even under the most difficult conditions. But the end never justifies the means, and basic ethical and human values must be maintained in the use of arms.

Among the responses to the commission from the public, there were those who expressed dissatisfaction with the holding of an inquiry on a subject not directly related to Israel's responsibility. The argument was advanced that in previous instances of massacre in Lebanon, when the lives of many more people were taken than those of the victims who fell in Sabra and Shatilla, world opinion was not shocked and no inquiry commissions were established. We cannot justify this approach to the issue of holding an inquiry, and not only for the formal reason that it was not we who decided to hold the inquiry, but rather the Israeli Government resolved thereon. The main purpose of the inquiry was to bring to light all the important facts relating to the perpetration of the atrocities; it therefore has importance from the perspective of Israel's moral fortitude and its functioning as a democratic state that scrupulously maintains the fundamental principles of the civilized world.

We do not deceive ourselves that the results of this inquiry will convince or satisfy those who have prejudices or selective consciences, but this inquiry was not intended for such people. We have striven and have spared no effort to arrive at the truth, and we hope that all persons of good will who will examine the issue without prejudice will be convinced that the inquiry was conducted without any bias.

PLO Chairman Yasir Arafat: Speech to Palestine National Council (February 14, 1983)

To those against whom war is made, permission is given to fight because they have been wronged; and truly God is most powerful for their aid. They are those who have been expelled from their homes in defiance of right, for no cause except that they say, our Lord is God.

. . . The struggle will continue until the aims of our Arab nation are achieved. It will continue so that its domain is protected. . . . This commitment is based on deep conviction and pan-Arab nobility and the revolutionary reunion which has driven and still drives our revolution in strength and gallantry to continue our militant road and our armed revolution until we achieve our firm national rights which are not open to disposal, including our right to return, self-determination, and the establishment of our independent Palestinian state on our national Palestinian soil and until our fluttering banners are raised over holy Jerusalem, capital of our independent Palestine, and over its minarets and over its churches and over its walls. . . .

. . . Our Palestine National Council is convened in these difficult and grave times through which our Arab nation is passing in the shadow of the fateful challenges to our civilization as an Arab nation, and not only as a Palestinian revolution and not as joint Lebanese-Palestinian forces, but as an Arab nation. It is a question of to be or not to be, in the shadow of the U.S. imperialist-Zionist onslaught whose nails and daggers pierce the body of our Arab nation. It tries to spread its domination over our entire Arab nation; it tries to control our resources and tries to annex us to its sphere of influence.

Here is the importance of the posture, the mighty posture displayed by the joint Lebanese-Palestinian forces, and the steadfastness which they continue to display in their confrontation of this all-embracing American onslaught. In the same vein is the unequalled steadfastness of our joint forces and our militant masses in face of the Israeli military operation, fully paid for by the United States, by the racist military clique in the Zionist invasion army, in order to commit these barbarous crimes against the ebanese and Palestinian people. These crimes reached the summit of barbarism and savagery as is clear from the massacres and butchery in the Sabra and Shatila camps after the gallant fighters of the joint forces had destroyed the arrogance and pomposity of the enemy and turned him back.

Your fighters stood fast in Beirut. Your masses stood fast in Beirut. Your nation stood fast by you in Beirut in the face of untiring attempts by the United States to exhaust the entire Arab nation and kneel before the aggressors, the Zionist invaders and the U.S. imperialists. In 88 days the pride of our contemporary Arab history . . . stood fast in the face of technological supremacy and challenged the superior and sophisticated U.S. military machine. . . .

Brother President, friends, brothers, by standing fast in Beirut a new phase began in our Arab history. Israel's blitzkrieg wars and its imaginary blitzkrieg victories have ended forever in the face of your mujahidin brothers who have died as martyrs for the existence and dignity of our entire Arab nation. Yes, brother, this is a new phase of our history which we enter with strength and belief after the volcano which erupted in Beirut. It is a phase of Arab transformation with all its values and concepts and with all that surrounds it. Imperialist balances and everything based upon them will not live long after the eruption of this volcano in Beirut.

Beirut has exposed everything. It has exposed everything and nothing is left to our Arab nation except the deep roots produced by the free and noble people and the mujahidin.

. . . For 18 years we have been fighting for our homeland through our Palestinian revolution. Through this last stage of our people's long march, that hard and difficult march, we have learned from our own experiences and those of revolutionaries all over the world that national unity is the guarantee for victory and that the independence of national decision away from all pressures and negative influences is the basis for crystallizing the national personality of our Palestinian people. We have learned that armed struggle complements political struggle in all fields. Despite all obstacles and hurdles and mines—and they are many—we have been guided by these bases. . . . The rallying of our Palestinian people, internally and externally, around their armed revolution is the protective shield on which the arrows of the aggressors and the plotters always fall. Whatever the disguises and however hard the parties to the plot hide or try to hide themselves, and whatever forms the plot takes, after the Beirut events, they cannot deceive our people and our masses. No force, however great and however much acclaimed, can transform the giant who stood fast in Beirut and Lebanon into a dwarf. . . . Our decision comes from our people and from the barrel of a gun. . . . These firm national objectives, which are not open to modification, are that our people shall live in their homeland, free and as masters.

I beg our Arab nation, and after the Arab summit in Fez approved the Arab peace plan and after the visit paid by the Arab seven-member committee to world capitals, I say to every Arab that peace is the peace of the strong. I say peace is the peace of the strong and there is no peace for the weak or for those who bend. Therefore, our Arab nation is called upon to mobilize all its energies and all its military and political and mass capabilities to confront the challenges of destiny imposed on us at this critical stage which our Arab nation is now experiencing. . . .

We do not fight for the sake of fighting and do not reject for the sake of rejection. We fight for the freedom of our homeland and people and for the sake of our dignity. We reject anything—far or near—that harms our firm national rights. On this basis, the PLO asks all countries in the world to stand beside it in the face of the Israeli aggression, stressing that there is no solution to the Middle East crisis, no peace, no stability, and no security in this region, without the firm national rights of the Palestinian people.

While clinging to the rifle and shouldering it in the face of aggression in order to defend our people and land and for the sake of our freedom, we are advocates of peace based on meeting our people's firm national rights, including the right to return, the right to self-determination, and the right to establish an independent Palestinian state on their natural soil with holy Jerusalem as the capital. Our choice to establish a confederation with our people in fraternal Jordan is a genuine expression of our conviction in comprehensive Arab unity. . . .

Our national unity is the basis of our action and movement, our independent national decision is our guide, which cannot be faulted in defining the target. It is inevitable that our National Council should lay down political programs which fulfill the requirements and reply to the challenges. Ultimately, it is inevitable that we should have absolute unity founded on a democratic and creative basis. Let thousands of flowers blossom but in the gardens of the revolution!

. . . The PLO, entering its new revolutionary stage with firm and strong steps, turns to all those who are free and honorable in the world to stand beside our people's just struggle. At the same time, when the revolution starts this new and regenerated uprising, it reaches out—as it has always done—to all the world's liberation movements. It clasps their hands and stands beside them with all our capabilities.

We turn, with greetings and appreciation, to our friends in the socialist bloc led by the friendly Soviet Union, to the nonaligned countries, to the Islamic countries, to the African countries, and to the friendly countries for their support and their stand beside the just and legitimate struggle of our people. We greet and stand beside the free and revolutionary people in South Africa and Namibia and warmly greet all the free and revolutionary people in America, Latin America, and Asia. We are with every struggler against imperialism, Zionism, and colonialism. We are with every struggler against oppression and racial discrimination and for a better life and future.

Palestine National Council: Political Statement (February 22, 1983)*

On the Palestinian Level:

1. Palestinian National Unity:

The battle of steadfastness of heroism in Lebanon and Beirut epitomizes Palestinian national unity in its best form. The PNC affirms continued adherence to independent Palestinian decisionmaking, its protection, and the resisting of all pressures from whatever source to detract from this independence.

Palestinian Armed Struggle:

The PNC affirms the need to develop and escalate the armed struggle against the Zionist enemy. It affirms the right of the Palestine revolution forces to carry out military action against the Zionist enemy from all Arab fronts. . . .

2. The Occupied Homeland:

The PNC salutes our steadfast masses in the occupied territory in the face of the occupation, colonization, and uprooting. It also salutes their comprehensive national unity and their complete rallying around the PLO, the sole legitimate representative of the Palestinian people, both internally and externally. The PNC condemns and denounces all the suspect Israeli and American attempts to strike at Palestinian national unanimity and calls on the masses of our people to resist them. . . .

The National Council salutes the steadfastness of its people living in the areas occupied in 1948 and is proud of their struggle, in the face of racist Zionism, to assert their national identity, it being an indivisible part of the Palestinian people. The council asserts the need to provide all the means of backing for them so as to consolidate their unity and that of their national forces.

Our Dispersed People:

The PNC asserts the need to mobilize the resources of our people wherever they reside outside our occupied land and to consolidate their rallying around the PLO as the sole legitimate representative of our people. It recommends to the Executive Committee to work to preserve the social and

---

*PNC Political Statement issued in Algiers at the concluding session.

economic interests of Palestinians and to defend their gained rights and their basic liberties and security.

Contacts with Jewish Forces:

. . . The PNC calls on the Executive Committee to study movement within this framework in line with the interest of the cause of Palestine and the Palestinian national interest.

On the Arab Level:

Deepening cohesion between the Palestinian revolution and the Arab national liberation movement throughout the Arab homeland so as to effectively stand up to the imperialist and Zionist plots and liquidation plans, particularly the Camp David accords and the Reagan plan, and also ending the Zionist occupation of the occupied Arab land, relations between the PLO and the Arab states shall be based on the following:

A. Commitment to the causes of the Arab struggle, first and foremost the cause of and struggle for Palestine.

B. Adherence to the rights of the Palestinian people, including their right to return, self-determination, and the establishment of their own independent state under the leadership of the PLO—rights that were confirmed by the resolutions of the Arab summit conferences.

C. Adherence to the question of sole representation and national unity and respect for national and independent Palestinian decisionmaking.

D. Rejection of all schemes aimed at harming the right of the PLO to be the sole representative of the Palestinian people through any formula such as assigning powers, acting on its behalf, or sharing its right to representation.

The Arab Peace Plan:

The PNC considers the Fez summit resolutions as the minimum for political moves by the Arab states, moves which must complement military action with all its requirements for adjusting the balance of forces in favor of the struggle and Palestinian and Arab rights. The council, in understanding these resolutions, affirms it is not in conflict with the commitment to the political program and the resolutions of the National Council.

Jordan:

Emphasizing the special and distinctive relations linking the Jordanian and Palestinian peoples and the need for action to develop them in harmony with the national interest of the two peoples and the Arab nation, and in order to realize the rights [as] the sole legitimate representative of the Palestinian people, both inside and outside the occupied land, the PNC deems that future relations with Jordan should be founded on the basis of a confederation between two independent states.

Lebanon:

1. Deepening relations with the Lebanese people and their National Forces and extending support and backing to them in their valiant struggle to resist the Zionist occupation and its instruments.

2. At the forefront of the current missions of the Palestinian revolution will be participation with the Lebanese masses and their National and democratic forces in the fight against and the ending of Zionist occupation.

Relations with Syria:

Relations with sister Syria are based on the resolutions of successive PNC sessions which confirm the importance of the strategic relationship between the PLO and Syria in the service of the nationalist and pan-Arab interests of struggle and in order to confront the imperialist and the Zionist enemy, in light of the PLO's and Syria's constituting the vanguard in the face of the common danger.

The Steadfastness and Confrontation Front:

The PNC entrusts the PLO Executive Committee to have talks with the sides of the pan-Arab Steadfastness and Confrontation Front to discuss how it should be revived anew on sound, clear, and effective foundations, working from the premise that the front was not at the level of the tasks requested of it during the Zionist invasion of Lebanon.

Egypt:

The PNC confirms its rejection of the Camp David accords and the autonomy and civil administrations plans linked to them. The council calls on the Executive Committee to develop PLO relations with Egyptian nationalist, democratic, and popular forces struggling against moves to normalize relations with the Zionist enemy in all their forms.

Reagan's Plan:

Reagan's plan, in style and content, does not respect the established national rights of the Palestinian people since it denies the right of return and self-determination and the setting up of the independent

Palestinian state and also the PLO—the sole legitimate representative of the Palestinian people—and since it contradicts international legality. Therefore, the PNC rejects the considering of this plan as a sound basis for the just and lasting solution of the cause of the Palestine and the Arab-Zionist conflict.

Barry Rubin: United It Stalls, The PLO (March 21, 1983)*

Can the Palestine Liberation Organization develop a pragmatic diplomatic policy following its crushing military defeat in Lebanon? The sixteenth Palestine National Council meeting in Algiers last month disappointed those who had hoped so. Although the PLO may be adapting to the new situation, its pace is so slow and hesitant as to throw into doubt its ability or desire to negotiate before it is too late. With Israel daily tightening its hold on the West Bank, and Jordan considering initiatives in its own right, the Palestinian leadership seems again to have thrown away opportunities, and to be further than ever from its goals.

In recent years the PLO has gradually shifted away from its old, unattainable objective of destroying Israel and replacing it with an Arab state. The PLO now proposes a Palestinian state in the West Bank and Gaza, though it persists in refusing to recognize Israel. Last September President Reagan suggested a plan for a Jordanian-Palestinian federation with a large measure of Palestinian self-rule. Since then the Administration has hoped—and a large segment of the media has grasped at straws to imply—that the PLO might accept this proposal. The current government of Israel opposes all these ideas, but President Reagan hopes to induce Prime Minister Begin to change his policy.

The result of the convention of the PNC, the PLO's parliamentary body, was both a clear-cut political victory for Yasir Arafat and a reminder of just how narrow is his room for maneuvering. The Reagan plan was rejected, and resolutions discouraged a proposed negotiating tactic to circumvent PLO-Israel mutual nonrecognition—the creation of a joint Jordanian-Palestinian delegation in which West Bank independents would represent the Palestinians, but take orders from PLO headquarters.

Observers have often overestimated Arafat's courage or ability to change PLO policy, given the caution bred by his constant struggle to mollify PLO factions and Arab regimes that use money, competing militancy, and even assassination in attempts to control the organization. Arafat's own weapons include cagey ambiguity in political positions and consensus

---

*The article was published in *The New Republic,* March 21, 1983, reprinted by permission of *The New Republic,* © 1983, The New Republic, Inc.

above all. These tools have served him well, but also block any moving away of the PLO from a maximalist and rejectionist stance.

There are thus two ironies in the PLO's politics. First, the very policies that preserve the organization also freeze it into self-defeating negativism. Second, Arafat's strong position as leader is best protected by minimum use of his potential leverage. With time no longer on its side and deprived of its base in Lebanon, the PLO may well find such flaws fatal.

PNC Chairman Khalid Fahum and Arafat themselves sketched out, in milder but equally determined language, the reasons why the Reagan plan was unacceptable to the PLO. They scorned it for disregarding refugees' "right to return" to what is now Israel, self-determination, establishment of an independent Palestinian state with East Jerusalem as its capital, and recognition of the PLO as its sole legitimate representative. These four points all concern major issues; the Reagan plan cannot be adjusted to meet them.

Thus the PNC political resolution rejected the U.S. proposal in fairly clear language: "Reagan's plan, in style and content, does not respect the established national rights of the Palestinian people. . . . Therefore, the PNC rejects the considering of this plan as a sound basis for the just and lasting solution of the cause of the Palestine and the Arab-Zionist conflict." Fatah leader Salah Khalif said in his speech—not quoted in the U.S. press—"I have not heard a single Palestinian say that he accepted Reagan's plan."

The PNC took a more favorable position on a confederation with Jordan, which Arafat even defended as an expression of Arab unity. But there was no question of accepting domination from Amman. The resolution called for "a confederation between two independent states." Our people shall live in their homeland, free and as masters," said Arafat. The PNC was suspicious about allowing the Jordanians or West Bank mayors to negotiate with the Americans or Israelis. The PNC final resolution called for: "Rejection of all schemes aimed at harming the right of the PLO to be the sole representative of the Palestinian people through any formula such as assigning powers, acting on its behalf, or sharing its right of representation."

If the PLO does change course, the Arab regimes will have a great deal to do with it. Despite Syria's negativism, the majority of involved Arab governments favor some accommodation with Israel for the first time in history. Egypt, Jordan, Saudi Arabia, and even Iraq take this "moderate" position. The Saudis, however, have been quite timid, even by their standards, in trying to influence the PLO. Their Fez summit resolution, endorsed by the PNC meeting, called for an independent Palestinian state in all the occupied territories with only the vaguest offer of recognition for Israel. So far they have not offered much encouragement to Reagan's efforts.

The PLO's anti-Americanism remains particularly strident. As PLO spokesmen repeatedly stress, the United States is Israel's main supplier of arms and aid, while U.S. guarantees to protect Palestinians in West Beirut proved worthless in the Sabra and Shatila massacres. Arafat's closing oration portrayed Lebanon as a PLO victory, and blamed setbacks on United States involvement. Washington received no thanks for saving the PLO leadership and troops in West Beirut from complete destruction. In Arafat's words, Ambassador Philip Habib and President Reagan decided "to destroy the foundation of the PLO." He even claimed, "The U.S. 6th fleet . . . was the one that carried out the Israeli military landings. . . . " But things in Lebanon were not really so bad: "They speak of this invincible [Israeli] army. But, brothers, by God I have not found it invincible. . . . I wish all my nation was with me to see the feebleness of this army."

Such rhetoric is aimed at building morale, but it also shapes thinking. PLO strategy is still tied to positions based on illusion or internal politics. Reporters and commentators like to suggest that the failure of the PLO or of Jordan to accept the Reagan plan results from a lack of U.S. credibility and an inability to bring rapid Israeli withdrawal from Lebanon or a settlement freeze on the West Bank. But aside from the misdeeds of the Begin government, the fact is that the PLO has principled differences with American objectives and the Jordanians are hard put to join in without an Arab mandate or PLO acquiescence. The PLO only offers Hussein the unattractive option of risking a great deal to establish a PLO-led state. Unless the Arab side can produce a better offer, Washington will have no incentive to put pressure on Israel, and the creeping annexation of the West Bank will continue. . . .

Jordanian Government: Refusal to Join the Reagan Peace Initiative (April 10, 1983)

Since the Israeli aggression of June 1967, and through our awareness of the dangers and repercussions of the occupation, Jordan has accepted the political option as one of the basic options that may lead to the recovery of Arab territories occupied through military aggression. Consequently, Jordan accepted Security Council Resolution 242 of November 22, 1967. When the October 1973 war happened, it underlined the importance of continuing work on the political option while in the same time building our intrinsic strength. This war brought about Security Council Resolution 338, which put a stop to military operations and implicitly reemphasized Security Council Resolution 242.

Based on Security Council Resolution 338, disengagement agreements were concluded between Israel on the one hand and Egypt and Syria on the other. This process completed the Arab circle immediately concerned with the recovery of the occupied lands through political means.

On this basis, Jordan, in cooperation with the Arab states, developed and adopted the concept of forming a unified Arab delegation that would attend an international conference for the purpose of achieving a just and comprehensive peace settlement to the Middle East problem.

In 1974, the Rabat Arab summit conference designated the Palestine Liberation Organization as the sole legitimate representative of the Palestinian people. Jordan went along with the Arab consensus and has been committed to that decision ever since.

The ensuing period saw the disjointment of Arab unity as evidenced by the Camp David accords. Further disintegration in the overall Arab position followed even between those directly affected by the Israeli occupation. All the while, Jordan kept sounding the alarm on the one hand and persevering in its course of action on the other.

Jordan warned repeatedly of the dangers inherent in the continuation of the no-war, no-peace situation, and of the exploitation by Israel of this situation to perpetuate the status quo by creating new facts in the occupied Arab territories, to realize its declared ambitions, aided by Arab disunity and by its military superiority.

Jordan has also cautioned against letting time pass by without concluding a just and comprehensive peace settlement because time was, and still is, essential to Israel's aim of creating new facts and bringing about a fait accompli.

Sixteen years have passed since the occupation, during which Israel established 146 colonies in the West Bank alone and has illegally expropriated more than 50 percent of that land.

Even today, Israel forges ahead in defiance of all international conventions and of the United Nations resolutions with a systematic policy of evacuating the inhabitants of the West Bank to change the demographic composition of the occupied Arab territories, thus realizing its designs to establish the Zionist state on the whole of Palestine.

From the early days of the occupation, and through awareness of the Zionist aims, Jordan made all these warnings and undertook the task of implementing all policies that may support the steadfastness of the Palestinian people and help them stay in their national soil.

With this objective in mind, we worked incessantly on all levels. Domestically, Jordan provides markets for the industrial and agricultural products of the West Bank and Gaza, and continues to extend support to the existing institutions in the West Bank. Also, we continue to attach great importance to building our intrinsic defense capability in cooperation with other Arab states, through the conviction held by all our nation of the great danger posed by Zionist ambitions, which threaten the Arab world and its future generations.

Within this context Jordan paid particular attention to building its armed forces, looked for new sources of arms within the available financial means and enacted the military service law to mobilize all its national resources for self-defense and for the defense of the Arab world because Jordan remains, by virtue of its geographic location, a constant target for Israeli aggression and the first line of defense on the east flank of the Arab world.

On the Arab level, Jordan sought to provide financial support for the steadfastness of the Palestinian people and formed a joint Jordanian Palestinian committee, which continues to implement the policy of supporting our people in the occupied lands.

On the international level, Jordan worked to mobilize world opinion to bring pressure to bear on Israel, and in the United Nations, through cooperation with Arab and friendly countries, Jordan succeeded in passing resolutions condemning, isolating and putting pressure on Israel.

All the while, Israel continued with its expansionist colonization program, evicting the Arab inhabitants of Palestine and replacing them by Jewish immigrants. We strive to confront this program, which stands to affect Jordan more than any other country and which threatens Jordan's identity and national security.

In June 1982, Israel launched its aggression on Lebanon, which resulted in that country joining the list of occupied Arab territories. Lebanon was not excluded from the ambitions of Israel, which had already annexed Jerusalem and the Golan Heights, and which works for the de facto annexation of the West Bank and Gaza.

Last September, the United States President Ronald Reagan declared his peace initiative to solve the Middle East crisis, and shortly after, the Fez Arab summit conference resumed its proceedings where the Arab peace plan was formulated. It is evident that both peace proposals were inspired by the provisions of Security Council Resolution 242 and by the United Nations resolutions that followed.

Jordan, as well as other Arab and friendly countries, found that the Reagan plan lacked some principles of the Fez peace plan, but in the same time it contained a number of positive elements. Given the realities of the international situation, on the other hand, the Arab peace plan lacked the mechanism that would enable it to make effective progress. The Reagan plan presented the vehicle that could propel the Fez peace plan forward, and Jordan proceeded to explore this possibility.

We believe, and continue to believe, that this aim can be achieved through an agreement between Jordan and the Palestine Liberation Organization on the establishment of a confederal relationship that would govern and regulate the future of the Jordanian and Palestinian peoples. This relationship would express itself, from the moment of its inception, through joint Jordanian-Palestinian action based on the Fez peace plan, Security

Council Resolution 242 and the principles of the Reagan initiative. In addition, such a confederal relationship would be sought if only through the faith Arabs have in their joint destiny and in recognition of the bonds that have linked the people of Jordan and Palestine throughout history.

These concepts, and the ideas and assessments that follow from them, formed the subject of intensive discussions held over several meetings between His Majesty King Hussein and PLO chairman Yasir Arafat, as well as between the Government of Jordan and a number of senior members of the PLO, within the framework of a higher committee which was formed for this purpose and which held its deliberations over the five months between October 1982 and the recent convention of the Palestinian National Council in 1982. In addition, a number of prominent Palestinians inside and outside the occupied territories took part in the discussions.

These deliberations resulted in the irrefutable conclusion that Jordan and Palestine are joined by undeniable objective considerations reflected by the common threat against them which united their interests and their goals. There also resulted a joint conviction in the soundness of our approach, and we agreed to form a joint stand capable of pursuing political action, which, with Arab support, can take advantage of the available opportunity to liberate our people, land and, foremost of which, Arab Jerusalem.

Then, upon the request of Mr. Yasir Arafat, we waited to see the results of the Palestinian National Council meeting, where Mr. Arafat assured us he would act to secure the support of the council for the envisaged joint political action, on whose basic elements we agreed, pending their developments in the Palestinian National Council by declaring confederate-union relationship between Jordan and Palestine.

In our latest meeting with Mr. Arafat, held in Amman between March 31 and April 5, we conducted a joint assessment of the realities of the Palestine problem in general, and in particular of the dilemma facing the Palestinian people under occupation.

We also discussed political action in accordance with the Arab and international peace plans, including President Reagan's peace initiative, bearing in mind the resolutions of the PNC. We held intensive talks on the principles and methods, and we reemphasized the importance of a confederal relationship between Jordan and Palestine as being a practical conceptualization from which to work for the implementation of this initiative. We agreed to work together in this delicate and crucial time to form a united Arab stand that would enable us to deal with the practical aspects of these initiatives, in the hope of achieving a just, permanent and comprehensive solution to the Middle East problem, especially the Palestinian problem.

We also agreed to start immediately joint political action on the Arab level to secure Arab support that would contribute enormously to the realization of the common goal of liberating the lands and people under occupation, thus fulfilling our duty to work in all possible ways and to take advantage of every possible opportunity to achieve our aims.

Together with PLO chairman Yasir Arafat, we laid the final draft of our agreement, which required us and Mr. Arafat to make immediate contacts with Arab leaders to inform them of its contents, seeking their blessing and support for the agreement.

The PLO executive committee deliberated on this issue in the course of several meetings, and finally Mr. Arafat decided to discuss the agreement with other PLO leaders outside Jordan and return to Amman after two days to conclude the joint steps necessary for the implementation of the agreement.

Five days later, a delegate was sent by the PLO executive committee chairman to Amman, to convey to us new ideas and to propose a new course of action that differed from our agreement and that did not give priority to saving the land, thus sending us back to where we were in October 1982.

In the light of this, it became evident that we cannot proceed with the course of political action which we had planned together and to which we had agreed in principle and in details, in answer to our historic responsibility to take the opportunities made available by Arab and international initiatives and save our land and people.

In view of the results of the efforts we made with the PLO, and in compliance with the 1974 Rabat summit resolution, and through the strict observance of the independence of the Palestinian decision, we respect the decision of the PLO, it being the sole legitimate representative of the Palestinian people. Accordingly, we leave it to the PLO and the Palestinian people to choose the ways and means for the salvation of themselves and their land, and for the realization of their declared aims in the manner they see fit.

We in Jordan, having refused from the beginning to negotiate on behalf of the Palestinians, will neither act separately nor in lieu of anybody in Middle East peace negotiations.

Jordan will work as a member of the Arab League, in compliance with its resolutions to support the PLO within our capabilities, and in compliance with the requirements of our national security.

Being consistent with ourselves, and faithful to our principles, Arab Jerusalem and holy shrines, we shall continue to provide support for our brothers in the occupied Palestinian territories and make our pledge to them before the Almighty that we shall remain their faithful brothers and side with them in their ordeal.

As for us in Jordan, we are directly affected by the results of the continued occupation of the West Bank and the Gaza Strip through the accelerating colonization program and through the economic pressures systematically being brought on the Palestinian people to force them out of their land.

In the light of these facts, and in the no-war and no-peace situation that prevails, we find ourselves more concerned than anybody else to confront the de facto annexation of the West Bank and Gaza Strip, which forces us to take all steps necessary to safeguard our national security in all its dimensions. Both Jordanians and Palestinians shall remain one family that cares for its national unity to the same extent that it cares to stay on this beloved Arab land.

May God assist us in our aspirations.

Lebanon and Israel: Truce Agreement (May 17, 1983)*

The government of the Republic of Lebanon and the government of the State of Israel, . . .

Having agreed to declare the termination of the state of war between them,

Desiring to ensure lasting security for both their states and to avoid threats and the use of force between them,

Desiring to establish their mutual relations in the manner provided for in this agreement, . . .

Have agreed to the following provisions:

ARTICLE 1

1. The parties agree and undertake to respect the sovereignty, political independence and territorial integrity of each other. They consider the existing international boundary between Lebanon and Israel inviolable.

2. The parties confirm that the state of war between Lebanon and Israel has been terminated and no longer exists.

3. Taking into account the provisions of paragraphs 1 and 2, Israel undertakes to withdraw all its armed forces from Lebanon in accordance with the annex of the present agreement.

ARTICLE 2

The parties, being guided by the principles of the Charter of the United Nations and of international law, undertake to settle their disputes by peaceful means in such a manner as to promote international peace and security and justice.

---

*Composed of the breakaway force of Major Saad Haddad.

ARTICLE 3

In order to provide maximum security for Lebanon and Israel, the parties agree to establish and implement security arrangements, including the creation of a security region, as provided for in the annex of the present agreement.

ARTICLE 4

1. The territory of each party will not be used as a base for hostile or terrorist activity against the other party, its territory, or its people.

2. Each party will prevent the existence or organization of irregular forces, armed bands, organizations, bases, offices or infrastructure, the aims and purposes of which include incursions or any act of terrorism into the territory of the other party, or any other activity aimed at threatening or endangering the security of the other party and safety of its people. To this end, all agreements and arrangements enabling the presence and functioning on the territory of either party of elements hostile to the other party are null and void.

3. Without prejudice to the inherent right of self-defense in accordance with international law, each party will refrain:

A. From organizing, instigating, assisting, or participating in threats or acts of belligerency, subversion, or incitement or any aggression directed against the other party, its population or property, both within its territory and originating therefrom, or in the territory of the other party.

B. From using the territory of the other party for conducting a military attack against the territory of a third state.

C. From intervening in the internal or external affairs of the other party.

4. Each party undertakes to ensure that preventive action and due proceedings will be taken against persons or organizations perpetrating acts in violation of this article.

ARTICLE 5

Consistent with the termination of the state of war and within the framework of their constitutional provisions, the parties will abstain from any form of hostile propaganda against each other.

ARTICLE 6

Each party will prevent entry into, deployment in, or passage through its territory, its air space and, subject to the right of innocent passage in accordance with international law, its territorial sea, by military forces, armament, or military equipment of any state hostile to the other party.

ARTICLE 7

Except as provided in the present agreement, nothing will preclude the deployment on Lebanese territory of international forces requested and accepted by the government of Lebanon to assist in maintaining its authority. New contributors to such forces shall be selected from among states having diplomatic relations with both parties to the present agreement.

ARTICLE 8

1. A. Upon entry into force of the present agreement, a Joint Liaison Committee will be established by the parties, in which the United States of America will be a participant, and will commence its functions. . . .

B. The Joint Liaison Committee will address itself on a continuing basis to the development of mutual relations between Lebanon and Israel, *inter alia* the regulation of the movement of goods, products and persons, communications, etc. . . .

2. During the six-month period after the withdrawal of all Israeli armed forces from Lebanon in accordance with Article 1 of the present agreement and the simultaneous restoration of Lebanese government authority along the international boundary between Lebanon and Israel, and in the light of the termination of the state of war, the parties shall initiate, within the Joint Liaison Committee, *bona fide* negotiations in order to conclude agreements on the movement of goods, products and persons and their implementation on a nondiscriminatory basis. . . .

ANNEX
SECURITY ARRANGEMENTS

A. A security region [in southern Lebanon] in which the government of Lebanon undertakes to implement the security arrangements agreed upon in this annex is hereby established. . . .

The Lebanese authorities will enforce special security measures aimed at detecting and preventing hostile activities as well as the introduction into or movement through the security region of unauthorized armed men or military equipment. . . .

B. Lebanese Police . . . may be stationed in the security region without restrictions as to their numbers. These forces and elements will be equipped only with personal and light automatic weapons. . . .

C. Two Lebanese Army brigades may be stationed in the security region. One will be the Lebanese Army territorial brigade. . . . The other will be a regular Lebanese Army brigade. . . .

D. The existing local units will be integrated as such into the Lebanese Army, in conformity with Lebanese Army regulations. . . .

Said Musa: Interview on Internal Dissent (May 26, 1983)*

. . . *Fatah*'s leadership knows that the Palestinian cause is not an issue of an officer or a group of officers, or an issue of a military group of elements in the arena of conflict in Al-Biqa' rebelling against military orders. Ours is a cry for correcting a mistaken political action that had begun to develop and emerge more clearly following our departure from Beirut. Frankly, there is a political conflict within *Fatah* that has been going on for years. This conflict has developed into a broad current that believes in political concepts that are committed to *Fatah*'s statutes and political program. . . .

Following our freeze in Beirut, several positive questions evolved. And these should have given us the incentive to stiffen our political stands in order to confront the U.S. imperialist plan and in order for this steadfastness not to become a catalyst for implementing the U.S. plot and program. Following the battle of Beirut, we should have also submitted a struggle plan that commits the Palestinian revolution to confront the U.S. plan on Lebanon's territory by virtue of the fact of the existing occupation and as a field of struggle through alliance with the nationalist movement and the honorable forces who are determined to continue the fight. However, this leadership went to Fez, and we consider that the Fez plan is actually Fahd's plan which stems from Camp David and from UN Resolution 242 despite the inclusion of certain points which at first glance appear positive, such as demanding the establishment of a Palestinian state, the return of refugees, regaining Jerusalem, and eliminating the settlements. But we wonder who is capable of translating this program or that plan. Are Arab summits capable of doing such a thing?

And I answer: No, because from our experience in Lebanon no one moved to provide Beirut's children with a single drink of water. We realize that the establishment of the Palestinian state and the return of the refugees is an issue that requires several wars. When the United States and Israel feel that their interests in the region are threatened, it is only at that moment that our voice as a Palestinian revolution will be heard. Then, the Arab countries can impose their plans, although they are supposed to be on the line of confrontation and in the middle of the conflict and not in a position to make deficient plans. Had these plans been offered by friends or allies or other parties, they could have been accepted, but not from the Arab countries because this is not what is expected of them. However, despite all this we say that whatever the matters may be, there is supposed to be a Palestinian option when there is a state of inability to implement these

*Excerpts from an interview by *Al-Watan* (Kuwait) with Said Musa (Abu Musa), of the anti-Arafat revolt in the PLO.

plans. Our Palestinian option since 1965 has been the option of armed struggle. However, the Palestinian leadership accepted the Arab option and dropped the option of armed struggle. . . .

And as for the Reagan plan, it was proposed on the day on which the last batch left Beirut. We heard the clauses of the plan when we were at sea. Its discussion in the *Fatah* movement began; we discussed its positive and negative sides. Through a simple political reading of the plan we find that it denies the existence of the Palestinian people and not only the Palestinian question. It also says no to the Palestinian state, no to the PLO, no to Jerusalem and its return, and yes to the settlements and to changing the borders. Despite all this, some voices within *Fatah* said there were positive points in the plan—that it recognized for the first time that the West Bank and Gaza Strip were under occupation. Is there anything new in this? Is there any justice in this? . . .

After the Reagan plan we plunged into a new whirlpool, the plan for a confederation with Jordan. We began to discuss the details before the state had been established—instead of first establishing the state and then discussing the confederation, which would be a direct result of establishing the state. Without going into all the details of this matter, I say that so far no clear decision has been made on this matter. We have not closed the door on it; it remains unresolved. There should be clear agreement that talks on a confederation are to be held after the establishment of an independent state. . . .

It is not a question of numbers. If it had been so I would have addressed an appeal to all our *fedayeen* and they would all have joined us. We are an indivisible part of *Fatah*. We are the conscience of *Fatah* who have raised their voice and thought aloud, and express the broad faithful base. . . . Therefore, it is necessary to stop and examine what we have achieved. What has this revolution achieved? Is it capable of shouldering the responsibility in confronting these big plans in light of its current reality or should it rearrange itself in a proper manner so that it can confront the coming stage? We say that the . . . National Council when it said yes to many of the political issues is neither a revolutionary nor a clear act. Political clarity is the major base. We understand that in the stages of retreat revolutionary movements adhere more closely to principles and bases.

What should I say to my father who fought in 1936 before the occupation of Palestine and the establishment of the Israeli state? What should I say to those who fought during these years to prevent the establishment of such a state? Are we fighting in order to recognize Israel? This is not reasonable, not reasonable and strange. These issues should be reexplained and corrected. Lastly, is it fair that the Central Committee issues decisions to put us under the command of the commander in chief together with Abu Hajim and Al-Haj Isma'il? Is it fair that it issues decisions to freeze our activity? . . .

Khalid al-Hasan: On the Dissident Rebellion (May 27, 1983)*

. . . Frankly and without exaggerating or underestimating what has been described as a rebellion, mutiny, or split within the *Fatah* movement, we ask: What did really happen, what were its causes, and what repercussions is it likely to have?

Answer: The group involved, including Abu Musa, Qadri, Abu Salih, and others, originally held political views characterized by rejection of the Fez resolutions and other policies. . . . This group, even before Fez, adopted certain political attitudes based on an idealistic rejection of everything or on conditional approval of many things. For example, Brother Abu Salih said that he would support the Fez summit [plan] if it included setting up a Palestinian state and would oppose it if it did not. So, fundamentally, this group has been adopting a certain political attitude for years. We could say that this attitude began to crystallize after the September events, and it has been applied to Jordan and to the recent Fez resolutions. The group included Naji 'Allush, Abu Nidal, and many others. Some of them left the movement and some continued to work within its framework. Even at the recent PNC meetings in Algiers, Abu Musa adopted certain attitudes which stemmed from a comprehensive theory which everyone wished it was possible to implement, even partially. The reason behind the declarations made in Al-Biqa' was certain military organizational decisions made with the approval of the Military Council. They believe that some of these decisions should not have been made, especially the appointment of Abu Hajim as officer in charge of the Al-Biqa' area and Al-Haj Isma'il as officer in charge of the north. Their position developed into a mutiny in the sense that they rejected the new military organizational steps. It was not made on political grounds, although the political aspect later came into it.

As far as discipline is concerned, this matter is serious. Democracy may be required on such matters, but at the level of the Central Committee, not the level of military officers. . . . That is the declared principle of the matter. The other fact is that, very regrettably, Brother Abu Salih overstepped the mark in *Fatah*'s democracy when he extended a hand for funds from a source outside *Fatah* and cooperated with two Arab states. . . . That money was paid before the PNC conference and it was agreed that five issues would be used to cause a split. They included rejection of the Fez summit, rejection of agreement with Jordan, and rejection of the Reagan initiative. There was no problem there, but to give the dissension a national character

*Excerpts from an Interview with Fatah Central committee member Khalid al-Hasan in *Al-Hawadith* (London).

they were to use these points and, in the event of failure, they were to raise the issue of the dialogue with Israeli democratic forces. . . .

Another issue had also been raised to cause disunity. That issue was the differences with Syria. . . . I believe that national unity is not unity of the organizations but rather unity of the people behind the leadership and the goals. This does in fact exist because the Palestinian people are united regardless of whether there is a leadership or not. It was the Palestinian people, not an organization or a leadership, who foiled the settlement plots in the fifties. This matter is too great to be undermined. The people are much more united than the organizations. The organizational numbers do not broadly and accurately reflect the real attitudes of the people. One organization or another may have some support here or there, but Abu 'Ammar's leadership is unquestionable and *Fatah*'s political line represents the mainstream. That is why I consider agreement among the organizations to be agreement among the instruments of work—and not national unity because unity is there. Our problem with the unity of the instruments is that some of them are not Palestinian, even though they are identified as such, because they do not take Palestinian orders. National unity or front relations under the National Charter, and in fact under any front regulations anywhere in the world, means agreement on a minimum plan of action with the minority accepting the views of the majority. It is very regrettable that the minority does not accept the opinion of the majority. . . .

King Hussein of Jordan: Speech to the Palestine National Council (November 22, 1984)

Brothers and sisters, the convocation of your council in Amman represents the unity of your will and the will of your people in the occupied homeland and elsewhere. It also represents the cohesion of the efforts and wills of two fraternal peoples, which have been demonstrated by their confrontation of the common challenge and danger. It is a natural return to what should and would continue to be. The Jordanian people have, more than and before anyone else, shared with the Palestinian people their sorrows, sufferings, and sacrifices and also carried with them their hope, determination, and resolution to regain their legitimate national rights on the land of Palestine. Jordan, and with it my family, have more than and before anyone else stood by the Palestinian people in confronting the Zionist danger in the early days just as we are confronting it today while it is at its peak. We are not saying this in order to outbid, maneuver, or seek praise, but to affirm an objective fact that has been made evident by actual participation in facing the common danger. . . .

I personally opened the first session of the PNC on May 28, 1964 in

Jerusalem. I told your brother representatives of the Palestinian people in that meeting, among other things, that your convention represented a unique, historic event in the entire history of the disaster. I said that it was the first meeting of the heroic struggler Palestinian people despite all the designs to scatter them to all the four corners of the globe. So you can see from the historical facts that we—as a Hashemite family and a country—have never disavowed, God forbid, the Palestinian identity and aspirations or tried to dominate Palestine and its people.

Brothers and sisters: Following Israel's occupation of the West Bank in 1967, we in Jordan and our brothers in Egypt devoted our efforts to achieving two objectives: first, rebuilding our Armed Forces which were destroyed by the war; and second, working politically for the sake of regaining the territory that was occupied by force. We cooperated with sister Egypt in issuing UN Security Council Resolution 242 which formed the basis of our political actions. The late leader President Jamal 'Abd al-Nasir urged me during our first meeting after the June war to do anything and exert every effort to regain the occupied territory. I did not need anyone to tell me to do that. By God, I have never showed cowardice and will not show cowardice when it comes to defending Jerusalem and Palestine. I have done all I could with God's help. I have spared no effort and pursued every course.

In the meantime, however, the PLO emerged as an effective party in the Palestinian arena. Its growth produced a natural tendency among the Palestinian people to manifest their national identity on their land. Their effort to regain the occupied territory was marred by doubts about the possibility of establishing their national authority on the land of Palestine once Jordan had regained the West Bank. A clear Palestinian trend evolved to relieve Jordan of this responsibility. This trend was nourished by an illusion that the restoration of the territory was around the corner. It was also nourished by all those who considered the Jordanian-Palestinian relationship as committing all Arabs equally to the fate of the Palestine question and to the duty of saving it, and, consequently, everyone who preferred to place the direct and primary responsibility on the Palestinian people, thereby placing the Arabs in the second rank. [sentence as heard] This was what we resisted as much as we could and considered as a relinquishment of a sacred duty at a time which did not permit such a thing. One could have imagined such a trend, if it had come before the entry of the Arab armies into the land of Palestine in 1984. But for this trend to come after all of the Palestinian territory had fallen to Israel, then it cannot but be construed as an attempt to let down the Palestinian people.

As a result of this, a secret conflict began between Jordan and the PLO. Because of the confused vision, this conflict led to a collision that resulted in regrettable incidents. We in Jordan faced a dilemma. If we capitulated to this approach, we would have improved the position of the enemy, who employed any pretext, however flimsy, in order to deceive world public opinion, strengthen its false claims, and annex the occupied territory. If we had continued our political work as we began it following the 1967 war, without paying attention to our Palestinian brothers' fear, our brothers' doubts concerning our aims would have increased. . . .

Brother and sister PNC members, the years go by, more than 17 years have passed, and the West Bank and Gaza Strip are still under occupation. The enemy continues to plan and implement. Jerusalem remains steadfast, patiently moaning whenever a Jewish castle is built upon it. The Al-Aqsa Mosque and the Dome of the Rock are being threatened with demolition and destruction and declared open to everyone by the delusions and thoughts of the fanatic. The holy and cherished land is being swallowed up every day through confiscation and appropriation or on the pretext of security and planning. The national character of the Palestinian economy is obliterated after becoming part of Israel's economy.

The future is just like the present, shrouded with doubt, anxiety, and uncertainty. As for the kinfolk, may God help them; despite every form of institutionalized pressure against them they remain steadfast. How long will we watch as the enemy exploits the time by greedily swallowing up another part of the remaining land every day while we wildly and thoughtlessly waste the time in arguments and vituperation. How long shall we heed those among us who say: Leave it for future generations. Is this not a clear abdication of responsibility? Is each generation not responsible for the era in which it lives? What makes them believe that the circumstances of future generations will be more conducive to achieving what they are avoiding to achieve? Can they stop time and progress for the enemy, and keep time and progress moving for themselves? What wisdom or morality is there in leaving future generations a heavy legacy more likely to grow than recede? Will the Palestinians, who are lost and suffering in the occupied land, accept such arguments when they know better than anyone else the meaning of giving the enemy more time and the impact of this on their existence and future?

The least that can be said of this argument is that it is escape from responsibility. The least that can be said of the advocates of this argument is that they are those who believe that the world is synonymous with their own existence. This is not the way the world works. Each generation has its own responsibilities. The justifications of the existence of any ruler depends on the wise and courageous fulfillment of his responsibilities and the sincere and vigorous implementation of his duties. If time has any meaning it is in properly using it and not in suspending it. . . .

Perhaps you share with me the view that the picture is bleak, and, consequently, requires a new outlook and course. The new outlook must necessarily start with defining future action. Perhaps the natural starting point is to emphasize the special relationship between Jordan and Palestine—a relationship forged by the purely objective factors of history, geography, and demography which have placed the two fraternal countries and peoples since the turn of the century in the same boat of suffering, hope, interest, harm, history, and destiny.

The special quality of our relationship is not a whimsical description that we have given to ourselves, but is a scientific fact which has made the Palestine question a central daily concern in our life and the pivot of our defense, foreign, and development policies. If the Palestine question is one of the first priorities of our brothers' foreign and defense policies, to us and to you the Palestine question is our top priority. Therefore, Palestine was never a political tool which we used to achieve our national or selfish aims. Palestine embraces Jerusalem, the cradle of Jesus, may peace be upon him; the place from which Muhammad, may peace be upon him, ascended to the heavens; the playground of Al-Shafi'i [founder of one of the four orthodox Islamic schools]; the battlefield of Salah al-Din; the resting place of Husayn ibn 'Ali; and the martyrs' ladder to glory. It is also the invaders' threshold to Jordan, just as Jordan is the conquest [fath] gateway to Palestine. Defending Palestine means defending Jordan and vice versa. This is the special relationship which has governed and will continue to govern our Jordanian policy. This is the distinguished policy which the enemy has tried to break up in order to achieve his designs. Some people tried to distort this relationship by giving it attributions it does not possess and that serve the tendency of one wing to dominate another.

This is the relationship within whose framework the first Palestinian conference was held 20 years ago and under whose canopy your council's 17th session is held in Amman today. This special relationship, brothers and sisters, encourages me to speak to you frankly. In order to eliminate any doubts about what I am going to say, I would like to affirm right from the beginning that nothing has been proposed to us in the efforts for a political settlement of the Palestine question. What I will say represents our opinion on the basis of our experience and analysis of the reality, possibilities, and circumstances. I am encouraged in this by the fact that you, too, are experienced people.

I hope that my speech will not be understood to mean that I, God forbid, will interfere in your affairs. The decision is yours. Jordan will not speak on your behalf, although it will remain fully ready to face its fate with you, because our fate is interconnected with yours. If the future seems too dark, as I have said, it is because one of the causes that made it so is that the special relationship binding Jordan with Palestine was eliminated from the Arab and Palestinian action. This has diverted the general effort from its correct course and has expended it in the wrong field.

If matters seem difficult now, it is because of the time we have wasted in differences, disputes, and vituperation. Although we have exerted sincere efforts to rectify matters, the Arab reality prevented us from achieving our aims. We thus enabled the enemy to exploit time in order to change reality on the land of Palestine in its favor. We failed to combine the justice of our cause with our financial and strategic resources in order to curtail the effect of the absolute U.S. support for Israel. We made our regional concerns dominate our pan-Arab responsibilities. All this has led to our present disunity and squandering of our resources.

Brothers and sisters, because we will be harmed the most as a result of the continuation of the present state of affairs, we shoulder the greatest responsibility for rectifying this situation. So far, we have succeeded in foiling attempts to paralyze our role and yours. Experience taught us to renounce immobility, which is no less harmful to your role than the attempts to undermine your legitimacy. Dealing with an issue like the Palestinian issue demands a great amount of flexibility and dynamism that is capable of adapting to circumstances and facing the challenges with the aim of reaching a clear aim—namely, liberating the land and freeing our kinfolk and sacred places. It is stagnation to be satisfied with saying: I want this or nothing. Even adopted positions need revision from time to time and a new look in light of changes and developments.

Dealing with the world necessitates permanent flexibility and dynamism. Let us remember that slogans will not be raised if they become chains which tie those who raise them and prevent them from moving and maneuvering. Principles would not have been embraced had they not been beacons of light to lead the way during work.

Let us be frank with you, brothers, about your sacred cause, which concerns us as much as it concerns you, and the ramifications of which affect us as much as they affect you. In general, the international stand believes that it is possible to regain the occupied territory through a Jordanian-Palestinian formula which gives both sides certain commitments the world considers essential for achieving a just and balanced peaceful settlement. If you are convinced of this option, notwithstanding our bonds as to families as well as the common destiny and common cause that unite us, we are ready to proceed together on this path and to present the world with a joint initiative for which we will rally backing and support.

However, if you believe that the PLO can proceed alone, we will tell you to go ahead, with God's blessing. And we will give you our backing and support. The decision will be first and last yours. And we will respect it, whatever the case. This is because it stems from your esteemed council, which represents the Palestinian people. [applause]

Brothers, if you decide to take the first option—the Jordanian-Palestinian option—then allow me to present to you our idea of how to get out of the present situation and into the arena of effective, rejuvenating action. The existing conditions in the Palestinian, Arab, and international arenas prompt us to adhere to Security Council Resolution 242 as a basis for a just, peaceful settlement. The principle of territory in exchange for peace is our guideline for any initiative we may present to the world. This principle is not a precondition, but the framework through which the negotiations would be held. Therefore, it is not negotiable.

The negotiations which we consider essential within the framework of an international conference for peace would revolve around the ways and means and the adequate guarantees for achieving the principle of territory in exchange for peace. As for the international conference, it shall be held under the supervision of the United Nations with the participation of the permanent member states of the UN Security Council and all the parties to the dispute. The PLO shall attend it on an equal basis with the other parties, because it is the party authorized to speak about the most serious and important dimension in the Middle East crisis—namely, the Palestinian dimension.

As for the question of regulating the Jordanian-Palestinian relationship, it is the primary responsibility of the Jordanian and Palestinian peoples. No one has the right to determine this relationship on their behalf or to interfere in it, be he enemy, brother, or friend. This is because this would be a detraction from Jordan's sovereignty and open interference in the Palestinian people's right to determine their own destiny. Furthermore, involving this issue in the efforts to regain the territory would enable the enemy to obstruct any serious effort to save this territory from the existing occupation and gradual annexation.

In our opinion, these general outlines can form the overall framework for a Jordanian-Palestinian initiative which we can present to the Arabs so that they can support it under the Fez summit resolutions. Then, we and our Arab brothers would present it to the world, giving it all our support. This would continue until the circle of support for this initiative expands to include the entire influential world. This is our own idea. We do not oblige you to accept it, and we do not impose it on you. The decision is yours, and the responsibility is yours. We are only presenting it to you for the viewpoint of our participation with you in the two states of security and danger, and benefit and harm. We are ready to do anything for the sake of your cause—which is our cause—except concluding a unilateral peace.. . .

Jordan-PLO: Joint Communiqué (February 11, 1985)

Emanating from the spirit of the Fez summit resolution, approved by Arab states, and from United Nations resolutions relating to the Palestinian question,

In Accordance with international legitimacy, and

Deriving from a common understanding on the establishment of a special relations between the Jordan and Palestinian peoples,

The Government of the Hashemite Kingdom of Jordan and the Palestine Liberation Organization have agreed to move together toward the achievement of a peaceful and just settlement of the Middle East crisis and the termination of Israeli occupation of the Occupied Arab Territories, including Jerusalem, on the basis of the following principles:

1. Total withdrawal from the territories occupied in 1967 for comprehensive peace as established in United Nations and Security Council resolutions.

2. Right of self-determination for the Palestinian people:

Palestinians will exercise their inalienable right of self-determination when Jordanians and Palestinians will be able to do so within the context of the formation of the proposed confederated Arab States of Jordan and Palestine.

3. Resolution of the problem of the Palestinian refugees in accordance with United Nations resolutions.

4. Resolution of the Palestinian question in all its aspects.

5. And on these bases, peace negotiations will be conducted under the auspices of an International Conference in which the five permanent members of the Security Council and all the parties to the conflict will participate, including the Palestine Liberation Organization, the sole legitimate representative of the Palestinian people, within a joint delegation (joint Jordanian-Palestinian delegation).

King Hussein of Jordan: Ending the Jordan-PLO Initiative (February 19, 1986)

In the past few days, Amman has been the center of attention for much of the world, drawing media people and journalists from all quarters. News coming out of Amman was reported on the front pages of world newspapers and occupied a prominent place in agency reports and news bulletins. But the content of these reports reflected mere speculation or expectations on the possible outcome of discussions held with us and with leading officials of our government by the Palestinian leadership while in Amman. Amman, along with concerned world circles, went through a period of expectation, but we preferred not to issue any declarations or communiqués until matters under intensive discussion, whether between us and the Palestinian leadership or among its own members, became clearer.

Now that a measure of clarity has become apparent, I consider it my duty as well as my responsibility towards you, being in the thick of events and in the eye of the hurricane, to appraise you of the most recent phase of political endeavor with regard to our foremost cause: Palestine, its land, its holy places, its people, and their identity. . . .

For a variety of reasons, there is a need for a thorough airing of this question. The shared destiny of Jordan and Palestine requires it. So does the time factor, in view of the fact that the West Bank, the Gaza Strip, and the Golan Heights have been occupied for close to 19 years. The situation is further aggravated by prolonged failure to find a solution by the growing threat to the Palestinians' true identity resulting from the gradual displacement of the Palestinian people. One also has to consider ramifications with regard to Jordan, the region, and the world. In the final analysis, a people without its land is nothing more than a disjointed community.

Identity without a homeland is but a reservoir of sad memories. Our aim should be the land itself. Now, as at the turn of the century, the Palestinian cause is inseparable from the Palestinian land, which today is the occupied West Bank and Gaza Strip. This being the case, the Palestinian people, steadfast on Palestinian territory, are our primary concern. For a different reason, they are also the primary concern of the enemy. They are the major obstacle to the advancement of expansionist Zionist programs. Their legitimate resistance poses an overt challenge to claims by Israel and its friends and supporters, be they states or communities, that Israel is a free and democratic society, and places it as an open test within the sight and hearing of the world.

Brothers and sisters, if most of us have so far failed to grasp these rudimentary facts, the enemy has not. It is on the basis of these facts that Israel's aims and policies were formulated from the very beginning: to occupy the land of Palestine and expand the territory of Israel. The Israeli leadership's motives were two-fold. Expanding Israeli territory, through occupation of Palestinian and other neighboring Arab lands, would fulfill one of Zionism's cherished aims while at the same time achieving, from their point of view, a security need arising more from psychological considerations than from those of space, distance, and topography, which Israel attempts to highlight whenever the security issue is raised. . . .

While it is true that Lebanon, Syria, Jordan, and Egypt share a geographical contiguity with Israel, Jordan is the prime target of Israel's step-by-step policy. Thus, the distinctive relationship between Jordan and Palestine is not a question we take lightly. We bring it up in order to draw attention to objective facts and conditions which the enemy attempts to exploit for the purpose of implementing its expansionist policy at the expense of the Jordanian and Palestinian peoples. The common links between the two peoples are not only a matter of shared history, experience, culture, economy, and social structure, but also a question of destiny. They represent a confluence of interest as well as of harm. . . .

The Palestinian people in the occupied territories are weak without the

PLO. By the same token, the Palestinian people and the PLO, which represents its aspirations, hopes and interests, are weaker without Jordan, and all three are weaker without the Arab nation as a whole. This has been our vision in all our endeavors. The components are as clear as the sun; and the position we occupy vis-à-vis the Palestinian issue on the one hand, and the Arab world on the other, provides us with no alternative vision. In Jordan we stand in two circles at once: one representing the Palestine tragedy and the other residing in national commitment. This has dictated our position on direct confrontation with Israel on military and political levels.

One facet of our conflict with Israel perhaps lies in the fact that Israel is attempting to dislodge us from the circle of national commitment into the sphere of tragedy. On our part, we are resisting this with all our might, attempting in the process to endow the circle of commitment with content which is both practical and effective. National commitment is not a one-way street, nor is it a passive or negative stance. Armed with true content, it leads to proper preparation and action. If national commitment is taken to mean a state of inaction in regard to declared positions and is characterized by fatalism, dependence, or expectancy of what lies in store, this would mean only one thing to us; acquiescence in the fait accompli as well as a willing acceptance of the loss of what remains of Palestinian land and of the resulting destructive consequences allowing greater room for expansionist Zionist designs.

It is for this reason, dear brothers, that Jordan had to act and must continue to act. We cannot possibly close down borders and deal with the issue as separate from us. Experience has shown that inaction leads to erosion in positions, as well as on the ground. The state of no war-no peace which has been imposed on us is a salient manifestation of this inaction. We must break out of its grasp. We must absolutely assert that the suffocation resulting from giving in to the state of no war-no peace is as reprehensible as the suicide arising from action leading to the relinquishing of rights. As we move towards peace, we reject the latter proposition as strongly as we do the former. . . .

The significance of setting up the PLO as a way station was that the Arab governments at the time wished to reaffirm that the Palestinian issue was an Arab issue while the Palestinian people had a say and a role to play in the struggle for liberation.

This decision represented the first turning point in the Arab position between 1947 and 1964. In other words, the PLO was established not with the purpose of giving the Palestinians an exclusive say, but to include the PLO, in its capacity as a representative of the Palestinian people, in Arab positions and action vis-à-vis the Palestine issue—as a means of keeping it alive. This was confirmed in the years immediately following the establishment of the PLO, when it had no significant weight in matters pertaining to the Palestine issue, since the Arab states continued to hold the reins and make decisions at will. The PLO itself was a tool used by this or that Arab state on the basis of its political positions, whether at the Arab or international levels. When the June war erupted, the PLO was still a form almost devoid of any real content.

But in the wake of the June war, Palestinian resistance to Israeli occupation experienced rapid growth, with the result that form and content became one and the PLO came to embody the resistance to occupation and the struggle for the rights of the Palestinian Arabs. Thus, the PLO rejected Security Council Resolution 242 because it dealt only with occupied Palestinian territory and not with the legitimate national rights of the Palestinian people. Because of our keen awareness of Israel's expansionist aims, it was natural that we should accord priority to restoring the territories occupied by Israel through war. Likewise, because of our sincere commitment to the restoration of the legitimate national rights of the Palestinians, we tried, along with Egypt, to persuade the PLO to separate the two objectives of our political action in the international arena. This separation would call for an attempt by the Arab states, whose territories had been occupied through war and were the subject of Resolution 242, to ensure Israeli withdrawal from these territories, while the PLO would continue to fulfill its role of representing the Palestinian people in their struggle for legitimate national rights above and beyond the mere withdrawal of Israel from the occupied territories.

The PLO, however, rejected this line of thinking, as it had rejected Resolution 242, and proceeded to make this dual rejection a basis for its political stand on the Arab and world scenes. It also became the basis of its dealings with Jordan in particular, on the grounds of the following suspicions. First: There was the probability that Jordan might succeed in restoring the West Bank by virtue of its good relations with the West, which had influence over Israel. Second: Jordan had territorial ambitions in the West Bank. Third: As long as the possibility of Jordan's restoration of the West Bank existed, who would guarantee that Jordan would relinquish the territory thus restored to the PLO?

It is to be noted from this position, which is based on suspicion, that, at the time, the PLO was not fully aware of a basic fact emphasized us and borne out by events, namely that Israel gave the utmost priority to territorial gain. It was also evident that the PLO based its dealings with Jordan on suspicion rather than trust. . . .

On November 22, 1984, I opened the 17th session of the PNC by delivering a speech which contained our assessment of prevailing Palestinian conditions and our conclusion that we needed to move politically outside the status quo of no peace-no war, which only helped to advance expansionist Zionist designs and posed serious dangers to the Palestinian issue, the Palestinian people, and Palestinian land, as well as a consequent threat to Jordan's national security. We proposed to the PNC members our view of future cooperation, should the PLO decide to work with Jordan to reach a joint Jordanian-Palestinian formula. . . .

In January 1985, we received the reply that the PLO Executive Committee had chosen to work with us on our proposal for joint political action. We started our consultations with Arafat's envoys on the third general outline—the Jordanian-Palestinian formula—since this formula constituted the base from which we were to move on the Arab and international arenas to convene an international peace conference.

In February 1985, Arafat, accompanied by other members of the Palestinian leadership, arrived in Amman. An expanded meeting was held in Al-Nadwah Palace which was concluded by the signing of the Jordanian-Palestinian agreement, known as the 11 February Accord. This accord incorporated the following principles:

1. Territory in return for peace as established in UN and Security Council resolutions.

2. The right of self-determination for the Palestinian people:

Palestinians will exercise their inalienable right of self-determination when it becomes possible to do so within the context of the formation of the proposed confederated Arab states of Jordan and Palestine.

3. Resolution of the problem of Palestinian refugees in accordance with UN resolutions.

4. Resolution of all aspects of the Palestine question.

5. On this basis, peace negotiations will be conducted under the auspices of an international conference in which the five permanent members of the Security Council and all parties involved in the conflict will participate, including the PLO, the sole legitimate representative of the Palestinian people, within a joint delegation—a joint Jordanian-Palestinian delegation. . . .

The accord became a mover for the peace process because of the principles it contained. These were:

1. The accord's affirmation of a peaceful resolution to the conflict in accordance with the UN Charter.

2. The accord's conformity with the principles of the Arab Peace Plan, derived from United Nations resolutions concerning the Arab-Israeli conflict in general and the Palestinian problem in particular.

3. The agreement between Jordan and the PLO, the sole legitimate representative of the Palestinian people, to form a confederation between Jordan and Palestine.

This last item, while it reflects the objective considerations which require close institutional links between Jordan and a free Palestine to mutual benefit of their peoples and the Arab nation at large, provides the key, or mechanism, to the peace process for two main reasons:

First, it justifies PLO participation in the proposed international conference within a joint Jordanian-Palestinian delegation. Since confederation is the ultimate objective, why not have the two parties concerned assume one of the confederation's functions before it is established as a reality on the ground, particularly since this function allows for the participation of the PLO in the international conference which in the past decade has posed one of the most difficult obstacles in convening an international peace conference?

Second, it lays the foundations for a responsible role for the PLO in realizing and safeguarding a just settlement through its links with Jordan, the sovereign state which enjoys credible international standing due to its serious and sincere efforts to achieve peace. . . .

Dear brethren, after signing the 11 February accord and the agreement of the PLO Executive Committee, which was empowered by the PNC to arrive at a joint formula with Jordan, we embarked with the Palestinian leadership upon drawing up a plan for our proposed action. Two objectives were defined for this purpose:

1. To rally international support for the convening of an international peace conference, to be attended by the five permanent members of the Security Council and all parties involved in the conflict. This conference would be convened under the auspices of the United Nations and called for by the UN secretary general.

2. To ensure that an invitation will be extended to the PLO, representing the Palestinian people, to attend the conference within a joint Jordanian-Palestinian delegation. . . .

We agree with the Palestinian leadership on the following procedures for joint action:

1. We asked the U.S. Administration to start a dialogue with a joint Jordanian-Palestinian delegation composed of Jordanian Government officials and members chosen by the PLO.

2. After this dialogue, the PLO would declare its acceptance of UN Security Council Resolutions 242 and 338.

3. If this took place, the United States would no longer be bound by its previous position not to conduct any talks with the PLO before the latter's acceptance of the two pertinent Security Council resolutions. Thus, the United States would recognize the PLO and a meeting between U.S. officials and members of the PLO could be held in Washington to discuss the issue of a peaceful settlement and relations between them would be normalized.

4. As a result of the normalization of U.S.-Palestinian relations a major political obstacle blocking the Arab Peace Plan, which gave an important role to the PLO, would have been removed. Arab efforts could then be channeled to pursue the efforts with the United States and other countries to convene an international peace conference.

After agreeing on this procedure with the Palestinian leadership, we accordingly contacted the officials in the U.S. Administration at the end of

March 1985 and presented them with the idea of meeting a joint delegation in preparation for the next two steps which would follow as a result of the meeting.

In early April 1985, we received the U.S. reply which, in principle, accepted this proposal provided that the Palestinian members of the joint delegation were not leading members of the PLO or any fedayeen organization.

We consulted with the Palestinian leadership, which provided us with the names of three candidates. The Americans refused them because they did not meet their criteria and asked that we provide them with the names of others who did.

In May 1985, we met with the U.S. secretary of state in Qaba, who reiterated the administration's position regarding the subject of the names. However, he did not exclude those who were members of the PNC.

The U.S. side expressed its government's doubts about the PLO's intentions and its government's fears that if the suggested meeting were to take place between a U.S. official and a joint Jordanian-Palestinian delegation—a meeting after that would not be followed by PLO's acceptance of Security Council Resolutions 242 and 338—the PLO would obtain a political weapon as a result of its member's meeting with an American official. The U.S. Government would then be left to face criticism and political troubles resulting from this in the U.S. arena. Thus, the serious political efforts would end at that point.

Our prime minister conveyed this recent U.S. stand to Yasir Arafat in a meeting held at the Prime Ministry on 18 May 1985. At that time, we were preparing for a visit to Washington. In order to remove the U.S. fears, the prime minister agreed with Yasir Arafat on the text of a press statement which we would make at the end of our talks with the U.S. President.

The statement which I made at the White House garden on 29 May 1985 says: I also asserted to President Reagan that, on the basis of the Jordanian agreement with the PLO signed on 11 February, as a result of the talks which I recently held with the PLO, and in view of our sincere desire to achieve peace, we are determined to negotiate to achieve a peaceful settlement within the framework of an international conference on the basis of the related UN resolutions, including Security Council Resolutions 242 and 338.

The U.S. officials affirmed, during my talks in Washington, their position regarding Palestinian participation in the joint delegation. They limited the number to four, two from the occupied territories and two from the outside. They requested that we provide them with these names in advance and as soon as possible so that the U.S. Administration could make its decision at the appropriate time.

Upon our return to Amman in June 1985, we conveyed to the Palestinian leadership our discussions in Washington. They in turn accepted this proposal and promised to provide us with the names of the candidates as soon as possible. We waited until 11 July 1985, when some names were provided to us. We were then told that a meeting of the PLO Executive Committee and the Fatah Central Committee had discussed this subject and had agreed upon the names of the candidates.

On 12 July 1985, we relayed a list of seven names to the U.S. Administration and waited for the administration to inform us of its approval of four of the names on that list. We agreed that no public announcement should be made on this issue. But a few days later, we were surprised when the world press began to discuss those names. Suddenly the issue turned into a U.S. political issue. The press began to discuss it and the Zionist lobby activated influential political institutions in opposition to it, culminating in pressure on the U.S. Administration to justify, defend, and finally retract its position. As a result, we received American approval of only two names from the list, instead of four: one from the West Bank and the other from the Gaza Strip. After inquiries we were told by U.S. officials that the administration was still not sure that the PLO would fulfill the second phase of the agreed scenario, namely, to accept Security Council Resolutions 242 and 338.

On 15 August 1985, a meeting was held at our prime minister's residence in Amman attended by the prime minister, the chief of the Royal Hashemite Court, the minister of the court and the foreign minister from the Jordanian side, and Yasir Arafat, accompanied by Khalil al-Wazir, Abd al-Razzaq al-Yahya and Muhammad Milhim from the Palestinian side. During that meeting, the prime minister again asked Arafat whether he was clear on the method of proceeding, particularly with regard to the second phase—PLO readiness to accept Security Council Resolutions 242 and 338. Arafat reaffirmed his acceptance of all steps and arrangements agreed upon between us, including the PLO's readiness to accept the abovementioned resolutions.

In light of Arafat's reply, we informed the U.S. Administration that the suspicions it had on this subject were not justified and that we were awaiting their positive reply concerning the date of the meeting between U.S. officials and a joint Jordanian-Palestinian delegation.

On 7 September 1985, we received the U.S. reply, which said that it was not possible to hold the meeting, thus terminating this scenario before the first step, originally expected in June, was taken. This came at the time we were preparing for a visit to New York to celebrate the 40th anniversary of the United Nations, and to Washington to discuss bilateral issues and the peace process with the U.S. Administration.

Assessment of the situation, prior to the visit, led us to believe that we could pursue our dialogue with the United States by concentrating this time on the second phase of the process, the international conference, since not much progress had been achieved on the issue of Palestinian represen-

tation. Our reading of the U.S. position led us to believe that further discussions could take place on that other issue, which was last discussed in
May 1985. I mentioned earlier that from the beginning our dialogue with
the Americans had dealt with two issues separately: Palestinian representation and the international conference, with emphasis on the subject of
Palestinian representation.

I will now turn to our efforts on the second issue, the convening of an
international conference.

In May 1985, in our discussions with the U.S. Administration in Washington, we raised the issue of convening such a conference because we
considered it to be the venue for all parties concerned to meet, including
the PLO. The U.S. position was a flat rejection of an international conference. Instead, the United States proposed that, after the PLO was brought
into the peace talks, a meeting should be set up between Israel and a joint
Jordanian-Palestinian delegation, under the auspices of the United States,
to be held in a U.S. city. Upon learning this, we decided to cut our visit
short and reaffirmed to them our definite and unequivocal rejection of
seeking a unilateral approach similar to that of Camp David in the negotiations.

The U.S. Administration then changed its position and proposed that
the talks could be held at the United Nations in Geneva. Once again, we informed the U.S. Administration that we rejected this proposal, like the one
before it, as we did not see that the problem was one of where the talks
should be held. We reiterated that Jordan's unwavering position was that it
sought to reach a comprehensive settlement through the convening of an
international conference attended by all the parties to the conflict, including the permanent members of the Security Council. As a result, the U.S.
Administration reconsidered its proposal and promised to seriously ponder
the issue of convening an international conference. We accepted this and
continued our discussions concerning the issue of Palestinian representation.

During talks in Washington in October 1985, we again raised the issue
of an international conference after having proposed it to the administration prior to our departure for the United States. Meetings were held
between Jordanian and U.S. officials in Washington. The United States
submitted a proposal concerning the international conference, which, after
careful examination, seemed to suggest a conference in name only. We on
the other hand insisted that the conference should have clear powers.

Among the various U.S. suggestions was the inclusion of the Soviet
Union in the conference only after it restored diplomatic relations with Israel, because this was an Israeli condition. We argued for the rejection of
this approach for the following reasons:

1. An international conference without the participation of the Soviet
Union would be a flawed conference.

2. If the reason to exclude the Soviet Union from the conference was that it had no diplomatic relations with Israel, which is a party to the conflict, the United States on its part does not recognize the PLO, which is equally a party to the conflict. Thus, in this regard, the Soviet Union and the United States were in the same position.

3. It would be futile to plan seriously to convene an international peace conference if any party had the right to place conditions on who could attend. This applies to the five permanent members of the Security Council as well as the parties involved in the conflict. Therefore, it was imperative that an invitation be extended to Syria, the PLO, and the Soviet Union to attend the conference if the peace process was to continue and the efforts for a just and comprehensive peace were to produce fruitful results.

After extensive discussions lasting three days, the United States accepted the following points which we proposed:

1. The UN secretary general would issue invitations to an international conference under UN auspices.

2. Invitations to attend the conference would be issued to the permanent members of the Security Council, including the Soviet Union, in addition to the parties involved in the conflict.

3. Security Council Resolutions 242 and 338 would form the basis for the international conference.

4. The Americans held to their position of requiring acceptance by the PLO of Security Council Resolutions 242 and 338, since these formed the basis for the convening of the international conference. We agreed to this understanding on the basis that Arafat had himself agreed to this last August.

We continued our intensive discussions with the U.S. Administration concerning the powers of the conference and we insisted that it should not be a conference in name only, but rather that it should be one that was effective and had a clear mandate. Despite prolonged discussions, we did not reach a final understanding with the U.S. Administration regarding this issue. We agreed to continue our discussions on this central point, and considered that what we had agreed upon constituted a basis from which to proceed. While we were still in Washington, the cycle of terrorism and counterterrorism began with the Larnaca incident, followed by the Israeli raid on the PLO headquarters in Tunis. This had a negative effect on the peace process and our efforts were once again jeopardized by fears and suspicions.

Upon our return to Amman in October 1985 we informed the Palestinian leadership of what we had accomplished during our talks in Washington. We informed them that the PLO would be required to accept Security Council Resolutions 242 and 338 in order to be invited to the international conference, to accept the principle of participating in negotiations with the Government of Israel as part of a joint Jordanian-Palestinian delegation within the context of the international conference, which would be convened to establish a comprehensive settlement, and to renounce terrorism. We also informed the Palestinian leadership that our discussions with the U.S. Administration regarding the question of the mandate of the conference were still inconclusive, and that further discussions would follow. We made it clear to the Palestinian leadership that a written statement of acceptance was needed from them, while leaving them to choose the appropriate time to announce that approval. The written acceptance was needed so that we could encourage the U.S. Administration to proceed earnestly to convene an international conference and to reassure them that the PLO was anxious to participate in the peace process. We had already made clear to the U.S. Administration that Jordan would not attend the conference unless invitations were extended to the PLO, sister Syria, and all other parties involved in the conflict, because we are after a comprehensive peace.

We also promised the Palestinian leadership that their acceptance would be kept confidential and shown only to the concerned U.S. officials until they themselves decided to announce it.

On 7 November 1985, after talks with President Husni Mubarak, Yasir Arafat issued a statement in Cairo denouncing terrorism in all its forms, irrespective of its source. The PLO Executive Committee then held a meeting in Baghdad, and as we were not officially notified of its decisions, we awaited Arafat's visit to Amman to hear from him, once again, the final position of the PLO on Security Council Resolution 242.

Meanwhile, I made a private visit to London on 7 January 1986 for medical reasons. While I was there, the assistant secretary of state for Near Eastern affairs [Richard Murphy] arrived in London with a U.S. delegation. He requested to see me to continue our discussions regarding the issue of the international conference. We held two rounds of talks in London, the first attended by the prime minister and the chief of the Royal Court on 18 January, and the second, on 20 January, attended by the chief of the Royal Court. Throughout both meetings the discussions focused on defining the mandate of the international conference and the participation of the PLO, as both issues had become interwoven as a result of progress achieved in the peace process. The American position had developed to the extent of agreeing to the right of the concerned parties to submit any disagreements between them to the conference. However, we could not reach full agreement regarding the role of the conference in settling disputes among the negotiating parties.

Concerning the issue of PLO participation in the conference, the American delegation reiterated its previous position requiring that the PLO should first accept Security Council Resolution 242 in order for the United States to start a dialogue with it. The United States did not commit itself to accepting the inviting of the PLO to the conference. Our reply was that we wanted the United States to agree to have the PLO invited to participate in the conference if it accepted Security Council Resolution 242. This point became the subject of extensive discussions, during which I asked for a clear American position to relay to the PLO. The American delegation agreed to take this up at the highest level on its return to Washington.

On 21 January 1986, I returned to Amman having achieved these results on the issues of an international conference and PLO participation. On 25 January 1986, our efforts bore fruit when I received a final reply from the U.S. Administration concerning PLO participation in the international conference. Their reply came in a written commitment which said:

When it is clearly on the public record that the PLO has accepted Resolutions 242 and 338, is prepared to negotiate peace with Israel, and has renounced terrorism, the United States accepts the fact that an invitation will be issued to the PLO to attend an international conference.

The United States would then start contacts with the Soviet Union with the purpose of having them participate, together with the other permanent members of the Security Council, in the international conference, which would be convened by the secretary general of the United Nations.

On that same day, Arafat arrived in Amman with a Palestinian leadership delegation. We held four extensive meetings in four days. I presided over three of these meetings. The discussion concentrated on the subject of American assurances and the PLO's position regarding those assurances. We assumed that the PLO would accept these since:

1. The assurances met the PLO's requirements.

2. They reflected a significant change in the U.S. position in favor of the PLO. The U.S. position regarding the PLO when we first started our intensive year-long dialogue had been that the United States would only enter into talks with the PLO after the latter's acceptance of Security Council Resolution 242. Now, by comparison, the present U.S. position was that it was willing to go one step beyond talking to the PLO by agreeing to have the PLO invited to the international conference.

But our brothers in the Palestinian leadership surprised us by refusing to accept Security Council Resolution 242 within this context, while acknowledging what they described as our "extraordinary effort," which had caused a significant change in the U.S. position, and which would not have been possible had it not been for the respect, credibility and trust which our country, Jordan, enjoyed in this world.

In spite of this, we continued our discussions with the PLO leadership in the hope of convincing them that their acceptance would cement a very important link in peace efforts leading to an international conference, which in the unanimous view of the Arabs and all peace-loving peoples constitutes the major venue for the establishment of a comprehensive, permanent, and just peace. It is towards the objective of convening such a conference that we have worked tirelessly for the past nine years, but to no avail. Now that the opportunity presented itself, we hoped that it would not be wasted like other missed opportunities if we were to remain faithful to our goals of saving our people and liberating our land and Holy Places.

The answer of the brothers in the Palestinian leadership was that they wanted an amendment to the proposed text in return for acceptance of Resolution 242. The amendment would require the addition of a statement indicating the agreement of the United States to the legitimate rights of the Palestinian people, including their right to self-determination within the context of a confederation between Jordan and Palestine, as stated in the February 11 accord. We reminded the Palestinian leadership that the subject of self-determination within the context of a confederation was a matter for Jordanians and Palestinians and that no other party had anything to do with it. Nothing was to be gained from the support of this or that state as long as we ourselves were committed to this text. The important thing was to achieve withdrawal first, then to proceed with what we had agreed upon. We reminded them that this had always been our position and that it had been clear all along, starting from my opening address in Amman at the 17th PNC session, in which I referred to the proposed Jordanian-Palestinian relationship, and continuing through all our discussions to date.

We also said to them that involving the United States, or others, in this matter meant that we were voluntarily opening the door to others to interfere in our common concerns and those of a people who had a sovereign right to their land and their own decisionmaking—unless they were dealing with us on a basis of lack of confidence. But despite this, our brothers in the Palestinian leadership insisted on their position. And despite the fact that the most recent American position had satisfied PLO demands, we agreed to resume contacts with officials in Washington through the American Embassy in Amman on the evening of 27 January 1986.

The American response was as follows:

1. The February 11 accord is a Jordanian-Palestinian accord which does not involve the United States.

2. The United States supports the legitimate rights of the Palestinian people as stated in the Reagan peace initiative.

3. The PLO, like any other party, has the right to propose anything it wishes, including the right of self-determination, at the international conference.

4. For all these reasons, the United States adheres to its position.

We relayed the American response to Yasir Arafat during an enlarged meeting at Al-Nawdah Palace on 28 January 1986, but he insisted that we try again. We indicated to him that we had gone as far as we could with the U.S. Administration at that stage, but he insisted. Thus, we got in touch once again and the reply was still that the United States adhered to its position.

On the morning of 29 January 1986, an enlarged meeting was held at the Prime Ministry and I headed the Jordanian side. I informed Yasir

Arafat and his party of the American position as reaffirmed to us once again. The meeting ended with a statement by Yasir Arafat saying that he needed to consult the Palestinian leadership. We asked him to give us the final answer on the PLO position with regard to Resolution 242 while he was still in Amman, although we had ascertained, only then, that the PLO's decision to reject Resolution 242 had been made during the meeting of the PLO leadership in Baghdad on 24 November 1985. We had not, however, officially been notified of that.

On the same evening, 29 January 1986, we received a suggestion from the U.S. Administration to the effect that the United States felt that since the PLO could not presently decide to accept Resolution 242, the PLO could wait until a time it considered appropriate. The United States felt that the peace process could still proceed with Palestinian participation from the occupied territories. The opportunity would remain available for the PLO to take part in the international conference the moment it accepted Resolution 242.

In our reply to the United States, we rejected this suggestion, indicating that this time the suggestion concerned not only the PLO but Jordan as well, since our unwavering position was: no separate settlement.

President Reagan wrote to me on 31 January 1986 explaining his inability to proceed in his efforts with Congress for the sale of sophisticated U.S. arms to Jordan. We had sought to acquire the arms since 1979 in the face of fierce Zionist opposition. I had received assurances from the President that our requirements would be met.

On the evening of the same day, the minister of the court informed Yasir Arafat of the latest American suggestion to proceed with the peace process without the PLO until it met the set conditions. He also informed him of our categorical refusal of this suggestion and apprised him of President Reagan's letter explaining his inability to meet Jordan's requirements.

On 5 February 1986, the American side presented a new text containing the approval by the United States to convene an international conference on the basis of Security Council Resolutions 242 and 338, including the realization of the legitimate rights of the Palestinian people. We met with Yasir Arafat on the same evening at Al-Nadwah Palace and we handed him the new American text. He promised to study it and at the same time gave us three differently worded texts which were the same in substance, reaffirming the same PLO position which we had heard from the start of this round of meetings.

On 6 February, Yasir Arafat had a meeting with our prime minister at his residence. The meeting was attended by the chief of the Royal Court and by 'Abd al-Razzaq al-Yahya and Hani al-Hasan from the Palestinian side. Arafat informed the prime minister that despite the positive development of the American position, recognition of the legitimate rights of the Palestinian people did not encompass the right to self-determination to which, the PLO insisted, the United States ought to give its prior approval.

On 7 February, Yasir Arafat left Amman still insisting on his position and on the reasons why the PLO was unable to accept Resolution 242. Hinging on this agreement, of course, was an immediate opening of a U.S.-Palestinian dialogue on the basis of which we would have continued our efforts to convene an international peace conference to which the PLO would be invited to participate as a representative of the Palestinian people.

Thus, another chapter came to an end in the search for peace. Another extremely important and significant round of Jordanian-Palestinian action was terminated—after a full year of serious and persistent efforts to transform the PLO role, referred to in the Arab Peace Plan, into a significant reality that would go beyond a mere statement of positions. It would have led to the presence and participation by the PLO in an international conference at the invitation of the UN secretary general, to represent its people and speak on their behalf with their adversary under the eyes of the world, side by side with the other parties concerned and the five permanent members of the Security Council. . . .

But if this phase of political action with the PLO has ended differently from what we had hoped for, the principles and tenets of the Jordanian-Palestinian accord will continue to embody the foundations governing relations between the Jordanian and Palestinian peoples with regard to equality of rights and obligations in facing our joint destiny.

Brothers, it has been my destiny to experience the various phases of the Palestine tragedy, as well as the results of the implementation of Zionist plans drawn up by forces which know what they want and carry out what they have planned, stage by stage. I have not seen or observed any emergence of the long-awaited Arab plan which would be capable of defending the most just cause of a brotherly and dear people who surely deserve better than their continued plight currently holds for them.

Israel and Jordan: "The London Document" (April 11, 1987)

Invitation by the UN Secretary General:

The UN Secretary General will send invitations to the five permanent members of the Security Council and to the parties involved in the Israeli-Arab conflict to negotiate an agreement by peaceful means based on UN resolutions 242 and 338 with the purpose of attaining comprehensive peace in the region and security for the countries in the area, and granting the Palestinian people their legitimate rights.

Decisions of the international conference:

The participants in the conference agree that the purpose of the negotiations is to attain by peaceful means an agreement about all aspects of the Palestinian problem. The conference invites the sides to set up regional bilateral committees to negotiate bilateral issues.

Nature of the agreement between Jordan and Israel: Israel and Jordan agree that:

1) the international conference will not impose a solution and will not veto any agreement reached by the sides;

2) the negotiations will be conducted in bilateral committees in a direct manner;

3) the Palestinian issue will be discussed in a meeting of the Jordanian, Palestinian, and Israeli delegations;

4) the representatives of the Palestinians will be included in the Jordanian-Palestinian delegation;

5) participation in the conference will be based on acceptance of UN resolutions 242 and 338 by the sides and the renunciation of violence and terror;

6) each committee will conduct negotiations independently;

7) other issues will be resolved through mutual agreement between Jordan and Israel.

This document of understanding is pending approval of the incumbent governments of Israel and Jordan. The content of this document will be presented and proposed to the United States.

PLO Executive Committee: On the Intifada (December 1987)

The PLO Executive Committee held a joint meeting with the Higher Committee for Occupied Homeland Affairs this morning to continue discussing the current giant uprising of our people in the occupied territory—the uprising which has entered its second week. The conferees expressed great pride in the struggle being waged by the Palestinian masses in the cities, villages, and camps of Gaza, the West Bank, and Jerusalem. The conferees also expressed their appreciation for the militant united stand exhibited by our masses in the Galilee, the Galilee Triangle, and the Negev.

This heroic steadfastness continues in the face of the Zionist and racist fascism and the tools of repression, killing, and crime used against our Palestinian people. This continuation proves that the iron will of the people to resist and confront occupation cannot soften or retreat until we extract our national inalienable rights, particularly our right to repatriation, self-determination, and an independent state under the leadership of the PLO, the sole, legitimate representative.

Our great masses in the occupied homeland today express, through their historical uprising, through the blood of the hundreds of martyrs and wounded, through their bravery, through the vigor of our prisoners, and through the struggle of all Palestinians—men, women, youths, and children—their determination to defeat the occupation forces and to expel them from the homeland regardless of the dear sacrifice and high price.

The entire world today looks with high appreciation and respect at this second uprising of all our people in our occupied territory for the sake of freedom, dignity, and independence. This uprising affirms that all fascist Zionist crimes, terrorism, and repression cannot save the criminal occupation from its inevitable crisis and fate; that is, their defeat and removal from the sacred Palestinian land, the land of fathers and grandfathers.

The names of our cities, villages, and camps have attracted the attention of all those who love and defend freedom in our Arab homeland and the entire world. These names have become symbols and titles of bravery and heroism to the entire world. Fascist crimes are perpetrated today by the Zionist occupation forces against women and children and against our defenseless people. The hospitals and places of worship are stormed. The camps and peaceful houses are treated as a battlefield. Thousands are arrested and put into mass detention camps. Children, old men, and women are killed. Tanks, planes, and combat units attack camp streets and homes. Herds of settlers are sent to practice bloody terrorism against our people. All these are crimes perpetrated by Zionist forces. These crimes disclose to human conscience and world public opinion the reality of this racist occupation and its objectives to annihilate our people, expel them from their homeland, and destroy all aspects of their existence.

The Zionist rulers today appear before the world as the inheritors of Nazism and fascism. However, crimes and terrorism cannot defeat our people's determination and steadfastness. Such crimes and terrorism will increase the Zionists' impasse and isolation and expose the collusion of their protectors in the U.S. Administration who have always mourned in defense of human rights. The Palestinian people are killed, tortured, and arrested. Their houses, hospitals, places of worship, and holy places are destroyed. Palestinian lands are seized. Palestinian water and food are stolen. Palestinian children are assassinated. While all this happens, those who claim to defend human rights do not even move to curb their tools and small agents, the Zionist rulers of Israel.

The powerful uprising has affirmed the strength and unity of all the factions of our people inside and outside occupied Palestine. It has also affirmed the people's rallying around the PLO and their strong rejection of all suspect calls and projects aimed at dominating our people, forging our people's will, and peddling the Zionist-U.S. plot to deprive them of their inalienable national rights. In their brave uprising, our people reject distributing roles, as well as any bribery for the so-called improvement of living, instead of ending the nightmare of the occupation and liberating the Al-Aqsa Mosque, from which the prophet descended and in which Christ was born.

By their brave uprising, our masses are defending the unity of all the Palestinian people inside and outside the homeland. They also defend the Palestinian people's unity of cause and rights and voice their adherence to every inch of their soil. They reject any attempt to divide the cause of the homeland, any encroachment on our established national rights, and adhere to the PLO's program for struggle to liberate the holy land. Our people also call for holding an international conference as urged by UN resolutions, the Arab summit, nonaligned countries, and socialist and friendly countries.

At these historical and fateful moments in our people's struggle, the PLO appeals to our Arab brothers—governments, parties, forces, institutions, and popular bodies—to increase their solidarity with and support for the uprising of our people. The pan-Arab responsibility and ties of brotherhood and solidarity are being shown today through support for our people by our brothers in our glorious Arab nation. This support asserts the unity of fate, struggle, and pan-Arab goals.

The PLO expresses its appreciation for the brotherly positions declared by many leaders, parties, and organizations. It also voices its pride in our nation's solidarity with and unity of position toward their brothers, the sons of the Palestinian people. The PLO also expresses its appreciation for the positions of friendly countries, forces, allies, all African countries, nonaligned countries, Islamic countries, socialist countries, friendly countries, and many friendly parties and forces. These groups hastened to announce their solidarity with the uprising of our people, their condemnation of the crimes of the Zionist occupiers, and their call for ending the Zionists' crimes against our people and terminating the nightmare of the Palestinian people's homeland.

Our people appreciate this support for their struggle against occupation. It encourages their struggle and reinforces their confidence in victory. The Security Council discussions express the depth and comprehensiveness of this support for our people's struggle, as well as the isolation, the disappointment, and the condemnation of the Zionist occupiers and their supporters. The PLO also voices appreciation for the positions of the democratic forces in Israel who voiced support for our people's uprising, condemned the crimes of the Zionist rulers and their fascist army, and called for ending the occupation of our homeland. The PLO calls on those who are concerned about just peace to take a responsible position required by these historic moments against the fascist military ruling clique whose hands are stained with the blood of our people and who ignore the facts of the age and the clear Palestinian reality.

O our glorious people inside and outside the occupied homeland. O you who continue steadfastness in Gaza, the West Bank, the Triangle, Galilee, and the Negev. O you who continue struggle in Lebanon's camps and in all areas of diaspora. Our people reiterate that the way of struggle and unity is the only way to victory, to regain their firm national rights, and to establish an independent state with Jerusalem as its capital. Your uprising in the occupied homeland enters human history because it expresses adherence to life, peace, freedom, honor, independence, the liberation of the homeland, and victory. Defenders of the Lebanon camps also support their brothers in the occupied homeland. They will retaliate for any Zionist aggression against southern Lebanon and the Palestinian camps side by side with the Lebanese national forces. They will stress with blood and martyrdom the people's unity, struggle, and steadfastness.

In light of this, the PLO Executive Committee has passed a series of resolutions and made arrangements to continue a large-scale movement in Arab and international arenas to provide all the requirements of steadfastness and resistance for our people in the occupied homeland. It has decided that the employees of the PLO and the revolution's institutions will donate a seven-day salary to the uprising. It also thanks President Saddam Husayn for his noble and brotherly initiative to support the families of the martyrs of the popular uprising and for calling on Palestinian and Arab masses to set up support committees. Glory to our people's struggle and righteous martyrs. Greetings to our imprisoned heroes. Victory for our great people's struggle. Revolution until victory.

West Bank-Gaza Palestinian Leaders: Fourteen Points (January 14, 1988)

During the past few weeks the Occupied Territories have witnessed a popular uprising against Israel's occupation and its oppressive measures. This uprising has so far resulted in the martyrdom of tens of our people, the wounding of hundreds more, and the imprisonment of thousands of unarmed civilians.

This uprising has come to further affirm our people's unbreakable commitment to its national aspirations. These aspirations include our people's firm national rights of self-determination and of the establishment of an independent state on our national soil under the leadership of the PLO, as our sole legitimate representative. The uprising also comes as further proof of our indefatigable spirit and our rejection of the sense of despair which has begun to creep to the minds of some Arab leaders who claim that the uprising is the result of despair.

The conclusion to be drawn from this uprising is that the present state of affairs in the Palestinian Occupied Territories is unnatural and that Israeli occupation cannot continue forever. Real peace cannot be achieved except through the recognition of Palestinian national rights, including the right of self-determination and the establishment of an independent Palestinian State on Palestinian national soil. Should these rights not be recognized, then the continuation of Israeli occupation will lead to further violence and bloodshed, and the further deepening of hatred. The opportunity for peace will also move farther away.

The only way to extricate ourselves from this scenario is through the convening of an international conference with the participation of all concerned parties including the PLO, the sole legitimate representative of the Palestinian people, as an equal partner, as well as the five permanent members of the Security Council, under the supervision of the two superpowers.

On this basis we call upon the Israeli authorities to comply with the following list of demands as a means to prepare the atmosphere for the convening of the suggested international peace conference, which conference will ensure a just and lasting settlement of the Palestinian problem in all its aspects, bringing about the realization of the inalienable national rights of the Palestinian people, peace and stability for the peoples of the region, and an end to violence and bloodshed:

1. To abide by the 4th Geneva Convention and all other international agreements pertaining to the protection of civilians, their properties and rights under a state of military occupation; to declare the Emergency Regulations of the British Mandate null and void, and to stop applying the iron fist policy;

2. The immediate compliance with Security Council Resolutions 605 and 607, which call upon Israel to abide by the Geneva Convention of 1949 and the Declaration of Human Rights; and which further call for the achievement of a just and lasting settlement of the Arab-Israeli conflict;

3. The release of all prisoners who were arrested during the recent uprising, and foremost among them our children. Also the rescinding of all proceedings and indictments against them;

4. The cancellation of the policy of expulsion, allowing all exiled Palestinians, including the four sent yesterday into exile, to return to their homes and families; also the release of all administrative detainees and the cancellation of the hundreds of house arrest orders. In this connection, special mention must be made of the several hundreds of applications for family reunions, which we call upon the authorities to accept forthwith;

5. The immediate lifting of the siege of all Palestinian refugee camps in

the West Bank and Gaza, and the withdrawal of the Israeli army from all population centres;

6. Carrying out a formal inquiry into the behaviour of the soldiers and settlers in the West Bank and Gaza, as well as inside jails and detention camps, and taking due punitive measures against all those convicted of having caused death or bodily harm to unarmed civilians;

7. A cessation of all settlement activity and land confiscation and the release of lands already confiscated, especially in the Gaza Strip, and an end to the harassments and provocations of the Arab population by settlers in the West Bank and Gaza as well as in the Old City of Jerusalem. In particular, the curtailment of the provocative activities in the old city of Jerusalem by Sharon and the ultra-religious settlers of Shuvu Banim and Ateret Cohanim;

8. Refraining from any act which might impinge on the Muslim and Christian holy sites or which might introduce change to the status quo in the city of Jerusalem;

9. The cancellation of the VAT and all other Israeli taxes which are imposed on Palestinian residents in Jerusalem, the rest of the West Bank, and in Gaza; and the putting to an end of the harassments caused to Palestinian business and tradesmen;

10. The cancellation of all restrictions on political freedoms, including the restrictions on meetings and conventions; also making provisions for free municipal elections under the supervision of a neutral authority;

11. The immediate release of monies deducted from the wages of labourers from the Occupied Territories who worked and still work inside the green line, which amount to several hundreds of millions of dollars. These accumulated deductions, with interest, must be returned to their rightful owners through the agency of the nationalist institutions headed by the worker's unions;

12. The removal of all restrictions on building permits and licences for industrial projects and artesian wells as well as agricultural development programs in the Occupied Territories, and the rescinding of all measures taken to deprive the Occupied Territories of their water resources;

13. The termination of the policy of discrimination being practised against industrial and agricultural produce from the Occupied Territories either by removing the restrictions on the transfer of goods to within the green line, or by placing comparable trade restrictions on the transfer of Israeli goods into the Occupied Territories.

14. The removal of the restrictions on political contacts between inhabitants of the Occupied Territories and the PLO, in such a way as to allow for the participation of Palestinians from the Occupied Territories in the proceedings of the Palestinian National Council, in order to ensure a direct input into the decision-making processes of the Palestinian Nation by the Palestinians under occupation.

Unified National Command of the Intifada: Call No. 6 (February 4, 1988)

Masses of our people, uprising multitudes in the camps, rural areas, and cities; you who by your will and determination have triumphed over the policy of entrenching the Zionist occupation and made your resounding voice heard throughout the world; creators of the mounting struggle action, which has snatched the initiative from the hands of the Tel Aviv rulers and put them under siege and in a position of international condemnation; you who by your struggle are paving every day and every hour the road to victory, the defeat of occupation, and the establishment of an independent national state under the leadership of the PLO, our sole, legitimate representative; our masses: In order to save the Zionist occupation from certain defeat, as well as to save Israel from a strangulating crisis and isolation on an international level, U.S. imperialism at this time is continuing to hatch plots in the region with the support of its collaborators. It is attempting to undermine the gains of the uprising by proposing plans for capitulatory solutions. Foremost among these plans are those related to the United States, such as the U.S. State Department's attempts to suggest that certain people produce an alternative to the PLO's leadership, our sole, legitimate leadership.

Our masses, in the name of our Palestinian people in the interior, who have made precious sacrifices represented by the martyrdom of scores of their most beloved sons and daughters, the thousands of detainees, the hundreds of injured, and the attacks on many of our camps, villages, and cities by the Zionists, we say in the name of our people, who have endured and are still enduring such sacrifices with courage and pride, that we affirm our rejection of all plots and all attempts by imperialism's envoys, including Philip Habib, to circumvent our legitimate leadership and to dictate surrender conditions such as recognition of Resolution 242. We affirm the determination of the people and the masses of the glorious uprising to foil all plots regardless of the different masks used by those behind them.

The PLO is our sole, legitimate representative. Therefore, whoever tries to represent the masses of the uprising from outside the PLO and to appoint a suspect leadership to make concessions and to surrender will be confronted by the Palestinian people. He will only face disappointment and miserable defeat.

Sons of our people, let us concert all efforts. Let all national key figures, organizations, and popular committees be united by a common will to escalate the uprising. Let all suitable organizations such as committees and units be formed in every area, on every street, and in every city, village, and camp in order to pave the road toward general civil disobedience as a more advanced struggle action. Disobedience means boycotting all enemy organs. It means boycotting the enemy economically and not paying taxes.

Therefore, let us climb another rung of the ladder by declaring this disobedience. Let us reinforce the spirit of sacrifice and common action following the war of molotov cocktails, stones, and the raising of flags. The disobedience will be a strong blow to the enemy, its economy, and its plunder of our people's wealth and resources. This lifeline must be cut off.

To pave the way for the implementation of this organized process, the Unified National Leadership of the Uprising calls on our workers to stop work immediately in the Israeli settlements of the Palestinian West Bank and Gaza Strip. It calls on our workers in institutions and factories to abide by the days of the general strike and to be prepared to declare a go-slow strike for a few days in all Israeli places and institutions.

O our heroic people, the Unified National Leadership of the Uprising, while greeting your heroism, sacrifices, and the epics of struggle being recorded by our people in Nabulus and in all parts of the homeland, and while emphasizing that struggle will continue, calls for the following:

The immediate resignation of the appointed municipal councils as a prelude to holding democratic elections at the appropriate time;

The [words indistinct] and abstain from paying taxes as a prelude to force the Zionist occupation authorities to cancel their [word indistinct] taxes; abstain from paying exorbitant and unfair fines imposed by the Zionist courts against the uprising detainees . . . the owners of real estate not to demand rents from shopowners due to the current circumstances;

Abidance by the boycott of the agent *al-Nahar* newspaper as mentioned in the previous call; and

Urging our masses to encourage the national economy and to boycott the Israeli goods and markets and use national goods instead.

O masses of the glorious uprising, let the confrontation escalate, let demonstrations and marches be staged next week, let the popular sit-in strikes and the burning of tires continue on every street, let the stones of the uprising and the molotov cocktails pour down on the heads of the Israeli occupation soldiers, let all the lines of settlements be cut off, let crowded prayers be performed in mosques and churches as a prelude to declaring a comprehensive strike on Sunday and Monday, 7 and 8 February 1988, to mark the elapse of 2 months of the successful uprising and commemorate the fall of the first group of uprising martyrs. . . .

U.S. Secretary of State George Shultz: Plan (March 6, 1988)

The agreed objective is a comprehensive peace providing for the security of all the States in the region and for the legitimate rights of the Palestinian people.

Negotiations will start on an early date certain between Israel and each of its neighbors which is willing to do so. Those negotiations could begin by May 1, 1988. Each of these negotiations will be based on United Nations Security Council Resolutions 242 and 338, in all their parts. The parties to each bilateral negotiation will determine the procedure and agenda of their negotiation. All participants in the negotiations must state their willingness to negotiate with one another.

As concerns negotiations between the Israeli delegation and Jordanian-Palestinian delegation, negotiations will begin on arrangements for a transitional period, with the objective of completing them within six months. Seven months after transitional negotiations begin, final status negotiations will begin, with the objective of completing them within one year. These negotiations will be based on all the provisions and principles of the United Nations Security Council Resolution 242. Final status talks will start before the transitional period begins. The transitional period will begin three months after the conclusion of the transitional agreement and will last for three years. The United States will participate in both negotiations and will promote their rapid conclusion. In particular, the United States will submit a draft agreement for the parties' consideration at the outset of the negotiations on transitional arrangements.

Two weeks before the opening of negotiations, an international conference will be held. The Secretary-General of the United Nations will be asked to issue invitations to the parties involved in the Arab-Israeli conflict and the five permanent members of the United Nations Security Council. All participants in the conference must accept United Nations Security Council Resolutions 242 and 338, and renounce violence and terrorism. The parties to each bilateral negotiations may refer reports on the status of their negotiations to the conference, in a manner to be agreed. The conference will not be able to impose solutions or veto agreements reached.

Palestinian representation will be within the Jordanian-Palestinian delegation. The Palestinian issue will be addressed in the negotiations between the Jordanian-Palestinian and Israeli delegations. Negotiations between the Israeli delegation and the Jordanian-Palestinian and Israeli delegations. Negotiations between the Israeli delegation and the Jordanian-Palestinian delegation will proceed independently of any other negotiations.

This statement of understandings is an integral whole. The United States understands that your acceptance is dependent on the implementation of each element in good faith.

PLO Executive Committee:
Statement on the Intifada (April 1988)

O masses of our great people, our people, through their continuous struggle and their blessed revolutionary uprising that is entering its 5th month, have scored additional achievements and victories. This has led to a deepening of the crisis of the Zionist occupation and its protectors in Washington. The entire world is now certain that this great people are determined to continue the way of jihad and struggle until, with the help of God, they achieve full victory and establish an independent Palestinian state on our sacred national soil.

The glorious Land Day, on which a total strike was observed throughout our occupied homeland, has proven that the solid and firm unity of our nation, the cohesion and solidarity of our ranks, and the firm insistence on the singleness of representation [*wihdaniyat al-tamthil*] are the strongest factors in confronting all Zionist-U.S. plots and all forms of oppression, slaughter, and destruction perpetrated by the Zionist occupation troops and the herds of the armed fascist settlers. Land Day was a day of cohesion and national solidarity among all the masses of our Palestinian people in the steadfast Galilee, the Triangle, and the Negev and in a position of clash and struggle in Lebanon and its south and in all areas of the diaspora.

It was another day of glory and confrontation in the steadfast West Bank and Gaza against all methods of fascist terrorism invented by Israel's rulers and generals including the war of starvation, the economic and media blockade, the perpetration of crimes and acts of slaughter against women, children, and defenseless citizens, and the demolishing of houses and communal arrests. Our heroic and faithful people have shown that these crimes can never weaken their escalating resistance or extinguish the flame of the uprising which is shaking the earth under the feet of the occupants and invaders.

The PLO Executive Committee, having discussed in detail all developments, tasks, and ways to escalate and develop the struggle of our people and their great uprising, stresses the following:

1. Extending a salutation of pride and appreciation to the struggling masses of the Palestinian people in the Galilee, the Triangle, and the Negev for their great actions on Land Day and throughout all of the days of the blessed uprising as they firmly and faithfully joined the masses of the West Bank and Gaza and their escalating continuous revolution which constitutes, through our nation inside and outside the occupied homeland, this unified innovative revolutionary fabric. The Executive Committee calls for further consolidation, entrenchment, and adherence to national unity and to further cohesion of the ranks of our peoples masses—children,

men, and women; cadres, heroes, and revolutionaries—on the path of liberation, return, and victory.

2. Emphasizing great appreciation for the role of the democratic forces which support the mammoth uprising of our people and firmly condemn the Nazi terrorism of Israel's rulers against our uprising masses who demand freedom and independence, the PLO Executive Committee calls for deepening and developing this role in all fields—political and media—to break the blockade that the Israeli rulers impose with the aim of concealing their barbaric crimes from the eyes of the world.

3. The PLO Executive Committee expresses, in the name of our entire people in all locations, the highest pride in the legendary steadfastness embodied by the blessed popular uprising through its daily epics in all sites. Every village, camp, neighborhood, and city in our occupied territory has provided its share of martyrdom, heroism, and sacrifice. They stood as a strong barrier before the enemy forces at a time when our masses in Lebanon and its south continue to pay the price of the confrontation and the clashes with more martyrs and sacrifices. All of our people proved that the banner of jihad will continue to fly high [words indistinct] with our blood, the souls of our martyrs, our captives, wounded, and detainees until the establishment of our independent state and the liberation of the precious soil of our homeland from the aggression and occupation of the Zionists.

4. The PLO Executive Committee emphasizes the need to continue to develop all forms of revolutionary cohesion, empathy, and support by the groupings of our Palestinian people outside the homeland for the blessed popular uprising and harness all struggle, political, media, and material capabilities and resources for that purpose on the Palestinian, Arab, and international levels.

5. The PLO Executive Committee emphasizes the need to adopt all measures and means to develop all forms of mass organization and action to maintain and escalate the uprising and to develop the role of the popular national committees in all positions under the banner of the PLO, the Unified National Command of the Uprising, until the uprising achieves its objectives of shattering the fascist racist terrorism inflicted upon the masses of our people and eliminating the abhorrent Zionist occupation and until the inalienable national rights of our struggling and persevering people are achieved.

6. The PLO Executive Committee emphasizes the stand on which our people are unanimous in confronting the serious U.S. plans: that a just and comprehensive solution must be based on the achievement of the national rights of our people and their right to national independence under the leadership of the PLO, their sole and legitimate representative.

The PLO reaffirms its complete rejection of all liquidatory plans and all forms of autonomy and the sharing of roles whatever their color and under whatever name. The PLO believes that the appropriate framework for a just solution is a UN-sponsored international conference with effective powers attended by the five permanent members of the Security Council and all the parties to the conflict in the region including the PLO, on an equal footing with the other parties and on the basis of international legality and UN resolutions on the Palestine question and the Middle East.

We are confident that U.S. imperialism and its ally the Zionist enemy, which is squatting on our land and sanctities, will not be able to bring our people to their knees or deprive them of their legitimate right to self-determination. Our people will wrest their inalienable national rights through blood and enormous sacrifices. Foremost among these rights are their right to repatriation, to self-determination, and to establish a free and independent state with Jerusalem as its capital.

7. The PLO Executive Committee, while it salutes the masses of our Arab nation, all of its forces, parties, institutions, and national bodies for their sincere stands in support of our people and their struggle, calls on the Arab masses to develop their support for our people's uprising and to stand firmly in opposing liquidatory U.S.-Israeli plans which they are trying to impose on our Arab nation and the entire region. The PLO Executive Committee appeals with confidence and faith to the entire Arab nation to achieve effective Arab solidarity based on implementing the resolutions that reject separate solutions and deals. The PLO Executive Committee calls for the consolidation of the inalienable national rights of the Palestinian people on the basis of Arab commitment and Arab resolutions.

8. The PLO Executive Committee affirms its great appreciation for the extensive solidarity with our people's valiant and just struggle which has embarrassed and isolated the rulers of Israel and exposed official U.S. collusion with the crimes of the racist Zionists and their savage terrorism against our people, children, and women.

In this regard the PLO Executive Committee salutes all friends and honorable people in the world who support our people and just cause, particularly in the African, nonaligned, and Muslim states as well as the socialist states, led by the Soviet Union and the PRC, and the friendly European countries.

9. In accordance with its responsibilities, the PLO Executive Committee will continue its efforts through all means, forms, and capabilities to maintain the continuity of our revolutionary march and to escalate our people's valiant uprising. The PLO Executive Committee calls upon international and friendly bodies to provide more support and backing for our struggling masses and our just cause, particularly in confronting the organized and official war of terrorism and the crimes perpetrated against our people by the fascist and racist Zionist occupation authorities.

O masses of our proud people, thanks to your enormous sacrifices the day of victory is approaching. With your great unity we face the enemy and his bloody terrorism. More struggle, more unity, and more organization. Dawn is definitely coming. Our independent state is definitely coming. Our victory will be achieved with God's blessing. In the name of God, the merciful, the compassionate. Say work, for God, His messenger, and the believers will see your work. [Koranic verse]

Long live our people's great uprising. Glory and immortality to the martyrs. Greetings to our detainees, prisoners, and wounded. Greetings to our valiant children, our struggling women, and our heroic men. Revolution until victory!

United National Command of the Intifada: Calls No. 12, 16, and 18 (April–May 1988)

Call No. 12 (April 1988)

In the name of God, the merciful, the compassionate. Call, call, call. No voice can rise above the voice of the uprising; no voice can rise above the voice of the Palestinian people, the voice of the PLO. Call No. 12, [word indistinct] issued by the PLO—the Unified National Leadership. We will die standing, we will not submit. They will not pass, and the uprising will triumph. O masses of our heroic people; O people of stones and Molotov cocktails; you are recording in blood and light the history of your Arab nation. You are making light with your blood to brighten the long darkness of the Arabs. O children of the triumphant uprising, our uprising is continuing, baptized in chaste blood day after day, watering the beloved soil of the homeland, realizing important achievements, and strengthened by the little triumphs which are accumulating one above the other to make great victories and establish the independent Palestinian state.

Despite the harshness of the Zionist enemy and its machine of repression and tyranny, the strong arms are challenging all military orders. The Zionist arrogance, which boasts of repressing the uprising, is being defied by our children, women, youths, and old men whose sacred stones and generous wrath are burning the occupation and its henchmen. . . .

Our triumphant uprising and popular revolution is in its 5th month. Our Palestinian masses are facing more than two-thirds of the Israeli Army and all the herds of the Zionist settlers whom the enemy sent to the streets of our camps, villages, and towns to confront our unarmed people. This overwhelming revolution cannot be ended or liquidated by the breaking of bones, fascist killing and terrorism, mass arrests, or economic harassment. Hundreds of thousands of Palestinians across our beloved homeland declare today there is no going back, that the stone revolution will not stop before the establishment of our independent state. This was demonstrated in the immortal Land Day when 2 million Palestinians identified themselves with the united people. Now they are rising united behind the banner which will never fall, the banner of the PLO, the banner of the unified national leadership, the banner of liberation and the independent homeland. To raise this banner over the hills of Jerusalem, the Palestinians in all towns, villages, camps, and streets are rising as one man.

O people of Palestine, O people of the PLO, O people of the unified national leadership. After its failure to put out the fires of the revolution through repression and terror, the occupation today is resorting to rumors and to spreading lies and forged statements allegedly signed by the Unified National Leadership in an attempt to cast doubt over our people—individuals and groups. The occupation is trying to sow the seeds of factionalism and sectarianism. It is spreading rumors about arresting the editors of the calls of the Unified National Leadership. All this is aimed at weakening the front of the burning uprising. The Unified National Leadership is certain that our people will be able to confront all the false rumors of the occupation. It affirms that the Unified National Leadership is the people of the uprising, represented by all its strata, groups, and sectors.

The Unified National Leadership includes the great martyrs whose blood is daily watering the soil of the homeland. This leadership consists of the children and youths of the stones and Molotov cocktails, the women who miscarried from the gas bombs and poison gas, the women whose husbands and sons are languishing in the Nazi prisons. The leadership consists of thousands of peasants and workers who stopped work in the Zionist settlements and who are protecting their villages, camps, and towns day and night against the tyranny and repression of the settlers and occupation soldiers.

O masses of our generous people, O mothers of martyrs, detainees, and wounded, O all mothers of Palestine, the rulers of the Zionist entity believe that by mass arrests and night stormings they can break our back and weaken our faith. But they do not know that our people are an inexhaustible store of generosity and are accustomed to making sacrifices for the sake of the homeland. So no matter how harsh Zionist repression and fascist measures are and no matter how many heroes and men of the uprising are detained, the Zionist enemy will not be able to put an end to this sweeping revolution—the revolution of the holy stones. Our people today are unified like a mighty giant destroying all the theories of the Zionist entity, intensifying the tribulation and dilemma of the Zionists, and increasing the confusion of their soldiers. More generosity means the breaking of the dawn of freedom forging its way in the darkness of coercion and heralding the independent Palestinian state.

While we are on the threshold of the 5th month of our glorious uprising and while we are hailing these days the 40th anniversary of the battle of heroism and sacrifice—the Battle of Al-Qastal and the commemoration of the martyrdom of hero commander 'Abd al-Qadir al-Husayni—the Unified National Leadership affirms the following:

1. Denouncing attempts to disrupt the convocation of the Arab summit in the first half of April. The summit should be held as soon as possible to back the struggle of the people of the uprising on the land of Palestine. We assure the Arab kings and presidents that we do not want funds. We would rather starve and remain destitute than bow down. We would rather die martyrs than concede our rights before final victory. However, we want the summit to abide in practice by its previous resolutions by asserting our people's inalienable rights to establish our independent state under the flag of the PLO, the leader of our struggle and our sole, legitimate representative, and abide by an international conference with full powers with the participation of all parties, including the PLO in an equal and independent manner. We also call on the summit to close all Arab doors to the Shultz plot, which seeks to liquidate the uprising, by categorically rejecting it and closing Arab airports before his shuttle tours as well as to all other U.S. envoys. Shultz and all those Arab regimes colluding with him should know that his only address is the PLO. It is the party concerned and the sole, legitimate representative.

2. The Unified National Leadership and the masses of the uprising denounce the oppressive authorities' recent measures represented by isolating the West Bank and Gaza, imposing a curfew on Gaza for 3 days, and considering the West Bank a closed area to the movement of citizens and journalists in a desperate attempt to prevent the people of the uprising from commemorating immortal Land Day. We tell them that all these desperate attempts are doomed to miserable failure. The will of the revolution of the stones and the uprising shall triumph over all their fascist and Nazi methods.

3. Denouncing the occupation authorities' decision to consider the youth movement [harakat al-shabibah] illegal and to close a number of trade union complexes and establishments and considering these measures as contrary to the most fundamental human rights and all international pacts and norms. The Unified National Leadership affirms that these measures will only make us more determined to continue the struggle.

4. The Unified National Leadership and the masses of the uprising evaluate the unified collective stand taken by merchants of the Ramallah area who pledged at a public meeting attended by 30 merchants not to pay taxes and who adhered to their pledge in practice. We consider this experiment an example that should be emulated by all merchants in all parts of the West Bank and Gaza.

5. The Unified National Leadership greets the stand taken by the members of the municipal and village committees who responded to the call for resignation by the Unified National Leadership and the masses of the uprising. The leadership announces the squandering of the blood and prop-

erty of the chairmen and members of the committees who have not resigned. We tell them that the masses of the uprising will trample upon whoever deviates from the stands of national unanimity and does not respond to the call and voice of the uprising.

6. The Unified National Leadership and the masses of the uprising evaluate the mass resignation of the tax and customs departments employees in Gaza and calls on the employees of these departments in the West Bank to follow their example. The leadership also evaluates the mass resignation of the policemen who responded to the call of the uprising and calls on municipality members to immediately resign from their posts. The Unified National Leadership urges all national popular committees to continue the work of setting up and generalizing cultivation, protection, and public order committees to prevent enemy authorities' attempts at sabotage and confusion. The Unified National Leadership also appeals to all our industrial firms to cooperation with the national popular committees in employing [resigning] policemen and tax and customs departments employees.

7. The Unified National Leadership urges agricultural engineers, owners of plant nurseries, and those with experience and capabilities to give every support and guidance to the masses of peasants, farmers, and striking workers to achieve maximum levels of self-sufficiency and to confront the measures of economic restriction used by the occupation authorities. Let us continue to reclaim and cultivate lands to meet our needs and support besieged areas. We should all realize the task of all the masses of the uprising is to intensify their work and to increase their production during our long struggle. We must realize that strike does not mean not working. The Unified National Leadership, while continuing on the long and difficult road of defeating the occupation and establishing our independent state, calls on the masses of the uprising to entrench the following struggle activities:

a. Declaring Monday, 4 April, a general strike day as an expression of the uprising masses' rejection of the plot by George Shultz, the secretary of U.S. imperialism. We reaffirm the PLO's stand and our determination to use the uprising to boycott any meetings with Shultz or any other U.S. envoy.

b. Declaring Monday, Tuesday, and Wednesday, 4, 5, and 6 April, days of various struggle activities by the uprising, masses, committees, striking groups, and various national frameworks against Shultz' visit and in solidarity with the uprising and detainees and wounded, including sit-ins and various public and women's demonstrations.

c. Considering Tuesday, 5 April, a day of national action in which all national establishments and factories shall operate at full capacity in the interests of those affected by the uprising, such as the families of martyrs, wounded, detainees, besieged areas, and workers who lost their jobs for ceasing to work in Zionist settlements and projects and also those who resigned in response to the call of the uprising. The national committees in every city, village, camp, and quarter shall distribute the revenues of this day.

d. On the occasion of World Health Day on 7 April, the Unified National Leadership greets all doctors, pharmacists, and nurses who have performed the duty of providing health care and relief work to the wounded of the uprising by returning to work in the camps, villages, and cities. The leadership calls on all those employed in the health care field to receive more patients and provide more medical treatment.

e. Declaring Thursday, 7 April, the anniversary of the Battle of Al-Qastal and the martyrdom of Palestinian commander 'Abd al-Qadir a day of violent clashes with the occupation forces and the cowardly settlers. Tumultuous demonstrations must come out in the streets and all our camps, villages, and cities must turn into fortresses of confrontation and fortification for the uprising.

f. Declaring Saturday, 9 April, which is the anniversary of the martyrdom of the first group of martyrs in the uprising as well as the martyrs of the Dayr Yasin massacre, and the beginning of the 5th month of our uprising, a day of people's authority in which processions shall proceed to the graves of the martyrs, sit-ins shall be organized in municipalities and establishments, and demonstrations shall be staged everywhere. It should be declared a day of sweeping indignation against the occupation authorities and their oppressive measures. Let the ground erupt like a volcano under the feet of the invader occupiers.

g. Considering Friday and Sunday, 8 and 10 April, days of prayer for the repose of the souls of the uprising's martyrs. Processions and demonstrations shall be staged and sit-ins shall be organized in mosques and churches.

8. Monday, 11 April, shall be a day of general strike and of guiding the masses of our people on volunteer work for cultivating lands, developing Palestinian rural areas, and promoting environmental economy. O people of the uprising continue to move forward. O cubs of the stones march ahead. They will not pass. The uprising shall triumph, shall triumph.

Call No. 16 (May 28, 1988)

In the name of God, the merciful, the compassionate. Call, call, call. No voice can rise above the voice of the uprising; no voice can rise above the voice of the Palestinian people, the people of the PLO.

O masses of our great people: Your triumphant uprising is now beginning its 6th month, defying the wounds; embracing the Palestinian sky through martyrdom and victory; challenging all kinds of oppression, tyranny, and killing which our enemy is pursuing; opening the door to our triumphant revolution and the originator of our struggle, the PLO; exposing our enemies' ugly faces before the whole world; foiling all the conspiratorial projects against our steadfast people; strengthening our people's unity around the PLO, the sole legitimate representative; and protecting our independent national decisionmaking. There will be no trusteeship or alternative except Palestine, the alternative which is baptized with the blood of our righteous martyrs.

O masses of our people, we are living the 40th anniversary of the Palestine disaster of 1948, the infamous day when tens of thousands of our people were expelled from their homeland and dispersed in all countries of the world, entrenching the presence of the colonialist Zionist occupation on our chaste soil under the shadow of Arab trusteeship over our people and through the defeated Arab regimes, which were under the influence of colonialist powers, especially Britain. Palestine was a victim of this trusteeship and weakness. From the bleeding wound emerged the Palestinian revolution, which declared at its birth in 1965 that there is no alternative to struggle against the usurping enemy through the methods of prolonged people's war and armed struggle until liberation and victory.

With the presence of the PLO and the continuation of the Palestinian struggle within its framework, and with the increasing number of martyrs, our triumphant revolution and our heroic masses were able to wrest their independent national decisionmaking at the 1974 Rabat summit conference. Our people won their independent decisionmaking, represented by declaring the PLO as the sole legitimate representative of the Palestinian people everywhere. And despite all the desperate attempts to strike at our triumphant revolution and our enemies' efforts to circumvent this representation, the Palestinian giant was able to confront all its enemies and to turn our Palestinian cause into a central cause for the whole world despite the wounds, the rivers of blood, the large number of martyrs, and our people's immense suffering.

Then came our sacred uprising to renew our people's resolve to attain their legitimate rights no matter what the sacrifices or how long the wait. It has grown into a giant, striking terror in the hearts of all enemies. Your glorious uprising is delivering painful blows to the Nazi occupation, foiling its measures against our struggling masses. Despite the fascist oppression, our masses are ever rallying around the uprising and its sacred slogans through a commitment to the PLO and the unified leadership of the uprising, withholding taxes, boycotting occupation goods, resigning en masse from the Zionist administration, economizing on expenses, intensifying local agriculture, land reclamation, and education, and building alternative bodies via popular committees, neighborhoods, education, and health as a key prelude to civil disobedience.

Having despaired of squelching and aborting the uprising, the rulers of Tel Aviv committed the crime of murdering the leader, the symbol Abu Jihad [Khalil al-Wazir], in Tunis in an attempt to end it. O our heroic masses, comrades, and brothers of the martyr hero Abu Jihad [words indistinct]. Abu Jihad's blood will not have been wasted. All our people are Abu Jihad. We will continue the march along the path of struggle until victory. This escalation has been crowned by the international consensus on denouncing the Zionist entity and its fascist policies, the Palestinian-Soviet agreement, reconciliation with Syria, and reopening the intra-Palestinian dialogue toward developing the unity of the PLO.

Then came the Algerian and Libyan efforts and Arab meetings to convene an Arab summit—the uprising summit to promote common Arab action in support of the uprising and build a wide Arab front in the face of conspiratorial plots led by the Shultz project, which our people have turned down. In the shadow of these great achievements, the Zionist enemy mounted an attack against Lebanon, laid a siege to some villages, and used repression and oppression against the innocent in renewed attempts to divert international attention from the uprising and in a desperate attempt to undo the militant, harmonious, integral relationship between the popular uprising in the occupied land and the Palestinian revolution on one hand and the Lebanese nationalist movement on the other.

At a time when the need to close ranks and train guns on the usurper enemy has never been greater, a handful of aberrant dissidents in Lebanon who have broken away from the will of our people made a wretched attempt to split and undermine the various efforts seeking to realize a national consensus within the PLO and direct the guns at the usurper enemy to consolidate the triumphant uprising of our people.

O our heroic Palestinian people, while marking these days—the 22d anniversary of the Arab regimes' defeat and of the occupation of the remainder of our dear homeland, amid the convening of the Moscow summit and the Arab summit and also in view of George Shultz' attempts to resume the conspiracy aimed at aborting the uprising—our people's masses are daily escalating their victorious uprising. There will be no return nor will there be any retreat until occupation is removed and an independent Palestinian state is established under the PLO's leadership.

Our masses know their path through revolution to obtain their rights. It is the path of persistent struggle. More than 20 years of coercion, persecution, oppression, and attempts to liquidate our identity and our people's national cause have created the generation of the uprising—the generation of freedom, independence, and of building an independent national state on its sacred national soil. This generation is determined to make occupation pay a dear price for desecrating our land and holy places. It is also determined to turn occupation into a hell that will burn the occupying soldiers and settlers.

The Unified National Leadership of the Uprising calls on our masses to further escalate the delivery of painful blows to the new Nazis and to further entrench and organize the generation of the uprising and its specialized committees and strike teams along the path of carrying out a comprehensive civil disobedience and fulfilling the slogans and just demands of the uprising as a basic introduction to wrest our people's national legitimate rights to repatriation, self-determination, and the establishment of an independent state.

These slogans and demands include the need to implement the four Geneva Conventions; dispatch international observers to provide the necessary protection for the sons of our people; withdraw the army from the cities, villages, and camps; lift the siege clamped on them; release the detainees; return deportees to their homeland; cancel the taxes and other laws and legislations enacted by the occupation authorities; hold democratic elections for the municipal and village councils; and remove restrictions imposed on our national production to allow for the building and developing of the industrial, agricultural, and services sectors.

The PLO, the Unified National Leadership, along with our people's masses, while waging a tough struggle within a firmly established national unity, calls on the Arab summit leaders to shoulder their responsibilities before their peoples and history by supporting this Palestinian struggle not through denunciation, condemnation, and verbal backing, but by:

1. Adopting a clear and unified political stand before the whole world in support of the PLO and the soleness and legitimacy of its representation of our people and providing all means of support enabling our people to continue their struggle.

2. Rejecting all liquidationist solutions, headed by the Shultz initiative, and insisting on the need to hold a fully empowered international conference with the participation of the PLO in an independent delegation just like the other parties.

3. Releasing political prisoners from Arab prisons, giving democratic freedoms to the Arab masses so they can act in solidarity and cohesion with our people's triumphant uprising, and allowing for fedayeen action across Arab borders in the direction of occupied Palestine.

Along the path of implementing a comprehensive civil disobedience, the Unified National Leadership of the Uprising, the PLO, emphasizes the following:

—The need for the immediate resignation of workers in traffic and licensing departments, organization and housing departments, and identity cards and people's registration offices. After the occupation authorities have been forced to reopen schools, it is essential to reprogram the curriculum to compensate the students for what they missed, especially secondary school students in their final year. We trust that schools will continue to be the strong citadels of the uprising. Popular education should play a complementary role in raising our students' efficiency.

—Total withholding of cooperation with the institutions through which the occupation seeks to restrict the movement of the population by boycotting certifications of good conduct and relevant official documents and refusing to have dealings with defeatists and appointed agent municipal committees. Here, it should be emphasized that the popular committees in every location are called upon to mobilize the population for a commitment to this patriotic stand.

—Banning the payment of all kinds of taxes, boycotting Zionist goods—industrial or agricultural—and completely withholding labor from Zionist settlements.

—Refusal by our sons in the [Gaza] Strip to receive the new identity cards. The popular committees are called upon to play a mobilizing role toward that end to consolidate the boycott and in compliance with PLO resolutions—the Unified Leadership of the Uprising.

—An intensification of the formation and organization of popular committees, neighborhood committees, health committees, sentry committees, security committees, agricultural committees, mobilization guidance committees, information committees, and strike forces—the militant arm of the Unified National Leadership of the Uprising—as well as the economic committees, and encouraging, developing, and entrenching household agriculture and rationalized consumption and spending.

—Directing and intensifying blows to dissenters from the will of our people in the appointed village and city council committees, customs offices, and police and intensifying the use of the means of popular struggle beginning with the stone and ending with the gasoline bomb against all the enemies.

O masses of our struggling people, the PLO—the Unified National Leadership—calls on all segments of our people to mark the following days with sweeping mass anger coinciding with forthcoming political events by executing and implementing the following militant activities:

First, dedicating 28 and 29 May to massive marches and rallies involving all national cadres, organizations, and personalities so our voice—the voice of the uprising—may be heard loud and clear by the superpower leaders in Moscow.

Second, dedicating 30 May to an all-out strike and raising the pitch of the militant struggle to mark the Gorbachev-Reagan summit and increasing the writing of nationalist slogans and raising flags in all villages, cities and camps.

Third, dedicating 1 June—International Children's Day—to children's demonstrations raising Palestinian slogans and flags. In the meantime, various committees, especially committees of solidarity with victims of our people, will distribute gifts to the children of the martyrs, the wounded, detainees, and deportees.

Fourth, dedicating 3, 4, 5, and 6 June to full-scale strikes to mark the [Mideast] visit of Shultz, the Lebanese invasion, and the 22d [as heard] anniversary of the Zionist occupation. In the meantime, our masses and strike forces will stage demonstrations and confrontations with occupiers and their agents. May the land scorch the feet of the usurping occupiers and their agents.

Fifth, dedicating 7 June to Arab solidarity with the glorious uprising of our people, holding massive demonstrations, and urging Arab masses to stage rallies of sympathy with our victorious uprising.

Call No. 18 (May 12, 1988)

O masses of our heroic people, who have destroyed the illusions of occupation in more than 20 years, who have refuted the claims about our people's coexistence with occupation, and who have destroyed all attempts to create feeble alternatives to our people's sole legitimate representative, the PLO, through destroying alternatives to the right to repatriation, to self-determination, and to an independent national state: You continue to proceed on the road through your suffering, through the huge sacrifices, and through the constant flow of blood on the road to achieving freedom and independence for our militant people.

Here is the victorious uprising destroying the apparatus and tools of the fascist occupation, which were established to serve the occupation's interests and to link the interests of our people's masses with the occupation. On the ruins of these tools you are building the apparatus of the heroic people's authority through the popular committees with their various tasks.

Here is the uprising restoring to our national cause its natural size as the cause of a people who are struggling for the sake of their legitimate national rights. This cause has thus become an important topic on the agenda of the Moscow summit as well as the major topic at the summit of the uprising in Algiers.

While saluting the combatants who returned to the ranks of the mother revolution, thereby rejecting the spilling of blood for the sake of achieving the objectives of those who reneged on our people's will, as well as those of Abu Musa [Sa'id Musa Muraghah], the one who reneged on this will, and his clique, the uprising masses appeal to the Lebanese nationalist movement to unify its ranks to confront the Zionist enemy and end their narrow differences, thus unifying the militant endeavors of the militant and pan-Arab Lebanese-Palestinian parties to make them serve as a significant factor and a principal pillar conducive to the achievement of victory.

At the same time, these masses appeal to all those exerting sincere efforts to accelerate the process of inter-Palestinian dialogue, to bolster the militant relationship with Syria, and to build an Arab base of steadfastness capable of achieving our nation's pan-Arab objectives. O you, masses of the valiant uprising. O you, people of martyrs. With steady and confident strides, we, along with you, are going through one phase after another in our popular uprising and revolt, strengthening the people's rules and authority on the road to general and comprehensive civil disobedience, which will take the form of securing a complete boycott between our people and the institutions of the occupying authority in all spheres.

This requires that we display further observance of the program of the phase and of that of the phases of the popular uprising, as well as of the decisions made by the Unified National Leadership, the PLO leadership.

We call upon our masses to remain alert and display serious and studied readiness to meet the requirements of civil disobedience. This readiness can materialize through providing the necessary supplies which can provide citizens' needs for at least one month. It includes enhancing self-sufficiency, displaying an eagerness to provide adequate quantities of water by preserving water wells, making available first aid, and enhancing the program of various committees—the popular, guard, information, and labor committees. Furthermore, this readiness can also materialize when emphasis is laid on the formation of further strike groups, the militant arm of our blessed popular revolution.

The PLO leadership, the Unified National Leadership of the Uprising, treading on the path of realizing comprehensive civil disobedience, emphasizes the following:

1. All sectors and walks of life are to enhance the complete boycott [of Israeli authorities] through their failure to pay all forms of taxes to the suckers of our people's blood.

2. The comprehensive boycott is to be enhanced and continued by our workers through their failure to head for their worksites inside the institutions of the Zionist entity and its crumbling organizations.

3. The Unified National Leadership calls upon our heroic masses in the proud Gaza Strip to boycott the receipt of identity cards, which the enemy authorities seek to force upon them with the objective of restricting the movement of citizens and forcing them to pay taxes. This hateful method seeks to weaken the growing flame of the uprising. Hence, we call upon you, our masses, to boycott completely this measure.

4. The Unified National Leadership of the Uprising calls upon the general directors working in the departments of the Civil Administration in the Gaza Strip to respond favorably to the call voiced by the uprising masses by tendering their resignations. We call upon the strike forces, the knights of the great clashes, and the faithful masses of our people to strike with an iron fist all those who refuse to carry out this decision. We also call upon the guard and security committees to maintain surveillance over these directors and to carry out their program in this regard.

5. The Unified National Leadership salutes the uprising masses and our valiant kinfolk in the camps of the Gaza Strip for their steadfastness and their legendary challenge, which took the form of breaking the curfews imposed on Palestinian camps and also the form of staging tumultuous demonstrations and violent clashes against the Nazi occupation troops.

6. The Unified Leadership of the Uprising calls upon our people's masses to form solidarity committees inside the occupied homeland to bolster the ties of social solidarity, cooperation, and mutual aid among our well-off families and our families that have been harmed.

7. The Unified National Leadership of the Uprising calls upon the lawyer's sector to form information and legal committees to work intensively to expose the Nazi methods being perpetrated by the occupation authorities against our masses, our prisoners, and our deportees—methods that contravene all international and human laws and norms. Special emphasis is to be laid on the methods being used by the occupation authorities in the new Nazi detention camps; namely, Ansar, the Negev desert prison, the Al-Zahiriyah prison, the Al-Fari'ah prison, and the remaining prisons.

8. The Unified National Leadership stresses the need to remain alert and to beware of forged statements which are being distributed by the well-known agent Hamadi al-Rishq by orders of Yitzhaq Rabin.

On the occasion of the blessed 'Id al-Fitr, the PLO leadership, the Unified National Leadership of the popular uprising, greets the masses of our people, detainees, wounded, and the families of our martyrs—the candles. It also greets the harmed families, our merchants, workers, deportees, and the revolution fighters in all arenas. It congratulates them on the blessed feast, which coincides with the escalation of our gigantic popular revolution and the victorious beginning of its 6th month. It greets our sons' heroic stands in their struggle over the recent months and during the blessed Al-Qadr night [the night between the 26th and 27th of Ramadan in which the Koran was revealed].

Naturally, the Unified Leadership calls for concealing all celebrations and to confine them to performing religious rites, prayers, and chants of God is great. It calls for formation of further committees and intensification of the following militant programs and activities on the path to a comprehensive civil disobedience:

1. On 13 May, the masses of our people shall head for mosques, perform prayers over the souls of our righteous martyrs, and take to the streets in massive demonstrations against the occupation and the herds of its armed settlers.

2. The 15th of May, the ill-omened day of the catastrophe, shall be considered a day for a comprehensive strike, a day of distinctive anger, and a new beginning in which Palestinian flags shall be hoisted over houses, poles, village council buildings, appointed municipalities, and everywhere. On this day the heroic strike groups shall confront the occupiers and all those departing from the will of our people, including the members of the appointed municipal councils, taxes, police, and misled criminal agents.

3. The 1st day of the blessed 'Id al-Fitr shall be announced as a day for national mourning in protest of Arab and Islamic silence and impotence and to honor and glorify the blood of our revolutionary martyr and symbol,

Brother Abu Jihad, and all the righteous uprising martyrs. On this day, our masses shall head [for mosques] to perform prayers and visit the tombs of martyrs and cemeteries and shall stage popular processions and massive, mammoth demonstrations in defiance of the Zionist means of repression and torture.

4. The Unified National Leadership calls on the masses of our people and various committees to pay solidarity visits to the families of our heroic martyrs, prisoners, wounded, and deportees on the 2d and 3d days of the blessed 'Id.

5. The 21st of May shall be declared a day of comprehensive strike and a day for enhancing popular teaching in all our cities, villages, and camps in protest of the inhuman arbitrary decisions of closing down various centers of learning. The teachers sector is called upon to organize protest processions.

6. The rest of the days and Fridays and Sundays shall be considered days for enhancing and intensifying the work of various militant activities, especially the strike forces, and for dealing painful blows to the flabby bodies of occupiers and their agents and setting ablaze the ground under the feet of the Zionist occupiers with fire and anger.

7. With the exception of what has been mentioned, our masses shall be committed to all the decisions declared in previous calls, especially regarding the hours of partial trade strike, which will be as usual.

O valiant sons of our people and makers of Palestinian glory. We will continue to resist with a strong will, profound belief, great sacrifices, and innovative and creative revolutionary action on the path of martyrs. We will continue to challenge all forms and means of systematic Zionist repression. O our heroic masses and strike forces, hurl more stones and flaming Molotov cocktails on all enemies and the forces of wickedness, injustice, and aggression. Continue using bows and arrows, poisoned nails, and all means of popular struggle.

Carry out further committee militant activities toward a stage of comprehensive civil disobedience on the path of an independent Palestinian state under the leadership of the PLO. Victory is undoubtedly imminent. Together, we will achieve our liberation and certain national independence on the soil of Palestine with Jerusalem as our everlasting capital. We will triumph.

King Hussein of Jordan: Disengagement from the West Bank (July 31, 1988)

Our decision as you know, comes after thirty-eight years of the unity of the two banks, and fourteen years after the Rabat summit resolution, designating the Palestine Liberation Organisation (PLO) as the sole legitimate representative of the Palestinian people. It also comes six years after the Fez summit resolution that agreed unanimously on the establishment of an independent Palestinian state in the occupied West Bank and the Gaza Strip, as one of the bases, and results of the peaceful settlement. . . .

We had never imagined that the preservation of the legal and administrative links between the two banks could constitute an obstacle to the liberation of the occupied Palestinian land. Consequently, during the period before adopting these measures we did not see a reason to do so, particularly since our position which calls for, and supports, the Palestinian people's rights to self-determination was clear beyond equivocation.

Lately, it has transpired that there is a general Palestinian and Arab orientation towards highlighting the Palestinian identity in a complete manner, in every effort or activity related to the Palestinian question and its developments. It has also become clear that there is a general conviction, that maintaining the legal and administrative links with the West Bank, and the ensuing Jordanian interaction with out Palestinian brothers under occupation, through Jordanian institutions in the occupied territories, contradicts this orientation. It is also viewed that these links hamper the Palestinian struggle to gain international support for the Palestinian cause, as the national cause of a people struggling against foreign occupation.

In view of this line of thought, which is certainly inspired by genuine Palestinian will, and Arab determination to support the Palestinian cause, it becomes our duty to be part of this direction, and to respond to its requirements. After all, we are a part of our nation, supportive of its causes, foremost among which is the Palestinian cause. Since there is a general conviction that the struggle to liberate the occupied Palestinian land could be enhanced by dismantling the legal and administrative links between the two banks, we have to fulfill our duty, and do what is required of us. At the Rabat summit of 1974 we responded to the Arab leaders appeal to us to continue our interaction with the occupied West Bank through the Jordanian institutions, to support the steadfastness of our brothers there. Today we respond to the wish of the Palestine Liberation Organisation, the sole legitimate representative of the Palestinian people, and to the Arab orientation to affirm the Palestinian identity in all its aspects. We pray God that this step be a substantive addition to the intensifying Palestinian struggle for freedom and independence. . . .

At the same time it has to be understood in all clarity and without any ambiguity or equivocation, that our measures regarding the West Bank, concern only the occupied Palestinian land and its people. They naturally do not relate in any way to the Jordanian citizens of Palestinian origin in the Hashemite Kingdom of Jordan. They all have the full rights of citizenship and all its obligations, the same as any other citizen irrespective of his origin. They are an integral part of the Jordanian state. They belong to it, they live on its land and they participate in its life and all its activities. Jordan is not Palestine; and the independent Palestinian state will be established on the occupied Palestinian land after its liberation, God willing. There the Palestinian identity will be embodied, and there the Palestinian struggle shall come to fruition, as confirmed by the glorious uprising of the Palestinian people under occupation.

National unity is precious in any country; but in Jordan it is more than that. It is the basis of our stability, and the spring-board of our development and prosperity. It is the foundation of our national security and the source of our faith in the future. It is the living embodiment of the principles of the Great Arab Revolt, which we inherited, and whose banner we proudly bear. It is a living example of constructive plurality, and a sound nucleus for wider Arab unity.

Based on that, safeguarding national unity is a sacred duty that will not be compromised. Any attempt to undermine it, under any pretext, would only help the enemy carry out his policy of expansion at the expense of Palestine and Jordan alike. Consequently, true nationalism lies in bolstering and fortifying national unity. Moreover, the responsibility to safeguard it falls on every one of you, leaving no place in our midst for sedition or treachery. With God's help, we shall be as always, a united cohesive family, whose members are joined by bonds of brotherhood, affection, awareness, and common national objectives.

It is most important to remember, as we emphasize the importance of safeguarding national unity, that stable and productive societies, are those where orderliness and discipline prevail. Discipline is the solid fabric that binds all members of a community in a solid, harmonious structure, blocking all avenues before the enemies, and opening horizons of hope for future generations.

The constructive plurality which Jordan has lived since its foundation, and through which it has witnessed progress and prosperity in all aspects of life, emanates not only from our faith in the sanctity of national unity, but also in the importance of Jordan's pan-Arab role. Jordan presents itself as the living example of the merger of various Arab groups on its soil, within the framework of good citizenship, and one Jordanian people. This paradigm that we live on our soil gives us faith in the inevitability of attaining Arab unity, God willing. In surveying contemporary tendencies, it becomes clear that the affirmation of national identity does not contradict the attainment of unitary institutional formats that can enjoin Arabs as a whole. There are living examples within our Arab homeland that attest to this, as there are living examples in foreign regions. Foremost among them is the European Community, which now seeks to realize European political unity, having successfully completed the process of economic complementarity among its members. It is well known that the bonds linking the Arabs are far greater than those linking European nations.

Citizens, Palestinian brothers in the occupied Palestinian lands, to dispel any doubts that may arise out of our measures, we assure you that these measures do not mean the abandonment of our national duty, either towards the Arab-Israeli conflict, or towards the Palestinian cause, nor do they mean relinquishing our faith in Arab unity. As I have stated, those steps were taken only in response to the wish of the Palestine Liberation Organisation, the sole legitimate representative of the Palestinian people, and the prevailing Arab conviction that such measures will contribute to the struggle of the Palestinian people and their glorious uprising. Jordan will continue its support for the steadfastness of the Palestinian people, and their courageous uprising in the occupied Palestinian land, within its capabilities. . . .

Hamas: Charter (August 1988)

ARTICLE SIX

The Islamic Resistance Movement is a distinct Palestinian Movement which owes its loyalty to Allah, derives from Islam its way of life and strives to raise the banner of Allah over every inch of Palestine. Only under the shadow of Islam could the members of all regions coexist in safety and security for their lives, properties and rights. In the absence of Islam, conflict arises, oppression reigns, corruption is rampant and struggles and wars prevail. . . .

ARTICLE NINE

Hamas finds itself at a period of time when Islam has waned away from the reality of life. For this reason, the checks and balances have been upset, concepts have become confused, and values have been transformed; evil has prevailed, oppression and obscurity have reigned; cowards have turned tigers, homelands have been usurped, people have been uprooted and are wandering all over the globe. The state of truth has disappeared and was replaced by the state of evil. Nothing has remained in its right place, for when Islam is removed from the scene, everything changes. These are the motives.

As to the objectives: discarding the evil, crushing it and defeating it, so that truth may prevail, homelands revert [to their owners], calls for prayer be heard from their mosques, announcing the reinstitution of the Muslim state. Thus, people and things will revert to their true place. . . .

ARTICLE ELEVEN

The Islamic Resistance Movement believes that the land of Palestine has been an Islamic Wakf throughout the generations and until the Day of Resurrection, no one can renounce it or part of it, or abandon it or part of it. No Arab country nor the aggregate of all Arab countries, and no Arab King or President nor all of them in the aggregate, have that right, nor has that right any organization or the aggregate of all organizations, be they Palestinian or Arab. . . .

ARTICLE TWELVE

Hamas regards Nationalism (*Wataniyya*) as part and parcel of the religious faith. Nothing is loftier or deeper in Nationalism than waging Jihad against the enemy and confronting him when he sets foot on the land of the Muslims. And this becomes an individual duty binding on every Muslim man and woman; a woman must go out and fight the enemy even without her husband's authorization, and a slave without his masters' permission.

This [principle] does not exist under any other regime, and it is a truth not to be questioned. While other nationalisms consist of material, human and territorial considerations, the nationality of Hamas also carries, in addition to all those, the all important divine factors which lend to it its spirit and life; so much so that it connects with the origin of the spirit and the source of life and raises in the skies of the Homeland the Banner of the Lord, thus inexorably connecting earth with Heaven. . . .

ARTICLE THIRTEEN

[Peace] initiatives, the so-called peaceful solutions, and the international conferences to resolve the Palestinian problem, are all contrary to the beliefs of the Islamic Resistance Movement. For renouncing any part of Palestine means renouncing part of the religion; the nationalism of the Islamic Resistance Movement is part of its faith, the movement educates its members to adhere to its principles and to raise the banner of Allah over their homeland as they fight their Jihad: "Allah is the all-powerful, but most people are not aware. . . . "

Those conferences are no more than a means to appoint the nonbelievers as arbitrators in the lands of Islam. Since when did the Unbelievers do justice to the Believers?

"And the Jews will not be pleased with thee, nor will the Christians, till thou follow their creed. Say: Lo! the guidance of Allah [himself] is the Guidance. And if you should follow their desires after the knowledge which has come unto thee, then you would have from Allah no protecting friend nor helper." *Sura II (the Cow), verse 120.*

There is no solution to the Palestinian problem except by Jihad. The initiatives, proposals and International Conferences are but a waste of time, an exercise in futility. The Palestinian people are too noble to have their future, their right and their destiny submitted to a vain game. . . .

ARTICLE FOURTEEN

The problem of the liberation of Palestine relates to three circles: the Palestinian, the Arab and the Islamic. Each one of these circles has a role to play in the struggle against Zionism and it has duties to fulfill. It would be an enormous mistake and an abysmal act of ignorance to disregard anyone of these circles. For Palestine is an Islamic land where the First Qibla and the third holiest site are located. That is also the place whence the Prophet, be Allah's prayer and peace upon him, ascended to Heavens.

> "Glorified be He who carried His servant by night from the Inviolable Place of worship to the Far Distant Place of Worship, the neighborhood whereof we have blessed, that we might show him of our tokens! Lo! He, only He, is the Hearer, the Seer." *Sura XVII (al-Isra'), verse 1.*

In consequence of this state of affairs, the liberation of that land is an individual duty binding on all Muslims everywhere. This is the base on which all Muslims have to regard the problem; this has to be understood by all Muslims. When the problem is dealt with on this basis, where the full potential of the three circles is mobilized, then the current circumstances will change and the day of liberation will come closer. . . .

ARTICLE TWENTY

Islamic society is one of solidarity. The Messenger of Allah, be Allah's prayer and peace upon him, said:

> What a wonderful tribe were the Ash'aris! When they were overtaxed, either in their location or during their journeys, they would collect all their possessions and then would divide them equally among themselves.

This is the Islamic spirit which ought to prevail in any Muslim society. A society which confronts a vicious, Nazi-like enemy, who does not differentiate between man and women, elder and young ought to be the first to adorn itself with this Islamic spirit. Our enemy pursues the style of collective punishment of usurping people's countries and properties, of pursuing them into their exiles and places of assembly. It has resorted to breaking bones, opening fire on women and children and the old, with or without reason, and to setting up detention camps where thousands upon thousands are interned in inhuman conditions. In addition, it destroys houses, renders children orphans and issues oppressive judgments against thousands of young people who spend the best years of their youth in the darkness of prisons. The Nazism of the Jews does not skip women and children, it scares everyone. They make war against people's livelihood, plunder their moneys and threaten their honour. In their horrible actions they mistreat people like the most horrendous war criminals. Exiling people from their country is another way of killing them. As we face this misconduct, we have no escape from establishing social solidarity among the people, from confronting the enemy as one solid body, so that if one organ is hurt the rest of the body will respond with alertness and fervor. . . .

The Powers Which Support the Enemy

ARTICLE TWENTY-TWO

The enemies have been scheming for a long time, and they have consolidated their schemes, in order to achieve what they have achieved. They took advantage of key elements in unfolding events, and accumulated a huge and influential material wealth which they put to the service of implementing their dream. This wealth [permitted them to] take over control of the world media such as news agencies, the press, publication houses, broadcasting and the like. [They also used this] wealth to stir revolutions in various parts of the globe in order to fulfill their interests and pick the fruits. They stood behind the French and the Communist Revolutions and behind most of the revolutions we hear about here and there. They also used the money to establish clandestine organizations which are spreading around the world, in order to destroy societies and carry out Zionist interests. Such organizations are: the Free Masons, Rotary Clubs, Lions Clubs, B'nai B'rith and the like. All of them are destructive spying organizations. They also used the money to take over control of the Imperialist states and made them colonize many countries in order to exploit the wealth of those countries and spread their corruption therein.

As regards local and world wars, it has come to pass and no one objected that they stood behind World War I, so as to wipe out the Islamic Caliphate. They collected material gains and took control of many sources of wealth. They obtained the Balfour Declaration and established the League of Nations in order to rule the world by means of that organization. They also stood behind World War II, where they collected immense benefits from trading with war materials, and prepared for the establishment of their state. They inspired the establishment of the United Nations and the Security Council to replace the League of Nations, in order to rule the world by their intermediary. There was no war that broke out anywhere without their fingerprints on it:

" . . . As often as they light a fire for war, Allah extinguishes it. Their efforts is for corruption in the land and Allah loves not corrupters." *Sura V (Al-Ma'ida—the Tablespread), verse 64.*

The forces of imperialism in both the Capitalist West and the Communist East support the enemy with all their might, in material and human terms, taking turns between themselves. When Islam appears, all the forces of Unbelief unite to confront it, because the Community of Unbelief is one.

"Oh ye who believe! Take not for intimates others than your own folk, who would spare no pain to ruin you. Hatred is revealed by [the utterance of] their mouth, but that which their breasts hide is greater. We have made plain for you the revelations if you will understand . . . " *Sura III, (Al-Imran), verse 118.*

It is not in vain that the verse ends with God's saying: "If you will understand. . . . "

ARTICLE TWENTY-SIX

The Hamas, while it views positively the Palestinian National Movements which do not owe their loyalty to the East or to the West, does not refrain from debating unfolding events regarding the Palestinian problem, on the local and international scenes. These debates are realistic and expose the extent to which [these developments] go along with, or contradict, national interests as viewed from the Islamic vantage point.

ARTICLE TWENTY-SEVEN

The PLO is among the closest to the Hamas, for its constitutes a father, a brother, a relative, a friend. Can a Muslim turn away from his father, his brother, his relative or his friend? Our homeland is one, our calamity is one, our destiny is one and our enemy is common to both of us. Under the influence of the circumstances which surrounded the founding of the PLO, and the ideological confusion which prevails in the Arab world as a result of the ideological invasion which has swept the Arab world since the rout of the Crusades, and which has been reinforced by Orientalism and the Christian Mission, the PLO has adopted the idea of a Secular State, and so we think of it. Secular thought is diametrically opposed to religious thought. Thought is the basis for positions, for modes of conduct and for resolutions. Therefore, in spite of our appreciation for the PLO and its possible transformation in the future, and despite the fact that we do not denigrate its role in the Arab-Israeli conflict, we cannot substitute it for the Islamic nature of Palestine by adopting secular thought. For the Islamic nature of Palestine is part of our religion, and anyone who neglects his religion is bound to lose.

"And who forsakes the religion of Abraham, save him who befools himself?" *Sura II (Al-Baqra—the Co), verse 130.*

When the PLO adopts Islam as the guideline for life, then we shall become its soldiers, the fuel of its fire which will burn the enemies. And until that happens, and we pray to Allah that it will happen soon, the position of the Hamas towards the PLO is one of a son towards his father, a brother towards his brother, and a relative towards his relative who suffers the other's pain when a thorn hits him, who supports the other in the confrontation with the enemies and who wishes him divine guidance and integrity of conduct. . . .

ARTICLE TWENTY-EIGHT

The Zionist invasion is a mischievous one. It does not hesitate to take any road, or to pursue all despicable and repulsive means to fulfill its desires. It relies to a great extent, for its meddling and spying activities, on the clandestine organizations which it has established, such as the Free Masons, Rotary Clubs, Lions, and other spying associations. All those secret organizations, some which are overt, act for the interests of Zionism and under its directions, strive to demolish societies, to destroy values, to wreck answerableness, to totter virtues and to wipe out Islam. It stands behind the diffusion of drugs and toxics of all kinds in order to facilitate its control and expansion.

The Arab states surrounding Israel are required to open their borders to the Jihad fighters, the sons of the Arab and Islamic peoples, to enable them to play their role and to join their efforts to those of their brothers among the Muslim Brothers in Palestine.

The other Arab and Islamic states are required, at the very least, to facilitate the movement of the Jihad fighters from and to them. We cannot fail to remind every Muslim that when the Jews occupied Holy Jerusalem in 1967 and stood at the doorstep of the Blessed Aqsa Mosque, they shouted with joy:

"Muhammed is dead, he left daughters behind."

Israel, by virtue of its being Jewish and of having a Jewish population, defies Islam and the Muslims. . . .

ARTICLE THIRTY-ONE

Hamas is a humane movement, which cares for human rights and is committed to the tolerance inherent in Islam as regards attitudes towards other religions. It is only hostile to those who are hostile towards it, or stand in its way in order to disturb its moves or to frustrate its efforts.

Under the shadow of Islam it is possible for the members of the three religions: Islam, Christianity and Judaism to coexist in safety and security. Safety and security can only prevail under the shadow of Islam, and recent and ancient history is the best witness to that effect. The members of other religions must desist from struggling against Islam over sovereignty in this region. For if they were to gain the upper hand, fighting, torture and up-rooting would follow; they would be fed up with each other, to say nothing of members of other religions. The past and the present are full of evidence to that effect.

"They will not fight you in body safe in fortified villages or from behind wells. Their adversity among themselves is very great. Ye think of them as a whole whereas their hearts are diverse. That is because they are a folk who have no sense." *Sura 59 (al-Hashr, the Exile), verse 14.*

Islam accords his rights to everyone who has rights and averts aggression against the rights of others. The Nazi Zionist practices against our people will not last the lifetime of their invasion, for "States built upon oppression last only one hour, states based upon justice will last until the hour of Resurrection."

"Allah forbids you not those who warred not against you on account of religion and drove you not out from your houses, that you should show them kindness and deal justly with them. Lo! Allah loves the just dealers." *Sura 60 (Al-Mumtahana), verse 8.*

The Attempts to Isolate the Palestinian People

ARTICLE THIRTY-TWO

World Zionism and Imperialist forces have been attempting, with smart moves and considered planning, to push the Arab countries, one after another, out of the circle of conflict with Zionism, in order, ultimately to isolate the Palestinian People. Egypt has already been cast out of the conflict, to a very great extent through the treacherous Camp David Accords, and she has been trying to drag other countries into similar agreements in order to push them out of the circle of conflict.

Hamas is calling upon the Arab and Islamic peoples to act seriously and tirelessly in order to frustrate that dreadful scheme and to make the masses aware of the danger of coping out of the circle of struggle with Zionism. Today it is Palestine and tomorrow it may be another country or other countries. For Zionist scheming has no end, and after Palestine they will covet expansion from the Nile to the Euphrates. Only when they have completed digesting the area on which they will have laid their hand, they will look forward to more expansion, etc. Their scheme has been laid out in the Protocols of the Elders of Zion, and their present [conduct] is the best proof of what is said there.

Leaving the circle of conflict with Israel is a major act of treason and it will bring curse on its perpetrators.

"Who so on that day turns his back to them, unless manoeuvering for battle or intent to join a company, he truly has incurred wrath from Allah, and his habitation will be hell, a hapless journey's end." *Sura VIII (Al-Anfal—spoils of war), verse 16.*

We have no escape from pooling together all the forces and energies to face this despicable Nazi-Tatar invasion. Otherwise we shall witness the loss of [our] countries, the uprooting of their inhabitants, the spreading of corruption on earth and the destruction of all religious values. Let everyone realize that he is accountable to Allah. . . .

"Whoever does a speck of good will [the consequences] and whoever does a speck of evil will see [the consequences]."

Within the circle of the conflict with world Zionism, the Hamas regards itself the spearhead and the avant-garde. It joins its efforts to all those who are active on the Palestinian scene, but more steps need to be taken by the Arab and Islamic peoples and Islamic associations throughout the Arab and Islamic world in order to make possible the next round with the Jews, the merchants of war. . . .

The greedy have coveted Palestine more than once and they raided it with armies in order to fulfill their covetousness. Multitudes of Crusades descended on it, carrying their faith with them and waving their Cross. They were able to defeat the Muslims for a long time, and the Muslims were not able to redeem it until they sought the protection of their religious banner; then, they unified their forces, sang the praise of their God and set out for Jihad under the Command of Saladin al-Ayyubi, for the duration of nearly two decades, and then the obvious conquest took place when the Crusaders were defeated and Palestine was liberated.

"Say (O Muhammed) unto those who disbelieve: ye shall be overcome and gathered unto Hell, an evil resting place." *Sura III (Allmran), verse 12.*

This is the only way to liberation, there is no doubt in the testimony of history. That is one of the rules of the universe and one of the laws of existence. Only iron can blunt iron, only the true faith of Islam can vanquish their false and falsified faith. Faith can only be fought by faith. Ultimately, victory is reserved to the truth, and truth is victorious. . . .

Palestine National Council: Political Resolution (November 15, 1988)

The primary features of our great people's *intifada* were obvious from its inception and have become clearer in the twelve months since then during which it has continued unabated: It is a total popular revolution that embodies the consensus of an entire nation—women and men, old and young, in the camps, in the villages, and the cities—on the rejection of the occupation and on the determination to struggle until the occupation is defeated and terminated.

This glorious *intifada* has demonstrated our people's deeply rooted national unity and their full adherence to the Palestine Liberation Organization, the sole, legitimate representative of our people, all our people, wherever they congregate—in our homeland or outside it. This was manifested by the participation of the Palestinian masses—their unions, their vocational organizations, their students, their workers, their farmers, their women, their merchants, their landlords, their artisans, their academics—in the *intifada* through its Unified National Command and the popular committees that were formed in the urban neighborhoods, the villages, and the camps. . . .

In addition to this Arab solidarity, our people's revolution and their blessed *intifada* have attracted widespread worldwide solidarity, as seen in the increased understanding of the Palestinian people's issue, the growing support of our just struggle by the peoples and states of the world, and the corresponding condemnation of Israeli occupation and the crimes it is committing, which has helped to expose Israel and increase its isolation and the isolation of its supporters.

Security Council resolutions 605, 607, and 608 and the resolutions of the General Assembly against the expulsion of the Palestinians from their land and against the repression and terrorism with which Israel is lashing the Palestinian people in the occupied Palestinian territories—these are strong manifestation of the growing support of international opinion, public and official, for our people and their representative, the Palestine Liberation Organization, and of the mounting international rejection of Israeli occupation with all the fascist, racist practices it entails.

The UN General Assembly's Resolution 21L/43/1 of 4/11/1988, which was adopted in the session dedicated to the *intifada,* is another sign of the stand the peoples and states of the world in their majority are taking against the occupation and with the just struggle of the Palestinian people and their firm right to liberation and independence. . . .

In addition to the rejection of the occupation and the condemnation of its repressive measures by the democratic and progressive Israeli forces, Jewish groups all over the world are no longer able to continue their defense of Israel or maintain their silence about its crimes against the Palestinian people. Many voices have risen among those groups to demand an end to these crimes and call for Israel's withdrawal from the occupied territories in order to allow the Palestinian people to exercise their right to self-determination.

The fruits that our people's revolution and their blessed *intifada* have borne on the local, Arab, and international levels have established the soundness and realism of the Palestine Liberation Organization's national program, a program aimed at the termination of the occupation and the achievement of our people's right to return, self-determination, and statehood. Those results have also confirmed that the struggle of our people is the decisive factor in the effort to snatch our national rights from the jaws of the occupation. It is the authority of our people, as represented in the Popular Committees, that controls the situation as we challenge the authority of the occupation's crumbling agencies.

The international community is now more prepared than ever before to strive for a political settlement of the Middle East crisis and its root cause, the question of Palestine. The Israeli occupation authorities, and the American administration that stands behind them, cannot continue to ignore the international will, which is now unanimous on the necessity of holding an international peace conference on the Middle East and enabling the Palestinian people to gain their national rights, foremost among which is their right to self-determination and national independence on their own national soil.

In the light of this, and toward the reinforcement of the steadfastness and blessed *intifada* of our people, and in accordance with the will of our masses in and outside of our homeland, and in fidelity to those of our people that have been martyred, wounded, or taken captive, the Palestine National Council resolves:

First: On the Escalation and Continuity of the Intifada:

A. To provide all the means and capabilities needed to escalate our people's *intifada* in various ways and on various levels to guarantee its continuation and intensification.

B. To support the popular institutions and organizations in the occupied Palestinian territories.

C. To bolster and develop the popular committees and other specialized popular and trade union bodies, including the attack groups and the popular army, with a view to expanding their role and increasing their effectiveness.

D. To consolidate the national unity that emerged and developed during the *intifada*.

E. To intensify efforts on the international level for the release of detainees, the return of those expelled, and the termination of the organized, official acts of repression and terrorism against our children, our women, our men, and our institutions.

F. To call on the United Nations to place the occupied Palestinian land under international supervision for the protection of our people and the termination of the Israeli occupation.

G. To call on the Palestinian people outside our homeland to intensify and increase their support, and to expand the family-assistance program.

H. To call on the Arab nation, its people, forces, institutions, and governments, to increase their political, material, and informational support for the *intifada*.

I. To call on all free and honorable people worldwide to stand by our people, our revolution, our *intifada* against the Israeli occupation, the repression, and the organized, fascist official terrorism to which the occupation forces and the armed fanatic settlers are subjecting our people, our universities, our institutions, our national economy, and our Islamic and Christian holy places.

Second: In the Political Arena:

Proceeding from the above, the Palestine National Council, being responsible to the Palestinian people, their national rights and their desire for peace as expressed in the Declaration of Independence issued on 15 November 1988; and in response to the humanitarian quest for international entente, nuclear disarmament, and the settlement of regional conflict by peaceful means, affirms the determination of the Palestine Liberation Organization to arrive at a comprehensive settlement of the Arab-Israeli conflict and its core, which is the question of Palestine, within the framework of the United Nations Charter, the principles and provisions of international legality, the norms of international law, and the resolutions of the United Nations, the latest of which are Security Council resolutions 605, 607, and 608, and the resolutions of the Arab summits, in such a manner that safeguards the Palestinian Arab people's rights to return, to self-determination, and the establishment of their independent national state on their national soil, and that institutes arrangements for the security and peace of all states in the region.

Toward the achievement of this, the Palestine National Council affirms:

1.—The necessity of convening the effective international conference on the issue of the Middle East and its core, the question of Palestine, under the auspices of the United Nations and with the participation of the permanent members of the Security Council and all parties to the conflict in the region including the Palestine Liberation Organization, the sole, legitimate representative of the Palestinian people, on an equal footing, and by considering that the international peace conference be convened on the basis of United Nations Security Council resolutions 242 and 338 and the attainment of the legitimate national rights of the Palestinian people, foremost among which is the right to self-determination and in accordance with the principles and provisions of the United Nations Charter concerning the right of peoples to self-determination, and by the inadmissibility of the acquisition of the territory of others by force or military conquest, and in accordance with the relevant United Nations resolutions on the question of Palestine.

2.—The withdrawal of Israel from all the Palestinian and Arab territories it occupied in 1967, including Arab Jerusalem.

3.—The annullment of all measures of annexation and appropriation and the removal of settlements established by Israel in the Palestinian and Arab territories since 1967.

4.—Endeavoring to place the occupied Palestinian territories, including Arab Jerusalem, under the auspices of the United Nations for a limited period in order to protect our people and afford the appropriate atmosphere for the success of the proceeding of the international conference toward the attainment of a comprehensive political settlement and the attainment of peace and security for all on the basis of mutual aquiescence and consent, and to enable the Palestinian state to exercise its effective authority in these territories.

5.—The settlement of the question of the Palestinian refugees in accordance with the relevant United Nations resolutions.

6.—Guaranteeing the freedom of worship and religious practice for all faiths in the holy places in Palestine.

7.—The Security Council is to formulate and guarantee arrangements for security and peace between all the states concerned in the region, including the Palestinian state.

The Palestine National Council affirms its previous resolutions concerning the distinctive relationship between the Jordanian and Palestinian peoples, and affirms that the future relationship between the two states of Palestine and Jordan should be on a confederal basis as a result of the free and voluntary choice of the two fraternal peoples in order to strengthen the historical bonds and the vital interests they hold in common.

The National Council also renews its commitment to the United Nations resolutions that affirm the right of peoples to resist foreign occupation, colonialism, and racial discrimination, and their right to struggle for their independence, and reiterates its rejection of terrorism in all its forms, including state terrorism, affirming its commitment to previous resolutions in this respect and the resolution of the Arab summit in Algiers in 1988, and to UN resolutions 42/195 of 1987, and 40/61 of 1985, and that contained in the Cairo declaration of 1985 in this respect.

Third: In the Arab and International Arenas:

. . . The Palestine National Council, as it hails the Arab states and thanks them for their support of our people's struggle, calls on them to honor the commitments they approved at the summit conference in Algiers in support of the Palestinian people and their blessed *intifada*. The Council, in issuing this appeal, expresses its great confidence that the leaders of the Arab nation will remain, as we have known them, a bulwark of support for Palestine and its people. . . .

The Palestine National Council expresses its deep gratitude to all the states and international forces and organizations that support the national rights of the Palestinians, and affirms its desire to strengthen the bonds of friendship and cooperation with the Soviet Union, the People's Republic of China, the other socialist countries, the nonaligned states, the Latin American states, and the other friendly states, and notes with satisfaction the signs of positive evolution in the position of some West European states and Japan in the direction of support for the rights of the Palestinian people, applauds this development, and urges intensified efforts to increase it. . . .

The Council notes with considerable concern the growth of the Israeli forces of fascism and extremism and the escalation of their open calls for the implementation of their policy of annihilation and individual and mass expulsion of our people from their homeland, and calls for intensified efforts in all arenas to confront this fascist peril. The Council at the same time expresses its appreciation of the role and courage of the Israeli peace forces as they resist and expose the forces of fascism, racism, and aggression; support our people's struggle and their valiant *intifada;* and back our people's right to self-determination and the establishment of an independent state. The Council confirms its past resolutions regarding the reinforcement and development of relations with these democratic forces.

The Palestine National Council also addresses itself to the American people, calling on them all to strive to put an end to the American policy that denies the Palestinian people's national rights, including their sacred right to self-determination, and urging them to work toward the adoption of policies that conform with the human rights character and the international conventions and resolutions and serve the quest for peace in the Middle East and security for all its peoples, including the Palestinian people. . . .

Palestine National Council:
Declaration of Independence
(November 15, 1988)

In the name of God, the Compassionate, the Merciful

Palestine, the Land of the three monotheistic faiths, is where the Palestinian Arab people was born, on which it grew, developed and excelled. The Palestinian people was never separated from or diminished in its integral bonds with Palestine. Thus the Palestinian Arab people ensured for itself an everlasting union between itself, its land and its history.

Resolute throughout that history, the Palestinian Arab people forged its national identity, rising even to unimagined levels in its defence, as invasion, the design of others, and the appeal special to Palestine's ancient and luminous place on that eminence where powers and civilizations are joined . . . All this intervened thereby to deprive the people of its political independence. Yet the undying connection between Palestine and its people, secured for the Land its character, and for the people its national genius.

Nourished by an unfolding series of civilizations and cultures, inspired by a heritage rich in variety and kind, the Palestinian Arab people added to its stature by consolidating a union between itself and its patrimonial Land. The call went out from Temple, Church and Mosque that to praise the Creator, to celebrate compassion and peace was indeed the message of Palestine. And in generation after generation, the Palestinian Arab people gave of itself unsparingly in the valiant battle for liberation and homeland. For what has been the unbroken chain of our people's rebellions but the heroic embodiment of our will for national independence? And so the people were sustained in the struggle to stay and to prevail.

When in the course of modern times a new order of values was declared with norms and values fair for all, it was the Palestinian Arab people that had been excluded from the destiny of all other peoples by a hostile array of local and foreign powers. Yet again had unaided justice been revealed as insufficient to drive the world's history along its preferred course.

And it was the Palestinian people, already wounded in its body, that was submitted to yet another type of occupation over which floated the falsehood that "Palestine was a land without people." This notion was foisted upon some in the world, whereas in Article 22 of the Covenant of the League of Nations (1919) and in the Treaty of Lausanne (1923), the community of nations had recognized that all the Arab territories, including Palestine, of the formerly Ottoman provinces, were to have granted to them their freedom as provisionally independent nations.

Despite the historical injustice inflicted on the Palestinian Arab people resulting in their dispersion and depriving them of their right to self-determination, following upon UN General Assembly Resolution 181 (1947), which partitioned Palestine into two states, one Arab, one Jewish, yet it is this resolution that still provides those conditions of international legitimacy that ensure the right of the Palestinian Arab people to sovereignty.

By stages, the occupation of Palestine and parts of other Arab territories by Israeli forces, the willed dispossession and expulsion from their ancestral homes of the majority of Palestine's civilian inhabitants was achieved by organized terror; those Palestinians who remained, as a vestige subjugated in its homeland, were persecuted and forced to endure the destruction of their national life.

Thus were principles of international legitimacy violated. Thus were the Charter of the United Nations and its resolutions disfigured, for they had recognized the Palestinian Arab people's national rights, including the right of Return, the right to independence, the right to sovereignty over territory and homeland.

In Palestine and on its perimeters, in exile distant and near, the Palestinian Arab people never faltered and never abandoned its conviction in its right of Return and independence. Occupation, massacres and dispersion achieved no gain in the unabated Palestinian consciousness of self and political identity, as Palestinians went forward with their destiny, undeterred and unbowed. And from out of the long years of trial in ever mounting struggle, the Palestinian political identity emerged further consolidated and confirmed. And the collective Palestinian national will forged for itself a political embodiment, the Palestine Liberation Organization, its sole, legitimate representative recognized by the world community as a whole, as well as by related regional and international institutions. Standing on the very rock of conviction in the Palestinian people's inalienable rights, and on the ground of Arab national consensus, and of international legitimacy, the PLO led the campaigns of its great people, moulded into unity and powerful resolve, one and indivisible in its triumphs, even as it suffered massacres and confinement within and without its home. And so Palestinian resistance was clarified and raised into the forefront of Arab and world awareness, as the struggle of the Palestinian Arab people achieved unique prominence among the world's liberation movements in the modern era.

The massive national uprising, the Intifada, now intensifying in cumulative scope and power on occupied Palestinian territories, as well as the unflinching resistance of the refugee camps outside the homeland, have elevated awareness of the Palestinian truth and right into still higher realms of comprehension and actuality. Now at last the curtain has been dropped around a whole epoch of prevarication and negation. The Intifada has set siege to the mind of official Israel, which has for too long relied exclusively upon myth and terror to deny Palestinian existence altogether. Because of the Intifada and its revolutionary irreversible impulse, the history of Palestine has therefore arrived at a decisive juncture.

Whereas the Palestinian people reaffirms most definitively its inalienable rights in the Land of its patrimony:

Now by virtue of natural, historical and legal rights, and the sacrifices of successive generations who gave of themselves in defence of the freedom and independence of their homeland;

In pursuance of Resolutions adopted by Arab Summit Conferences and relying on the authority bestowed by international legitimacy as embodied in the resolutions of the United Nations Organization since 1947;

And in exercise by the Palestinian Arab people of its rights to self-determination, political independence, and sovereignty over its territory;

The Palestine National Council, in the name of God, and in the name of the Palestinian Arab people; hereby proclaims the establishment of the State of Palestine on our Palestinian territory with its capital Holy Jerusalem (Al-Quds Ash-Sharif).

The State of Palestine is the state of Palestinians wherever they may be. The state is for them to enjoy in it their collective national and cultural identity, theirs to pursue in it a complete equality of rights. In it will be safeguarded their political and religious convictions and their human dignity by means of a parliamentary democratic system of governance, itself based on freedom of expression and the freedom to form parties. The rights of minorities will duly be respected by the majority, as minorities must abide by decisions of the majority. Governance will be based on principles of social justice, equality and non-discrimination in public rights of men or women, on grounds of race, religion, colour or sex under the aegis of a constitution which ensures the rule of law and an independent judiciary. Thus shall these principles allow no departure from Palestine's age-old spiritual and civilizational heritage of tolerance and religious coexistence.

The State of Palestine is an Arab state, an integral and indivisible part of the Arab nation, at one with that nation in heritage and civilization, with it also in its aspiration for liberation, progress, democracy and unity. The State of Palestine affirms its obligation to abide by the Charter of the League of Arab States, whereby the coordination of the Arab states with each other shall be strengthened. It calls upon Arab compatriots to consolidate and enhance the emergence in reality of our state, to mobilize potential, and to intensify efforts whose goal is to end Israeli occupation.

The State of Palestine proclaims its commitment to the principles and purposes of the United Nations, and to the Universal Declaration of Human Rights. It proclaims its commitment as well to the principles and policies of the Non-Aligned Movement.

It further announces itself to be a peace-loving State, in adherence to the principles of peaceful coexistance. It will join with all states and peoples in order to assure a permanent peace based upon justice and the respect of rights so that humanity's potential for well-being may be assured, an earnest competition for excellence may be maintained, and in which confidence in the future will eliminate fear for those who are just and for whom justice is the only recourse.

In the context of its struggle for peace in the Land of Love and Peace, the State of Palestine calls upon the United Nations to bear special responsibility for the Palestinian Arab people and its homeland. It calls upon all peace- and freedom-loving peoples and states to assist it in the attainment of its objectives, to provide it with security, to alleviate the tragedy of its people, and to help it terminate Israel's occupation of the Palestinian territories.

The State of Palestine herewith declares that it believes in the settlement of regional and international disputes by peaceful means, in accordance with the UN Charter and resolutions. Without prejudice to its natural right to defend its territorial integrity and independence, it therefore rejects the threat or use of force, violence and terrorism against its territorial integrity or political independence, as it also rejects their use against the territorial integrity of other states.

Therefore, on this day unlike all others, November 15, 1988, as we stand at the threshold of a new dawn, in all honour and modesty we humbly bow to the sacred spirits of our fallen ones, Palestinian and Arab, by the purity of whose sacrifice for the homeland our sky has been illuminated and our land given life. Our hearts are lifted up and irradiated by the light emanating from the much blessed Intifada, from those who have endured and have fought the fight of the camps, of dispersion, of exile, from those who have borne the standard for freedom, our children, our aged, our youth, our prisoners, detainees and wounded, all those whose ties to our sacred soil are confirmed in camp, village and town. We render special tribute to that brave Palestinian woman, guardian of sustenance and life, keeper of our people's perennial flame. To the souls of our sainted martyrs, to the whole of our Palestinian Arab people, to all free and honorable peoples everywhere, we pledge that our struggle shall be continued until the occupation ends, and the foundation of our sovereignty and independence shall be fortified accordingly.

Therefore, we call upon our great people to rally to the banner of Palestine, to cherish and defend it, so that it may forever be the symbol of our freedom and dignity in that homeland, which is a homeland for the free, now and always. In the name of God, the Compassionate, the Merciful:

"Say:

O God, Master of the Kingdom,
Thou givest the Kingdom to whom Thou wilt,
and seizest the Kingdom from whom Thou wilt,
Thou exaltest whom Thou wilt,
and Thou abasest whom Thou wilt;
in Thy hand is the good;
Thou art powerful over everything."

Egyptian President Hosni Mubarak: The Inevitability of Peace (January 21, 1989)

. . . I hope this year will be a year of peace. In fact, we are exerting the utmost efforts for the sake of peace. All our contacts with the friendly and European states are also channeled in the direction of peace because peace is the only path leading to a real solution to all key issues. I believe that wars have not decisively resolved any issue, as best proved by the war of Vietnam with the United States. That war continued for many years and was settled only through negotiations. We hope that 1989 will be a year of peace, and we, together with our brothers in the Arab countries, are exerting our utmost efforts to promote the Middle East peace process. We are helped in this regard by the European states, the big powers, and the peace-loving forces in Israel itself. As long as we have confidence in peace, the opposing forces will certainly respond because the current of peace is sweeping and nobody can stop it. . . .

Enough of "wars." I once again ask what is wrong with peace? Has it prevented any steps in our or the Arab nation's favor? We are helping the Palestine question more than anyone else. I will speak frankly and without resentment. For example, when I visited the United States last January, I did not forget Syria. Asked about Syria, I said verbatim: We will not forget Syria. During the visit, Richard Murphy and Philip Habib visited Syria and I was told in Dallas about the meeting and what took place during it. We are helping movement toward all the Arab nation's issues.

As for Libya, they say there is nothing called Israel although the world's countries, including the two superpowers and the European, Asian, and African states, recognize Israel. The Soviet Union has recognized it and even helped it join the other members of the United Nations. The colonel [Al-Qadhdhafi] is free not to recognize it, but this does not mean that it is not recognized. He asks the entire Arab world to wage war. God has granted us a mind with which to think. We fought for many years, but where did we get? We also spent 100 billion [currency not specified] on wars, apart from thousands of martyrs, until we reached the present situation from which we are now suffering. I am therefore not ready to take more risks. Moreover, wars have generally not solved any problem. Regardless of the difficulties or obstacles surrounding the present peace process, our real effort focuses on removing these obstacles and bringing viewpoints closer. We are not at all pessimistic. Today's world is one of peace, peaceful negotiations, and fruitful dialogue, which leads to real results away from blood and fire.

All world public opinion supports the international conference with the exception of Yitzhak Shamir, who does not agree to it. He should respond to the call of peace because the peace-loving forces in Israel and elsewhere are increasing. War has exhausted the region's forces, including Israel. It has also lowered the people's standard of living in Israel itself and the entire region. Let me ask: Is it possible for this situation to continue? Shamir must respond to the call of peace sooner or later because this is the will of the people. Peace will come even though it seems to be a long way ahead. Israel will sooner or later respond to the international conference, and I am optimistic that peace is coming. . . .

Israeli Prime Minister Yitzhak Shamir: Peace Plan (May 14, 1989)

Basic Premises

3.—The initiative is founded upon the assumption that there is a national consensus for it on the basis of the basic guidelines of the Government of Israel, including the following points:

a) Israel yearns for peace and the continuation of the political process by means of direct negotiations based on the principles of the Camp David Accords.

b) Israel opposes the establishment of an additional Palestinian state in the Gaza district and in the area between Israel and Jordan.

c) Israel will not conduct negotiations with the PLO.

d) There will be no change in the status of Judea, Samaria and Gaza other than in accordance with the basic guidelines of the Government.

Subjects to Be Dealt with in the Peace Process

4.—Israel views as important that the peace between Israel and Egypt, based on the Camp David Accords, will serve as a cornerstone for enlarging the circle of peace in the region, and calls for a common endeavour for the strengthening of the peace and its extension, through continued consultation.

b) Israel calls for the establishment of peaceful relations between it and those Arab states which still maintain a state of war with it for the purpose of promoting a comprehensive settlement for the Arab-Israeli conflict, including recognition, direct negotiations, ending the boycott, diplomatic relations, cessation of hostile activity in international institutions or forums and regional and bilateral cooperation.

c) Israel calls for an international endeavour to resolve the problem of the residents of the Arab refugee camps in Judea, Samaria and the Gaza district in order to improve their living conditions and to rehabilitate them. Israel is prepared to be a partner in this endeavour.

d) In order to advance the political negotiation process leading to peace, Israel proposes free and democratic elections among the Palestinian Arab inhabitants of Judea, Samaria and the Gaza district in an atmosphere devoid of violence, threats and terror. In these elections a representation will be chosen to conduct negotiations for a transitional period of self-rule. This period will constitute a test for co-existence and cooperation. At a later stage, negotiations will be conducted for a permanent solution during which all the proposed options for an agreed settlement will be examined, and peace between Israel and Jordan will be achieved.

e) All the above-mentioned steps should be dealt with simultaneously.

f) The details of what has been mentioned in (*d*) above will be given below.

The Principles Constituting the Initiative Stages

5.—The initiative is based on two stages
   a) Stage A—A transitional period for an interim agreement.
   b) Stage B—Permanent Solution.
6.—The interlock between the Stages is a timetable on which the Plan is built: the peace process delineated by the initiative is based on Resolutions 242 and 338 upon which the Camp David Accords are founded.

Timetable

7.—The transitional period will continue for 5 years.
8.—As soon as possible, but not later than the third year after the beginning of the transitional period, negotiations for achieving a permanent solution will begin.

Parties Participating in the Negotiations in Both Stages

9.—The parties participating in the negotiations for the First Stage (the interim agreement) shall include Israel and the elected representation of the Palestinian Arab inhabitants of Judea, Samaria and the Gaza district. Jordan and Egypt will be invited to participate in these negotiations if they so desire.

10.—The parties participating in the negotiations for the Second Stage (Permanent Solution) shall include Israel and the elected representation of the Palestinian Arab inhabitants of Judea, Samaria and the Gaza district, as well as Jordan: furthermore, Egypt may participate in these negotiations. In negotiations between Israel and Jordan, in which the elected representation of the Palestinian Arab inhabitants of Judea, Samaria and the Gaza district will participate, the peace treaty between Israel and Jordan will be concluded.

Substance of Transitional Period

11.—During the transitional period the Palestinian Arab inhabitants of Judea, Samaria and the Gaza district will be accorded self-rule by means of which they will, themselves, conduct their affairs of daily life. Israel will continue to be responsible for security, foreign affairs and all matters concerning Israeli citizens in Judea, Samaria and the Gaza district. Topics involving the implementation of the plan for self-rule will be considered and decided within the framework of the negotiations for an interim agreement.

Substance of Permanent Solution

12.—In the negotiations for a permanent solution every party shall be entitled to present for discussion all the subjects it may wish to raise.

13.—The aim of the negotiations should be:

a) The achievement of a permanent solution acceptable to the negotiating parties.

b) The arrangements for peace and borders between Israel and Jordan.

Details of the Process for the Implementation of the Initiative

14.—First and foremost dialogue and basic agreement by the Palestinian Arab inhabitants of Judea, Samaria and the Gaza district, as well as Egypt and Jordan if they wish to take part, as abovementioned, in the negotiations, on the principles constituting the initiative.

15.—*a*) Immediately afterwards will follow the stage of preparations and implementation of the election process in which a representation of the Palestinian Arab inhabitants of Judea, Samaria and Gaza will be elected. This representation:

I) Shall be a partner to the conduct of negotiations for the transitional period (interim agreement).

II) Shall constitute the self-governing authority in the course of the transitional period.

III) Shall be the central Palestinian component, subject to agreement after three years, in the negotiations for the permanent solution.

b) In the period of the preparation and implementation there shall be a calming of the violence in Judea, Samaria and the Gaza district.

16.—As to the substance of the elections, it is recommended that a proposal of regional elections be adopted, the details of which shall be determined in further discussions.

17.—Every Palestinian Arab residing in Judea, Samaria and the Gaza districts, who shall be elected by the inhabitants to represent them—after having submitted his candidacy in accordance with the detailed document which shall determine the subject of the elections—may be a legitimate participant in the conduct of negotiations with Israel.

18.—The elections shall be free, democratic and secret.

19.—Immediately after the election of the Palestinian representation, negotiations shall be conducted with it on an interim agreement for a transitional period which shall continue for 5 years, as mentioned above. In these negotiations the parties shall determine all the subjects relating to the substance to the self-rule and the arrangements necessary for its implementation.

20.—As soon as possible, but not later than the third year after the establishment of the self-rule, negotiations for a permanent solution shall begin. During the whole period of these negotiations until the signing of the agreement for a permanent solution, the self-rule shall continue in effect as determined in the negotiations for an interim agreement.

Egyptian President Hosni Mubarak: Ten-Point Plan (September 4, 1989)

1.—The necessity for the participation of all citizens of the West Bank and Gaza (including the residents of East Jerusalem) in the elections both in the voting and in the right to stand as a candidate for any person who has not been convicted by a court of committing a crime. This allows for the participation of those under administrative detention.

2.—Freedom to campaign before and during the elections.

3.—Acceptance of international supervision of the election process.

4.—Prior commitment of the government of Israel that it will accept the results of the elections.

5.—Commitment of the government of Israel that the elections will be part of the efforts which will lead not only to an interim phase, but also to a final settlement and that all efforts from beginning to end will be based on the principles of solution according to the U.S. conception, namely resolutions 242 and 338, territory for peace, insuring the security of all the states of the region including Israel, and Palestinian political rights.

6.—Withdrawal of the Israeli army during the election process at least one kilometer outside the perimeters of the polling stations.

7.—Prohibition of Israelis from entering the West Bank and Gaza on election day with permission to enter only for those who work there and the residents of the settlements.

8.—The preparatory period for the elections should not exceed two months. These preparations shall be undertaken by a joint Israeli-Palestinian committee. (The U.S. and Egypt may assist in forming this committee).

9.—Guarantee by the U.S. of all the above points together with a prior declaration to that effect on the part of the government of Israel.

10.—A halt to settlement.

PLO Chairman Yasir Arafat: Speech on the Intifada (September 1989)

In the name of God, the merciful, the compassionate. So lose not heart, nor fall into despair: For ye must gain mastery if ye are true in faith. If a wound hath touched you, be sure a similar wound hath touched the others. Such days (for varying fortunes) we give to men and men by turns: That God may know that those believe, and that He may take to Himself from your ranks martyr-witnesses (to truth). And God loveth not those who do wrong.

O the great masses of our Palestinian people, O the epic of the brave *intifada* [uprising] on the soil of the homeland, O steadfast heroes in the camps and on the borders of the homeland, O struggles in every field of struggle inside and outside the beloved homeland, victory is yours, as you are making your dear sacrifices on the path of national independence. Freedom and victory are yours as you daily create events of unique heroism and distinguished experience for your giant *intifada,* which has occupied its lofty peak since its first waves in the history of mankind as a major landmark and a new contribution to the experience of peoples struggling against the forces of colonialism, Zionism, racism, coercion, and injustice.

O women of my country; O heroes of my country; O brave and heroic youths and men of my country; you continue the march with more resolution and stronger will as you are entering the 22d month of the sacred stones *intifada.* Despite all repressive and terrorist attempts and despite the great sacrifices, you have continued—with legendary courage—to raise the banner of resistance. And, with your stones, you are pounding the structure of the transient occupation and building our forthcoming Palestinian state, making the certain date of independence and freedom nearer for our people. Who in the world, beloved ones, could have believed or predicted—in those days of January 1987—that the *intifada* would continue and escalate? Who in the world was ready to admit our people's great ability to continue the march to achieve the goal which we will not relinquish, the goal of independence, freedom, and victory. Many people refused to believe our signs. Many people were not interested in our talk about the escalating volcano inside and outside the homeland. Many people were also not interested in our talk about the gathering storm throughout the region. Then the *intifada* came, the *intifada* came so that we could storm the walls of the world's conscience. Its news also reached every house around the world and our people's cause has recorded its shining and prominent regional and international presence. The phoenix has set out each day to occupy new positions, which would not have existed without the great sacrifices and the procession of martyrs who fill the path of heroism and glory—the path of the dear sons and righteous beloved ones. This is in addition to the sacrifices and heroism of our wounded, prisoners, and detainees that emerged through this mammoth popular momentum of the great people of the *intifada,* through their inspiring legendary steadfastness, and through this firmness and resistance of our heroes in the positions of combat and conflict. . . .

The masses of the blessed *intifada* were affirming, every moment and in every way before the whole world, that whoever for one moment thinks of the possibility of peddling the settlement project, which does not provide for our people's firm and national rights, is dreaming and cannot read the revolutionary reality or know the revolutionary will of our people. They do not know how to observe the current course of history flowing to the delta of liberty and independence.

They are still haunted by the ghosts and delusions of the old eras of occupation, control, and expansion. These delusions are extinct and the blessed stones of our women, children, and men are now declaring the end of these extinct delusions. Nay, this forces many of these deluded to recognize the impossibility of torpedoing the unity of the Palestinian stand which manifests a unique example of the revolutionary world march through creating splits and divisions in its ranks, casting doubts, or liquidation. This is a great revolutionary example of unity and revolutionary cohesion. . . .

O masses of the blessed *intifada;* O heroes of the stones and songs; O courageous strike forces; O you steadfast people in every location: The fascist occupation have been trying—since the outbreak of the *intifada*—to impose a media blackout on the *intifada* activities to prevent the arrival of your brave voice to world conscience and to prevent the exposure of their racist crimes and crazy terrorism. However, despite all their repressive measures, the Palestinian blood has infiltrated the siege while the Palestinian shout reached the heart and conscience of the world.

You, courageous heroes, knew that confronting the campaigns of siege and news blackout will escalate the defiance and steadfastnes and with more jihad and struggle that are entrenched on the ground in the form of daily effective blows which had their effect in shaking and shattering the authority and might of the enemy. The power of the people, the power of the *intifada* and the power of revolution, which has been entrenched by Qawim, will emerge along with our broad, believing masses, the effectiveness of the popular committees, and the activities of the strike forces. This power has also been entrenched by this accurate popular organization that has gathered all factions of our people and forces in the crucible of a firm national unity to entrench the foundations of national independence. In the name of God, the merciful, the compassionate: God truly loves those who fight in his cause in battle array, as if they were a solid cemented structure.

Hence, my brothers, your boycott of Israeli goods has succeeded, and your organized strikes have affected labor in Israeli concerns and the enemy's labor activity and economy. The national agricultural, industrial, and vocational projects have succeeded in supporting the national and local production and in bolstering the home economy. Therefore, we have to work actively and confidently to promote national institutions and all their projects, to support national production, and to boost family economy. We should also work toward expanding the activity of mass institutions, specialized committees, popular education, national media, and others. In addition, we should concentrate on mass education and establishing well-being committees to solve the problems of peoples, and there are many problems.

Revolutionary discipline should also be practiced to prevent the negative aspects and crush deviations, because the enemy will try to push his secret agents among us to intensify these negative points and deviations in order to make people hate the march and to distract them from their blessed intifada. So, you are urged to show more and more revolutionary discipline, more and more fight against anarchy, and more and more serious work to end the negative aspects and increase the positive ones.

No revolution can emerge victorious unless supported by its masses, and no militant march can continue without sound revolutionary discipline. It cannot continue without bolstering the unity of its ranks, commitment to the calls of the Unified National Leadership, supporting the structure of the popular committees, and firmly confronting all attempts to create divisions, especially in the way of dealing with the sons of our people who lost their way and fell in the trap of the enemy. We should push them toward repentance, first, second, and third; "Let he who is without sin cast the first stone." Otherwise we will fall in the trap that our enemy is making for us, as happened to the revolution of 1936. I therefore appeal to you to commit yourselves to this fraternal and revolutionary policy; "Strong against unbelievers, (but) compassionate among each other" [part of Koranic verse]. I also appeal to you to be alert against falsehoods against the march of the intifada and the discipline of the masses, which make a unified whole. Hence came the orientation not to issue statements in the names of the various frameworks of the intifada and its unified strike force. This was a clear reference to the statements issued to disintegrate and undermine the firmness of the intifada and its unified strike forces, which are remote from organizational bragging and nonsense. We all have the heart of one man. In the name of God, the merciful, the compassionate: Our Lord, decide thou between us and our people in truth, for thou art the best to decide.

We realize, my beloved brothers, that this great revolutionary achievement, which is daily being entrenched on the ground, exasperates the fascist occupiers, who fully understand its significance and essence. They, therefore, intensify their terrorist campaigns and attempts to infiltrate our ranks, confuse our minds, and undermine our unity. They declare the war of murder in cold blood; they also declare the war of starvation, blockade, and detention in an unsuccessful attempt to crush the blessed intifada. "Fain would they extinguish God's light with their mouths, but God will not allow but that His light should be perfected, even though the unbelievers may detest (it)."

By this, they prove their failure to learn the lesson and absorb the bright fact. This intifada will continue, continue, with God's help, despite all difficulties, wave after wave, until the hateful Israeli occupation of our land and sacred places is ended. There are endless queues of heroes proceeding one after the other to receive the banner whenever a struggler falls or another is imprisoned in occupation jails.

O courageous people of the intifada, O hero strugglers of the Unified National Leadership, popular committees, and strike force. O strugglers of mass institutions—women, youths, students, workers, peasants, professionals, vocationalists, academicians, landowners, farmers, and, especially,

the cubs of the revolution: O captive heroes, makers of the epic of steadfastness in prisons; our valiant wounded, who lift the banners of triumph
over your wounds; O steadfast people in all positions of struggle in the
homeland and abroad; O masses of the great Arab nation: Our *intifada* today enters its 22d month with full confidence in the inevitability of victory,
God willing. Freedom has never been so near and within reach as it seems
to us now. It needs the efforts of friends, support of brothers, and sacrifices
of revolutionaries. After we imposed our existence on the political map, it
is inevitable that we impose it on the geographical map. Let us boost the
unity of our ranks and the cohesion of our front. Unity, unity among all,
among our broad masses, all our organizations—Hamas, Fatah, the Popular Front [for the Liberation of Palestine], the Democratic Front [for the
Liberation of Palestine], the Jihad, the communists, the [Palestinian Popu-
lar] Struggle Front, the Palestinian Front, and all and trade unions, popular
forces and the institutions—all united in one framework. Let us affirm
strong commitment to the calls of the Unified National Leadership of the
intifada, and escalate the war of the sacred stones with utmost vigor and
strength, and let the strike forces escalate their struggle with firmness and
solidity against the occupiers, all of whose weapons cannot conceal their
political and historical crisis. Your *intifada* is continuing until the state is
established, and your steadfastness will continue until victory is achieved.
The state is within a stone's throw, the victory is coming, and our Palestinian flag will be raised, God willing, over Jerusalem, the capital of our city,
the first of the two qiplas [direction in which Muslims position themselves
during prayer—Jerusalem and Mecca] and the third sacred shrines, the
birthplace of the Messiah and the city to where Prophet Muhammad made
his night journey. In the name of God, the merciful, the compassionate:
"And another (favor will He bestow, which ye do love—help from God
and a speedy victory. So give the glad tidings to the believers."

U.S. Secretary of State James Baker: Five-Point Plan (October 10, 1989)

1.—The United States understands that because Egypt and Israel have
been working hard on the peace process, there is agreement that an Israeli
delegation should conduct a dialogue with a Palestinian delegation in
Cairo.

2.—The United States understands that Egypt cannot substitute itself
for the Palestinians and Egypt will consult with Palestinians on all aspects
of that dialogue. Egypt will also consult with Israel and the United States.

3.—The United States understands that Israel will attend the dialogue
only after a satisfactory list of Palestinians has been worked out.

4.—The United States understands that the Government of Israel will come to the dialogue on the basis of the Israeli Government's May 14 initiative. The United States further understands that Palestinians will come to the dialogue prepared to discuss elections and the negotiating process in accordance with Israel's initiative. The U.S. understands, therefore, that Palestinians would be free to raise issues that relate to their opinions on how to make elections and the negotiating process succeed.

5.—In order to facilitate this process, the U.S. proposes that the Foreign Ministers of Israel, Egypt, and the U.S. meet in Washington within two weeks.

Iraqi President Saddam Hussein: Speech to the Arab Cooperation Council (February 1990)

We Arabs, Iraqis included, have a habit of either underrating or overrating our power. I believe that through cooperation among ourselves and the prevalence of a brotherly spirit, we will reach a way of thinking that will prevent us from overestimating ourselves to the point of delirium, or underestimating ourselves to the point of missing our chance to play an influential role.

The Arabs possess an extraordinary ability to accelerate the creation of an international balance because, in addition to the known traditional elements including the known strategic elements involving the region's geography and their influence, there is an additional element: the possession of an energy source unparalleled in the world. All the major influential powers are affected by this, be it the United States, Japan, or Europe, or even the Soviet Union. Consequently, when Arab influence, by virtue of this extra element, reaches this point, then we can speed up the creation of a balance that at least does not make Arab interests vulnerable. . . .

The Arabs should not only settle their differences, but also organize their course of action by adopting positive steps. The more their course is organized through positive action, the more their influence will be. But, if we concern ourselves only with extinguishing fires, we will lose much of our energy inasmuch as we will be handicapped and unable to move forward.

Praise be to God, we hope that the new spirit in the Arab League will bring about leaders' meetings and other meetings and produce fraternal cooperation at the level of the three groupings—the Arab Maghreb Union, the Gulf Cooperation Council, and the ACC. All these are positive signs. At the same time, our enemies will take the positive steps we announce into their calculations of the balances of power. They will take into account that behind every statement we make there is real action they have to deal with. They will assume that we mean what we say. When we do not translate what we say we will be the losers because our enemy will be aware that we are only making statements and not taking action.

What draws attention in the Americans' behavior is the quick appearance of the spirit of unilateralism although the international imbalance is not old. An example of this is encouraging Jewish emigration, particularly Soviet Jewish immigration to the occupied territory, although the declared U.S. position is that it works for peace and that it is in touch with Egypt and the Palestinians on the basis that it wants to establish peace. Would someone who wants to achieve peace act this way? It is a superpower and it has become the first-ranking superpower, while the USSR, as a superpower, is undergoing a series of changes. In addition to this, we have taken note of U.S. statements on the Gulf and the assertions that the Israelis can use weapons stored in Israel. None of these signs is good.

In case of danger, there are always early signs. Israel always takes international changes and their effect into consideration. Israel has never lost an opportunity to take advantage of the atmosphere of change. Since the establishment of Israel—and even before it was established when it opened contacts with the Ottoman Empire and until the Balfour Declaration—the Jews who believe in the establishment of the State of Israel have always exploited opportunities. We must expect Israel to exploit the opportunity resulting from the current changes in the world.

Israel now is facing a clear question; that is, in light of its present situation time is not on its side. Tension in relations among the Arabs has begun to ease; the Arabs want to understand, resolve their problems, and cooperate among themselves. There is a real desire to know about the changes in the world and their effect on their situation; they want to know what they should do to become effective in the world. Arab scientific cadres are being formed and our intrinsic military capabilities are growing. The Israelis say that the news of Arab capabilities have surprised them.

Therefore, all this makes the Israelis realize that time is against them in terms of topography and politics, as well as other factors. Let us not rule out that some Israeli strategists will say that time is against us in this situation. If we can change this situation and change the military geography, time might be on our side.

Therefore, we should be alert over the next five years because when Israel wants to embark on military aggression it will take new land; it might launch a new attack to come out of its deadlock. Who will oppose them internationally?

The answer is no one, even if no one offered direct support to encourage it to launch aggression, no one will stand against Israeli aggression, as happened in the wars of 1967 and 1973 because the United States has remained alone in the arena of the big powers, and the U.S. policy is the policy we are now experiencing. Will the Soviet Union be capable of confronting the aggression if it takes place, or will it be Europe that confronts the aggression? All this makes us wonder what then is the situation?

The most influential stand *vis-à-vis* such a situation should come from within ourselves and our capabilities. There is no better way than this to remove the minefields that mar Arab relations. The second best way under these circumstances is also to push ahead joint action as expeditiously as possible. Faced with the quick developments, we should have a joint policy as Arabs on the regional level. It is not sufficient that Iraq has a policy, whether this policy is viewed as sound, or wrong in varying degrees, or that Egypt has such a policy, or Kuwait and Saudi Arabia, and Algeria too. We are dutybound as Arabs to have a joint regional policy. The basic pillars of this joint regional policy are to reduce the number of the Arab nation's enemies, or to reduce the frictions that will add further enemies. Our relations with Ethiopia should not be bad. We must try to solve our problems with Iran as Arabs and within boundaries that safeguard our rights and do not encroach on its rights.

All these elements limit the Israeli ability to make inroads during the mentioned five-year period not only in the Arab land but also in terms of influencing the Arabs in the technological, political and military fields with its own efforts or with the help of Jewish influence in the world. If the Arabs take all these elements into consideration, they will find themselves in an excellent position and will prevent the wave from destroying their barriers. The wave will merely move from one place to another because their barriers are high and impregnable. The wave will thus be forced to change direction and to destroy barriers in other places. . . . Moreover, when interest in the Palestine question diminishes, the Arabs will not act either. When a long time passes without effective action, interest in an issue fades away. There is another important issue, which is the situation in the occupied territories and the valiant popular resistance there.

It is not enough to show Arab solidarity with the *intifada* in a traditional manner that may become ineffective if it remains unchanged. It is necessary to overhaul the means and formulas of attention and support. At the top of the list is extending real financial support to the militant Palestinian people and enhancing organized and meaningful political action in the international arena. . . . the *intifada* and its actions represent an Arab army corps that is carrying out the task of weakening the Zionists in the occupied territories by using stones. We must provide the *intifada* with its needs out of pan-Arab principles and regional security considerations. Let us then provide it with what an army corps needs in supplies and ammunition. Then, and only then, will we ensure the strength of the *intifada*.

What weakens the enemy most is psychological exhaustion. Israel used to say that its soldier was invincible and some of us even believed it. Now, and due to the *intifada,* that soldier looks weak and undisciplined. He no longer wears his beret or helmet and does not rise to salute his officers when they pass by. This, and other things, show that he lacks discipline. It is well known that the soldier's strength lies in his discipline.

The *intifada* of the young people and valiant women has shown us the true, pathetic state of the Israeli soldier. They have told us: Here you see the Israeli soldier—a man whom we can defeat if we exhaust him. If we, the little ones and women, have destroyed the Israeli soldiers' morale, then Arabs, united and with greater power, are able to defeat the enemy and regain their rights.

Now we see certain new factors emerging on the ground that affect the residents of the West Bank and Gaza. Immigration to Israel has made some of them leave their lands and go to Jordan. Last year, Mr. President, 55,000 young Palestinians left the West Bank and Gaza and came to Jordan. This should make us think about maintaining, through resistance, what is left of Arab rights on the land until such time as we can use more effective methods to regain more than what we can regain now. We know that 80 percent of Israelis live on the Mediterranean coast and do not care about the *intifada*. As for us, we are affected by the *intifada*. The Israeli people have become used to the fact that there are children throwing stones, and the one who is really affected is the Israeli soldier who returns to his home town at the weekend. What I mean, Mr. President, is that without real, constant, and strong support for the *intifada*, it may become ineffective in the future. Immigration itself and the absorption of thousands of new immigrants into Palestinian territory—whether in Israel or in the occupied territories—aim to end the Arab presence in Palestinian territory.

Palestine was usurped through deliberate planning, and it can only be restored through deliberate planning backed by determination to achieve justice. The struggler sons of Palestine have proved to be an example of determination and readiness for sacrifice. The loss of Palestine was not essentially due to the Zionists' faith in the Zionist cause, but due to the Arabs' abandonment of the Arab cause. It was also not essentially due to Zionist strength, but to Arab weakness. Now that the Arabs have realized—through different factors and reasons, including their triumph over their enemies and the enemies of God on the eastern front and the heroic stand of the people of the deadly stones—that they are capable of taking action, then Palestine will return. Light will chase out darkness and the banners of justice shall fly over holy Jerusalem, God willing. . . .

Among the most important developments since the international conflict in World War II has been the fact that some countries which used to enjoy broad international influence, such as France and Britain, have declined, while the influence and impact of two countries expanded until they became the two superpowers among the countries of the world—I mean the United States and the Soviet Union. Of course, with these results, two axis have developed: the Western axis under the leadership of the United

States, with its known capitalist approach and its imperialist policy; or the East bloc under the leadership of the Soviet Union and its communist philosophy.

Among the results of World War II: The Zionist state has become a reality, and the original owners of the land, the Palestinians, have become refugees. While the imperialist Western world helped the expansionist scheme and aggression of the Zionist entity in 1967, the communist bloc sided with the Arabs in the concept of balance of interests in the context of the global competition between the two blocs, and sought to secure footholds for the East bloc against the Western interests in the Arab homeland. The East bloc, led by the USSR, supported the Arabs' basic rights, including their rights in the Arab-Zionist conflict. The global policy continued on the basis of the existence of two poles that were balanced in term of force. They are the two superpowers, the United States and the USSR.

And suddenly, the situation changed in a dramatic way. The USSR turned to tackle its domestic problems after relinquishing the process of continuous conflict and its slogans. The USSR shifted from the balanced position with the United States in a practical manner, although it has not acknowledged this officially so far. The USSR went to nurse the wounds that were inflicted on it as a result of the principles and the mistaken policy it followed for such a long time, and as a result of the wave of change it embarked on, which began to depart from the charted course. It has become clear to everyone that the United States has emerged in a superior position in international politics. This superiority will be demonstrated in the U.S. readiness to play such a role more than in the predicted guarantees for its continuation.

We believe that the world can fill the vacuum resulting from the recent changes and find a new balance in the global arena by developing new perspectives and reducing or adding to this or that force. The forces that laid the ground for filling the vacuum and for the emergence of the two superpowers, the U.S. and the USSR, after World War II at the expense of France, Britain, and Germany can develop new forces, which we expect will be in Europe and Japan. America will lose its power just as quickly as it gained it by frightening Europe, Japan, and other countries through the continuous hinting at the danger of the USSR and communism. The United States will lose its power as the fierce competition for gaining the upper hand between the two superpowers and their allies recedes.

However, we believe that the U.S. will continue to depart from the restrictions that govern the rest of world throughout the next five years until new forces of balance are formed. Moreover, the undisciplined and irresponsible behavior will engender hostility and grudges if it embarks on rejected stupidities.

Given the relative erosion of the role of the Soviet Union as the key champion of the Arabs in the context of the Arab-Zionist conflict and globally, and given that the influence of the Zionist lobby on U.S. policies is as powerful as ever, the Arabs must take into account that there is a real possibility that Israel might embark on new stupidities within the five-year span I have mentioned. This might take place as a result of direct or tacit U.S. encouragement. On the other hand, the Arabs have a plus, and that is Arab solidarity that will be effective if the Arabs work out a well-defined plan of action and devise regional policies *vis-à-vis* neighboring foreign countries, and if they forge fruitful cooperation based on strong foundations oriented toward clear goals. The cooperation will have to encompass culture, politics, economics, and other areas. Recent American utterances and behavior as far as pan-Arab security and Palestinian Arab rights to their homeland are concerned inevitably cause alarm and warrant Arab vigilance, or are supposed to evoke such a reaction on our part. One may cite recurrent statements by U.S. officials about their intention to keep their fleets in the Gulf for an unlimited period of time, and their support for an unprecedented exodus of Soviet Jews to Palestinian territory, neither of which would have been possible solely under the cover of the human rights slogan had not the Americans put pressure on the Soviets, exploiting the latter's special circumstances so as to incorporate the issue into their bilateral agreements with the Soviets. Add to that the increasing support for the Zionist entity's strategic arms stockpiles and giving it license to deploy them when necessary, the judgment on when to use them being left up to Israel. This is above and beyond U.S. assistance to Israel in other areas.

We all remember, as does the whole world, the circumstances under which the United States deployed and bolstered its fleets in the Gulf. Most important of these circumstances: The war that was raging between Iraq and Iran; Iranian aggression had extended to other Arabian Gulf countries, most notably the sisterly state of Kuwait. At the time, beyond the conflicting views regarding the presence of foreign fleets in Arab territorial waters and foreign bases on their territory and their repercussions for pan-Arab security, that excessive deployment was somehow comprehensible. But now, and against the background of the recent world developments and the cessation of hostilities between Iraq and Iran, and with Kuwait no longer being the target of Iranian aggression, the Arabian Gulf states, including Iraq, and even the entire Arabs would have liked the Americans to state their intention to withdraw their fleets.

Had they said that under the same circumstances and causes they would have returned to the Gulf, it might have been understandable also. But U.S. officials are making such statements as if to show that their immediate and longer-term presence in Gulf waters and, maybe, on some of its territory, is not bound to a time frame. These suspect policies give Arabs reason to feel suspicious of U.S. policies and intentions as to whether it is officially and actually interested in a termination of the Iraq-Iran war and thus contribute to much needed regional stability.

The other side is the immigration of Soviet Jews to the occupied Palestinian land. How can we explain the Americans' support and backing for Jewish immigration to the occupied Arab territories, except that the United States does not want peace as it claims and declares. If it really and actually wants peace, the United States would not have encouraged Israel and the aggressive trends in it to adopt such policies, which enhance Israel's capability to commit aggression and carry out expansion.

We the Arabs, proceeding from a long-standing friendship with the Soviet Union, did not expect that the Soviets would give in to this U.S. pressure in such a way that it would lead to these grave consequences for the Arabs and their pan-Arab security. As we tackle these challenges, it would be just as compromising to the destiny and cause of the Arabs to feel fear as it would be to be lax in our evaluating and working out a reaction to them. Therefore, there is no place among the ranks of good Arabs for the fainthearted who would argue that as a superpower, the United States will be the decisive factor, and others have no choice but to submit. At the same time, there is no place in our midst for those who fail to take note of recent developments that have added to U.S. strength, thus prompting it to the possible commission of follies against the interests and national security of the Arabs—either directly or by fanning and encouraging conflicts detrimental to the Arabs, irrespective of their source. We are not thus out to antagonize or to incite public opinion against the United States on the strength of mere speculation over potential developments. We are only making the point that the Arabs seek peace and justice throughout the world and want to forge relations of friendship with those who show respect to what friendship is all about—be it the United States or any other nation. It is only natural that the Arabs take a realistic approach to the new posture and power of the United States that has led the Soviet Union to abandon its erstwhile position of influence. However, America must respect the Arabs and respect their rights, and should not interfere in their internal affairs under any cover. The United States must not forget that the Arab nation is a great nation that taught humanity things it had been ignorant of. Otherwise, there is no room for unilateral friendship or unilateral respect, and there will be no consideration for the interests and rights of any party unless it is capable of understanding and respecting the Arabs' rights, interests, dignity, options, and pan-Arab security. Against the backdrop of the vital issues related to the substance of national Arab security, the question arises as to what we the Arabs have to do.

One of certain indisputable things, brothers, is that the correct description for a certain situation is not necessarily the correct solution to that situation, but an inevitable introduction leading to the correct solution.

Therefore, in all cases, a solution does not merely consist of defining which issues are rejected, both concerning our behavior or the behavior and thinking of others who harm our pan-Arab security and national and pan-Arab interests. Another thing over which there is no room for dispute is that the policy of the age is not set by concerned foreign parties on any basis other than policies and strategies whose expected final result is to serve the interest of their countries.

Zionism realized these facts and concentrated its international effort here and there in accordance with an accurate perception and longer-lasting knowledge than that of the Arabs. The Zionists were progressive initiators in fields where they would disrupt the calculations and influences of the Arabs. In accordance with this basis, and not only on the basis of developing public opinion, Zionism directed its special concentration on the United States of America to involve it in its strategy, after realizing that the future of its goals and joint action with the Europeans would come up against special obstacles. The United States accepted the concept of joining interests and action with Zionism out of its concept of its own interests, after the United States had taken over the role of the European colonialists following World War II.

Despite all the harm the United States inflicted upon the Arabs due to its alliance with Zionism, there remained the fear of communism, the Soviet Union, and the Arab friends and allies of the Soviet Union in the region, in addition to other factors. This continued to prevent the Arabs from taking influential stands towards U.S. policy, with minor exceptions. Their stands became restricted to a mere ineffective rejection or an ineffective silence and acceptance. The United States began not to take Arab stances seriously. The United States may have the famous red lines beyond which it does not tread concerning the interests of other nations that deal peacefully with it, but its policy so far has no red lines warning the concerned sides in the United States not to tread beyond them where Arab interests are concerned.

Realizing Arab solidarity on the basis of pan-Arab interests, correctly defining Arab interests, clearly and accurately defining everything that threatens their security and stability, and proceeding from this basis of capability, frankness, and solidarity with the United States, or other countries in general, prevents these countries from exceeding the proper bounds with the Arab nation and thus becoming a threat.

This might be a realistic basis for the establishment of Arab relations with the United States and other states, based on the principles I have mentioned. These are mutual respect, noninterference in internal affairs, and respect for the requirements of pan-Arab security and common interests on a legitimate and agreed-upon basis.

Brothers, Zionism and its entity, Israel, have been used to embark upon areas and affairs to which the Arabs do not pay attention. The Arabs have also been used on occasion to rise all together to counter the Zionists' political, informational, or any other offensive for which Zionism has prepared all requirements through effective work over a long period of time. The Arabs would launch a counteroffensive without being fully prepared and soon their rising would dwindle and vanish. Therefore, the Arab reaction is often verbal or ineffective even if part of it takes the form of real action. In politics as well as in war, responsibility and experience have taught us that the counteroffensive should not necessarily be on the same axis that is always chosen by the enemy, especially when the encounter lasts a long time and when it is possible to choose one or more axis or one or more places other than those from which the enemy began its offensive and for which it prepared the requirements of confrontation and took into consideration Arab reaction. In such a case it might be enough to preoccupy the enemy on the axis selected for its offensive against us, and then we would attack it from another axis if the desired results were possible on the other axis. Accordingly, the direct offensive on the harmful plans and means used by the U.S. and Zionism against the Arabs in a certain field might not be always the right solution if we use all of our potential at one time in a manner that takes us away from other fields.

The big does not become big nor does the great earn such a description unless he is in the arena of comparison or fighting with someone else on a different level. The big powers became big only when small and medium-sized countries were found on this earth around these big powers. The big powers do not become big unless they are influential in small and medium-sized countries. Accordingly, among the means to weaken hostile policies and the harmful influence of those who harm us is to weaken the one who harms us inside or outside his national soil. Accordingly, and because interest is the basis of the Soviet Union's new policy, as well as the policy of the East European states, as it has always been the basis of the policy of other states, we are dutybound to ask and answer accurately how we can approach these states in order to weaken our enemies' influence on them or how we can benefit from our common financial, economic, political, informational, and other powers to achieve better results.

It has been proven that Arabs are capable of being influential when they make a decision and set their minds to it for actual application purposes. We have much evidence of how effective they can be; for example, the joint Iraqi-Saudi resolution of 6 August, 1980, and the warning the two countries issued together that embassies must not be moved to Jerusalem, one of whose direct results in less than a month—the duration of the warning—was not only that the concerned countries did not transfer their embassies to Jerusalem, but also that embassies that had already long been transferred to the city returned to Tel Aviv.

The reason the United States stays in the Gulf is that the Gulf has become the most important spot in the region and perhaps the whole world due to developments in international policy, the oil market, and increasing demands from the United States, Europe, Japan, Eastern Europe, and perhaps the Soviet Union, for this product. The country that will have the greatest influence in the region through the Arab Gulf and its oil will maintain its superiority as a superpower without an equal to compete with it. This means that if the Gulf people, along with all Arabs, are not careful, the Arab Gulf region will be governed by the U.S. will. If the Arabs are not alerted and the weakness persists, the situation could develop to the extent desired by the United States; that is, it would fix the amount of oil and gas produced in each country and sold to this or that country in the world. Prices would also be fixed in line with a special perspective benefitting U.S. interests and ignoring the interests of others.

If this possibility is there and it is convincing, those who are convinced by it must conclude that peace in the Middle East is remote from the U.S. point of view because U.S. strategy, according to this analysis, needs an aggressive Israel, not a peaceful one. Peace between Iraq and Iran could be far off as long as Iran does not react favorably from an aware and responsible position and with the peace initiatives proposed by Iraq. The region could witness inter-Arab wars or controlled wars between the Arabs and some of their neighbors, if tangible results are not achieved on the basis of the principles of noninterference in others' internal affairs and nonuse of military force in inter-Arab relations.

Agreement should be reached over clear and widespread pan-Arab cooperation programs among Arab countries in the economic, political, and educational fields, as well as other fields. Love and peace of mind will take the place of suspicion, doubt, mistrust, and giving in to information and speculation propagated by rumormongers such as prejudiced Westerners and some rootless Arabs.

Brothers, the weakness of a big body lies in its bulkiness. All strong men have their Achilles' heel. Therefore, irrespective of our known stand on terror and terrorists, we saw that the United States as a superpower departed Lebanon immediately when some Marines were killed, the very men who are considered to be the most prominent symbol of its arrogance. The whole U.S. Administration would have been called into question had the forces that conquered Panama continued to be engaged by the Panamanian Armed Forces. The United States has been defeated in some combat arenas for all the forces it possesses, and it has displayed signs of fatigue, frustration, and hesitation when committing aggression on other peoples' rights and acting from motives of arrogance and hegemony. This is a natural outcome for those who commit aggression on other peoples' rights. Israel, once dubbed the invincible country, has been defeated by some of the Arabs. The resistance put up by Palestinian and Lebanese militia against Israeli invasion forces in 1982 and before that the heroic Egyptian crossing of the Suez Canal in 1973 have had a more telling psychological and actual impact than all Arab threats. Further, the threat to use Arab oil in 1973 during the October war proved more effective than all political attempts to protest or to beg at the gates of American decisionmaking centers. The stones in occupied Palestine now turn into a virtual and potentially fatal bullet if additional requirements are made available. It is the best proof of what is possible and indeed gives us cause to hold our heads high.

Just as Israel controls interests to put pressure on the U.S. Administration, hundreds of billions invested by the Arabs in the United States and the West may be similarly deployed. Indeed, for instance, some of these investments may be diverted to the USSR and East European countries. It may prove even more profitable than investment in the West, which has grown saturated with its national resources. Such a course of action may yield inestimable benefits for the Arabs and their national causes.

Our purported weakness does not lie in our ideological and hereditary characteristics. Contemporary experience has shown our nation to be distinguished and excellent, just as our nation's history over the centuries has shown this to be the case. Our purported weakness lies in a lack of mutual trust among ourselves, our failure to concentrate on the components of our strength, and our failure to focus on our weaknesses with a view to righting them. Let our motto be: All of us are strong as long as we are united, and all of us are weak as long as we are divided. Then we will see how all of us will reach safe shores, God willing, so we can take off together on the road of stability and prosperity, heartening our people and ourselves. We will also see how Satan will grow weaker wherever he may be and the evil will depart our homeland and our nation. We are proceeding with resolve and firmness, God willing, to reach this goal through brotherly cooperation that would serve as a model for common Arab action and developed brotherly cooperation. Let us go forward.

Brother leaders of the ACC countries; brother members of the audience. These are ideas and concepts that we are proposing for brotherly dialogue in the context of an exchange of views and experience among us on all issues of concern to our Arab countries and nation. We ask success from God toward the good. The peace and blessings of God be upon you, brothers.

PLO Chairman Yasir Arafat: The PLO and the Gulf Crisis (December 13, 1990)*

Do not forget that I was continually warning about the constant possibility of an escalation in this region. Most specifically, last April I pointed out

*Interview with *Vjesnik* (Zagreb), December 8, 1990.

two possible explosive points: On the one hand this involved increased U.S.-Israeli threats to Iraq and the Palestinians in southern Lebanon, and on the other the mass settlement of Jews into our occupied Palestine—a problem that I was constantly pointing out and to which I was trying to attract the world's attention because it involved a move with unpredictable consequences. I also said that the Arab summit in Baghdad in March this year should be a summit to straighten things out. Anyway, I will give you the letter the Americans sent us at that time through the Arab League. This is the dangerous letter that no one has wanted to talk about. I will give you a copy: go ahead and publish it if you wish. In this letter they openly announce that they will increase their presence in the Gulf and warned the Arabs that they will not tolerate any resistance to their presence. When I spoke about this on 17 May, two lines concerning the U.S. intentions were already apparent among the Arabs. One line approved of their presence and the other did not.

Another issue was the question of Israel and its expansion. The letter itself was a classic ultimatum. They issued a metal coin—here, I will give you one—with a sketch on it of the map of Israel as they see it. This Israel contains half of Iraq, half of Syria, the whole of Lebanon, Jordan, the whole of Palestine, a part of Saudi Arabia, and a good part of Sinai. They have not forsaken this dream. When I left Beirut in 1982, I said that the storm that had overtaken that city would not stop. The storm at that point had one center, one "eye" as we would say: Palestine. Today that storm has two eyes—one in the Gulf and the other in Palestine. . . .

A few days ago, when I was with Saddam Husayn, it seemed to me that the chances of peace were great. What the Americans have prepared through the Security Council, however . . . this is some kind of declaration of war. This is an ultimatum. Really, there is the danger of the Middle East's exploding, not only in the Gulf but on all sides. If Israel is in this war—and it certainly will be—we will fight against it as well as against the Americans. They must know that not one single Arab soldier—neither Egyptian, nor Syrian, nor Saudi—will agree to be in the same trench as Israeli soldiers. This is the reality.

There is no doubt about it. No matter what the outcome of the war, the Arab order as a whole will collapse. . . .

We are the greatest losers even now. Our people in Kuwait were the richest. The total losses of the Palestinian colony in Kuwait amounted to $8.5 billion. Our people had almost $3 billion in the banks there alone. Look what happened. The U.S.-European committee discussed, and to a considerable extent has already paid, compensation to the whole world for the money lost in Kuwait, but the Palestinians did not receive anything. What is this meant to be? A punishment for the Palestinians? Where are the principles here? Are they not ashamed of this? Or do they really only want to ignite a new explosion? Viewed in the long term, perhaps there is cause for optimism. In the shorter term, the situation is exceptionally difficult. It seems that we have definitely come closer to a war which will leave behind nothing but catastrophe. Both Asia and Europe will feel the repercussions. In order for people to come to their senses, it is necessary for a lot of effort to be made throughout the world. But there is no sense. Look at the Security Council—what is its duty? To foment war or to seek peaceful solutions? I cannot accept this. As regards the solution, it is very strange that, for example, it is being demanded of the Palestinians that they talk with the Israelis while they are occupying the Palestinians' country, but at the same time we are not being allowed to ask that Arabs look for a solution among themselves for the new problem in the Gulf. So one can have negotiations among enemies but not among Arabs. What do they want? That I reject one occupation but accept another, or something like this? I cannot accept a foreign presence in this region. I know that they are literally punishing the Palestinians because of this, but I will not sell my opinion for any sum of money. I could easily say that I support the Saudis or the Americans. You know, however, that I have fought for principles, and I will not betray them.

Palestine National Council: Political Communiqué (September 28, 1991)

In the name of God, the merciful, the compassionate. From the date of its beginning in 1965, the Palestinian revolution has embarked on a long, bitter, and strenuous struggle during which our people have made huge sacrifices. This beginning came after years of excluding the Palestinian question and considering it a refugee question.

The long years of struggle in all forms, under the PLO leadership, the sole legitimate representative of our people, have again posed the question of Palestine to the international community on the grounds that it is the national cause of a people entitled to liberation, self-determination, and independence.

The question of Palestine occupied a central position in the Arab-Israeli conflict. Peace, security, and stability in the Middle East cannot be secured unless this conflict is resolved.

Then came the blessed *intifada*, with its popular and democratic depth, as a creative continuation of the Palestinian national struggle. It has constituted a distinct phase which has left its imprint on the whole world and reverberated around it. It has consolidated international recognition of our people's rights and of the PLO, which has always and immediately put such international support and polarization to use.

Thus, our National Council convened its 19th session and launched the Palestinian peace initiative, and the historic birth of the state of Palestine was proclaimed on 15 November 1988.

The world had welcomed our peace initiative through the resolutions of the UN General Assembly in its 43rd session, which was held in Geneva. Also, most countries recognized the state of Palestine and established diplomatic and political relations with it.

Despite the international welcome with which the Palestinian initiative and the historic speech by the president of the state of Palestine, brother Yasir' Arafat, who demonstrated to the whole world our wish for a just peace, was met—thus for the first time the United States announced the opening of an official dialogue with the PLO—the Israeli policy of stubbornness and pressure led to the failure of all initiatives and peaceful efforts, bringing them down a dead-end street.

Afterwards, there came regional and international developments, most prominent of which was the Gulf war and the changes that occurred in the socialist bloc. This resulted in a substantial change in the balance of power. Thus, the cold war came to an end, and the features of a new age in international relations began to develop, especially in the field of U.S.-Soviet relations and cooperation between the two nations to resolve regional conflicts and problems peacefully.

The PLO has closely monitored the course of events in the world and their effect on the Palestinian question and the Arab-Israeli conflict. If the Palestinian people have had their homeland usurped as a result of the prejudices of the old world order, it is impermissible, according to any logic, that they be denied these rights in a phase witnessing the emergence of the new world order that raises slogans of democracy, human rights, and the sanctity of peoples' right to self-determination.

The current situation requires us to deal with it in the spirit of political responsibility and national realism and to examine the new regional and international developments. This situation also requires us to learn the lessons and experience from the popular *intifada* that has turned the aim of Palestinian independence into a feasible program.

In harmony with the Palestinian initiative proposed in 1989 and with international and Arab legitimacy, the PLO has dealt positively and effectively with international and peaceful ideas, proposals, and initiatives that relied on international legality. The PLO also welcomed the positive elements mentioned in the declaration of U.S. President George Bush and the positions of the EEC, the Soviet Union, the Nonaligned Movement states, and other international quarters.

The PLO, which had welcomed the current peaceful efforts and initiatives and dealt with them positively, including the call launched by Presidents Bush and Gorbachev for convening a peace conference related to settling the conflict in the Middle East, believes that the success of the efforts aimed at holding the peace conference requires the continuation of work with the other sides so as to achieve the following foundations:

1. The peace conference should rely on international legitimacy and its resolutions, including UN Security Council Resolutions 242 and 338, and should undertake to implement them. These resolutions secure a full Israeli withdrawal from Arab and Palestinian occupied territories, including sacred Jerusalem; the realization of the land-for-peace exchange principle; and the national and political rights of the Palestinian people.

2. It must be stressed that Jerusalem is an indivisible part of occupied Palestinian territory and that what applies to the rest of the occupied territories applies to it, as stipulated by the resolutions of the Security Council and the United Nations.

3. Halting settlement in the occupied territories, including holy Jerusalem, is an indispensable necessity to start the peace process, and international guarantees must be provided to achieve that.

4. The PLO, as the legitimate and sole representative of the Palestinian people, has the right to form the Palestinian delegation from within and outside the homeland, including Jerusalem, and to define the formula of their participation in the peace process on an equitable basis and in a way that stresses its authority.

5. Arab positions should be coordinated to ensure the realization of a comprehensive settlement, excluding unilateral solutions, in accordance with the resolutions of Arab summits.

6. The connection between the stages of the settlement toward reaching a comprehensive settlement should be ensured according to the resolutions of international legitimacy.

The PLO, which starts from these bases and premises on the peace efforts, aims to accomplish the following:

1. The right to self-determination must be secured for our Palestinian people in a way that guarantees the right to freedom and national independence.

2. There must be a full Israeli withdrawal from all Palestinian and Arab lands occupied in 1967, including Holy Jerusalem.

3. The problem of Palestinian refugees driven out of their homeland by force and against their will must be resolved, in accordance with UN resolutions, especially Resolution 194, issued by the UN General Assembly.

4. Any provisional arrangements must include the right of our people to sovereignty of land, water, natural resources, and all political and economic affairs.

5. International protection for the Palestinian people, in preparation for the exercise of the right to self-determination, must be provided.

6. Full guarantees must be provided for an effort to remove the existing settlements by declaring them illegal, in accordance with the resolutions of international law, including UN Security Council Resolution No. 465.

The National Council charges the Executive Committee to continue current efforts to provide the best conditions for guaranteeing the success of the peace process in accordance with the resolution of the Palestine National Council [PNC]. However, the committee will submit the results to the Central Council to make a final decision in light of the supreme national interest of our people.

The PLO, which in the previous phase made all possible efforts to propel the peace process, hopes that the other parties, especially the United States and the USSR, will also make efforts to help ease the obstacles placed by Israel before this ongoing political process and to leave the door open for a return to the UN Security Council so as to implement the resolutions of international legitimacy.

Working toward the achievement of our national objectives in the next phase and toward facing up to obstacles marring our struggle requires the consolidation and entrenchment of national unity in various fields. It requires developing the contribution of all national forces, bodies, and personalities inside and outside the occupied homeland—along with the political leadership of the PLO—to all issues related to our people's future and the ongoing political process, and to finding the appropriate formula for achieving this purpose.

In this respect, the PNC calls for increasing the activities and role of the PLO Central Council in monitoring and implementing the resolutions of the National Council as a way of consolidating democracy and its practice. The council considers promoting the *intifada* and consolidating its popular and democratic character and the participation of our entire people in backing and supporting it to be the real guarantee for securing the political and national objectives in the next phase of our national struggle.

In this respect, the Council addresses its struggle greetings to the masses of the brave *intifada* and stresses the consolidation of the role and prestige of the Unified National Command of the *Intifada,* the development of its struggle wings, the continuation of the formation of cadres, and the setting up of supreme sectorial councils.

The Council reaffirms that the protection and support of the *intifada* and the provision of all requirements for its development are at the forefront of Palestinian national action.

The Council extends greetings to our heroic prisoners in the detention centers of Zionist occupation and to our brave wounded who are watching over the path of the *intifada,* which was built by our pure martyrs.

The National Council extends its struggle greetings to the masses of our steadfast people in Galilee, the Triangle, Negev, and the coast, and reaffirms its appreciation of their struggle in defense of their rights against the policies of persecution and segregation and their active support for the brave *intifada*.

The council also affirms that guaranteeing the realization of the objectives of our people and Arab nation, through the peace process, in order to secure a full Israeli withdrawal from Arab and Palestinian lands, and to guarantee the right of return, the self-determination to our people, and the setting up of a Palestinian state with Holy Jerusalem as its capital, require the restoration of inter-Arab solidarity in order to protect the Arab future in light of current international and regional changes.

In this respect, the council invites the five Arab states concerned in the peace process to achieve the highest levels of political and diplomatic coordination between them, in order to face up to the requirements of the coming stage and to reinforce the Arab negotiating position, so as to guarantee the realization of a comprehensive solution at all levels and prevent any separate solutions at the expense of the national rights of our people and the rights of our Arab nation. . . .

The PNC urges the international community to deal with the issue of Jewish colonizing emigration in a way that ensures that Israel does not use it to serve its objectives of expansion, colonization, and depriving our people of the right to decide their destiny in the territory of their homeland. The Council believes that the continuation of this emigration, in accordance with Israeli plans to intensify settlement in our occupied land, constitutes a direct obstacle, a danger threatening the future of peace in the region, and a violation of the Palestinian people's rights and international conventions.

The PNC draws attention to the attempts and endeavors currently under way in some international circles to repeal the UN General Assembly's resolution on Zionism as a form of racism. The Council urges the Executive Committee to work with the friendly and fraternal states to face up to these attempts and to abort them. . . .

Finally, the PNC addresses greetings, compassion, and love to our steadfast and patient Palestinian people, both inside our occupied land and in the diaspora, and to the masses of our Arab nation and its influential forces for their positions supporting and backing the jihad of our Palestinian people and their national, inalienable rights. The Council urges them to stand firmly in the face of the conspiracies hatched by the enemies of our Arab nation in order to preserve our Arab nation, its existence, pride, dignity, and national security.

U.S. Letter of Assurances
to the Palestinians (October 18, 1991)

The Palestinian decision to attend a peace conference to launch direct negotiations with Israel represents an important step in the search for a comprehensive, just and lasting peace in the region. The United States has long believed that Palestinian participation is critical to the success of our efforts.

In the context of the process on which we are embarking, we want to respond to your requests for certain assurances related to this process. These assurances constitute U.S. understandings and intentions concerning the conference and ensuring negotiations.

These assurances are consistent with United States policy and do not undermine or contradict United Nations Security Council Resolutions 242 and 338. Moreover, there will be no assurances provided to one party that are not known to all the others. By this we can foster a sense of confidence and minimize chances for misunderstandings.

As President Bush stated in his March 6, 1991, address to Congress, the United States continues to believe firmly that a comprehensive peace must be grounded in United Nations Security Council Resolutions 242 and 338 and the principle of territory for peace. Such an outcome must also provide for security and recognition for all states in the region, including Israel, and for the legitimate political rights of the Palestinian people. Anything else, the President noted, would fail the twin tests of fairness and security.

The process we are trying to create offers Palestinians a way to achieve these objectives. The United States believes that there should be an end to the Israeli occupation which can occur only through genuine and meaningful negotiations. The United States also believes that this process should create a new relationship of mutuality where Palestinians and Israelis can respect one another's security, identity, and political rights. We believe Palestinians should gain control over political, economic and other decisions that affect their lives and fate.

Direct bilateral negotiations will begin four days after the opening of the conference; those parties who wish to attend multilateral negotiations will convene two weeks after the opening of the conference to organize those negotiations. In this regard, the United States will support Palestinian involvement in any bilateral or multilateral negotiations on refugees and in all multilateral negotiations. The conference and the negotiations that follow will be based on UN Security Council Resolutions 242 and 338. The process will proceed along two tracks through direct negotiations between Israel and Arab states and Israel and Palestinians. The United States is determined to achieve a comprehensive settlement of the Arab-Israeli conflict and will do its utmost to ensure that the process moves forward along both tracks toward this end.

In pursuit of a comprehensive settlement, all the negotiations should proceed as quickly as possible toward agreement. For its part, the United States will work for serious negotiations and will also seek to avoid prolongation and stalling by any party.

The conference will be co-sponsored by the United States and the Soviet Union. The European Community will be a participant in the conference alongside the United States and the Soviet Union and be represented by its Presidency. The conference can reconvene only with the consent of all the parties.

With regard to the role of the United Nations, the UN Secretary General will send a representative to the conference as an observer. The cosponsors will keep the Secretary General apprised of the progress of the negotiations. Agreements reached between the parties will be registered with the UN Secretariat and reported to the Security Council, and the parties will seek the Council's endorsement of such agreements. Since it is in the interest of all parties for this process to succeed, while this process is actively ongoing, the United States will not support a competing or parallel process in the United Nations Security Council.

The United States does not seek to determine who speaks for Palestinians in this process. We are seeking to launch a political negotiation process that directly involves Palestinians and offers a pathway for achieving the legitimate political rights of the Palestinian people and for participation in the determination of their future. We believe that a joint Jordanian Palestinian delegation offers the most promising pathway toward this end.

Only Palestinians can choose their delegation members, which are not subject to veto from anyone. The United States understands that members of the delegation will be Palestinians from the territories who agree to negotiations on two tracks, in phases, and who are willing to live in peace with Israel. No party can be forced to sit with anyone it does not want to sit with.

Palestinians will be free to announce their component of the joint delegation and to make a statement during the opening of the conference. They may also raise any issue pertaining to the substance of the negotiations during the negotiations.

The United States understands how much importance Palestinians attach to the question of east Jerusalem. Thus, we want to assure you that nothing Palestinians do in choosing their delegation members in this phase of the process will affect their claim to east Jerusalem, or be prejudicial or precedential to the outcome of negotiations. It remains the firm position of the United States that Jerusalem must never again be a divided city and that its final status should be decided by negotiations. Thus, we do not recognize Israel's annexation of east Jerusalem or the extension of its municipal boundaries, and we encourage all sides to avoid unilateral acts that would exacerbate local tensions or make negotiations more difficult or preempt their final outcome. It is also the United States position that a Palestinian resident in Jordan with ties to a prominent Jerusalem family would be eligible to join the Jordanian side of the delegation.

Furthermore, it is also the United States position that Palestinians of east Jerusalem should be able to participate by voting in the elections for an interim self-governing authority. The United States further believes that Palestinians from east Jerusalem and Palestinians outside the occupied territories who meet the three criteria should be able to participate in the negotiations on final status. And, the United States supports the right of Palestinians to bring any issue, including east Jerusalem, to the table.

Because the issues at stake are so complex and the emotions so deep, the United States has long maintained that a transitional period is required to break down the walls of suspicion and mistrust and lay the basis for sustainable negotiations on the final status of the occupied territories. The purpose of negotiations on transitional arrangements is to effect the peaceful and orderly transfer of authority from Israel to Palestinians. Palestinians need to achieve rapid control over political, economic, and other decisions that affect their lives and to adjust to a new situation in which Palestinians exercise authority in the West Bank and Gaza. For its part, the United States will strive from the outset and encourage all parties to adopt steps that can create an environment of confidence and mutual trust, including respect for human rights.

As you are aware with respect to negotiations between Israel and Palestinians, negotiations will be conducted in phases, beginning with talks on interim self-government arrangements. These talks will be conducted with the objective of reaching agreement within one year. Once agreed, the interim self-government arrangements will last for a period of five years. Beginning the third year of the period of interim government arrangements, negotiations will take place on permanent status. It is the aim of the United States that permanent status negotiations will be concluded by the end of the transitional period.

It has long been our position that only direct negotiations based on UN Security Council Resolutions 242 and 338 can produce a real peace. No one can dictate the outcome in advance. The United States understands that Palestinians must be free, in opening statements at the conference and in the negotiations that follow, to raise any issue of importance to them. Thus, Palestinians are free to argue for whatever outcome they believe best meets their requirements. The United States will accept any outcome agreed by the parties. In this regard and consistent with longstanding U.S. policies, confederation is not excluded as a possible outcome of negotiations on final status.

The United States has long believed that no party should take unilateral actions that seek to predetermine issues that can only be resolved through negotiations. In this regard the United States has opposed and will continue to oppose settlement activity in the territories occupied in 1967, which remains an obstacle to peace.

The United States will act as an honest broker in trying to resolve the Arab-Israeli conflict. It is our intention, together with the Soviet Union, to play the role of a driving force in this process to help the parties move forward toward a comprehensive peace. Any party will have access to the co-sponsors at any time. The United States is prepared to participate in all stages of the negotiations, with the consent of the parties to each negotiation.

These are the assurances that the United States is providing concerning the implementation of the initiative we have discussed. We are persuaded that we have a real opportunity to accomplish something very important in the peace process. And we are prepared to work hard together with you in the period ahead to build on the progress we have made. There will be difficult challenges for all parties. But with Palestinians' continued commitment and creativity, we have a real chance of moving to a peace conference and to negotiation and then on toward the broader peace that we all seek.

Israeli Prime Minister Yitzhak Shamir and Palestinian Delegation Leader Haydar Abd al-Shafi: Speeches at the Madrid Peace Conference (October 31, 1991)

Israeli Prime Minister Yitzhak Shamir

We pray that this meeting will mark the beginning of a new chapter in the history of the Middle East; that it will signal the end of hostility, violence, terror, and war; that it will bring dialogue, accommodation, coexistence, and above all, peace.

Ladies and gentlemen, to appreciate the meaning of peace for the people of Israel, one has to view today's Jewish sovereignty in the Land of Israel against the background of our history. Jews have been persecuted throughout the ages in almost every continent. Some countries barely tolerated us; others oppressed, tortured, slaughtered, and exiled us. This century saw the Nazi regime set out to exterminate us. The Shoah—the Holocaust, the catastrophic genocide of unprecedented proportions which destroyed a third of our people—became possible because no one defended us. Being homeless, we were also defenseless. But it was not the Holocaust which made the world community recognize our rightful claim to the Land of Israel. In fact, the rebirth of the State of Israel so soon after the Holocaust has made the world forget that our claim is immemorial. We are the only people who have lived in the Land of Israel without interruption for nearly 4,000 years. We are the only people, except for a short Crusader kingdom, who have had an independent sovereignty in this land. We are the only people for whom Jerusalem has been a capital. We are the only people whose sacred places are only in the Land of Israel. No nation has expressed its bond with its land with as much intensity and consistency as we have. For millennia, our people repeated at every occasion the cry of the psalmist: If I forget thee, Jerusalem, may my right hand lose its cunning. For millennia, we have encouraged each other with the greeting: Next year in Jerusalem. For millennia, our prayers, literature, and folklore have expressed powerful longing to return to our land. Only Eretz Yisra'el, the Land of Israel, is our true homeland.

Any other country, no matter how hospitable, is still a diaspora, a temporary station on the way home. To others, it was not an attractive land; no one wanted it. Mark Twain described it only 100 years ago as a desolate country which sits in sackcloth and ashes—a silent, mournful expanse which not even imagination can grace with the pomp of life.

The Zionist movement gave political expression to our claim to the Land of Israel, and in 1922, the League of Nations recognized the justice of this claim. They understood the compelling historic imperative of establishing a Jewish homeland in the Land of Israel. The United Nations organization reaffirmed this recognition after World War II.

Regrettably, the Arab leaders, whose friendship we wanted most, opposed a Jewish state in the region. With a few distinguished exceptions, they claimed that the Land of Israel is part of the Arab domain that stretches from the Atlantic to the Persian Gulf. In defiance of international will and legality, the Arab regimes attempted to overrun and destroy the Jewish state even before it was born. The Arab spokesmen at the United Nations declared that the establishment of a Jewish state would cause a bloodbath which would make the slaughters of Genghis Khan pale into insignificance. In its declaration of independence on May 15, 1948, Israel stretched out its hand in peace to its Arab neighbors, calling for an end to war and bloodshed. In response, seven Arab states invaded Israel. The UN resolution that partitioned the country was thus violated and effectively annulled.

The United Nations did not create Israel. The Jewish state came into being because the tiny Jewish community in what was Mandatory Palestine rebelled against foreign imperialist rule. We did not conquer a foreign land; we repulsed the Arab onslaught, prevented Israel's annihilation, declared its independence, and established a viable state and government institutions within a very short time.

After their attack on Israel failed, the Arab regimes continued their fight against Israel with boycott, blockade, terrorism, and outright war. Soon after the establishment of Israel, they turned against the Jewish communities in Arab countries. A wave of oppression, expropriation, and expulsion caused a mass exodus of some 800,000 Jews from lands they had inhabited from before the rise of the Islam. Most of the Jewish refugees, stripped of their considerable possessions, came to Israel. They were welcomed by the Jewish state, they were given shelter and support, and they were integrated into Israeli society, together with half a million survivors of the European Holocaust.

The Arab regimes' rejection of Israel's existence in the Middle East and the continuous war they have waged against it are part of history. There have been attempts to rewrite this history, which depicts the Arabs as victims and Israel as the aggressor. Like attempts to deny the Holocaust, they will fail. With the demise of totalitarian regimes in most of the world, this perversion of history will disappear.

In their war against Israel's existence, the Arab governments took advantage of the cold war. They enlisted the military, economic, and political support of the communist world against Israel, and they turned a local regional conflict into an international powder keg. This caused the Middle East to be flooded with arms, which fueled wars and turned the area into a dangerous battleground and a testing arena for sophisticated weapons. At the UN, the Arab states mustered the support of other Muslim countries and the Soviet bloc. Together, they had an automatic majority for countless resolutions that perverted history, paraded fiction as fact, and made a travesty of the UN and its charter.

Arab hostility to Israel has also brought tragic human suffering to the Arab people. Tens of thousands have been killed and wounded; hundreds of thousands of Arabs who lived in Mandatory Palestine were encouraged by their own leaders to flee from their homes. Their suffering is a blot on humanity. No decent person—least of all a Jew of this era—can be oblivious to this suffering. Several hundreds of thousands of Palestinian Arabs live in slums known as refugee camps in Gaza, Judaea, and Samaria. Attempts by Israel to rehabilitate and house them have been defeated by Arab objections. Nor has their fate been any better in Arab states. Unlike the Jewish refugees who came to Israel from Arab countries, most Arab refugees were neither welcomed nor integrated by their hosts. Only the Kingdom of Jordan awarded them citizenship. Their plight has been used as a political weapon against Israel. The Arabs who have chosen to remain in Israel—Christian and Muslim—have become full-fledged citizens, enjoying equal rights and representation in the legislature, in the judiciary, and in all walks of life.

We, who over the centuries were denied access to our holy places, respect the religion of all faiths in our country. Our law guarantees freedom of worship and protects the holy places of every religion.

Distinguished co-chairmen, ladies, and gentlemen, I stand before you today in yet another quest for peace—not only on behalf of the State of Israel, but in the name of the entire Jewish people that has maintained an unbreakable bond with the Land of Israel for almost 4,000 years. Our pursuit of accommodation and peace has been relentless. For us, the ingathering of Jews into their ancient homeland, their integration into our society, and the creation of the necessary infrastructure are at the very top of our national agenda.

A nation that faces such a gigantic challenge would most naturally desire peace with all its neighbors. Since the beginning of Zionism, we formulated innumerable peace proposals and plans. All of them were rejected. The first crack in the wall of hostility occurred in 1977, when the late President Anwar al-Sadat of Egypt decided to break the taboo and come to Jerusalem. His gesture was reciprocated with enthusiasm by the people and Government of Israel, headed by Menahem Begin. This development led to the Camp David accords and a treaty of peace between Egypt and Israel. Four years later, in May 1983, an agreement was signed with the lawful government of Lebanon. Unfortunately, this agreement was not fulfilled because of outside intervention. But a precedent was set, and we look forward to courageous steps, similar to those of Anwar al-Sadat. Regrettably, not one Arab leader has seen fit to come forward and respond to our call for peace.

Today's gathering is a result of a sustained American effort based on our own peace plan of May 1989, which in turn was founded on the Camp David accords. According to the American initiative, the purpose of this meeting is to launch direct peace negotiations between Israel and each of its neighbors and multilateral negotiations on regional issues among all the countries of the region. We have always believed that only direct bilateral talks can bring peace. We have agreed to precede such talks with this ceremonial conference, but we hope that Arab consent to direct bilateral talks indicates an understanding that there is no other way to peace. In the Middle East, this has special meaning, because such talks imply mutual acceptance, and the root cause of the conflict is the Arab refusal to recognize the legitimacy of the State of Israel.

The multilateral talks that would accompany the bilateral negotiations are a vital component in the process. In these talks, the essential ingredients of coexistence and regional cooperation will be discussed. There cannot be genuine peace in our region unless these regional issues are addressed and resolved.

We believe the goal of the bilateral negotiations is to sign peace treaties between Israel and its neighbors and to reach an agreement on interim self-government arrangements with the Palestinian Arabs. But nothing can be achieved without goodwill. I appeal to the Arab leaders—those who are here and those who have not yet joined the process: Show us and the world that you accept Israel's existence. Demonstrate your readiness to accept Israel as a permanent entity in the region. Let the people in our region hear you speak in the language of reconciliation, coexistence, and peace with Israel. In Israel, there is an almost total consensus for the need for peace. We only differ on the best ways to achieve it. In most Arab countries, the opposite seems to be true. The only differences are over the ways to push Israel into a defenseless position and, ultimately, to destruction. We would like to see in your countries an end to poisonous preachings against Israel. We would like to see an indication of the kind of hunger for peace which characterizes Israeli society.

We appeal to you to renounce the jihad against Israel; we appeal to you to denounce the PLO Covenant which calls for Israel's destruction; we appeal to you to condemn declarations that call for Israel's annihilation, like the one issued by the rejectionist conference in Tehran last week; we appeal to you to let Jews who wish to leave your countries go. And we address a call to the Palestinian Arabs: Renounce violence and terrorism. Use the universities in the administered territories, whose existence was made possible only by Israel, for learning and development, not agitation and violence. Stop exposing your children to danger by sending them to throw bombs and stones at soldiers and civilians.

Just two days ago, we were reminded that Palestinian terrorism is still rampant, when the mother of seven children and the father of four were slaughtered in cold blood. We cannot remain indifferent and be expected to talk with people involved in such repulsive activities.

We appeal to you to shun dictators like Saddam Husayn who aim to destroy Israel. Stop the brutal torture and murder of those who do not agree with you. Allow us and the world community to build decent housing for the people who now live in refugee camps. Above all, we hope you finally realize that you could have been at this table long ago, soon after the Camp David accords were first concluded, had you chosen dialogue instead of violence, coexistence instead of terrorism.

Ladies and gentlemen, we come to this process with an open heart, sincere intentions, and great expectations. We are committed to negotiating without interruption, until an agreement is reached. There will be problems, obstacles, crises, and conflicting claims, but it is better to talk than to shed blood. Wars have not solved anything in our region; they have only caused misery, suffering, bereavement, and hatred.

We know our partners to the negotiations will make territorial demands on Israel but, as an examination of the conflict's long history makes clear, its nature is not territorial. It raged well before Israel acquired Judaea, Samaria, Gaza, and the Golan in a defensive war. There was no hint at recognition of Israel before the war in 1967, when the territories in question were not under Israel's control.

We are a nation of 4 million. The Arab nations from the Atlantic to the Gulf number 170 million. We control only 28,000 square km. The Arabs possess a land mass of 14 million square km. The issue is not territory, but our existence. It will be regrettable if the talks focus primarily and exclusively on territory. It is the quickest way to an impasse.

What we need, first and foremost, is the building of confidence, the removal of the danger of confrontation, and the development of relations in as many spheres as possible. The issues are complex, and the negotiations will be lengthy and difficult. We submit that the best venue for the talks is in our region, in close proximity to the decisionmakers, not in a foreign land. We invite our partners to this process to come to Israel for the first round of talks. On our part, we are ready to go to Jordan, to Lebanon, and to Syria for the same purpose. There is no better way to make peace than to talk in each other's home. Avoiding such talks is a denial of the purpose of the negotiations. I would welcome a positive answer from the representatives of these states here and now. We must learn to live together. We must learn to live without war, without hatred.

Judaism has given the world not only the belief in one god, but the idea that all men and women are created in God's image. There is no greater sin than to ravage this image by shedding blood. I am sure that there is no Arab mother who wants her son to die in battle, just as there is no Jewish mother who wants her son to die in war. I believe every mother wants her children to learn the art of living, not the science of war.

For many hundreds of years, wars, deep antagonisms, and terrible suffering cursed this continent on which we meet. The nations of Europe saw the rise of dictators and their defeat after lengthy and painful struggles. Now they are together, former bitter enemies, in a united community. They are discussing the good of the community, cooperating in all matters, acting almost as one unit. I envy them. I would like to see such a community rise in the Middle East, and I believe that despite all differences between us we should be able, gradually, to build a united regional community. Today it is a dream, but we have seen in our own lifetimes some of the most fantastic dreams become reality. Today the gulf separating the two sides is still too wide, the Arab hostility to Israel too deep, the lack of trust too immense to permit a dramatic, quick solution, but we must start on the long road to reconciliation with this first step in the peace process.

We are convinced that human nature prefers peace to war and belligerence. We, who have had to fight seven wars and sacrifice many thousands of lives, glorify neither death nor war. The Jewish faith exalts peace, even to the extent that it considers it a synonym for the Creator himself. We yearn for peace; we pray for peace.

We believe the blessing of peace can turn the Middle East into a paradise, a center of cultural, scientific, medical, technological creativity. We can foresee a period of great economic progress that would put an end to misery, hunger, and illiteracy. It could put the Middle East, the cradle of civilization, on the road to a new era. Such a goal merits our devotion and dedication for as long as it is necessary, until, in the words of the prophet

Isaiah, we shall be able to turn swords into plowshares and bring the blessings of peace to all the peoples of our region. . . .

Palestine Delegation Leader Haydar Abd al-Shafi

. . . We, the people of Palestine, stand before you in the fullness of our
pain, our pride, and our anticipation, for we long harbored a yearning for
peace and a dream of justice and freedom. For too long, the Palestinian
people have gone unheeded, silenced and denied. Our identity negated by
political expediency; our right for struggle against injustice maligned; and
our present existence subdued by the past tragedy of another people. For
the greater part of this century we have been victimized by the myth of a
land without a people and described with impunity as the invisible Palestinians. Before such willful blindness, we refused to disappear or to accept
a distorted identity. Our *intifada* is a testimony to our perseverance and re-
silience waged in a just struggle to regain our rights. It is time for us to nar-
rate our own story, to stand witness as advocates of truth which has long
lain buried in the consciousness and conscience of the world. We do not
stand before you as supplicants, but rather as the torchbearers who know
that, in our world of today, ignorance can never be an excuse. We seek neither an admission of guilt after the fact, nor vengeance for past inequities,
but rather an act of will that would make a just peace a reality.

We speak out, ladies and gentlemen, from the full conviction of the
rightness of our cause, the verity of our history, and the depth of our commitment. Therein lies the strength of the Palestinian people today, for we
have scaled walls of fear and reticence, and we wish to speak out with the
courage and integrity that our narrative and history deserve. The cosponsors have invited us here today to present our case and to reach out to the
other with whom we have had to face a mutually exclusive reality on the
land of Palestine. But even in the invitation to this peace conference, our
narrative was distorted and our truth only partially acknowledged.

The Palestinian people are one, fused by centuries of history in Palestine, bound together by a collective memory of shared sorrows and joys,
and sharing a unity of purpose and vision. Our songs and ballads are full of
tales and children's stories, the dialect of our jokes, the image of our po-
ems, that hint of melancholy which colors even our happiest moments, are
as important to us as the blood ties which link our families and clans. Yet,
an invitation to discuss peace, the peace we all desire and need, comes to
only a portion of our people. It ignores our national, historical, and organic
unity. We come here wrenched from our sisters and brothers in exile to
stand before you as the Palestinians under occupation, although we maintain that each of us represents the rights and interests of the whole.

We have been denied the right to publicly acknowledge our loyalty to
our leadership and system of government. But allegiance and loyalty can-

not be censored or severed. Our acknowledged leadership is more than [the] justly democratically chosen leadership of all the Palestinian people. It is the symbol of our national unity and identity, the guardian of our past, the protector of our present, and the hope of our future. Our people have chosen to entrust it with their history and the preservation of our precious legacy. This leadership has been clearly and unequivocally recognized by the community of nations, with only a few exceptions who had chosen for so many years shadow over substance. Regardless of the nature and conditions of our oppression, whether the disposition and dispersion of exile or the brutality and repression of the occupation, the Palestinian people cannot be torn asunder. They remain united—a nation wherever they are, or are forced to be.

And Jerusalem, ladies and gentlemen, that city which is not only the soul of Palestine, but the cradle of three world religions, is tangible even in its claimed absence from our midst at this stage. It is apparent, through artificial exclusion from this conference, that this is a denial of its right to seek peace and redemption. For it, too, has suffered from war and occupation. Jerusalem, the city of peace, has been barred from a peace conference and deprived of its calling. Palestinian Jerusalem, the capital of our homeland and future state, defines Palestinian existence, past, present, and future, but itself has been denied a voice and an identity. Jerusalem defies exclusive possessiveness or bondage. Israel's annexation of Arab Jerusalem remains both clearly illegal in the eyes of the world community, and an affront to the peace that this city deserves.

We come to you from a tortured land and a proud, though captive people, having been asked to negotiate with our occupiers, but leaving behind the children of the *intifada* and a people under occupation and under curfew who enjoined us not to surrender or forget. As we speak, thousands of our brothers and sisters are languishing in Israeli prisons and detention camps, most detained without evidence, charge, or trial, many cruelly mistreated and tortured in interrogation, guilty only of seeking freedom or daring to defy the occupation. We speak in their name and we say: Set them free. As we speak, the tens of thousands who have been wounded or permanently disabled are in pain. Let peace heal their wounds. As we speak, the eyes of thousands of Palestinian refugees, deportees, and displaced persons since 1967, are haunting us, for exile is a cruel fate. Bring them home. They have the right to return. As we speak, the silence of demolished homes echoes through the halls and in our minds. We must rebuild our homes in our free state.

And what do we tell the loved ones of those killed by army bullets? How do we answer the questions and the fear in our children's eyes. For one out of three Palestinian children under occupation has been killed, injured, or detained in the past four years. How can we explain to our children that they are denied education or schools are so often closed by the army fate? [sentence as heard] Or why their life is in danger for raising a flag in a land where even children are killed or jailed? What requiem can be sung for trees uprooted by army bulldozers? And most of all, who can explain to those whose lands are confiscated and clear waters stolen, a message of peace? Remove the barbed wire. Restore to the land and its life-giving water. The settlements must stop now. Peace cannot be waged while Palestinian land confiscated in myriad ways and the status of the occupied territories is being decided each day by Israeli bulldozers and barbed wire. This is not simply a position. It is an irrefutable reality. Territory for peace is a travesty when territory for illegal settlement is official Israeli policy and practice. The settlements must stop now.

In the name of the Palestinian people, we wish to directly address the Israeli people with whom we have had a prolonged exchange of pain: Let us share hope, instead. We are willing to live side by side on the land and the promise of the future. Sharing, however, requires two partners, willing to share as equals. Mutuality and reciprocity must replace domination and hostility for genuine reconciliation and coexistence under international legality. Your security and ours are mutually dependent as entwined as the fears and nightmares of our children. We have seen some of you at your best and at your worst. For the occupier can hide no secrets from the occupied, and we are witness to the toll that occupation has exacted from you and yours.

We have seen you agonize over the transformation of your sons and daughters into instruments of a blind and violent occupation. And we are sure that at no time did you envisage such a role for the children whom you thought would forge your future. We have seen you look back in deepest sorrow at the tragedy of your past, and look on in horror at the disfigurement of the victim-turned-oppressor. Not for this have you nurtured your hopes, dreams, and your offspring. This is why we have responded with solemn appreciation to those of you who came to offer consolation to our bereaved, to give support to those whose homes were being demolished, and to extend encouragement and counsel to those detained behind barbed wire and iron bars. And we have marched together, often choking together in the nondiscriminatory tear gas or crying out in pain as the clubs descended on both Palestinian and Israeli alike, for pain knows no national boundaries, and no one can claim a monopoly on suffering. We once formed a human chain around Jerusalem, joining hands and calling for peace. Let us today form a moral chain around Madrid and continue that noble effort for peace and a promise of freedom for our sons and daughters. Break through the barriers of mistrust and manipulated fears. Let us look forward in magnanimity and in hope.

To our Arab brothers and sisters, most of whom are represented here in this historic occasion, we express our loyalty and gratitude for their lifelong support and solidarity. We are here together seeking a just and lasting peace, whose cornerstone is freedom for Palestine, justice for the Palestinians, and an end to the occupation of all Palestinian and Arab lands. Only then can we really enjoy together the fruits of peace, prosperity, security, and human dignity and freedom.

In particular, we address our Jordanian colleagues in our joint delegation: Our two peoples have a very special historic and geographic relationship. Together, we shall strive to achieve peace. We will continue to strive for our sovereignty, while proceeding freely and willingly to prepare the grounds for a confederation between the two states of Palestine and Jordan, which can be a cornerstone for our security and prosperity.

To the community of nations on our fragile planet, to the nations of Africa and Asia, to the Muslim world, and particularly to Europe, on whose southern and neighborly shores we meet today, from the heart of our collective struggle for peace, we greet you and acknowledge your support and recognition. You have recognized our rights and our government, and have given us real support and protection. You have penetrated the distorting mist of racism, stereotyping, and ignorance, and committed the act of seeing the invisible and listening to the voice of the silenced. Palestinians under occupation and in exile have become a reality in your eyes, and with courage and determination, you have affirmed the truth of our narrative. You have taken up our cause and our case, and we have brought you into our hearts. We thank you for caring and daring to know the truth, the truth which must set us all free.

To the co-sponsors and participants in this occasion of awe and challenge, we pledge our commitment to the principle of justice, peace, and reconciliation based on international legitimacy and uniform standards. We shall persist in our quest for peace to place before you the substance and determination of our people, often victimized but never defeated. We shall pursue our people's right to self-determination to the exhilaration of freedom and to the warmth of the sun as a nation among equals.

This is the moment of truth. You must have the courage to recognize it and the will to implement it, for our truth can no longer be hidden away in the dark recesses of inadvertency or neglect. People of Palestine look at you with a straightforward, direct gaze, seeking to touch your heart, for you have dared to stir up hopes that cannot be abandoned. You cannot afford to let us down, for we have lived up to the values you espouse, and we have remained true to our cause.

We, the Palestinian people, made the imaginative leap in the Palestine National Council of November 1988, during which the Palestine Liberation Organization launched its peace initiative based on Security Council Resolution 242 and 338, and declared Palestinian independence based on Resolution 181 of the United Nations, which gave birth to two states in 1948, Israel and Palestine. December 1988, a historic speech before the United Nations in Geneva led directly to the launching of the Palestinian-

American dialogue. Ever since then, our people have responded positively to every serious peace initiative and has done its utmost to ensure the success of this process. Israel, on the other hand, has placed many obstacles and barriers in the path of peace to negate the very validity of the process. Its illegal and frenzied settlement activity is the most glaring evidence of its rejectionism, the latest settlement being erected just two days ago. These historic decisions of the Palestine National Council wrench the course of history from inevitable confrontation and conflict towards peace and mutual recognition. With our own hands and in an act of sheer will, we have molded the shape of the future of our people. Our parliament has articulated the message of the people, with the courage to say yes to the challenge of history, just as it provided the reference in its resolutions last month in Algiers and in the Central Council meeting this month in Tunis to go forward to this historic conference. We cannot be made to bear the brunt of other people's noes. We must have reciprocity. We must have peace.

Ladies and Gentlemen: In the Middle East, there is no superfluous people outside time and place, but rather a state sorely missed by time and place. The state of Palestine must be born on the land of Palestine to redeem the injustice of the destruction of its historical reality and to free the people of Palestine from the shackles of their victimization.

Our homeland has never ceased to exist in our minds and hearts, but it has to exist as a state on all the territories occupied by Israel in the war of 1967 with Arab Jerusalem as its capital in the context of that city's special status and its non-exclusive character.

This state, in a condition of emergence, has already been a subject of anticipation for too long, should take place today rather than tomorrow. However, we are willing to accept the proposal for a transitional stage provided interim arrangements are not transformed into permanent status. The time frame must be condensed to respond to the dispossessed Palestinian's urgent need for sanctuary and to the occupied Palestinians' right to gain relief from oppression and to win recognition of their authentic will.

During this phase, international protection for our people is most urgently needed. And the dejure application of the Fourth Geneva Convention is a necessary condition. The phases must not prejudice the outcome. Rather, they require an internal momentum and motivation to lead sequentially to sovereignty. Bilateral negotiations on the withdrawal of Israeli forces, the dissolution of Israeli administration, and the transfer of authority to the Palestinian people cannot proceed under coercion or threat in the current asymmetry of power. Israel must demonstrate its willingness to negotiate in good faith by immediately halting all settlement activity and land confiscation while implementing meaningful confidence-building measures.

Without genuine progress, tangible constructive changes and just agreements during the bilateral talks, multilateral negotiations will be meaningless. Regional stability, security, and development are the logical outcome of an equitable and just solution to the Palestinian question, which remains the key to the resolution of wider conflicts and concerns.

In its confrontation of wills between the legitimacy of the people and the illegality of the occupation, the *intifada*'s message has been consistent: to embody the Palestinian state and to build its institutions and infrastructure. We seek recognition for this creative impulse which nurtures within it the potential nascent state.

We have paid a heavy price for daring to substantiate our authenticity and to practice popular democracy in spite of the cruelty of occupation. It was a sheer act of will that brought us here; the same will which asserted itself in the essence of the *intifada* as the cry for freedom, an act of civil resistance and people's participation and empowerment.

The *intifada* is our drive towards nation-building and social transformation. We are here today with the support of our people, who have given itself the right to hope and to make a stand for peace. We must recognize as well that some of our people harbor serious doubts and skepticism about this process. Within our democratic, social, and political structures, we have evolved a respect for pluralism and diversity and we shall guard the opposition's right to differ within the parameters of mutual respect and national unity.

The process launched here must lead us to the light at the end of the tunnel. And this light is the promise of a new Palestine—free, democratic, and respectful of human rights and the integrity of nature.

Self-determination, ladies and gentlemen, can neither be granted nor withheld at the will of the political self-interest of others. For it is enshrined in all international charters and humanitarian law. We claim this right; we firmly assert it here before you and in the eyes of the rest of the world. For it is a sacred and inviolable right which we shall relentlessly pursue and exercise with dedication and self-confidence and pride.

Let's end the Palestinian-Israeli fatal proximity in this unnatural condition of occupation, which has already claimed too many lives. No dream of expansion or glory can justify the taking of a single life. Set us free to reengage as neighbors and as equals on our holy land.

To our people in exile and under occupation, who have sent us to this appointment, laden with their trust, love, and aspirations, we say that the load is heavy and the task is great, but we shall be true. In the words of our great national poet Mahmud Darwish: *My homeland is not a suitcase, and I am no traveler.*

To the exiled and the occupied we say you shall return and you shall remain and we will prevail, for our cause is just. We will put on our embroidered robes and kafiyehs [traditional headdresses] in the sight of the world and celebrate together on the day of liberation.

Refugee camps are not fit for people who were raised on the land of Palestine in the warmth of the sun and freedom. The hail of Israeli bombs almost daily pouring down on our defenseless civilian population in the refugee camps of Lebanon is no substitute for the healing rain of the homeland. Yet, the international will had ensured their return in United Nation Resolution 194—a fact willfully ignored and unenacted. Similarly, all other resolutions pertinent to the Palestinian question beginning with Resolution 181, through Resolutions 242 and 338, and ending with Security Council Resolutions 681, have until now been relegated to the domain of public debate rather than real implementation. They formed a larger body of legality, including all relevant provisions of international law within which any peaceful settlement must proceed. If international legitimacy and the rule of law are to prevail and govern relations among nations, they must be respected and impartially and uniformly implemented. We as Palestinians require nothing less than justice.

Palestinians everywhere: Today we bear in our hands the precious gift of your love and your pain, and we shall set it down gently here before the eyes of the world and say there is a right here which must be acknowledged—the right to self-determination and statehood. There is strength and there is the scent of sacred incense in the air. Jerusalem, the heart of our homeland and the cradle of the soul, is shimmering through the barriers of occupation and deceit.

The deliberate violation of its sanctities is also an act of violence against the collective human, cultural, and spiritual memory and an aggression against its enduring symbols of tolerance, magnanimity, and respect for cultural and religious authenticity.

The cobbled streets of the old city must not echo with the discordant beat of Israeli military boots. We must restore to them the chant of the muezzin, the chimes of the church, the call of the ram, and the prayers of all the faithful calling for peace in the city of peace.

From Madrid let's light the candle of peace and let the olive branch blossom. Let's celebrate the rituals of justice and rejoice in the hymns of truth, for the awe of the moment is a promise to the future, which we all must redeem.

Palestinians will be free and will stand tall among the community of nations in the fullness of the pride and dignity which, by right, belongs to all people. Today, our people under occupation are holding high the olive branch of peace. In the words of Chairman Arafat in 1974 before the UN General Assembly: *Let not the olive branch of peace fall from my hands. Let not the olive branch of peace fall from the hands of the Palestinian people.* May God's mercy, peace, and blessings be upon you.

Part IV

The Apparent Approach of Peace

Israeli Prime Minister Yitzhak Rabin: Inaugural Speech (July 13, 1992)

. . . This government is determined to embrace every possible effort, pave every road, and do every possible and impossible thing for the sake of national and personal security, for the sake of peace and of preventing war, for the sake of eliminating unemployment, for the sake of *aliyah* and its absorption, for the sake of economic growth, to enhance the foundations of democracy and the rule of law, and for the sake of ensuring equality for all citizens, while upholding human rights.

We will change the national order of priorities. We know well that the road we are about to tread will be fraught with obstacles; crises will erupt, and there will be disappointment, tears, and pain. After all this is over, however, once we come to the end of this road, we will have acquired a strong country, a good country, a country in which we all share in the big efforts and are proud to be its citizens. As the poet Rahel put it: *Will a concerted, stubborn, and persistent effort of a thousand arms not move mountains?* The answer lies with us and is up to us.

. . . In the last decade of the 20th century, the atlases and the history and geography books no longer depict reality. Walls of hatred have crumbled, borders have been erased, superpowers have collapsed, ideologies have broken down, countries have been born and passed away, and the gates have opened to immigration to Israel. It is our duty, both to ourselves and to our children, to see the new world as it is today, to examine the risks and explore the chances, and to do everything so that the State of Israel becomes part of the changing world. We are no longer an isolated nation, and it is no longer true that the entire world is against us. We must rid ourselves of the feeling of isolation that has afflicted us for almost 50 years. We must join the campaign of peace, reconciliation, and international cooperation that is currently engulfing the entire globe, lest we miss the train and be left alone at the station.

This is why the new government made its main goal to promote the attainment of peace for Israel and to launch vigorous steps to bring about the termination of the Arab-Israeli conflict. We will do this on the basis of recognition by the Arab countries and the Palestinians of Israel as a sovereign state and of its right to live in peace and security. We sincerely believe that this is possible, imperative, and will come to be. As the poet Saul Tchernichowsky wrote: *"Believe I in the future. Though it may be far off, the day will yet come when peace shall be spoken and nation will bless nation."* I would like to believe that this day is not far off.

The government will propose to the Arab countries and to the Palestinians to pursue the peace negotiations based on the format consolidated at the Madrid conference. As a first step on the way to the permanent solution, we will discuss the implementation of autonomy in Judea, Samaria, and the Gaza district. It is not our intention to waste valuable time. The first directive the government will issue to the negotiating teams will be to accelerate the talks and to conduct intensive deliberations between the sides.

Within a short period of time, we will reopen the talks to dampen the flame of hatred between the Palestinians and the State of Israel. As a first step, and in order to demonstrate our integrity and goodwill, I wish to invite the Palestinian-Jordanian delegation for an informal meeting here in Jerusalem, to hear them and to let them hear us, in order to create the proper atmosphere for a good partnership.

From this podium I want to send a message to you, the Palestinians in the territories: We have been destined to live together on the same piece of land in the same country. Our life proceeds alongside yours, with you, and against you. You have failed in the wars against us. A hundred years of bloody terror on your part only inflicted suffering, pain, and bereavement upon you. You have lost thousands of your sons and daughters, and you have constantly lost ground. For over 44 years you have been deluding yourselves, your leaders have been leading you by the nose with falsehoods and lies. They missed all the opportunities, they rejected all our proposed solutions, and they led you from one disaster to another. You, the Palestinians in the territories, living in miserable exile in Gaza and Khan Yunus and in the refugee camps in Nabulus and Hebron, you who have never in your lives known even one day of freedom and happiness: You had better listen to us, if only this time. We are offering you the most fair and realistic offer we can put forth today: autonomy, self-rule, with its advantages and limitations. You will not get all that you want. We, too, may not get everything we want. Once and for all, take your fate into your own hands. Do not once again miss the opportunity which may never recur. Take our proposal seriously, give it the seriousness it deserves to spare yourselves yet more suffering and bereavement. Enough of tears and blood!

Today the new government proposes to the Palestinians in the territories to give peace a chance and to stop all violent and terrorist activities during the autonomy negotiations. We know very well that the Palestinians are not of one mind and that some of them think differently, but the people have been suffering for years.

To the troublemakers in the territories we propose to drop the stones and the knives and await the outcome of the talks which may engender peace in the Middle East. If the Palestinians accept this proposal, we will pursue the talks. Nevertheless, we will deal with the territories as if there were no negotiations going on between us. Instead of stretching out a friendly hand, we will enforce all the measures to prevent terror and violence. The choice is in the hands of the Palestinians in the territories.

We have lost our best sons and daughters in the struggle over this land and in the wars against the Arab armies. My longtime comrades in the IDF [Israel Defense Forces] and I, as a former military man who fought in Israel's wars, carry their memory in our hearts with great love. We share the grief of the families whose nights are sleepless and for whom all days of the year are one long memorial day, because only those who have lost their best friends can understand the feeling. Our heart also goes out to the disabled whose bodies are marked with the scars of war and terror. Even at this festive time, we do not forget the Israeli MIA's and POW's. We will continue to wage every possible effort to bring them back home. Our thoughts today, as always, are with their families.

Members of the Knesset, we will continue to fight for our right to live here in peace and tranquility. No knife, stone, firebomb, or mine will stop us. The government being presented here today sees itself responsible for the security of each and every Israeli citizen, Jew and Arab alike, in the State of Israel, in Judaea, Samaria, and the Gaza Strip. We will strike hard and relentlessly at the terrorists and their henchmen. There will be no compromises in the war against terror. The IDF and the other security forces will prove to the bloodthirsty men that our lives are not expendable. We will take action to reduce hostile activities as much as possible and safeguard the personal safety of the inhabitants of Israel and the inhabitants of the territories while meticulously upholding the law and individual freedoms.

Members of the Knesset, on your behalf, too, allow me to seize this occasion to convey our gratitude to the soldiers and commanders of the IDF, to the secret warriors of the Shin Bet, to the men of the Border Police and the Israel Police for the nights spent in pursuit and lying in ambush, for the days spent on guard and on the alert. On behalf of all of us, I shake your hand.

Members of the Knesset, the plan for Palestinian self-rule in Judaea, Samaria, and Gaza—the autonomy—included in the Camp David accords involves a five-year interim arrangement. No later than three years after its establishment, discussions will begin on the permanent solution. By definition, the very fact that this issue is being discussed arouses concern among those of us who chose to settle in Judaea, Samaria, and the Gaza district. I hereby inform you that the government, by means of the IDF and the other security forces, will be responsible for the security and welfare of the residents in Judaea, Samaria, and the Gaza Strip. At the same time, the government will avoid moves and acts that would disturb the proper conduct of the peace negotiations. We would like to emphasize that the government will continue to strengthen and build up Jewish settlement along the confrontation lines, due to their security importance, and in metropolitan Jerusalem.

This government, just like all its predecessors, believes there are no differences of opinion within this House concerning the eternalness of Jerusalem as the capital of Israel. Jerusalem, whole and united, has been and will remain the capital of the Israeli people under Israeli sovereignty, the place every Jew yearns and dreams of. The government is resolute in its position that Jerusalem is not a negotiable issue. The coming years, too, will witness the expansion of construction in metropolitan Jerusalem. Every Jew, both religious and secular, vows: If I forget thee, O Jerusalem, let my right hand wither! This vow unites all of us and certainly applies to me, being a native of Jerusalem.

The government will uphold the freedom of worship of members of all other faiths in Jerusalem. It will meticulously maintain free access to the holy sites of all faiths and sects and will make a normal and comfortable life possible for all those visiting and living in it.

Members of the Knesset, the winds of peace that have been blowing recently from Moscow to Washington, from Berlin to Beijing; the voluntary elimination of weapons of mass destruction; and the abrogation of military pacts have decreased the risks of war in the Middle East as well. Nevertheless, this region—made up of Syria, Jordan, Iraq, and Lebanon—is still rife with dangers, which is why we will not make even the slightest concession on issues of security. As far as we are concerned, security comes even before peace.

Several countries in our region have recently stepped up their efforts to develop and export nuclear weapons. According to reports, Iraq was very close to possessing nuclear arms. Fortunately, the Iraqi nuclear capability was exposed in time and, according to various testimonies, it was affected and damaged in and after the Gulf war. The possibility that nuclear weapons may make their appearance in the Middle East in the next few years is a negative and very serious development from Israel's point of view. Already in its initial steps, the government—possibly with the cooperation of other countries—will give its attention to the foiling of every possibility that any of Israel's enemies should get a hold on nuclear weapons. For a long time, Israel has been ready for the danger of the existence of nuclear weapons. Nevertheless, this reality requires us to give additional thought to the urgent need to terminate the Arab-Israeli conflict and to attain peace with our neighbors.

Members of the House, from this moment on, the term "peace process" is no longer relevant. Starting today we will not talk of a process, but of making peace. In making peace, we would like to employ the good services of Egypt, whose late leader Anwar al-Sadat mustered the courage and had the wisdom to award his people and us the first peace treaty. The government will seek other ways to improve neighborly relations and to enhance the ties with Egypt and its president, Husni Mubarak.

I call on the leaders of the Arab countries to follow in the footsteps of Egypt and its presidents, to make the move that will bring peace to us and them. I invite the king of Jordan and the Syrian and Lebanese presidents to come here to this podium, here in Israel's Knesset in Jerusalem, and talk peace. I am willing to travel today, tomorrow, to Amman, Damascus, Beirut on behalf of peace, because there is no greater triumph than the triumph of peace. In wars, there are victors and vanquished. In peace, all are victors.

In making peace, we will also be joined by the United States, whose friendship and special closeness we sincerely appreciate and hold dear. We will spare no effort to tighten and improve the special relations we have with the only superpower in the world. Although we will receive its advice, the decisions will be ours only—of Israel as a sovereign and independent state.

PLO Chairman Yasir Arafat: Speech for Fatah's Anniversary (December 31, 1992)

O revolutionaries in all the posts of the revolution, inside and outside the homeland; O masses of our fighting Palestinian people; O masses of our militant Arab nation, on such a day 28 years ago, the Palestinian people announced the start of the armed Palestinian revolution, which was ignited by the bullets of your pioneering movement—namely, the *Fatah* movement—on 1 January 1965. . . .

The road to victory and freedom, which our free men and revolutionaries are building day after day with their bare hands and pure blood, is the road to Palestine, which the faithful are longing for with their hearts.

Our people, O brothers and friends, are the active volcano in the Middle East which will only calm itself when one of the youths of the revolution and the *intifada* hoists the flag of your state over Jerusalem, and our homeland Palestine; an independent Palestine. . . .

Our battle to free the Palestinian will has been decided in favor of the Palestinian people, away from guardianship, dependence, and containment. The battle of the Palestinian will as expressed by the bullets of your leading movement, *Fatah,* early in 1965 was a hard and bitter one, but the few believers remained true to the oath and continued with resolve and strength.

The vanguard of your revolution, the *Fatah* movement, has proven that there is no going back on the jihad for Palestine, on the homeland, or on martyrdom. . . .

Masses of our glorious Arab nation. Ideological, political, and economic changes have swept our contemporary world. What was yesterday an established fact has today become something of the past. These changes have reached our region in the Middle East, bringing in the wake of their first wave the Gulf crisis and the Gulf war. This has dealt our Arab nation a great blow, hit Arab solidarity, and paralyzed the Arab position toward the Palestinian question, and as a result, lost us an historic opportunity to exploit those world changes for the national and the Palestinian interest. . . .

Then, my brothers, came the second wave, with the collapse of the Soviet Union and the domination by the single uni-polar American power over the fate of international politics.

This new world order brings great, real, and manifest dangers that pose a challenge for the Arab nation—peoples as well as states. These risks keep our nation bogged down in the whirlwind of the conflicts of the new world order. We either live or we will have to die, especially as Israel, world Zionism, and their allies are lying in wait for any serious Arab trend aimed at building our national destiny in light of the new world situation. . . .

We must stand by our brothers in Iraq—its people and its children, lift their siege and their suffering, and thwart the conspiracy being perpetrated against Iraq's territorial integrity and its unity. Likewise, the sanctions against Libya and its fraternal people must be lifted and their suffering must be brought to an end. And what about Somalia and our absence, as one Arab nation, when dealing with its problems, of which others have had to take charge? . . .

This is a clear declaration in the name of the entire nation: This land will remain Arab, will remain Arab, and will remain Arab. History will not register that the present generation of Palestinians squandered an atom of the soil of its homeland or of Jerusalem—or of Jerusalem.

Sons of our heroic Palestinian people, heroes in the positions of revolution, brothers, I want it to be clear to us all that the distance between us and the enemy at the negotiations table is too wide. . . .

Likewise, the distance is wide between us and the enemy in the field of conflict and the battle. But it is our political battle that covers our land and sanctities, and that will determine our fate and future. After more than a year since the start of the Madrid negotiations, which we attended despite the unjust conditions, our negotiators find themselves still at the same point at which they began. This is because the Israeli enemy is bent on maneuvering and not on negotiating. He tries to gain more time so that the conditions that forced him to sit face to face before the delegation of Palestine—the delegation of the owners of the land the enemy usurped and the land of the people he is persecuting and denies existence—may change. . . .

We have entered the negotiations in highly complicated Arab and international conditions and under unjust circumstances that are aimed at obstructing Palestinian participation. But thanks to our trust in ourselves and in our people, and our bold participation, we overcame the unjust conditions the Israeli enemy imposed.

International support for the Palestine right grew, and then came the Israeli elections, which brought the government of Yitzhaq Rabin, whom the U.S. Administration has given loan guarantees of $10 billion and guarantees for Israeli military supremacy. And so the Israeli Government continued with its policy of the iron fist, beatings, deportation, collective punishments, and crimes against our Islamic and Christian sanctities. The Israeli Government thus persisted in the confiscation of lands and the building of settlements for the new settlers in our land.

The policy of double dealing and measures that govern American attitudes toward the Arab-Israeli conflict have so far frustrated all opportunities for forcing the Israeli enemy to abide by the resolutions of international legitimacy and the withdrawal of its aggressor enemies from the Palestinian and Arab territories in implementation of these international resolutions, on whose basis the invitations to the Madrid peace conference were given, and for the implementation of which, talks were held in Washington and elsewhere.

The chronic fault in the pro-Israel U.S. stance alone explains the failure of the peace process in the Middle East. It is clear that successive American administrations make Israel a state above the law and above the resolutions of international legitimacy, and provide it with international protection and unlimited support.

Militant brothers, O sons of our brave *intifada,* our Palestinian delegation, the delegation of the Palestinian people, the PLO delegation, from the premise of our national constants approved by our national and central councils tightly tied Palestinian flexibility with the Palestinian national constants. [sentence as heard] With what brothers? With the national constants. Thus it rejected the enemy's sayings and submissions. Our delegation held fast to our national constants and the resolutions of international legitimacy, especially UN Security Council Resolutions 242 and 338, because they are the terms of reference of the peace process, from the moment it started until its conclusion with Israeli withdrawal from all the Arab and Palestinian territories, including holy Jerusalem, and the implementation of the principle of land for peace and the legitimate rights of the Palestinian people, including our right to return, to self-determination, and to establish an independent state with Jerusalem as its capital, on the way to Palestinian-Jordanian confederation in accordance with the voluntary and free choice of the two fraternal peoples: The Palestinian and the Jordanian.

Israel remaining an aggressive state, above the law and international legitimacy, only opens the door before lasting wars and total chaos. Yes, this only opens the door before lasting wars and total chaos in the region, which harms all. . . .

More steadfastness, more all-out confrontations in the sixth year of our blessed *intifada* in the towns, villages, camps, streets, fields, and mountains. The battle for national deliverance has begun with these solid Palestinian human blocs, who fill our lands and defy the bullets of the Israeli occupation and ferocity with their strong and profound faith and deeprooted will and great sacrifices, and with national unity our staunch shield in the melting pot of the PLO, the sole legitimate representative of our people and revolution. . . .

The Palestinian people remain the secure fence for the unity of the revolution and the unity of the PLO, and for preserving its national program and its future decisions with patience, wisdom, and persistence, and on the basis of democratic principles and democratic dialogue, common denominators, political and organizational programs approved by our national councils, in order to consolidate this national unity. Those democratic principles have foiled crude intervention in our internal affairs of our Palestinian house. Hence, from here and in this blessed year, the sixth year of our *intifada* and the 29th of our revolution, we renew the call to all the brothers active in the national field, from all political orientations, to consolidate this national unity. . . .

I say to those I love in the Israeli prisons and detention camps that the day of freedom is nigh. Your brothers have been pounding at the doors of the great prison and you are pounding at the walls of your prisons and detention camps. Your voices roar to the world. Be patient. Victory is from God. Victory needs no more than an hour's patience. . . .

Be patient. You are the spark that has inflamed anew the wrath of the masses of the Palestinian people in the face of the Israeli occupation. You are the free sons of this struggling people who have exposed the falsehood of Rabin and his Labor government with regard to the peace process. There will be no peace while you remain away from your homeland and kinsmen and your *intifada*. . . .

Your organization, the PLO, has acted on all fronts throughout the world to prevent the plot of the transfer—from the UN Security Council in New York to Europe, to Russia, to the Islamic and African summits at Dakar, to the Arab foreign ministers' conference in Cairo, to the Nonaligned Movement in Indonesia, to China, and to Japan. The action continues. . . .

Sons of the great Palestinian revolution, proud struggling people of Palestine, let the 29th year of the Palestine revolution and the sixth year of our blessed *intifada* be the year of challenge and victorious confrontation. What year, brothers? The year of challenge and victorious confrontation under the shadow of our solid national unity and the confidence of the PLO, our national unity, for routing the forces of Israeli dictatorship and the liberation of our Palestinian land and our holy Jerusalem.

Let us all stand like one man with one heart and one goal against our enemy, who occupies our land and homeland and sanctities.

The greater the darkness the closer the dawn!

Mahmoud Darwish: Resigning from the PLO Executive Committee (August 1993)

I will shock you. This organization, complete with its hierarchy and structure and figures and perhaps its content—this organization is finished. Yes, it is finished, and you must admit this and act accordingly. [You must] put all your imaginative resources to work to see what comes next and to nurture the infant that it [the PLO] has given birth to, whether some of us weep for it [the PLO] or others rejoice at its demise.

This organization is finished whether you go with the settlement to the end or drop out of the settlement now. The organization's remaining role is to sign the agreement with Israel. The moment it signs, it will be transformed into something else. What is this something else? Think about it as of now, and think of the fate of the cadres standing in the wind. . . .

We are approaching a grave decision relating to an imminent agreement with the Israeli government on Gaza and Jericho. When will this matter be discussed? When?

Some will say: Israel does not want to keep Gaza, and handing it over to the Palestinians solves an Israeli problem caused by the Gaza's unsolvable problems and caused by the *intifada* and by Israel's inability to annex because it wants to preserve Israel's Jewish character. Some will say that the Israeli-Palestinian agreement will eliminate the obstacle standing in the way of the Arab-Israeli peace train, and that the agreement will cool down the Arab-Israeli conflict and divide the Palestinian cause and the Palestinian people, and, and. . . . All this is true, but we cannot say that Gaza and Jericho don't concern us. Whether the proposal promises us full self-government or incomplete independence, we must take our time studying it in order to avoid leaping into thin air, in order not to take risks. We must carefully examine the details and the principles before we take this step, and the examination must involve all the groups and trends of the Palestinian people.

Have we obtained answers to the questions, including the following questions:

Is this deal part of a comprehensive peace settlement . . . ?

Is it clear that this is the first stage of the implementation of [Security

Council] Resolution 242 in accordance with a clear timetable linked with a clear commitment and a clear recognition that this land is occupied land?

Who will run this experimental self-government in Gaza and Jericho? The PLO, whose role is going to end? Or an elected council?

Will the PLO go there, or will its chairman, in his capacity as its chairman or the president of something else?

What are the parameters of the experimental interim stage? Will it be self-government if the experiment and the test are a success? And what if it fails? Here, allow me to warn that our current conditions and present structure provide a negative answer to this question.

Is there a clear bridge linking the interim stage with the final stage, to reassure us that the interim stage will not be the final one?

Is the popular base ready to plunge into this experiment? Or is it charged with dangerous, explosive elements?

Can we ignore the fears, real or contrived, that our Arab 'neighbors' are expressing about the agreement with our Israeli 'neighbors'?

What international economic guarantees are there that to make Gaza viable and build its infrastructure . . . ?

What forms of national self-expression will be allowed in resisting the occupation, which will remain there through general security, the settlements, the borders, the right of foreign representation, the crossings and the bridges and other forms of Israeli sovereignty?

Those questions make me think we are about to take an historic risk. I hope it works, but I have fears about its failure and its destructive national effects, which could lead to disaster.

My conscience will not tolerate participation in this adventurous decision as long as I cannot answer the questions posed. For that reason, I stand by my resignation from the decision-making body, placing myself at the disposal of the Palestinian people and their higher national interests.

Forgive me if I say that I am under no obligation to take part in this gamble. . . .

It is your right to ask me: Why [resign from the PLO Executive Committee] now? Why at this particular time?

Among the easy, ready-made charges: Isn't this abandoning ship?

I will respond immediately. . . . I don't see a ship now, if the ship is the PLO. Look around you carefully: its institutions, departments and bureaus are unoperational. They are up for auction.

It would be a crime to ignore the objective element in the crisis we are going through, but it is arrogant to ignore the subjective element. I am asking for no more than good management of the ending, in a manner that preserves people's dignity and humanity. We have taken two generations to their death in the project of liberation and independence, and it now appears as if we are abandoning them completely, leaving them to the winds of the new wilderness. No, the martyrs were not stupid, as some angry people are saying. The martyrs were right. They believed their blood and their nation. We are the ones to blame, we who have no answer to any question relating to their children. . . .

We see a ship's captain in a fluid image driven by a mysterious force towards an unknown fate at sea. On the shore, we see thousands of the martyrs' children waving to him: wait for us, or take us with you. . . .

We are bidding a chaotic farewell to an historic stage and entering another stage for which we have not prepared ourselves. This is the question that haunts me. . . .

Israel and PLO: Declaration of Principles on Interim Self-Government Arrangements ["Oslo Agreement"](September 13, 1993)

The Government of the State of Israel and the P.L.O. team (in the Jordanian-Palestinian delegation to the Middle East Peace Conference) (the "Palestinian Delegation"), representing the Palestinian people, agree that it is time to put an end to decades of confrontation and conflict, recognize their mutual legitimate and political rights, and strive to live in peaceful coexistence and mutual dignity and security and achieve a just, lasting and comprehensive peace settlement and historic reconciliation through the agreed political process. Accordingly, the two sides agree to the following principles:

ARTICLE I

Aim of the Negotiations

The aim of the Israeli-Palestinian negotiations within the current Middle East peace process is, among other things, to establish a Palestinian Interim Self-Government Authority, the elected Council (the "Council"), for the Palestinian people in the West Bank and the Gaza Strip, for a transitional period not exceeding five years, leading to a permanent settlement based on Security Council Resolutions 242 and 338.

It is understood that the interim arrangements are an integral part of the whole peace process and that the negotiations on the permanent status will lead to the implementation of Security Council Resolutions 242 and 338.

ARTICLE II

Framework for the Interim Period

The agreed framework for the interim period is set forth in this Declaration of Principles.

ARTICLE III

Elections

1. In order that the Palestinian people in the West Bank and Gaza Strip may govern themselves according to democratic principles, direct, free and general political elections will be held for the Council under agreed supervision and international observation, while the Palestinian police will ensure public order.

2. An agreement will be concluded on the exact mode and conditions of the elections in accordance with the protocol attached as Annex I, with the goal of holding the elections not later than nine months after the entry into force of this Declaration of Principles.

3. These elections will constitute a significant interim preparatory step toward the realization of the legitimate rights of the Palestinian people and their just requirements.

ARTICLE IV

Jurisdiction

Jurisdiction of the Council will cover West Bank and Gaza Strip territory, except for issues that will be negotiated in the permanent status negotiations. The two sides view the West Bank and the Gaza Strip as a single territorial unit, whose integrity will be preserved during the interim period.

ARTICLE V

Transitional Period and Permanent Status Negotiations

1. The five-year transitional period will begin upon the withdrawal from the Gaza Strip and Jericho area.

2. Permanent status negotiations will commence as soon as possible, but not later than the beginning of the third year of the interim period, between the Government of Israel and the Palestinian people representatives.

3. It is understood that these negotiations shall cover remaining issues, including: Jerusalem, refugees, settlements, security arrangements, borders, relations and cooperation with other neighbors, and other issues of common interest.

4. The two parties agree that the outcome of the permanent status negotiations should not be prejudiced or preempted by agreements reached for the interim period.

ARTICLE VI

Preparatory Transfer of Powers and Responsibilities

1. Upon the entry into force of this Declaration of Principles and the withdrawal from the Gaza Strip and the Jericho area, a transfer of authority from the Israeli military government and its Civil Administration to the authorised Palestinians for this task, as detailed herein, will commence. This transfer of authority will be of a preparatory nature until the inauguration of the Council.

2. Immediately after the entry into force of this Declaration of Principles and the withdrawal from the Gaza Strip and Jericho area, with the view to promoting economic development in the West Bank and Gaza Strip, authority will be transferred to the Palestinians on the following spheres: education and culture, health, social welfare, direct taxation, and tourism. The Palestinian side will commence in building the Palestinian police force, as agreed upon. Pending the inauguration of the Council, the two parties may negotiate the transfer of additional powers and responsibilities, as agreed upon.

ARTICLE VII

Interim Agreement

1. The Israeli and Palestinian delegations will negotiate an agreement on the interim period (the "Interim Agreement").

2. The Interim Agreement shall specify, among other things, the structure of the Council, the number of its members, and the transfer of powers and responsibilities from the Israeli military government and its Civil Administration to the Council. The Interim Agreement shall also specify the Council's executive authority, legislative authority in accordance with Article IX below, and the independent Palestinian judicial organs.

3. The Interim Agreement shall include arrangements, to be implemented upon the inauguration of the Council, for the assumption by the Council of all of the powers and responsibilities transferred previously in accordance with Article VI above.

4. In order to enable the Council to promote economic growth, upon its inauguration, the Council will establish, among other things, a Palestinian Electricity Authority, a Gaza Sea Port Authority, a Palestinian Development Bank, a Palestinian Export Promotion Board, a Palestinian Environmental Authority, a Palestinian Land Authority and a Palestinian Water Administration Authority, and any other Authorities agreed upon, in accordance with the Interim Agreement that will specify their powers and responsibilities.

5. After the inauguration of the Council, the Civil Administration will be dissolved, and the Israeli military government will be withdrawn.

ARTICLE VIII

Public Order and Security

In order to guarantee public order and internal security for the Palestinians of the West Bank and the Gaza Strip, the Council will establish a strong police force, while Israel will continue to carry the responsibility for defending against external threats, as well as the responsibility for overall security of Israelis for the purpose of safeguarding their internal security and public order.

ARTICLE IX

Laws and Military Orders

1. The Council will be empowered to legislate, in accordance with the Interim Agreement, within all authorities transferred to it.

2. Both parties will review jointly laws and military orders presently in force in remaining spheres.

ARTICLE X

Joint Israeli-Palestinian Liaison Committee

In order to provide for a smooth implementation of this Declaration of Principles and any subsequent agreements pertaining to the interim period, upon the entry into force of this Declaration of Principles, a Joint Israeli Palestinian Liaison Committee will be established in order to deal with issues requiring coordination, other issues of common interest, and disputes.

ARTICLE XI

Israeli-Palestinian Cooperation in Economic Fields

Recognizing the mutual benefit of cooperation in promoting the development of the West Bank, the Gaza Strip and Israel, upon the entry into force of this Declaration of Principles, an Israeli-Palestinian Economic Cooperation Committee will be established in order to develop and implement in a cooperative manner the programs identified in the protocols attached as Annex III and Annex IV.

ARTICLE XII

Liaison and Cooperation with Jordan and Egypt

The two parties will invite the Governments of Jordan and Egypt to participate in establishing further liaison and cooperation arrangements between the Government of Israel and the Palestinian representatives, on the one hand, and the Governments of Jordan and Egypt, on the other hand, to promote cooperation between them. These arrangements will include the constitution of a Continuing Committee that will decide by agreement on the modalities of admission of persons displaced from the West Bank and Gaza Strip in 1967, together with necessary measures to prevent disruption and disorder. Other matters of common concern will be dealt with by this Committee.

ARTICLE XIII

Redeployment of Israeli Forces

1. After the entry into force of this Declaration of Principles, and not later than the eve of elections for the Council, a redeployment of Israeli military forces in the West Bank and the Gaza Strip will take place, in addition to withdrawal of Israeli forces carried out in accordance with Article XIV.

2. In redeploying its military forces, Israel will be guided by the principle that its military forces should be redeployed outside populated areas.

3. Further redeployments to specified locations will be gradually implemented commensurate with the assumption of responsibility for public order and internal security by the Palestinian police force pursuant to Article VIII above.

ARTICLE XIV

Israeli Withdrawal from the Gaza Strip and Jericho Area

Israeli will withdraw from the Gaza Strip and Jericho area, as detailed in the protocol attached as Annex II.

ARTICLE XV

Resolution of Disputes

1. Disputes arising out of the application or interpretation of this Declaration of Principles, or any subsequent agreements pertaining to the interim period, shall be resolved by negotiations through the Joint Liaison Committee to be established pursuant to Article X above.

2. Disputes which cannot be settled by negotiations may be resolved by a mechanism of conciliation to be agreed upon by the parties.

3. The parties may agree to submit to arbitration disputes relating to the interim period, which cannot be settled through conciliation. To this end, upon the agreement of both parties, the parties will establish an Arbitration Committee.

ARTICLE XVI

Israeli-Palestinian Cooperation Concerning Regional Programs

Both parties view the multilateral working groups as an appropriate instrument for promoting a "Marshall Plan," the regional programs and other programs, including special programs for the West Bank and Gaza Strip, as indicated in the protocol attached as Annex IV.

ARTICLE XVII

Miscellaneous Provisions

1. This Declaration of Principles will enter into force one month after its signing.

2. All protocols annexed to this Declaration of Principles and Agreed Minutes pertaining thereto shall be regarded as an integral part hereof.

ANNEX I

Protocol on the Mode and Conditions of Elections

1. Palestinians of Jerusalem who live there will have the right to participate in the election process, according to an agreement between the two sides.

2. In addition, the election agreement should cover, among other things, the following issues:

   a. the system of elections;

   b. the mode of the agreed supervision and international observation and their personal composition; and

   c. rules and regulations regarding election campaign, including agreed arrangements for the organizing of mass media, and the possibility of licensing a broadcasting and TV station.

3. The future status of displaced Palestinians who were registered on 4th June 1967 will not be prejudiced because they are unable to participate in the election process due to practical reasons.

ANNEX II

Protocol on Withdrawal of Israeli Forces from the Gaza Strip and Jericho Area

1. The two sides will conclude and sign within two months from the date of entry into force of this Declaration of Principles, an agreement on the withdrawal of Israeli military forces from the Gaza Strip and Jericho area. This agreement will include comprehensive arrangements to apply in the Gaza Strip and the Jericho area subsequent to the Israeli withdrawal.

2. Israel will implement an accelerated and scheduled withdrawal of Israeli military forces from the Gaza Strip and Jericho area, beginning immediately with the signing of the agreement on the Gaza Strip and Jericho area and to be completed within a period not exceeding four months after the signing of this agreement.

3. The above agreement will include, among other things:

a. Arrangements for a smooth and peaceful transfer of authority from the Israeli military government and its Civil Administration to the Palestinian representatives.

b. Structure, powers and responsibilities of the Palestinian authority in these areas, except: external security, settlements, Israelis, foreign relations, and other mutually agreed matters.

c. Arrangements for the assumption of internal security and public order by the Palestinian police force consisting of police officers recruited locally and from abroad (holding Jordanian passports and Palestinian documents issued by Egypt). Those who will participate in the Palestinian police force coming from abroad should be trained as police and police officers.

d. A temporary international or foreign presence, as agreed upon.

e. Establishment of a joint Palestinian-Israeli Coordination and Cooperation Committee for mutual security purposes.

f. An economic development and stabilization program, including the establishment of an Emergency Fund, to encourage foreign investment, and financial and economic support. Both sides will coordinate and cooperate jointly and unilaterally with regional and international parties to support these aims.

g. Arrangements for a safe passage for persons and transportation between the Gaza Strip and Jericho area.

4. The above agreement will include arrangements for coordination between both parties regarding passages:

a. Gaza—Egypt; and

b. Jericho—Jordan.

5. The offices responsible for carrying out the powers and responsibilities of the Palestinian authority under this Annex II and Article VI of the Declaration of Principles will be located in the Gaza Strip and in the Jericho area pending the inauguration of the Council.

6. Other than these agreed arrangements, the status of the Gaza Strip and Jericho area will continue to be an integral part of the West Bank and Gaza Strip, and will not be changed in the interim period.

ANNEX III

Protocol on Israeli-Palestinian Cooperation in Economic and Development Programs

The two sides agree to establish an Israeli-Palestinian Continuing Committee for Economic Cooperation, focusing, among other things, on the following:

1. Cooperation in the field of water, including a Water Development Program prepared by experts from both sides, which will also specify the mode of cooperation in the management of water resources in the West Bank and Gaza Strip, and will include proposals for studies and plans on water rights of each party, as well as on the equitable utilization of joint water resources for implementation in and beyond the interim period.

2. Cooperation in the field of electricity, including an Electricity Development Program, which will also specify the mode of cooperation for the production, maintenance, purchase and sale of electricity resources.

3. Cooperation in the field of energy, including an Energy Development Program, which will provide for the exploitation of oil and gas for industrial purposes, particularly in the Gaza Strip and in the Negev, and will encourage further joint exploitation of other energy resources. This Program may also provide for the construction of a Petrochemical industrial complex in the Gaza Strip and the construction of oil and gas pipelines.

4. Cooperation in the field of finance, including a Financial Development and Action Program for the encouragement of international investment in the West Bank and the Gaza Strip, and in Israel, as well as the establishment of a Palestinian Development Bank.

5. Cooperation in the field of transport and communications, including a Program, which will define guidelines for the establishment of a Gaza Sea Port Area, and will provide for the establishing of transport and communications lines to and from the West Bank and the Gaza Strip to Israel and to other countries. In addition, this

Program will provide for carrying out the necessary construction of roads, railways, communications lines, etc.

6. Cooperation in the field of trade, including studies, and Trade Promotion Programs, which will encourage local, regional and inter-regional trade, as well as a feasibility study of creating free trade zones in the Gaza Strip and in Israel, mutual access to these zones, and cooperation in other areas related to trade and commerce.

7. Cooperation in the field of industry, including Industrial Development Programs, which will provide for the establishment of joint Israeli-Palestinian Industrial Research and Development Centers, will promote Palestinian-Israeli joint ventures, and provide guidelines for cooperation in the textile, food, pharmaceutical, electronics, diamonds, computer and science-based industries.

8. A program for cooperation in, and regulation of, labor relations and cooperation in social welfare issues.

9. A Human Resources Development and Cooperation Plan, providing for joint Israeli-Palestinian workshops and seminars, and for the establishment of joint vocational training centers, research institutes and data banks.

10. An Environmental Protection Plan, providing for joint and/or coordinated measures in this sphere.

11. A program for developing coordination and cooperation in the field of communication and media.

12. Any other programs of mutual interest.

Annex IV

Protocol on Israeli-Palestinian Cooperation Concerning Regional Development Programs

1. The two sides will cooperate in the context of the multilateral peace efforts in promoting a Development Program for the region, including the West Bank and the Gaza Strip, to be initiated by the G-7. The parties will request the G-7 to seek the participation in this program of other interested states, such as members of the Organisation for Economic Cooperation and Development regional Arab states and institutions, as well as members of the private sector.

2. The Development Program will consist of two elements:

a) An Economic Development Program for the West Bank and the Gaza Strip.

b) A Regional Economic Development Program.

A. The Economic Development Program for the West Bank and the Gaza Strip will consist of the following elements:

(1) A Social Rehabilitation Program, including a Housing and Construction Program.

(2) A Small and Medium Business Development Plan.

(3) An Infrastructure Development Program (water, electricity, transportation and communications, etc.)

(4) A Human Resources Plan.

(5) Other programs.

B. The Regional Economic Development Program may consist of the following elements:

(1) The establishment of a Middle East Development Fund, as a first step, and a Middle East Development Bank, as a second step.

(2) The development of a joint Israeli-Palestinian-Jordanian Plan for coordinated exploitation of the Dead Sea area.

(3) The Mediterranean Sea (Gaza)—Dead Sea Canal.

(4) Regional Desalinization and other water development projects.

(5) A regional plan for agricultural development, including a co-ordinated regional effort for the prevention of desertification.

(6) Interconnection of electricity grids.

(7) Regional cooperation for the transfer, distribution and industrial exploitation of gas, oil and other energy resources.

(8) A Regional Tourism, Transportation and Telecommunications Development Plan.

(9) Regional cooperation in other spheres.

3. The two sides will encourage the multilateral working groups, and will coordinate towards their success. The two parties will encourage intersessional activities, as well as pre-feasibility and feasibility studies, within the various multilateral working groups.

Israel and PLO: Agreed Minutes to the Declaration of Principles on Interim Self-Government Arrangements (September 13, 1993)

Any powers and responsibilities transferred to the Palestinians pursuant to the Declaration of Principles prior to the inauguration of the Council will be subject to the same principles pertaining to Article IV, as set out in these Agreed Minutes below.

B. Specific Understandings and Agreements

ARTICLE IV

It is understood that:

1. Jurisdiction of the Council will cover West Bank and Gaza Strip territory, except for issues that will be negotiated in the perma-

nent status negotiations: Jerusalem, settlements, military locations, and Israelis.

2. The Council's jurisdiction will apply with regard to the agreed powers, responsibilities, spheres and authorities transferred to it.

ARTICLE VI (2)

It is agreed that the transfer of authority will be as follows:

1. The Palestinian side will inform the Israeli side of the names of the authorized Palestinians who will assume the powers, authorities and responsibilities that will be transferred to the Palestinians according to the Declaration of Principles in the following fields: education and culture, health, social welfare, direct taxation, tourism, and any other authorities agreed upon.

2. It is understood that the rights and obligations of these offices will not be affected.

3. Each of the spheres described above will continue to enjoy existing budgetary allocations in accordance with arrangements to be mutually agreed upon. These arrangements also will provide for the necessary adjustments required in order to take into account the taxes collected by the direct taxation office.

4. Upon the execution of the Declaration of Principles, the Israeli and Palestinian delegations will immediately commence negotiations on a detailed plan for the transfer of authority on the above offices in accordance with the above understandings.

ARTICLE VII (2)

The Interim Agreement will also include arrangements for coordination and cooperation.

ARTICLE VII (5)

The withdrawal of the military government will not prevent Israel from exercising the powers and responsibilities not transferred to the Council.

ARTICLE VIII

It is understood that the Interim Agreement will include arrangements for cooperation and coordination between the two parties in this regard. It is also agreed that the transfer of powers and responsibilities to the Palestinian police will be accomplished in a phased manner, as agreed in the Interim Agreement.

ARTICLE X

It is agreed that, upon the entry into force of the Declaration of Principles, the Israeli and Palestinian delegations will exchange the names of the individuals designated by them as members of the Joint Israeli-Palestinian Liaison Committee.

It is further agreed that each side will have an equal number of members in the Joint Committee. The Joint Committee will reach decisions by agreement. The Joint Committee may add other technicians and experts, as necessary. The Joint Committee will decide on the frequency and place or places of its meetings.

ANNEX II

It is understood that, subsequent to the Israeli withdrawal, Israel will continue to be responsible for external security, and for internal security and public order of settlements and Israelis. Israeli military forces and civilians may continue to use roads freely within the Gaza Strip and the Jericho area.

September 9, 1993

Mr. Prime Minister,

The signing of the Declaration of Principles marks a new era in the history of the Middle East. In firm conviction thereof, I would like to confirm the following PLO commitments:

The PLO recognizes the right of the State of Israel to exist in peace and security.

The PLO accepts United Nations Security Council Resolutions 242 and 338.

The PLO commits itself to the Middle East peace process, and to a peaceful resolution of the conflict between the two sides and declares that all outstanding issues relating to permanent status will be resolved through negotiations.

The PLO considers that the signing of the Declaration of Principles constitutes a historic event, inaugurating a new epoch of peaceful coexistence, free from violence and all other acts which endanger peace and stability. Accordingly, the PLO renounces the use of terrorism and other acts of violence and will assume responsibility over all PLO elements and personnel in order to assure their compliance, prevent violations and discipline violators.

In view of the promise of a new era and the signing of the Declaration of Principles and based on Palestinian acceptance of Security Council Resolutions 242 and 338, the PLO affirms that those articles of the Palestinian Covenant which deny Israel's right to exist, and the provisions of the Covenant which are inconsistent with the commitments of this letter are now inoperative and no longer valid. Consequently, the PLO undertakes to submit to the Palestinian National Council for formal approval the necessary changes in regard to the Palestinian Covenant.

Sincerely,
Yasser Arafat
Chairman
The Palestine Liberation Organization

September 9, 1993

Mr. Chairman,

In response to your letter of September 9, 1993, I wish to confirm to you that, in light of the PLO commitments included in your letter, the Government of Israel has decided to recognize the PLO as the representative of the Palestinian people and commence negotiations with the PLO within the Middle East peace process.

Sincerely,
Yitzhak Rabin
Prime Minister of Israel

U.S. President Bill Clinton, Israeli Prime Minister Yitzhak Rabin, and PLO Chairman Yasir Arafat:Speeches at the Signing of the Israel-PLO Declaration of Principles (September 13, 1993)

U.S. President Bill Clinton

We have been granted the great privilege of witnessing this victory for peace. Just as the Jewish people this week celebrate the dawn of a new year, let us all go from this place to celebrate the dawn of a new era—not only for the Middle East but for the entire world.

The sound we heard today, once again as in ancient Jericho, was of trumpets toppling walls, the walls of anger and suspicion between Israeli and Palestinian, between Arab and Jew. This time, praise God, the trumpets herald not the destruction of that city but its new beginning.

Now let each of us here today return to our portion of that effort. Uplifted by the spirit of the moment, refreshed in our hopes and guided by the wisdom of the Almighty, who has brought us to this joyous day. Go in peace. Go as peacemakers.

Israeli Prime Minister Yitzhak Rabin

President Clinton, the President of the United States, your excellencies, ladies and gentlemen. This signing of the Israeli-Palestinian declaration of principles here today is not so easy, neither for myself as a soldier in Israel's wars, nor for the people of Israel, nor for the Jewish people in the Diaspora who are watching us now with great hope mixed with apprehension. It is certainly not easy for the families of the victims of the wars, violence, terror, whose pain will never heal, for the many thousands who defended our lives with their own and have even sacrificed their lives for our own. For them, this ceremony has come too late.

Today, on the eve of an opportunity for peace, and perhaps an end to violence and wars, we remember each and every one of them with everlasting love. We have come from Jerusalem, the ancient and eternal capital of the Jewish people. We have come from an anguished and grieving land. We have come from a people, a home, a family that has not known a single year, not a single month, in which mothers have not wept for their sons. We have come to try and put an end to the hostilities so that our children, and our children's children, will no longer experience the painful cost of war, violence and terror. We have come to secure their lives and to ease the sorrow and the painful memories of the past, to hope and pray for peace.

Let me say to you, the Palestinians, we are destined to live together on the same soil in the same land. We, the soldiers who have returned from battles stained with blood; we who have seen our relatives and friends killed before our eyes; we who have attended their funerals and cannot look into the eyes of their parents; we who have come from a land where parents bury their children: we who have fought against you, the Palestinians, we say to you today in a loud and a clear voice, enough of blood and tears. Enough!

We have no desire for revenge. We harbor no hatred towards you. We, like you, are people—people who want to build a home, to plant a tree, to love, live side by side with you in dignity, in affinity, as human beings, as free men. We are today giving peace a chance and saying again to you, "Enough." Let us pray that a day will come when we all will say farewell to arms. We wish to open a new chapter in the sad book of our lives together—a chapter of mutual recognition, of good neighborliness, of mutual respect, of understanding. We hope to embark on a new era in the history of the Middle East.

Today here in Washington at the White House, we will begin a new reckoning in the relations between peoples, between parents tired of war, between children who will not know war. President of the United States, ladies and gentlemen, our inner strength, our higher moral values have been derived for thousands of years from the Book of the Books, in one of which, Koheleth (Ecclesiastes), we read, "To every thing there is a season and a time to every purpose under heaven. A time to be born and time to die, a time to kill and a time to heal. A time to weep and a time to laugh. A time to love and a time to hate, a time of war and a time of peace." Ladies and gentlemen, the time for peace has come.

PLO Chairman Yasir Arafat

In the name of God, the most merciful, the passionate, Mr. President, ladies and gentlemen, I would like to express our tremendous appreciation to President Clinton and to his administration for sponsoring this historic event which the entire world has been waiting for.

Mr. President, I am taking this opportunity to assure you and to assure the great American people that we share your values for freedom, justice and human rights—values for which my people have been striving.

My people are hoping that this agreement which we are signing today marks the beginning of the end of a chapter of pain and suffering which has lasted throughout this century.

My people are hoping that this agreement which we are signing today will usher in an age of peace, coexistence and equal rights. We are relying on your role, Mr. President, and on the role of all the countries which believe that without peace in the Middle East, peace in the world will not be complete.

Enforcing the agreement and moving toward the final settlement, after two years, to implement all aspects of U.N. resolutions 242 and 338 in all of their aspects, and resolve all the issues of Jerusalem, the settlements, the refugees and the boundaries will be a Palestinian and an Israeli responsibility. It is also the responsibility of the international community in its entirety to help the parties overcome the tremendous difficulties which are still standing in the way of reaching a final and comprehensive settlement.

Now as we stand on the threshold of this new historic era, let me address the people of Israel and their leaders, with whom we are meeting today for the first time, and let me assure them that the difficult decision we reached together was one that required great and exceptional courage.

We will need more courage and determination to continue the course of building coexistence and peace between us. This is possible and it will happen with mutual determination and with the effort that will be made with all parties on all the tracks to establish the foundations of a just and comprehensive peace.

Our people do not consider that exercising the right to self-determination could violate the rights of their neighbors or infringe on their security. Rather, putting an end to their feelings of being wronged and of having suffered an historic injustice is the strongest guarantee to achieve coexistence and openness between our two peoples and future generations. Our two peoples are awaiting today this historic hope, and they want to give peace a real chance.

Such a shift will give us an opportunity to embark upon the process of economic, social and cultural growth and development. And we hope that international participation in that process will be extensive as it can be. This shift will also provide an opportunity for all forms of cooperation on a broad scale and in all fields. . . .

I wish to thank the Russian Federation and President Boris Yeltsin. Our thanks also go to Secretary Christopher and Foreign Minister Kozyrev, to the government of Norway and to the Foreign Minister of Norway for the positive part they played in bringing about this major achievement. I extend greetings to all the Arab leaders, our brothers, and to all the world leaders who contributed to this achievement.

Ladies and gentlemen, the battle for peace is the most difficult battle of our lives. It deserves our utmost efforts because the land of peace, the land of peace yearns for a just and comprehensive peace.

Israeli Prime Minister Yitzhak Rabin: Speech to Knesset (September 21, 1993)

Honorable President of the State, Mr. Speaker, distinguished Knesset: The government today submitted to the Knesset the declaration of principles about the interim arrangements on self-government for the Palestinians in the territories, as well as the letters exchanged between Israel and the PLO and the agenda for the negotiations between Israel and Jordan. All the documents pertaining to the issue have been placed before the members of the House, and there is no other, secret agreement. Everything is out in the open and aboveboard. The government will ask for the Knesset's endorsement and will regard the Knesset's decision as a vote of confidence in the government and its resolutions.

Distinguished Knesset, in three days every Jew, wherever he may be, will observe the sanctity of Yom Kippur. On this day of national and personal reckoning, as the sun sets and we say the concluding prayer, millions of Jews in every corner of the earth, from Casablanca and Buenos Aires to Melbourne and Qiryat Shemona, will utter the prayer: As you close the gates, open them anew because a new day has dawned.

The Israeli government today believes that with the beginning of the new year, a gate has opened—a gate of peace, a gate of blessing. As the prayer goes: Bestow peace, good, blessings, life, favor and grace, charity and mercy upon us and all the people of Israel. On the eve of Yom Kippur 5754, the Israeli government presents the Israeli people with a chance for peace and, perhaps, for an end to the wars, violence, and terror. In the high holidays prayers we also say: who will live and who will die, who will perish and who will not, who will die by water, fire, or sword.

On this bitter day twenty years ago, we felt death by fire and sword on our flesh and skin. All of us, both religious and secular, left-wing or right-wing, Jewish and non-Jewish citizens of Israel experienced one of the toughest hours in our history as a state. In the sands of the Chinese Farm in the Sinai Peninsula, on the cliffs of the Mount Hermon on the Golan Heights, IDF soldiers in the regular army and in the reserves, our best sons, used their bodies to block the waves of tanks and columns of soldiers that threatened our existence. In the battle to defend our lives and homes against the Egyptian and Syrian armies, 2,569 IDF soldiers and officers fell.

Today, too, twenty years later, we anguish over the deaths of our dear ones and we share in the sorrow of the bereaved families, whose pain does not abate or the scars of their tragedy heal as years go by. On the eve of Yom Kippur, our hearts are with them, and so it will be forever.

Distinguished Knesset, the Yom Kippur War taught us as well as our enemies the limitations of military power and the possibilities entailed in a political solution. In the wake of the disengagement agreements we signed with Egypt and Syria, the interim agreement we signed with Egypt, and the IDF's withdrawal from Egypt and the heart of Syria, we knew and we know to this day long years of peace, quiet, and tranquility in those two cores of fire and war. Thanks to the determination and initiative of the late Prime Minister Menahem Begin—and here with us is the Honorable President of the State, who was a full partner to it—the Israeli government signed the first and unprecedentedly important peace treaty with Egypt. As for the Israeli-Syrian border, quiet and security have prevailed for almost twenty years, and are enjoyed by the population of the Golan Heights.

Mr. Speaker, distinguished Knesset, for over 100 years we have been seeking to build ourselves a home in the only place on earth that was and will be our home: here, in the land of Israel. For over 100 years we have been seeking to live here in peace and tranquility, to plant a tree, to pave a road. For over 100 years we have been seeking good relations with our neighbors, a life without fear and dread. For over 100 years we have been dreaming and fighting. In 100 years of colonization, this land experienced a great deal of suffering and blood. We who came back home after 2,000 years in exile, after the Holocaust which sent the best of the Jewish people to the crematoriums, we who look for a harbor in the storm, a place to rest our head, we stretched out our hand to our neighbors, but this hand was rejected time and again. Time and again it was rejected, but our soul did not tire of seeking peace. Our life in this suffering land was accompanied by salvos of fire, mines, and grenades. We planted and they uprooted, we built and they destroyed, we defended and they attacked. Almost every day we buried our dead. One hundred years of terror and war harmed us, but it did not destroy our dream. We dreamed of peace for 100 years.

Distinguished Knesset, when it assumed office over a year ago, this government decided to put an end to the terror and war, to try to build a new world in the state, at home, in the family which did not know even one year or one month of its life in which mothers did not cry for their sons. This government decided to put an end to the hatred so that our children and grandchildren will no longer suffer the painful price of wars, terror, and violence. This government decided to safeguard their lives and security, to ease the pain and horrible memories, to pray and hope for peace. When we presented the government to the Knesset over a year ago, we said—and I quote: This government is determined to do everything in its power, to forge any path, to do everything possible and impossible for the sake of national and personal security, for the sake of peace and preventing war. We said then—and I quote: The road we will tread will be fraught with obstacles, crises, disappointments, tears, and pain. After all these, however, when we come to the end of this road, we will have a strong country, a good country, a country in which we all share in the big effort and whose citizens we are proud to be.

We said then: The new government shares the current feeling among the people that this is an hour of great opportunities, and we will do everything not to miss the opportunities. We said then: We owe it to ourselves and our children to see the new world as it is, to study the dangers, check out the chances, and do everything so that the State of Israel becomes part of the changing world. We must rid ourselves of the feeling of isolation that gripped us for almost a quarter of a century. We must join the international march of peace, reconciliation, and cooperation that is currently storming across the entire globe. Otherwise, we will be the last and only ones waiting behind at the station.

We said then that the main goal of the new government will be to promote the making of peace and to take feverish steps to bring about the end of the Arab-Israeli conflict. We will do that on the basis of the Arab states' and the Palestinians' recognition of Israel as a sovereign state and of its right to live in peace and security. We sincerely believe that this is possible and imperative, and that it will come.

Members of the Knesset, we said then the following words—and I quote: The government will propose to the Arab states and the Palestinians to pursue the peace negotiations based on the format consolidated in the Madrid conference as the first step on the way to a permanent solution. We will discuss the implementation of autonomy in Judea, Samaria, and the Gaza District. We do not intend to waste precious time. Within a short period of time, we will open and pursue the talks in order to lower the flame of hostility between the Palestinians and the State of Israel.

The day we presented our government we also said: Holding such negotiations on the issue worry those among us who chose to settle in Judea, Samaria, and the Gaza District. I hereby inform you that this government, by means of the IDF and the other security forces, will be responsible for the security and welfare of the inhabitants of those areas.

On the question of Jerusalem, we said that this government, just like all its predecessors, believes there are no differences of opinion in this House over the eternalness of Jerusalem as Israel's capital. United and unified Jerusalem is not negotiable and will be the capital of the Israeli people under Israel's sovereignty and the subject of every Jew's yearnings and dreams for ever and ever.

Members of the Knesset, fourteen months ago we presented an IOU to the Knesset, the voters, and the Israeli people. We promised to try to bring peace to this land. In the time that has elapsed since then, we did not close any doors or miss any opportunity. We checked out every crack and hint. We did not forestall any chance of attaining peace or interim arrangements that would offer a normal life to both peoples in this land.

We conducted negotiations with the delegations of Syria, Lebanon, Jordan, and the Palestinians. During the negotiations, and in fact from their beginning, it transpired that the only address for negotiations with the Palestinians was PLO-Tunis. We could have behaved like ostriches; we could have lied to ourselves and buried our heads in the sand. We could have claimed that Faisal Husseini, Hanan Ashrawi, and others represent the residents of the territories while ignoring the real party that stood behind them. We decided not to behave in this manner. We knew very well who stood behind them, and the Israeli public is also perfectly aware of this. We have no desire to deny the fact that this is a merciless terrorist organization, an organization that dispatched the terrorists who murdered the children in Avivim and Ma'alot, who shot the guests in Tel Aviv's Savoy Hotel, who attacked the innocent victims riding the bus on the Tel Aviv-Haifa coastal road, and who committed hundreds of other acts of murder and terror. This organization has shed the blood of hundreds of our beloved citizens: the blood of Smadar Haran's family in Nahariyya; the blood of 'Ofra and Tal Moses, members of the family of Abie Moses from Alfey Menashe; the blood of innocent people whose only fault was being Jewish.

Knesset members, we cannot choose our neighbors and our enemies, including the cruelest of them. We must deal with what we have: the PLO, which has fought against us and against whom we fought. Today we are looking for a way to achieve peace together with this organization. We can shut all the doors, cease any attempt to achieve peace. Morally, we are entitled not to sit at the negotiating table with the PLO, not to shake the hands of those who have wielded knives or pulled the trigger. We could have rejected the proposals of the PLO with disgust, in which case we would have unwittingly been among those responsible for the continuation of the vicious circle in which we have been forced to live so far: war, terrorism, and violence.

We chose to adopt another way, one which offers a chance and hope. We decided to recognize the PLO as the representative of the Palestinian people to the negotiations in the framework of the peace talks. We have known, and we still know, what a heavy load we are carrying from the past. We took this step only after the PLO undertook, in its letters to the prime minister, the following: recognition of Israel's right to live in peace and security and a commitment to settle any future controversy by peaceful means and through negotiations. The PLO has undertaken to denounce and put an end to terrorism and violence in Israel, in the territories, and elsewhere. I want to say here that since the agreements were signed, the PLO has not carried out even one act of terrorism. The PLO has undertaken to enforce an end to terrorism and violence by its members and to punish the violators. The PLO has undertaken to renounce the clauses of the Palestinian Covenant that negate Israel's right to exist and the peace process and to bring about their formal cancellation by the pertinent institution.

In Washington, Foreign Minister Shimon Peres signed on Israel's behalf the declaration of principles agreement for the interim period only. This agreement, which permits the Palestinians to run their affairs, safeguards the following issues for Israel: Unified Jerusalem remains under Israel's rule, and the body that will run the lives of the Palestinians in the territories will have no authority over it. The Israeli settlements in Judea, Samaria, and Gaza will remain under Israel's rule without any change whatsoever in their status. The authority of the Palestinian council will not apply to any Israeli in the areas of Judea, Samaria, and Gaza. The IDF will continue to bear overall responsibility for the security of the Israeli settlements in the territories, the security of every Israeli staying in the territories, and for external security—namely, for the defense of the current confrontation lines along the Jordan River and for the Egyptian border. The IDF will deploy in all areas of Judea, Samaria, and the Gaza District on the basis of these missions. All the issues pertaining to the permanent arrangement will be put off for the negotiations that will begin two years after the date stipulated in the agreement, while preserving the Israeli government's freedom to determine its positions regarding the permanent solution. This means that the declaration of principles leaves all the options open on this issue.

The agreement on the interim period in Gaza and Jericho will be implemented before the establishment of the elected Palestinian council, which will direct the affairs of the Palestinians in Judea, Samaria, and the Gaza Strip. The council will be established only after we agree with the Palestinians about its structure, composition, and functions. The target date for elections is nine months after the declaration of principles goes into effect. Israel will regard the Gaza-Jericho First stage as a sort of test of the Palestinians' ability to implement the agreement on the declaration of principles.

I would like to repeat here what I said in Washington last week—and I quote: We are destined to live together on the same soil, in the same land. We, the soldiers who have returned from the battles stained with blood;

we, who have seen our relatives and best friends killed before our eyes; we, who have attended their funerals and cannot look into the eyes of their parents and their orphans; we, who have come from a land where parents bury their children; we, who have fought against you, the Palestinians; we say to you today in a loud and clear voice: enough of blood and tears, enough. We harbor no hatred towards you. We have no desire for revenge. We, like you, are people who want to build a home, to plant a tree, to love, to live with you side by side, in dignity, in empathy, as human beings, as free men. Today we are giving peace a chance and saying to you in a clear voice: enough, no more.

Mr. Speaker, distinguished Knesset, we have no intention or desire to hide the truth from the Knesset members and the Israeli public. In addition to the great advantages, the expected peace also harbors dangers. We are aware of these dangers and will do everything necessary to minimize them. At the same time, we believe the risks are calculated and will not harm Israel's security and existence. In any event, the might of the IDF—the best army in the world—is available for our use if, God forbid, we are faced with such a challenge. Today we are looking forward to the good chances, to days without worries and nights without fears, to a developing economy and a prosperous society. If and when the long-desired peace arrives, our lives will completely change. We will no longer live only by our swords.

On the eve of the New Year, after 100 years of violence and terrorism, after wars and suffering, today there is a good chance to open a new chapter in Israel's history. There is a chance for putting an end to tears. Flower buds and new horizons are opening up for the Israeli economy and society. Above all, I want to tell you that this is a victory for Zionism, which is now recognized by its most adamant and bitter enemies. There are chances for good relations with our neighbors, for an end to the bereavement which has afflicted our homes, for an end to war.

Syrian President Hafiz al-Asad: Reaction to Israel-PLO Agreement (October 1, 1993)

The PLO was the Arab party pressing most for coordination among Arab parties. We have also stood for coordination, because we thought intra-Arab coordination could propel the peace process forward toward its objectives and firm up the steps leading in that direction. So, meetings to coordinate Arab moves were held between the bilateral rounds. The foreign ministers of the Arab states involved in the peace process used to meet to assess the previous round and devise tactics that might advance the peace process in the next round. In addition, the Arab delegations that held talks with the Israeli teams in Washington used to meet every week or so to compare notes. Each party, then, had a picture of how and what the others were doing. Thus, the Arabs moved in tandem toward a common objective.

All of a sudden, we hear that a secret agreement was reached between some PLO members and Israel. It turns out that the agreement was worked out in many months of secret negotiations, when, meanwhile, Arab states were meeting at the levels I have noted. The Palestinian side was engaged in talks with Israel, without the coordination it had pressed for. To my mind, this is not their best option, nor the best route to the establishment of peace. Yet, we decided not to obstruct the agreement. We said this is up to the Palestinian people and their organizations. However, no one should expect us to wax enthusiastic over a secret agreement concluded behind our backs. . . .

What is the justification for the unilateral decision that has been taken? We are all together. We all participated in the preliminary talks that laid the foundations of the Madrid conference. But, suddenly, one party began following a separate path. As we have always done, we will continue to urge and hope that the Palestinian Arab people regain their legitimate rights.

I said we decided not to obstruct the agreement. I did not say we will obstruct those who oppose it. We will not obstruct it, although we are not satisfied with it, especially since it deviates from the consensus. : . .

It is not our specialty, responsibility, or right to repress those who oppose this agreement or those who oppose anything else. . . .

We must carry on with the peace process that began in Madrid. . . .

If I struck the deal Arafat did, I would come up against many real problems. This has nothing to do with how the masses feel about Arafat or me. If I were to conclude such a deal, the Syrian people would conclude I had compromised my cause and abandoned the cause of another Arab people. . . . You know, there are those who paid with their lives for individual actions the masses perceived as not being in their best interests. I don't want to lead you to think I have just one individual in mind, but more than one.

Arafat and I and every Arab know that the masses will conduct themselves according to their perception of their leaders. This is not to be interpreted as encouragement on my part for such a course of action; nor do I see it as a solution; if anything, it will further complicate matters. This is my personal opinion.

We have repeatedly said that, many times. The Syrian delegation to the negotiations said that, and I, too, have said that in some statements. I said three elements should be dealt with, although they are classified under the title of peace. They are withdrawal, peace, and security. We should discuss all these. Each side will attain what we all agree is its right, and which will provide security and peace of mind for it. We know peace has its requirements. We do not expect to take what we believe to be our right while others do not take theirs. We also believe we should take our rights and give others their rights. . . .

As long as this occupation remains, its results, including the boycott, must remain. I heard some statements by Israelis, including Peres while he was at the United Nations. In his statements, both in the U.N. General Assembly and to the press, he says, effectively: Why are you Arabs boycotting us? You have been saying the Palestine question is the core of the conflict. Here we are now, we have reached an agreement. It seems to me he is either insulting the intelligence of the others, specifically the Arabs, or he wants to fill the occasion, or the paper he is reading, with any words. Of course, we have said, and we still say, that the Palestine question is the core of the conflict. It is the core of the conflict in that it was the starting point of hostility. Hence, we called it the core of the conflict, but it is not the conflict. The Palestine question is the core of the conflict, but it is not the conflict. The Israelis know they have fought states. All the wars that were fought between Arabs and Israel were wars with states bordering Palestine. As a result of these wars, the core of the conflict that started in Palestine expanded to mean that every occupied Arab territory has become the core of the conflict.

Hani al-Hasan: Opposition to the Israel-PLO Accord (October 9, 1993)*

I personally thought from the outset that the letter of invitation to the October 1991 Madrid peace conference would only lead to the consecration of Israeli control over Palestinian land and the Palestinian people. In my view, what happened now amounts to the consecration of this control.

Indeed, Israel did recognize the PLO, but only after stripping the organization of all that it represents. The PLO which Israel has recognized is one that has submitted to Israeli demands. It is no longer the PLO that embodies the Palestinian people's aspirations to independent statehood after a full Israeli withdrawal from the West Bank and Gaza Strip and upholds the rights of the Palestinian refugees.

The Palestinian negotiator knows full well that Israel has no intention of withdrawing to the pre-June 1967 borders, and the proposed accord is therefore aimed at deceiving the Palestinian people.

Israel's intention to keep 20 percent of the West Bank in addition to East Jerusalem when a permanent solution is supposed to be in place five years down the line was spelled out during Palestinian-Israeli "security talks" held in London in late 1992. . . .

At another secret PLO-Israel meeting, this one in Cairo around two months ago, Israeli Environment Minister Yossi Sarid made clear to Nabil

*Interview with *Mideast Mirror,* October 9, 1993

Shaath, an Arafat adviser, that even his own Meretz faction supported the official Israeli position on Jerusalem (that it will remain Israel's undivided capital) and that the Jerusalem issue can only be discussed from a religious angle. Hence East Jerusalemites who will take part in elections to the proposed Palestinian Council will do so as candidates or electors from other West Bank towns.

Those who concluded the accord with Israel, agreeing to stop the *intifada*, are banking on the Jewish state's good will. The accord treats the occupied lands as disputed territories and is a recipe for the establishment of a federation between the State of Israel and a Palestinian "entity." PLO negotiators Abu-Mazen and Ahmad Krai (Abu-Ala'a) were told as much during the Oslo talks. That is how Israel plans to keep its army in the West Bank even if a Palestinian "entity" emerges there.

As to the refugee issue, it was decided at the last meeting in Oslo that the multilateral committee on refugees would deal with seven areas none of which features UN Resolution 194 calling for the repatriation or compensation of 1948 refugees. This is a step towards ending the refugee issue and striking it off the United Nations' agenda.

That is why we, the 1948 exiles, categorically reject what is happening. The PLO leaders who concluded the deal with Israel have all but buried the refugees' right of return.

This is why someone like myself opposes what is happening now—even though I do not belong to the school of rejectionism and fully belong to the school of political settlements. But settlements are based on balance, whereas the proposed solution is one imposed by Israel as the victor.

As Israeli Prime Minister Yitzhak Rabin's remarks after he recognized the PLO indicate, proponents of the Gaza-Jericho deal have been entrusted with the task of punishing anyone who resorts to violence. It is strange that a Palestinian leader should undertake to stop the resistance in, say, Nablus or Hebron (on the West Bank) which will remain under Israeli occupation for at least five years. Hence Gaza-Jericho advocates will be the allies of the Israeli security forces over the next five years.

It is true that we will get a handful of billions of dollars and that we will build power stations in Gaza and a sewage system on the West Bank. But this is not what the PLO is about.

West Bank-Gaza Palestinian Leaders: Memorandum to Chairman Yasir Arafat (November 1993)

Mr. President of Palestine and Chairman of the PLO Executive Committee; Members of the PLO Executive Committee:

Greetings from Palestine:

Since the signing of the Declaration of Principles and the mutual recognition agreement between the PLO and the Israeli Government, the Palestinian people, together with their national forces, have been facing a new situation that has imposed new challenges. This is because the Declaration of Principles is an event that separates a militant stage, which aimed at underscoring Palestinian presence on the political map of the region and the world, from another militant stage that moves toward a greater and more advanced achievement; namely, the setting up of an independent Palestinian state on the land of Palestine by Palestinian hands.

Your Excellency the President: We assume that our Palestinian people, together with their national forces, have studied the agreement in terms of preambles, texts, and prospects as the various national institutions did in order to endorse it constitutionally through the PLO Executive Committee and the PLO Central Council. However, the agreement has produced an opposition that has different principles and objectives. And this is natural in an arena which pioneered the entrenching of democratic dialogue and relations among its forces as the only way to govern national life in the various fields.

The signatories to this memorandum believe that the Palestinian-Israeli agreement is a decisive political event which should be dealt with in a positive and responsible way in order to develop what is positive in it and besiege what is negative.

In light of all this, we declare:

First, our total affiliation with our people's potentials to build our new entity on the ground;

Second, our commitment to the PLO and its legitimate institutions as the sole representative of the Palestinian people and the national framework to which there is no alternative in order to organize and lead the national potentials toward achieving all the national legitimate objectives of the Palestinian people.

Proceeding from this, and in order to benefit from our democratic right of taking the initiative to propose ideas and procedures which are important and vital in this qualitative stage of our national struggle, we reiterate the following:

First: We are not satisfied with the political leadership's method of work in this stage, either in terms of running the difficult and delicate negotiations with the Israeli side or in terms of the preparations to embark on the stage of national construction in the interim period. It is obvious to everybody that the political leadership is practicing its role in a manner that is close to improvisation and without prior preparation for the necessary practical steps toward embodying the national interests through a planned implementation of our obligations to what was signed.

Second: The political leadership has not made sufficient effort to invigorate the required national dialogue whether on the level of the national forces, which adopted the agreement as an opportunity that would provide serious possibilities to proceed toward our national objectives, or on the level of the principled opposition to the agreement. Our national traditions require that we expeditiously launch such dialogue and work seriously to render it a success. The objective is to create a reasonable level of national harmony that will entrench Palestinian national security and create a healthy atmosphere for further mobilization toward the new tasks of the Palestinian people.

Third: The political leadership failed to present the agreement in an objective way to the Palestinian people so that this people would be aware of the prospects and potentials of their present and future moves. Consequently, this increased the confusion, ambiguity, and concern, particularly when the Palestinian people receive various and contradictory interpretations, not only on the level of the PLO and Israel, but also within the PLO itself.

Fourth: If we return to the statements and comments of the majority who voted, during the recent meeting of the PLO Central Council, in favor of the Declaration of Principles agreement, we will find that their support was on condition that the leadership performance will develop, Palestinian potentials will be mobilized, Palestinian skills and expertise will be exploited in the best way possible, and that the peace process will be dealt with as a militant process, not an administrative or bureaucratic one. As many of the PLO Central Council members said, whether the result of the Declaration of Principles agreement will be good or bad for the Palestinian people, and whether it will pave the way for national independence and an independent state, or whether it will consecrate the occupation, this result will be basically decided through the materialization of the previous conditions.

While we present these general remarks as a first step, we ask the political leadership to shoulder its responsibilities in dealing with the negative aspects in a manner that guarantees a balanced, viable, and responsible performance during the next stage.

Based on this, we present the following urgent demands:

1. The political leadership should set up specialized councils in all fields of political action, whether on the level of building the new entity or on the level of organizing moves in the Arab and international arenas.

2. The political leadership should appeal to all specialists in various sectors to join these councils and their working groups, whether through planning or implementation. In order to regulate this great process, a department should be set up in the PLO assigned with following up this issue and working out the appropriate action frameworks.

3. Adopting the principle of professional and political efficiency

in forming the working groups, establishments, negotiating committees, and other bodies, and abandoning the fractional mentality and
appeasement at the expense of efficiency.

4. Working out an integrated negotiating plan that is based on the
Declaration of Principles and that ensures integration and harmony
of the working groups and the various negotiating teams.

5. Forming a mini-leadership team to lead the entire negotiating
process, supervise and follow it up, and coordinate between the various committees and groups.

6. Forming the Palestinian Development and Reconstruction
Council according to certain specifications that ensure sound performance, planning, follow up and monitoring, and the credibility of
our people with the donor countries and in order to develop the infrastructure of our national economy. Any delay in the formation of
this council will waste more time and weaken the credibility of the
Palestinians with the international parties that assist our people.

7. Completing the work of the Legal Committee assigned with
drafting the bylaw of the Palestinian national authority (the constitutional document) in a manner that emphasizes its democratic nature
and commitment to all principles contained in the Palestinian Declaration of Principles. This constitutional document should then be
presented for broad deliberations by the Palestinian people as soon
as possible.

8. The political leadership should immediately form a higher
leadership authority that will start a national dialogue and work for
the continuation and success of this dialogue. The political leadership should benefit from its previous mistakes in this respect, since
the committees that used to be formed did not work with sufficient
seriousness.

9. Setting up a higher planning, consulting, and guidance authority of experts that operates alongside the Executive Committee and
assists it in carrying out its major tasks in this stage.

While making such a proposal, we are not undermining the role and jurisdiction of the first executive authority. We present these proposals because
we know how this authority has been adversely affected by the resignation
of some of its members and the possibility that others may resign or freeze
their membership. . . .

The signatories: Dr. Haydar 'Abd al-Shafi, Bashir al-Barghuthi, Ibrahim
Abu 'Ayyash, Dr. Anis Fawzi al-Qasim, Tawfiq Abu Bakr, Dr. Taysir
'Aruri, Samih 'Abd al-Fattah, known as Abu Hisham, Lawyer 'Ali al-
Safarini, Faysal Hurani, Lawyer Muhammad 'Ayyash Milham, Nabil
'Amr, the Reverend Ibrahim 'Ayyad, Dr. Mundhir Salah, Dr. 'Izz al-Din al-
Manasirah, and Ghazi al-Sa'di.

Syrian President Hafiz al-Asad and U.S. President Bill Clinton: Statement on Their Meeting (January 16, 1994)

Syrian President Hafiz al-Asad

I wish to express my deep satisfaction for what these talks have affected in terms of U.S. determination to do all it can in order to bring the peace process to its desired objective—the objective of establishing a just and comprehensive peace in the region through the implementation of UN Security Council Resolutions 242, 338, and 425 as well as the principle of land for peace.

In this respect, I appreciate the fact that not withstanding the great importance that President Clinton attaches to the internal affairs of his country, he has attached a special importance as a full partner and honest intermediary to helping the parties reach a comprehensive peace that is in the interest not only of the peoples of the region, but also the people of the world at large.

Today's meeting between President Clinton and myself came to crown a number of exchanges and telephone communications between us over the last year. I hope that our meeting today will contribute to the realization of the aspirations of the peoples in the region; mainly, that this new year will be the year of achieving a just and comprehensive peace which puts an end to the tragedies of violence and wars endured by them for several decades.

During our meeting, I had the opportunity to stress to President Clinton Syria's firm commitment to the principles and bases of the peace process and our strong conviction that peace cannot be genuine and lasting unless it is comprehensive and based on the principles of international legitimacy and justice. This means endeavoring to reach a just solution on all tracks.

Historical evidence, both past and present, has proved that separate peace and partial solutions are not conducive to the establishment of real peace in the region. In this regard, I would like to express my satisfaction that President Clinton himself has committed to the objective of comprehensive peace.

On this basis, we have agreed to work together for successful efforts aimed at putting an end to the Arab-Israeli conflict and at reaching a genuine and comprehensive peace that enables the peoples of the region to focus on development, progress, and prosperity.

This meeting has also provided us with the opportunity to exchange views on a number of issues, including those related to bilateral relations between our countries. We have agreed that the noble objective toward which we are working requires a qualitative move in these relations.

We have also discussed questions related to the regional situation as well as all matters that might constructively contribute to the achievement of security and stability in the Middle East. Syria seeks a just and comprehensive peace with Israel as a strategic choice that secures Arab rights; ends the Israeli occupation; and enables all peoples in the region to live in peace, security, and dignity. In honor we fought; in honor we negotiate; and in honor we shall make peace. We want an honorable peace for our people and for the hundreds of thousands who paid their lives in defense of their countries and their rights.

There is hardly a home in Syria in which there is no martyr who has fallen in defense of his country, nation, and Arab pride. For the sake of all those, for our sons, daughters, and families, we want the peace of the brave—a genuine peace which can survive and last, a peace which secures the interests of each side and renders to all their rights. If the leaders of Israel have sufficient courage to respond to this kind of peace, the new era of security and stability in which normal peaceful relations among all shall dawn anew.

U.S. President Bill Clinton

I believe you could tell from that statement that I have just completed a constructive and encouraging meeting with President Asad. From the first days of my Administration, the achievement of a comprehensive peace between Israel and its Arab neighbors, based on Security Council Resolutions 242 and 338 and the principle of territory for peace, has been one of my highest foreign policy objectives.

In pursuit of that priority, I have always viewed Syria's involvement as critical. That is why, from the outset of our Administration, I have engaged President Asad in regular correspondence by telephone and letter, and why I am now pleased to have had this opportunity to hear, personally, President Asad's views about how best to make this a year of breakthroughs on all fronts.

During our meeting, I told President Asad that I was personally committed to the objective of a comprehensive and secure peace that would produce genuine reconciliation among the peoples of the Middle East. I told him of my view that the agreement between Israel and the PLO constitutes an important first step by establishing an agreed basis for resolving the Palestinian problem. I also told him that I believe Syria is the key to the achievement of an enduring and comprehensive peace that finally will put an end to the conflict between Israel and her Arab neighbors.

President Asad, as you have just heard, shares this objective—not just an end to war, but the establishment of real and comprehensive peace with

Israel that will ensure normal, peaceful relations among good neighbors.

Crucial decisions will have to be made by Syria and Israel if this common objective is to be achieved. That is why President Asad has called for a peace of the brave. And it is why I join him now in endorsing that appeal. Accordingly, we pledged today to work together in order to bring the negotiations that started in Madrid over two years ago to a prompt and successful conclusion.

Critical issues remain to be resolved, especially the question of relating withdrawal to peace and security. But as a result of our conversation today, I am confident that we laid the foundations for real progress in the negotiations between heads of delegation that will begin again next week in Washington.

President Asad and I also discussed the state of relations between the United States and Syria and agreed on the desirability of improving them. This requires honestly addressing the problems in our relationship. Accordingly, we've instructed the Secretary of State and the Syrian Foreign Minister to establish a mechanism to address these issues in detail and openly.

For too long, the Middle East has been denied the benefits of peace. And yet, it is within our power to create the conditions that will enable Israeli and Arab, Muslim, Christian, and Jew to live together in peace. Today's meeting was an important step toward fulfilling that vision. We have a lot of work to do, but we are closer to our goal.

Israel and PLO: Cairo Agreement (March 4, 1994)

The Government of the State of Israel and the Palestine Liberation Organization (hereinafter "the PLO"), the representative of the Palestinian people;

PREAMBLE

Within the framework of the Middle East peace process initiated at Madrid in October 1991;

Reaffirming their determination to live in peaceful coexistence, mutual dignity and security, while recognizing their mutual legitimate and political rights;

Reaffirming their desire to achieve a just, lasting and comprehensive peace settlement through the agreed political process;

Reaffirming their adherence to the mutual recognition and commitments expressed in the letters dated September 9, 1993, signed by and exchanged between the Prime Minister of Israel and the Chairman of the PLO;

Reaffirming their understanding that the interim self-government arrangements, including the arrangements to apply in the Gaza Strip and the Jericho Area contained in this Agreement, are an integral part of the whole peace process and that the negotiations on the permanent status will lead to the implementation of Security Council Resolutions 242 and 338;

Desirous of putting into effect the Declaration of Principles on Interim Self-Government Arrangements signed at Washington, D.C., on September 13, 1993, and the Agreed Minutes thereto (hereinafter "the Declaration of Principles"), and in particular the Protocol on withdrawal of Israeli forces from the Gaza Strip and the Jericho Area;

Hereby agree to the following arrangements regarding the Gaza Strip and the Jericho Area:

ARTICLE I

Definitions

For the purpose of this Agreement:

a. The Gaza Strip and the Jericho Area are delineated on Map Nos. 1 and 2 attached to this Agreement;

b. "The Settlements" means the Gush Katif and Erez settlement areas, as well as the other settlements in the Gaza Strip, as shown on attached Map No. 1;

c. "The Military Installation Area" means the Israeli military installation area along the Egyptian border in the Gaza Strip, as shown on Map No. 1; and

d. The term "Israelis" shall also include Israeli statutory agencies and corporations registered in Israel.

ARTICLE II

Scheduled Withdrawal of Israeli Military Forces

1. Israel shall implement an accelerated and scheduled withdrawal of Israeli military forces from the Gaza Strip and from the Jericho Area to begin immediately with the signing of this Agreement. Israel shall complete such withdrawal within three weeks from this date.

2. Subject to the arrangements included in the Protocol concerning withdrawal of Israeli military forces and security arrangements attached as Annex I, the Israeli withdrawal shall include evacuating all military bases and other fixed installations to be handed over to the Palestinian Police, to be established pursuant to Article IX below (hereinafter "the Palestinian Police").

3. In order to carry out Israeli's responsibility for external secu-

rity and for internal security and public order of Settlements and Is-raelis, Israel shall, concurrently with the withdrawal, redeploy its remaining military forces to the Settlements and the Military Installation Area, in accordance with the provisions of this Agreement. Subject to the provisions of this Agreement, this redeployment shall constitute full implementation of Article XIII of the Declaration of Principles with regard to the Gaza Strip and the Jericho Area only.

4. For the purposes of this Agreement, "Israeli military forces" may include Israeli police and other Israeli security forces.

5. Israelis, including Israeli military forces, may continue to use roads freely within the Gaza Strip and the Jericho Area. Palestinians may use public roads crossing the Settlements freely, as provided for in Annex I.

6. The Palestinian Police shall be deployed and shall assume responsibility for public order and internal security of Palestinians in accordance with this Agreement and Annex I.

ARTICLE III

Transfer of Authority

1. Israel shall transfer authority as specified in this Agreement from the Israeli military government and its Civil Administration to the Palestinian Authority, hereby established, in accordance with Article V of this Agreement, except for the authority that Israel shall continue to exercise as specified in this Agreement.

2. As regards the transfer and assumption of authority in civil spheres, powers and responsibilities shall be transferred and assumed as set out in the Protocol concerning civil affairs attached as Annex II.

3. Arrangements for a smooth and peaceful transfer of the agreed powers and responsibilities are set out in Annex II.

4. Upon the completion of the Israeli withdrawal and the transfer of powers and responsibilities as detailed in Paragraphs 1 and 2 above and in Annex II, the Civil Administration in the Gaza Strip and the Jericho Area will be dissolved and the Israeli military government will be withdrawn. The withdrawal of the military government shall not prevent it from continuing to exercise the powers and responsibilities specified in this Agreement.

5. A Joint Civil Affairs Coordination and Cooperation Committee (hereinafter "the CAC") and two Joint Regional Civil Affairs Subcommittees for the Gaza Strip and the Jericho Area respectively shall be established in order to provide for coordination and cooperation in civil affairs between the Palestinian Authority and Israel, as detailed in Annex II.

6. The offices of the Palestinian Authority shall be located in the Gaza Strip and the Jericho Area pending the inauguration of the Council to be elected pursuant to the Declaration of Principles.

ARTICLE IV

Structure and Composition of the Palestinian Authority

1. The Palestinian Authority will consist of one body of 24 members which shall carry out and be responsible for all the legislative and executive powers and responsibilities transferred to it under this Agreement, in accordance with this Article, and shall be responsible for the exercise of judicial functions in accordance with Article VI, subparagraph 1.b of this Agreement.

2. The Palestinian Authority shall administer the departments transferred to it and may establish, within its jurisdiction, other departments and subordinate administrative units as necessary for the fulfillment of its responsibilities. It shall determine its own internal procedures.

3. The PLO shall inform the Government of Israel of the names of the members of the Palestinian Authority and any change of members. Changes in the membership of the Palestinian Authority will take effect upon an exchange of letters between the PLO and the Government of Israel.

4. Each member of the Palestinian Authority shall enter into office upon undertaking to act in accordance with this Agreement.

ARTICLE V

Jurisdiction

1. The authority of the Palestinian Authority encompasses all matters that fall within its territorial, functional and personal jurisdiction, as follows:

a. The territorial jurisdiction covers the Gaza Strip and the Jericho Area territory, as defined in Article I, except for Settlements and the Military Installation Area.

Territorial jurisdiction shall include land, subcoil and territorial waters, in accordance with the provisions of this Agreement.

b. The functional jurisdiction encompasses all powers and responsibilities as specified in this Agreement. This jurisdiction does not include foreign relations, internal security and public order of Settlements and the Military Installation Area and Israelis, and external security.

c. The personal jurisdiction extends to all persons within the territorial jurisdiction referred to above, except for Israelis, unless otherwise provided in this Agreement.

2. The Palestinian Authority has, within its authority, legislative, executive and judicial powers and responsibilities, as provided for in this Agreement.

3. a. Israel has authority over the Settlements, the Military Installation Area, Israelis, external security, internal security and public order of Settlements, the Military Installation Area and Israelis, and those agreed powers and responsibilities specified in this Agreement.

b. Israel shall exercise its authority through its military government, which, for that end, shall continue to have the necessary legislative, judicial and executive powers and responsibilities, in accordance with international law. This provision shall not derogate from Israel's applicable legislation over Israelis in personam.

4. The exercise of authority with regard to the electromagnetic sphere and airspace shall be in accordance with the provisions of this Agreement.

5. The provisions of this Article are subject to the specific legal arrangements detailed in the Protocol Concerning Legal Matters attached as Annex III. Israel and the Palestinian Authority may negotiate further legal arrangements.

6. Israel and the Palestinian Authority shall cooperate on matters of legal assistance in criminal and civil matters through the legal subcommittee of the CAC.

Article VI

Powers and Responsibilities of the Palestinian Authority

1. Subject to the provisions of this Agreement, the Palestinian Authority, within its jurisdiction:

a. has legislative powers as set out in Article VII of this Agreement, as well as executive powers;

b. will administer justice through an independent judiciary;

c. will have, *inter alia,* power to formulate policies, supervise their implementation, employ staff, establish departments, authorities and institutions, sue and be sued and conclude contracts; and

d. will have, *inter alia,* the power to keep and administer registers and records of the population, and issue certificates, licenses and documents.

2. a. In accordance with the Declaration of Principles, the Palestinian Authority will not have powers and responsibilities in the sphere of foreign relations, which sphere includes the establishment abroad of embassies, consulates or other types of foreign missions and posts or permitting their establishment in the Gaza Strip or the Jericho Area, the appointment of or admission of diplomatic and consular staff, and the exercise of diplomatic functions.

b. Notwithstanding the provisions of this paragraph, the PLO may conduct negotiations and sign agreements with states or international organizations for the benefit of the Palestinian Authority in the following cases only: (1) economic agreements, as specifically provided in Annex IV of this Agreement; (2) agreements with donor countries for the purpose of implementing arrangements for the provision of assistance to the Palestinian Authority; (3) agreements for the purpose of implementing the regional development plans detailed in Annex IV of the Declaration of Principles or in agreements entered into in the framework of the multilateral negotiations; and (4) cultural, scientific and educational agreements.

c. Dealings between the Palestinian Authority and representatives of foreign states and international organizations, as well as the establishment in the Gaza Strip and the Jericho Area of representative offices other than those described in subparagraph 2.a. above, for the purpose of implementing the agreements referred to in subparagraph 2.b. above, shall not be considered foreign relations.

ARTICLE VII

Legislative Powers of the Palestinian Authority

1. The Palestinian Authority will have the power, within its jurisdiction, to promulgate legislation, including basic laws, laws, regulations and other legislative acts.

2. Legislation promulgated by the Palestinian Authority shall be consistent with the provisions of this Agreement.

3. Legislation promulgated by the Palestinian Authority shall be communicated to a legislation subcommittee to be established by the CAC (hereinafter "the Legislation Subcommittee"). During a period of 30 days from the communication of the legislation, Israel may request that the Legislation Subcommittee decide whether such legislation exceeds the jurisdiction of the Palestinian Authority or is otherwise inconsistent with the provisions of this Agreement.

4. Upon receipt of the Israeli request, the Legislation Subcommittee shall decide, as an initial matter, on the entry into force of the legislation pending its decision on the merits of the matter.

5. If the Legislation Subcommittee is unable to reach a decision with regard to the entry into force of the legislation within 15 days, this issue will be referred to a Board of Review. This Board of Review shall be comprised of two judges, retired judges or senior jurists (hereinafter "Judges"), one from each side, to be appointed from a compiled list of three Judges proposed by each.

In order to expedite the proceedings before this board of review, the two most senior Judges, one from each side, shall develop written informal rules of procedure.

6. Legislation referred to the Board of Review shall enter into force only if the Board of Review decides that it does not deal with a security issue which falls under Israel's responsibility, that it does not seriously threaten other significant Israeli interests protected by this Agreement and that the entry into force of the legislation could not cause irreparable damage or harm.

7. The Legislation Subcommittee shall attempt to reach a decision on the merits of the matter within 30 days from the date of the Israeli request. If this Subcommittee is unable to reach such a decision within this period of 30 days, the matter shall be referred to the Joint Israeli-Palestinian Liaison Committee referred to in Article XV below (hereinafter "the Liaison Committee"). This Liaison Committee will deal with the matter immediately and will attempt to settle it within 30 days.

8. Where the legislation has not entered into force pursuant to paragraphs 5 or 7 above, this situation shall be maintained pending the decision of the Liaison Committee on the merits of the matter, unless it has decided otherwise.

9. Laws and military orders in effect in the Gaza Strip or the Jericho Area prior to the signing of this Agreement shall remain in force, unless amended or abrogated in accordance with this Agreement.

Article VIII

Arrangements for Security and Public Order

1. In order to guarantee public order and internal security for the Palestinians of the Gaza Strip and the Jericho Area, the Palestinian Authority shall establish a strong police force, as set out in Article IX below. Israel shall continue to carry the responsibility for defense against external threats, including the responsibility for protecting the Egyptian border and the Jordanian line, and for defense against external threats from the sea and from the air, as well as the responsibility for overall security of Israelis and Settlements, for the purpose of safeguarding their internal security and public order, and will have all the powers to take the steps necessary to meet this responsibility.

2. Agreed security arrangements and coordination mechanisms are specified in Annex I.

3. A joint Coordination and Cooperation Committee for mutual security purposes (hereinafter "the JSC"), as well as three joint District Coordination and Cooperation Offices for the Gaza district, the

Khan Younis district and the Jericho district respectively (hereinafter "the DCOS") are hereby established as provided for in Annex I.

4. The security arrangements provided for in this Agreement and in Annex I may be reviewed at the request of either Party and may be amended by mutual agreement of the Parties. Specific review arrangements are included in Annex I.

ARTICLE IX

The Palestinian Directorate of Police Force

1. The Palestinian Authority shall establish a strong police force, the Palestinian Directorate of Police Force (hereinafter "the Palestinian Police"). The duties, functions, structure, deployment and composition of the Palestinian Police, together with provisions regarding its equipment and operation, are set out in Annex I, Article III. Rules of conduct governing the activities of the Palestinian Police are set out in Annex I, Article VIII.

2. Except for the Palestinian Police referred to in this Article and the Israeli military forces, no other armed forces shall be established or operate in the Gaza Strip or the Jericho Area.

3. Except for the arms, ammunition and equipment of the Palestinian Police described in Annex I, Article III, and those of the Israeli military forces, no organization or individual in the Gaza Strip and the Jericho Area shall manufacture, sell, acquire, possess, import or otherwise introduce into the Gaza Strip or the Jericho Area any firearms, ammunition, weapons, explosives, gunpowder or any related equipment, unless otherwise provided for in Annex I.

ARTICLE X

Passages

Arrangements for coordination between Israel and the Palestinian Authority regarding the Gaza-Egypt and Jericho-Jordan passages, as well as any other agreed international crossings, are set out in Annex I, Article X.

ARTICLE XI

Safe Passage Between the Gaza Strip and the Jericho Area

Arrangements for safe passage of persons and transportation between the Gaza Strip and the Jericho Area are set out in Annex I, Article IX.

ARTICLE XII

Relations Between Israel and the Palestinian Authority

1. Israel and the Palestinian Authority shall seek to foster mutual understanding and tolerance and shall accordingly abstain from incitement, including hostile propaganda, against each other and, without derogating from the principle of freedom of expression, shall take legal measures to prevent such incitement by any organizations, groups or individuals within their jurisdiction.

2. Without derogating from the other provisions of this Agreement, Israel and the Palestinian Authority shall cooperate in combating criminal activity which may affect both sides, including offenses related to trafficking in illegal drugs and psychotropic substances, smuggling, and offenses against property, including offenses related to vehicles.

ARTICLE XIII

Economic Relations

The economic relations between the two sides are set out in the Protocol on Economic Relations signed in Paris on April 29, 1994 and the Appendices thereto, certified copies of which are attached as Annex IV, and will be governed by the relevant provisions of this Agreement and its Annexes.

ARTICLE XIV

Human Rights and the Rule of Law

Israel and the Palestinian Authority shall exercise their powers and responsibilities pursuant to this Agreement with due regard to internationally-accepted norms and principles of human rights and the rule of law.

ARTICLE XV

The Joint Israeli-Palestinian Liaison Committee

1. The Liaison Committee established pursuant to Article X of the Declaration of Principles shall ensure the smooth implementation of this Agreement. It shall deal with issues requiring coordination, other issues of common interest and disputes.

2. The Liaison Committee shall be composed of an equal number of members from each Party. It may add other technicians and experts as necessary.

3. The Liaison Committee shall adopt its rules of procedure, including the frequency and place or places of its meetings.

4. The Liaison Committee shall reach its decisions by Agreement.

ARTICLE XVI

Liaison and Cooperation with Jordan and Egypt

1. Pursuant to Article XII of the Declaration of Principles, the two Parties shall invite the Governments of Jordan and Egypt to participate in establishing further Liaison and Cooperation Arrangements between the Government of Israel and the Palestinian Representatives on the one hand, and the Governments of Jordan and Egypt on the other hand, to promote cooperation between them. These arrangements shall include the constitution of a Continuing Committee.

2. The Continuing Committee shall decide by agreement on the modalities of admission of persons displaced from the West Bank and the Gaza Strip in 1967, together with necessary measures to prevent disruption and disorder.

3. The Continuing Committee shall deal with other matters of common concern.

ARTICLE XVII

Settlement of Differences and Disputes

Any difference relating to the application of this Agreement shall be referred to the appropriate coordination and cooperation mechanism established under this Agreement. The provisions of Article XV of the Declaration of Principles shall apply to any such difference which is not settled through the appropriate coordination and cooperation mechanism, namely:

1. Disputes arising out of the application or interpretation of this Agreement or any subsequent agreements pertaining to the interim period shall be settled by negotiations through the Liaison Committee.

2. Disputes which cannot be settled by negotiations may be settled by a mechanism of conciliation to be agreed between the Parties.

3. The Parties may agree to submit to arbitration disputes relating to the interim period, which cannot be settled through conciliation. To this end, upon the agreement of both Parties, the Parties will establish an Arbitration Committee.

Article XVIII

Prevention of Hostile Acts

Both sides shall take all measures necessary in order to prevent acts of terrorism, crime and hostilities directed against each other, against individuals falling under the other's authority and against their property, and shall take legal measures against offenders. In addition, the Palestinian side shall take all measures necessary to prevent such hostile acts directed against the Settlements, the infrastructure serving them and the Military Installation Area, and the Israeli side shall take all measures necessary to prevent such hostile acts emanating from the Settlements and directed against Palestinians.

Article XIX

Missing Persons

The Palestinian Authority shall cooperate with Israel by providing all necessary assistance in the conduct of searches by Israel within the Gaza Strip and the Jericho Area for missing Israelis, as well as by providing information about missing Israelis. Israel shall cooperate with the Palestinian Authority in searching for, and providing necessary information about, missing Palestinians.

Article XX

Confidence-Building Measures

With a view to creating a positive and supportive public atmosphere to accompany the implementation of this Agreement, and to establish a solid basis of mutual trust and good faith, both Parties agree to carry out confidence-building measures as detailed herewith:

1. Upon the signing of this Agreement, Israel will release, or turn over, to the Palestinian Authority within a period of 5 weeks, about 5,000 Palestinian detainees and prisoners, residents of the West Bank and the Gaza Strip. Those released will be free to return to their homes anywhere in the West Bank or the Gaza Strip. Prisoners turned over to the Palestinian Authority shall be obliged to remain in the Gaza Strip or the Jericho Area for the remainder of their sentence.

2. After the signing of this Agreement, the two Parties shall continue to negotiate the release of additional Palestinian prisoners and detainees, building on agreed principles.

3. The implementation of the above measures will be subject to the fulfillment of the procedures determined by Israeli law for the release and transfer of detainees and prisoners.

4. With the assumption of Palestinian Authority, the Palestinian side commits itself to solving the problem of those Palestinians who were in contact with the Israeli authorities. Until an agreed solution is found, the Palestinian side undertakes not to prosecute these Palestinians or to harm them in any way.

5. Palestinians from abroad whose entry into the Gaza Strip and the Jericho Area is approved pursuant to this Agreement, and to whom the provisions of this Article are applicable, will not be prosecuted for offenses committed prior to September 13, 1993.

Article XXI

Temporary International Presence

1. The Parties agree to a temporary international or foreign presence in the Gaza Strip and the Jericho Area (hereinafter "the TIP"), in accordance with the provisions of this Article.

2. The TIP shall consist of 400 qualified personnel, including observers, instructors and other experts, from 5 or 6 of the donor countries.

3. The two Parties shall request the donor countries to establish a special fund to provide finance for the TIP.

4. The TIP will function for a period of 6 months. The TIP may extend this period, or change the scope of its operation, with the agreement of the two Parties.

5. The TIP shall be stationed and operate within the following cities and villages: Gaza, Khan Younis, Rafah, Deir al-Balah, Jabalya, Absan, Beit Hanun and Jericho.

6. Israel and the Palestinian Authority shall agree on a special Protocol to implement this Article, with the goal of concluding negotiations with the donor countries contributing personnel within two months.

Article XXII

Rights, Liabilities and Obligations

1. a. The transfer of all powers and responsibilities to the Palestinian Authority, as detailed in Annex II, includes all related rights, liabilities and obligations arising with regard to acts or omissions which occurred prior to the transfer. Israel will cease to bear any financial responsibility regarding such acts or omissions and the Palestinian Authority will bear all financial responsibility for these and for its own functioning.

b. Any financial claim made in this regard against Israel will be referred to the Palestinian Authority.

c. Israel shall provide the Palestinian Authority with the information it has regarding pending and anticipated claims brought before any court or tribunal against Israel in this regard.

d. Where legal proceedings are brought in respect of such a claim, Israel will notify the Palestinian Authority and enable it to participate in defending the claim and raise any arguments on its behalf.

e. In the event that an award is made against Israel by any court or tribunal in respect of such a claim, the Palestinian Authority shall reimburse Israel the full amount of the award.

f. Without prejudice to the above, where a court or tribunal hearing such a claim finds that liability rests solely with an employee or agent who acted beyond the scope of the powers assigned to him or her, unlawfully or with willful malfeasance, the Palestinian Authority shall not bear financial responsibility.

2. The transfer of authority in itself shall not affect rights, liabilities and obligations of any person or legal entity, in existence at the date of signing of this Agreement.

ARTICLE XXIII

Final Clauses

1. This Agreement shall enter into force on the date of its signing.

2. The arrangements established by this Agreement shall remain in force until and to the extent superceded by the Interim Agreement referred to in the Declaration of Principles or any other agreement between the Parties.

3. The five-year Interim Period referred to in the Declaration of Principles commences on the date of the signing of this Agreement.

4. The Parties agree that, as long as this Agreement is in force, the security fence erected by Israel around the Gaza Strip shall remain in place and that the line demarcated by the fence, as shown on attached Map No. 1, shall be authoritative only for the purpose of this Agreement.

5. Nothing in this Agreement shall prejudice or preempt the outcome of the negotiations on the Interim Agreement or on the Permanent Status to be conducted pursuant to the Declaration of Principles. Neither Party shall be deemed, by virtue of having entered into this Agreement, to have renounced or waived any of its existing rights, claims or positions.

6. The two Parties view the West Bank and the Gaza Strip as a single territorial unit, the integrity of which will be preserved during the Interim Period.

7. The Gaza Strip and the Jericho Area shall continue to be an integral part of the West Bank and the Gaza Strip, and their status shall not be changed for the period of this Agreement. Nothing in this Agreement shall be considered to change this status.

8. The Preamble to this Agreement, and all Annexes, Appendices and Maps attached hereto, shall constitute an integral part hereof.

Israeli Prime Minister Yitzhak Rabin and PLO Chairman Yasir Arafat: Speeches at the Signing of the Cairo Agreement (March 4, 1994)

Israeli Prime Minister Yitzhak Rabin

We witnessed, you witnessed, the world witnessed the tip of the iceberg of problems that we shall have to overcome in the implementation of even the first phase of the Declaration of Principles [DOP]. To overcome 100 years of animosity, suspicion, bloodshed, it's not so simple. There is an opposition on both sides to what we are doing today, and it will require a lot, a lot on both sides to make sure that we will succeed and achieve peaceful coexistence and, in addition to the coexistence, to bring a permanent solution.

Today we signed the Gaza-Jericho First agreement, which is the first phase of implementation. It's a very daring project, and we are committed by signature today to make sure that it will work. We will achieve our goals; we will be able to overcome all these problems.

In 1889, 105 years ago, Avraham Jablonsky, a blacksmith, was murdered in his clay hut in Wadi Khalil. Avraham Jablonsky was the first victim in the history of the Jewish settlement in Eretz Yisra'el in modern times. He was the first victim of the bloody conflict between us and the Palestinian people since our return to the land of our forefathers after 2,000 years of exile. Since Avraham Jablonsky's death, the experience of our grandparents, parents, ourselves, and even our children and grandchildren has been almost solely one of blood and bereavement. For 100 years, this blood gave us no rest. What did we want? We wanted to return to the land of our forefathers, to the land of the Bible. We wanted a homeland; we wanted a home; we wanted a safe haven; we wanted a place to call our own; we wanted to live as all men live, to be like other nations. We wanted to live.

The war for the land of our forefathers took our best sons and daughters. It drained us of spiritual and physical energies and channeled our entire spiritual and physical existence to paths we did not want, to paths of pain. We deplore that. Even in our most difficult times, our hearts ached at the sights of devastation, hatred, and death. Even in our most bitter moments, we knew that the tears of a bereaved mother from within our midst are no different from the tears of another bereaved mother; that they are equally piercing and painful in any family; that the cries of despair are the same even when uttered in other languages.

We decided to try to put an end to this terrible circle of pain. We decided to look ahead at a different future. On 13 September 1993, on the White House lawn in Washington, we decided to embark on a new road. Tomorrow we will begin implementing the DOP. The DOP and its implementation—in Gaza and Jericho, at this point—is designed to attain a dual purpose: to enable the Palestinian authority to administer the lives of the Palestinians and to uphold public law and order in their places of residence. Our goal is to uphold security for Israelis wherever they may be, particularly in the wake of the change that is scheduled to take place in Gaza and Jericho. If the security of the Israelis is not ensured and if the Palestinians are not given new hope, the goal of the agreement will not be attained.

A great deal depends on the Palestinians. We are embarking on this new road with a lot of hope and with strong will, and we know that it entails wonderful chances as well as serious risks. We are convinced that both peoples can live on the same strip of land, every man under his vine and under his fig tree, as the Biblical prophets envisioned; to give this land, the land of stones and graves, the taste of milk and honey it deserves.

At this hour, I appeal to the Palestinian people and say to them: Palestinian neighbors, 100 bloody years have instilled in us hatred for each other. For 100 years, we wanted to see you dead and you wanted to see us dead. We killed you and you killed us. Thousands of our graves and yours dot the mountains and the valleys, and they are painful landmarks in your history and ours. Today, you and we are extending our hands in peace. Today we are opening a new account. The Israeli people expect you not to let them down. Let the new hope flourish. It is not easy to forget the past, but let us try to overcome the rancors and obstacles in order to open a new, unique, and historic horizon; an opportunity which may never recur for a different life, a life that is not fraught with fear, a life that is not fraught with hatred, a life that does not involve the frightened eyes of children, a life that does not entail pain; a life in which we will build a home, plant a vineyard, and live to a ripe old age alongside our fellow men. . . .

On a spring day of 1994, two weeks ago, the late Second Lieutenant Shahar Simani was murdered. He was 21 years old and a resident of Ashqelon. His bullet-riddled body was found by the roadside on the way to Jerusalem. A thread of blood links the Israeli people from the murder of Avraham Jablonsky, the blacksmith, 105 years ago, to the murder of Second Lieutenant Shahar Simani two weeks ago. I pray: May Shahar Simani be the last fatality among all of us, Israelis and Palestinians.

The new hope we are taking with us as we leave this place is immeasurable. There is no limit to our goodwill, to the will to see a historic reconciliation between two peoples that have lived so far by their swords. In the alleyways of Khan Yunus and on the outskirts of Ramat Gan, in the houses of Gaza, in the squares of Hadera, Rafah, and 'Afula, a new reality is being born today. One hundred years of the Palestinian-Israeli conflict and millions of people who want to live are watching us. May God be with us.

PLO Chairman Yasir Arafat

In the name of every Palestinian man and woman, I look with great confidence and hope at our brothers and our people's friends who are participating in this historic occasion and I think of those who could not come. I thank them all and stress to them that our people today in the West Bank, Gaza, holy Jerusalem, and in all the diaspora are looking more than ever toward your role so that this first step in Gaza and Jericho will become the real start for completing the peace process, guaranteeing our Palestinian people's legitimate rights, achieving justice and equality by ending the occupation of our Palestinian territories, and building the Palestinian future based on democracy, development, and progress, a future linked with the tradition of its glorious Arab nation. . . .

The withdrawal from Gaza and Jericho is the prelude; it opens the door to removing the entire occupation and to establishing new relations between our peoples, Prime Minister Rabin, between our Israeli and Palestinian peoples, for the sake of our children and yours.

Completing this step required Herculean courage after long periods of war and violence. The coming stage will require still greater courage, a thorough insight, real farsightedness, and firm patience so that we can establish a firm and unshakable peace, the peace of the bold.

The Palestinian people have lived on their land throughout history. They helped to create civilization and raise the voice of peace, the voice of the only all-powerful God, the creator, the lord of the universe and of the three heavenly religions, calling for praising God's blessings, giving, and his name on this sacred land.

The people of Palestine, based on their deep historical heritage, today express their loyalty to the just and comprehensive peace. Thus our people demonstrated faithfulness to the heritage of their successive generations; to the sweat of the Palestinian people, mixed as it is with the soil of the earth; to the Palestinian maker's determination to build life and let it flourish; and to the creativity of the Palestinian intellectual, who always believes that history will never go off its track no matter how much time passes.

Our people, gentlemen, have struggled long to see the beginning of the peace era. For peace to be achieved, our people offered dear sacrifices. To achieve this recognition of our national rights, the eyes of bereaved mothers and of children who were raised to know that love and loyalty to the homeland are the highest values of life looked forward. Also looking forward to this were the prisoners, whose hope of freedom, for themselves and for their people, is renewed every day, and the refugee camp residents, who never lost confidence that a new era of freedom would come.

Nothing has gone in vain. Alive and great nations make their wounds, the sacrifice of their martyrs, and their long suffering the motives for the future and the banners for building a new era based on justice under the shadow of tolerance and coexistence among the three religions of Judaism, Christianity, and Islam over centuries.

We have offered a great deal to reach this day. We confronted patiently and persistently every hindrance and doubt and we always thought that every step in the peace negotiations, despite all the pain, was a move away from the era of war and violence nearer to the era of equal rights and the implementation of international legitimacy. While today we celebrate the signing of the first step, we must all realize that all those concerned about peace, including our people at home and in the diaspora, measure the seriousness of this step by one criterion: honest and precise implementation and the change it will make to the reality on the ground. It is the right of our people and of everybody concerned with genuine peace to point to the measures isolating holy Jerusalem from its surroundings and preventing the Palestinians from entering it and the other sacred Islamic and Christian places. These measures obstruct life in the city, paralyze its economy, and separate the sons of the same family.

All this is incompatible with the spirit of the just and real peace, with the course of equality, justice, and human rights that we are aspiring to adopt as the basis for free and positive relations between the two neighboring peoples, as Mr. Peres said, between the Palestinian and Israeli peoples. The suffering of the city of Hebron following the bloody massacre cannot continue. It is still suffering encirclement and siege both inside and outside it.

The continuation of the settlement and the attempt to impose the fait accompli in Jerusalem and in other areas conflict with the essence, clauses, and the short- and long-term objectives of the peace process.

The boldness of peace prompts me today to adopt the policy of frankness on peace without which we cannot end the age of confrontation and start the age of constructive and real cooperation. The Arab peoples and millions of Muslims and Christians will observe our practical steps tomorrow to pass judgment on the possibility of coexistence and of opening a new chapter in normal relations. All those who want the success of the Palestinian-Israeli peace experiment realize the importance of the great steps facing this peace, including the settlements, the refugee problem, holy Jerusalem, and the need to solve it later, as we agreed, so as to help create a new era of protecting the future of the entire region and ensuring openness between their peoples and countries on the basis of respect for the rules and resolutions of international legitimacy.

Ladies and gentlemen, I am confident today that the Palestinian people will receive this new stage with a desire to provide a real opportunity for building real peace with the same desire it has for its national identity and its independent national being. Our people extends its hand to the Israeli people to start this era and end the whirlpool of violence for the sake of our real interests today and the interests of our coming generations.

Coexistence is possible. It is inevitable. It is our common fate to live together as neighbors governed by the rules of justice, democracy, and national and human dignity.

Hatred, bigotry, and extremism will only lead to more squandering of our creative and brilliant resources. We are proposing the alternative today, namely equality, joint building, and respect for every people's right and independent choice and security.

Today again I also address our great Arab nation, leaders and peoples, on the threshold of the first step of the return to the homeland and stress to them that their pain, sacrifice, and determination to uphold our Palestinian people's national legitimate rights prompt us today to strengthen our fraternal ties in every field so that peace for Palestine will, as always, be a peace for all the Arabs.

Yes, gentlemen, our peace is a peace for our Arab nation. It is a peace for Israel, for the Middle East region, for the whole world. Yes, it is a peace for the whole world.

O God, you are peace, peace comes from you, and peace is for you. Blessed are you God, full of majesty, bounty, and honor. Glory to God in the highest, peace on earth, and goodwill toward men. Peace be with you.

Israeli Prime Minister Yitzhak Rabin: Speech to Knesset (April 18, 1994)

Last week, we celebrated the forty-sixth anniversary of the establishment of the State of Israel and its independence. Today, we return to our regular lives; but we are all permitted to look back with pride—and forward, with great hope.

Forty-six difficult years of struggle for life, and of building an economy and society have brought about the great accomplishments of the State of Israel. Despite its deficiencies, it is today one of the more enchanting and beautiful countries of the world; one of those in which it is good to live. I want to take advantage of this opportunity, of the opening of the Knesset's summer session, to again congratulate the citizens of Israel on the occasion of Independence Day.

The last Independence Day took place in the shadow of the terrorist attacks, and of the most recent attack—just before the Memorial Day siren. Five civilians and soldiers died in the explosion of a bomb at the central bus station in Hadera.

The bomb was planted by a degenerate murderer, a member of Hamas, who apparently chose to perish with his innocent victims. This House, the entire country, joins in the mourning and agony of the bereaved families . . . to offer our condolences for their suffering. This House, the Government, also wishes a speedy recovery to the wounded.

Last September, we embarked on a new path. We set forth on an honest attempt to turn a page of history that is fraught with the blood of both Jews—later Israelis—and Palestinians. We decided not to deal with past accounts. We decided to overcome the accumulations of hatred and blood. We decided to try and create a new and better future for both peoples who have been summoned to the same tract of land by fate and history.

We came with a desire to make peace and I must tell you, members of Knesset, that we also found a willingness for peace on the other side, that of the Palestinians—who have also known great suffering for generations. Both we and the Palestinians knew that we would not receive everything we wanted. The Palestinians will not get everything they want. That is the nature of negotiations. That is the nature of compromise. That is the nature of peace.

The negotiations with the Palestinians on "Gaza-Jericho first" continue even today and, in my opinion, we are at an advanced stage. I hope that it will be possible to conclude the negotiations in a short time.

It is our current assessment that, shortly after the agreement is signed, IDF forces and other security branches will be able to conclude their redeployment—I mean in the wake of the Gaza-Jericho negotiations—and the attempt to create peaceful co-existence with the Palestinians will be tested.

I say: I am waiting for this moment when I will feel more comfortable as Defense Minister, not sending IDF soldiers to patrol in metropolitan Gaza City—which contains 250,000 Palestinians, in refugee camps, in Khan Yunis, in Rafiah, in Dir al-Balah.

I want to add: In the wake of reports that have been published—true or not—I wish to clarify that any PLO agreement or accord with Hamas on the possibility of continuing Hamas terror with the approval of the PLO will prevent the achievement of an agreement and its implementation.

This Government, which promised to make every effort for peace, also intends to continue talks with Syria, Lebanon and Jordan.

Towards the end of April and the beginning of May, the bilateral talks in Washington will resume, and Secretary of State Warren Christopher will apparently come to the region to prepare for the talks—in order to enable progress toward the signing of a peace treaty between us and the neighboring countries.

At the peace talks, and as of today, we have still not discovered an appropriate measure of openness and flexibility on the part of the Syrians which would enable a breakthrough and a substantive discussion with respect to a peace agreement. Even the efforts of our American friends, who so want to see peace come to our region, have been unsuccessful.

At the same time, the position of the current government is known. We are making a great effort so that the precedent of the price we paid for peace with Egypt—comprehensive withdrawal, the removal of any Israeli presence—will not be repeated as a condition for achieving peace with Syria. Still, we are seriously preparing for the negotiations and working on various possibilities relating to the character of peace, the depth of the withdrawal on the Golan Heights, security arrangements and the phases for the implementation of peace—so that there will be time to examine the normalization before completing the withdrawal from the Golan Heights as well as what we will require from our friend the United States in the wake of peace. If and when we reach a viable agreement with the Syrians, and should it require a significant withdrawal, we will call a referendum. The people, and nobody else, will decide.

The negotiations with Lebanon are connected to the negotiations with Syria, and we know that Beirut will not lift a finger without the approval of Damascus. Despite this, we repeat—even today—our offer to the authority in Beirut. We have proposed that, in the first phase, the Lebanese military be deployed up to the northern border of the security zone. For six months, it must prove its ability to maintain total calm and to disarm Hizballah in southern Lebanon. If this is proven and total quiet reigns on the northern border of the security zone, we will begin peace negotiations that I hope will continue for three months. We will be prepared to withdraw to the international border between Lebanon and Israel on three conditions: full peace and normalization; appropriate security arrangements; and, of course—our commitment to the SLA and the residents of southern Lebanon—the integration of the SLA within the Lebanese army and a guarantee to residents of southern Lebanon that they will not be harmed.

In the negotiations with Jordan, a resolution is possible. But, unfortunately, I get the impression that it will not come before an agreement with Syria, the big brother who watches over all.

I want to tell the truth. For twenty-seven years, we have controlled another people that does not want our rule. For twenty-seven years, the Palestinians—who now number 1,800,000—have risen in the morning and cultivated a burning hatred for us as Israelis and as Jews. Every morning, they awake to a difficult life and it is partly our fault . . . but not completely. It cannot be denied: The continued rule of a foreign people who does not want us has a price. There is first of all a painful price, the price of constant confrontation between us and them.

For six and one-half years, we have witnessed a popular Palestinian uprising against our rule—the *intifada*. They are trying, through violence and terror, to harm us, to cause us casualties and to break our spirit.

I would like to present some data, provided to me by the IDF. Since the beginning of the uprising, 219 Israelis have been killed, murdered; 68 were security forces personnel and 151 were civilians. A heavy price.

It is difficult for me to recall the War of Independence. In the brigade which I had the privilege to command, in the battle for besieged Jerusalem and the road to Jerusalem, during six months, from one of the ten Haganah brigades which became the Israel Defense Forces, the same number of people fell. One of the outstanding commanders of the brigade and of the IDF, MK Rafael Eitan, is sitting here, and he certainly remembers this. One of 10 brigades, from slightly more than 600,000 civilians. Not one of those people's spirit was broken then. No one rejoiced over the blood.

Our wounded: 7,872, of whom 5,062 were security force personnel and 2,810 were civilians.

1,045 Palestinians have been killed by our forces, those of the IDF and the security branches. 69 have been killed by Israeli civilians. 922 Palestinians have been killed by their own people. 99 have been killed in unknown circumstances. 21 have blown themselves up while handling explosives. A total of 2,156.

Palestinians wounded, according to IDF figures: 18,967. I estimate that at least 25,000 have been wounded. Between 120,000 and 140,000 have been detained and imprisoned.

These are the figures of the struggle over the past six and a half years.

What are the possibilities which face us after twenty-seven years of ruling—and I do not want to use other terms—a different entity than us: religiously, politically, nationally, another people?

The first possibility is to perpetuate the situation as it is, to make proposals with no partner—there never were, and there is no settlement without a partner. To try and eternalize the rule of another people, to continue on a course of never-ending violence and terrorism, which will bring about a political impasse.

Governments of Israel, all Governments of Israel—certainly since the Yom Kippur War—have well-understood the danger contained in freezing the situation. Accordingly, all the governments have sought the second option. The second option is to try and find a political solution. The first phase—in separation agreements. The Government of Menachem Begin went this way, with the peace agreement with Egypt. The Government of Yitzhak Shamir also went this way, in consenting to the Madrid peace conference. We have also gone this way since the Oslo discussion and the Washington signing.

Today, peace seems closer than ever. There is a chance, a great chance, to put an end to wars, to one hundred years of terror and blood, one hundred years of animosity. When we embarked on the journey to peace, we knew that it would be impossible to erase one hundred years of hatred with one signature. We knew that it would be impossible to alter concepts and education from the moment of birth. We knew that this peace would have enemies. We knew there would be people and organizations—whose very existence is founded on hostility between peoples—that would continue to enflame passions to the best of their abilities.

On the Palestinian side, the opposition to peace is led by Hamas along with Islamic Jihad, the rejectionist organizations. The emissaries of this organization have carried out most of the recent acts of terror and murder, some of them in suicide operations. Over the past two or three years, we have encountered radical Islamic terror reminiscent of Hizballah, which was created in Lebanon and carried out attacks—including suicide attacks.

There is no end to the goals of Hamas and other terrorism—every citizen, every Israeli in the territories and within the Green Line, every bus and every home is a target for its murderous intentions.

And, without separating the two populations, the current situation creates endless possibilities for the Hamas murderers. According to our estimate, about 40,000 vehicles move about daily in Judea, Samaria and Gaza. Tens of thousands of soldiers and civilians move about on the roads. IDF soldiers safeguard hundreds of vehicles in the territories, mostly buses, every day.

Hundreds of thousands, Jews and Arabs, thousands of vehicles are intermingled each day. One population within the other.

There are endless possibilities of moving for the territories to Israel. Fewer from Gaza, more from Judea and Samaria. Thousands of hidden and exposed paths lead from the territories into Israel. We cannot hermetically seal the territory.

We are making every effort to ensure the security of Israeli citizens—Jews and Arabs—within the Green Line zone territories, everywhere. I reveal to the Knesset today that a significant part of the standing force of the IDF is now engaged in missions protecting and defending Israeli citizens everywhere.

In this situation, where Hamas has endless targets, it embarks on operations of murder—declaring that its foremost aim is to murder Israelis. And, politically, to destroy the peace talks, not to allow them to

At first, Hamas murderers operated against the Israeli residents of Judea, Samaria and the Gaza Strip. The political intent of Hamas members was that the Israeli residents of Judea, Samaria and Gaza—who were harmed by terror—would demonstrate and act against the Israeli government, in an effort to halt peace efforts.

When this attempt was unsuccessful, and we continued our peace efforts, Hamas directed its primary effort to attacks against the Israeli population within the sovereign territory of Israel, including united Jerusalem.

Since 1 January 1994, twenty-three Israeli civilians, Jews and Arabs, have been killed. Twenty of them were killed within sovereign Israel, including united Jerusalem. Three were killed in the territories.

It is no secret how sensitive we are to casualties, and the Hamas murderers are trying to break us through attacks—with knives, explosive devices, shots from ambushes, car bombs.

They have no chance. We already learned about knives during the bloody incidents of the 1930s. We already learned about car bombs during the War of Independence. We learned about buses filled with bloodshed: in Ma'aleh Akrabim, in Avivim, on the coastal road. We learned about massacres in Ma'alot, and we learned about massacres at the airport in Lod, at the Savoy Hotel, in Kfar Yuval, in Kiryat Shmona, in Misgav Am, in Nahariya. Time and again. We are not panicked. It is painful, but we recover and continue. Even acts of terrorism will not stop the peace convoy.

It is difficult for me to determine that the extent of the risk to our security has increased of late, in the wake of the despicable massacre committed by the Jewish murderer from Hebron. Even though Arab terror had one thousand reasons and excuses to harm us, this man came and added some.

We have found that one of the concentrations of Hamas activity is in Jordan. We are convinced that the Jordanian security authorities are aware of this and, nevertheless, they have enabled information and operational activities in Amman.

Thus, we have seen fit to warn the Jordanian authorities about the continuation of Hamas activity there, and we expect that the King will act against the Hamas murderers—who will attempt to challenge and bring down his regime and rule there as well.

We have also taken a series of measures, including strengthening the terms of closure. We are aware of the suffering being caused to residents of the territories as a consequence of the closure, but we have no other choice. If we wish to live, we must be stricter. And, if reality requires us to do so, we will be even stricter.

And above all, IDF forces, the GSS, the Israel Police and Border Police officers are engaged in an all-out war against all those continuing the violence and terror. There is no limitation to the activity of these forces against terrorism and violence, obviously within the framework of the law.

The Hizballah terrorist organization is also a partner to in the effort to destroy the chance for peace. The Lebanon war did not eradicate terror from Lebanon. Hizballah is the leader in attacks on IDF and SLA forces in the security zone and, sometimes, even against targets in Israel. IDF and SLA soldiers guarantee that northern communities and residents will lead normal lives.

From this platform, I wish to offer my heartfelt praise to IDF commanders and IDF soldiers, to the Israel Police and the Border Police, and particularly to members of the GSS, who are playing a significant role in the difficult war on the murderous terrorism waged by the enemies of Israel and of peace.

This is the situation for now. The path to peace is laid with our good intentions, and with their murderous attacks. It may be even more difficult; we may not manage to prevent more terror attacks. But peace will be victorious.

Israeli Prime Minister Yitzhak Rabin: Accepting the UNESCO Peace Prize (July 6, 1994)

For over a hundred years, we have fought over the same strip of land: the country in which we, the sons of Abraham, have been fated to live together. Both peoples, Israelis and Palestinians, have known suffering, pain, and bereavement.

Now the fanfares and festivals are over. Now the vapors of euphoria are slowly settling into grains of dust, and the echoes of celebration are being scattered by the hot southern wind. Now the flags have been folded, the trumpets silenced, the stages dismantled—now, the more difficult, more dangerous part has come. And both sides must calculate their steps slowly, with prudence and care. For a century of hatred does not dissolve suddenly, with a handshake in Washington. All the bloodshed can't be covered by the beating of drums. Peace will be built slowly, day by day, through modest deeds, and countless spontaneous details. It will be built, step by step, by people.

From now on, the making of peace is not a matter for spotlights, for elegant halls, and ball gowns. From now on, the baking sun in Jericho and Na'ama, in Khan Yunis and Netzer Hazani, will replace the spotlights in Washington, Cairo, and Paris. The handshakes on the lawn in Washington, the stage in Cairo, and here in Paris must be repeated by the residents of Gaza and Ashkelon, of Jericho and Ma'ale Adumim. What we have acknowledged here in this beautiful setting in Paris must be transferred to the markets in Gaza, where Israelis will buy fruit from Palestinian vendors.

Peace will be tasted in the Palestinian coffee poured into the cups of Israeli friends. It will be heard in the applause of Israeli audiences for the performance of a Palestinian theater troupe, and in the jeers of the rival soccer fans when Khan Yunis plays against Tel Aviv.

Peace will be seen when an Israeli driver yields the right of way to his Palestinian counterpart—vice versa: when a Palestinian policeman gives a ticket to an Israeli driver—and the other way around. Peace lies in the grin of an Israeli doctor delivering Palestinian newborn, and in the smile of a Palestinian lifeguard toward Israeli bathers on the beach.

That, ladies and gentlemen, is peace.

We are going along slowly and cautiously, one step at a time, because the enemies of peace are even more numerous than we imagine. Because extremists on both sides are lying in wait for us, and we—Israelis and Palestinians, alike—must not fail. At every step, we must think, consider, we—Israelis and Palestinians, alike—must not fail. At every step, we must think, consider, weigh, check, and beware.

We are in a hurry because we have waited over a hundred years for this day, in Gaza and Jerusalem, in Jericho and Netanya, in Rafiah and Rosh Pinah.

We are in a hurry to spare another Israeli mother weeping tears of pain and another Palestinian mother from shedding bitter sobs.

We are in a hurry in order to see a light in the eyes of neighbors who, until now, have never seen a single day of freedom and joy. We are hastening in order to hike, drive, tour, and enjoy life in every corner of this land.

We are in a hurry so that children can be born into a new world—a world where 'hostility' and 'war' are just dead words, found only in the dictionary.

We are in a hurry, Ladies and Gentlemen—and therefore we are proceeding slowly. We are moving very carefully. For not all of us will have another chance. . . .

Ladies and Gentlemen, peace is an abstract concept. Prime Ministers tend to see the essential things—the 'big picture'—and it's said that they don't have time for details. I translate peace into people: men and women, flesh and blood, with names and addresses. Sometimes when I have to make a decision, there are certain people I think of, and I contemplate their fate.

There was a family in Israel that symbolizes, in our eyes, the bond of generations to the Land of Israel, Jewish moral and cultural values, a return to the soil after two thousand years of exile, security, and the dream of peace.

The mother of the family, Rachel Kaplan, was the daughter of the Chief Rabbi of Jerusalem—the offspring of a family deeply rooted, for generations, between the Western Wall—the walls of the Old City—and the new city of Jerusalem, the City of Peace.

The father, Yisrael, came to the land that had been promised to the Patriarch Abraham, the father of the Jewish People, from exile in Poland. Hundreds of thousands came like him, and after him, from seventy countries of dispersion, and set down roots in their ancient home.

Avner was the eldest son of Rachel and Yisrael Kaplan. He chose to settle the land and to work the soil as a way of life as another expression of the Jewish ties to the Land of Israel. Avner Kaplan died in a fire in his house, on Kibbutz Tel Katzir, facing the Golan Heights.

Yossi was the Kaplans' second son. He chose defense as a way of life and served as an outstanding officer in the paratroops. Yossi was killed while in pursuit of terrorists in the Jordan Valley. He entered a cave where a woman was sitting with her baby. A moral man, a humanist whom circumstances had made into a tough soldier, Yossi believed her when she said that she was alone. But when he turned to leave, he was shot by the man hiding there. That's how Yossi Kaplan died.

Yoni was their third son. He chose university studies and army service. Although he was entitled to be exempt from combat, because of the death of his brothers, he did not waive his right to serve on the front line, the vanguard of attack. Yoni Kaplan was killed in the bitter fighting against the Egyptian Army in the Yom Kippur War.

The mother of this wonderful family, Rachel, was struck down by cancer.

The father, Yisrael, died of a broken heart over the loss of his sons, one after the other.

There remains the fourth, last son: Amiram Kaplan.

For your sake, Amiram—for you, for our children and their children, we are moving toward peace. We are proceeding slowly, and we shall hurry to bring it to you. That is our vow to you.

Israel and Jordan:
The Washington Agreement (July 26, 1994)

A. After generations of hostility, blood, and tears and in the wake of years of pain and wars, His Majesty King Hussein and Prime Minister Yitzhak Rabin are determined to bring an end to bloodshed and sorrow. It is in this spirit that His Majesty King Hussein of the Hashemite Kingdom of Jordan and Prime Minister and Minister of Defense, Mr. Yitzhak Rabin of Israel, met in Washington today at the invitation of President William J. Clinton of the United States of America. The initiative of President William J. Clinton constitutes an historic landmark in the United States untiring efforts in promoting peace and stability in the Middle East. The personal involvement of the president has made it possible to realize agreement on the content of this historic declaration. The signing of this declaration bears testimony to the president's vision and devotion to the cause of peace.

B. In their meeting, His Majesty King Hussein and Prime Minister Yitzhak Rabin have jointly reaffirmed the five underlying principles of their understanding on an Agreed Common Agenda designed to reach the goal of a just, lasting, and comprehensive peace between the Arab States and the Palestinians, with Israel.

1. Jordan and Israel aim at the achievement of just, lasting, and comprehensive peace between Israel and its neighbors and at the conclusion of a Treaty of Peace between both countries.

2. The two countries will vigorously continue their negotiations to arrive at a state of peace, based on Security Council Resolutions 242 and 338 in all their aspects, and founded on freedom, equality and justice.

3. Israel respects the present special role of the Hashemite Kingdom of Jordan in Moslem holy shrines in Jerusalem. When negotiations on the permanent status will take place, Israel will give high priority to the Jordanian historic role in these shrines. In addition, the two sides have agreed to act together to promote interfaith relations among the three monotheistic religions.

4. The two countries recognize their right and obligation to live in peace with each other as well as with all states within secure and recognized boundaries. The two states affirmed their respect for and acknowledgment of the sovereignty, territorial integrity, and political independence of every state in the area.

5. The two countries desire to develop good neighborly relations of cooperation between them to ensure lasting security and to avoid threats and the use of force between them.

C. The long conflict between the two states is now coming to an end. In this spirit, the state of belligerency between Jordan and Israel has been terminated.

D. Following this declaration and in keeping with the Agreed Common Agenda both countries will refrain from actions or activities by either side that may adversely affect the security of the other or may prejudice the final outcome of negotiations. Neither side will threaten the other by use of force, weapons, or any other means against each other and both sides will thwart threats to security resulting from all kinds of terrorism.

E. His Majesty King Hussein and Prime Minister Yitzhak Rabin took note of the progress made in the bilateral negotiations within the Jordan-Israel track last week on the steps decided to implement the sub-agendas on borders, territorial matters, security, water, energy, environment, and the Jordan Rift Valley.

In this framework, mindful of items of the Agreed Common Agenda (borders and territorial matters) they noted that the boundary subcommission has reached agreement in July 1994 in fulfillment of part of the role entrusted to it in the subagenda. They also noted that the subcommission for water, environment, and energy agreed to mutually recognize, as the role of their negotiations, the rightful allocations of the two sides in Jordan River and Yarmouk River waters and to fully respect and comply with the negotiated rightful allocations, in accordance with agreed acceptable principles with mutually acceptable quality.

Similarly, His Majesty King Hussein and Prime Minister Yitzhak Rabin expressed their deep satisfaction and pride in the work of the trilateral commission in its meeting held in Jordan on Wednesday, July 20, 1994, hosted by the Jordanian Prime Minister, Dr. Abdessalam Majali, and attended by Secretary of State Warren Christopher and Foreign Minister Shimon Peres. They voiced their pleasure at the association and commitment of the United States in this endeavor.

F. His Majesty King Hussein and Prime Minister Yitzhak Rabin believe that steps must be taken to both overcome psychological barriers and to break with the legacy of war. By working with optimism towards the dividends of peace for all the people in the region, Jordan and Israel are determined to shoulder their responsibilities towards the human dimension of peace making. They recognize imbalances and disparities are a root cause of extremism which thrives on poverty and unemployment and the degradation of human dignity. In this spirit, His Majesty King Hussein and Prime Minister Yitzhak Rabin have today approved a series of steps to symbolize the new era which is now at hand:

1. Direct telephone links will be opened between Jordan and Israel.

2. The electricity grids of Jordan and Israel will be linked as part of a regional concept.

3. Two new border crossings will be opened between Jordan and Israel—one at the southern tip of Akaba-Eilat and the other at a mutually agreed point in the North.

4. In principle, free access will be given to third country tourists traveling between Jordan and Israel.

5. Negotiations will be accelerated on opening an international air corridor between both countries.

6. The police forces of Jordan and Israel will cooperate in combating crime with emphasis on smuggling and particularly drug smuggling. The United States will be invited to participate in this joint endeavor.

7. Negotiations on economic matters will continue in order to prepare for future bilateral cooperation, including the abolition of all economic boycotts.

All these steps are being implemented within the framework of regional infrastructural development plans and in conjunction with the Jordan-Israel bilaterals on boundaries, security, water and related issues and without prejudice to the final outcome of the negotiations on the items included in the Agreed Common Agenda between Jordan and Israel.

G. His Majesty King Hussein and Prime Minister Yitzhak Rabin have agreed to meet periodically or whenever they feel necessary to review the progress of the negotiations and express their firm intention to shepherd and direct the process in entirety.

H. In conclusion, His Majesty King Hussein and Prime Minister Yitzhak Rabin wish to express once again their profound thanks and appreciation to President William J. Clinton and his administration for their untiring efforts in furthering the cause of peace, justice, and prosperity for all the peoples of the region.

King Hussein of Jordan and Israeli Prime Minister Yitzhak Rabin: Speeches on Signing the Washington Agreement (July 26, 1994)

King Hussein of Jordan

We in Jordan have always sought a bold peace. We have been conscious of our responsibilities towards the coming generations to ensure that they will have the certainty of leading a dignified and fulfilled life. We have sought a peace that can harness the creative energies to allow them to realize their true potential and build their future with confidence, devoid of fear and uncertainty. None of this can be achieved without establishing a direct dialogue at the highest level of leadership.

This meeting in Washington, at the invitation of President Clinton, represents the beginning of a new phase in our common journey towards peace between Jordan and Israel. It is a milestone on the road toward comprehensive peace in our region. This meeting was preceded by a trilateral Jordanian-American-Israeli meeting at which my brother, Crown Prince Hassan, represented myself and the Hashemite Kingdom of Jordan, and Foreign Minister Shimon Peres represented Israel.

The trilateral working group was established under an agreement completed at the meeting hosted by President Clinton at the White House in October 1993.

Following my recent visit to the United States, in light of the status of negotiations, I decided to share with my people the realities affecting our search for peace. In a meeting with members of our parliament, I addressed the entire Jordanian nation. I have been rewarded by their approval and support. Their expression of confidence has always been the foremost consideration in my life. All of Jordan is here with me today.

We also remember today the three generations of gallant Jordanians and so many others who sacrificed themselves for the cause of Palestine. Every household in Jordan has sent a son to answer the Arab call. Many have not returned. Their sacrifice has made it possible for me to be here today.

My family has also paid a heavy price. My great grandfather, the leader of the great Arab revolt for freedom, independence and unity, lies buried next to the blessed Al Aqsa Mosque in Jerusalem. I was by the side of my grandfather, King Abdallah, at the doors of Al Aqsa Mosque when he was martyred. He was a man of peace who gave his life for this ideal. I have pledged my life to fulfilling his dream. He, too, is here today.

Mr. Speaker, at our meeting today I hope you will find a clear message to the American nation and to the world.

We are, together, committed to work tirelessly, to banish forever the abnormal conditions which have dominated our people's lives. We want normality and humanity to become the prevailing order.

Although we have labored for so long under conditions of hostility, I am certain that we can see these conditions for what they are: emblems of an unnatural and sinister state. We have all known the portents of the state—the fear of death, the silence of isolation—and we have all felt the fear that has mesmerized us, preventing us from moving forward to create together a bright future for the coming generations. What we are witnessing today, God willing, is a progression from a state of war to a state of peace.

These unique circumstances allow us to take bold steps. Our meeting now represents a revolt against all that is unnatural. It is unnatural not to have direct and open meetings between our respective officials and their leaders in order to grapple with all aspects of the conflict and, God willing, to resolve them. It is unnatural not to wish to bridge this gulf across which we have all paid a shattering toll in blood and tears, the waste of our youth, and the grief of our forefathers. We have suffered this loss together, and it will leave its impact on all of us far into the future.

The two Semitic people, the Arabs and the Jews, have endured bitter trials and tribulations during the journey of history. Let us resolve to end this suffering forever and to fulfill our responsibilities as leaders of our peoples and our duty as human beings towards mankind. I come before you today fully conscious of the need to secure a peace for all the children of Abraham. Our land is the birthplace of the divine faiths and the cradle of the heavenly messages to all humanity.

I also come before you today as a soldier who seeks to bear arms solely in the defense of his homeland, a man who understands the fears of his neighbors and who wishes only to live in peace with them, a man who wishes to secure democracy, political pluralism and human rights for his nation.

I come before you today encouraged in the knowledge that the prime minister of Israel and his government have responded to the call for peace. They have recognized the Palestinian people and their rights and are negotiating with their chosen leadership in accordance with United Nations Security Council Resolutions 242 and 338.

For our part, we will never forget Palestine, not for a moment. We in Jordan were the first to shoulder our responsibility, and we were the most adversely affected by the legacy of the Palestinian tragedy. And still our people in Jordan remain one united family irrespective of their origins, sharing equally, free to choose our political future and destiny.

My religious faith demands that sovereignty over the holy places in Jerusalem reside with God, and God alone. Dialogue between the faiths should be strengthened. Religious sovereignty should be accorded to all believers of the three Abrahamic faiths in accordance with their religions, and this way Jerusalem will become the symbol of peace and its embodiment as it must be for both Palestinians and Israelis when their negotiations determine the final status of Arab East Jerusalem.

I come before you today fully confident that progress will be made on the Syrian-Israeli and Lebanese-Israeli tracks of the peace process and towards achievement of comprehensive peace. . . .

The state of war between Israel and Jordan is over.

We have accepted United Nations Security Council Resolution 338, which calls for negotiations between the parties concerned under appropriate auspices to establish a just and durable peace in the Middle East. We have accepted United Nations Security Council Resolution 242, which sought acknowledgement of the sovereignty, territorial integrity and political independence of every state in the area and thereby to live in peace within secure and recognized boundaries, free from threats or acts of force.

I want to reaffirm, without any reservation, that we, together with other parties concerned, have exercised our sovereign right to make peace.

We are moving forward and tackling, one by one, all the problems listed in our common agenda. We have great faith in our joint progress towards the ultimate goal, the culmination of all our efforts, a Jordanian-Israeli peace treaty.

In this we take courage from the words of God in his holy book, the Koran, that if they should be inclined to make peace, do thou incline towards it also, and put thy trust in Allah. Surely it is he who is all hearing, all knowing.

I value the long friendship between Jordan and the United States inherited from the era of my grandfather. I have strived over 34 years since the presidency of Dwight Eisenhower to ensure that it be honest and true.

It has been a friendship built on mutual respect and common interests, and I am proud to remind how we stood shoulder to shoulder during the long years of the Cold War. And now, together we share a great hope to establish a lasting peace in the Middle East.

We believe that an enduring partnership for cooperation and development between Jordan and the United States is essential to the realization of this dream. We aim to build a better future under peace, to change the pattern of life for our people from despair and hopelessness to honor and dignity. We want to fashion a new commonwealth of hope on our ancient soil. We want all voices to be heard in shaping a new regional order. If we are to achieve our aims, all of us must be given the opportunity and the tools to play our part in this historic endeavor.

The creative drive of our region has been crippled by the conflict. The healing hand of the international community is now essential. It should never be forgotten that peace resides ultimately not in the hands of governments but in the hands of the people, for unless peace can be made real to the men, women and children of the Middle East, the best efforts of negotiators will come to naught.

I have come before you today to demonstrate that we are ready to open a new era in our relations with Israel. With the help and cooperation of this august body, the peace we all want can be achieved. With your help, I am certain that the imbalances between our societies can be remedied and that the sources of frustration and enmity can be eradicated. It is in this spirit and with these hopes that I share this platform with Prime Minister Yitzhak Rabin.

Israeli Prime Minister Yitzhak Rabin

Each year, on Memorial Day for the Fallen of Israel's Wars, I go to the cemetery on Mount Herzl in Jerusalem. Facing me are the graves and headstones, the colorful flowers blooming on them—and thousands of pairs of weeping eyes. I stand there, in front of the large silent crowd—and read in their eyes the words of "The Young Dead Soldiers"—as the famous American poet Archibald MacLeish entitled the poem from which I take these lines:

> *They say:*
> *Whether our lives and our deaths*
> *were for peace and a new hope,*
> *or for nothing,*
> *we cannot say;*
> *it is you who must say this.*

We have come from Jerusalem to Washington because it is we who must say, and we are here to say: Peace is our goal. It is peace we desire.

With me here in this House today are my partners in this great dream. Allow me to refer to some Israelis who are here with me, here with you:

• Amiram Kaplan, whose first brother was killed in an accident, whose second brother was killed in pursuit of terrorists, whose third brother was killed in war, and whose parents died of heartbreak. And today he is a seeker of peace.
• Moshe Sasson, who, together with his father, was an emissary to the talks with King Abdallah and to other missions of peace. Today he is also an emissary of peace.
• With me, a classmate of mine, Chana Rivlin of Kibbutz Gesher, which faces Jordan, who endured bitter fighting and lost a son in war. Today she looks out her window onto Jordan, and wants the dream of peace to come true.
• Avraham Daskal, almost 90 years old, who worked for the Electric Company in Trans-Jordan and was privileged to attend the celebrations marking King Hussein's birth, is hoping for peace in his lifetime.
• And Dani Matt, who fought against Jordan in the War of Independence, was taken prisoner of war, and devoted his life to the security of the State of Israel. He hopes that his grandchildren will never know war.
• Mrs. Penina Herzog, whose husband wove the first threads of political ties with Jordan.

With us here in this hall are:

• Mr. Gabi Kadosh, the mayor of Eilat, which touches the frontier with Jordan and will be a focus of common tourism.
• And Mr. Shimon Cahaner, who fought against the Jordanians, memorializes his fallen comrades, and hopes that they will have been the last to fall.
• And Mr. Talal al-Krienawi, the mayor of a Bedouin town in Israel, who looks forward to renewing the friendship with their brothers in Jordan.
• And Mr. David Coren, a member of a kibbutz which was captured by the Jordanians in 1948, who awaits the day when the borders will be open.
• And Dr. Asher Susser, a scholar who has done research on Jordan throughout his adult life.
• And Dr. Sharon Regev, whose father was killed while pursuing terrorists in the Jordan Valley, and who yearns for peace with all his heart.

Here they are before you. All of them wanted to come. Here they are, people who never rejoiced in the victories of war, but whose hearts are now filled with joy in peace.

I have come here from Jerusalem on behalf of those thousands of bereaved families—though I haven't asked their permission. I stand here on behalf of the parents who have buried their children; of the children who have no fathers; and of the sons and daughters who are gone, but return to us in our dreams. I stand here today on behalf of those youngsters who wanted to live, to love, to build a home.

I have come from Jerusalem in the name of our children, who began their lives with great hope—and are now names on graves and memorial stones; old pictures in albums; fading clothes in closets.

Each year as I stand before the parents whose lips are chanting "Kaddish", the Jewish memorial prayer, ringing in my ears are the words of Archibald MacLeish, who echoes the plea of the young dead soldiers:

> *They say: We leave you our deaths.*
> *Give them their meaning.*

Let us give them meaning. Let us make an end to bloodshed. Let us make true peace. Let us today be victorious in ending war.

The debate goes on: Who shapes the face of history?—leaders or circumstances?

My answer to you is: We all shape the face of history. We, the people. We, the farmers behind our plows, the teachers in our classrooms, the doctors saving lives, the scientists at our computers, the workers on the assembly lines, the builders on our scaffolds.

We, the mothers blinking back tears as our sons are drafted into the army; we, the fathers who stay awake at night worried and anxious for our children's safety. We, Jews and Arabs. We, Israelis and Jordanians. We, the people, we shape the face of history.

And we, the leaders, hear the voices, and sense the deepest emotions and feelings of the thousands and the millions, and translate them into reality.

If my people did not desire peace so strongly, I would not be standing here today. And I am sure that if the children of Amman, and the soldiers of Irbid, the women of Saltt and the citizens of Aqaba did not seek peace, our partner in this great quest, the King of Jordan, would not be here now, shaking hands, calling for peace.

We bear the responsibility. We have the power to decide. And we dare not miss this great opportunity. For it is the duty of leaders to bring peace and well-being to their peoples. We are graced with the privilege of fulfilling this duty for our peoples. This is our responsibility.

The complex relations between Israel and Jordan have continued for a generation. Today, so many years later, we carry with us good memories of the special ties between your country, your Majesty, and mine, and we carry with us the grim reminders of the times we found ourselves at war. We remember the days of your grandfather, King Abdallah, who sought avenues of peace with the heads of the Jewish people and the leaders of the young State of Israel.

There is much work before us. We face psychological barriers. We face genuine practical problems. Walls of hostility have been built on the River Jordan which runs between us. You in Amman, and we in Jerusalem, must bring down those barriers and walls, must solve those concrete problems. I am sure that we will do it.

Yesterday we took a giant step towards a peace which will embrace it all: borders and water, security and economics, trade without boycotts, tourism and environment, diplomatic relations. We want peace between countries, but above all, between human beings.

Beyond the ceremonies, after the festivities, we will move on to the negotiations. They will not be easy. But when they are completed, a wonderful, common future awaits us. The Middle East, the cradle of the great monotheistic civilizations—Judaism, Christianity, and Islam; the Middle East, which was a valley of the shadow of death, will be a place where it is a pleasure to live.

We live on the same stretch of land. The same rain nourishes our soil; the same hot wind parches our fields. We find shade under the same fig tree. We savor the fruit of the same green vine. We drink from the same well. Only a 70-minute journey separates these cities—Jerusalem and Amman—and 46 years. And just as we have been enemies, so can we be good and friendly neighbors.

Since it is unprecedented that in this joint meeting two speakers are invited, allow me to turn to His Majesty.

Your Majesty, We have both seen a lot in our lifetime. We have both seen too much suffering. What will you leave to your children? What will I leave to my grandchildren? I have only dreams: to build a better world— a world of understanding and harmony, a world in which it is a joy to live. This is not asking too much.

The State of Israel thanks you: thanks you for accepting our hand in peace; for your political wisdom and courage; for planting new hope in our hearts, in the hearts of your subjects, and the hearts of all peace-loving people. And I know that you enjoy the highest esteem of the United States—this great America which is helping the bold to make a peace of the brave. . . .

I do so because no words can express our gratitude to you and to the American people for your generous support, understanding, and cooperation which are beyond compare in modern history. Thank you, America. God bless America.

Tomorrow I shall return to Jerusalem, the capital of the State of Israel and the heart of the Jewish people. Lining the road to Jerusalem are rusting hulks of metal—burnt-out, silent, cold. They are the remains of convoys which brought food and medicine to the war-torn and besieged city of Jerusalem 46 years ago.

For many of Israel's citizens, their story is one of heroism, part of our national legend. For me and for my comrades-in-arms, every scrap of cold metal lying there by the wayside is a bitter memory. I remember it as though it were just yesterday.

I remember them. I was their commander in war. For them this ceremony has come too late. What endures are their children, their comrades, their legacy.

Allow me to make a personal note. I, military I.D. number three-zero-seven-four-three, retired general in the Israel Defense Forces in the past, consider myself to be a soldier in the army of peace today. I, who served my country for 27 years as a soldier, I say to you, Your Majesty, the King of Jordan, and I say to you, American friends:

Today we are embarking on a battle which has no dead and no wounded, no blood and no anguish. This is the only battle which is a pleasure to wage: the battle for peace.

Tomorrow, on the way up to Jerusalem, thousands of flowers will cover the remains of those rusting armored vehicles, the ones that never made it to the city. Tomorrow, from those silent metal heaps, thousands of flowers will smile to us with the word peace: "shalom."

In the Bible, our Book of Books, peace is mentioned, in its various idioms, 237 times. In the Bible, from which we draw our values and our strength, in the Book of Jeremiah, we find a lamentation for Rachel the Matriarch. It reads:

> *Refrain your voice from weeping, and your eyes from tears:*
> *for their work shall be rewarded, says the Lord.*

I will not refrain from weeping for those who are gone. But on this summer day in Washington, far from home, we sense that our work will be rewarded, as the prophet foretold.

The Jewish tradition calls for a blessing on every new tree, every new fruit, on every new season. Let me conclude with the ancient Jewish blessing that has been with us in exile, and in Israel, for thousands of years:

"Blessed are You, O Lord, who has preserved us, and sustained us, and enabled us to reach this time."

Israel and Jordan: Peace Treaty (October 26, 1994)

PREAMBLE

The government of the Hashemite Kingdom of Jordan and the government of the State of Israel:

Bearing in mind the Washington Declaration, signed by them on 25 July 1994 and which they are both committed to honor.

Aiming at the achievement of a just, lasting, and comprehensive peace in the Middle East based on Security Council resolutions 242 and 318 in all their aspects;

Bearing in mind the importance of maintaining and strengthening peace based on freedom, equality, justice, and respect for fundamental and human rights: thereby overcoming psychological barriers and promoting human dignity;

Reaffirming their faith in the purposes and the principles of the Charter of the United Nations and recognizing their right and obligation to live in peace with each other as well as with all states, within secure and recognized boundaries;

Desiring to develop friendly relations and cooperation between them in accordance with the principles of international law governing international relations in times of peace;

Desiring as well to ensure lasting security for both their states and, in particular, to avoid threats and the use of force between them;

Bearing in mind that in their Washington Declaration of 25 July 1994, they declared the termination of the state of belligerency between them;

Deciding to establish peace between them in accordance with this treaty of peace;

Have agreed as follows:

ARTICLE 1 — ESTABLISHMENT OF PEACE

Peace is hereby established between the Hashemite Kingdom of Jordan and the State of Israel (the parties) effective from the exchange of the instruments of ratifications of this treaty.

ARTICLE 2 — GENERAL PRINCIPLES

The parties will apply between them the provisions of the Charter of the United Nations and the principles of international law governing relations among states in times of peace. In particular:

a. They recognize and will respect each other's sovereignty, territorial integrity, and political independence.

b. They recognize and will respect each other's right to live in peace within secure and recognized boundaries.

c. They will develop good neighborly relations of cooperation between them to ensure lasting security, will refrain from the threat or use of force against each other, and will settle all disputes between them by peaceful means.

d. They respect and recognize the sovereignty, territorial integrity, and political independence of every state in the region.

e. They respect and recognize the pivotal role of human development and dignity in regional and bilateral relationships.

f. They further believe that within their control, involuntary movements of persons in such a way as to adversely prejudice the security of either party should not be permitted.

ARTICLE 3 — INTERNATIONAL BOUNDARY

a. The international boundary between Israel and Jordan is delimited with reference to the boundary definition under the Mandate as is shown in Annex I (a), on the mapping materials attached thereto and coordinates specified therein.

b. The boundary, as set out in Annex I (a), is the permanent, secure, and recognized international boundary between Israel and Jordan, without prejudice to the status of any territories that came under Israeli military government control in 1967.

c. The parties recognize the international boundary, including the territorial waters and airspace, as inviolable, and will respect and comply with them.

d. The demarcation of the boundary will take place as set forth in the Appendix I to Annex I (a) and will be concluded no later than nine months after the signing of the treaty.

e. It is agreed that where the boundary follows a river, in the event of natural changes in the course of the flow of the river as described in Annex I (a), the boundary shall follow the new course of the flow. In the event of any other changes, the boundary shall not be affected unless otherwise agreed.

f. Immediately upon the exchange of the instruments of ratification of this treaty, each party will deploy on each side of the international boundary as defined in Annex I (a).

g. The parties shall, upon the signature of the treaty, enter into the negotiations to conclude, within nine months, an agreement on the delimitation of their maritime boundary in the Gulf of Akaba.

h. Taking into account the special circumstances of the Bakura/Naharayim area, which is under Jordanian sovereignty, with Israeli private ownership rights, the parties agreed to apply the provisions set out in Annex I (b).

i. With respects to the Tzofar area the provisions set out in Annex I (c) will apply.

ARTICLE 4 — SECURITY

1. a. Both parties, acknowledging that mutual understanding and cooperation in security-related matters will form a significant part of their relations and will further enhance the security of the region, take upon themselves to base their security relations on mutual trust,

advancement of joint interests and cooperation, and to aim towards a regional framework of partnership in peace.

b. Towards that goal, the parties recognize the achievements of the European Community and European Union in the development of the Conference on Security and Cooperation in Europe (CSCE) and commit themselves to the creation, in the Middle East, of a CSCME (Conference on Security and Cooperation in the Middle East).

This commitment entails the adoption of regional models of security successfully implemented in the post World War era (along the lines of the Helsinki process) culminating in a regional zone of security and stability.

2. The obligations referred to in this article are without prejudice to the inherent right of self-defense in accordance with the United Nations Charter.

3. The parties undertake, in accordance with the provisions of this article, the following:

a. To refrain from the threat or use of force or weapons, conventional, non-conventional, or of any other kind, against each other or of other actions or activities that adversely affect the security of the other party;

b. To refrain from organizing, instigating, inciting, assisting, or participating in acts or threats of belligerency, hostility, subversion, or violence against the other party;

c. To take necessary and effective measures to ensure that acts or threats of belligerency, hostility, subversion, or violence against the other party do not originate from, and are not committed within, their territory (hereinafter the term "territory" includes the airspace and territorial waters), or through or over their territory.

4. Consistent with the era of peace and with the efforts to build regional security and to avoid and prevent aggression and violence, the parties further agree to refrain from the following:

a. Joining or in any way assisting, promoting, or cooperating with any coalition, organization, or alliance with a military or security character with a third party, the objectives or activities of which include launching aggression or other acts of military hostility against the other party, in contravention of the provisions of the present treaty;

b. Allowing the entry, stationing, and operating on their territory, or through it, of military forces, personnel, or material of a third party, in circumstances which may adversely prejudice the security of the other party.

5. Both parties will take necessary and effective measures, and will cooperate in combating terrorism of all kinds. The parties undertake:

a. To take necessary and effective measures to prevent acts of terrorism, subversion, or violence from being carried out from their territory or through it, and to take necessary and effective measures to combat such activities and all their perpetrators;

b. Without prejudice to the basic rights of freedom of expression and association, to take necessary and effective measures to prevent the entry, presence and operations in their territory of any group or organization, and its infrastructure, which threatens the security of the other party by the use or incitement to the use of violent means;

c. To cooperate in preventing and combating cross-boundary infiltrations.

6. Any question as to the implementation of this article will be dealt with through a mechanism of consultation which will include a liaison system, verification, supervision, and where necessary, other mechanisms, and higher level consultation. The details of the mechanism of consultation will be contained in an agreement to be concluded by the parties within three months of the exchange of the instruments of ratification of this treaty.

7. To work as a matter of priority and as soon as possible in the context of the multilateral working groups on arms control and regional security, and jointly, toward the following:

a. The creation in the Middle East of a region free from hostile alliances and coalitions;

b. The creation of a Middle East free from weapons of mass destruction, both conventional and non-conventional, in the context of a comprehensive, lasting, and stable peace, characterized by the renunciation of the use of force, reconciliation, and goodwill.

ARTICLE 5 — DIPLOMATIC AND OTHER BILATERAL RELATIONS

1. The parties agree to establish full diplomatic and consular relations and to exchange resident ambassadors within one month of the exchange of the instruments of ratification of this treaty.

2. The parties agree that the normal relationship between them will further include economic and cultural relations.

ARTICLE 6 — WATER

With the view to achieving a comprehensive and lasting settlement of all the water problems between them:

1. The parties agree mutually to recognize the rightful allocations of both of them in Jordan River, Yarmuk River waters, and Arab/Arava ground water in accordance with the agreed acceptable princi-

ples, quantities, and quality as set out in Annex II, which shall be fully respected and complied with;

2. The parties, recognizing the necessity to find a practical, just, and agreed solution to their water problems and with the view that the subject of water can form the basis for the advancement of cooperation between them, jointly undertake to ensure that the management and development of their water resources do not, in any way, harm the water resources of the other party;

3. The parties recognize that their water resources are not sufficient to meet their needs. More water should be supplied for their use through various methods, including projects of regional and international cooperation;

4. In light of paragraph 2a, with the understanding that the cooperation in water-related subjects would be to the benefit of both parties, and will help alleviate their water shortages, and that water issues along their entire boundary must be dealt with in their totality, including the possibility of trans-boundary water transfers, the parties agreed to search for ways to alleviate water shortages and to cooperate in the following fields:

a. Development of existing and new water resources increasing the water availability, including on a regional basis, as appropriate, and minimizing wastage of water resources through the chain of their uses;

b. Prevention of contamination of water resources;

c. Mutual assistance in the alleviation of water shortages;

d. Transfer of information and joint research and development in water-related subjects, and review of the potentials for enhancement of water resources development and use;

5. The implementation of both countries' undertakings under this article is detailed in Annex II.

ARTICLE 7 — ECONOMIC RELATIONS

1. Viewing economic development and prosperity as pillars of peace, security, and harmonious relations between states, peoples, and individual human beings, the parties, taking note of understandings reached between them, affirm their mutual desire to promote economic cooperation between them, as well as within the framework of wider regional economic cooperation.

2. In order to establish this goal, the parties agree to the following:

a. To remove all discriminatory barriers to normal economic relations, to terminate economic boycotts directed at each other, and to cooperate in terminating boycotts against each other by third parties;

b. Recognizing that the principle of free and unimpeded flow of goods and services should guide their relations, the parties will enter into negotiations with a view to concluding agreements on economic cooperation, including trade and the establishment of a free trade area, investment, banking, industrial cooperation, and labor, for the purpose of promoting beneficial economic relations, based on principles to be agreed upon, as well as on human development considerations on a regional basis. These negotiations will be concluded no later than six months from the exchange the instruments of ratification of the treaty;

c. To cooperate bilaterally, as well as in multilateral forums, toward the promotion of their respective economies and of their neighborly economic relations with other regional parties.

ARTICLE 8 — REFUGEES AND DISPLACED PERSONS

1. Recognizing the massive human problems caused by both parties by the conflict in the Middle East, as well as the contribution made by them towards the alleviation of human suffering. The parties will seek to further alleviate those problems arising on a bilateral level.

2. Recognizing that the above human problems caused by the conflict in the Middle East cannot be fully resolved on the bilateral level, the parties will seek to resolve them in appropriate forums, in accordance with international law, including the following:

a. In the case of displaced persons, in a quadripartite committee together with Egypt and the Palestinians;

b. In the case of refugees,

(i) in the framework of the work of the Multilateral Group on Refugees;

(ii) in negotiations, in a framework to be agreed, bilateral or otherwise, in conjunction with and at the same time as the permanent status negotiations pertaining to the territories referred to in Article 3 of this treaty.

3. Through the implementation of agreed United Nations programs and other agreed international economic programs concerning refugees and displaced persons, including assistance to their settlement.

ARTICLE 9 — PLACES OF HISTORICAL AND RELIGIOUS SIGNIFICANCE

1. Each party will provide freedom of access to places of religious and historical significance.

2. In this regard, in accordance with the Washington Declaration, Israel respects the present special role of the Hashemite Kingdom of

Jordan in Moslem holy shrines in Jerusalem. When negotiations on the permanent status will take place, Israel will give high priority to the Jordanian historic role in these shrines.

3. The parties will act together to promote interfaith relations among the three monotheistic religions, with the aim of working towards religious understanding, moral commitment, freedom of religious worship, and tolerance and peace.

ARTICLE 10—CULTURAL AND SCIENTIFIC EXCHANGES

The parties, wishing to remove biases developed through periods of conflict, recognize the desirability of cultural and scientific exchanges in all fields, and agree to establish normal cultural relations between them. Thus, they shall, as soon as possible and not later than nine months from the exchange of the instruments of ratification of this treaty, conclude the negotiations on cultural and scientific agreements.

ARTICLE 11—MUTUAL UNDERSTANDING AND GOOD NEIGHBORLY RELATIONS

1. The parties will seek to foster mutual understanding and tolerance based on shared historic values, and accordingly undertake:

a. To abstain from hostile or discriminatory propaganda against each other, and to take all possible legal and administrative measures to prevent the dissemination of such propaganda by any organization or individual present in the territory of either party;

b. As soon as possible, and not later that three months from the exchange of the instruments of ratification of this treaty, to repeal all adverse or discriminatory references and expressions of hostility in their respective legislation;

c. To refrain in all government publications from any such reference or expressions;

d. To ensure mutual enjoyment by each other's citizens of due process of law within their respective legal systems and before their courts.

2. Article 1 (a) is without prejudice to the right to freedom of expression as contained in the International Covenant on Civil and Political Rights.

3. A joint committee shall be formed to examine incidents where one party claims there has been a violation of this article.

ARTICLE 12—COMBATING CRIME AND DRUGS

The parties will cooperate in combating crime, with an emphasis on smuggling, and will take all necessary measures to combat and prevent such activities as the production of, as well as the trafficking in illicit drugs, and will bring to trial perpetrators of such acts. In this regard, they take note of the understandings reached between them in the above spheres, as per Annex III and undertake to conclude all relevant agreements no later than nine months from the date of the exchange of the instruments of ratification of this treaty.

ARTICLE 13 — TRANSPORTATION AND ROADS

Taking note of the progress already made in the area of transportation, the parties recognize the mutuality of interest in good neighborly relations in the area of transportation and agree to the following means to promote relations between them in this sphere:

a. Each party will permit the free movement of nationals and vehicles of the other into and within its territory according to the general rules applicable to nationals and vehicles or other states. Neither party will impose discriminatory taxes or restrictions on the free movement of persons and vehicles from its territory to the territory of the other;

b. The parties will open and maintain roads and border-crossings between their countries and will consider further road and rail links between them;

c. The parties will continue their negotiations concerning mutual transportation agreements in the above and other areas, such as joint projects, traffic safety, transport standards and norms, licensing of vehicles, land passages, shipment of goods and cargo, and meteorology, to be concluded not later than six months from the exchange of the instruments of ratification of this treaty;

d. The parties agree to continue their negotiations for a highway to be constructed and maintained between Egypt, Israel, and Jordan near Eilat. . . .

ARTICLE 14 — FREEDOM OF NAVIGATION AND ACCESS TO PORTS

. . . 3. The parties consider the Strait of Tiran and the Gulf of Akaba to be international waterways open to all nations for unimpeded and non-suspendable freedom of navigation and overflight. The parties will respect each other's right to navigation and overflight for access to either party through the Strait of Tiran and the Gulf of Akaba.

ARTICLE 15 — CIVIL AVIATION

1. The parties recognize as applicable to each other the rights, privileges, and obligations provided for by the multilateral aviation agreements to which they are both party. . . .

ARTICLE 16 — POSTS AND TELECOMMUNICATIONS

The parties take note of the opening between them, in accordance with the Washington Declaration, of direct telephone and facsimile lines. Postal links, the negotiations on which having been concluded, will be activated upon the signature of this treaty. The parties further agree that normal wireless and cable communication and television relay services by cable, radio, and satellite, will be established between them, in accordance with all relevant international conventions and regulations. The negotiations on these subjects will be concluded not later than nine months from the exchange of the instruments of ratification of this treaty.

ARTICLE 17 — TOURISM

The parties affirm their mutual desire to promote cooperation between them in the field of tourism. . . .

ARTICLE 19 — ENERGY

1. The parties will cooperate in the development of energy resources, including the development of energy-related projects, such as the utilization of solar energy.

2. The parties, having concluded their negotiations on the interconnecting of their electric grids in the Eilat-Akaba area, will implement the interconnecting upon the signature of this treaty. The parties view this step as a part of a wider bi-national and regional concept. They agree to continue their negotiations as soon as possible to widen the scope of their interconnected grids. . . .

ARTICLE 20 — RIFT VALLEY DEVELOPMENT

The parties attach great importance to the integrated development of the Jordan Rift Valley area, including joint projects in the economic, environmental, energy-related, and tourism fields. Taking note of the terms of reference developed in the framework of the trilateral Israel-Jordan-US economic committee towards the Jordan Rift Valley Development Master Plan . . . they will vigorously continue their efforts towards the completion of planning and towards implementation. . . .

Israeli Prime Minister Yitzhak Rabin, PLO Chairman Yasir Arafat, and Israeli Foreign Minister Shimon Peres: Speeches Accepting the Nobel Peace Prize (December 10, 1994)

Israeli Prime Minister Yitzhak Rabin

At an age when most youngsters are struggling to unravel the secrets of mathematics and the mysteries of the Bible; at an age when first love blooms; at the tender age of sixteen, I was handed a rifle so that I could defend myself.

That was not my dream. I wanted to be a water engineer. I studied in an agricultural school and I thought being a water engineer was an important profession in the parched Middle East. I still think so today. However, I was compelled to resort to the gun.

I served in the military for decades. Under my responsibility, young men and women who wanted to live, wanted to love, went to their deaths instead. They fell in the defense of our lives.

In my current position, I have ample opportunity to fly over the State of Israel, and lately over other parts of the Middle East as well. The view from the plane is breathtaking: deep-blue seas and lakes, dark-green fields, dune-colored deserts, stone-gray mountains, and the entire countryside peppered with white-washed, red-roofed houses.

And also cemeteries. Graves as far as the eye can see. Hundreds of cemeteries in our part of the world, in the Middle East—in our home in Israel, but also in Egypt, in Syria, Jordan, Lebanon. From the plane's window, from the thousands of feet above them, the countless tombstones are silent. But the sound of their outcry has carried from the Middle East throughout the world for decades.

Standing here today, I wish to salute our loved ones—and past foes. I wish to salute all of them—the fallen of all the countries in all the wars; the members of their families who bear the enduring burden of bereavement; the disabled whose scars will never heal. Tonight, I wish to pay tribute to each and every one of them, for this important prize is theirs. . . .

Of all the memories I have stored up in my seventy-two years, what I shall remember most, to my last day, are the silences: The heavy silence of the moment after, and the terrifying silence of the moment before.

As a military man, as a commander, as a minister of defense, I ordered many military operations. And together with the joy of victory and the grief of bereavement, I shall always remember the moment just after taking such decisions: the hush as senior officers or cabinet ministers slowly rise from their seats; the sight of their receding backs; the sound of the closing door; and then the silence in which I remain alone.

That is the moment you grasp that as a result of the decision just made, people might go to their deaths. People from my nation, people from other nations. And they still don't know it.

At that hour, they are still laughing and weeping; still weaving plans and dreaming about love; still musing about planting a garden or building a house—and they have no idea these are their last hours on earth. Which of them is fated to die? Whose picture will appear in the black frame in tomorrow's newspaper? Whose mother will soon be in mourning? Whose world will crumble under the weight of the loss?

As a former military man, I will also forever remember the silence of the moment before: the hush when the hands of the clock seem to be spinning forward, when time is running out and in another hour, another minute, the inferno will erupt.

In that moment of great tension just before the finger pulls the trigger, just before the fuse begins to burn; in the terrible quiet of the moment, there is still time to wonder, to wonder alone: Is it really imperative to act? Is there no other choice? No other way?

"God takes pity on kindergartners," wrote the poet Yehudah Amichai, who is here with us this evening—and I quote his:

"God takes pity on kindergartners, Less so on the schoolchildren, And will no longer pity their elders, Leaving them to their own, And sometimes they will have to crawl on all fours, Through the burning sand, To reach the casualty station, Bleeding."

For decades, God has not taken pity on the kindergartners in the Middle East, or the schoolchildren, or their elders. There has been no pity in the Middle East for generations.

I was a young man who has now grown fully in years. And of all the memories I have stored up in my seventy-two years, I now recall the hopes.

Our people have chosen us to give them life. Terrible as it is to say, their lives are in our hands. Tonight, their eyes are upon us and their hearts are asking: How is the power vested in these men and women being used? What will they decide? Into what kind of morning will we rise tomorrow? A day of peace? Of war? Of laughter? Of tears?

A child is born in an utterly undemocratic way. He cannot choose his father and mother. He cannot pick his sex or color, his religion, nationality or homeland. Whether he is born in a manor or a manger, whether he lives under a despotic or democratic regime is not his choice. From the moment he comes, close-fisted, into the world, his fate—to a large extent—is decided by his nation's leaders. It is they who will decide whether he lives in comfort or in despair, in security or in fear. His fate is given to us to resolve—to the governments of countries, democratic or otherwise.

Just as no two fingerprints are identical, so no two people are alike, and every country has its own laws and culture, traditions and leaders. But there is one universal message which can embrace the entire world, one precept which can be common to different regimes, to races which bear no resemblance, to cultures that are alien to each other.

It is a message which the Jewish people has carried for thousands of years, the message found in the Book of Books: "Therefore take good heed of yourselves"—or, in contemporary terms, the message of the sanctity of life.

The leaders of nations must provide their peoples with the conditions—the infrastructure, if you will—which enables them to enjoy life: freedom of speech and movement; food and shelter; and most important of all: life itself. A man cannot enjoy his rights if he is not alive. And so every country must protect and preserve the key element in its national ethos: the lives of its citizens.

Only to defend those lives, we can call upon our citizens to enlist in the army. And to defend the lives of our citizens serving in the army, we invest huge sums in planes and tanks, and other means. Yet despite it all, we fail to protect the lives of our citizens and soldiers. Military cemeteries in every corner of the world are silent testimony to the failure of national leaders to sanctify human life.

There is only one radical means for sanctifying human life. The one radical solution is a real peace.

The profession of soldiering embraces a certain paradox. We take the best and the bravest of our young men into the army. We supply them with equipment which costs a virtual fortune. We rigorously train them for the day when they must do their duty—and we expect them to do it well. Yet we fervently pray that that day will never come—that the planes will never take off, the tanks will never move forward, the soldiers will never mount the attacks for which they have been trained so well.

We pray that it will never happen, because of the sanctity of life.

History as a whole, and modern history in particular, has known harrowing times when national leaders turned their citizens into cannon fodder in the name of wicked doctrines: vicious Fascism, terrible Nazism. Pictures of children marching to slaughter, photos of terrified women at the gates of the crematoria must loom before the eyes of every leader in our generation, and the generations to come. They must serve as a warning to all who wield power.

Almost all regimes which did not place the sanctity of life at the heart of their worldview, all those regimes have collapsed and are no more. You can see it for yourselves in our own time.

Yet this is not the whole picture. To preserve the sanctity of life, we must sometimes risk it. Sometimes there is no other way to defend our citizens than to fight for their lives, for their safety and freedom. This is the creed of every democratic state.

In the State of Israel, from which I come today; in the Israel Defense Forces, which I have had the privilege to serve, we have always viewed the sanctity of life as a supreme value. We have never gone to war unless a war was forced on us.

The history of the State of Israel, the annals of the Israel Defense Forces, are filled with thousands of stories of soldiers who sacrificed themselves—who died while trying to save wounded comrades; who gave their lives to avoid causing harm to innocent people on their enemy's side.

In the coming days, a special commission of the Israel Defense Forces will finish drafting a Code of Conduct for our soldiers. The formulation regarding human life will read as follows, and I quote:

"In recognition of its supreme importance, the soldier will preserve human life in every way possible and endanger himself, or others, only to the extent deemed necessary to fulfill this mission.

"The sanctity of life, in the point of view of the soldiers of the Israel Defense Forces, will find expression in all their actions."

For many years ahead—even if wars come to an end, after peace comes to our land—these words will remain a pillar of fire which goes before our camp, a guiding light for our people. And we take pride in that.

We are in the midst of building the peace. The architects and the engineers of this enterprise are engaged in their work even as we gather here tonight, building the peace, layer by layer, brick by brick. The job is difficult, complex, trying. Mistakes could topple the whole structure and bring disaster down upon us.

And so we are determined to do the job well—despite the toll of murderous terrorism, despite the fanatic and cruel enemies of peace.

We will pursue the course of peace with determination and fortitude. We will not let up. We will not give in. Peace will triumph over all its enemies, because the alternative is grimmer for us all. And we will prevail.

We will prevail because we regard the building of peace as a great blessing for us, for our children after us. We regard it as a blessing for our neighbors on all sides, and for our partners in this enterprise—the United States, Russia, Norway—which did so much to bring the agreement that was signed here, later on in Washington, later on in Cairo, that wrote a beginning of the solution to the longest and most difficult part of the Arab-Israeli conflict: the Palestinian-Israeli one. We thank others who have contributed to it, too.

We wake up every morning, now, as different people. Peace is possible. We see the hope in our children's eyes. We see the light in our soldiers' faces, in the streets, in the buses, in the fields. We must not let them down. We will not let them down.

I stand here not alone today, on this small rostrum in Oslo. I am here to speak in the name of generations of Israelis and Jews, of the shepherds of

Israel—and you know that King David was a shepherd; he started to build Jerusalem about 3,000 years ago—the herdsmen and dressers of sycamore trees, and as the Prophet Amos was; of the rebels against the establishment, as the Prophet Jeremiah was; and of men who went down to the sea, like the Prophet Jonah.

I am here to speak in the name of the poets and of those who dreamed of an end to war, like the Prophet Isaiah.

I am also here to speak in the names of sons of the Jewish people like Albert Einstein and Baruch Spinoza, like Maimonides, Sigmund Freud and Franz Kafka.

And I am the emissary of millions who perished in the Holocaust, among whom were surely many Einsteins and Freuds who were lost to us, and to humanity, in the flames of the crematoria.

I am here as the emissary of Jerusalem, at whose gates I fought in the days of siege; Jerusalem which has always been, and is today, the eternal capital of the State of Israel and the heart of the Jewish people, who pray toward Jerusalem three times a day.

And I am also the emissary of the children who drew their visions of peace; and of the immigrants from St. Petersburg and Addis Ababa.

I stand here mainly for the generations to come, so that we may all be deemed worthy of the medal which you have bestowed on me and my colleagues today.

I stand here as the emissary today—if they will allow me—of our neighbors who were our enemies. I stand here as the emissary of the soaring hopes of a people which has endured the worst that history has to offer and nevertheless made its mark—not just on the chronicles of the Jewish people but on all mankind.

With me here are five million citizens of Israel—Jews, Arabs, Druze and Circassians—five million hearts beating for peace, and five million pairs of eyes which look at us with such great expectations for peace.

I wish to thank, first and foremost, those citizens of the State of Israel, of all the generations, of all the political persuasions, whose sacrifices and relentless struggle for peace bring us steadier closer to our goal.

I wish to thank our partners—the Egyptians, the Jordanians, and the Palestinians, that are led by the Chairman of the Palestinian Liberation Organization, Mr. Yasir Arafat, with whom we share this Nobel Prize—who have chosen the path of peace and are writing a new page in the annals of the Middle East.

I wish to thank the members of the Israeli government, but above all my partner the Foreign Minister, Mr. Shimon Peres, whose energy and devotion to the cause of peace are an example to us all. . . .

Allow me to close by sharing with you a traditional Jewish blessing which has been recited by my people, in good times and bad ones, as a token of their deepest longing:

"The Lord will give strength to his people; the Lord will bless his people—and all of us—in peace."

PLO Chairman Yasir Arafat

In the name of God, the merciful, the compassionate. "But if the enemy incline toward peace, do thou also incline toward peace, and trust in God." [Koranic quotation]

Since my people entrusted me with the hard task of searching for our lost home, I have been filled with warm faith that those who carried their keys in the diaspora as they carry their own limbs, and that those who endured their wounds in the homeland and maintained their identity will be rewarded by return and freedom for their sacrifices. I have also been filled with faith that the arduous trek on the long path of pain will end in our home's yard.

As we celebrate together the first sight of the crescent of peace, I, at this podium stare into the open eyes of the martyrs within my conscience. They ask me about the national soil and their vacant seats there. I conceal my tears from them and tell them: How true you were; your generous blood has enabled us to see the holy land and to take our first steps in a difficult battle, the battle of peace, the peace of the brave.

As we celebrate together, we invoke the powers of creativity within us to reconstruct a home destroyed by war, a home overlooking our neighbor's, where our children will play with their children and will compete in picking flowers. Now, I have a sense of national and human pride in my Palestinian Arab people's patience and sacrifice, through which they have established an uninterrupted link between the homeland, history and the people, adding to the old legends of the homeland an epic of hope. For them, for the children of those good-natured and tough people, who are made of oaks and dews, of fire and sweat, I present this Nobel Prize, which I will carry to our children, who have a promise of freedom, security and safety in a homeland not threatened by an invader from outside or an exploiter from inside.

I know that this highly indicative prize has not been granted to me and my partners, Israel's Prime Minister Yitzhak Rabin and Foreign Minister Shimon Peres, to crown a mission that we have fulfilled, but to encourage us to complete a path which we have started with larger strides, deeper awareness, and more honest intentions. This is so we can transfer the option of peace, the peace of the brave, from words on paper to practices on the ground, and so we will be worthy of carrying the message that both our peoples and the world and human conscience have asked us to carry. Like their Arab brethren, the Palestinians, whose cause is the guardian of the gate of the Arab-Israeli peace, are looking forward to a comprehensive, just, and durable peace on the basis of land for peace and compliance with international legitimacy and its resolutions.

Peace, to us, is a value and an interest. Peace is an absolute human value which will help man develop his humanity with freedom that cannot be limited by regional, religious, or national restrictions. It restores to the Arab-Jewish relationship its innocent nature and gives the Arab conscience the opportunity to express—through absolute human terms—its understanding of the European tragedy of the Jews. It also gives the Jewish conscience the opportunity to express the suffering of the Palestinian peoples which resulted from this historical intersection and to find an echo for this suffering in the pained Jewish soul. The pained people are more capable than others of understanding the suffering of other people.

Peace is an interest because, in an atmosphere of just peace, the Palestinian people will be able to achieve their ambitions for independence and sovereignty, to develop their national and cultural existence through relations of good neighborliness, mutual respect, and cooperation with the Israeli people. Peace will enable the Israeli people to define their Middle East identity and to enjoy economic and cultural openness toward their Arab neighbors, who are eager to develop their region, which was kept by the long war from finding its real position in today's world in an atmosphere of democracy, pluralism, and prosperity.

As war is an adventure, peace is also a challenge and a gamble. If we do not fortify peace to stand against storms and wind, and if we do not support it and strengthen it, the gamble will then be exposed to blackmail, perhaps to fall. Therefore, I call on my partners in peace on this high platform to expedite the peace process, achieve early withdrawal, pave the road for elections, and to move to the second stage in record time, so that peace will grow and become a firm reality.

We have started the peace process based on land for peace, on UN Resolutions 242 and 338, and on the other international resolutions calling for achieving the legitimate rights of the Palestinian people. While the peace process has not yet reached its target, the new atmosphere of confidence and the modest achievements of the first and second year of the peace process are promising. Therefore, the parties are urged to abandon their reservations, facilitate measures, and achieve the remaining goals, foremost of which are transferring powers and taking steps toward an Israeli withdrawal in the West Bank and the settlements. This will finally lead to a comprehensive withdrawal and will enable our society to build its infrastructure and utilize its status, heritage, knowledge, and awareness to formulate our new world.

In this context, I call on Russia and the United States, sponsors of the peace process, to accelerate the steps of this process, to take part in its formulation and to overcome its obstacles. I urge Norway and Egypt, in their capacity as hosts to the Palestinian-Israeli agreement, to continue their good initiative, which started from Oslo and reached Washington and Cairo. Oslo, as well as the names of the other states that have been hosting the multilateral talks, will remain shining names linked to the peace of the courageous. I also urge all countries, foremost of which are the donor countries, to make their contributions quickly to enable the Palestinian people to overcome their economic and social problems, to rebuild themselves and to establish their infrastructure. Peace cannot grow and the peace process cannot be entrenched unless their necessary material conditions are met.

I then urge my partners in peace to view the peace process in a comprehensive and strategic way. Confidence alone cannot make peace, but only recognizing the rights, together with confidence, can make peace. Encroaching on rights generates a sense of injustice, keeps the fire under the ashes, and will push peace to a dangerous point and toward quicksand that may destroy it. We view peace as a strategic option, rather than a tactical option influenced by temporary calculations of loss and profit. The peace process is not only a political one, but also an integrated process in which national awareness and economic, scientific, and technological development play an important role. The interaction of cultural, social, and creative elements also play basic roles in strengthening the peace process.

I view all this as I recall the difficult peace march, in which we have covered only a short distance. We should have courage and move as far as possible to cover the greater distance based on just and comprehensive peace and to absorb the strength of creativity which is contained in the deeper lesson of peace.

As long as we have decided to coexist and live in peace, then we should coexist on a solid basis that can last through all time and that is acceptable to the future generations. In this context, full withdrawal from the West Bank and the Gaza Strip requires deep discussions about the settlements that cut through geographic and political unity, prevent free movement between the areas of the West Bank and the Strip, and create hotbeds of tension that conflict with the spirit of peace, which we want to be free of anything that spoils its purity.

As for Jerusalem, it is the spiritual home of Christians, Muslims, and Jews. To Palestinians, it is the city of cities. The Jewish shrines in the city are our shrines, the same as the Islamic and Christian shrines. So let us make Jerusalem an international symbol of this spiritual harmony, this cultural brightness, and this religious heritage of humanity as a whole.

There is an urgent task that activates the peace mechanism and enables it to overcome the problem that is troubling hearts, the question of prisoners. It is important to release them so smiles can return to their children, their mothers, and their wives. Let us together protect this little baby from the winter's winds, and let us provide it with the milk and honey it deserves in the land of milk and honey in the land of Salim, Ibrahim, Isma'il, and Ishaq—the holy land, the land of peace.

Finally, I again congratulate my partners in peace—Israeli Prime Minister Yitzhak Rabin and Israeli Foreign Minister Simon Peres—for winning the Nobel Peace Prize. . . . I emphasize to you that we will discover ourselves through peace more than we did through confrontation and conflict. I am certain that Israelis will find themselves through peace more than they did in war.

Glory to God in the highest, and on Earth peace, and good will toward men.

Israeli Foreign Minister Shimon Pères

I am pleased to be receiving this prize together with Yitzhak Rabin, with whom I have labored for long years for the defense of our country and with whom I now labor together in the cause of peace in our region. This is a salute to his daring leadership.

I believe it is fitting that the prize has been awarded to Yasir Arafat. His quitting the path of confrontation in favor of the path of dialogue has opened the way to peace between ourselves and the Palestinian people, to whom we wish all the best in the future. . . .

From my earliest youth, I have known that while obliged to plan with care the stages of our journey, we are entitled to dream, and keep dreaming, of its destination. A man may feel as old as his years, yet as young as his dreams. The laws of biology do not apply to sanguine aspiration.

I was born in a small Jewish town in White Russia. Nothing Jewish remains of it. From my youngest childhood, I related to my place of birth as a mere way station. My family's dream, and my own, was to live in Israel, and our voyage to the port of Jaffa was a dream that came true. Had it not been for this dream and this voyage, I would probably have perished in the flames, as did so many of my people, among them most of my own family.

I went to school at an agricultural youth village in the heart of Israel. The village and its fields were enclosed by barbed wire which separated their greenness from the bleakness of the enmity all around. In the morning, we would go out to the fields with scythes on our backs to harvest the crop. In the evening, we went out with rifles on our shoulders to defend our lives. On Shabbat we would go out to visit our Arab neighbors. On Shabbat, we would talk with them of peace, though the rest of the week we traded rifle fire across the darkness!

From the Ben Shemen Youth village, my comrades and I went to Kibbutz Alumot in the Lower Galilee. We had no houses, no electricity, no running water. But we had a magnificent view and a lofty dream: to build a new, egalitarian society that would ennoble each of its members.

Not all of it came true, but not all of it went to waste. The part that came true created a new landscape. The part that did not come true resides in our hearts to this very day.

For two decades, in the Ministry of Defense, I was privileged to work closely with a man who was and remains, to my mind, the greatest Jew of our time. From him I learned that the vision of the future should shape the agenda for the present; that you can overcome obstacles by dint of faith; that you may feel disappointed—but never despair. And above all, I learned that the wisest consideration is the moral one. David Ben-Gurion has passed away, yet his vision continues to flourish: to be a singular people, to live at peace with our neighbors.

The wars we fought were forced upon us. Thanks to the Israel Defence Forces, we won them all, but we did not win the greatest victory that we aspired to: release from the need to win victories.

We proved that aggressors do not necessarily emerge as the victors, but we learned that victors do not necessarily win peace.

It is no wonder that war, as a method of conducting human affairs, is in its death throes, and that the time has come to bury it.

The sword, as the Bible teaches us, consumes flesh, but it cannot provide sustenance. It is not rifles but people who triumph, and the conclusion from all the wars is that we need better people, not better rifles—to avoid wars, to win peace.

There was a time when war was fought for lack of choice. Today peace is the "no-choice" option for all of us. The reasons for this are profound and incontrovertible. The sources of material wealth and political power have changed. No longer are they determined by the size of territory won by war. Today they are a consequence of intellectual potential, obtained principally by education.

Israel, essentially a desert country, has achieved remarkable agricultural yields by applying science to its fields, without expanding its territory or its water resources.

Science must be learned; it cannot be conquered. An army that can occupy knowledge has yet to be built. And that is why armies of occupation are passé. Indeed, even for the defense of the country you cannot rely on the army alone. Territorial frontiers are no obstacle to ballistic missiles, and no weapon can shield a nation from a nuclear device. Today, the battle for survival must be based on political wisdom and moral vision no less than on military might.

Science, technology, information are—for better or for worse—universal, not national. They are universally available. Their availability is not contingent on color of skin or place of birth. Past distinctions between West and East, North and South, have lost their importance in the face of a new distinction: between those who move ahead in pace with new opportunities, and those who lag behind.

Countries used to divide the world into their friends and foes. No longer.

The foes now are universal—poverty, famine, religious radicalization, desertification, drugs, proliferation of nuclear weapons, ecological devastation. They threaten all nations, just as science and information are the potential friends of all nations.

Classical diplomacy and strategy were aimed at identifying enemies and confronting them. Now they have to identify dangers, global and local, to tackle them before they become disasters.

As we leave a world of enemies, as we enter a world of dangers, the future wars which may break out will not be, probably, the wars of the strong against the weak for conquest, but the wars of the weak against the strong for protest.

The Middle East must never lose pride in having been the cradle of civilization. But though living in the cradle, we cannot remain infants forever.

Today as in my youth, I carry dreams. I would mention two: the future of the Jewish people and the future of the Middle East.

In history, Judaism has been far more successful than the Jews themselves. The Jewish people remained small, but the spirit of Jerusalem—the capital of Jewish life, the city holy and open to all religions—went from strength to strength. The Bible is to be found in hundreds of millions of homes. The moral majesty of the Book of Books has been undefeated by the ups and downs of history.

Moreover, time and again, history has succumbed to the Bible's immortal ideas. The message that the one, invisible God created man in His image, and hence there are no higher and lower orders of man, has fused with the realization that morality is the highest form of wisdom and, perhaps, of beauty and courage, too.

Slings, arrows, gas chambers can annihilate man, but they cannot destroy human values, the dignity and freedom of the human being.

Jewish history presents an encouraging lesson for mankind. For nearly four thousand years, a small nation carried a great message. Initially, the nation dwelt in its own land; later, it wandered in exile. This small nation swam against the tide and was repeatedly persecuted, banished, downtrodden. There is no other example in all history—neither among the great empires nor among their colonies and dependencies—of a nation, after so long a saga of tragedy and misfortune, rising up again, shaking itself free, gathering together its dispersed remnants, and setting out anew on its national adventure. Defeating doubters within and enemies without. Reviving its land and its language. Rebuilding its identity, and reaching toward new heights of distinction and excellence.

The message of the Jewish people to mankind is that faith and moral vision can triumph over all adversity.

The conflicts shaping up as our century nears its close will be over the content of civilization, not over territory. Jewish culture has lived over many centuries; now it has taken root again in its own soil. For the first time in our history, some five million people speak Hebrew as their native language. That is both a lot and a little: a lot, because there have never been so many Hebrew-speaking people; but a little, because a culture based on five million people can hardly withstand the pervasive, corrosive effect of the global television culture.

In the five decades of Israel's existence, our efforts have focused on re-establishing our territorial center. In the future, we shall have to devote our main effort to strengthen our spiritual center. Judaism—or Jewishness—is a fusion of belief, history, land, and language. Being Jewish means to belong to a people that is both unique and universal. My greatest hope is that our children, like our forefathers, will not make do with the transient and the sham, but will continue to plow the historic Jewish furrow in the fields of human spirit, that Israel will become the center of our heritage, not merely a homeland for our people; that the Jewish people will be inspired by others, but at the same be to them a source of inspiration.

The second dream is about the Middle East. In the Middle East most people are impoverished and wretched. A new scale of priorities is needed, with weapons on the bottom and regional market economy at the top. Most inhabitants of the region—more than sixty percent—are under the age of eighteen. The Middle East is a huge kindergarten, a huge school. A new future can be and should be offered to them. Israel has computerized its education and has achieved excellent results. Education can be computerized throughout the Middle East, allowing young people, Arabs and others, to progress not just from grade to grade but from generation to generation.

Israel's role in the Middle East should be to contribute to a great, sustained regional revival:

A Middle East without wars, without enemies, without ballistic missiles, without nuclear warheads.

A Middle East in which men, goods and services can move freely without the need for customs clearance or police licenses.

A Middle East in which every believer will be free to pray in his own language—Arabic, Hebrew, Latin, or whatever language he chooses—and in which the prayers will reach their destination without censorship, without interference, and without offending anyone.

A Middle East in which nations strive for economic equality and encourage cultural pluralism.

A Middle East where young men and women can attain university education. A Middle East where living standards are in no way inferior to those in the world's most advanced countries—may I say, a Middle East very much like Scandinavia.

A Middle East where waters flow to slake thirst, to make crops grow and deserts bloom, in which no hostile borders bring death, hunger, despair, or shame.

A Middle East of competition, not of domination. A Middle East in which men are each other's hosts, not hostages.

A Middle East that is not a killing field, but a field of creativity and growth.

A Middle East that honors so much its history, that it strives to add to it new noble chapters.

A Middle East which will serve as a spiritual and cultural focal point for the entire world.

While thanking you, for the Prize, thanking the many people in uniform and civil dress in many nations, for arriving to this moment of happiness and hope, I believe that all of us remain committed to the process. I thank my family, that stood behind me for such a long journey, and are convinced as I am that this is the best option.

We have reached the age where dialogue is really the only way to run the world.

Sufyan Abu-Zayidah: Interview
(January 27, 1995)*

[Levitzky]: People here in Gaza were seen rejoicing after the terrorist attack. This kind of behavior by your people is unacceptable and quite simply denies them the right to consider themselves part of the human race.

[Abu-Zayidah]: I did not see any rejoicing. But let us say that some of the people here were not particularly upset. This is because the Palestinian people do not feel that the Israelis are giving them anything in return. Neither territory nor honor. The Palestinians are bitterly disappointed. There has been no improvement in their economic and social well-being.

If you were to ask any Palestinian immediately after the agreement, he would have told you that the war between our peoples is over. Now he realizes that nothing has really changed. Except for the abolishment of the night curfew and your army's withdrawal from the refugee camps, nothing has changed. The Palestinians in the Gaza Strip are asking what kind of peace is this, with 5,000 settlers controlling 25 percent of the land. What kind of logic dictates that 20 families from Netzarim should control a larger slice of territory than all of Jabalyah, with its 80,000 residents. The Palestinian refugees know they are living in the most crowded place on earth, while 20 settler families are ensconced in luxury a few meters away. I cannot understand why Rabin does not remove Netzarim. What is this stupidity?

[Levitzky]: I think you have gone too far this time. Even a moderate man like Ezer Weizman, who supports reaching an arrangement, has

*Yediot Ahronof January 27, 1995; FBIS January 30, 1995.

called for a suspension of the process. This should be viewed as a serious warning.

[Abu-Zayidah]: Not only Ezer Weizman. I, too, sometimes have doubts about the process. The problem begins with Oslo. The fact that Israelis and Palestinians met in such a secret fashion in Oslo gave the impression that just by sitting down together, we had already made the required concessions, and now everything would work out. But this was followed by all the mistakes in the world.

[Levitzky]: How, then, can we totally eliminate this hatred?

[Abu-Zayidah]: In the past, I thought that Israelis, or at least the majority of them, were thinking straight and did not hate us. I believed that most of your public understood the situation. Apparently, I must have been wrong. Despite the Oslo agreement, most Israelis still think that the Palestinians as a people do not deserve the same rights as them.

The majority of Israelis think that whatever the Palestinians get is a privilege. It reminds me of prison. That is how relations between the guards and prisoners work. If you behave nicely, you will get half of the Gaza Strip. If you behave even better, we will let you have all of the Gaza Strip. What is this? Is it impossible for you to understand that the Palestinian people have a right to their own state, flag, and passport.

The Israelis see all of us as construction workers, dishwashers, and street cleaners in Tel Aviv and Jerusalem. You consider us an inferior people. We are prepared to reach a compromise with you. Most of the Palestinian people are ready to accept a Palestinian state alongside with Israel. How much more blood must be spilled before Israel accepts such a compromise?

[Levitzky]: You Palestinians are shooting yourselves in the foot. Why not learn from Israel's history? Why does Arafat not follow Ben-Gurion's example? You were given a one-time opportunity, and you are wasting it. You cannot get everything at once.

[Abu-Zayidah]: We are not Israel, and Arafat is not Ben-Gurion. You were given a state; we were granted limited autonomy over part of the land. I agree that we had an opportunity to achieve something and that we have occasionally supplied you with excuses to delay the process and to avoid implementing subsequent stages of the agreement.

We also tell *Fatah* members who have reservations about the process that violence will get us nowhere. We tell them that it only exacerbates hatred between our two peoples. We opted for the way of peace and must stick to it. There is no other choice. We constantly say the same thing to Hamas and the Islamic Jihad. We really want to stop the cycle of hatred and bloodshed.

[Levitzky]: You say that to Hamas and the Islamic Jihad? That is really a laugh. These are not the kind of people you can just talk to. Bassam Abu-

Sharif told [Israel television's Arab affairs correspondent] Ehud Ya'ari that these organizations should be outlawed.

[Abu-Zayidah]: Abu-Sharif should stop shooting his mouth off. What law is he talking about? Does he not know that we have no constitution and no laws? There are not even regulations. We have failed to formulate any rules of behavior here. We are having a hard time making the transition from an underground movement to the building of national institutions. Here in Gaza, we still act as though we were in Lebanon.

[Levitzky]: You sound very disappointed in Arafat. So are we. He does not talk to us, convince us, or take any steps to win the confidence of the Israeli public. What is the matter with him?

[Abu-Zayidah]: I am very disappointed by our inability to create the basis for our future state. Arafat busies himself with small details, which he should not be handling. He should not be issuing building permits for another house or floor. He should not be holding meetings with all and sundry. He is having a bad influence on the behavior of his ministers. He constantly interferes with their work and the work of the senior bureaucracy.

I agree with you that some of those who came from Tunis do not understand the Israelis. The gap is too wide; they do not understand the dynamics or what the Israelis are feeling. This poses a big problem for me and my friends from *Fatah*, who operate in the field. We keep on trying to persuade Arafat to speak to the Israeli public and build trust between the two peoples. So far, we have been unsuccessful.

[Levitzky]: But you, the field operatives, can do something. Where is the Palestinian equivalent of Peace Now? Why did you not demonstrate in the street against the Bet Lid murders? We demonstrated against Sabra and Shatila.

[Abu-Zayidah]: The entire *Fatah* organization is basically Peace Now. Our "Peace Now" is the governing authority. You do not understand what is holding the Palestinians back. The people still feel that you are stepping on their necks and trampling their honor. Although a lot of people told me they were shocked by the Bet Lid murders, the day when we can stage such demonstrations is still a long way off. I wish we could, but this is the result of the harsh reality in which we live.

[Levitzky]: In the end, you will bring about the downfall of Rabin, the man who was willing to sit down and negotiate with you. You will get Binyamin Netanyahu instead. What will happen then?

[Abu-Zayidah]: I am not so certain that it would really be so bad if Rabin were replaced by Netanyahu. What will Netanyahu do? Will he refuse to meet with Arafat? Will he revoke the agreement? Will he reenter the Gaza Strip? . . . If Rabin falls, it is because he did not know how to explain to the Israeli public that full Peace demands concessions. Rabin and the

Labor Party cannot go farther than they have come today. This is the most the Israeli public will allow them. When the Likud experiences a few bombings in central Israel, then the Israeli people will ask it what it is doing to guarantee security and why it is not stopping the attacks. What has Israel conceded in this agreement? You make me laugh. So you gave up the Gaza Strip. What a pity. You should have stayed here and eaten shit with us.

[Levitzky]: If Arafat would take the steps required of a leader, calm down the street, and talk to the Palestinian public about reconciliation, then maybe things would be different.

[Abu-Zayidah]: No soothing words will do the trick here. Even if Arafat spoke about reconciliation, his words would be meaningless. There are hundreds of Palestinians in prison. True, they are accused of killing Israelis. They have been imprisoned for 10 or 20 years. But Arafat dispatched them. They remain in prison today, although they support peace. They have thousands of relatives. Can you not understand how destructive this is?

I recognize the fact that we Palestinians are not implementing any confidence-building measures. I would like us to do more, but you Israelis still behave like conquerors, and it is difficult. Approximately 45 days ago, I visited male and female prisoners at a prison in the central part of the West Bank. Believe me, I left frustrated. I felt so small, a member of the PA, sitting opposite female Palestinian prisoners and talking to them about peace.

Then I went to see the male prisoners. They were my reception committee in the prison. They are in prison, and I come in a suit and tie. How can you talk about reconciliation like this? You ask us to forgive all your soldiers, pilots, and officers, who have so much blood on their hands that it reaches their neck. You ask us to pardon them, while you refuse to forgive Palestinians who fought you and have blood on their hands.

Israeli and Palestinian Authority: Interim Agreement on the West Bank and Gaza Strip (September 28, 1995)

PREAMBLE

The Government of the State of Israel and the Palestine Liberation Organization (hereinafter "the PLO"), the representative of the Palestinian people.

Within the framework of the Middle East peace process initiated at Madrid in October 1991;

Reaffirming their determination to put an end to decades of confrontation and to live in peaceful coexistence, mutual dignity and security, while recognizing their mutual legitimate and political rights;

Reaffirming their desire to achieve a just, lasting and comprehensive peace settlement and historic reconciliation through the agreed political process;

Recognizing that the peace process and the new era that it has created, as well as the new relationship established between the two Parties as described above, are irreversible, and the determination of the two Parties to maintain, sustain and continue the peace process;

Recognizing that the aim of the Israel-Palestinian negotiations within the current Middle East peace process is, among other things, to establish a Palestinian Interim Self-Government Authority, i.e. the elected Council (hereinafter "the Council" or "the Palestinian Council"), and the elected Ra'ees of the Executive Authority; for the Palestinian people in the West Bank and the Gaza Strip, for a transitional period not exceeding five years from the date of signing the Agreement on the Gaza Strip and the Jericho Area (hereinafter "the Gaza-Jericho Agreement") on May 4, 1994, leading to a permanent settlement based on Security Council Resolutions 242 and 338;

Reaffirming their understanding that the interim self-government arrangements contained in this Agreement are an integral part of the whole peace process, that the negotiations on the permanent status, that will start as soon as possible but not later than May 4, 1996, will lead to the implementation of Security Council Resolutions 242 and 338, and that the Interim Agreement shall settle all the issues of the interim period and that no such issues will be deferred to the agenda of the permanent status negotiations;

Reaffirming their adherence to the mutual recognition and commitments expressed in the letters dated September 9, 1993, signed by and exchanged between the Prime Minister of Israel and the Chairman of the PLO;

Desirous of putting into effect the Declaration of Principles on Interim Self-Government Arrangements signed at Washington, D.C. on September 13, 1993, and the Agreed Minutes thereto (hereinafter "the DOP") and in particular Article III and Annex I concerning the holding of direct, free and general political elections for the Council and the Ra'ees of the Executive Authority in order that the Palestinian people in the West Bank, Jerusalem and the Gaza Strip may democratically elect accountable representatives;

Recognizing that these elections will constitute a significant interim preparatory step toward the realization of the legitimate rights of the Palestinian people and their just requirements and will provide a democratic basis for the establishment of Palestinian institutions;

Reaffirming their mutual commitment to act, in accordance with this

Agreement, immediately, efficiently and effectively against acts or threats of terrorism, violence or incitement, whether committed by Palestinians or Israelis;

Following the Gaza-Jericho Agreement; the Agreement on Preparatory Transfer of Powers and Responsibilities signed at Erez on August 29, 1994 (hereinafter "the Preparatory Transfer Agreement"); and the Protocol on Further Transfer of Powers and Responsibilities signed at Cairo on August 27, 1995 (hereinafter "the Further Transfer Protocol"); which three agreements will be superseded by this Agreement;

Hereby agree as follows:

CHAPTER I—THE COUNCIL

Article I—Transfer of Authority

1. Israel shall transfer powers and responsibilities as specified in this Agreement from the Israeli military government and its Civil Administration to the Council in accordance with this Agreement. Israel shall continue to exercise powers and responsibilities not so transferred.

2. Pending the inauguration of the Council, the powers and responsibilities transferred to the Council shall be exercised by the Palestinian Authority established in accordance with the Gaza-Jericho Agreement, which shall also have all the rights, liabilities and obligations to be assumed by the Council in this regard. Accordingly, the term "Council" throughout this Agreement shall, pending the inauguration of the Council, be construed as meaning the Palestinian Authority.

3. The transfer of powers and responsibilities to the police force established by the Palestinian Council in accordance with Article XIV below (hereinafter "the Palestinian Police") shall be accomplished in a phased manner, as detailed in this Agreement and in the Protocol concerning Redeployment and Security Arrangements attached as Annex I to this Agreement (hereinafter "Annex I").

4. As regards the transfer and assumption of authority in civil spheres, powers and responsibilities shall be transferred and assumed as set out in the Protocol Concerning Civil Affairs attached as Annex III to this Agreement (hereinafter "Annex III").

5. After the inauguration of the Council, the Civil Administration in the West Bank will be dissolved, and the Israeli military government shall be withdrawn. The withdrawal of the military government shall not prevent it from exercising the powers and responsibilities not transferred to the Council.

6. A Joint Civil Affairs Coordination and Cooperation Committee (hereinafter "the CAC"), Joint Regional Civil Affairs Subcommittees, one for the Gaza Strip and the other for the West Bank, and District Civil Liaison Offices in the West Bank shall be established in order to provide for coor-

dination and cooperation in civil affairs between the Council and Israel, as detailed in Annex III.

7. The offices of the Council, and the offices of its Ra'ees and its Executive Authority and other committees, shall be located in areas under Palestinian territorial jurisdiction in the West Bank and the Gaza Strip.

Article II—Elections

1. In order that the Palestinian people of the West Bank and the Gaza Strip may govern themselves according to democratic principles, direct, free and general political elections will be held for the Council and the Ra'ees of the Executive Authority of the Council in accordance with the provisions set out in the Protocol concerning Elections attached as Annex II to this Agreement (hereinafter "Annex II").

2. These elections will constitute a significant interim preparatory step towards the realization of the legitimate rights of the Palestinian people and their just requirements and will provide a democratic basis for the establishment of Palestinian institutions.

3. Palestinians of Jerusalem who live there may participate in the election process in accordance with the provisions contained in this Article and in Article VI of Annex II (Election Arrangements concerning Jerusalem).

4. The elections shall be called by the Chairman of the Palestinian Authority immediately following the signing of this Agreement to take place at the earliest practicable date following the redeployment of Israeli forces in accordance with Annex I, and consistent with the requirements of the election timetable as provided in Annex II, the Election Law and the Election Regulations, as defined in Article I of Annex II.

Article III—Structure of the Palestinian Council

1. The Palestinian Council and the Ra'ees of the Executive Authority of the Council constitute the Palestinian Interim Self-Government Authority, which will be elected by the Palestinian people of the West Bank, Jerusalem and the Gaza Strip for the transitional period agreed in Article I of the DOP.

2. The Council shall possess both legislative power and executive power, in accordance with Articles VII and IX of the DOP. The Council shall carry out and be responsible for all the legislative and executive powers and responsibilities transferred to it under this Agreement. The exercise of legislative powers shall be in accordance with Article XVIII of this Agreement (Legislative Powers of the Council).

3. The Council and the Ra'ees of the Executive Authority of the Council shall be directly and simultaneously elected by the Palestinian people of the West Bank, Jerusalem and the Gaza Strip, in accordance with the pro-

visions of this Agreement and the Election Law and Regulations, which shall not be contrary to the provisions of this Agreement.

4. The Council and the Ra'ees of the Executive Authority of the Council shall be elected for a transitional period not exceeding five years from the signing of the Gaza-Jericho Agreement on May 4, 1994.

5. Immediately upon its inauguration, the Council will elect from among its members a Speaker. The Speaker will preside over the meetings of the Council, administer the Council and its committees, decide on the agenda of each meeting, and lay before the Council proposals for voting and declare their results.

6. The jurisdiction of the Council shall be as determined in Article XVII of this Agreement (Jurisdiction).

7. The organization, structure and functioning of the Council shall be in accordance with this Agreement and the Basic Law for the Palestinian Interim Self-Government Authority, which Law shall be adopted by the Council. The Basic Law and any regulations made under it shall not be contrary to the provisions of this Agreement.

8. The Council shall be responsible under its executive powers for the offices, services and departments transferred to it and may establish, within its jurisdiction, ministries and subordinate bodies, as necessary for the fulfillment of its responsibilities.

9. The Speaker will present for the Council's approval proposed internal procedures that will regulate, among other things, the decision-making processes of the Council.

Article IV—Size of the Council

The Palestinian Council shall be composed of 82 representatives and the Ra'ees of the Executive Authority, who will be directly and simultaneously elected by the Palestinian people of the West Bank, Jerusalem and the Gaza Strip.

Article V—The Executive Authority of the Council

1. The Council will have a committee that will exercise the executive authority of the Council, formed in accordance with paragraph 4 below (hereinafter "the Executive Authority").

2. The Executive Authority shall be bestowed with the executive authority of the Council and will exercise it on behalf of the Council. It shall determine its own internal procedures and decision-making processes.

3. The Council will publish the names of the members of the Executive Authority immediately upon their initial appointment and subsequent to any changes.

4.a. The Ra'ees of the Executive Authority shall be an ex officio member of the Executive Authority.

b. All of the other members of the Executive Authority, except as provided in subparagraph c. below, shall be members of the Council, chosen and proposed to the Council by the Ra'ees of the Executive Authority and approved by the Council.

c. The Ra'ees of the Executive Authority shall have the right to appoint some persons, in number not exceeding 20 percent of the total membership of the Executive Authority, who are not members of the Council, to exercise executive authority and participate in government tasks. Such appointed members may not vote in meetings of the Council.

d. Non-elected members of the Executive Authority must have a valid address in an area under the jurisdiction of the Council.

Article VI—Other Committees of the Council

1. The Council may form small committees to simplify the proceedings of the Council and to assist in controlling the activity of its Executive Authority.

2. Each committee shall establish its own decision-making processes within the general framework of the organization and structure of the Council.

Article VII—Open Government

1. All meetings of the Council and of its committees, other than the Executive Authority, shall be open to the public, except upon a resolution of the Council or the relevant committee on the grounds of security, or commercial or personal confidentiality.

2. Participation in the deliberations of the Council, its committees and the Executive Authority shall be limited to their respective members only. Experts may be invited to such meetings to address specific issues on an ad hoc basis.

Article VIII—Judicial Review

Any person or organization affected by any act or decision of the Ra'ees of the Executive Authority of the Council or of any member of the Executive Authority, who believes that such act or decision exceeds the authority of the Ra'ees or of such member, or is otherwise incorrect in law or procedure, may apply to the relevant Palestinian Court of Justice for a review of such activity or decision.

Article IX—Powers and Responsibilities of the Council

1. Subject to the provisions of this Agreement, the Council will, within its jurisdiction, have legislative powers a set out in Article XVIII of this Agreement, as well as executive powers.

2. The executive power of the Palestinian Council shall extend to all matters within its jurisdiction under this Agreement or any future agreement that may be reached between the two Parties during the interim period. It shall include the power to formulate and conduct Palestinian policies and to supervise their implementation, to issue any rule or regulation under powers given in approved legislation and administrative decisions necessary for the realization of Palestinian self-government, the power to employ staff, sue and be sued and conclude contracts, and the power to keep and administer registers and records of the population, and issue certificates, licenses and documents.

3. The Palestinian Council's executive decisions and acts shall be consistent with the provisions of this Agreement.

4. The Palestinian Council may adopt all necessary measures in order to enforce the law and any of its decisions, and bring proceedings before the Palestinian courts and tribunals.

5.a. In accordance with the DOP, the Council will not have powers and responsibilities in the sphere of foreign relations, which sphere includes the establishment abroad of embassies, consulates or other types of foreign missions and posts or permitting their establishment in the West Bank or the Gaza Strip, the appointment of or admission of diplomatic and consular staff, and the exercise of diplomatic functions.

b. Notwithstanding the provisions of this paragraph, the PLO may conduct negotiations and sign agreements with states or international organizations for the benefit of the Council in the following cases only:

(1) economic agreements, as specifically provided in Annex V of this Agreement,

(2) agreements with donor countries for the purpose of implementing arrangements for the provision of assistance to the Council,

(3) agreements for the purpose of implementing the regional development plans detailed in Annex IV of the DOP or in agreements entered into in the framework of the multilateral negotiations, and

(4) cultural, scientific and educational agreements. Dealings between the Council and representatives of foreign states and international organizations, as well as the establishment in the West Bank and the Gaza Strip of representative offices other than those described in subparagraph 5.a above, for the purpose of implementing the agreements referred to in subparagraph 5.b above, shall not be considered foreign relations

6. Subject to the provisions of this Agreement, the Council shall, within its jurisdiction, have an independent judicial system composed of independent Palestinian courts and tribunals.

CHAPTER 2 — REDEPLOYMENT AND SECURITY ARRANGEMENTS

Article X—Redeployment of Israeli Military Forces

1. The first phase of the Israeli military forces redeployment will cover populated areas in the West Bank—cities, towns, villages, refugee camps and hamlets—as set out in Annex I, and will be completed prior to the eve of the Palestinian elections, i. e., 22 days before the day of the elections.

2. Further redeployments of Israeli military forces to specified military locations will commence after the inauguration of the Council and will be gradually implemented commensurate with the assumption of responsibility for public order and internal security by the Palestinian Police, to be completed within 18 months from the date of the inauguration of the Council as detailed in Articles XI (Land) and XIII (Security), below and in Annex I.

3. The Palestinian Police shall be deployed and shall assume responsibility for public order and internal security for Palestinians in a phased manner in accordance with XIII (Security) below and Annex I.

4. Israel shall continue to carry the responsibility for external security, as well as the responsibility for overall security of Israelis for the purpose of safeguarding their internal security and public order.

5. For the purpose of this Agreement, "Israeli military forces" includes Israel Police and other Israeli security forces.

Article XI—Land

1. The two sides view the West Bank and the Gaza Strip as a single territorial unit, the integrity and status of which will be preserved during the interim period.

2. The two sides agree that West Bank and Gaza Strip territory, except for issues that will be negotiated in the permanent status negotiations, will come under the jurisdiction of the Palestinian Council in a phased manner, to be completed within 18 months from the date of the inauguration of the Council, as specified below:

a. Land in populated areas (Areas A and B), including government and Al Waqf land, will come under the jurisdiction of the Council during the first phase of redeployment.

b. All civil powers and responsibilities, including planning and zoning, in Areas A and B, set out in Annex III, will be transferred to and assumed by the Council during the first phase of redeployment.

c. In Area C, during the first phase of redeployment Israel will transfer to the Council civil powers and responsibilities not relating to territory, as set out in Annex III.

d. The further redeployments of Israeli military forces to specified military locations will be gradually implemented in accordance with the DOP in three phases, each to take place after an interval of six months, after the inauguration of the Council, to be completed within 18 months from the date of the inauguration of the Council.

e. During the further redeployment phases to be completed within 18 months from the date of the inauguration of the Council, powers and responsibilities relating to territory will be transferred gradually to Palestinian jurisdiction that will cover West Bank and Gaza Strip territory, except for the issues that will be negotiated in the permanent status negotiations.

f. The specified military locations referred to in Article X, paragraph 2 above will be determined in the further redeployment phases, within the specified time-frame ending not later than 18 months from the date of the inauguration of the Council, and will be negotiated in the permanent status negotiations.

3. For the purpose of this Agreement and until the completion of the first phase of the further redeployments:

a. "Area A" means the populated areas delineated by a red line and shaded in brown on attached map No. 1;

b. "Area B" means the populated areas delineated by a red line and shaded in yellow on attached map No. 1, and the built-up area of the hamlets listed in Appendix 6 to Annex I, and

c. "Area C" means areas of the West Bank outside Areas A and B, which, except for the issues that will be negotiated in the permanent status negotiations, will be gradually transferred to Palestinian jurisdiction in accordance with this Agreement.

Article XII—Arrangements for Security and Public Order

1. In order to guarantee public order and internal security for the Palestinians of the West Bank and the Gaza Strip, the Council shall establish a strong police force as set out in Article XIV below. Israel shall continue to carry the responsibility for defense against external threats, including the responsibility for protecting the Egyptian and Jordanian borders, and for defense against external threats from the sea and from the air, as well as the responsibility for overall security of Israelis and Settlements, for the purpose of safeguarding their internal security and public order, and will have all the powers to take the steps necessary to meet this responsibility.

2. Agreed security arrangements and coordination mechanisms are specified in Annex I.

3. A Joint Coordination and Cooperation Committee for Mutual Security Purposes (hereinafter "the JSC"), as well as Joint Regional Security Committees (hereinafter "RSCs") and Joint District Coordination Offices (hereinafter "DCOs"), are hereby established as provided for in Annex I.

4. The security arrangements provided for in this Agreement and in An-

nex I may be reviewed at the request of either Party and may be amended by mutual agreement of the Parties. Specific review arrangements are included in Annex I.

5. For the purpose of this Agreement, "the Settlements" means, in the West Bank the settlements in Area C; and in the Gaza Strip—the Gush Katif and Erez settlement areas, as well as the other settlements in the Gaza Strip, as shown on attached map No. 2.

Article XIII—Security

1. The Council will, upon completion of the redeployment of Israeli military forces in each district, as set out in Appendix 1 to Annex I, assume the powers and responsibilities for internal security and public order in Area A in that district.

2. a. There will be a complete redeployment of Israeli military forces from Area B. Israel will transfer to the Council and the Council will assume responsibility for public order for Palestinians. Israel shall have the overriding responsibility for security for the purpose of protecting Israelis and confronting the threat of terrorism.

b. In Area B the Palestinian Police shall assume the responsibility for public order for Palestinians and shall be deployed in order to accommodate the Palestinian needs and requirements in the following manner:

(1) The Palestinian Police shall establish 25 police stations and posts in towns, villages, and other places listed in Appendix 2 to Annex I and as delineated on map No. 3. The West Bank RSC may agree on the establishment of additional police stations and posts, if required.

(2) The Palestinian Police shall be responsible for handling public order incidents in which only Palestinians are involved.

(3) The Palestinian Police shall operate freely in populated places where police stations and posts are located, as set out in paragraph b(1) above.

(4) While the movement of uniformed Palestinian policemen in Area B outside places where there is a Palestinian police station or post will be carried out after coordination and confirmation through the relevant DCO, three months after the completion of redeployment from Area B, the DCOs may decide that movement of Palestinian policemen from the police stations in Area B to Palestinian towns and villages in Area B on roads that are used only by Palestinian traffic will take place after notifying the DCO.

(5) The coordination of such planned movement prior to confirmation through the relevant DCO shall include a scheduled plan, including the number of policemen, as well as the type and number of weapons and vehicles intended to take part. It shall also include details of arrangements for ensuring continued coordination through appropriate communication links, the exact schedule of movement to the area of the planned operation, including

the destination and routes thereto, its proposed duration and the schedule for returning to the police station or post. The Israeli side of the DCO will provide the Palestinian side with its response, following a request for movement of policemen in accordance with this paragraph, in normal or routine cases within one day and in emergency cases no later than two hours.

(6) The Palestinian Police and the Israeli military forces will conduct joint security activities on the main roads as set out in Annex I.

(7) The Palestinian Police will notify the West Bank RSC of the names of the policemen, number plates of police vehicles and serial numbers of weapons, with respect to each police station and post in Area B.

(8) Further redeployments from Area C and transfer of internal security responsibility to the Palestinian Police in Areas B and C will be carried out in three phases, each to take place after an interval of six months, to be completed 18 months after the inauguration of the Council, except for the issues of permanent status negotiations and of Israel's overall responsibility for Israelis and borders.

(9) The procedures detailed in this paragraph will be reviewed within six months of the completion of the first phase of redeployment.

Article XIV—The Palestinian Police

1. The Council shall establish a strong police force. The duties, functions, structure, deployment and composition of the Palestinian Police, together with provisions regarding its equipment and operation, as well as rules of conduct, are set out in Annex I.

2. The Palestinian police force established under the Gaza-Jericho Agreement will be fully integrated into the Palestinian Police and will be subject to the provisions of this Agreement.

3. Except for the Palestinian Police and the Israeli military forces, no other armed forces shall be established or operate in the West Bank and the Gaza Strip.

4. Except for the arms, ammunition and equipment of the Palestinian Police described in Annex I, and those of the Israeli military forces, no organization, group or individual in the West Bank and the Gaza Strip shall manufacture, sell, acquire, possess, import or otherwise introduce into the West Bank or the Gaza Strip any firearms, ammunition, weapons, explosives, gunpowder or any related equipment unless otherwise provided for in Annex I.

Article XV—Prevention of Hostile Acts

1. Both sides shall take all measures necessary in order to prevent acts of terrorism, crime and hostilities directed against each other, against individuals falling under the other's authority and against their property and shall take legal measures against offenders.

2. Specific provisions for the implementation of this Article are set out in Annex I.

Article XVI—Confidence Building Measures

With a view to fostering a positive and supportive public atmosphere to accompany the implementation of this Agreement, to establish a solid basis of mutual trust and good faith, and in order to facilitate the anticipated cooperation and new relations between the two peoples, both Parties agree to carry out confidence building measures as detailed herewith:

1. Israel will release or turn over to the Palestinian side, Palestinian detainees and prisoners, residents of the West Bank and the Gaza Strip. The first stage of release of these prisoners and detainees will take place on the signing of this Agreement and the second stage will take place prior to the date of the elections. There will be a third stage of release of detainees and prisoners. Detainees and prisoners will be released from among categories detailed in Annex VII (Release of Palestinian Prisoners and Detainees). Those released will be free to return to their homes in the West Bank and the Gaza Strip.

2. Palestinians who have maintained contact with the Israeli authorities will not be subjected to acts of harassment, violence, retribution or prosecution. Appropriate ongoing measures will be taken, in coordination with Israel, in order to ensure their protection.

3. Palestinians from abroad whose entry into the West Bank and the Gaza Strip is approved pursuant to this Agreement, and to whom the provisions of this Article are applicable, will not be prosecuted for offenses committed prior to September 13, 1993.

Chapter 3—Legal Affairs

Article XVII—Jurisdiction

1. In accordance with the DOP, the jurisdiction of the Council will cover West Bank and Gaza Strip territory as a single territorial unit, except for:

a. issues that will be negotiated in the permanent status negotiations: Jerusalem, settlements, specified military locations, Palestinian refugees, borders, foreign relations and Israelis; and

b. powers and responsibilities not transferred to the Council.

2. Accordingly, the authority of the Council encompasses all matters that fall within its territorial, functional and personal jurisdiction, as follows:

a. The territorial jurisdiction of the Council shall encompass Gaza Strip territory, except for the Settlements and the Military Installation Area shown on map No. 2, and West Bank territory, except for Area C which, except for the issues that will be negotiated in the permanent status negotiations, will be gradually transferred to Palestinian jurisdiction in three phases, each to take place after an interval of six months, to be completed 18 months after the inauguration of the Council. At this time, the jurisdiction of the Council will cover West Bank and Gaza Strip territory, except for the issues that will be negotiated in the permanent status negotiations. Territorial jurisdiction includes land, subsoil and territorial waters, in accordance with the provisions of this Agreement.

b. The functional jurisdiction of the Council extends to all powers and responsibilities transferred to the Council, as specified in this Agreement or in any future agreements that may be reached between the Parties during the interim period.

c. The territorial and functional jurisdiction of the Council will apply to all persons, except for Israelis, unless otherwise provided in this Agreement.

d. Notwithstanding subparagraph a. above, the Council shall have functional jurisdiction in Area C, as detailed in Article IV of Annex III.

3. The Council has, within its authority, legislative, executive and judicial powers and responsibilities, as provided for in this Agreement.

4. a. Israel, through its military government, has the authority over areas that are not under the territorial jurisdiction of the Council, powers and responsibilities not transferred to the Council and Israelis.

b. To this end, the Israeli military government shall retain the necessary legislative, judicial and executive powers and responsibilities, in accordance with international law. This provision shall not derogate from Israel's applicable legislation over Israelis in personam.

5. The exercise of authority with regard to the electromagnetic sphere and air space shall be in accordance with the provisions of this Agreement.

6. Without derogating from the provisions of this Article, legal arrangements detailed in the Protocol Concerning Legal Matters attached as Annex IV to this Agreement (hereinafter "Annex IV") shall be observed. Israel and the Council may negotiate further legal arrangements.

7. Israel and the Council shall cooperate on matters of legal assistance in criminal and civil matters through a legal committee (hereinafter "the Legal Committee"), hereby established.

8. The Council's jurisdiction will extend gradually to cover West Bank and Gaza Strip territory, except for the issues to be negotiated in the permanent status negotiations, through a series of redeployments of the Israeli military forces. The first phase of the redeployment of Israeli military forces will cover populated areas in the West Bank—cities, towns, refugee camps and hamlets, as set out in Annex I—and will be completed prior to the eve of the Palestinian elections, i.e. 22 days before the day of the elections. Further redeployments of Israeli military forces to specified military locations will commence immediately upon the inauguration of the Council and will be effected in three phases,

each to take place after an interval of six months to be concluded no later than eighteen months from the date of the inauguration of the Council.

Article XVIII—Legislative Powers of the Council

1. For the purposes of this Article, legislation shall mean any primary and secondary legislation, including basic laws, laws, regulations and other legislative acts.

2. The Council has the power, within its jurisdiction as defined in Article XVII of this Agreement, to adopt legislation.

3. While the primary legislative power shall lie in the hands of the Council as a whole, the Ra'ees of the Executive Authority of the Council shall have the following legislative powers:

a. the power to initiate legislation or to present proposed legislation to the Council;

b. the power to promulgate legislation adopted by the Council; and

c. the power to issue secondary legislation, including regulations, relating to any matters specified and within the scope laid down in any primary legislation adopted by the Council.

4. a. Legislation, including legislation which amends or abrogates existing laws or military orders, which exceeds the jurisdiction of the Council or which is otherwise inconsistent with the provisions of the DOP, this Agreement, or of any other agreement that may be reached between the two sides during the interim period, shall have no effect and shall be void *ab initio*.

b. The Ra'ees of the Executive Authority of the Council shall not promulgate legislation adopted by the Council if such legislation falls under the provisions of this paragraph.

5. All legislation shall be communicated to the Israeli side of the Legal Committee.

6. Without derogating from the provisions of paragraph 4 above, the Israeli side of the Legal Committee may refer for the attention of the Committee any legislation regarding which Israel considers the provisions of paragraph 4 apply, in order to discuss issues arising from such legislation. The Legal Committee will consider the legislation referred to it at the earliest opportunity.

Article XIX—Human Rights and the Rule of Law

Israel and the Council shall exercise their powers and responsibilities pursuant to this Agreement with due regard to internationally-accepted norms and principles of human rights and the rule of law.

Article XX—Rights, Liabilities and Obligations

1. a. The transfer of powers and responsibilities from the Israeli military government and its civil administration to the Council, as detailed in Annex III, includes all related rights, liabilities and obligations arising with regard to acts or omissions which occurred prior to such transfer. Israel will cease to bear any financial responsibility regarding such acts or omissions and the Council will bear all financial responsibility for these and for its own functioning.

b. Any financial claim made in this regard against Israel will be referred to the Council.

c. Israel shall provide the Council with the information it has regarding pending and anticipated claims brought before any court or tribunal against Israel in this regard.

d. Where legal proceedings are brought in respect of such a claim, Israel will notify the Council and enable it to participate in defending the claim and raise any arguments on its behalf.

e. In the event that an award is made against Israel by any court or tribunal in respect of such a claim, the Council shall immediately reimburse Israel the full amount of the award.

f. Without prejudice to the above, where a court or tribunal hearing such a claim finds that liability rests solely with an employee or agent who acted beyond the scope of the powers assigned to him or her, unlawfully or with willful malfeasance, the Council shall not bear financial responsibility.

2. a. Notwithstanding the provisions of paragraphs 1.d through 1.f above, each side may take the necessary measures, including promulgation of legislation, in order to ensure that such claims by Palestinians including pending claims in which the hearing of evidence has not yet begun, are brought only before Palestinian courts or tribunals in the West Bank and the Gaza Strip, and are not brought before or heard by Israeli courts or tribunals.

b. Where a new claim has been brought before a Palestinian court or tribunal subsequent to the dismissal of the claim pursuant to subparagraph a. above, the Council shall defend it and, in accordance with sub-paragraph 1.a above, in the event that an award is made for the plaintiff, shall pay the amount of the award.

c. The Legal Committee shall agree on arrangements for the transfer of all materials and information needed to enable the Palestinian courts or tribunals to hear such claims as referred to in subparagraph b. above, and, when necessary, for the provision of legal assistance by Israel to the Council in defending such claims.

3. The transfer of authority in itself shall not affect rights, liabilities and obligations of any person or legal entity, in existence at the date of signing of this Agreement.

4. The Council, upon its inauguration, will assume all the rights, liabilities and obligations of the Palestinian Authority. . . .

Article XXI—Settlement of Differences and Disputes

Any difference relating to the application of this Agreement shall be referred to the appropriate coordination and cooperation mechanism established under this Agreement. The provisions of Article XV of the DOP shall apply to any such difference which is not settled through the appropriate coordination and cooperation mechanism, namely:

1. Disputes arising out of the application or interpretation of this Agreement or any related agreements pertaining to the interim period shall be settled through the Liaison Committee.

2. Disputes which cannot be settled by negotiations may be settled by a mechanism of conciliation to be agreed between the Parties.

3. The Parties may agree to submit to arbitration disputes relating to the interim period, which cannot be settled through conciliation. To this end, upon the agreement of both Parties, the Parties will establish an Arbitration Committee.

CHAPTER 4—COOPERATION

Article XXII—Relations between Israel and the Council

1. Israel and the Council shall seek to foster mutual understanding and tolerance and shall accordingly abstain from incitement, including hostile propaganda, against each other and, without derogating from the principle of freedom of expression, shall take legal measures to prevent such incitement by any organizations, groups or individuals within their jurisdiction.

2. Israel and the Council will ensure that their respective educational systems contribute to the peace between the Israeli and Palestinian peoples and to peace in the entire region, and will refrain from the introduction of any motifs that could adversely affect the process of reconciliation.

3. Without derogating from the other provisions of this Agreement, Israel and the Council shall cooperate in combating criminal activity which may affect both sides, including offenses related to trafficking in illegal drugs and psychotropic substances, smuggling, and offenses against property, including offenses related to vehicles.

Article XXIII—Cooperation with Regard to Transfer of Powers and Responsibilities

In order to ensure a smooth, peaceful and orderly transfer of powers and responsibilities, the two sides will cooperate with regard to the transfer of security powers and responsibilities in accordance with the provisions of

Annex I, and the transfer of civil powers and responsibilities in accordance with the provisions of Annex III.

Article XXIV—Economic Relations

The economic relations between the two sides are set out in the Protocol on Economic Relations signed in Paris on April 29, 1994, and the Appendices thereto, and the Supplement to the Protocol on Economic Relations all attached as Annex V, and will be governed by the relevant provisions of this Agreement and its Annexes.

Article XXV—Cooperation Programs

1. The Parties agree to establish a mechanism to develop programs of cooperation between them. Details of such cooperation are set out in Annex VI.

2. A Standing Cooperation Committee to deal with issues arising in the context of this cooperation is hereby established as provided for in Annex VI.

Article XXVI—The Joint Israeli-Palestinian Liaison Committee

1. The Liaison Committee established pursuant to Article X of the DOP shall ensure the smooth implementation of this Agreement. It shall deal with issues requiring coordination, other issues of common interest and disputes.

2. The Liaison Committee shall be composed of an equal number of members from each Party. It may add other technicians and experts as necessary.

3. The Liaison Committee shall adopt its rules of procedures, including the frequency and place or places of its meetings.

4. The Liaison Committee shall reach its decisions by agreement.

5. The Liaison Committee shall establish a subcommittee that will monitor and steer the implementation of this Agreement (hereinafter "the Monitoring and Steering Committee"). It will function as follows:

a. The Monitoring and Steering Committee will, on an ongoing basis, monitor the implementation of this Agreement, with a view to enhancing the cooperation and fostering the peaceful relations between the two sides.

b. The Monitoring and Steering Committee will steer the activities of the various joint committees established in this Agreement (the JSC, the CAC, the Legal Committee, the Joint Economic Committee and the Standing Cooperation Committee) concerning the ongoing implementation of the Agreement, and will report to the Liaison Committee.

c. The Monitoring and Steering Committee will be composed of the heads of the various committees mentioned above.

d. The two heads of the Monitoring and Steering Committee will establish its rules of procedures, including the frequency and places of its meetings.

Article XXVII—Liaison and Cooperation with Jordan and Egypt

1. Pursuant to Article XII of the DOP, the two Parties have invited the Governments of Jordan and Egypt to participate in establishing further liaison and cooperation arrangements between the Government of Israel and the Palestinian representatives on the one hand, and the Governments of Jordan and Egypt on the other hand, to promote cooperation between them. As part of these arrangements a Continuing Committee has been constituted and has commenced its deliberations.

2. The Continuing Committee shall decide by agreement on the modalities of admission of persons displaced from the West Bank and the Gaza Strip in 1967, together with necessary measures to prevent disruption and disorder.

3. The Continuing Committee shall also deal with other matters of common concern.

Article XXVIII—Missing Persons

1. Israel and the Council shall cooperate by providing each other with all necessary assistance in the conduct of searches for missing persons and bodies of persons which have not been recovered, as well as by providing information about missing persons

2. The PLO undertakes to cooperate with Israel and to assist it in its efforts to locate and to return to Israel Israeli soldiers who are missing in action and the bodies of soldiers which have not been recovered.

Chapter 5 — Miscellaneous Provisions

Article XXIX—Safe Passage Between the West Bank and the Gaza Strip

Arrangements for safe passage of persons and transportation between the West Bank and the Gaza Strip arse set out in Annex I.

Article XXX—Passages

Arrangements for coordination between Israel and the Council regarding passage to and from Egypt and Jordan, as well as any other agreed international crossings, are set out in Annex I.

Article XXXI—Final Clauses

1. This Agreement shall enter into force on the date of its signing.

2. The Gaza-Jericho Agreement, except for Article XX (Confidence-Building Measures), the Preparatory Transfer Agreement and the Further Transfer Protocol will be superseded by this Agreement.

3. The Council, upon its inauguration, shall replace the Palestinian Authority and shall assume all the undertakings and obligations of the Pales-

tinian Authority under the Gaza-Jericho Agreement, the Preparatory Transfer Agreement, and the Further Transfer Protocol.

4. The two sides shall pass all necessary legislation to implement this Agreement.

5. Permanent status negotiations will commence as soon as possible, but not later than May 4, 1996, between the Parties. It is understood that these negotiations shall cover remaining issues, including: Jerusalem, refugees, settlements, security arrangements, borders, relations and cooperation with other neighbors, and other issues of common interest.

6. Nothing in this Agreement shall prejudice or preempt the outcome of the negotiations on the permanent status to be conducted pursuant to the DOP. Neither Party shall be deemed, by virtue of having entered into this Agreement, to have renounced or waived any of its existing rights, claims or positions.

7. Neither side shall initiate or take any step that will change the status of the West Bank and the Gaza Strip pending the outcome of the permanent status negotiations.

8. The two Parties view the West Bank and the Gaza Strip as a single territorial unit, the integrity and status of which will be preserved during the interim period.

9. The PLO undertakes that, within two months of the date of the inauguration of the Council, the Palestinian National Council will convene and formally approve the necessary changes in regard to the Palestinian Covenant, as undertaken in the letters signed by the Chairman of the PLO and addressed to the Prime Minister of Israel, dated September 9, 1993 and May 4, 1994.

10. Pursuant to Annex I, Article IX of this Agreement, Israel confirms that the permanent checkpoints on the roads leading to and from the Jericho Area (except those related to the access road leading from Mousa Alami to the Allenby Bridge) will be removed upon the completion of the first phase of redeployment.

11. Prisoners who, pursuant to the Gaza-Jericho Agreement, were turned over to the Palestinian Authority on the condition that they remain in the Jericho Area for the remainder of their sentence, will be free to return to their homes in the West Bank and the Gaza Strip upon the completion of the first phase of redeployment.

12. As regards relations between Israel and the PLO, and without derogating from the commitments contained in the letters signed by and exchanged between the Prime Minister of Israel and the Chairman of the PLO, dated September 9, 1993 and May 4, 1994, the two sides will apply between them the provisions contained in Article XXII, paragraph 1, with the necessary changes.

13. a. The Preamble to this Agreement, and all Annexes, Appendices and maps attached hereto, shall constitute an integral part hereof.

b. The Parties agree that the maps attached to the Gaza-Jericho Agreement as: i. map No. 1 (The Gaza Strip), an exact copy of which is attached to this Agreement as map No. (in this Agreement "map No. 2"); ii. map No. 4 (Deployment of Palestinian Police in the Gaza Strip), an exact copy of which is attached to this Agreement as map No. 5 (in this Agreement "map No. 5"); and iii. map No. 6 (Maritime Activity Zones), an exact copy of which is attached to this Agreement as map No. 8 (in this Agreement "map No. 8"; are an integral part hereof and will remain in effect for the duration of this Agreement.

14. While the Jeftlik area will come under the functional and personal jurisdiction of the Council in the first phase of redeployment, the area's transfer to the territorial jurisdiction of the Council will be considered by the Israeli side in the first phase of the further redeployment phases.

Israeli Prime Minister Yitzhak Rabin: Speech at Peace Rally (November 4, 1995)

Allow me to say, I am also moved. I want to thank each and every one of you who stood up here against violence and for peace. This government, which I have the privilege to lead, together with my friend Shimon Peres, decided to give peace a chance. A peace that will solve most of the problems of the State of Israel. I was a military man for twenty-seven years. I fought as long as there were no prospects for peace. Today I believe that there are prospects for peace, great prospects. We must take advantage of it for the sake of those standing here, and for the sake of those who do not stand here. And they are many among our people. I have always believed that the majority of the people want peace, are prepared to take risks for peace. And you here, by showing up at this rally, prove it, along with the many who did not make it here, that the people truly want peace and oppose violence. Violence is undermining the very foundations of Israeli democracy. It must be condemned, denounced, and isolated. This is not the way of the State of Israel. Controversies may arise in a democracy, but the decision must be reached through democratic elections, just as it happened in 1992, when we were given the mandate to do what we are doing, and to continue to do it. I want to thank from here the President of Egypt, the King of Jordan, and the King of Morocco, whose representatives are present here, conveying their partnership with us on the march toward peace. But above all the people of Israel, who have proven, in the three years this government has been in office, that peace is attainable, a peace that will provide an opportunity for a progressive society and economy. Peace exists first and foremost in our prayers, but not only in prayers. Peace is what the Jewish People aspire to, a true aspiration. Peace entails difficulties, even pain. Israel knows no path devoid of pain. But the path of peace is preferable to the path of war. I say this to you as one who was a military man and minister of defense, and who saw the pain of the families of IDF soldiers. It is for their sake, and for the sake of our children and grandchildren, that I want this government to exert every effort, exhaust every opportunity, to promote and to reach a comprehensive peace. This rally must send a message to the Israeli public, to the Jewish community throughout the world, to many, many in the Arab world and in the entire world, that the people of Israel want peace, support peace, and for that, I thank you very much.

Israel and Palestinian Authority: Hebron Accords (January 15, 1997)

The following "Note for the Record," prepared by U.S. Special Middle East Coordinator Dennis Ross and appended to the Hebron Accords, set the agenda for the peace process during the next three years.

The two leaders [Israeli Prime Minister Benjamin Netanyahu and Chairman Yasir Arafat] agreed that the Oslo peace process must move forward to succeed. Both parties to the Interim Agreement have concerns and obligations. Accordingly, the two leaders reaffirmed their commitment to implement the Interim Agreement on the basis of reciprocity and, in this context, conveyed the following undertakings to each other:

ISRAELI RESPONSIBILITIES

The Israeli side reaffirms its commitments to the following measures and principles in accordance with the Interim Agreement:

ISSUES FOR IMPLEMENTATION

1. Further Redeployment Phases
The first phase of further redeployment
2. Prisoner Release Issues
Prisoner release issues will be dealt with in accordance with the Interim Agreement's provisions and procedures, including Annex VII.
3. Issues for Negotiation. Outstanding Interim Agreement Issues Negotiations on the following outstanding issues from the Interim Agreement will be immediately resumed. Negotiations on these issues will be conducted in parallel:
a) Safe Passage
b) Gaza Airport
c) Gaza port
d) Passages

e) Economic, financial, civilian and security issues

f) People-to-people

4. Permanent Status Negotiations

Permanent status negotiations will be resumed within two months after implementation of the Hebron Protocol.

PALESTINIAN RESPONSIBILITIES

The Palestinian side reaffirms its commitments to the following measures and principles in accordance with the Interim Agreement:

1. Complete the process of revising the Palestinian National Charter

2. Fighting terror and preventing violence

a) Strengthening security cooperation

b) Preventing incitement and hostile propaganda, as specified in Article XXII of the Interim Agreement.

c) Combat systematically and effectively terrorist organizations and infrastructure

d) Apprehension, prosecution and punishment of terrorists

e) Requests for transfer of suspects and defendants will be acted upon in accordance with Article II(7)(f) of Annex IV to the Interim Agreement

f) Confiscation of illegal firearms

3. Size of Palestinian Police will be pursuant to the Interim Agreement.

4. Exercise of Palestinian governmental activity, and location of Palestinian governmental offices, will be as specified in the Interim Agreement. The aforementioned commitments will be dealt with immediately and in parallel.

OTHER ISSUES

Either party is free to raise other issues not specified above related to implementation of the Interim Agreement and obligations of both sides arising from the Interim Agreement.

U.S. Secretary of State Warren Christopher: Letter to Israeli Prime Minister Benjamin Netanyahu (January 15, 1997)

Dear Mr. Prime Minister,

I wanted personally to congratulate you on the successful conclusion of the "Protocol Concerning the Redeployment in Hebron." It represents an important step forward in the Oslo peace process and reaffirms my conviction that a just and lasting peace will be established between Israelis and Palestinians in the very near future.

In this connection, I can assure you that it remains the policy of the United States to support and promote full implementation of the Interim

Agreement in all of its parts. We intend to continue our efforts to help ensure that all outstanding commitments are carried out by both parties in a cooperative spirit and on the basis of reciprocity. As part of this process, I have impressed upon Chairman Arafat the imperative need for the Palestinian Authority to make every effort to ensure public order and internal security within the West Bank and Gaza Strip. I have stressed to him that effectively carrying out this major responsibility will be a critical foundation for completing implementation of the Interim Agreement, as well as the peace process as a whole. I wanted you to know that, in this context, I have advised Chairman Arafat of U.S. views on Israel's process of redeploying its forces, designating specified military locations and transferring additional powers and responsibilities to the Palestinian Authority. In this regard, I have conveyed our belief, that the first phase of further redeployments should take place as soon as possible, and that all three phases of the further redeployments should be completed within twelve months from the implementation of the first phase of the further redeployments but not later than mid-1998.

Mr. Prime Minister, you can be assured that the United States' commitment to Israel's security is ironclad and constitutes the fundamental cornerstone of our special relationship. The key element in our approach to peace, including the negotiation and implementation of agreements between Israel and its Arab partners, has always been a recognition of Israel's security requirements. Moreover, a hallmark of U.S. policy remains our commitment to work cooperatively to seek to meet the security needs that Israel identifies. Finally, I would like to reiterate our position that Israel is entitled to secure and defensible borders, which should be directly negotiated and agreed with its neighbors.

Alessandra Antonelli: From the Battlefield to the Table (February 27, 1998)

Marwan Barghouti, Husam Khader, Hisham Abdul Razik all belong to the same past of struggle, weapons and jail detentions, and all of them, once wartime was over, left the battlefield to sit in the designated place where statebuilding was to occur: the Palestine Legislative Council.

The battle began when they were very young. Husam Khader was 10 years old when his friend, Khader Daoud, held his hand in Balata Camp and took him to a demonstration. At 14, he entered prison for the first time. He was to go through those prison doors another 22 times. Abdul Razik was 16 when he was first jailed. His first incarceration, under administrative detention, was short, but the second, because of the bomb he was carrying in his car, (which exploded and injured him) lasted two decades.

Marwan Barghouti's personal memories also count many years in and out of prison, starting from school age, and a lengthy deportation.

The peace talks shifted the struggle from weapons to a democratic parliament, from the battleground to the table and from stone and violence to peaceful rallies. The struggle, indeed, is not over, yet. We are still striving to regain the human rights which have been stolen from Palestinians. We are still working for peace, and want to support it in this difficult time, says Hisham Abdul Razik. Marwan Barghouti feels the same. He points out that, in the past years, during, before and after the intifada, we were fighting to end the occupation. We got an agreement in 1993, but the occupation still persists. We change our way of fighting, but the goal is the same. If there is disappointment because of the continuing dispute with the Israelis, there is also disappointment from the Palestinian reality. We have been given the opportunity to start a new country, but we haven't done it well. Some people misinterpreted the power they were given; they have forgotten the honesty and loyalty of the years of the struggle for independence, so the battle now is also to stop corruption, says Husam Khader. Sometimes it is extremely hard because you confront people you shared important resistance moments with.

In some ways, it was easier to oppose a well-defined, external enemy before than to deal with political adversaries now.

Opposition is a natural part of a democratic society. We should worry if there wasn't any. But it has to express itself in the Parliament. And respecting each other the majority and the minority should join together in a common effort to establish a Palestinian state and a lasting and fair peace, says Hisham Abdul Razik.

It is not so simple to fully adopt a democratic system at the drop of a hat. Palestinians under occupation looked at and dreamt of the Israeli near democracy; those in the Diaspora experienced life in democratic nations. But to implement democracy within such a short period has turned out to be quite a complicated matter.

I would like to see more respect for political pluralism, more respect for the political institutions and for the Parliament's activities, says Marwan Barghouti. And also greater freedom of press. The point is, according to Khader, that the Palestinian Authority does not take into enough consideration the decisions and recommendations of the Legislative Council. Often, they simply put our suggestions away in a drawer. He also suggests the establishment of a Council of Ministries, a clearer definition of their powers and the creation of a steering committee to oversee political activities and procedures.

The Oslo agreement underlined the fact that, for these three, Palestinians had achieved a certain historical maturity which called for a change in our minds and in the means we were using. Or, as Abdul Razik puts it, "Palestinians have been living with slogans for 100 years. But with peace the time came to put them aside, because we realized that peace would be the only solution to getting some of our rights back and to be able to start living like any other nation." Since then, the same hands that held guns and threw stones have been holding briefcases and signing papers. It was easy to have unconditional respect from people when I was a freedom fighter, says Barghouti. But now it is much more difficult. At that time, we were only focused on the war against the occupiers. I didn't pay too much attention to the needs of the people, to the disastrous situation of electricity, sewage system, roads. But as a politician, I need to be aware of the people's priorities, of their needs. And sometime it's hard to meet all their expectations, to earn their full trust and understanding.

From the 74 meetings he held last year, Barghouti says Palestinians' biggest concerns are—in that order—the confiscation of lands which is still going on to expand and ensure the presence of settlements; the lack of jobs; and the inadequacy of the infrastructure. The close contact with people makes them aware that this is the vital moment to create a social and economic environment that responds to the demands of the population. This has became a must for this generation of fighters transformed into politicians by historical reasons. The best tools they can put to work in the service of Palestine are the tolerance, the patience, the respect of the people, and the stubborn will to reach a goal that they acquired during the occupation years, as Barghouti says. But they must also possess the ability to listen carefully, because there is a changing ground swell that needs to be heard, says Khader, who believes that the PLO's political system, which fit in the intifada period, is no longer suitable to these new circumstances.

And all of them are striving to guarantee a true democracy that grants everyone rights, and freedom of expression, and which is able to protect any person in the society, beginning with the family, as Abdul Razik puts it. Obstinate activists and efficient leaders during their youth, all three men are now husbands and fathers. Their striving for a better Palestine assumes then a deeper meaning, because to accomplish the agenda they set to free the country before, and to fairly build it later, will become part of the precious heritage they will leave to their sons and daughters.

The picture they have of a future Palestine is one that is no longer in flames, no longer watered with blood, but a country resting in peace, the real peace that the land which hosts three religions deserves, as Abdul Razik vividly and poetically describes it. More concretely, they want a Palestine where the values of respect, for individuals, for ethnic, religious or political minorities, for established social, legal and economic institutions as well as those being built, and respect for a multi-party parliament. That respect is the only way for the values of freedom and peace to take root, the only ground on which a truly independent country can blossom.

Hasan Asfour and Mahmud Abbas (Abu Mazin): Reflections on the Oslo Agreement's 5th Anniversary (September 11, 1998)

We cannot give up on these accords because we paid a price for this agreement when we agreed to partition Palestine into two states. The Palestinians made historic concessions in order to achieve specific national goals. . . . The agreement could work with an Israeli partner, and has not worked because of the lack of an Israeli partner. We lost the one partner who participated in setting up the accords with the PLO, and later with the PA. . . . We did have problems with the Labor government in terms of implementation; these problems stemmed from attempts to change portions of the agreement but were nonetheless still within the framework of the agreement. The real obstacle arose with the arrival of a government which from the very beginning did not believe in a peace agreement with the Palestinians. It does not believe that there is a Palestinian people and Palestinian land, or that this people has legitimate political rights. However, because it can't say this openly, it goes around the agreement by making verbal commitments to all the while trying to kill it. This is the real political problem. It is not the text of the agreement itself that is the problem, but the lack of an Israeli partner willing to stick to the peace process and reach the political goal "a historic reconciliation" guaranteed by the accords on the principle of mutual recognition of political rights.

It constituted a huge turning point on the road to establishment of a Palestinian state, an adjustment to the path of the Palestinian political movement, and a reassessment of the sociopolitical status and entity of the Palestinian people after their long journey of desolation and dispersion, the Palestinian revolution, the PLO and Palestinian armed struggle. The struggle now has a legitimate political role far beyond the importance of the PLO, which is still considered the spiritual nation. However, the Palestinian land remains under occupation, and hopes are still centered on the land and people. The accords helped to make this adjustment, and the dynamics of the Oslo process served as the basic foundation for this new perspective on the Palestinian entity and nation.

There is no agreement which is good for one side alone. An agreement is a compromise between two sides . . . The one point which people sometimes hold against the agreement is that the binding mechanism for implementation is unclear. We tried to maintain a balance between the time agenda for implementation and the force of implementation. Perhaps the gap between the obligation to implement and actual implementation within the time frame was not guaranteed in one way or the other. However, this issue was not as easy five years ago, as historians or readers seem to think. The Israelis also realized that they needed to change parts of the agreement but were in a better position to do so. Both sides felt that there were things which should have been amended. But the Palestinians do not have the power to make changes, while the Israelis do. This is the political problem but again, there is no agreement which is good for one side alone. Either both sides benefit or both sides do not, no agreement is bad for both sides unless it is one of surrender . . .

Abu Mazin: One cannot say that implementation has been 100 percent good or 100 percent bad. This experiment is new to us from beginning to end. We are ruling ourselves for the first time. There are many complex problems. Like other newly liberated peoples, we are facing specific relevant obstacles, but I say that we have the advantage of having a foothold and yet unexploited qualifications. Some other nations achieved independence with not even 5 percent of their population able to read and write. We enter the phase of independence with less than 5 percent illiteracy. That is the difference which justifies better expectations for us. But let me sum up what has been happening as follows: Over the past 50 years the clock was ticking but now, after Oslo, it is moving forward and the train is moving forward on its tracks. We may not reach the final station in one or several years but we will reach it eventually. For 50 years before Oslo the Palestinians used to leave the homeland. After Oslo their direction was reversed and they have begun returning to the homeland.

. . . That is why this experiment of negotiation, reconstruction, repatriation, and everything else is a unique experiment. Inasmuch as I maintain that we have great capabilities and qualifications, I also blame us for the mistakes that are bound to occur sometimes.

I am not in favor of negotiations through the media where every time we come out of a negotiation session we hold a press conference and say what went on in the negotiations. That method is harmful to the negotiators and the negotiations. Why? Because each side wants to appear to its public as the side which made no concession and would want to stick to certain forms which it would abandon inside the negotiating chamber. . . .

My feeling is that with that agreement we got the maximum possible to put the Palestinian people on the road to independence. But I always tell my brothers: We should not exaggerate what we achieved lest we lose it, and we should not underestimate what we achieved lest we waste it. There is no harm in being a little late because we have no right, in the interest of time, to accept just any solution with a low ceiling. . . . We have time and there is no need to rush. We were late before, so let us be a little late again. What is the problem, if we want to achieve a solution to our advantage? Furthermore, we are negotiating for our rights. I say that the Oslo agreement is not an ideal agreement. It does not give us what we want but it also does not give them everything they want. As we have signed the agreement I am not prepared to concede any right guaranteed for me under the agreement.

Israel and Palestinian Authority: The Wye River Memorandum (October 23, 1998)

The following are steps to facilitate implementation of the Interim Agreement on the West Bank and Gaza Strip of September 28, 1995 (the "Interim Agreement") and other related agreements including the Note for the Record of January 17, 1997 (hereinafter referred to as "the prior agreements") so that the Israeli and Palestinian sides can more effectively carry out their reciprocal responsibilities, including those relating to further redeployments and security respectively. These steps are to be carried out in a parallel phased approach in accordance with this Memorandum and the attached time line. They are subject to the relevant terms and conditions of the prior agreements and do not supersede their other requirements.

I. FURTHER REDEPLOYMENTS

A. Phase One and Two Further Redeployments

1. Pursuant to the Interim Agreement and subsequent agreements, the Israeli side's implementation of the first and second F.R.D. will consist of the transfer to the Palestinian side of 13% from Area C as follows: 1% to Area (A) 12% to Area (B). The Palestinian side has informed that it will allocate an area/areas amounting to 3% from the above Area (B) to be designated as Green Areas and/or Nature Reserves. The Palestinian side has further informed that they will act according to the established scientific standards, and that therefore there will be no changes in the status of these areas, without prejudice to the rights of the existing inhabitants in these areas including Bedouins; while these standards do not allow new construction in these areas, existing roads and buildings may be maintained. The Israeli side will retain in these Green Areas/Nature Reserves the overriding security responsibility for the purpose of protecting Israelis and confronting the threat of terrorism. Activities and movements of the Palestinian Police forces may be carried out after coordination and confirmation; the Israeli side will respond to such requests expeditiously.

2. As part of the foregoing implementation of the first and second F.R.D., 14.2% from Area (B) will become Area (A).

B. Third Phase of Further Redeployments

With regard to the terms of the Interim Agreement and of Secretary Christopher's letters to the two sides of January 17, 1997 relating to the further redeployment process, there will be a committee to address this question. The United States will be briefed regularly.

II. SECURITY

In the provisions on security arrangements of the Interim Agreement, the Palestinian side agreed to take all measures necessary in order to prevent acts of terrorism, crime and hostilities directed against the Israeli side, against individuals falling under the Israeli side's authority and against their property, just as the Israeli side agreed to take all measures necessary in order to prevent acts of terrorism, crime and hostilities directed against the Palestinian side, against individuals falling under the Palestinian side's authority and against their property. The two sides also agreed to take legal measures against offenders within their jurisdiction and to prevent incitement against each other by any organizations, groups or individuals within their jurisdiction. Both sides recognize that it is in their vital interests to combat terrorism and fight violence in accordance with Annex I of the Interim Agreement and the Note for the Record. They also recognize that the struggle against terror and violence must be comprehensive in that it deals with terrorists, the terror support structure, and the environment conducive to the support of terror. It must be continuous and constant over a long-term, in that there can be no pauses in the work against terrorists and their structure. It must be cooperative in that no effort can be fully effective without Israeli-Palestinian cooperation and the continuous exchange of information, concepts, and actions. Pursuant to the prior agreements, the Palestinian side's implementation of its responsibilities for security, security cooperation, and other issues will be as detailed below during the time periods specified in the attached time line:

A. Security Actions

1. Outlawing and Combating Terrorist Organizations

(a) The Palestinian side will make known its policy of zero tolerance for terror and violence against both sides.

(b) A work plan developed by the Palestinian side will be shared with the U.S. and thereafter implementation will begin immediately to ensure the systematic and effective combat of terrorist organizations and their infrastructure.

(c) In addition to the bilateral Israeli-Palestinian security cooperation, a U.S.-Palestinian committee will meet biweekly to review the steps being taken to eliminate terrorists calls and the support structure that plans, finances, supplies and abets terror. In these meetings, the Palestinian side will inform the U.S. fully of the actions it has taken to outlaw all organizations (or wings of organizations, as appropriate) of a military, terrorist or violent character and their support structure and to prevent them from operating in area under its jurisdiction.

(d) The Palestinian side will apprehend the specific individuals suspected of perpetrating acts of violence and terror for the purpose of further investigation, and prosecution and punishment of all persons involved in acts of violence and terror.

(e) A U.S.-Palestinian committee will meet to review and evaluate information pertinent to the decisions on prosecution, punishment or other legal measures which affect the status of individuals suspected of abetting or perpetrating acts of violence and terror.

2. Prohibiting Illegal Weapons

(a) The Palestinian side will ensure an effective legal framework is in place to criminalize, in conformity with the prior agreements, any importation, manufacturing or unlicensed sale, acquisition or possession of firearms, ammunition or weapons in areas under Palestinian jurisdiction.

(b) In addition, the Palestinian side will establish and vigorously and continuously implement a systematic program for the collection and appropriate handling of all such illegal items in accordance with the prior agreements. The U.S. has agreed to assist in carrying out this program.

(c) A U.S.-Palestinian-Israeli committee will be established to assist and enhance cooperation in preventing the smuggling or other unauthorized introduction of weapons or explosive materials into areas under Palestinian jurisdiction.

3. Prevention Incitement

(a) Drawing on relevant international practice and pursuant to Article XXII (1) of the Interim Agreement and the Note for the Record, the Palestinian side will issue a decree prohibiting all forms of incitement to violence or terror, and establishing mechanisms for acting systematically against all expressions or threats of violence or terror. This decree will be comparable to the existing Israeli legislation which deals with the same subject.

(b) A U.S.-Palestinian-Israeli committee will meet on a regular basis to monitor cases of possible incitement to violence or terror and to make recommendations and reports on how to prevent such incitement. The Israeli, Palestinian and U.S. sides will each appoint a media specialist, a law enforcement representative, an educational specialist and a current or former elected official to the committee.

B. Security Cooperation

The two sides agree that their security cooperation will be based on a spirit of partnership and will include, among other things, the following steps:

1. Bilateral Cooperation

There will be full bilateral security cooperation between the two sides which will be continuous, intensive and comprehensive.

2. Forensic Cooperation

There will be an exchange of forensic expertise, training, and other assistance.

3. Trilateral Committee

In addition to the bilateral Israeli-Palestinian security cooperation, a high-ranking U.S.-Palestinian-Israeli committee will meet as required and not less than biweekly to assess current threats, deal with any impediments to effective security cooperation and coordination and address the steps being taken to combat terror and terrorist organizations. The committee will also serve as a forum to address the issue of external support for terror. In these meetings, the Palestinian side will fully inform the members of the committee of the results of its investigations concerning terrorist suspects already in custody and the participants will exchange additional relevant information. The committee will report regularly to the leaders of the two sides on the status of cooperation, the results of the meetings and its recommendations.

C. Other Issues

(a) The Palestinian side will provide a list of its policemen to the Israeli side in conformity with the prior agreements.

(b) Should the Palestinian side request technical assistance, the U.S. has indicated its willingness to help meet those needs in cooperation with other donors.

(c) The Monitoring and Steering Committee will, as part of its functions, monitor the implementation of this provision and brief the U.S.

2. PLO Charter

The Executive Committee of the Palestine Liberation Organization and the Palestinian Central Council will reaffirm the letter of 22 January 1998 from PLO Chairman Yasir Arafat to President Clinton concerning the nullification of the Palestinian National Charter provisions that are inconsistent with the letters exchanged between the PLO and the Government of Israel on 9–10 September 1993. PLO Chairman Arafat, the Speaker of the Palestine National Council, and the Speaker of the Palestinian Council will invite the members of the PNC, as well as the members of the Central Council, the Council, and the Palestinian Heads of Ministries to a meeting to be addressed by President Clinton to reaffirm their support for the peace process and the aforementioned decisions of the Executive Committee and the Central Council. . . .

4. Human Rights and the Rule of Law Pursuant to Article XI

(1) of Annex I of the Interim Agreement, and without derogating from

the above, the Palestinian Police will exercise powers and responsibilities to implement this Memorandum with due regard to internationally accepted norms of human rights and the rule of law, and will be guided by the need to protect the public, respect human dignity, and avoid harassment.

III. INTERIM COMMITTEES AND ECONOMIC ISSUES

1. The Israeli and Palestinian sides reaffirm their commitment to enhancing their relationship and agree on the need actively to promote economic development in the West Bank and Gaza. In this regard, the parties agree to continue or to reactivate all standing committees established by the Interim Agreement, including the Monitoring and Steering Committee, the Joint Economic Committee (JEC), the Civil Affairs Committee (CAC), the Legal Committee, and the Standing Cooperation Committee.

2. The Israeli and Palestinian sides have agreed on arrangements which will permit the timely opening of the Gaza Industrial Estate. They also have concluded a "Protocol Regarding the Establishment and Operation of the International Airport in the Gaza Strip During the Interim Period."

3. Both sides will renew negotiations on Safe Passage immediately. As regards the southern route, the sides will make best efforts to conclude the agreement within a week of the entry into force of this Memorandum. Operation of the southern route will start as soon as possible thereafter. As regards the northern route, negotiations will continue with the goal of reaching agreement as soon as possible. Implementation will take place expeditiously thereafter.

4. The Israeli and Palestinian sides acknowledge the great importance of the Port of Gaza for the development of the Palestinian economy, and the expansion of Palestinian trade. They commit themselves to proceeding without delay to conclude an agreement to allow the construction and operation of the port in accordance with the prior agreements. The Israeli-Palestinian Committee will reactivate its work immediately with a goal of concluding the protocol within 60 days, which will allow commencement of the construction of the port.

5. The two sides recognize that unresolved legal issues adversely affect the relationship between the two peoples. They therefore will accelerate efforts through the Legal Committee to address outstanding legal issues and to implement solutions to these issues in the shortest possible period. The Palestinian side will provide to the Israeli side copies of all of its laws in effect.

6. The Israeli and Palestinian sides also will launch a strategic economic dialogue to enhance their economic relationship. They will establish within the framework of the JEC and Ad Hoc Committee for this purpose. The committee will review the following four issues:

(1) Israeli purchase taxes;

(2) cooperation in combating vehicle theft;

(3) dealing with unpaid Palestinian debts; and

(4) the impact of Israeli standards as barriers to trade and the expansion of the A1 and A2 lists. The committee will submit an interim report within three weeks of the entry into force of this Memorandum, and within six weeks will submit its conclusions and recommendations to be implemented.

7. The two sides agree on the importance of continued international donor assistance to facilitate implementation by both sides of agreements reached. They also recognize the need for enhanced donor support for economic development in the West Bank and Gaza. They agree to jointly approach the donor community to organize a Ministerial Conference before the end of 1998 to seek pledges for enhanced levels of assistance.

IV. Permanent Status Negotiations

The two sides will immediately resume permanent status negotiations on an accelerated basis and will make a determined effort to achieve the mutual goal of reaching an agreement by May 4, 1999. The negotiations will be continuous and without interruption. The United States has expressed its willingness to facilitate these negotiations.

V. Unilateral Actions

Recognizing the necessity to create a positive environment for the negotiations, neither side shall initiate or take any step that will change the status of the West Bank and the Gaza Strip in accordance with the Interim Agreement.

King Hussein of Jordan: Remarks at Wye River Agreement Signing Ceremony (October 23, 1998)

. . . . I recall in discovering past events over many years, and one thing that remained with me throughout those many years was a total commitment to the cause of peace. We quarrel, we agree; we are friendly, we are not friendly. But we have no right to dictate through irresponsible action or narrow-mindedness the future of our children and their children's children. There has been enough destruction. Enough death. Enough waste. And it's time that, together, we occupy a place beyond ourselves, our peoples, that is worthy of them under the sun, the descendants of the children of Abraham. . . .

I think that we passed a crossroad. We have made our commitment to the welfare and happiness and security and future of our peoples in all the times to come. And now our partners are numerous, and we wish them every success in their endeavors and we'll do everything we can to help them. I think such a step as is concluded today will inevitably trigger those who want to destroy life, destroy hope, create fear in the hearts and minds of people, trigger in them their worst instincts. They will be skeptical on the surface, but if they can, they will cause damage, wherever they are and wherever they belong. Let's hope that the overwhelming majority of us— those who are committed to the future, those who know what responsibilities they hold now—will be able, through steady progress and a determined combined joint effort, be able to thwart their aims and their objectives and move—and maybe, God willing, witness the dawn that we are always seeking of a comprehensive peace in our entire region. . . .

U.S. President Bill Clinton: Speech to the Palestinian Leadership (December 14, 1998)

. . . . I am profoundly honored to be the first American President to address the Palestinian people in a city [Gaza City] governed by Palestinians. I have listened carefully to all that has been said. I have watched carefully the reactions of all of you to what has been said. I know that the Palestinian people stand at a crossroads; behind you a history of dispossession and dispersal, before you the opportunity to shape a new Palestinian future on your own land.

I know the way is often difficult and frustrating, but you have come to this point through a commitment to peace and negotiations. You reaffirmed that commitment today. I believe it is the only way to fulfill the aspirations of your people and I am profoundly grateful to have had the opportunity to work with Chairman Arafat for the cause of peace, to come here as a friend of peace and a friend of your future, and to witness you raising your hands, standing up tall, standing up not only against what you believe is wrong, but for what you believe is right in the future.

I was sitting here thinking that this moment would have been inconceivable a decade ago—no Palestinian Authority, no elections in Gaza and the West Bank, no relations between the United States and Palestinians, no Israeli troop redeployments from the West Bank and Gaza, no Palestinians, in charge in Gaza, Ramallah, Bethlehem, Hebron, Tulkarem, Jenin, Nablus, Jericho and so many other places. There was no Gaza International Airport. Today, I had the privilege of cutting the ribbon on the International Airport.

Hillary and I, along with Chairman and Mrs. Arafat, celebrated a place that will become a magnet for planes from throughout the Middle East and beyond, bringing you a future in which Palestinians can travel directly to the far corners of the world; a future in which it is easier and cheaper to bring materials, technology and expertise in and out of Gaza; a future in which tourists and traders can flock here, to this beautiful place on the Mediterranean; a future, in short, in which the Palestinian people are connected to the world. I am told that just a few months ago, at a time of profound pessimism in the peace process, your largest exporter of fruit and flowers was prepared to plow under a field of roses, convinced the airport would never open. But Israelis and Palestinians came to agreement at Wye River, the airport has opened, and now I am told that company plans to export roses and carnations to Europe and throughout the Gulf, a true flowering of Palestinian promise.

I come here today to talk about that promise, to ask you to rededicate yourselves to it, to ask you to think for a moment about how we can get beyond the present state of things where every step forward is like, as we say in America, pulling teeth. Where there is still, in spite of the agreement at Wye, achieved because we don't need much sleep and we worked so hard, and Mr. Netanyahu worked with us, and we made this agreement. But I want to talk to you about how we can get beyond this moment, where there is still so much mistrust and misunderstanding and quite a few missteps. You did a good thing today in raising your hands. You know why? It has nothing to do with the government in Israel. You will touch the people of Israel. I want the people of Israel to know that for many Palestinians, five years after Oslo, the benefits of this process remain remote; that for too many Palestinians lives are hard, jobs are scarce, prospects are uncertain and personal grief is great.

I know that tremendous pain remains as a result of losses suffered from violence, the separation of families, the restrictions on the movement of people and goods. I understand your concerns about settlement activity, land confiscation and home demolitions. I understand your concerns, and theirs, about unilateral statements that could prejudge the outcome of final status negotiations. I understand, in short, that there's still a good deal of misunderstanding five years after the beginning of this remarkable process. It takes time to change things and still more time for change to benefit everyone. It takes determination and courage to make peace and sometimes even more to persevere for peace. But slowly, but surely, the peace agreements are turning into concrete progress the transfer of territories, the Gaza industrial estate and the airport. These changes will make a difference in many Palestinian lives.

I thank you, I thank you, Mr. Chairman, for your leadership for peace and your perseverance, for enduring all the criticism from all sides, for being willing to change course and for being strong enough to stay with what is right. You have done a remarkable thing for your people.

America is determined to do what we can to bring tangible benefits of peace. I am proud that the roads we traveled on to get here were paved, in part, with our assistance, as were hundreds of miles of roads that knit together towns and villages throughout the West Bank and Gaza. Two weeks ago, in Washington, we joined with other nations to pledge hundreds of millions of dollars toward your development, including health care and clean water, education for your children, rule of law projects that nurture democracy. Today I am pleased to announce we will also fund the training of Palestinian health care providers, and airport administrators, increase our support to Palestinian refugees. And next year I will ask the Congress for another several hundred million dollars to support the development of the Palestinian people.

But make no mistake about it, all this was made possible because of what you did because five years ago you made a choice for peace, and because through all the tough times since, when in your own mind you had a hundred good reasons to walk away, you didn't. Because you still harbor the wisdom that led to the Oslo Accords, that led to the signing in Washington in September of '93, you still can raise your hand and stand and lift your voice for peace.

Mr. Chairman, you said some profound words today in embracing the idea that Israelis and Palestinians can live in peace as neighbors. Again I say you have led the way, and we would not be here without you. I say to all of you, I can come here and work, I can bring you to America and we can work, but in the end, this is up to you. You and the Israelis. For you have to live with the consequences of what you do. I can help because I believe it is my job to do so; I believe it is my duty to do so; because America has Palestinian Americans, Jewish Americans, other Arab Americans who desperately want us to be helpful. But in the end, you have to decide what the understanding will be, and you have to decide whether we can get beyond the present moment where there is still, for all the progress we have made, so much mistrust. And the people who are listening to us today in Israel, they have to make the same decisions.

Peace must mean many things: legitimate rights for Palestinians, real security for Israel. But it must begin with something even more basic—mutual recognition, seeing people who are different, with whom there have been profound differences, as people.

I've had two profoundly emotional experiences in the last less than 24 hours. I was with Chairman Arafat and four little children came to see me whose fathers are in Israeli prisons. Last night, I met some little children whose fathers had been killed in conflict with Palestinians, at the dinner that Prime Minister Netanyahu had for me. Those children brought tears to my eyes. We have to find a way for both sets of children to get their lives back and to go forward.

Palestinians must recognize the right of Israel and its people to live safe and secure lives today, tomorrow and forever. Israel must recognize the right of Palestinians to aspire to live free today, tomorrow and forever.

And I ask you to remember these experiences I had with these two groups of children. If I had met them in reverse order I would not have known which ones were Israeli and which Palestinian. If they had all been lined up in a row and I had seen their tears, I could not tell whose father was dead and whose father was in prison, or what the story of their lives were, making up the grief that they bore. We must acknowledge that neither side has a monopoly on pain or virtue.

At the end of America's Civil War, in my home state, a man was elected governor who had fought with President Lincoln's forces, even though most of the people in my home state fought with the secessionist forces. And he made his inaugural speech after four years of unbelievable bloodshed in America, in which he had been on the winning side, but in the minority in our home. And everyone wondered what kind of leader he would be. His first sentence was, "We have all done wrong." I say that because I think the beginning of mutual respect after so much pain is to recognize not only the positive characteristics of people on both sides, but the fact that there has been a lot a lot of hurt and harm. The fulfillment of one side's aspirations must not come at the expense of the other. We must believe that everyone can win in the new Middle East.

It does not hurt Israelis to hear Palestinians peacefully and pridefully asserting their identity, as we saw today. That is not a bad thing. And it does not hurt Palestinians to acknowledge the profound desire of Israelis to live without fear. It is in this spirit that I ask you to consider where we go from here. I thank you for your rejection fully, finally and forever of the passages in the Palestinian Charter calling for the destruction of Israel. For they were the ideological underpinnings of a struggle renounced at Oslo. By revoking them once and for all, you have sent, I say again, a powerful message not to the government, but to the people of Israel. You will touch people on the street there. You will reach their hearts there. I know how profoundly important this is to Israelis. I have been there four times as President. I have spent a lot of time with people other than the political leaders Israeli school children who heard about you only as someone who thought they should be driven into the sea. They did not know what their parents or grandparents did that you thought was so bad. They were just children, too. Is it surprising that all this has led to the hardening of hearts on both sides; that they refuse to acknowledge your existence as a people and that led to a terrible reaction by you? By turning this page on the past you are taking the lead in writing a new story for the future. And you have issued a challenge to the government and the leaders of Israel to walk down that path with you. I thank you for doing that. The children of all the Middle East thank you.

But declaring a change of heart still won't be enough. Let's be realistic here. First of all, there are real differences. And secondly, a lot of water has flowed under the bridge, as we used to say at home. An American poet has written, "To long a sacrifice can make a stone of the heart." Palestinians and Israelis and their pasts both share a history of oppression and dispossession; both have felt their hearts turn to stone for living too long in fear and seeing loved ones die too young. You are two great people of strong talent and soaring ambition, sharing such a small piece of sacred land. The time has come to sanctify your holy ground with genuine forgiveness and reconciliation. Every influential Palestinian, from teacher to journalist, from politician to community leader, must make this a mission to banish from the minds of children glorifying suicide bombers; to end the practice of speaking peace in one place and preaching hatred in another; to teach school children the value of peace and the waste of war; to break the cycle of violence. Our great American prophet, Martin Luther King, once said, "The old law of an eye for an eye leaves everybody blind." I believe you have gained more in five years of peace than in 45 years of war. I believe that what we are doing today, working together for security, will lead to further gains and changes in the heart. I believe that our work against terrorism, as you stand strong, will be rewarded for that must become a fact of the past. It must never be a part of your future. Let me say this as clearly as I can: no matter how sharp a grievance or how deep a hurt, there is no justification for killing innocents.

Mr. Chairman, you said at the White House that no Israel mother should have to worry if her son or daughter is late coming home. Your words touched many people. You said much the same thing today. We must invest those words with the weight of reality in the minds of every person in Israel and every Palestinian. I feel this all the more strongly because the act of a few can falsify the image of the many. How many times have we seen it? How many times has it happened to us? We both know it is profoundly wrong to equate Palestinians in particular and Islam in general with terrorism, or to see a fundamental conflict between Islam and the West. For the vast majority of the more than one billion Muslims in the world, tolerance is an article of faith and terrorism a travesty of faith.

I know that in my own country, where Islam is one of the fastest growing religions, we share the same devotion to family and hard work and community. When it comes to relations between the United States and Palestinians, we have come far to overcome our misperceptions of each other. Americans have come to appreciate the strength of your identity and the dept of your aspirations. And we have learned to listen to your grievances as well. I hope you have begun to see America as your friend.

I have tried to speak plainly to you about the need to reach out to the people of Israel, to understand the pain of their children, to understand the history of their fear and mistrust, their yearning, gnawing desire for security, because that is the only way friends can speak and the only way we can move forward. I took the same liberty yesterday in Israel. I talked there about the need to see one's own mistakes, not just those of others; to recognize the steps others have taken for peace, not just one's own; to break out of the politics of absolutes; to treat one's neighbors with respect and dignity. I talked about the profound courage of both peoples and their leaders which must continue in order for a secure, just and lasting peace to occur; the courage of Israelis to continue turning over territory for peace and security; the courage of Palestinians to take action against all those who resort to and support violence and terrorism; the courage of Israelis to guarantee safe passage between the West Bank and Gaza and allow for greater trade and development; the courage of Palestinians to confiscate illegal weapons of war and terror; the courage of Israelis to curtail closures and curfews that remain a daily hardship; the courage of Palestinians to resolve all differences at the negotiating table; the courage of both peoples to abandon the rhetoric of hate that still poisons public discourse and limits the vision of your children; and the courage to move ahead to final status negotiations together, without either side taking unilateral steps or making unilateral statements that could prejudice the outcome whether governing refugee settlements, borders, Jerusalem, or any other issue encompassed by the Oslo Accord. Now, it will take good faith, mutual respect and compromise to forge a final agreement. I think there will be more breakdowns, frankly; but I think there will be more breakthroughs, as well. There will be more challenges to peace from its enemies. And so I ask you today never to lose sight of how far you have come. With Chairman Arafat's leadership already you have accomplished what many said was impossible. The seemingly intractable problems of the past can clearly find practical solutions in the future. But it requires a consistent commitment and a genuine willingness to change heart.

As we approach this new century, think of this: think of all the conflicts in the 20th century that many people thought were permanent that have been healed or are healing. Two great world wars between the French and the Germans; they're best friends. The Americans and the Russians, the whole Cold War, now we have a constructive partnership. The Irish Catholics and Protestants; the Chinese and the Japanese; the black and white South Africans; the Serbs, the Croats and the Muslims in Bosnia all have turned from conflict to cooperation. Yes, there is still some distrust; yes, there's still some difficulty but they are walking down the right road together. And when they see each other's children, increasingly they only see children, together. When they see the children crying they realize the pain is real, whatever the child's story. In each case there was a vision of greater peace and prosperity and security.

In biblical times, Jews and Arabs lived side by side. They contributed to the flowering of Alexandria. During the Golden Age of Spain, Jews, Muslims and Christians came together in an era of remarkable tolerance and learning a third of the population laid down its tools on Friday, a third on

Saturday, a third on Sunday. They were scholars and scientists, poets, musicians, merchants and statesmen, setting an example of peaceful coexistence that we can make a model for the future. There is no guarantee of success or failure today, but the challenge of this generation of Palestinians is to wage an historic and heroic struggle for peace.

Again I say this is an historic day. I thank you for coming. I thank you for raising your hands. I thank you for standing up. I thank you for your voices. I thank you for clapping every time I said what you were really doing was reaching deep into the heart of the people of Israel. Chairman Arafat said he and Mrs. Arafat are taking Hillary and Chelsea and me, we're going to Bethlehem tomorrow. For a Christian family to light the Christmas tree in Bethlehem is a great honor. It is an interesting thing to contemplate that in this small place, the home of Islam, Judaism and Christianity the embodiment of my faith was born a Jew and is still recognized by Muslims as a prophet. He said a lot of very interesting things. But in the end he was known as the Prince of Peace. And we celebrate at Christmastime the birth of the Prince of Peace. One reason He is known as the Prince of Peace is he knew something about what it takes to make peace. And one of the wisest things He ever said was, "We will be judged by the same standard by which we judge; but mercy triumphs over judgment."

In this Christmas season, in this Hanukkah season, on the edge of Ramadan, this is a time for mercy and vision and looking at all of our children together. You have reaffirmed the fact that you now intend to share this piece of land without war, with your neighbors, forever. They have heard you. They have heard you. Now, you and they must now determine what kind of peace you will have. Will it be grudging and mean-spirited and confining, or will it be generous and open? Will you begin to judge each other in the way you would like to be judged? Will you begin to see each other's children in the way you see your own? Will they feel your pain and will you understand theirs? Surely, to goodness, after five years of this peace process, and decades of suffering, and after you have come here today and done what you have done, we can say, enough of this gnashing of teeth, let us join hands and proudly go forward together.

Israeli Prime Minister Ehud Barak: Presentation of the Government to the Knesset (July 6, 1999)

. . . . Now it is our duty to complete the mission, and establish a comprehensive peace in the Middle East which has known so much war. It is our duty to ourselves and our children to take decisive measures to strengthen Israel by ending the Arab-Israeli conflict. This government is determined to make every effort, pursue every path and do everything necessary for Israel's security, the achievement of peace and the prevention of war. We have an historic obligation to take advantage of the "window of opportunity" which has opened before us in order to bring long-term security and peace to Israel. We know that comprehensive and stable peace can be established only if it rests, simultaneously, on four pillars: Egypt, Jordan, and Syria and Lebanon, in some sense as a single bloc, and of course the Palestinians. As long as peace is not grounded on all these four pillars, it will remain incomplete and unstable.

The Arab countries must know that only a strong and self-confident Israel can bring peace. Here, today, I call upon all the leaders of the region to extend their hands to meet our outstretched hand, and toward a "peace of the brave," in a region which has known so much war, blood and suffering. To our neighbors the Palestinians, I wish to say: the bitter conflict between us has brought great suffering to both our peoples. Now, there is no reason to settle accounts over historical mistakes. Perhaps things could have been otherwise, but we cannot change the past; we can only make the future better. I am not only cognizant of the sufferings of my people, but I also recognize the sufferings of the Palestinian people.

My ambition and desire is to bring an end to violence and suffering, and to work with the elected Palestinian leadership, under Chairman Yasser Arafat, in partnership and respect, in order to jointly arrive at a fair and agreed settlement for coexistence in freedom, prosperity and good neighborliness in this beloved land where the two peoples will always live. To Syrian President Hafez Assad, I say that the new Israeli government is determined, as soon as possible, to advance the negotiations for the achievement of full, bilateral treaty of peace and security, on the basis of Security Council Resolutions 242 and 338. We have been tough and bitter adversaries on the battlefield. The time has come to establish a secure and courageous peace which will ensure the futures of our peoples, our children and our grandchildren. It is my intention to bring an end to the IDF presence in Lebanon within one year, to deploy the IDF, through agreement, along the border, and to bring our boys home while also taking the necessary measures to guarantee the welfare and security of residents along the northern border, as well as the future of the Lebanese security and civilian assistance personnel who have worked alongside us, over all these years, for the sake of the residents of the region. I wish to take advantage of this opportunity to praise the residents of Kiryat Shmona and communities along the confrontation line for their firm stand in the face of the Katyushas. From here, on behalf of us all, I offer my support to them. Their determination and the strength of the IDF are what will enable us to create the new situation. . . .

The Government's objective will be to act, at the same time, to bring peace closer on all fronts, but without compromising on Israel's security needs and most vital interests first and foremost among them, a united Jerusalem, the eternal capital of Israel, under our sovereignty. We will not be deterred by the difficulties. I know very well that difficult negotiations, replete with crises and ups and downs, await us before we reach our desired goal. I can only promise that, if the other side displays the same degree of determination and good will to reach an agreement as on our side, no force in the world will prevent us from achieving peace here. In this context, I attach the greatest importance to the support of our partners to peace treaties: Egypt and Jordan. I believe that President Hosni Mubarak and King Abdullah can play a vital role in creating the dynamics and an atmosphere of trust so needed for progress toward peace. They can also advance education for peace among the children of Egypt and Jordan, the Palestinians and, in the future, also of Syria and Lebanon education for peace, which is a condition for any longterm, stable peace. I am convinced that King Hassan of Morocco can also contribute to this, as can other countries who already, in the past, opened channels of communication with Israel, cooperating with the peace process in various spheres. My aspiration will be to firmly resume these contacts in order to create a favorable regional atmosphere that can assist the negotiations. The guarantee of the peace agreements and their implementation lies in the strength of the Israel Defense Forces. As such, we will attend to bolstering the IDF, the quality of its commanders and soldiers, its equipment with the best educational and technological systems training and fitness, its ability to always be prepared to deter and provide a response to distant and near dangers, and to all kinds of threats, whether conventional or otherwise. . . .

Israeli Government: Basic Guidelines
(July 1999)

. . . .

1.2 The Government of Israel will act to bring an end to the Arab-Israeli conflict through peaceful means, and by standing firm on Israel's national security, integrity and development. The Government will strive to establish peace based on mutual respect, ensuring the security and other vital interests of the State and offering personal security for all its citizens. . . .

2.1 The Government views peace as a basic value of life in Israel, whose sources draw on the vision of the Prophets, as expressed in the Declaration of Independence and in the continued yearning of the Israeli people for peace and security. The Government believes that it is possible to bring an end to the cycle of blood-shed in our region. Making peace is grounded in the strength of the IDF and on the overall strength of Israel, on the deterrent capabilities of the State, and on the desire for stability in the

Middle East that will allow resources to be directed toward economic and social development.

2.2 Peace is a component in the national security conception and the foreign relations of Israel. The arrangements and peace treaties to which Israel will be a partner will be grounded in the preservation of the security and national interests of Israel, resting on the broad support of the people in Israel.

2.3 The Government will cultivate the strength of the IDF as the defensive and deterrent force of Israel.

2.4 The Government will conduct an all-out war against terrorist organizations and the initiators and perpetrators of terrorism, and guarantee the personal security of all residents of Israel.

2.5 As part of its policy to bring about and establish peace in the Middle East, the Government will act toward the development of mechanisms for political, economic, scientific and cultural cooperation between peoples of the region.

2.6 The Government will act to accelerate the negotiations with the Palestinians, based on the existing process, with a view toward ending the conflict with a permanent settlement that guarantees the security and vital interests of Israel. The permanent settlement with the Palestinians will be submitted for approval in a referendum.

2.7 The Government will honor and implement the agreements which Israel has signed with the Palestinians, while, at the same time, insisting that the Palestinian Authority also honor and implement these agreements.

2.8 The Government will resume the negotiations with Syria with a view toward concluding a peace treaty therewith full peace that bolsters the security of Israel, grounded in UN Security Council Resolutions 242 and 338 and on the existence of a normal relationship between two neighboring states, living side by side in peace. The peace treaty with Syria will be submitted for approval in a referendum.

2.9 The Government will act toward bringing the IDF out of Lebanon, while guaranteeing the welfare and security of residents of the north, and aspiring to conclude a peace treaty with Lebanon.

2.10 The Government views Egypt, Jordan and the Palestinian Authority as important partners in the effort to establish peace in our region, and will conduct an ongoing political dialogue with each of them. The Government will also work to advance understanding and friendship, as well as the development of the economy, commerce and tourism between the Israeli people and the Egyptian, Jordanian and Palestinian peoples.

2.11 The Government will conduct an ongoing dialogue with the United States with regard to its positions on the permanent settlement. The dialogue will also relate to American political, economic and defense assistance to Israel. The Government will work to intensify the special

friendship between the United States and Israel, and to continue and cultivate the strategic cooperation with the United States. . . .

3.1 Greater Jerusalem, the eternal capital of Israel, will remain united
and complete under the sovereignty of Israel.

3.2 Members of all religions will be guaranteed free access to the holy
places, and freedom of worship.

3.3 The Government will work toward the development and prosperity
of Jerusalem, and for continued construction therein for the welfare of all
its residents.

4.1 The Government views all forms of settlement as a valued social
and national enterprise, and will work to improve its ability to contend
with the difficulties and challenges it faces.

4.2 Until the status of the Jewish communities in Judea, Samaria and
Gaza is determined, within the framework of the permanent settlement, no
new communities will be built and no existing communities will be detri-
mentally affected.

4.3 The Government will work to ensure the security of the Jewish residents in Judea, Samaria and Gaza, and to provide regular Government and
municipal services equal to those offered to residents of all other communities in Israel. . . .

U.S. President Bill Clinton, Israeli Prime Minister Ehud Barak, and Syrian Foreign Minister Faruk al-Shara: Speeches at the Renewal of Syrian-Israeli Negotiations (December 15, 1999)

U.S. President Bill Clinton

When the history of this century is written, some of its most illustrious
chapters will be the stories of men and women who put old rivalries and
conflicts behind them and looked ahead to peace and reconciliation for
their children. What we are witnessing today is not yet peace, and getting
there will require bold thinking and hard choices. But today is a big step
along that path. Prime Minister Barak and Foreign Minister Shara are
about to begin the highest level meeting ever between their two countries.
They are prepared to get down to business. For the first time in history,
there is a chance of a comprehensive peace between Israel and Syria and
indeed all its neighbors. That Prime Minister Barak and Foreign Minister
Shara chose to come here to Washington reminds us of one other fact, of
course, which is the United States' own responsibility in this endeavor.
Secretary Albright and I and our entire team will do everything we possi-

bly can to help the parties succeed. For a comprehensive peace in the Middle East is vital not only to the region, it is also vital to the world and to the security of the American people. For we have learned from experience that tensions in the region can escalate, and the escalations can lead into diplomatic, financial and ultimately military involvement far more costly than even the costliest peace. We should be clear, of course. The success of the enterprise we embark upon today is not guaranteed. The road to peace is no easier and in many ways it is harder than the road to war.

There will be challenges along the way, but we have never had such an extraordinary opportunity to reach a comprehensive settlement. Prime Minister Barak, an exceptional hero in war, is now a determined soldier for peace. He knows a negotiated peace, one that serves the interests of all sides, is the only way to bring genuine security to the people of Israel, to see that they are bound by a circle of peace. President Assad too has known the cost of war. From my discussion with him in recent months, I am convinced he knows what a true peace could do to lift the lives of his people and give them a better future. And Foreign Minister Shara is an able representative of the president and the people of Syria.

Let me also say a brief word about the continuing progress of the Palestinian track. Chairman Arafat also has embarked on a courageous quest for peace and the Israelis and the Palestinians continue to work on that. We see new leaders with an unquestioned determination to defend and advance the interest of their own people, but also determined to marshal the courage and creativity, the vision and resolve to secure a bright future based on peace rather than a dark future under the storm clouds of continuing, endless conflict. At the close of this millennium and in this season of religious celebration for Jews, for Muslims, for Christians, Israelis, Palestinians, Syrians, Lebanese, all have it within their power to end decades of bitter conflict. Together they can choose to write a new chapter in the history of our time. Again, let me say that today's meeting is a big step in the right direction, and I am profoundly grateful for the leaders of both nations for being here. We have just talked and agreed that it would be appropriate for each leader to say a few brief words on behalf of the delegation. We will take no questions in keeping with our commitment to do serious business and not cause more problems than we can solve out here with you and all your helpful questions.

Israeli Prime Minister Ehud Barak

We came here to put behind us the horrors of war and to step forward toward peace. We are fully aware of the opportunity of the building of responsibility and of the seriousness, determination and devotion that will be needed in order to begin this march together with our Syrian partners to make a different Middle East where nations are living side by side in peaceful relationship and in mutual respect and good neighborliness. We are determined to do whatever we can to put an end and to bring about the dreams of children and mothers all around the region to see a better future of the Middle East at the entrance to the new millennium.

Syrian Foreign Minister Farouk al-Shara

. . . . Your announcement, Mr. President, was warmly welcomed, both in Syria and in the Arab world, and its positive echoes resonated in the world at large. That is because it promises for the first time the dawn of a real hope to achieve an honorable and just peace in the Middle East. And as you have mentioned in your letter of Oct. 12, 1999, to President Assad, the issues have crystallized and difficulties defined. That is why, if these talks are to succeed as rapidly as we all desire, no one should ignore what has been achieved until now or what still needs to be achieved.

It goes without saying that peace for Syria means the return of all its occupied land, while for Israel, peace will mean the end of the psychological fear which the Israelis have been living in as a result of the existence of occupation, which is undoubtedly the source of all adversities and wars. Hence, ending occupation will be balanced for the first time by eliminating the barrier of fear and anxieties, and exchanging it with a true and a mutual feeling of peace and security.

Thus, the peace which the parties are going to reach will be established on justice and international legitimacy, and thus peace will be the only triumphant after 50 years of struggle. Those who reject to return the occupied territories to their original owners in the framework of international legitimacy send a message to the Arabs that the conflict between Israel and Arabs is a conflict of existence in which bloodshed can never stop, and not a conflict about borders which can be ended as soon as parties get the rights, as President Assad has stressed to these meetings more than once before and after Middle East peace conference.

We are approaching the moment of truth, as you have said, and there is no doubt that everyone realizes that a peace agreement between Syria and Israel and between Lebanon and Israel would indeed mean for our region the end of a history of wars and conflicts, and may well usher in a dialogue of civilization and an honorable competition in various domains the political, cultural, scientific and economy. Peace will certainly pose new questions to all sides, especially for the Arab side, who will wonder, after reviewing the past 50 years, whether the Arab-Israeli conflict was the one who solely defied the Arab unity or the one which frustrated it.

During the last half-century, in particular, the vision of the Arabs and their sufferings were totally ignored due to the lack of immediate opportunity for them which conveys their points of view to international opinion. And the last example of this is what we have witnessed during the last four days of attempts to muster international sympathy with a few thousand of settlers in the Golan, ignoring totally more than half a million Syrian people who were uprooted from tens of villages on the Golan where their fore-fathers lived for thousands of years and their villages were totally wiped out from existence.

The image formulated in the minds of Western people and which formulated in public opinion was that Syria was the aggressor and Syria was the one who shelled settlements from the Golan prior to the 1967 war. These claims carry no grain of truth in them. As Moshe Dayan has explained in his memoirs, that it was the other side who insisted on provoking the Syrians until they clashed together and then claimed that the Syrians are the aggressors. Mr. President, the peace talks between Israel and Syria have been ongoing for the last eight years with off and on, of course.

We hope that this is going to be the last resumption of negotiations which will be concluded with a peace agreement, a peace based on justice and comprehensivity, an honorable peace for both sides that preserves rights, dignity and sovereignty. Because only honorable and just peace will be embraced by future generations. And it is the only peace that shall open new horizons for totally new relations between peoples of the region.

President Assad has announced many years ago that peace is the strategic option of Syria, and we hope that peace has become the strategic option for others today in order to have or to leave future generations a region that is not torn with wars, a region whose sky is not polluted by the smell of the blood and destruction. We all here agree that we are at a threshold of a historic opportunity, an opportunity for the Arabs and Israelis alike, and for the United States and the world at large. Therefore, we all have to be objective and show a high sense of responsibility in order to achieve a just and comprehensive peace, a peace that has been so long awaited by all the peoples of our region and the world at large.

UN Security Council:
Israel's Withdrawal from Lebanon
(June 19, 2000)

The Security Council welcomes the report of the Secretary-General of 16 June 2000 (S/2000/590) . . . [that] Israel has withdrawn its forces from Lebanon in accordance with resolution 425 (1978) of 19 March 1978.

. . . . The Council notes that Israel and Lebanon have confirmed to the Secretary-General, as referred to in his report of 16 June 2000 (S/2000/590), that identifying the withdrawal line was solely the responsibility of the United Nations and that they will respect the line as identified. . . .

The Security Council calls on all parties concerned to continue to cooperate fully with the United Nations and the United Nations Interim Force in Lebanon (UNIFIL) and to exercise utmost restraint. The Council reemphasizes the need for strict respect for the territorial integrity, sovereignty and political independence of Lebanon within its internationally recognized boundaries.

The Security Council, recalling resolution 425 (1978) and resolution 426 (1978) of 19 March 1978, calls on the Government of Lebanon to ensure the return of its effective authority and presence in the south. The Council notes that the United Nations cannot assume law and order functions which are properly the responsibility of the Government of Lebanon. In this regard, the Council welcomes the first steps taken by the Government of Lebanon and calls upon it to proceed with the deployment of the Lebanese armed forces as soon as possible, with the assistance of UNIFIL, into the Lebanese territory recently vacated by Israel.

The Security Council welcomes the measures taken by the Secretary-General and the troop-contributing countries relating to UNIFIL augmentation, in accordance with paragraph 32 of the report of the Secretary-General of 22 May 2000. The Council stresses that the redeployment of UNIFIL should be conducted in coordination with the Government of Lebanon and with the Lebanese armed forces. . . .

Israeli Prime Minister Ehud Barak: Leaving for the Camp David Talks (July 10, 2000)

. . . . The moment of truth is close and I am prepared for it.

One hundred years of enmity and struggle meet at this point in time. We have buried too many; there has been suffering and anguish on both sides because of the unbearably high price not only for defeat but also for victory. The time has now come to put an end to the conflict, and to give our children the opportunity to flourish in peace.

The time has come to make decisions and to bequeath a better future for our children; a different reality from that of our generation and our parents' generation.

This is the time to devote our best resources to education, to reducing unemployment, to bridging social gaps, to equal opportunities, and fully utilizing the enormous potential of our young and gifted generation.

This is the meaning of peace and security!

There is no peace without a price, just as there is no peace at any price. The dream and the ideal are lofty, and they will never be straightforward and perfect. The reality of life is highly complex and complicated. Painful compromise is required. There is no choice. . . .

The negotiations will be heart-rending and difficult because they will involve not only distant maps and locations, but also our beloved homeland. They will involve roots entrenched deep in the hills, and the love of the homeland to which I am bound and committed. This is a love that cannot be divided.

If we do reach an agreement that will put an end to the conflict, there will be a heavy but necessary price to pay. As Menahem Begin said, "The difficulties of peace are better than the agonies of war."

If there is an agreement, it will only be one that will strengthen the security of Israel, its economy, and its regional and international standing. Otherwise, there will be no agreement.

If there is an agreement, it will only be one that will comply with the principles to which I committed myself before I was elected, and principles that I have consistently and clearly stressed:

- –A united Jerusalem under Israeli sovereignty;
- –The 1967 borders will be amended;
- –The overwhelming majority of the settlers in Judea, Samaria and the Gaza Strip will be in settlement blocs under Israeli sovereignty;
- –No foreign army in the entire area west of the Jordan River;
- –A solution to the problem of refugees outside Israeli sovereign territory.

These are the principles—these and no others. If there is an agreement, I will submit it, as I promised, to the Israeli people for decision. It is the Israeli people who will decide on the agreement in a referendum. I will sign the agreement only if I am convinced that it strengthens Israel and its future. Such an agreement will, I am sure, be approved and endorsed by an overwhelming majority of the Israeli people, and I am sure by a majority of the Israeli residents of Judea, Samaria and the Gaza Strip.

If there is an agreement, it will require painful compromise, not only by us, but also by the Palestinians; otherwise, there will be no agreement.

I would like to take this opportunity, on the eve of the summit, to address the Palestinian leadership and people and ask them to clear the air of accusations, threats and gloomy prophecies, and to rise to the greatness of the hour.

We are arriving at a decisive crossroads in the future relationship between us. The choice between us is between the peace of the brave, which will put the relationship between us on a positive track of good neighborliness and prosperity; or, God forbid, will lead to violent conflict, which in turn will lead to further suffering and victims, and will not solve anything.

The State of Israel does not wish to control you or your future. We want good neighborly relations with you based on respect and liberty, on broad coordination, on shared interests, and on a separation that will allow you and us to maintain independent identities, development and free choice.

And I look forward to Yasir Arafat coming to Camp David with the full backing of the Palestinian people to achieve a historic peace. I expect him to come full of resolution and the ability to make a decision in order that together we may achieve our common goal. Together, with the help of the President of the United States, we will be able to bring peace and security to our peoples. . . .

U.S. President Bill Clinton: Statement after the Camp David Peace Talks (July 25, 2000)

After 14 days of intensive negotiations between Israelis and Palestinians, I have concluded with regret that they will not be able to reach an agreement at this time. As I explained on the eve of the summit, success was far from guaranteed—given the historical, religious, political and emotional dimensions of the conflict.

Still, because the parties were not making progress on their own and the September deadline they set for themselves was fast approaching, I thought we had no choice. We can't afford to leave a single stone unturned in the search for a just, lasting and comprehensive peace.

Now, at Camp David, both sides engaged in comprehensive discussions that were really unprecedented because they dealt with the most sensitive issues dividing them; profound and complex questions that long had been considered off limits.

Under the operating rules that nothing is agreed until everything is agreed, they are, of course, not bound by any proposal discussed at the summit. However, while we did not get an agreement here, significant progress was made on the core issues. I want to express my appreciation to Prime Minister Barak, Chairman Arafat and their delegations for the efforts they undertook to reach an agreement.

Prime Minister Barak showed particular courage and vision, and an understanding of the historical importance of this moment. Chairman Arafat made it clear that he, too, remains committed to the path of peace. The trilateral statement we issued affirms both leaders' commitment to avoid violence or unilateral actions which will make peace more difficult and to keep the peace process going until it reaches a successful conclusion.

At the end of this summit, I am fully aware of the deep disappointment that will be felt on both sides. But it was essential for Israelis and Palestinians, finally, to begin to deal with the toughest decisions in the peace process. Only they can make those decisions, and they both pledged to make them, I say again, by mid-September.

Now, it's essential that they not lose hope, that they keep working for peace, they avoid any unilateral actions that would only make the hard task ahead more difficult. The statement the leaders have made today is encouraging in that regard.

Israelis and Palestinians are destined to live side by side, destined to have a common future. They have to decide what kind of future it will be. Though the differences that remain are deep, they have come a long way in the last seven years, and, notwithstanding the failure to reach an agreement, they made real headway in the last two weeks.

Now, the two parties must go home and reflect, both on what happened at Camp David and on what did not happen. For the sake of their children, they must rededicate themselves to the path of peace and find a way to resume their negotiations in the next few weeks. They've asked us to continue to help, and as always, we'll do our best. But the parties themselves, both of them, must be prepared to resolve profound questions of history, identity and national faith—as well as the future of sites that are holy to religious people all over the world who are part of the Islamic, Christian and Judaic traditions. . . .

[Jerusalem] was the most difficult problem. And I must tell you that we tried a lot of different approaches to it, and we have not yet found a solution. But the good news is that there is not a great deal of disagreement—and I want to emphasize this—it seemed to me, anyway, there was not a great deal of disagreement in many of these areas about what the facts on the ground would be after an agreement were made—that is, how people would live.

For example, everyone conceded that Jerusalem is a place that required everyone to have access to the holy sites and the kinds of things you've heard, and lot of other things in terms of how, operationally, the Israelis and the Palestinians have worked together; there was actually more agreement than I had thought there would be.

But obviously, the questions around Jerusalem go to the core identity of both the Palestinians and the Israelis. There were some very, as I said—it has been reported Prime Minister Barak took some very bold decisions, but we were in the end unable to bridge the gaps. I think there will be a bridge, because I think the alternative is unthinkable. . . .

But I think it is fair to say that at this moment in time, maybe because they had been preparing for it longer, maybe because they had thought through it more, that the Prime Minister moved forward more from his initial position than Chairman Arafat, on—particularly surrounding the questions of Jerusalem.

Now, these are hard questions. And as I said to both of them, none of us, no outsider can judge for another person what is at the core of his being, at the core of his sense of national essence. But we cannot make an agreement here without a continuing effort of both sides to compromise. . . .

Oh, yes, there were always side papers—even going back to 1993—about how these final issues would be solved. There were always speculation, there were always the odd conversation between Palestinians and Israelis who were friends and part of the various—the different government operations. But these folks really never had to come together before, and in an official setting put themselves on the line. And it is profoundly difficult. . . .

Of all the peace groups I ever worked with, these people know each other, they know the names of each other's children, they know how many grandchildren the grandparents have, they know their life stories, they have a genuine respect and understanding for each other. It is truly extraordinary and unique in my experience in almost eight years of dealing with it. . . . They couldn't get there. But this was the first time in an organized, disciplined way they had to work through, both for themselves and then with each other how they were going to come to grips with issues that go to the core of their identity. . . .

One of the things that often happens in a very difficult peace process is that people, if they're not careful, will gravitate to the intense position rather than the position that will make peace. And it's very often that people know that a superficially safe position is to say no, that you won't get in trouble with whoever is dominating the debate back home wherever your home is, as long as you say no. . . .

The Palestinians changed their position; they moved forward. The Israelis moved more from the position they had. I said what I said; I will say again: I was not condemning Arafat, I was praising Barak. But I would be making a mistake not to praise Barak because I think he took a big risk. And I think it sparked, already, in Israel a real debate, which is moving Israeli public opinion toward the conditions that will make peace. So I thought that was important, and I think it deserves to be acknowledged.

But the overriding thing you need to know is that progress was made on all fronts, that significant progress was made on some of the core issues, that Jerusalem, as you all knew it would be, remains the biggest problem for the reasons you know.

But what we have to find here, if there is going to be an agreement—by definition, an agreement is one in which everybody is a little disappointed and nobody is defeated, in which neither side requires the other to say they have lost everything and they find a way to—a shared result. . . .

Keep in mind: When the Oslo Agreement was drafted, these things were put down as final status issues because the people that drafted them knew it would be hard. And they took a gamble. And their gamble was that if the Israelis and the Palestinians worked together over a seven-year period and they began to share security cooperation, for example . . . and if they kept making other specific agreements, that by the time we got to the end of the road, there would be enough knowledge and trust and understanding of each other's positions that these huge, epochal issues could be resolved.

Israeli Prime Minister Ehud Barak: Statement after the Camp David Talks (July 25, 2000)

The Government of Israel, and I as Prime Minister, acted in the course of the Camp David Summit out of moral and personal commitment, and supreme national obligation to do everything possible to bring about an end to the conflict—but not at any price—while at the same time, strengthening the State of Israel, and Jerusalem its capital. In the course of the negotiations, we touched the most sensitive nerves, ours and the Palestinians, but regretfully—with no result.

We were not prepared to relinquish three things: the security of Israel, those things that are holy to Israel, and the unity of our people. If we will be faced with the alternative between compromising one of these and a confrontation, the choice is clear to every Israeli.

We've known how to face such situations in the past, and we will in the future. Yet, if we will find ourselves in a confrontation, we will be able to look straight into the eyes of our children and to say that we have done everything to prevent it. In the face of the dangers and risks before us, we must put aside all our differences and unite, as we have known to do so many times in the past.

All my life I fought for Israeli security, and I reiterate: I will not agree to relinquish the vital interests of Israeli security; I will not agree to give up the strengthening of Israel and the bolstering of greater Jerusalem, with a solid Jewish majority, for future generations.

Israel was prepared to pay a painful price to bring about an end to the conflict, but not any price. We sought a stable balance, and peace for generations to come, not headlines in tomorrow's paper. The summit was a major—and for now the latest—milestone in the intensive and exhaustive negotiating process to achieve a framework agreement for the permanent status accord with the Palestinians, which my government has been striving to achieve.

We can today look in the mirror and say: In the past year, we have exhausted every possibility to bring an end to the 100-year-old conflict between us and the Palestinians, but regrettably the conditions were not yet ripe.

I understand the disappointment of many in Israel, who believe in coexistence and extending a hand in peace to our Palestinian neighbors. I even join them in their disappointment. However, we will not cease our effort to achieve peace and will continue to work to bring it about—yet not at any price.

Arafat was afraid to make the historic decisions necessary at this time in order to bring about an end to the conflict. Arafat's positions on Jerusalem are those which prevented the achievement of the agreement. . . .

We must not lose hope. The vision of peace is not dead, but it suffered a heavy blow because of the Palestinian stubbornness. The Palestinians must deal with their extremist elements, and both sides must work together to prevent a deterioration into violence. . . .

We have done our best, out of a moral and personal and government responsibility, to do whatever we can to put an end to a conflict of 100 years, not at any cost, and in a way, of course, that will strengthen Israel. But unfortunately, in spite of being ready to touch the most sensitive nerves, we have ended with no results.

We will emphasize, under whatever circumstances, the security of Israel, the sacred values and interests of Israel, and the unity of our people. And if we have to face the challenge and fight for one of those, we will be ready to fight to the end. We were ready to end the conflict; we looked for an equilibrium point that will provide a peace for generations. But unfortunately, Arafat somehow hesitated to take the historic decisions that were needed in order to put an end of it. . . .

We have considered, and some ideas were raised, that in order to make Jerusalem wider and stronger than at any time, in any previous time in the history of the city, we should consider annexing to Jerusalem cities within the West Bank beyond the 1967 border, like Maale Adumin and Givat Ze'ev and Gush Etzion, and in exchange for this to give to the Palestinians the sovereignty over certain villages or small cities that had been annexed to Jerusalem just after 1967. These ideas were raised, they were contemplated. But as the whole summit was run under the rules of "Nothing is agreed until everything is agreed," even those ideas are now null and void. . . .

It's painful to realize that the other side is not ripe for peace, but it's always better to know the realities than to delude ourselves. And I still hope that when they will consider what are the real alternatives what await all of us down the stream, they will have an opportunity to make up their minds once again.

The major, toughest kind of debate, or inability to bridge the gaps were about issues that have to do with Jerusalem. We believe that the ideas raised by the president was far-reaching and justified a kind of positive response from Arafat. They didn't. And I should admit that even on other issues—especially the refugees—there are still wide gaps of a kind of conceptual nature, not just technical nature.

So I believe that we made a long way, and the public debate within the Israeli public and within the Palestinian delegation is very important for the future contact. But unfortunately, we have to admit reality: we were unable as of now, basically as a result of unripeness on the Palestinian side, to achieve a deal, or strike a deal. . . .

A year ago, I stood here—in Washington, in fact—and told that we—our government, my government—will do whatever it takes, and we'll leave no stone unturned on the way to check whether it's possible to make a peace with our neighbors without violating our vital interest. But I emphasized that it takes two to tango. We cannot impose it upon them. We are ready, and if a partner will be there, there will be peace.

Now we did exactly this. We checked it. It's very important for us, first of all, out of our responsibility, to make peace if it's possible, but on the other end, at the same time, in order to be able to face the challenges of no peace with a united Israeli people that knows that its government made whatever it could to put an end to the conflict—and if there is no end to the conflict, somehow the responsibility is upon the other side. This is our basic position—and of course, the fact that such an attempt to touch for the first time in the whole history of the conflict the very core issues—refugees, Jerusalem—tried to solve that.

When we find that it's still unripe—of course I say with a certain kind of sorrow that it will influence, of course, the third further redeployment or the comprehensive agreement negotiations, since we cannot delude ourselves that we have not seen what we have seen in the last 12 days. And there is a need to continue from this point forward, not from a different kind of approach or track.

PLO Chairman Yasir Arafat: Speech at the Arab Summit (October 21, 2000)

. . . . The direct reason for holding this extraordinary summit is the wave of savage violence that our Palestinian people have been subjected to. This wave started when [Israeli opposition leader Ariel] Sharon desecrated the Al-Aqsa mosque and its compound [by visiting it on September 28, 2000]. With this premeditated step, that was conducted in concert with the Israeli government, Sharon set off a spark that spread from Jerusalem to every Arab, Muslim, and Christian city and village, including the cities and villages of Galilee and the Triangle.

This visit was not simply a passing act like those committed by the settlers against our holy shrines; instead, it created a new dimension in the Arab-Israeli struggle. I remind you that when he was defense minister, and a minister in past governments before that, as well as an army commander, he was barred from visiting such holy shrines. Therefore, what took place was planned in collusion with the Israeli Government.

A new, religious, dimension was added to the Arab-Israeli struggle. Everyone is well aware of the critical nature of this dimension, and knows how difficult it is to contain it and control its repercussions. The Israeli delegation detonated this dimension at the end of our talks in the second Camp David summit. When I say this step was premeditated, I say it because as soon as Sharon's intention to conduct this visit was announced, we warned the Israeli Government of the dangers of what Sharon intended to do. We also warned the United States of this and informed our brothers, friends, and international forces of this.

Instead of taking our warning seriously, the Israeli Government granted Sharon special permission to conduct the visit and even provided him with full military and security protection. He did not pay such a visit when he was defense minister and army commander in past governments. This reveals what was being planned against us.

Our people, who were worshipping in Al-Aqsa, countered Sharon with their chests and naked fists, and prevented him from conducting this dangerous visit, forcing him to leave the holy place. The Israeli Government, however, did not forgive the Palestinian worshippers for their steadfastness, and committed a new massacre during Friday prayers in the Al-Aqsa mosque compound on the very next day. We all saw the bloody chapters of this massacre in the media.

Your Majesties, Excellencies, and Highnesses, innocent blood was shed abundantly on the pure Al-Aqsa land. A new procession of honorable people of this nation was added to the martyrs who defend the holy places and who stand fast on this blessed land and defend its purity with faith and pride. There is no inch of Palestinian territory that has not been saturated with Arab blood that is dear to all of us. The blood that was shed in Al-Aqsa definitely unleashed the wrath in the hearts of our Palestinian masses everywhere in the homeland. The unarmed citizens rose to express their feelings in a legitimate spontaneous *intifada* to uphold Arab, Islamic, and Christian values in accordance with the Umarite Covenant. The Israelis cancelled this covenant, by claiming sovereignty over Al-Haram al-Sharif and forging its history and reality and saying it is the place where the temple was built, by licentiously attacking the worshippers in its mosques and those defending its honor and sanctity, or by attempting to Judaize holy Jerusalem and its Christian and Islamic holy places and imposing a siege on Bethlehem. We have repeatedly warned the United States, the European countries, and the friendly countries against the serious consequences of this rejected hypothesis. We also contacted all the peace-loving forces about this and told them that this would lead the region to religious wars with untold consequences. Since the eruption of Al-Aqsa *intifada*, our unarmed people have been facing the broadest collective extermination campaign and barbaric bombardment, coupled with an iron-clad and stifling siege by the Israeli war machine against more than 3 million Palestinians.

The Israeli Government, supported by some international quarters, tried to portray the mass extermination campaign against our people as a military engagement between two military sides, and the expression of the need to reach a framework for cease-fire between the two sides unjustly surfaced. However, this attempt failed as proved by the issuance of the recent UN Security Council Resolution 1322 condemning the Israeli aggression and calling for the formation of an international investigation committee whose task is to find mechanisms to prevent the recurrence of this unjust aggression. . . .

Most of the Israeli political and military leaders admitted that they have been planning for more than one year to ignite this fire, that has not stopped until now and which inflicted more than 7,000 wounded and [193] martyrs . . . in addition to a large number of prisoners and missing, not to mention the economic and financial losses and the banning of our workers from working, thus placing more than 150,000 workers among the ranks of the unemployed. Large quantities of agricultural produce were destroyed, houses and establishments were demolished with missiles, and many colleges and even command and presidential centers and many other sites were set on fire and attacked. And do thou be patient, for thy patience is but from God. . . .

We should . . . put a final end to all causes of aggression, killing, and suffering. This will happen only when Israel is forced to submit to international legitimacy, implement the signed agreements, stop aggression, open the international border posts, lift the siege on our cities and people, and withdraw from all the occupied Palestinian and Arab territories, including the Syrian territories and the last Lebanese territory in Shab'a.

Israel should lift the siege on our cities and people and withdraw from all the Palestinian and Arab territories, including holy Jerusalem, the capital of our independent Palestinian state. It should also solve the issue of refugees justly on the basis of Resolution 194 and the other international resolutions.

Brothers, I recall at this important meeting the fact that the Arab summits have always been the first to raise the banner of a just, permanent, and comprehensive peace. The Arab summits are the advocate of the loftiest and most important plan for peace in the Middle East, particularly after the Madrid peace conference.

It is true that part of the just and comprehensive peace has been achieved on parts of our beloved Arab land, but the territory still under occupation in Palestine, Syria, and Lebanon made the issue of peace in the Middle East a constantly explosive issue putting the region on the verge of danger. All that has been achieved will collapse if not complemented by what has not been achieved.

This requires us all to examine with a great degree of seriousness and responsibility the means to provide real support for our Arab view of peace and our legitimate rights, while reminding the world, of which we are a vital part, that regional and international stability depends on fulfilling all Arab rights stipulated by international legitimacy resolutions. The international community, especially the peace process sponsors, the EU, China,

Japan, Norway, the nonaligned countries, and all those who support the peace process, must shoulder their responsibilities toward the peace process.

The bloody events that resulted from the Israeli aggression against our Palestinian people have shown that the dangers of the absence of a just and lasting peace are not limited to a specific geographical area; instead these dangers spread and threaten international security and stability.

Allow me, dear brothers, to say more than this, and address the United States, not just because it is a peace process sponsor, but also because it is the world power with distinguished responsibilities on the universal level and because it is directly interested in all areas of conflict in our world. The Middle East peace process has suffered from the absence of the balance needed to offer real chances for the progress of this process and the reaching of effective results in it.

The world undoubtedly clearly sees that the Middle East peace sponsor must not give any leeway in adopting international legitimacy as the legal bases of rights and obligations. Moreover, the sponsor must not stop the contributions of states interested in peace in our region.

I would like to draw attention to an issue where political dimensions mix with morals, where the concept of impartial sponsorship of the peace process does not go in line with the excessively harsh stands against the Palestinian people. These stands are embodied in many of the U.S. Congress's decisions, which adopt a stand hostile to the Palestinian people and their rights. Despite our extreme bitterness toward these stands, I objectively note U.S. President Bill Clinton's positive stands, for whom we have respect and whose continuous work and initiatives to protect the peace process and push it forward we appreciate.

Your majesties, your excellencies, your highnesses: Speaking from the highest Arab forum, I reiterate that despite all the scars and disappointments of the difficult trek of peace on the Palestinian track, we choose a just, lasting, and comprehensive peace. I reiterate that our goals are the liberation of our land, the establishment of our independent state on the blessed land of Palestine with holy Jerusalem as its capital, and the return of refugees based on international legitimacy resolutions, especially Resolutions 181 and 194.

These goals, which our Palestinian People and Arab and Muslim nations agree on, and which the entire world and the UN support, must be realized this year. We have a natural right to self-determination. It is also the responsibility of our Arab nation and its struggling peoples, who support us and all Arab causes with strength, to offer all means of support to achieve these goals. Our people of revolutionary struggle, the people of the glorious *intifada,* whose waves will only stop with victory, pledge to every Arab, Muslim, Christian, and friend to continue their struggle using all legitimate means to reach victory.

We call on you to take a true Arab stand of pride that is in line with the history of this glorious Arab nation, its capabilities, and the sacrifices of its steadfast peoples in protection of their holy shrines, land, and future. I would like to thank all our brothers and friends in the world who support our just struggle and cause. I would also like to thank them for their help at all levels.

I conclude my speech by conveying the message of my people to you, the Arab leaders, calling on you to disregard all differences and reach inter-Arab reconciliation which will put the corner stone for a new Arab era that is in line with the status of our nation and the greatness of our pan-Arab goals. This also requires us all to end the siege imposed on the Iraqi people and make way for real and comprehensive Arab reconciliation and openness within our single Arab nation. For the sake of the children of Palestine, Iraq, Lebanon, Syria, and the rest of the Arab nation, we call on you to entrench unity and integration. . . .

Marwan Barghuti: "The Israelis Must Leave the Territories" (October 26, 2000)*

The *intifada* is a decision of the Palestinian people—not *Fatah*. Everything happens first on the ground. [We do not] determine what people do. . . . If tens of thousands of people have mobilized, it is on nobody's orders. The Israelis have made me the *intifada*'s leader because I am seen in the media. President Yasir Arafat remains the nation's leader; he takes the political decisions. And he support us. Without his support, the *intifada* could not continue. But he does not deal with the day-to-day details. People follow me only because I express what they expect. We have set up local coordinating committees of the movement. Some 30 parties are represented on them, from the Communists to the Islamists. Those committees determine the *intifada*'s progress from day to day. . . . The decisions are collective, but *Fatah* holds the majority on them. . . .

Perhaps some people believed at the outset that this movement would stop quickly, but nobody can stop it. Perhaps some people among us still believe that the message sent by the *intifada* to Israel and the international community is now sufficient. But that is not my opinion. The movement will continue and must continue. . . .

What would be the point of a return to calm? We were calm for seven years in order to give a chance to the negotiations, of which I have been a keen supporter.

*Interview with the *Fatah* secretary-general of the West Bank by *Le Monde*, October 26, 2000, reprinted with permission.

But the Israelis used that time in order to negotiate interim agreements which were never implemented and to continue their policy of a fait accompli on the ground: The new settlements, the expropriations, the confiscation of land, the keeping of prisoners in the jails. Why should calm now be restored? So that they can resume the same policy? We have the right to self-determination, like all the peoples of the world.

Some people believe: If Marwan al-Barghuthi gives the order to stop everything, everything will stop. That is wrong. People do not support me because I give orders but because I support them. They will stay with me as long as I express their opinion. If I no longer do so, they will be against me. . . .

A withdrawal from the territories conquered by Israel in 1967 is our demand. And ending the occupation is the real reason for the current *intifada*. The *intifada* will last as long as the occupation lasts. After seven years, we have experience of the Israelis; we have had hundreds of meetings with them: They never let go of anything without being obliged to do so by force. I have nothing against the negotiations—on the contrary. But the rules of the game must now be changed. In the first place, they should agree to negotiate during the confrontations. Second, the monopoly exercised by the Americans must be broken, because the United States is not an honest mediator. The United Nations, the Europeans, and Russia should also be directly involved. . . .

The Islamists—Hamas and Jihad—are in the local committees' coordinating body called the "Committee of National and Islamic Political Forces." Sometimes they have their own activities, as we do, but, on the whole, we cooperate well; we are very united. *Fatah* is leading the movement not because it is afraid of being outflanked by the Islamists but because it is its duty. . . .

The Islamists sometimes shout slogans taken from the Koran referring to the Jews, but not "death to the Jews." That is absolutely not in the tradition of Islam. Listen: I was first imprisoned at the age of 17. Between 1978 and 1988 I served six and a half years in prison for political activities, plus six months' house arrest. I was expelled in 1987 by an order signed by Mr. Barak. I stayed in exile for seven years, until my return in 1994. What kind of life have I had? I was a keen supporter of Oslo. I want reconciliation with the Israelis. We are not extremists. The vast majority of the Palestinians still want peace and coexistence with Israel, which is and will remain our neighbor forever. But I do not want my children to experience what I have experienced.

They will live in a free, unoccupied country. The Israelis want everything: Peace, security, stability, the settlements, and a Palestinian state without Jerusalem and without real sovereignty. That is impossible. They must leave the territories, and there will be no more confrontations. . . .

There will never again be either a 1948 or a 1967; they will not be able to expel us *en masse*. The Israelis will eventually realize that the occupation also works against them. I am very optimistic.

U.S. President Bill Clinton: The Clinton Plan (December 23, 2000)*

TERRITORY:

Based on what I heard, I believe that the solution should be in the mid-90 percents, between 94–96 percent of the West Bank territory of the Palestinian State. The land annexed by Israel should be compensated by a land swap of 1–3 percent in addition to territorial arrangements such as a permanent safe passage. The parties also should consider the swap of leased land to meet their respective needs. . . . The parties should develop a map consistent with the following criteria:

- –80 percent of settlers in blocks;
- –Contiguity;
- –Minimize the annexed areas;
- –Minimize the number of Palestinians affected.

SECURITY:

The key lies in an international presence that can only be withdrawn by mutual consent. This presence will also monitor the implementation of the agreement between both sides. . . .

My best judgment is that the Israeli presence would remain in fixed locations in the Jordan Valley under the authority of the international force for another 36 months. This period could be reduced in the event of favorable regional developments that diminish the threat to Israel.

On early warning stations, Israel should maintain three facilities in the West Bank with a Palestinian liaison presence. The stations will be subject to review every 10 years with any changes in the status to be mutually agreed.

Regarding emergency developments, I understand that you will still have to develop a map of the relevant areas and routes. . . . I propose the following definition:

Imminent and demonstrable threat to Israel's national security of a military nature that requires the activation of a national state emergency.

Of course, the international forces will need to be notified of any such determination.

On airspace, I suggest that the state of Palestine will have sovereignty

Ha'aretz, December 31, 2000.

over its airspace but that the two sides should work out special arrangements for Israeli training and operational needs.

I understand that the Israeli position is that Palestine should be defined as a "demilitarized state" while the Palestinian side proposes "a state with limited arms." As a compromise, I suggest calling it a "non-militarized state." This will be consistent with the fact that in addition to a strong Palestinian security force, Palestine will have an international force for border security and deterrent purposes. . . .

JERUSALEM:

The general principle is that Arab areas are Palestinian and Jewish ones are Israeli. This would apply to the Old City as well. I urge the two sides to work on maps to create maximum contiguity for both sides.

Regarding the Haram Temple Mount, I believe that the gaps are not related to practical administration but to symbolic issues of sovereignty and to finding a way to accord respect to the religious beliefs of both sides.

I know you have been discussing a number of formulations. . . . I add to these two additional formulations guaranteeing Palestinian effective control over the Haram while respecting the conviction of the Jewish people. Regarding either one of those two formulations will be international monitoring to provide mutual confidence.

Palestinian sovereignty over the Haram and Israeli sovereignty over a) the Western Wall and the space sacred to Judaism of which it is a part or b) the Western Wall and the Holy of Holies of which it is a part. There will be a firm commitment by both not to excavate beneath the Haram or behind the Wall.

Palestinian sovereignty over the Haram and Israeli sovereignty over the Western Wall and shared functional sovereignty over the issue of excavation under the Haram and behind the Wall such that mutual consent would be requested before any excavation could take place.

REFUGEES:

I sense that the differences are more relating to formulations and less to what will happen on a practical level. I believe that Israel is prepared to acknowledge the moral and material suffering caused to the Palestinian people as a result of the 1948 war and the need to assist the international community in addressing the problem. . . .

The fundamental gap is on how to handle the concept of the right of return. I know the history of the issue and how hard it will be for the Palestinian leadership to appear to be abandoning the principle.

The Israeli side could not accept any reference to a right of return that would imply a right to immigrate to Israel in defiance of Israel's sovereign policies and admission or that would threaten the Jewish character of the state.

Any solution must address both needs. The solution will have to be consistent with the two state approach. . . . the state of Palestine as the homeland of the Palestinian people and the state of Israel as the homeland of the Jewish people.

Under the two-state solution, the guiding principle should be that the Palestinian state should be the focal point for the Palestinians who choose to return to the area without ruling out that Israel will accept some of these refugees.

I believe that we need to adopt a formulation on the right of return that will make clear that there is no specific right of return to Israel itself but that does not negate the aspiration of the Palestinian people to return to the area.

I propose two alternatives:

1. both sides recognize the right of Palestinian refugees to return to historic Palestine,
2. both sides recognize the right of Palestinian refugees to return to their homeland.

The agreement will define the implementation of this general right in a way that is consistent with the two-state solution. It would list the five possible homes for the refugees:

1. The State of Palestine
2. Areas in Israel being transferred to Palestine in the land swap
3. Rehabilitation in host country
4. Resettlement in third country
5. Admission to Israel

In listing these options, the agreement will make clear that the return to the West Bank, Gaza Strip and area acquired in the land swap would be right to all Palestinian refugees, while rehabilitation in host countries, resettlement in third countries and absorption into Israel will depend upon the policies of those countries.

Israel could indicate in the agreement that it intends to establish a policy so that some the refugees would be absorbed into Israel consistent with Israel sovereign decision.

I believe that priority should be given to the refugee population in Lebanon. The parties would agree that this implements Resolution 194.

THE END OF CONFLICT:

I propose that the agreement clearly mark the end of the conflict and its implementation put an end to all claims. This could be implemented through a UN Security Council Resolution that notes that resolutions 242 and 338 have been implemented and through the release for Palestinian prisoners.

Yoel Marcus: "If They Want It, They'll Take It" (December 26, 2000)*

The Palestinian leaders are starting to get on people's nerves. These leaders, who negotiate while shooting their six-guns, are getting things that they never even dreamed of getting. Yet they incite their public to attack us, while they never stop whining and complaining. Purposely overlooking what they have already obtained or what is already within their grasp, they are never satisfied. They just want us to keep on trying and making concessions—otherwise, they threaten, they'll refuse to sign a peace treaty with us. They remind many people of the legendary Hershel of Ostropol who threatened that, if he were not given a free meal, he would have to do what his father used to do—namely, go to bed hungry. Israel is a strong nation that has emerged victorious from every war it has ever fought. Furthermore, Israel can live with the status quo for many years and with much less trouble than the Palestinians. They need our approval if they want to set up an independent state and they need us as partners in every possible sphere. Who knows, one day they might find themselves needing our military umbrella to protect them from their own Arab brothers and sisters. In our generation, more Arabs have been killed by other Arabs than by Jews.

In the Oslo agreement and in the White House lawn parties, it was Israel that resurrected a Yasser Arafat who had become a pariah among the leaders of the Arab world for his support of Iraqi President Saddam Hussein and it was Israel that freed him from the status of persona non grata. The Oslo agreement, which returned Arafat to his homeland from his life of exile and ceaseless wandering, was designed to bring about conciliation between the Palestinians and the Israelis.

However, to this day, Arafat has not managed, has not wanted or has not been able to break the habit of constantly using the slogan about Palestine being redeemed only through blood and fire. Instead of leading his people down the road to conciliation with Israel, he is leading them down the road to terrorism, murder and anti-Semitic incitement.

Has a speaker of the Knesset ever walked upon the Palestinian flag? Yet Abu Ala, speaker of the Palestinian Parliament, his head held erect, walked on a "carpet" consisting of Israeli flags. Arafat missed his chance with Yitzhak Rabin, and he missed his chance with Shimon Peres.

Now the only Israeli leader with whom Arafat can arrive at an agreement is Prime Minister Ehud Barak. "After me, the flood!" seems to be Arafat's motto.

The Palestinians have been offered things that the Labor Party, in its

Ha'aretz, reprinted with permission.

various historical metamorphoses and in all its election campaigns, promised never to give to them. From Arafat's standpoint, this is a golden opportunity that might never recur in his lifetime.

He should pay attention to what the leaders of the Likud are saying. They want an immediate halt to the Palestinian-Israeli talks and they also want to sabotage the anticipated peace treaty right now, so that if their party wins the next general election, it will not be forced to honor that agreement. Their solution is an iron-fist policy and war on the Palestinians.

Arafat would have to be out of his mind not to grab with both hands what he is being offered. Barak has gone to the very limits of the concessions he is prepared to make. Even Peres admits that Barak has conceded too much. Yet what was Arafat's reaction after Israel's major concession at Camp David? He instructed his people to launch an *Intifada* and thus he planted among the members of Israeli society the seeds of distrust. "What," Israelis began asking themselves, "after declaring ourselves ready to make such concessions, we're being 'rewarded' with the deaths of our fellow Israelis?"

Politically speaking, Barak could have taken the easy way out: He could have set up a national unity government with Likud chief Ariel Sharon, thereby saying, in effect, "To hell with the peace process!" Instead, he risked his political skin, lost his partners in the coalition and has reached the point where his reelection is in doubt.

Barak has repeatedly warned the Israeli public that failure to arrive at a peace treaty with the Palestinians could ultimately plunge Israel into a regional war where non-conventional weapons will be used. Why is Arafat not broadcasting a similar message of urgency and catastrophe to his own people?

The Palestinians could not ask for a better time to get the best possible peace treaty than right now. But they want more. They want sovereignty. More than anything else, they want the right of return to be recognized and fulfilled. The Palestinian refugee problem was not caused by Israel; it was caused by the Arab states, which have tried, time and again, to use brute force to wipe us off the map. Israel bears no responsibility whatsoever for the tragic plight of the Palestinian refugees.

Israel has never demanded compensation for the thousands of Israeli citizens killed because of Arab aggression and has not received even one penny in compensation for the integration of hundreds of thousands of Jewish refugees from the Arab states and for the Jewish property that those states confiscated. Fulfillment of the right of return would mean the end of Israel as a Jewish state, and thus Israel will never agree to this demand.

If the Palestinians have included the clause on the right of return as a ploy intended simply to enhance their bargaining position, they would be wise to withdraw it right now—because time is running out. Even the most patient of suitors gives up trying to capture a hard-to-get virgin. Arafat lost his virginity a long time ago, and we've had it with his game-playing and with his arm-twisting attempts. If they want it, they'll take it.

If they fail to grab hold of these offers now, instead of Barak, they'll get Sharon, Limor Livnat, Avigdor Lieberman and Natan Sharansky. Already, instead of Bill Clinton, they'll get George W. Bush, who will first have to learn to find Palestine on the map.

Palestinian Negotiating Team: Remarks and Questions Regarding the Clinton Plan (January 2, 2001)

. . . . We wish to explain why the latest United States proposals, taken together and as presented without clarification, fail to satisfy the conditions required for a permanent peace. As it stands now, the United States proposal would:

1) divide a Palestinian state into three separate cantons connected and divided by Jewish-only and Arab-only roads and jeopardize the Palestinian state's viability;

2) divide Palestinian Jerusalem into a number of unconnected islands separate from each other and from the rest of Palestine;

3) force Palestinians to surrender the right of return of Palestinian refugees. It also fails to provide workable security arrangements between Palestine and Israel, and to address a number of other issues of importance to the Palestinian people. The United States proposal seems to respond to Israeli demands while neglecting the basic Palestinian need: a viable state.

The United States proposals were couched in general terms that in some instances lack clarity and detail. A permanent status agreement, in our view, is not merely a document that declares general political principles. It is, rather, a comprehensive instrument that spells out the details, modalities, and timetables of ending the Palestinian-Israeli conflict. For such an agreement to be effective, it must be backed by clear, effective international implementation guarantees. We believe that a general, vague agreement at this advanced stage of the peace process will be counterproductive. This conviction has resulted from our past experiences with vague agreements and from Israel's history of noncompliance with signed agreements. The permanent status agreement must be a truly final agreement rather than an agreement to negotiate.

The United States side presented proposals regarding four primary issues: territory, Jerusalem, refugees, and security.

TERRITORY OF THE PALESTINIAN STATE

On the issue of territory, the United States proposed that Israel annex 4 to 6 percent of the West Bank; that the annexation be compensated through a "land swap" of 1 to 3 percent; and that the Parties also consider a swap of leased land. The United States recommended that the final map be drawn in a manner that would place 80 percent of Israeli settlers in annexed settlement blocs, but that would nevertheless promote territorial contiguity, minimize annexed areas and minimize the number of Palestinians affected.

This proposal poses a number of serious problems. As the proposal is not accompanied by a map, and because the total area from which the percentages are calculated is not defined, it is difficult to imagine how the percentages presented can be reconciled with the goal of Palestinian contiguity. This is especially worrisome in light of the fact that the Israeli side continues to insist, and the United States has never questioned, that Jerusalem, as defined by Israel, the "no-man's land," and the Dead Sea are not part of the total area from which the percentages are calculated. Moreover, the United States proposal calls for the "swap of leased land." It is not entirely clear if Palestinian interests are served by such a swap since the Palestinian side has no territorial needs in Israel, except for a corridor linking the West Bank and the Gaza Strip, which will be covered in a land swap. This proposal, taken together with the map presented by the Israeli side in the most recent round of negotiations in Washington (see attached map), provides Israel with control over large swaths of land, rendering the Palestinian state unviable and lacking direct access to international borders.

Without a map clarifying the above ambiguities, the United States proposal does nothing to foreclose a return by Israel to its proposals at Camp David which leaves 10 percent of the West Bank under Israeli sovereignty and an additional 10 percent under Israeli control pursuant to ill-defined security arrangements. It is important to bear in mind that all of the settlements in the West Bank currently occupy approximately 2 percent of the West Bank.

In this context, the Palestinian side rejects the use of "settlement blocs" as a guiding principle as recommended by the United States proposal. The use of this criterion subordinates Palestinian interests in the contiguity of their state and control over their natural resources to Israeli interests regarding the contiguity of settlements, recognized as illegal by the international community. It also contradicts the United States proposal's criteria concerning minimizing annexed areas and the number of Palestinians affected. In addition, the Palestinian side needs to know exactly which settlements Israel intends to annex.

Ultimately, it is impossible to agree to a proposal that punishes Palestinians while rewarding Israel's illegal settlement policies. A proposal involving annexation of 4 to 6 percent (not to mention 10 percent) of the land would inevitably damage vital Palestinian interests. Under such a proposal, a number of Palestinian villages will be annexed to Israel, adding to the already great number of displaced Palestinians.

Moreover, as the attached map demonstrates, a large quantity of unsettled land in key development areas such as Jerusalem and Bethlehem will also be annexed by Israel, destroying the territorial contiguity of the State of Palestine. In addition to compromising Palestinians' freedom of movement within their own state, this would also have serious ramifications for the state's development potential. In addition, any such large-scale annexation will inevitably prejudice Palestinian water rights.

As for the "land swap," the United States proposal does not identify which areas within Israel are to compensate for the annexed land. The Palestinian side continues to insist that any annexed land must be compensated with land of equal size and value. No argument has been presented as to why this should not be the case. However, the United States proposal explicitly rejects the principle that compensation of land must be of equal size and remains silent on the issue of the location and quality of the compensated land. All previous Israeli and United States proposals concerning compensated land have referred to land near the Gaza Strip in exchange for valuable real estate in the West Bank. In addition to being desert areas, the lands being offered near the Gaza Strip are currently being used by Israel to dump toxic waste. Obviously, we cannot accept trading prime agricultural and development land for toxic waste dumps.

JERUSALEM

On the issue of Jerusalem, President Clinton articulated a general principle that "Arab areas are Palestinian and Jewish areas are Israeli," but urged the two sides to work on maps to create maximum contiguity for both. Two alternative formulations were presented addressing each State's sovereignty over and rights to the Haram al-Sharif ("Haram") and the "Western Wall" ("Wall"). Both formulations provide for Palestinian sovereignty over the Haram and Israeli sovereignty over the Wall, resticting the Parties from excavating beneath the Haram or behind the Wall.

The United States formulations on the Haram are problematic. First, the proposal appears to recognize Israeli sovereignty under the Haram by implying that it has a right, which it voluntarily relinquishes, to excavate behind the Western Wall (i.e., the area under the Haram). Moreover, the "Western Wall" extends to areas beyond the Wailing Wall, including the tunnel opened in 1996 by Israel's former Prime Minister Benjamin Netanyahu which caused widespread confrontations.

The territorial aspects of the United States proposals concerning Jerusalem also raise very serious concerns and call for further clarification. As the attached map shows, as a result of Israel's internationally condemned settlement policy in occupied East Jerusalem, the United States formulation "that Arab areas are Palestinian and Jewish ones are Israeli" will be impossible to reconcile with the concept of "maximum contiguity for both," presented in the proposal. Rather, the formulation will inevitably result in Palestinian islands within the city separated from one another. Israel, however, will be able to maintain contiguity.

Therefore, the proposal is actually calling for "maximum contiguity for both" translates in practice into "maximum contiguity for Israel."

Israel's continued demand for sovereignty over a number of geographically undefined "religious sites" in Jerusalem, and its refusal to present maps clearly showing its territorial demands in Jerusalem only compounds the Palestinian concerns. Any formulation that will be acceptable by the Palestinian side must guarantee the contiguity of Palestinian areas within the city as well as the contiguity of Jerusalem with the rest of Palestine.

A key element of the Palestinian position on Jerusalem is its status as an Open City with free access for all. This status is imperative not only to ensure access to and worship in all holy sites for all those who hold the city sacred, but also to guarantee free movement through the State of Palestine. Unfortunately, the United States proposal makes no reference to this essential concept.

PALESTINIAN REFUGEES

On the issue of Palestinian refugees, driven from their homes as a result of the establishment of the State of Israel, the United States proposed that both sides recognize the right of Palestinian refugees to return either to "historic Palestine" or to "their homeland," but added that the agreement should make clear that there is no specific right of return to what is now Israel. Instead, it proposed five possible final homes for the refugees: (1) the State of Palestine; (2) areas in Israel transferred to Palestine in the "land swap"; (3) rehabilitation in the host countries; (4) resettlement in third countries; and (5) admission to Israel. All refugees would have the right to "return" to the State of Palestine; however, rehabilitation in host countries, resettlement in third countries, and admission to Israel all would depend on the policies of those individual countries.

The United States proposal reflects a wholesale adoption of the Israeli position that the implementation of the right of return be subject entirely to Israel's discretion. It is important to recall that Resolution 194, long regarded as the basis for a just settlement of the refugee problem, calls for the return of Palestinian refugees to "their homes," wherever located not to their "homeland" or to "historic Palestine."

The essence of the right of return is choice: Palestinians should be given the option to choose where they wish to settle, including return to the homes from which they were driven. There is no historical precedent for a people abandoning their fundamental right to return to their homes whether they were forced to leave or fled in fear. We will not be the first people to do so. Recognition of the right to return and the provision of choice to refugees is a prerequisite for the closure of the conflict.

The Palestinians are prepared to think flexibly and creatively about the mechanisms for implementing the right of return. In many discussions with Israel, mechanisms for implementing this right in such a way so as to end the refugee status and refugee problem, as well as to otherwise accommodate Israeli concerns, have been identified and elaborated in some detail. The United States proposal fails to make reference to any of these advances and refers back to earlier Israeli negotiating positions.

In addition, the United States proposal fails to provide any assurance that refugee rights to restitution and compensation will be fulfilled.

SECURITY

On the issue of security, the United States proposed that there be an international presence to guarantee the implementation of the agreement. The United States proposal suggests that the Israeli withdrawal should be carried out over a three-year period, with international forces phased in on a gradual basis. Then, at the end of this period, an Israeli military presence would be allowed to remain in the Jordan Valley for another three years under the authority of the international force.

The United States also proposed that Israel be permitted to maintain three early warning stations for at least ten years and that it be given the right to deploy its forces in Palestinian territory during "a national state of emergency." In addition, the United States has suggested that Palestine be defined as a "nonmilitarized State," and, while acknowledging Palestinian sovereignty over its own airspace, it has proposed that the two sides develop special arrangements for Israeli training and operational needs.

Although the United States proposals place less burdens on Palestinian sovereignty than earlier Israeli proposals, they nevertheless raise a number of concerns. There is no reason why Israel would require three years to withdraw from the West Bank and Gaza Strip. In view of the fact that Israel resettled more than one million immigrants from the former Soviet Union in a few years, one year is more than enough time to resettle less than 60,000 Israeli settlers. It is moreover unclear from the United States proposal that the withdrawal period relates to both soldiers and settlers, both of whom are considered part of the occupation forces in the Palestinian Territories. A protracted withdrawal process could jeopardize the peaceful implementation of the agreement and would create a continued source of friction.

There are other Palestinian concerns. Israel has yet to make a persuasive case regarding why it would require either a standing force in the Jordan Valley or emergency deployment rights much less both. This is especially the case given that international forces will be present in these areas. Furthermore, Israel requires no more than one early warning station in the West Bank to satisfy its strategic needs. The maintenance of stations at current locations near Ramallah and Nablus and in East Jerusalem will seriously inhibit Palestinian development. Moreover, the United States proposal would give Israel sole discretion for determining how long these stations will be operational.

The United States proposal's suggestion that special arrangements be made for Israeli training and operational needs in Palestinian airspace is also extremely problematic. Without specific clarification, this might be used to defend a right for Israel to use Palestinian airspace for military training exercises with all the accompanying dangers to the Palestinian civilian population and the environment while sparing Israeli citizens from any similar infringement. Palestinians remain committed to working out regional agreements concerning aviation in line with commonly accepted international regulations. Any arrangement to the contrary would infringe on Palestinian sovereignty and harm relations with neighboring countries.

OTHER ISSUES

The United States proposal remains silent on a number of issues that are essential for the establishment of a lasting and comprehensive peace. By focusing solely on the four issues above, the United States proposal not only neglects relating to ending the conflict, but also disregards ways to ensure that the future relations between the two peoples will be mutually beneficial. Specifically, the proposal does not address water, compensation for damages resulting from over thirty years of occupation, the environment, future economic relations, and other state-to-state issues.

END OF CONFLICT

While we are totally committed to ending the Palestinian-Israeli conflict, we believe that this can only be achieved once the issues that have caused and perpetrated the conflict are resolved in full. This in turn can only be achieved by a comprehensive agreement that provides detailed modalities for the resolution of the issues at the core of the conflict. It must be remembered that in reaching a settlement between Israel and, respectively, Egypt and Jordan, the end of conflict came only after the final, detailed peace treaty.

Even putting aside the requirements of international law and justice, the United States proposals—unless clarified to take into account the above concerns—do not even allow for a pragmatic resolution of the conflict. If no such solutions are reached in practice, we believe that any formalistic pronouncement of the end of conflict would be meaningless.

CONCLUSION

We would like, once again, to emphasize that we remain committed to a peaceful resolution of the Palestinian-Israeli conflict in accordance with

UN Security Council Resolutions 242 and 338 and international law. In view of the tremendous human cost caused by each delay in negotiations, we recognize the need to resolve this conflict as soon as possible. We cannot, however, accept a proposal that secures neither the establishment of a viable Palestinian state nor the right of Palestinian refugees to return to their homes.

U.S. President Bill Clinton: Summarizing His Experience with the Peace Process (January 7, 2001)*

Prime Minister Barak . . . came to office with absolute conviction that in the end, Israel could not be secure unless a just and lasting peace could be reached with its neighbors, beginning with the Palestinians. That if that turned out not to be possible, then the next best thing was to be as strong as possible and as effective in the use of that strength.

But his knowledge of war has fed a passion for peace. And his understanding of the changing technology of war has made him more passionate, not because he thinks the existence of Israel is less secure—if anything, it's more secure—but because the sophisticated weapons available to terrorists today mean even though they still lose, they can exact a higher price along the way. . . .

But no dilemma I have ever faced approximates in difficulty or comes close to the choice that Prime Minister Barak had to make when he took office. He realized that he couldn't know for sure what the final intentions of the Palestinian leadership were without testing them. He further realized that even if the intentions were there, there was a lot of competition among the Palestinians and from outside forces, from people who are enemies of peace because they don't give a rip how the ordinary Palestinians have to live and they're pursuing a whole different agenda.

He knew nine things could go wrong and only one thing could go right. But he promised himself that he would have to try. And as long as he knew Israel in the end could defend itself and maintain its security, he would keep taking risks. And that's what he's done, down to these days. There may be those who disagree with him, but he has demonstrated as much bravery in the office of Prime Minister as he ever did on the field of battle and no one should ever question that . . .

All the dreams we had in 1993 that were revived when we had the peace with Jordan, revived again when we had the Wye River accords—

*Speech at the Israel Policy Forum in New York.

that was, I think, the most interesting peace talks I was ever involved in. My strategy was the same used to break prisoners of war, I just didn't let anybody sleep for nine days and, finally, out of exhaustion, we made a deal—just so people could go home and go to bed. I've been looking for an opportunity to employ it again, ever since.

There have been a lot of positive things, and I think it's worth remembering that there have been positive developments along the way. But this is heartbreaking, what we've been through these last few months, for all of you who have believed for eight years in the Oslo process; all of you whose hearts soared on September 19, 1993, when Yasir Arafat and Yitzhak Rabin signed that agreement.

For over three months we have lived through a tragic cycle of violence that has cost hundreds of lives. It has shattered the confidence in the peace process. It has raised questions in some people's minds about whether Palestinians and Israelis could ever really live and work together, support each other's peace and prosperity and security. It's been a heartbreaking time for me, too. But we have done our best to work with the parties to restore calm, to end the bloodshed and to get back to working on an agreement to address the underlying causes that continuously erupt in conflicts. . . .

From my first day as president, we have worked to advance interests in the Middle East that are long standing and historically bipartisan. . . . Along the way since 1993, through the positive agreements that have been reached between those two sides, through the peace between Israel and Jordan, through last summer's withdrawal from Lebanon in which Israel fulfilled its part of implementing UN Security Counsel resolution 425— along this way we have learned some important lessons, not only because of the benchmarks of progress, because of the occasional eruption of terrorism, bombing, death and then these months of conflict. I think these lessons have to guide any effort, now or in the future, to reach a comprehensive peace. Here's what I think they are. Most of you probably believed in them, up to the last three months. I still do. First, the Arab-Israeli conflict is not just a morality play between good and evil. It is a conflict with a complex history, whose resolution requires balancing the needs of both sides, including respect for their national identities and religious beliefs.

Second, there is no place for violence, and no military solution to this conflict. The only path to a just and durable resolution is through negotiation. Third, there will be no lasting peace or regional stability without a strong and secure Israel, secure enough to make peace, strong enough to deter the adversaries which will still be there, even if a peace is made in complete good faith. And clearly that is why the United States must maintain its commitment to preserving Israel's qualitative edge in military superiority.

Fourth, talks must be accompanied by acts—acts which show trust and partnership. For goodwill at the negotiating table cannot survive forever ill intent on the ground. And it is important that each side understands how the other reads actions.

For example, on the one hand, the tolerance of violence and incitement of hatred in classrooms and the media in the Palestinian communities, or on the other hand, humiliating treatment on the streets or at checkpoints by Israelis are real obstacles to even getting people to talk about building a genuine peace.

Fifth, in the resolution of remaining differences, whether they come today or after several years of heartbreak and bloodshed, the fundamental, painful, but necessary choices will almost certainly remain the same whenever the decision is made. The parties will face the same history, the same geography, the same neighbors, the same passions, the same hatreds. This is not a problem time will take care of. . . . because there are all these independent actors . . . independent of the Palestinian Authority and not under the direct control of any international legal body—who don't want this peace to work. So that even if we can get an agreement, and the Palestinian Authority works as hard as they can, and the Israelis works as hard as they can, we're all going to have to pitch in, send in an international force like we did in the Sinai, and hang tough, because there are enemies of peace out there, number one.

Number two, because the enemies of peace know they can drive the Israelis to close the borders if they can blow up enough bombs. They do it periodically to make sure that the Palestinians in the street cannot enjoy the benefits of peace that have come to the people in Northern Ireland. So as long as they can keep the people miserable, and they can keep the fundamental decisions from being made, they still have a hope, the enemies of peace, of derailing the whole thing. . . .

The fundamental realities are not going to be changed by delays. . . . We can wait until [a whole generation] and we've got a whole lot more bodies and a lot more funerals, a lot more crying and a lot more hatred, and I'll swear the decisions will still be the same ones that will have to be made today. . . .

I'm a little concerned that we could draw the wrong lessons from this tragic, still relatively brief, chapter in the history of the Middle East. The violence does not demonstrate that the quest for peace has gone too far or too fast. It demonstrates what happens when you've got a problem that is profoundly difficult and you never quite get to the end, so there is no settlement, no resolution, anxiety prevailed, and at least some people never get any concrete benefits out of it.

And I believe that the last few months demonstrate the futility of force or terrorism as an ultimate solution. . . . I believe that the violence confirms the need to do more to prepare both publics for the requirements of peace, not to condition people for the so-called glory of further conflict.

Now, what are we going to do now? The first priority, obviously, has got to be to drastically reduce the current cycle of violence. But beyond that, on the Palestinian side, there must be an end to the culture of violence and the culture of incitement that, since Oslo, has not gone unchecked. Young children still are being educated to believe in confrontation with Israel, and multiple militia-like groups carry and use weapons with impunity. Voices of reason in that kind of environment will be drowned out too often by voices of revenge.

Such conduct is inconsistent with the Palestinian leadership's commitment to Oslo's nonviolent path to peace and its persistence sends the wrong message to the Israeli people, and makes it much more difficult for them to support their leaders in making the compromises necessary to get a lasting agreement.

For their part, the Israeli people also must understand that they're creating a few problems, too; that the settlement enterprise and building bypass roads in the heart of what they already know will one day be part of a Palestinian state is inconsistent with the Oslo commitment that both sides negotiate a compromise.

And restoring confidence requires the Palestinians being able to lead a normal existence, and not be subject to daily, often humiliating reminders that they lack basic freedom and control over their lives.

These, too, make it harder for the Palestinians to believe the commitments made to them will be kept. Can two peoples with this kind of present trouble and troubling history still conclude a genuine and lasting peace? . . . They share such a small piece of land with such a profound history of importance to more than a billion people around the world. So I believe with all my heart not only that they can, but that they must.

At Camp David, I saw Israeli and Palestinian negotiators who knew how many children each other had, who knew how many grandchildren each other had, who knew how they met their spouses, who knew what their family tragedies were, who trusted each other in their word. It was almost shocking to see what could happen and how people still felt on the ground when I saw how their leaders felt about each other and the respect and the confidence they had in each other when they were talking.

The alternative to getting this peace done is being played out before our very eyes. But amidst the agony, I will say again, there are signs of hope. And let me try to put this into what I think is a realistic context.

Camp David was a transformative event, because the two sides faced the core issue of their dispute in a forum that was official for the first time. And they had to debate the tradeoffs required to resolve the issues. Just as Oslo forced Israelis and Palestinians to come to terms with each other's existence, the discussions of the past six months have forced them to come to terms with each other's needs and the contours of a peace that ultimately they will have to reach.

That's why Prime Minister Barak, I think, has demonstrated real courage and vision in moving toward peace in difficult circumstances while trying to find a way to continue to protect Israel's security and vital interests.

So that's a fancy way of saying we know what we have to do and we've got a mess on our hands. So where do we go from here? Given the impasse and the tragic deterioration on the ground, a couple of weeks ago both sides asked me to present my ideas. So I put forward parameters that I wanted to be a guide toward a comprehensive agreement; parameters based on eight years of listening carefully to both sides and hearing them describe with increasing clarity their respective grievances and needs.

Both Prime Minister Barak and Chairman Arafat have now accepted these parameters as the basis for further efforts. . . . The parameters I put forward contemplate a settlement in response to each side's essential needs, if not to their utmost desires. A settlement based on sovereign homelands, security, peace and dignity for both Israelis and Palestinians. These parameters don't begin to answer every question, they just narrow the questions that have to be answered.

Here they are. First, I think there can be no genuine resolution to the conflict without a sovereign, viable, Palestinian state that accommodates Israeli's security requirements and the demographic realities. That suggests Palestinian sovereignty over Gaza, the vast majority of the West Bank, the incorporation into Israel of settlement blocks, with the goal of maximizing the number of settlers in Israel while minimizing the land annex for Palestine to be viable must be a geographically contiguous state.

Now, the land annexed into Israel into settlement blocks should include as few Palestinians as possible, consistent with the logic of two separate homelands. And to make the agreement durable, I think there will have to be some territorial swaps and other arrangements.

Second, a solution will have to be found for the Palestinian refugees who have suffered a great deal—particularly some of them. A solution that allows them to return to a Palestinian state that will provide all Palestinians with a place they can safely and proudly call home. All Palestinian refugees who wish to live in this homeland should have the right to do so. All others who want to find new homes, whether in their current locations or in third countries, should be able to do so, consistent with those countries' sovereign decisions. And that includes Israel.

All refugees should receive compensation from the international community for their losses, and assistance in building new lives.

Now, you all know what the rub is. That was a lot of artful language for saying that you cannot expect Israel to acknowledge an unlimited right of return to present day Israel, and at the same time, to give up Gaza and the West Bank and have the settlement blocks as compact as possible, because of where a lot of these refugees came from. We cannot expect Israel to make a decision that would threaten the very foundations of the state of Israel, and would undermine the whole logic of peace. And it shouldn't be done.

But I have made it very clear that the refugees will be a high priority, and that the United States will take a lead in raising the money necessary to relocate them in the most appropriate manner. . . . But there cannot be an unlimited language in an agreement that would undermine the very foundations of the Israeli state or the whole reason for creating the Palestinian state. So that's what we're working on.

Third, there will be no peace, and no peace agreement, unless the Israeli people have lasting security guarantees. These need not and should not come at the expense of Palestinian sovereignty, or interfere with Palestinian territorial integrity. So my parameters rely on an international presence in Palestine to provide border security along the Jordan Valley and to monitor implementation of the final agreement. They rely on a non-militarized Palestine, a phased Israeli withdrawal, to address Israeli security needs in the Jordan Valley, and other essential arrangements to ensure Israel's ability to defend itself.

Fourth, I come to the issue of Jerusalem, perhaps the most emotional and sensitive of all. It is a historic, cultural and political center for both Israelis and Palestinians, a unique city sacred to all three monotheistic religions. And I believe the parameters I have established flow from four fair and logical propositions.

First, Jerusalem should be an open and undivided city, with assured freedom of access and worship for all. It should encompass the internationally recognized capitals of two states, Israel and Palestine. Second, what is Arab should be Palestinian, for why would Israel want to govern in perpetuity the lives of hundreds of thousands of Palestinians? Third, what is Jewish should be Israeli. That would give rise to a Jewish Jerusalem, larger and more vibrant than any in history. Fourth, what is holy to both requires a special care to meet the needs of all. I was glad to hear what the Speaker said about that. No peace agreement will last if not premised on mutual respect for the religious beliefs and holy shrines of Jews, Muslims and Christians.

I have offered formulations on the Haram Ash-Shareef, and the area holy to the Jewish people, an area which for 2,000 years, as I said at Camp David, has been the focus of Jewish yearning, that I believed fairly addressed the concerns of both sides.

Fifth and, finally, any agreement will have to mark the decision to end the conflict, for neither side can afford to make these painful compromises, only to be subjected to further demands. They are both entitled to know that if they take the last drop of blood out of each other's turnip, that's it. It really will have to be the end of the struggle that has pitted Palestinians and Israelis against one another for too long. And the end of the conflict must manifest itself with concrete acts that demonstrate a new attitude and a new approach by Palestinians and Israelis toward each other, and by other states in the region toward Israel, and by the entire region toward Palestine, to help it get off to a good start.

The parties' experience with interim accords has not always been happy—too many deadlines missed, too many commitments unfulfilled on both sides. So for this to signify a real end of the conflict, there must be effective mechanisms to provide guarantees of implementation. . . .

Now, I still think the benefits of the agreement, based on these parameters, far outweigh the burdens. For the people of Israel, they are an end to conflict, secure and defensible borders, the incorporation of most of the settlers into Israel, and the Jewish capital of Jerusalem, recognized by all, not just the United States, by everybody in the world. It's a big deal, and it needs to be done.

For the Palestinian people, it means the freedom to determine their own future on their own land, a new life for the refugees, an independent and sovereign state with al-Quds as its capital, recognized by all. And for America, it means that we could have new flags flying over new embassies in both these capitals. . . .

Let me say those who believe that my ideas can be altered to one party's exclusive benefit are mistaken. I think to press for more will produce less. There can be no peace without compromise. . . . I have said what I have out of a profound lifetime commitment to and love for the state of Israel, out of a conviction that the Palestinian people have been ignored or used as political footballs by others for long enough, and they ought to have a chance to make their own life with dignity. And out of a belief that in the homeland of the world's three great religions that believe we are all the creatures of one God, we ought to be able to prove that one person's win is not, by definition, another's loss; that one person's dignity is not, by definition, another's humiliation; that one person's work of God is not, by definition, another's heresy. There has to be a way for us to find a truth we can share. There has to be a way for us to reach those young Palestinian kids who . . . don't imagine a future in which they would ever put on clothes like this and sit at a dinner like this.

There has to be a way for us to say to them, struggle and pain and destruction and self-destruction are way overrated, and not the only option. There has to be a way for us to reach those people in Israel who have paid such a high price and believe, frankly, that people who embrace the ideas I just outlined are nuts, because Israel is a little country and this agreement would make it smaller; to understand that the world in which we live and the technology of modern weaponry no longer make defense primarily a matter of geography and of politics and the human feeling and the interdependence and the cooperation and the shared values and the shared interests are more important and worth the considered risk, especially if the United States remains committed to the military capacity of the state of Israel.

So I say to the Palestinians: there will always be those who are sitting outside . . . urging you to hold out for more, or to plant one more bomb. But all the people who do that, they're not the refugees languishing in those camps—you are. They're not the ones with children growing up in poverty whose income is lower today than it was the day we had the signing on the White House Lawn in 1993—you are.

All the people that are saying to the Palestinian people: Stay on the path of no, are people that have a vested interest in the failure of the peace process that has nothing to do with how those kids in Gaza and the West Bank are going to grow up and live and raise their own children.

To the citizens of Israel who have returned to an ancient homeland after 2,000 years, whose hopes and dreams almost vanished in the Holocaust, who have hardly had one day of peace and quiet since the state of Israel was created, I understand, I believe, something of the disillusionment, the anger, the frustration that so many feel when, just at the moment peace seemed within reach, all this violence broke out and raised the question of whether it is ever possible.

The fact is that the people of Israel dreamed of a homeland. The dream came through; but when they came home, the land was not all vacant. Your land is also their land, it is the homeland of two people. And, therefore, there is no choice but to create two states and make the best of it.

If it happens today, it will be better than if it happens tomorrow, because fewer people will die. And after it happens, the motives of those who continue the violence will be clearer to all than they are today. . . . New York has its own high-tech corridor called "Silicon Alley." The number one foreign recipient of venture capital from Silicon Alley is Israel. Palestinians who have come to the United States, to Chile, to Canada, to Europe, have done fabulously well—in business, in the sciences, in academia.

If we could ever let a lot of this stuff go and realize that . . . the enemies of peace in the Middle East are overlooking . . . what has happened to the state of Israel since its birth, and how fabulously well the people of Palestinian descent have done everywhere else in the world except in their homeland—where they are in the grip of forces that have not permitted them to reconcile with one another and with the people of Israel—listen, if you guys ever got together, ten years from now we would all wonder what the heck happened for thirty years before.

And the center of energy and creativity and economic power and political influence in the entire region would be with the Israelis and the Palestinians because of their gifts. It could happen. But somebody has got to take the long leap, and they have to be somebodies on both sides. . . .